Chapter 8	Chapter 9	Chapter 10	Chapter 11	Chapter 12	Chapter 13	Chapter 14	Chapter 15	Chapter 16	Chapter 17
Ego Psychology Anna Freud Heinz Hartmann Erik Erikson									Reprise
									Reprise
	Trait Theory Gordon Allport Raymond Cattell Hans Eysenck The Big Five								Reprise
		R.D. Laing							Reprise
			Theory of the Person Carl Rogers **Personal Construct Theory** George Kelly						Reprise
				S-R Theory John Dollard & Neal Miller	**Radical Behaviourism** B.F. Skinner	**Social Learning Theory** Julian Rotter	**Social Cognitive Learning Theory** Albert Bandura Walter Mischel		Reprise
								Genes, Behaviour, Personality	Reprise

Personality
theory

Personality theory

DOUGLAS P. CROWNE

OXFORD

UNIVERSITY PRESS

OXFORD
UNIVERSITY PRESS

70 Wynford Drive, Don Mills, Ontario M3C 1J9
www.oup.com/ca

Oxford University Press is a department of the University of Oxford.
It furthers the University's objective of excellence in research, scholarship,
and education by publishing worldwide in

Oxford   New York

Auckland   Cape Town   Dar es Salaam   Hong Kong   Karachi
Kuala Lumpur Madrid   Melbourne   Mexico City   Nairobi
New Delhi   Shanghai   Taipei   Toronto

With offices in

Argentina   Austria   Brazil   Chile   Czech Republic   France   Greece
Guatemala   Hungary   Italy   Japan   Poland   Portugal   Singapore
South Korea   Switzerland   Thailand   Turkey   Ukraine   Vietnam

Oxford is a trade mark of Oxford University Press
in the UK and in certain other countries

Published in Canada
by Oxford University Press

Library and Archives Canada Cataloguing in Publication

Crowne, Douglas P.
Personality theory / Douglas P. Crowne.

Includes bibliographical references and index.
ISBN-13: 978-0-19-542218-4
ISBN-10: 0-19-542218-X

1. Personality—Textbooks. I. Title.

BF698.C76 2006   155.2   C2006-904950-5

1 2 3 4 - 10 09 08 07

Cover Design: Andrea Katwaroo
Cover Image: Gandee Vasan/Getty Images

This book is printed on permanent (acid-free) paper ∞.
Printed in Canada

Contents

Preface   xiv

1   The Scientific Study of Personality   1

Personality and the Nature of Human Nature   1
Paradigms in Personality   3
Observing People and Asking Questions   8
Personality Theory in Psychology and Personality Theory as Science   9
The Assumptions and Methods of Science   9
Research Methods In Personality   14
The Experiment   14
The Clinical Method   15
An Introduction to the Nature of Personality   17
Defining Personality   19
Persons and Situations   20
Theories of Personality from Study of the Disturbed?   21
The Nature of Personality Theory   22
Theory and Fiction   23
Falsifiability   24
Summary   24
To Test Your Understanding   27

2   The Beginnings of Personality Theory   29

Introduction   29
Sigmund Freud: Personal History and Context   29
The First Discoveries   38
Resistance   38
Repression   39
Symptom Irrationality   39
The Unconscious   39
Childhood Origins of Neurosis   40
A Theory of Neurosis   40
A New Theory of Neurosis   41
Summary   43
To Test Your Understanding   45

3   Psychoanalysis: Sigmund Freud   46

Introduction   46
Emphases   46
Traumatic Events and the Symptoms of Neurosis   46

Instincts, the Unconscious, and Defences   47
Three Parts of Personality   47
Personality Development   48
The Broad Sweep of Psychoanalysis   48
The Major Concepts of Psychoanalysis   48
The Structure of Personality   48
The Stages of Personality Development   54
Adult Character Structure   60
Dreams and Symbolic Expression   62
What Is a Dream?   62
Why Do We Dream?   62
The Ego as Dream Censor   63
Dream Symbolism   63
Dream Work and Ego Defences   64
The Sources of Dream Theory   66
Some Extended Implications of Psychoanalysis   69
Creative Expression   69
Aggression   70
Transference   70
Wit and Humour   71
Psychoanalysis in Literature   71
Research   71
Repression   73
Unconscious Processes   76
Psychoanalytic Research and Psychoanalysis   80
Psychoanalysis in Perspective   80
Modern Revisions   80
Object Relations   81
Summary   82
To Test Your Understanding   87

4   Analytic Psychology: Carl Jung   88

Introduction   88
Carl Jung: Personal History   93
Emphases   93
Teleology   93
The Collective Unconscious   93
Psychic Energy   94
Ego and Self   94
Religion   94
The Principle of Synchronicity   94
The Major Concepts of Analytic Psychology   95
The Ego   95
The Personal Unconscious   95
The Collective Unconscious   96
Libido   102
Four Functions   103

Personality Typologies   104
Personality Development   106
Research   107
Analytic Psychology in Perspective   111
Summary   111
To Test Your Understanding   113

5   The Neo-Freudians: Alfred Adler   114

Introduction   114
Alfred Adler: Personal History   115
Emphases   120
Practicality   120
A Conscious Ego   121
The Individual in Society   121
Individual Uniqueness   121
Pursuing Future Goals   121
The Family as a Social Group   121
How Personality is Expressed   122
The Major Concepts of Individual Psychology   122
Organ Inferiority and Compensation   122
Feelings of Inferiority   123
Superiority Striving   123
The Style of Life   124
Fictional Finalism   125
Social Interest   125
The Creative Self   126
Personality Development   126
Expressions of Personality   130
Dreams   130
Earliest Memories   132
The Meaning of Symptoms   132
Research   133
Affiliation When Afraid   133
Intelligence   134
Adler in Perspective   135
Summary   137
To Test Your Understanding   141

6   The Neo-Freudians: Harry Stack Sullivan
and Karen Horney   142

Introduction   142
Harry Stack Sullivan: Introduction   142
Harry Stack Sullivan: Personal History   143
Emphases   145
American Psychiatry and Sociology   145
An Interpersonal View of Personality   146

Parataxic Thinking and Distortion   146
The Self   147
Needs   147
The Major Concepts of the Interpersonal Theory of Psychiatry   147
Tension   147
Dynamisms   148
Cognitive Processes   150
Communication   151
Personality Development   152
Infancy   152
Childhood   153
Juvenile Era   154
Preadolescence   154
Early Adolescence   155
Late Adolescence   155
Adulthood   155
Research   155
Sullivan in Perspective   160
Karen Horney: Introduction   161
Karen Horney: Personal History   161
Emphases   162
Clinical Evidence   162
The Psychology of Women   163
Personality Development   163
The Self   163
The Analytic Situation   163
Neurotic Needs   165
The Major Concepts of Horney's Theory   165
Basic Anxiety   165
The Vicious Circle   165
The Basic Nature of Human Needs   166
The Ego as Self   167
Personality Development   169
Feminine Psychology   169
Research   170
Horney in Perspective   170
Summary   171
To Test Your Understanding   175

7   The Neo-Freudians: Erich Fromm   176

Introduction   176
Erich Fromm: Personal History   176
Emphases   177
The Personality–Society–Culture Relation   177
The Emphases and Major Concepts of Fromm's Theory   179
Fromm's Basic Propositions   179

Expressions of Personality: The Dream 188
**Personality Development: How We Get to Be the
    Way We Are** 188
Research 189
Fromm in Perspective 191
Summary 194
To Test Your Understanding 196

8   Ego Psychology: Anna Freud, Heinz Hartmann,
     and Erik Erikson   197

Introduction 197
Anna Freud 197
Heinz Hartmann 198
Erik Erikson 200
    Erik Erikson: Personal History 200
    Emphases 202
The Major Concepts of Erikson's Ego Psychology 204
    The Eight Ages of Man 204
    Ritualization, Ritual, and Ritualism 209
    Research 212
Ego Psychology in Perspective 218
Summary 220
To Test Your Understanding 223

9   Trait Theory: Gordon Allport, Raymond Cattell,
     Hans Eysenck, and the Big Five   224

Introduction 224
The Trait Theory of Gordon Allport 226
    Gordon Allport: Personal History 226
    Personality and the Trait 228
    Allport in Perspective 230
Raymond Cattell and Factor-Analytic Trait Theory 231
    Introduction 231
    Raymond Cattell: Personal History 233
    Emphases and Major Concepts 234
    Personality Development 238
    Research 241
    Implications 241
    Cattell's Factor-Analytic Theory in Perspective 241
The Type-Trait Theory of Hans Eysenck 242
    Introduction 242
    Hans Eysenck: Personal History 245
    Type-Trait Theory: Emphases and Major Concepts 246
    Research 251
    Implications 252
    Type-Trait Theory in Perspective 252

Big Five Theory 253
   Big Five Measurement 254
   Validity of Measurement and Theory 255
   A Causal Five-Factor Model 257
A Final Perspective on Trait Theories 260
   Trait and Situation 260
Summary 261
To Test Your Understanding 264

10 Existentialism: R.D. Laing 265

Introduction 265
R.D. Laing: Personal History 267
Emphases and Major Concepts 270
   Ontological Insecurity and Schizophrenia 271
   Ontological Insecurity and Anxiety 273
   Self-Consciousness 274
Implications 275
Research 278
Existentialism in Perspective 278
Summary 279
To Test Your Understanding 280

11 Phenomenology: Carl Rogers' Theory of the Person and George Kelly's Personal Construct Theory 281

Introduction 281
Carl Rogers' Person-Centred Theory 282
   Carl Rogers: Personal History 282
Emphases 286
   The Major Concepts of Person-Centred Theory 287
   A Theory of Therapy and Personality Change 291
   Personality Development 294
   Implications 295
   Research 296
   Person-Centred Theory in Perspective 299
George Kelly's Personal Construct Theory 300
   George Kelly: Personal History 300
   Emphases and Major Concepts 302
   Implications 306
   Research 307
   Personal Construct Theory in Perspective 308
Positive Psychology 309
   Emphases 310
Summary 312
   To Test Your Understanding 315

12 Learning Theories of Personality: The S-R Theory of John Dollard and Neal Miller   316

Introduction   316
An Introduction to S-R Theory   317
John Dollard & Neal Miller: Personal Histories   320
Emphases   322
    The Principles and Conditions of Learning   322
    The Stimuli of Drives   322
    The Concept of Habit   323
    Internal Responses   323
The Major Concepts of S-R Theory   323
    What is a Neurosis?   324
    The Variables in S-R Theory   326
    S-R Theory Principles and the Explanation of Neurosis   329
    A Theory of Conflict   332
    Personality Development   338
    Four Child-Training Situations   340
    The Damaging Effects of Mislabelling   341
Research   342
    Conflict   342
    Studies of Displacement   342
S-R Theory in Perspective   344
Summary   346
To Test Your Understanding   349

13 Learning Theories of Personality: The Radical Behaviourism of B.F. Skinner   350

Introduction   350
B.F. Skinner: Personal History   355
Emphases   358
    The Control of Behaviour   358
    Functional Analysis   359
    Skinner's 'Theory' Is Not a Theory   359
    What Is Personality?   359
The Major Concepts of Skinnerian Behaviourism   360
    Respondent and Operant Conditioning   360
    Shaping   361
    The Control of Operant Responding   362
    The Nature of Reinforcement   363
Personality Development   366
    Shaping Again   366
    Punishment   366
    Language   367
Research and Applications   367
Radical Behaviourism in Perspective   371

Summary   374
To Test Your Understanding   376

14   Learning Theories of Personality: The Social Learning Theory of Julian Rotter   377

Introduction   377
Julian Rotter: Personal History   378
Emphases   380
The Major Concepts of Social Learning Theory   383
Implications of the Theory   385
   The Psychological Situation   388
Research   389
   The Locus of Control of Reinforcement   389
Social Learning Theory in Perspective   395
Summary   398
To Test Your Understanding   400

15   Learning Theories of Personality: The Social Cognitive Learning Theories of Albert Bandura and Walter Mischel   401

Albert Bandura   401
   Introduction   401
   Albert Bandura: Personal History   404
   Emphases and Major Concepts of Social Cognitive Theory   405
   The Major Concepts of Social Cognitive Theory: Reprise   414
   Implications   415
   Research   422
   Social Cognitive Learning Theory in Perspective   422
Walter Mischel   423
   Introduction   423
   Walter Mischel: Personal History   424
   Emphases and Major Concepts of the Cognitive-Affective Personality System   425
   The Reinforcement Principle   426
   The Elements of the Cognitive-Affective Personality System   426
   The Cognitive-Affective Personality System in Perspective   429
Summary   430
To Test Your Understanding   433

16   Genes, Behaviour, and Personality   434

Introduction   434
What Is a Gene?   435
   The DNA Code   436

Some Genetic History 437
  Gregor Mendel 439
  Huntington's Disease 440
Research Methods in the Genetics of Personality 443
  Family Studies 443
  Twin Studies 446
  Adoption Studies 453
Personality Theory, Genetics, and Environment 455
  The Importance of the Nonshared Environment 456
A Final Word 457
Summary 458
To Test Your Understanding 461

17 Personality Theory in Perspective 462

Introduction 462
  The Age of Theory 462
Paradigms in Personality: Reprise and Prospects 464
  Psychodynamic 465
  Family, Society, and Culture 466
  Learning and Personality 466
  Phenomenology and Humanism 467
  Existentialism 468
  Traits 468
  The Inheritance of Behaviour 469
An Alternative: Miniature Theories 470
  Sensation-Seeking 470
  The Achievement Need 474
Some Concluding Thoughts about Personality Theory 478
Summary 479
To Test Your Understanding 481

Appendix 483
Glossary 485
References 493
Index 509

Preface

I have three feet of texts on personality theory on my bookshelf, and they are not all of them. Some publishers have four or five on their lists, selling to a large market the way Proctor and Gamble peddles competing brands of soap. Why another text, then? Surely in three feet my fellow authors—I may now include myself in their number—must have said all there is to say about theories of personality, their strong points and foibles. Indeed, collectively, they have come close. Taken together, personality theory texts do cover a great part of the obligatory material with, however, some notable omissions. Several of the neo-Freudians—especially Sullivan, Fromm, and, not infrequently, Adler—get passed over, not fit, so it seems, to survive into the modern world. So, here's the first hint about what a new book might deal with.

Individually, no book on my personality shelf is comprehensive. Although many have remarkable strengths and are books I admire, they include theories and topics I would not have chosen and omit some with which students should become acquainted. The problem facing someone who wishes to add to the collection is how to go about it. There are, basically, two ways to write a text on theories of personality. The original model was Calvin Hall and Gardner Lindzey's *Theories of Personality*, which appeared in 1957 and went through the several editions from which we textbook writers were mostly taught. Hall and Lindzey presented the major theories one by one, giving a brief biography and stating the case for each theorist. As other texts appeared, a whole new way of presenting personality theories emerged. Many new authors did not follow Hall and Lindzey's path, choosing instead to embed each theory in a conceptual scaffold of personality, and this is very much the case today. In large measure, contemporary texts are built around these paradigms, as if theories themselves could not stand on their own—or, perhaps, as if personality theories, tired and old, needed renewing by a novel context.

Texts written in this way, emphasizing concepts and paradigms at the expense of the theories they have been devised to explain, are really texts about schemes for thinking about personality; they are less (or sometimes hardly at all) about the classic psychological theories of the person. The approach encourages the author to omit theories that don't fit comfortably in the paradigm he or she believes in, leaving the student—who expects to be taught about the great theories of personality—puzzled and in the end disappointed.

I believe that a theory-by-theory account of personality shows each theory in its underwear and makes it, in its exposure, speak for itself. To present the study of personality theory in this way is friendly to students, both giving them the text they expected and challenging them to hold each theory up to standards and judge its adequacy. Instructors benefit as well. They are on familiar ground and get to shine as they explain what they know so intimately. And if instructors have paradigms to give their students, so much the better, for their own views of the organization of theory and personality will stand out in sharper relief. None among our theories is perfect. Each one needs a fair hearing, each needs to be defended. In this necessary (and enjoyable) process, we instructors are like lawyers with an unpopular and possibly guilty client, who must get the best defence possible, our students empanelled as the jury.

There are also two avenues to the research on each theory. One approach favours the review article, with citation after citation documenting finding upon finding that students at their stage in learning will not (and need not) remember. A preferable approach is to provide a selection, a carefully drawn list of articles, presenting research that exemplifies the findings and methods of each theory, a list of articles that students *should* know about and remember.

Now, finally, comes the question of which theories to include which to exclude. The answer is simple in principle: the author must decide which theories in a long list have had a major influence on research, new theory, clinical practice, and cultural life. This will be easy enough with many, but the writer will have to be sufficiently wise and judicious to avoid the trap of banishing the older theory (Sullivan's, say, or Fromm's) in favour of newer ones that have yet to make their mark. New does not necessarily mean influential and deserving of a place among the giants. I don't by any means intend to imply that because a theory is hoary it also deserves to be taught. I do say that smaller, less inclusive approaches that are offshoots of major theories—extensions that don't supplant their forebears—may not merit inclusion simply because they have come on the scene more recently. If I have erred here, it is in giving the nod to the established and influential in the belief that students will benefit most from exposure to the ideas that have dominated our field. Those students who choose to go on will soon enough learn about the contributions of newer views.

This book is the result of more than thirty years of teaching personality theory to large undergraduate classes. I had been content to do that, not thinking at all of writing a text, until it came time to make a major revision in my course, renewing and updating it with substantial revisions to existing lectures and the addition of new ones. Not long into that process, it became evident that, whether I had meant to or not, I was actually writing my own textbook, and there was nothing else to do but to get on with it. There were some things to commend such a venture. I have been closely involved with personality theory and theorists for all of a long career. Students and instructors will discover that I was a colleague of two major theorists, Julian Rotter and George Kelly during a halcyon era at The Ohio State University. I revered—and still do—Rotter as my teacher and friend, and readers will see the influence of his social learning theory in my thinking and approach. In due course, my reservations about Kelly will make their appearance. In 1949, I was a young Antioch College student on a co-operative job at Chestnut Lodge Sanitarium, the private psychiatric hospital that was the clinical expression of Sullivan's interpersonal theory of psychiatry. This was the year that Sullivan suddenly died, and I saw the bereavement of his colleagues at first hand. I date my appreciation of Sullivan's theory to that brief period at the Lodge and to the keen sense of loss his distinguished fellow psychiatrists could not hide. How could I not look on these brushes with theorists as preparation for this book?

When all the hours at the keyboard are at an end and it is time for the publisher to take over and turn the product of those keyboard hours into bound, printed pages, writers have one more task to complete before indulging in the well-earned pleasure of self-congratulation. It is the happy one of acknowledgement, of recording our indebtedness to those who have given aid and advice, who have corrected our errors and turned our infelicities into more graceful prose. My list begins with my wife, Dr Sandra Crowne. Through draft after draft she has read every word, and contributed many a perfect one. Her medical knowledge was invaluable in helping me to get my account straight, especially of genetics in Chapter 16. But her contribution was not at all limited to that. Her cartoon of the three Freudian voices of personality appears in Chapter 3. My biologist colleague Dr Jack Pasternak read several chapters but outdid himself in his illuminating critique of Chapter 16, 'Genes, Behaviour, and Personality'. Department of Psychology colleagues and chair have been supportive. Their collective refrain over the trial of writing—'How's the book coming?'—warmly cheered me on. Finally, I am pleased to acknowledge the consistent encouragement and great help given by my team of Oxford University Press editors, Lisa Meschino, Roberta Osborne, Eric Sinkins, and Marta Tomins. *Personality Theory* would not have come to existence without them.

Douglas Crowne
St Agatha, Ontario
February, 2006

CHAPTER ONE

The Scientific Study of Personality

Personality and the Nature of Human Nature

The way to begin a study like this is with a straightforward declarative sentence setting out the subject to be covered. A definition. *Botany is . . .* (if that's what the book is about). *Organic chemistry is the study of . . .* Right? So, with your highlighter underline the following statement—it will give you the essence of personality. Well, sorry, there won't be just one, so you'd better limber up your fingers. There will be several.

> 'Personality is the dynamic organization within the individual of those psychophysical systems that determine his characteristic behavior and thought' (Allport, 1961, p. 28).

> 'In psychoanalytic theory, [personality] is defined as a configuration of traits. But . . . [it] often stands as the organization of inner conflicts rather than their resolution' (Gay, 1988, p. 336).

> Personality '. . . is the study of phenomena that occur in interpersonal situations, in configurations made up of two or more people all but one of whom may be more or less completely illusory' (Sullivan, 1964, p. 33).

> '*Personality is that which permits a prediction of what a person will do in a given situation*' (Cattell, 1950, p. 2).

> Personality '. . . is simply a device for representing *a functionally unified system of responses*' (Skinner, 1953, p. 285).

> 'Personality refers to those characteristics of the person that account for consistent patterns of feeling, thinking, and behaving' (Pervin, Cervone, & John, 2005, p. 6).

Starting with a definition, a good, firm step into our subject, just isn't going to work, is it? I've already listed six and barely scratched the surface. The trouble is that each personality theorist sees personality differently and will define it according to his or her theoretical lights. There will be as many definitions, very nearly, as there are theories. Sorry again. That was a good idea of mine, but it just dug us into a hole. We had better back out and start over with something that won't put us deep in the middle of our exploration before we're ready. Something basic: What are personality theories all about, anyway?

Most simply said, personality theories are concerned with the nature of human nature. They consider

- motives, feelings, thinking, and action—the forces that drive us and order our emotional and cognitive life;
- the recognizable continuity of personality from situation to situation and over the life span;
- how humans develop, with emphasis on the psychological attributes that make each person unique;
- how we reach productive maturity and cope with aging;
- what stress and damaging disorders of personality do to us.

Wondering about and worrying over the nature of the human animal is an age-old practice. It was the occupation of the great philosophers of Athens, Socrates, Plato, and Aristotle. We shall see, however, that our present study differs from ancient questioning, and the modern philosophy descended from it, in two ways. First, personality theory takes a *psychological* perspective, using concepts and methods of psychology to study how humans develop and how we may understand their actions. Second, personality theory is a *scientific* enterprise: almost all personality theorists have been men and women of science who have adopted a scientific approach and applied the methods of science.

In this text we'll study theories themselves, their concepts, and how in each theory those concepts are linked together to form a cohesive account of the psychology of the person. Another part of our inquiry will be the observations and evidence that led to the *development* of each theory, and the evidence—naturalistic, clinical, and experimental—bearing on the implications of each theory. For each theory, we'll want to consider how well it enables us to **predict**, **understand**, and **control**★ (not in a sinister Machiavellian way but in the sense of exercising control over observations the theory's concerned with) significant human behaviour. *Personality Theory* will take up twenty-two major theories of personality, the ones that have had the greatest influence. That sounds like a big undertaking, but these twenty-two theories fall into a more manageable-sounding seven paradigms, within which there are important commonalities that will simplify our study.

Some theorists we'll study: Freud (© Bettmann/CORBIS); Adler (© Bettmann/CORBIS); Fromm (Ullstein Bild/The Granger Collection, New York); Horney (© Bettmann/CORBIS).

Some theorists we'll study: Sullivan (© Bettmann/CORBIS); Erikson (courtesy Jon Erikson); Jung (© Bettmann/CORBIS); Skinner (© Bettmann/CORBIS).

Paradigms in Personality

To the Greeks of the ancient world, **paradigm**★ meant a pattern or example shown side by side with an object or instance held up in comparison to it. 'See, it's like this,' the demonstrator might say. So the meaning of paradigm, signifying a model, remained until it was adopted by scientific disciplines late in the nineteenth century to stand for an established set of ideas or body of thought. Scientific theories became paradigms, models of the phenomena they were designed to explain, as did accepted experimental procedures. In well-studied and settled disciplines, there may be one paradigm or a very few of them; in less developed areas of inquiry, a number of paradigms may compete, each holding up a different account. This is the case in personality theory: seven paradigms offer contesting views of the origin and organization of human behaviour.

With one exception, all got their start after the appearance of the first paradigm, psychoanalysis, which became recognizable as theory in the early years of the twentieth century. As they developed, these paradigms adopted, modified, criticized, or flatly rejected their parent, presenting new schemes to explain personality, each a distinctive analysis of the psychology of the person. They remain viable as theoretical accounts, attract and hold adherents, and seek to convince scientists and practitioners of their validity. Persuasive though they may be, some of these seven paradigms rest on shaky empirical ground, their evidence gleaned from clinical diagnosis and treatment. We shall soon see how much of a

Some theorists we'll study: Dollard (Yale University Library Manuscripts and Archives); Miller (Courtesy of the Rockefeller University Archives); Rotter (Homer Babbidge Library, University of Connecticut); Rogers (Donald C. Davidson Library, University of California, Santa Barbara)]

problem such a limitation represents. The exception to the Freudian origin of personality paradigms is the genetics of behaviour and behaviour disorders which, although lacking adequate research methods and a good scientific database, predates psychoanalysis. The great strides of the behaviour genetics paradigm have been taken in more recent times. Now, let's see how twenty-two theories can be represented by seven paradigms.

Psychodynamic

Combine the word *dynamic* with the root of *psychology*, *psycho-*, and we have the term for the first paradigm. Inherent in the dynamic view of personality is the view that behaviour—both the overt behaviour we can see and the covert that we cannot— derive from motive forces in the person. Both the word and the approach it represents come from physics: dynamics is the study of forces that produce motion or action. It is no big leap to take this conception and apply it to behaviour and its sources. In the nineteenth century, biological scientists adopted the physics of motion and other physical principles as a way of viewing the body and bodily processes. Among them were distinguished physiologists and medical men who taught Freud. They saw the human body as a machine—a hugely complicated and finely tuned one to be sure, but a machine nonetheless—the workings of which could be understood by systematically applying the 'physical-mathematical method'. Freud admired these pioneering scientists greatly and took their scientific teaching beyond the body to the mind. We shall explore this 'scientific world view', as Freud called it, an influence that shaped the very foundation of psychoanalysis and formed the basis of psychodynamics, in chapters 2 and 3. Four other theories, covered in succeeding chapters, are in the lineage of this paradigm: three ego psychologies and the analytic psychology of Carl Gustav Jung.

Freud founded the psychodynamic approach in psychology by taking the mind to be no less a scientific object than the structures of the body. Mind isn't corporeal: it doesn't have substance as a part of the body does. But treating mind as if were material opens up a whole vista of possibilities to explain how it is that people are captive to wishes, urgings, and inhibitions that drive and thwart their behaviour. When motives are aroused and energized they are imperious, demanding instant gratification. Human social living, however, requires the disciplining and modulation of motive states. No society has a long future if its members insist on the immediate gratification of needs for sex or to aggress against a source of frustration, nor are tissue needs for food and fluid exempt from controlling social rules. Societies thus erect barriers, specifying when and where motives may be satisfied, how and how much. Psychodynamic theories see that motives and the controls on them come into conflict; psychological distress and symptoms of disturbance may result when motives are strong and the barriers, which become internalized and part of each person's psychology, are insuperable.

Structures in personality have the roles of ensuring motive gratification, finding realistic ways of achieving it, and imposing restraint. They engage in dynamic processes to carry out their missions and never let up, are never quiet. Even in sleep we are not internally peaceful and at rest. View the human in dynamic terms and this is what you get.

To summarize, psychodynamics is the story of the driving forces that impel people to act, the regulating forces that hold impulsive action back, and how the two direct behaviour toward less fulfilling but allowable actions. If the psychodynamic view of personality reminds you of the vectors of physics that express the magnitude of forces and their direction, then you have a nice beginning grasp of this approach to personality.

Family, Society, and Culture

Personality develops in the family and is expressed throughout life in a sociocultural context. The four theorists who introduced this paradigm—Alfred Adler, Erich Fromm, Harry Stack Sullivan, and Karen Horney—began with psychoanalysis, honouring Freud's psychodynamics, but arrived at the understanding that locating personality entirely within the individual fails to recognize the pervasive and enduring influences of the social world. They saw psychodynamics as incomplete and misleading: the course of instinctual (motivational) life could not possibly account for all the twists and turns of personality development, individual variation, and the visible effects of societies and their childrearing practices on behaviour.

Three of these theorists—Adler, Sullivan, and Horney—emphasized the role of the family. Being engaged, like the psychodynamic theorists, in the treatment of disturbed people, they pointed to the damage that psychological pathology (or sheer ignorance of how to nurture children) in parents can do to growing and vulnerable young personalities. The fourth, Fromm, was a social theorist, examining the effects of society and culture on the person, beginning with early life in the family—the agent of society—and continuing throughout life. Improve the ways in which societies fulfill elemental human needs, and happier, more loving, and more productive individual personalities will result. You can see in this paradigm a great corrective influence on psychodynamics and person-based theorists by showing how much the psychology of the person is moulded by parents in early life and channelled in adulthood by the social world.

Learning and Personality

In this paradigm, the modifiability of human behaviour is the key to understanding personality, and the processes by which behaviour is acquired, maintained, and altered provide the principles. Personality attributes are no different from any learned behaviour, and applying the rules of learning enables us to see how they develop and how maladaptive personalities may be helped to develop more satisfying and socially appropriate ways of thinking and acting.

Five theorists represent this paradigm: John Dollard and Neal Miller in collaboration, Julian Rotter, Albert Bandura, Walter Mischel, and B.F. Skinner. They draw on the major theories of learning for **process concepts** of behaviour change and, with one exception, stay well clear of personality structures. A single theory proposes a part of personality responsible for carrying out person-centred duties.

The theorists associated with this paradigm appreciate that learning does not occur in a vacuum. They see the social context as fundamental to the development of new behaviour and the replacement of outworn and useless or harmful behaviour. Two of these theorists, Rotter and Bandura, identify their approaches as social learning theories to give emphasis to this point. They differ from family, society, and culture theorists in recognizing the need to specify learning situations in detail if behaviour, simple or complex, is to be understood.

As chapters 9 through 12 will show, the theories of the learning paradigm are especially effective in the treatment of personality disorders, particularly those called the neuroses. They have trouble discovering the antecedents of current behaviour (neurotic symptoms, for example) because they must recover and reconstruct learning histories often buried deep in the past. Without knowledge of the situations in which behaviour was acquired—the conditions of learning—the learning theorist has one hand tied behind his back. Sometimes, however, a knowledge of common family or social practices will supply the missing evidence.

We must give the theorists of this paradigm high marks for their forthright attempts to take on personality by applying the rigorous concepts of theories of learning to the complexities of social behaviour, the unique individual histories and contemporary situations, and the frequently puzzling nature of personality disorder. They also merit recognition for their strong emphasis on research to test theoretical hypotheses in the laboratory and in the life contexts.

Phenomenology and Humanism

It would seem to be a truism that all people, no exceptions granted, make sense of the world through their own experience. Take that proposition with great seriousness, as earnest philosophers have, and it becomes a significant view of human nature with momentous implications. The *phenomenal* world of the person—the world as perceived through the senses—is the only world, the only reality. The phenomenological philosopher looks inward to examine his own consciousness of the objects that make up the external world.

The phenomenological psychologist adopts this basic conception of mind and turns it into a personality paradigm. One of two major approaches, Carl Rogers' person-centred theory, focuses on the self and processes leading toward individual growth and development ('self-actualization'). In this view, the experiences of self and the relation of self to others are central to personality; each individual's unique reality, his or her perceptions of self and self in relation to the world, is no less valid than any other's. A theory of psychotherapy proposes the conditions and therapeutic processes to enable people whose selves have been damaged to regain self-worth and to achieve their potential. The second approach, George Kelly's personal construct theory, is entirely concerned with the ways in which people construe their reality, with the constructs they develop to predict the world around them. In this version of the phenomenological paradigm, personality *is* the unique set of constructs developed by each and every person to account for the social events and the inanimate world he or she encounters.

As a personality paradigm, phenomenology leads quite directly to a deep respect for the experience of the individual. It endows everyone with an essential humanity. Humanistic psychology begins here, taking two of the principles above as givens: reality as defined by the person, and the potential for personal growth in all people. The humanistic view, expressed most clearly and forcefully by Abraham Maslow, upbraids psychology, particularly personality psychology, for dwelling in a negative, neurosis- and symptom-bound way on human inadequacy and personal failure. Humanism not only takes people as they are but sees the possibilities for them to become what they might be. It is a welcome corrective to a dark and pessimistic conception of human nature that appears especially in classical psychodynamic theory.

Existentialism

The philosophical movement known as existentialism was the child of nineteenth- and early twentieth-century European philosophers, phenomenologists notable among them. It took individual experience as its subject matter and, under the influence of its major protagonist, Martin Heidegger, the nature of being. Humans *are*, Heidegger held, by virtue of their being-in-the-world. World exists because there are beings to experience it and reveal their experience; human existence is defined in the only way it can be, said Heidegger, by being-in-the-world. This is elusive and not easy to get one's mind around. I think what Heidegger meant to emphasize is the immediacy of experience, the nature of it and of our existence, and what our experience and existence mean.

From here, existentialism arrives at some very difficult questions: Why am I here, born into a world and at a time I didn't choose? What shall I do? How shall I choose what to do, and what will guide my choices? How can I face my inevitable end? Existential ontology (the inquiry into the nature of being) doesn't let us off the hook. This is what life is like, it tells us, and we might as well face it. Reasoned, responsible choices, keeping faith, living authentically, and doing something with our open-ended freedom offer the best possibilities but do not—emphatically do not—confer immunity against anxiety, loneliness, and despair over the void of existence.

Existentialism came into its own in the years following the Second World War, appealing to those who had deeply suffered from the years of Nazi tyranny, the Holocaust, and the fear and privation brought by the war and its desolate aftermath. From a formal philosophy, it became a movement in psychology—a paradigm claiming to be a more honestly human psychology than any of its established rivals—and a form of psychotherapy to help people to live the tough life. Existentialists disparage the scientific analysis of human behaviour; more fundamentally, they do not believe that causation plays any role in human affairs. They offer a paradigm for understanding the human condition but not a theory.

Traits

The trait paradigm is the easiest of the seven to grasp because every person in the world makes use of it. All of us have the tools to identify consistencies in the behaviour of others: they are the trait words of our languages, and there are thousands of them. Each of us is an amateur trait psychologist, picking the words to describe the behaviour of the people we encounter: stingy, forgiving, affectionate, aggressive, trustworthy . . . We are often right, and our chosen trait words agree with those of others, but we can also fail to agree on the trait descriptions that characterize a person. And we have to acknowledge that amateur trait psychologists are not scientists we can depend on to develop a systematic trait theory of personality. We amateurs have contributed a beginning, however, giving scientists the body of words to characterize recognizable and consistent behaviour. Our contribution is the idea that everyday language contains all the information to construct a trait theory of personality.

The several thousand words in everyday language to describe people are too many to deal with, so this huge set has to be reduced. Then, with a manageable number, trait descriptions of large samples of people can be subjected to the sophisticated statistical techniques discussed in Chapter 15. The result is a small set of traits that represent all the dimensions of personality. Note that they are attributes of persons, not persons acting in, being influenced by, and influencing their environments. It is possible to incorporate the behavioural context—situations—in trait theories of personality, as Chapter 15 will show, but for the most part the trait paradigm is sharply focused on the enduring characteristics of people. Research in this paradigm applies personality traits to the prediction of trait-relevant behaviour, asking such questions as, 'Do persons scoring high in conscientiousness, agreeableness, or neuroticism behave in ways consistent with these traits?' 'Do the traits found among North Americans appear in Chinese, Germans, or Israelis, and do they predict the same behaviours?'

The Inheritance of Behaviour

It is certainly not new to propose that the major features of personality might be inherited. Until recently, personality theorists were hardly interested at all in the heritability of personal attributes, though the idea was a staple of nineteenth-century psychiatry and originated much earlier. Psychiatric disorder was commonly thought to be born of a 'hereditary taint'. The trouble was that there were no satisfactory methods at hand to investigate the inheritance of personality. In the late nineteenth century the amateur English scientist and psychologist Sir Francis Galton proposed the study of twins to explore the heritability of physical and psychological characteristics, but he misapplied the study and no one set him straight.

The genetics of personality needed viable research methods and robust measures to characterize personal dispositions. With the development of these after the middle of the twentieth century, behaviour genetics began to take giant steps. Personality tests for measuring traits and methods involving the study of twins and adoption provided the essentials, now complemented by the new methods of investigating genes described in Chapter 16. The behaviour genetics paradigm has established that many personality traits have substantial genetic contributions. We have only hints about what is actually inherited; the study of biochemical processes linked to personality traits and to genes, for example, is at an early stage. But stay tuned to this paradigm.

Observing People and Asking Questions

Before we dig into personality theory, here are descriptions of two episodes and some questions to suggest the kinds of things our theorists are concerned with and try to explain. Note that the incidents described do not come from the world of the comfortably normal. The people observed are in the grip of strong and uncontrolled feeling and are not managing it well. The questions that follow are mostly about significantly distressing experience. My choices are deliberate: I want to alert you to a major point that will come up later in this chapter—that we can learn about the perfectly normal from studying people who are beset by psychological difficulties.

(1)

A man and his wife, the pair of them sixty or so, are arguing in full view and hearing of their neighbours about the best way to pick up their grass cuttings. Their battle grows more furious by the moment. He stumps after his wife, gesticulating and red-faced in his rage, shaking the grass catcher at her. She literally runs from him, pushing the lawnmower as she goes, gasping at the effort required to move her ample bulk with such speed. What set off this argument? Was it one episode in a continuing story of domestic anger? What started it this time? Some almost innocent trigger? How did it escalate? And with such enmity between them, how do they remain together?

(2)

A large woman, ten-year-old daughter in tow, crosses the parking lot of a supermarket screaming obscenities at her child for opening her purse. The child, expressionless, tags along saying nothing. But the mother continues to berate, ugly words streaming from her mouth, across the lot to her car. Was this the pattern of her childrearing? Did it always take something trivial and inoffensive to set her off? And what was the effect on the child? What was she learning from her mother's lack of control over her anger? How would she turn out? What kind of parent will she make?

- Have you ever known someone who broke down, life in disarray, who couldn't function for a time? Someone who became severely depressed, say?
- Have you ever been temporarily crippled by anxiety, unable to contend with the situation facing you?
- Have you been touched by a loving and trusting relationship between two children, perhaps three and five years old, holding hands and happily chattering as they walk along with their mother? What is it in their development that has made them happy and loving?
- Have you wondered what makes each of us the way we are, what shapes our thinking and feeling, how we acquire the distinctive characteristics that make us both individual and like other humans?

Personality Theory in Psychology and Personality Theory as Science

To begin, we're going to look at the two distinctive attributes of the psychological study of personality: a *psychological perspective* and a *basis in science*. The second of these is the more fundamental, and we should take it up first.

Psychology, like all other sciences, subscribes to a set of beliefs about how we may best gain understanding of nature. Some of these beliefs constitute a set of assumptions about reality and how we may approach it, and other beliefs concern the best way to subject the world of objects and organisms to study. All sciences share a common core of assumptions and a procedural code, the scientific method. They begin with a kind of institutionalized skepticism, a way of suspending belief until the facts are clear. This is familiar territory, but it is of such importance that I want to risk going over old ground. Perhaps, though, this will be a review of the nature of science from a perspective that's not so well known to you and will give you a new view to consider.

The Assumptions and Methods of Science

Science requires a set of assumptions about events in nature, about how they occur and how to approach the study of them. These assumptions, outlined below, are absolutely essential, ones that, as scientists, we simply have to make. If we're not willing to grant them, there's no point in proceeding further.

Determinism

A cardinal belief in science is that the universe and all the things and organisms within it act in lawful and orderly ways. This assumption of determinism establishes the basis on which all scientific inquiry rests, and it is no less true of human action than any other

Figure 1.1 Some
assumptions of science

- **_Determinism:_** All events in nature act in lawful ways.
  - Is human behaviour lawfully determined?
  - What about free will?
- **_Discoverability:_** In principle, the laws governing all events are potentially discoverable.·
- **_Scientific method:_** A way of going about it.
- **_Potential human benefit:_** It is part of the scientific credo that knowledge gained by science is potentially beneficial to humans and to nonhuman creatures.

events. So, we believe that all human behaviour—the overt things we can observe and the covert ones like thinking and feeling that take place unobserved—is lawfully determined. We may not know all the laws, but our behaviour is nonetheless obedient to them.

The test of any assumption lies in its consequences, and there are two that follow from the assumption of psychological determinism. The first is that humans are biological organisms, and it is difficult to believe that human behaviour, which we know to be registered in and controlled by the brain, somehow rises above lawfulness. The second consequence is found in the answer to the question _Is human behaviour predictable?_. Most of our personality theorists take it as given that with the relevant facts in hand we can predict behaviour accurately.

We have no objection to the idea that dogs, cats, or laboratory animals act in predictable ways, nor do we object to the idea that our bodies are lawfully regulated biological systems. Indeed, we're thankful that they are, for it means that medicine can treat us scientifically. But when it comes to how we think, feel, and act, the determinism assumption challenges our faith in _free will_, questioning our freedom to make any choice we wish at any moment. We don't want to concede that how we think, feel, and act is determined by heredity, our nervous systems, our past experience right up to the present moment, and the immediate situation. We pin our faith on the idea—no vain conceit, this—that we are our own masters, capable of conscious and deliberate choice.

If it is true that our thought, feeling, and action are determined—and I can sense your reluctance—then just what is 'free will'? Free will is a belief, a personal theory, about our individual freedom of choice. Calling it a belief is not to diminish its importance to us; we're deeply committed to the idea that we are free to choose how we act. We have personal theories about a lot of things, not only free will. Why we made a certain choice, why we did badly in a course, how it was that we got along especially well with someone. . . . But while personal theories explain and usually satisfy us with their accounts, they are not examined, not subjected to critical observation and test. Scientific theories are.

Freud was emphatic in his insistence that our behaviour and our cognitive and emotional lives are determined by biological makeup and experience. Why, he demanded, should **psychic energy★**, the energy behind thought, feeling, and action, differ in principle from the physical energy of bodily processes except in the form of its expression? Freud held that there are no accidents in thought or behaviour. Most other personality theorists agree. Not all, however. We'll encounter a couple who believe that humans can rise above their individual biology and the past.

Some final questions for you on the issue of free will: Could biological organisms behave _non_-lawfully? Is human behaviour predictable? What evidence can you think of? What's the problem when we can't predict behaviour? Throughout this book, theory by theory, you will need to be alert to the determinism assumption and how each theorist handles it.

Discoverability

Discoverability is the assumption that the laws controlling the events we study are *potentially* discoverable—in other words, there are, in principle, no closed doors. Consider what this means for the claim we sometimes hear people make: 'Oh, you'll never understand that. People can never really be understood.' Of course, at any time there is an enormity of questions we cannot answer and an infinity of them we can't even formulate. Science, however, is always looking for new ways to think about phenomena and new approaches to study them. It is, if you'll permit an operatic simile, like Don Giovanni in constant search of new conquests. The discoverability assumption is a way of thinking about our prospects. Nothing, it asserts, is potentially inexplicable.

Scientific Method

There is a set of methods by which we can submit hypotheses (the beliefs or ideas that theories generate) to the test of sense experience to determine whether they are true or false. This assumption means that we can set questions and devise procedures in such a way as to generate answers in the form of observations that may be checked and repeated. This way of asking questions and answering them is the scientific method.

Potential Human Benefit

The accumulation of scientific knowledge offers the potential to improve and enhance life. Science can also, as we're well aware, introduce dangers. We know about the perils revealed by nuclear fission and fusion. We have serious questions about some current research in molecular biology and genetics—research that makes it possible to alter heredity. Psychological techniques of influence, in the hands of unscrupulous demagogues, may be used to brainwash, inflame, or prejudice. A particular source of controversy surrounds investigations into ethnic differences in intelligence, with some psychologists asking how far we should pursue this research. Herrenstein and Murray, in a book titled *The Bell Curve* (1994), argued that there are such differences and that the effect of them on American society is disastrous. Whatever the merit of such an argument and the evidence adduced in its favour (the argument has critical flaws and the evidence doesn't support it), is it inflammatory and socially destructive? There may well be a risk from both well-supported and questionable science, but risks from expanding knowledge cannot be avoided. We generally believe that it is better to know and to keep seeking. The closed mind is worse.

Having reviewed the assumptions of science, we'll now examine its methods. This set of scientific beliefs is about how to go about scientific inquiry; it constitutes a code of procedure. Science is a prescription for telling someone how to experience what we have observed. This prescription is not in principle different from things we all do in our daily lives and that humans have always done in making sense of their environments. But science goes further. At the heart of the scientific method are six basic attributes— the *essential ingredients* of the prescription.

An Attitude of Willingness to Submit Ideas to Test

This sounds so obvious and easy that we hardly need think about it—but it isn't. Sometimes, even in science, we see the triumph of belief—personal conviction—over an honest and fair scientific test. A notorious example in psychology is the monumental fraud of Englishman Sir Cyril Burt, who was utterly convinced that intelligence is inherited (Hearnshaw, 1979). The only method then (and one on which we still rely) was to compare by correlation the IQs of pairs of subjects of varying degrees of biological relationship (see Chapter 16). The most critical data come from identical twins (who are genetic duplicates of each other) reared apart from an early age. Identical twins are a rare population, and separation makes it rarer. Studies do exist, but there aren't a great many of them and only a few in the period from the 1930s to the 1960s. It was discovered after Burt's death that the impressive twin studies he reported, showing very high IQ correspondence, were fabricated. He had even made up a research assistant, 'Miss Jane Conway', with whom he published!

Fortunately, we do have safeguards. A shared passion in science for true knowledge is one of them. Another is that there are usually many scientists investigating a given question, and it is most unlikely that numbers of them will be so committed to a particular belief as to bend the data to support it.

A Way of Putting Ideas into Questions that Observation Can Answer

Ideas are abstract, and we have to find a way to put them into the form of questions that will yield empirical answers. These are usually *how* questions rather than *why* questions. The reason is that *how* questions direct us to look at processes—how, for example, motives develop in young children, rather than why.

Operationism

Science requires us to translate abstract ideas into specific procedures capable of being measured and described. We define ideas by the procedures (called *operations*) we use to measure them. Concepts are thus tied to reality, to things we can actually observe.

Theories of personality are full of abstract concepts, and the operational trick is to make them concrete, unambiguous, and testable. There are concepts in some theories that resist operational definition; they are imprecisely stated and do not clearly imply specific measurement procedures. Look out for those and mark down any theory in which you find them. In other theories, concepts are explicitly defined and operational. They deserve full marks.

Observation of the Relevant Events

Good procedure demands that we have objective, systematic, standardized observations that can be repeated by others. At the same time, we need to be alert to the new and unexpected—as James Watson and Francis Crick were in the discovery of the double helix form of the DNA molecule. At the time (1953), other investigators were close, but Watson and Crick had the edge in seeing DNA's ladder-like arrangement. It couldn't but have helped that late one night Crick ran down a spiral staircase to tell Watson, below, of his solution to the DNA riddle (Watson, 1968). This is a demanding ingredient.

Careful Description

We need an objective, precise, 'thing-oriented' language, a language that points to the objects of our observation. Everyday language is often subjective and impression-oriented; derived from popular culture, it is hardly a language for testable hypotheses. Most personality theorists agree on the need for a precise scientific language, but not all.

THE SCIENTIFIC STUDY OF PERSONALITY

Some are preoccupied with subjective meaning rather than objectivity. This is another issue on which to scrutinize theories closely.

Logical Inference

Science is the union of **induction★** (observation and accumulation of sense experience) and **deduction★** (logical derivation by strict rules). The deduction of hypotheses—predictions about consequences yet to be observed—and the conclusions we may draw from verified (or disconfirmed) predictions must follow strict rules of logic. Logical inference must also guide generalization from a limited set of observations to all relevant instances, including instances not yet observed. We don't want to restrict our conclusions to the specific subjects, time, and place of a given set of observations—for instance, well-to-do Viennese patients in psychoanalysis, a sample of students at a particular university serving in an experiment on repression. Our interest is in personality processes and motivated forgetting in *all* people. This is the issue of **external validity★**. Another element in this ingredient is *logical analysis*: we need to think of the relation of ideas to observable things. Logical analysis is the process by which we clarify the relation of concepts to observables.

The essential ingredients get us a long way, but they are not infallible. Two *higher-order ingredients* greatly improve on the essentials.

Higher-Order Ingredients: The Experiment

The experiment introduces rigorous procedures that enable us to draw more certain conclusions about the conditions under which an event occurs and about the causal connections between events. The experiment makes it possible for us to **manipulate★** the variable(s) that we think are responsible for a phenomenon. Here is an example. Schachter (1959) tested the hypothesis that people who were the first born in their families want the reassuring company of others when afraid. He induced anxiety in experimental participants by telling them the experiment would involve strong electric shock; he then looked for birth-order differences in the desire to be with others while waiting for the experiment to begin. If the hypothesis were true, anxious first-born participants should want company; first-born participants in a control group (not frightened) shouldn't care, nor should the later-born in either group. We'll consider this research in greater detail in Chapter 4.

When we manipulate a variable to study it experimentally, we're controlling it. This is the principle of **control★**. We also hold constant (that is, control) other variables that might affect the outcome so that we can see what the experimental variable alone does. This kind of control is exercised over variables whose effects might be mixed up, or *confounded*, with those of the variable in which we are interested. In many experiments, control appears in the form of a control group that provides a baseline against which to compare the experimental group receiving the manipulation. The control group receives exactly the same treatment as the experimental group except for the experimental manipulation.

The controlled experiment gives us the critical possibility of replicating complex observations. To achieve control of the variables in an experiment we try to simplify the complex real world, paring it down to the essential features we wish to study. An

Figure 1.2 The methods of science: A prescription

Essential ingredients	Higher-order ingredients
• *Willingness* to test ideas	• The *experiment*
• Putting ideas into *questions*	– The principle of *control*
• *Operationism:* how we define ideas	• *Quantification*
• *Observation*	
• *Careful description*	
• *Logical inference*	

experiment, thus, is an abstraction from nature, nature without all the confusing details that could obscure the real cause of the behaviour under investigation.

Higher-order Ingredients: Quantification

Science introduces another higher-order ingredient: **quantification★**, the precision of quantifying data and mathematically analyzing them to determine the probability that research findings are not determined by chance. There is inevitable variability, even in the data of carefully controlled experiments, and statistical probabilities tell us the likelihood that differences in an experiment (between experimental and control groups, for example) are within or outside that variability. Further, in some areas of psychology, mathematical psychologists have developed models of basic processes—conditioning and learning, for example, and artificial intelligence. Trait theories (discussed in Chapter 15) make extensive use of quantitative techniques to discover the essential dimensions of personality.

Research Methods In Personality

The Experiment

We'll start our look at research methods in personality by considering the place of the experiment, that most powerful of all investigative methods. To control and manipulate cause is to know it. There are, however, many questions for which we cannot design an experiment. An experiment may be premature when we try to apply it to a little-understood problem. And an experiment is often impossible because we can't ethically or practically impose its treatment techniques on people—we can't, for example, make people *very* angry or *very* afraid. Further, experimental techniques to produce the effect we predict may simply not exist. For instance, we can't *create* personality characteristics in the laboratory by experimental manipulations, nor can experimental manipulations change longstanding and deeply rooted personality characteristics. An experiment is not the procedure of choice when we wish to see the natural development of behaviour—children's acquisition of language, say, or how they develop elemental operations of thinking and reasoning. Or again, we won't look to the experiment to tell us how children acquire important and powerful social motives, or the processes by which some children become disturbed or predisposed to break down later in adulthood. Finally, the laboratory no longer suffices when we reach the point in research on some experimental problem when we want to *verify* the experimental findings to see how they occur in life situations. Of necessity, then, non-experimental approaches have an important place in psychology and a very important place in the study of human personality.

The experimental study of personality is a formidable challenge. Each person has a distinctive profile of psychological attributes—motives, ways of organizing experience in perception and thought, beliefs and attitudes, and actions. How could that profile be reduced to dimensions that experiments could cope with? Personality is also enduring: we begin to acquire the distinctive characteristics that make us individuals early in life, and those characteristics become firmly resistant to change. How could we hope to modify personality by experimental manipulation?

The experimental study of personality *is* indeed possible, but it requires that we investigate one or at most a very few variables at a time. But this means we surrender a good part of the richness and vitality that come with studying the striving, the loving and hating, the emotional extremes, and even the failures of people living their lives. These are serious deterrents to the experimental study of persons, and partly because of them the study of personality developed elsewhere.

So what kinds of situations *would* lend themselves to the close and intimate observation necessary to see the expression of individual personality? The answer is, not many. It's hard to find observational vantage points from which to study individual persons close up. One such vantage point stands out, however, because it uniquely affords the opportunity to listen to people talking about their lives in the fullest detail. In this situation, people do not talk casually or abstractly. They talk, rather, with all the emotional intensity and coloration that come from lives marred by psychological symptoms and conflict. This is the clinical relationship of patient and psychotherapist, and the form of the psychological inquiry is known as the **clinical method★**.

Personality theory began as clinical theory, growing out of the treatment of psychologically disturbed persons. The research method is the **case study★**, the study in depth of individual persons. Much of contemporary personality theory was built on the foundation of the clinical method. Here is where the observations came from. Here is where hypotheses were formulated and tested. Since the clinical method has been so important to the development of personality theory, we necessarily have to ask about its adequacy as a research method.

The Clinical Method

The word *clinical*, from a Greek word for *bed*, refers to the bedside treatment of patients; it also refers to the course of a patient's disease. It was at the patient's sickbed that disease ran its course, and so it was here that medicine was most often practised. In the beginning of his work with neurotic patients, Freud often treated them in their bedchambers. Home visitation is a relic of a genteel past: modern psychological and psychiatric practice takes place in offices, but the adjective *clinical* still retains the sense of the old meaning. In psychology and psychiatry, the word denotes contact with people who are disturbed or ill, contact with them for the broad purpose of diagnosis and treatment. The word *clinical* distinguishes psychologists and psychiatrists who practice professionally, but I want to emphasize that clinicians often do research, contributing to applied—and sometimes theoretical—knowledge.

The clinical method is a general term for a body of techniques used to study individuals in depth, and a context or setting with special attributes. It relies on many techniques:

- the interview, often specialized to explore personality in depth;
- tests, both psychological and physical (the neurological examination, for example);
- observation of behaviour;

- simply listening to people as they struggle to express feelings and relate experiences;
- the interpretations that clinicians may make to clarify and guide the process of self-understanding, and how patients react to them.

To summarize, the important attributes of the clinical method are both a general context and focus on understanding individual persons *and* the specific techniques used. In the hands of an accomplished clinician, the tools of the clinical method can become instruments of discovery, instruments turned to the problem of understanding the meaning of disturbed behaviour and to the more general problem of understanding human personality.

The clinical situation is an unparalleled 'window to mental life', as two of our theorists, John Dollard and Neal Miller, once characterized it (Dollard & Miller, 1950, p. 3). This is true even though we most often use it as a window to look in on disturbed, damaged personalities. The idea that we use the study of disturbed persons to make inferences about human personality may be disquieting to you. I'd like you to consider that this may not be the disadvantage it seems at first to be. There are powerful reasons to believe that disturbed personalities differ from the normal only in *degree*, not in kind. The same laws are at work in all individuals, but what we see are more extreme expressions of them in abnormal persons. This is a point to which we'll return later in the chapter.

What can we say about the clinical method as science? Is it really scientific? And if we conclude that it is, is it good science? I think there is little question that when the clinical method is well conducted the essential ingredients are there:

- the attitude of willingness to submit ideas to test
- the formulation of potentially answerable questions
- operationally defined concepts
- careful observation
- objective description
- the logical pursuit of generalizations

Each of these ingredients is part of the clinical process.

The clinical method requires both astute observation and the ability to tease general principles out of apparently unrelated details. But the sheer mass of data to be assimilated in clinical interactions with persons is formidable, and the clinical task is both observationally and conceptually demanding. In an ongoing interaction, it is very difficult to keep sharply attuned to all the things the patient may be saying or doing and, hardly a breath later, to think about what these words and actions might signify. Consider the following, an experience of psychoanalyst Frieda Fromm-Reichmann (1959):

> One day, this patient urinated, before I came to see her, on the seat of the chair on which I was supposed to be seated during our interview. I did not see that the chair was wet. The patient did not warn me, and I sat down. I became aware of the situation only after the dampness had penetrated my clothing (p. 202).

What to do? She couldn't ignore it, even if she had been willing to endure the discomfort. The patient knew that her analyst had to know. What to say, not in a matter of seconds, but immediately? And what to say that would ideally recognize a hostile intent without therapeutic damage? Fromm-Reichmann went on:

I thereupon expressed my disgust in no uncertain terms. Then I stated that I had to go home. The patient asked anxiously about my coming back, which I refused with the explanation that the time allotted to our interview would be over by the time I had taken a bath and attended to my soiled clothes (p. 202).

To say this, she had to be certain—with no time to reflect on it—that her patient could take the rebuke and loss of her therapy hour. Thankfully, clinical interactions don't often confront us with the sudden and revolting, but they do present, moment-by-moment, great demands on our ability to observe, remember, think, and respond.

How adequate is the clinical method? Does it produce evidence that withstands exacting examination? The question is a necessary one. It is to ask about the adequacy of a research method. The first thing to note is that while the clinical method includes the essential ingredients discussed earlier, it lacks the most important feature of the higher-order ingredients—*control*. The clinician simply cannot bring under control all the potential influences on the behaviour and talking he or she observes and hears. We have to acknowledge that the clinical method is vulnerable on this point. The wonderfully intimate view of people that the clinical method affords comes at a stiff price: acceptance of largely uncontrolled observation. With that comes some serious difficulty in enabling others to see what we may have seen. We have another problem, then, with the *replicability* of clinical observations. Please don't take this as an argument to eliminate the clinical method from the scientist's bag of techniques. Intelligently used, it provides a great wealth of observational data. I want to persuade you that we need *both* the clinical and experimental methods.

The clinical method provides observational detail that is otherwise impossible to obtain, detail that cannot be gained from experimental study. It is also fertile soil in which to cultivate hypotheses. The experimental method provides a rigorous testing ground in which we can carefully manipulate variables we think may be significant and hold potentially confounding ones constant. Often, we can then come back to life situations (or the clinical situation) to determine whether experimental findings are borne out in complex, ongoing behaviour. Later, when we study the learning theory of Dollard and Miller, Rotter's social learning theory, and Bandura's social cognitive theory, we'll see how elegantly the clinical method and the experimental method can be combined.

An Introduction to the Nature of Personality

Perspective 1.1   Will the Real John Crowen Please Stand Up?

My grandfather was christened John H. Crowen, the second son of Irish immigrant parents. He was born in New York City, in the infamous lower east side ghetto known as the Five Points. His year of birth was 1854, although as an adult he would variously claim it as 1855, 1856, 1857, 1858, or 1860. His father had arrived from Ireland only a few years before and taken a job as a porter, one of the menial jobs available to Irishmen. Six years after John's birth, he opened a small fancy goods and upholstery shop, later expanding to furniture, in Brooklyn. As they grew up, his sons—four of them—joined him as clerks in the store.

In his early twenties, John was still living at home and working for his father, but at twenty-six he had a new occupation as a signpainter. At thirty, he moved out, to a place of his own nearby. Four years later, on the death of his mother, he returned home to care for his father, in the terminal stages of syphilis, looking after him for the last two years of his life.

We seem to have a picture of a dutiful son in a close-knit family, and that may have been the case. Was there, though, a simmering resentment—at his brothers for failing to pitch in when help was sorely needed, and at his father for the humiliation of his disease? No sooner had his father died than John moved out, changed his surname by inverting the last two letters, and completely turned his back on his brothers. He would have nothing to do with them for the rest of his life. The break wasn't his fault, he insisted—one of his brothers had switched the family name from Crowne to Crowen! John couldn't abide being in the wrong and made the Crowens the villains of the piece.

There is more. We have to ask an inevitable question about John's change of name and rejection of his family: had he come to hold in contempt his whole working-class, Irish immigrant background? A carpenter, an upholsterer, and a printer as brothers, a father paying the ultimate penance for sexual licence? And how could a man who believed himself destined to be someone of substance stand to be the butt of then popular Irish jokes and caricatures? Ireland? The country of his father's birth was itself a joke. Abject poverty and famine had driven its young away; what could possibly inspire pride of origin in the immigrant sons of a poor benighted country like that?

Married at thirty-seven, he left Brooklyn for Queens, only ten miles but a whole world away, and started a family—a daughter in 1893 and a son, my father, in 1896. The new John Crowne was a gifted signpainter who could letter in gold leaf, but his aims were higher. Proud to a fault, he began to identify himself as a designer—no longer just a renderer of signs but an imaginative creator of them. His fancy title, uncommon in those days, elevated him to the level of a professional. He taught himself drafting and became highly skilled in mechanical drawing. When, in the 1920s, my father was invited to submit an entry for the *Encyclopaedia Britannica* on electromagnetism, he asked his father to do the drawings.

The new John Crowne established more than a high-flown occupation. No connection to his family name or Irish heritage remained, and he began to claim that he was born in a covered wagon on the way to California. This was his story to the end of his life. My father never knew that he was, but for the reversing of those letters, a Crowen, one generation removed from the old sod. John Crowne was diligent and creative in his work and provided an adequate living for his family. Measured against a burning need for stature and recognition, though, life at the lower end of the middle class was a constant disappointment. Try as he might, this was as high as he could reach. He had never been a warm and easygoing man, and a certain dour quality that could border on bitterness became more and more evident.

He survived the Great Depression, but it did him no favours; there was a small market for the design of handsome signs in an economy with a quarter of its work force unable to find a job. Just scraping by, he was unable to set money aside for retirement. So, in his late seventies, no longer able to find steady work, he and his wife were forced to take the third-floor bedroom in his daughter and son-in-law's house and to rely on them wholly for support. He did get the occasional sign to paint, but that was for pin money. His days were spent in telling ever-taller tales of his youth and exploits to his grandson, who became his captive audience. The stories were thrilling, if doubtful, and young boys need their freedom. It was not an easy relationship. He lived into the 1940s, a sad and embittered old man. Even his son did not go to visit him.

Who was John Crowne—or John Crowen? How shall we capture him in a personality portrait? Can we look to the fourteen personality theories that are to come for help in describing him? We certainly can, but we shall have to accept not one but fourteen different versions. From psychoanalysis to radical behaviourism, no two theories will etch the same profile of this complex man. It's not necessarily a bad thing to question the science of personality. With sketchy data (all I can supply, unfortunately) and a person who showed many faces over his lifetime, it should be no surprise that theories with unique emphases and concepts would each see him differently. Could all fourteen John Crownes be equally he? I venture to say that every one of them would accurately represent some features and minimize or fail to recognize others. I don't think that should discourage you as you begin the study of personality theory. Rather, you should be impressed with the difficulty of the task, with how complicated an undertaking it is to depict personality. Remember John Crowne as we go along and try to picture him in the terms of each theory.

Defining Personality

In everyday usage, the term *personality* refers to our impressions of someone. We say such things as 'He has an abrasive personality,' or 'She has a shy, retiring personality.' This makes personality a kind of shorthand for a person's **social stimulus value★**—a way of summarizing how that person strikes us. The trouble with this sort of definition is that it defines personality by the subjective impressions of others (observers), whose relationships to the person characterized may often be quite different and may be coloured by the preferences and feelings of each observer. How someone's personality is described by others may also strongly reflect the observational situation. Hockey games, classrooms, or an interview with a psychologist are just not going to produce identical behaviour in the same person.

Although personality impressions can provide interesting and provocative data about how people form judgements of others, they aren't useful in helping us to get beneath the surface and to think about the origins of human action. For psychologists, personality has a more challenging and more elemental meaning. It refers to those inferred attributes and processes, visible in behaviour or not, that make each person individually unique. We're good behaviourists, we personality psychologists, and we are interested in how people behave. But we—except for the radical behaviourists we'll encounter later on—want to know more than that. We want to know what's behind action—what we refer to as the **potentialities★** for action—and how those potentialities are organized and integrated.

Behaviour is what we have to observe and what we seek to predict. But nearly all personality theorists think that simply to describe behaviour is too limiting. Radical behaviourists like B.F. Skinner have wished to limit psychology to describing the behaviour of organisms (people no less than rats and pigeons) and the stimulus conditions under which behaviour is emitted, and they do not exempt the psychology of personality. There are powerful things that can be done with such an approach, but it is also severely restricting. Most personality psychologists, then, seek to understand the motives that impel people to act and that direct their choices of action. That means developing procedures—observational, clinical, experimental, and those techniques used to elicit self-descriptive responses from people that we call personality tests—to provide sources of inference about motivational processes.

Persons and Situations

The study of personality is also the study of **situations**⋆—the specific contexts in which behaviour takes place. We might say that personality is expressed in the meeting of person and situation. While it may seem odd to suggest that potentialities for action and the unique way they are organized within a person should be strongly influenced by the situations in which behaviour takes place, that's the way it is. We can't understand personality without understanding important life situations and how individuals interpret them. So in the modern study of personality, we say that it is the study of person–situation interactions.

Previous experience and individual motives are shapers of our thoughts, feelings, and actions, but so, too, are situations. Learning about important life situations starts in infancy, and experiences throughout development vastly extend, fill in, and colour the understanding of situations. The infant whose cries and restlessness subside moments *before* sucking begins shows by that small anticipatory act an important achievement in learning about feeding and its relation to security. In the first year of school, children master some basic features of achievement situations—hand-raising to speak, to ask questions, or for permission to leave the room; turn-taking; and what we might call a format for behaviour that sometimes tends to make individual accomplishment a pursuit of social conformity and approval. Children first acquire their appreciation of male–female relationships and sex-defined roles by observation of their parents, and adolescent interactions amplify, alter, and sometimes overturn what has been learned from parental models about how we get along with the opposite sex. Not every person

Is this classroom situation the same for each of these children? (© Royalty-Free/CORBIS)

learns the same things from the same kinds of situations. Individuals react distinctively, showing the influence of their past experiences on their perceptions of new situations.

As we consider each personality theory, you should ask how adequately each theorist deals with this important concept of person–situation interaction. You will find some theorists who fail to recognize the principle of person–situation interaction, who don't grasp the essential idea, and you will find some who clearly do understand and whose theories reflect that understanding. The theories of this second group are able to account for the varied outcomes of persons experiencing and acting in different situations.

Theories of Personality from Study of the Disturbed?

We need to consider one further aspect of the nature of personality. It is that many of the important concepts in present-day personality theory reflect an origin in the study and treatment of disturbed behaviour. Concepts like anxiety, conflict, stress, defence mechanisms, and displacement are just a few examples. Personality psychologists make an assumption—I referred to it earlier—that there is no discontinuity between disturbed or abnormal behaviour and behaviour that we would consider normal. There is, rather, a continuum—a continuous distribution or gradual shading of normal into disturbed. That is to say, the same psychological processes found among the disturbed will be seen among normal people in less extreme form. The differences, then, are differences in *degree*, not differences in *kind* (or qualitative differences). This was a major point of Freud's, one we'll see represented in almost all of the personality theories we study. We may call it the **continuity assumption★**. Let me illustrate it for you by taking two concepts as examples, concepts that apply over the whole span from perfectly normal to extremely disturbed.

First, let's consider fantasy. We all spend considerable time each day in fantasy. We plan, we anticipate pleasant occurrences or problems, we work out disappointments and frustrations, and we deal with periods in which our moods are down. Fantasy—imaginative activity—is both a delight and a way of working through the painful and difficult. Imagine, now, fantasy expressed in a more extreme way, fantasy that involves withdrawal from active participation with others, self-preoccupation, and utter absorption in a private world. Try imagining this to the degree that is called *autism*—an immersion in fantasy so intense that the line between fantasy and reality becomes blurred and indistinct. Can you accept that there is no sharp dividing line between the fantasy in which we all engage and this 'abnormal' version? A shy schoolchild, turned inward and disdaining relationships with other children, may fall somewhere toward the abnormal end of the fantasy continuum. A schizophrenic patient might be at the far end, lost in fantastic and bizarre thoughts and unable to test reality.

My second example concerns the harbouring of beliefs that others do not share. A number of years ago, Cameron (1959) proposed an intriguing idea about the origin of

Figure 1.3 The continuity assumption: Differences in degree, not differences in kind, between normal and psychologically disturbed persons

Differences in degree, not in kind, between normal and disturbed
We can draw conclusions about normal personality from studying disturbed persons

paranoid delusion. To illustrate Cameron's notion, let's think of a common experience, one most of us have had. We come upon a group of acquaintances who suddenly stop talking as we approach. This is certainly upsetting; most of us are inclined to jump immediately to the conclusion that the discussion was about us and was surely not complimentary. But we often find that a first impression like this was based on a misperception. We're able to ask a member of the group just what or who was being talked about, or we might be able to take the perspective of members of the group and figure out the topic of the conversation. We all have experiences of social misperception, but in the course of our development most of us have acquired considerable skill in role-taking that helps to recognize the meaning of a huge variety of social situations, to take perspective on our own behaviour, and to approach others when there is a misunderstanding to straighten out.

Suppose, however, that someone has had defective experience in testing reality so effectively and has no skill in correcting misperceptions. This person is likely to have the same kinds of experiences that you and I have had in sometimes misinterpreting the behaviour and motives of others. Because of his or her limited social knowledge and ability, however, there isn't any way to recover from the error. Here may be the beginning of suspicion and mistrust and the insidious origin of a more extreme development—a paranoid delusion. We can't let distressing things go without explanation, and the delusional idea is just such an attempt to explain and understand. I'd like you to appreciate that a role-taking accomplishment we take for granted is a matter of degree: some have it in spades, most are reasonably good, and then there are a few who are badly lacking. The least adept are at risk to develop suspiciousness of others and, in more extreme form, paranoid delusion.

I hope these examples may help to persuade you that in the study of disturbed persons we can learn about human behaviour in general—about *both* disturbed *and* normal behaviour. It is important that you give a fair hearing to the continuity assumption; it is a pillar on which theories of personality rest.

The Nature of Personality Theory

Personality theories are general behaviour theories. They are concerned in principle with *all* human behaviour. We could say that a personality theory develops a model of the human, but we have to be clear about an important point: not every personality theory presents a complete model, and we'll see that each theory has its own special emphasis. Some theories are good at explaining some things and not good at all at explaining others. For example, we can have a personality theory that gives a clear account of the development of social relationships in childhood on the basis of modelling parental behaviour. Such a theory could help us to understand how it is that some children become aggressive through observation of their parents. Another theory may do an excellent job with clinical phenomena such as crippling anxiety, sadism and masochism, or how maladaptive behaviour patterns develop. This theory might have less to say about parent–child relationships and their influence on personality development, focusing instead on inferred processes within the developing child. Each theory has—as my one-time colleague George Kelly was fond of saying—a 'focus of convenience', a range of events it is specifically devised to deal with (Kelly, 1955, p. 11). Outside its focus, there are likely to be areas in which any theory is not very explicit.

The model of humankind that most personality theories develop is a *representation* of the real flesh-and-blood person. We need to be very clear about this. Theories make assumptions about the nature of the world (in our case, the human being), assumptions that are 'as if' constructions. 'Suppose reality [human nature] followed this plan,' they say. 'What consequences would then ensue?' The model envisioned by psychoanalysis, for example, assumes that people are forever at war within themselves. Against their own instinctual impulses, which are inevitably socially destructive, are arrayed powerful repressive forces that represent the view of society. Within the first few years of life, these repressive forces are incorporated within individual personality. This model sees humans as perpetual victims of inner conflict. Psychoanalysis goes on to make further assumptions about how these conflicting forces are balanced and controlled. Other theories make different assumptions and arrive at different consequences. They do not model the person in the same way.

Theory and Fiction

To extend what I have just said about representations, assumptions, and models, let me add this: that the concepts of any theory are *fictions,* inventive constructions of the theorist. Is the nature of theory, then, only a less fanciful version of the fictional creations of a novel? Let's compare the two. Fiction evolves from the experiences of the writer. So, too, do scientific concepts. They come from the experience of the scientist/theorist, from his or her observations, which suggest concepts to explain things that are puzzling, that we don't understand. Second, the novel gives order and meaning to experience. So, also, do scientific concepts. Third, fiction paints a picture of reality. The novelist tells it like it is, but 'how it is' is merely how he or she sees the world; other pictures exist. Scientific concepts do no less. They are also ways of capturing reality.

Here, the parallel ends. Scientific concepts have two other attributes. First, they are phrased in precise, objective language (ideally, anyway), as we earlier considered. And, second, scientific concepts entail a check: predictions can be derived about events not yet observed, in order to test whether the outcomes confirm or refute the concepts.

Now what, more exactly, does this notion of the fictional nature of scientific concepts mean? Just this: each personality theory is made up of constructions invented by the theorist to account for behaviour. Freud's concept of the ego as the executor of personality, the planner, the mediator, was intended to explain a whole class of observations about

Table 1.1   Scientific concepts and fiction share several attributes, but scientific concepts go further.

Fiction	Scientific Concepts
1. Evolves from experience	1. Evolve from experience
2. Order & meaning	2. Order & meaning
3. How things 'work'	3. How things 'work'
	4. Precise language
	5. A 'check:' prediction of new events

behaviour and how it is regulated. We can't see the ego nor can we measure it directly. It has no reality. Ego is an abstraction, a shorthand way of summarizing and thinking about many varieties of thought, feeling, and action. And this is so with all theories: their concepts are similarly abstractions. It's very important to remember, then, that the scientific test of a theoretical concept really concerns its *usefulness*. That is, does the concept enable us to predict behaviour, the specific behaviour the concept is supposed to account for? Psychoanalysis as a theory is a set of assumptions about the dynamic interactions of three processes labelled *id*, *ego*, and *superego* and how they emerge in personality in the course of development. As a set of assumptions, psychoanalytic theory (or any other theory) can neither be proved nor disproved. Rather, we try to derive from the theory predictions or truth claims (*hypotheses*) about observations to be made that are relevant to the theory.

Falsifiability

The real check on theory is what we call **falsifiability**★. Falsifiability means simply that the truth claims of a theory are potentially *disconfirmable*, that they can be disproved. This is very strict but—if we truly want to know—inescapable. The doctrine of falsifiability demands that we genuinely put theoretical concepts to test. We let observations decide whether the prediction is true or false by going out of our way to give the theoretical prediction a chance to be wrong if it really is. We don't want to 'baby' the theory by setting up our tests in such a way that the theory could never be proved wrong. For each of the theories we study, a question that must be asked is whether it sets up truth claims that are truly falsifiable, or whether its claims are nonspecific and could not be honestly tested.

SUMMARY

1. Personality theories are concerned with the most significant questions about human behaviour, thought, and emotion. They focus on motivation as well as action, and each theory specifies the ways in which human cognitive and emotional life are determined. Theories of personality are also, in part, theories of development from childhood to maturity and old age. They are especially concerned with the psychological characteristics that make each person unique. Most theories address questions of stress and the processes behind personality disorders. It is important to understand that personality theories are scientific theories; their accounts of personality and its development ideally generate hypotheses that can be empirically tested. Some are more successful as scientific theories than others, however.

2. Twenty-two major theories of personality are covered in this book. They fall into seven paradigms that offer distinct views of the psychological makeup of the human animal. Each paradigm represents a common theme, a general theoretical framework that the theories within it share. The paradigms are the following:
   - *Psychodynamic*, beginning with psychoanalysis and including the ego psychologies of Anna Freud, Heinz Hartmann, and Erik Erikson and the Analytic Psychology of Carl Gustav Jung.
   - *Family, Society, and Culture*, the theories of Alfred Adler, Erich Fromm, Harry Stack Sullivan, and Karen Horney, each proposing that personality structures are moulded by family and social/cultural influences.
   - *Learning and Personality*, a set of theories derived from the psychology of learning that make use of process concepts to account for the acquisition, maintenance, and change of behaviour. The theories are Stimulus–Response (John Dollard and Neal Miller), Social–Cognitive (Julian Rotter, Albert Bandura, and Walter Mischel), and Radical Behaviourism (B.F. Skinner).

- *Phenomenology and Humanism*, the theories of Carl Rogers and George Kelly, emphasizing the proposition that all behaviour derives from the personal experience of the individual, and stressing the human potential for growth and development.
- *Existentialism*, represented by the theory of R.D. Laing, which focuses on the challenges of life, the severe dilemmas faced by the self-reflective human organism, and the possibilities for coping with the inevitable anxieties of existence.
- *Trait* theories, which define personality by a small constellation of attributes characteristic of each person, shown in consistent behaviour across situations. The theorists are Gordon Allport, Raymond Cattell, Hans Eysenck, and several who propose five-factor (trait) versions.
- *The Inheritance of Behaviour*, a theoretical approach that uses a variety of genetic methods to discover the heritability of personality traits.

3. The scientific discipline of psychology subscribes—like all sciences—to a set of assumptions about how to study its particular subject matter. These assumptions are absolutely essential to scientific study. There are four of them:
   - *Determinism*, the assumption that events in nature are lawfully regulated and act in orderly ways. This assumption extends to human behaviour, thought, and feeling, despite our belief in free will. In a scientific sense, free will is a *personal* theory that accounts for the way we choose to act, think, and feel.
   - *Discoverability*, the assumption that the laws regulating the events studied by any science are *potentially* discoverable. Personality psychologists hold as a matter of principle that no aspect of human behaviour is beyond explanation.
   - *Scientific method*, the assumption that there is a procedure by which questions about events can be submitted to empirical test. This procedure is the scientific method.
   - *Potential human benefit*, the assumption that scientific knowledge has potential benefits. Despite the dangers that scientific findings sometimes introduce, it is held that knowledge is better than ignorance.

4. Accompanying these assumptions are the specific attributes of the scientific method, which can be thought of as a prescription telling someone else how to observe what we have observed. There are six *essential* ingredients:
   - *An attitude of willingness to submit beliefs to empirical test.* Science has to be willing to accept evidence, even if it contradicts the results we're hoping for.
   - *A way of putting ideas into questions that observation can answer.* This is a requirement to translate abstract ideas into concrete questions so that specific observations can be made.
   - *Operationism.* Concepts in theories are abstract. Not only do they have to be put as questions that make observation possible, they have to be defined by specific measurement procedures (operations).
   - *Observation of the relevant events.* Science demands objective and standardized observations that can be made systematically so that one observer can reproduce the observations of another.
   - *Careful description.* The terms used to describe concepts and observations need to be objective and precise. Everyday language is inadequate as a theoretical and observational language.
   - *Logical inference.* Science unites induction (observation) with deduction (logical derivation from theoretical premises of empirical consequences). Hypotheses are deduced and conclusions drawn from evidence according to strict rules of inference. Logical analysis concerns the relation of concepts to observable events.

5. Two *higher-order ingredients* extend the power of these essentials.
   - The *experiment* and the *principle of control.* Controlled experiments will typically manipulate the variable or variables hypothesized to be responsible for a phenomenon, and hold constant other variables that might influence the outcome of the experiment. A control group matches the experimental group in every respect except for the experimental manipulation. It provides the baseline against which to compare the effects of the treatment given to the experimental group.
   - *Quantification* makes possible the precise analysis of data, and statistical techniques and reasoning enable us to determine the probability that the results of an experiment are not due to chance.

6. In some areas of psychology, it is often not possible to apply experimental methods to study questions of

interest. One of these areas is personality. Observational methods have a critical place in personality study, and one of them in particular—the clinical method—has provided the basic data for the development of theories. The clinical method includes the essential ingredients of the scientific prescription but not the possibility of controlled observations.

7. There are many research questions in personality to which experimental methods can be applied, but there are also many that we are unable to study experimentally. Experiments are not appropriate when the natural development of personality characteristics (social motives, for example, or the processes leading to personality disturbance) is the question, and we rely on observational methods.

8. There are very few situations in which personality can be studied close up and in detail. One stands out: the clinical interaction of patient and psychotherapist, in which people reveal the intimate details of their lives. This is the *clinical* or *case study* method, and it is the research method on which personality theory was founded. The clinical method has provided the observations on which many personality theories are based. It has been both the source of hypotheses and the situation in which they are tested.

9. A number of techniques are part of the clinical method. They include the interview, the use of tests (psychological and such physical tests as the neurological exam), observing behaviour, listening to people as they express feelings and relate experiences, and clinical interpretations and the way patients react to them. The clinical method is a general term that identifies both a context and focus on understanding individuals, and a body of techniques. The procedures of the clinical method can also be used in discovery—to find the basis of personality disorders and to formulate personality theories.

10. Is the clinical method scientific, and is it good science? When carried out capably, it has the essential ingredients of science, but it does not include the rigorous use of control. Clinical interactions are often fast-moving and present the clinician with a mass of detail that must be acted on immediately. Moreover, the clinician cannot control all the potential influences on the behaviour he or she observes. There is, thus, a tradeoff between a rich and intimate view of individuals and the kind of controlled observation that the experiment entails. The clinical method is a fertile source of hypotheses, but a fallible situation in which to test them.

11. The psychological use of the term *personality* differs from the way we use it in everyday life. In ordinary language, personality is a shorthand way of characterizing a person (e.g. a pleasant personality, an irritating personality). To psychologists, personality refers to the inferred attributes and processes responsible for behaviour—*potentialities* for action. Personality psychologists must necessarily call on methods to study the motives that drive and direct behaviour.

12. Personality study also focuses on the *situations* in which behaviour occurs. Situation strongly influences behaviour, thought, and emotion. Although many situations (male–female relationships, the classroom, the workplace) elicit similar behaviour from people, there are significant individual differences in the way people interpret them. Each individual has a unique way of interpreting the myriad situations he or she encounters. Accordingly, the modern study of personality is the study of *person–situation interactions*. Not all personality theories account well for the interaction of person and situation, and this is one of the criteria on which theories should be judged.

13. Personality theories began with the clinical study and treatment of disturbed behaviour and only later became full-fledged theories of personality. The core concepts were based on patients afflicted with neurosis. Personality theorists generally assume that theoretical principles derived from clinical study of the disturbed may be applied to the understanding of normal personality. This is the *continuity* assumption—that the same psychological processes observed in disturbed persons will be found in people who are normal (but will have less extreme expression). Freud was a firm advocate of the continuity assumption, and subsequent personality theorists have agreed. To cite an example, fantasy, in which everyone engages, extends from normal imaginative activity to the exceptional degree seen in schizophrenia, in which self-absorption blurs reality testing. Paranoid delusion is another example. Cameron proposed that delusions begin in deficiencies in role-taking and correcting misperceptions. The to-be-paranoid person lacks the social skills to discover that the misperceived motives of others are actually benign and begins to construct

an explanation shared by no one else. He or she has now created a pseudocommunity, from which delusional beliefs develop.

14. Personality theories are general behaviour theories that develop psychological models of the human. However, the model of every personality theory is incomplete; each theory has its own particular emphasis, areas in which it is more complete and adequate, and each is unable to deal well with certain other aspects of personality. It is important to understand that the model presented by a theory is a *representation* of reality and is not to be taken as a description of reality itself. Theoretical concepts are 'as if' constructions that present the consequences of thinking about features of personality in a given way. The constructions of personality theory are inventive ideas of the theorist—fictions—that like the fictional creations of a novelist derive from experience. But while both novelist and scientist represent reality and give it meaning, scientific concepts entail a check on the validity of their claims about how reality works. The test lies in predictions that can be tested to determine whether they are true or false. In its strictest form, this check on theory is called *falsifiability*, which means that the claims of a theory are potentially disconfirmable. Thus, if a prediction is actually wrong, we want to be sure to find that out. This is a critical standard on which to evaluate personality theories.

TO TEST YOUR UNDERSTANDING

1. Can you find any common elements in the six definitions of personality with which this chapter began? What, if anything, do these several definitions share? Why are they so different?

2. Seven paradigms and twenty-two theories is a lot. What does it mean that there are so many? Do you think that the psychology of personality is badly fractured, with many theorists going off in different directions, unwilling to seek each other out to find areas of common agreement? Or is this a healthy state of theoretical controversy, one that promotes the development and exploration of new ideas? What's your view on this question at the beginning of your study of personality theory?

3. Which of the assumptions of science do you think is most fundamental? Put the assumptions that science makes in order from most basic to least. Do the same thing for the ingredients of the scientific prescription.

4. How would personality theories have been different had they developed from the experimental study of persons and not from clinical observation? What would you expect an experimentally derived theory of personality to look like?

5. One personality theorist believes that personality is real, that it is the actuality of the person. Personality, he says, *is* something and *does* something. How does his view differ from the views of theorists who regard the concepts of personality as constructions, as representations of the psychology of the human? Which of these approaches to personality most appeals to you?

CHAPTER TWO

The Beginnings of Personality Theory

Introduction

Suppose we were going to set out to create a theory of personality. How would we begin, and what would we begin with? We'd start, inescapably, with the knowledge of our time—the science, the psychology, and the personality psychology of the early twenty-first century—which we would adapt, embellish, and modify as our own ideas and the data we collected would direct. We'd also bring to the process of theory formation the important features of our culture and society and family upbringing that shaped us, channelling our thinking and causing us to follow some lines rather than others. We would not be bound inextricably to the scientific and social currency that nurtured us, but we would certainly be powerfully influenced. Our theory would bear the stamp, whether we wished it or not, of our time and place in the history of ideas and of culture.

Some have argued that great minds take giant leaps beyond their contemporaries, outstripping the conceptions on which they themselves were raised to create something altogether new and unprecedented. The opposing view is that ideas are embedded in their *Zeitgeist*, a wonderful German word meaning 'the spirit of the times' (on this question, see Boring, 1950; Hilgard, 1987). There are unconvinced critics, but few historians of modern thought doubt that Freud belongs with Darwin, Pavlov, and Einstein as one who took the giant steps. That said, it is also beyond question that we can better understand theories of personality—or of anything else—if we have some appreciation of the sources of their development, sources from which the theorist took his sustenance. With a modern theory—like the one we're going to contrive—there will be many strands to trace. These will include scientific concepts, current beliefs on theory and how theories are best constructed, and notions about personality, the theory's substance. There will also be the cultural and social strands, less easily understood because we are so close to them.

We can see the wellsprings of personality theory in sharper relief, stripped of modern complexity, if we go back to the very beginning of a science of personality. So, to explore the way in which personality theories are developed, we're going to look in some detail at how the primordial theory of personality, Freud's psychoanalysis, emerged from the science and culture of its time. We shall see the database, the processes of hypothesis formation and test, the rejection of hypotheses bared by evidence as wrong, and the gradual merging of *fractional hypotheses*—part theories—into a grand and inclusive picture of the human person. We'll pursue psychoanalysis in this and the next chapter to follow its birth and development, bring it to the present, and evaluate it. We shall see the ghosts of Freud's teachers—notably Ernst Brücke, after whom Freud named his youngest son, and Jean Martin Charcot, honoured in the name of Freud's first son, Martin—and find Viennese science and culture peeking through. As if it were somehow embossed on the theory itself, we'll discover that it was 'Made in Vienna', the date of manufacture circa 1900.

'Now just a minute,' I can almost hear you cry. 'Freud? Two chapters? Why two chapters on psychoanalysis? Isn't this an outmoded and discredited theory?' Not exactly. Psychoanalysis is still full of life and has made a number of adaptations in response to the criticisms levied at it. This, the first scientific theory of personality, came to hold vast sway, in one way or another, over virtually every other personality theory, over literature and literary criticism, over philosophy, and over popular culture. Psychoanalytic ideas and language have become part of the way we think and speak about ourselves and others: words and concepts like *anxiety*, *repression*, psychological *conflict*, *catharsis* (which refers to getting pent-up emotion out of your system), not to mention the very notion of an unconscious mind.

Freud took the common idea that we are the products of our childhood and made it the psychological basis of our personalities. The strange, quixotic, and sometimes ugly things that people do became understandable in his hands. We act from motives we're unaware of and, because of Freud, are aware that we do. Life in Western culture would be very different without Freud's influence.

Sigmund Freud: Personal History and Context

Freud was born in May of 1856 in the small town of Freiberg in Moravia, the northern-most part of the sprawling Habsburg empire that spanned central Europe. Freiberg is now Příbor in the Czech Republic. He was given the names Sigismund Schlomo but changed 'Sigismund' to 'Sigmund' after entering the University of Vienna in 1873. He died in London, England, in September 1939, a refugee from Nazi Austria. One of the most renowned men in the world, the Nazis had not dared to refuse him leave to go. He had greatly suffered for sixteen years from the pain of advancing cancer of the jaw and palate and the monstrous discomfort from the oral prosthesis it obliged him to wear. He remained, though, active and creative nearly to the end.

Freud's father, Jacob, was a struggling and improvident wool merchant, and the family was very poor. They occupied one room, in which Freud was born, over a smithy. The blacksmith, Zajic, was their landlord. Freud's mother, Amalia, was Jacob's third wife and twenty years his junior. Although they lived in Freiberg only briefly after Freud's birth, he retained fond memories of the town and its wooded countryside, and returned there frequently on holidays during his school years. In 1931, when Freud was seventy-five and world famous, a plaque honouring him was erected in Freiberg. Acknowledging the honour, Freud wrote, 'Deep within me, covered over, there still lives that happy child from Freiberg, the first-born son of a youthful mother, who had received the first indelible impressions from this air, from this soil' (Freud, 1961, p. 259).

The Freuds moved in 1860 to Vienna and took up residence in the Jewish ghetto. These were not easy times. Many years later Freud wrote, 'Then

Freud as a young man, about 1885. (CORBIS)

came long hard years. I think nothing about them was worth remembering' (Freud, 1962, p. 312). The family's circumstances did eventually improve, however, although they were crowded into a small apartment with not enough bedrooms for everyone. Sigmund, the family favourite and a talented student, was given his own bedroom.

The Habsburg Empire, which became the Dual Monarchy, the Austro–Hungarian Empire in 1867, brought together nearly a dozen peoples, many with national aspirations of their own, speaking different languages, and practising half a dozen religions. German was the official language. When the Freuds left provincial Freiberg for Vienna, they became part of an urban and urbane, sophisticated world. Freud professed to hate it, but despite opportunities to leave (to immigrate to England, for example) he remained. This was a liberal period in the history of the empire, and anti-Semitism, always present, was at a low ebb. Many opportunities were afforded to Jews—in business, in culture and the arts, in medicine, and in other professions. But anti-Semitic feeling never altogether vanished, and before the close of the century it would rear its head again. In the 1880s, it would play a role in denying Freud the academic career he dreamed of. And in 1938, when the Nazis took over Austria, it would send him into exile in London, England, and take the lives of his four sisters who remained in Vienna. I think we cannot underestimate the effects of a society that was fundamentally intolerant and unaccepting of Jews on Freud himself and more than likely on the dark and pessimistic view of humankind that inarguably colours psychoanalysis.

Vienna, with all its trials for a minority group, did give Freud an education, with admission to the University of Vienna and to medical school and the research career (however badly paid and without prospects) that got him started. Vienna gave him the intelligent patients from well-to-do families on whose experiences with **neurosis**★ the theory of psychoanalysis was founded. And there is another influence we have to consider, that of the sexually repressive culture of Freud's time, which cast women in a subservient, homemaking, maternal role and accepted no frankness in matters of sexual activity. That's not to say that illicit sexual behaviour did not occur. It certainly did, but very covertly.

Freud was a brilliant student, the first in his class at the Gymnasium, and this gained him entry to the University of Vienna, where he excelled. In medical school, he continued to shine. He was taken on as an assistant—a research assistant, as we would say today—to the great Viennese physiologist Ernst Brücke. Brücke was one of the most distinguished proponents of **positivism**★ in biological science, which sought to apply the experimental rigour of astronomy, physics, and chemistry—the paragons of the natural sciences—to biology, physiology, and medicine. There was to be no metaphysical speculation, none of the vitalism that imputed mysterious powers of nature to living things, vital forces that animated bodily processes and action. Instead, the biological sciences—and medicine—were to be strictly empirical, relying for explanation on known physical and chemical processes. Freud was hugely indebted to Brücke and from him wholeheartedly adopted the view that disordered human behaviour, no less than disease, could be understood in physical terms. He would go well beyond his teacher and intellectual father as he came to see material processes in the body and the dynamics of energy systems as the fundamentals of personality. It was the essence of the positivist position that Freud wrote in 1932 that psychoanalysis 'is a piece of science and can adhere to the scientific world view' (Freud, 1964, p. 181).

Brücke was a hero to Freud, but he was also a stern taskmaster who had once severely upbraided his young assistant. But he knew talent when he saw it, and Freud had that in spades—as a physiologist, neuroanatomist, neurologist, and yet to come, as a psychological theorist. And he clearly appreciated the devotion of his pupil: Freud took in his teaching like mother's milk. His mentor was forty years older than Freud and would soon retire. Could a brilliant and productive young scholar aspire to his professorship? Not in Freud's case. The senior assistant in Brücke's laboratory, Sigmund Exner, was Freud's senior by ten years and on Brücke's death stood to become the professor. Then, there was the endemic anti-Semitism, which was becoming increasingly virulent. Freud's path to academic advancement was utterly blocked.

After Brücke advised him to turn elsewhere, Freud worked for three years in psychiatric and pediatric neurological clinics, barely scraping by and unable to put aside enough money to get married. Then, with Brücke's and another professor's backing, he was awarded a small travelling fellowship to spend a few months in Paris at the clinic of the distinguished French neurologist Jean Martin Charcot. Freud was captivated by the charismatic Charcot, who was a compelling lecturer. Freud's first son became Charcot's namesake, as we have just seen, and an engraving of a famous painting by the artist André Brouillet, *La Leçon clinique du Dr Charcot*, signed by Charcot, hung in Freud's consulting room. He later liked to say that he had spent a year with Charcot, when in fact his sojourn was four months.

At this time, the mid-1880s, Charcot and his colleagues were caught up in the problem of **hysteria***, a neurosis appearing to mimic neurological symptoms like the loss of sensory or motor functions. In the Brouillet painting, Charcot demonstrates to colleagues and students the symptoms of a patient with hysteria. Charcot, the neurologist, was fundamentally concerned with impaired functioning of the nervous system. In the neurological clinic, one saw—far more often in those times than today—patients with

La leçon clinique du Dr Charcot, by André Brouillet. (© Bettmann/CORBIS)

symptoms of central nervous system disorders that had no demonstrable neurological basis. Paralysis of limbs, loss of feeling or distorted sensation in parts of the body, epileptic-like seizures, painful muscular contractions, and even on occasion blindness might appear in these patients. There were also some distinctive personality characteristics—a tendency to overdramatize, a certain naïveté and gullibility, dependency, and—most striking of all—an indifference on the part of these patients to their crippling and life-restricting symptoms called *la belle indifference*. Hysteria has been supplanted in our modern psychiatric lexicon by the term **conversion disorder***. Today, we are more likely to see *chronic fatigue syndrome* and *somatoform pain disorder* (a complaint, which can't be confirmed by physical evidence, of chronic pain), which are more apt to find belief in our medically sophisticated age (Shorter, 1992).

The phenomenon of hysteria was not a new one in Charcot's era. It had been known since ancient times, and it was the Greeks who named it *hysteria*, meaning 'wandering womb'. So in the ancient world of classical Greece there first arose the suspicion that this disorder had something to do with sex. It is important here to point out a few things concerning this condition. First, the hysterical patient is not deliberately putting on symptoms—malingering—to evade some awkward, impossibly difficult, or mortally embarrassing situation. Some hysterical patients are genuinely unaware of their symptoms. In one form of hysteria, the person has tunnel vision in which the outer reaches of the visual fields are lost. This hysterical tunnel vision is often not noticed by the patient and only comes to light with a doctor's examination. Second, hysterical patients suffer real and severe restrictions in their lives because of their symptoms—confinement in bed is an example. Third, as Freud was to show, the symptoms of the hysteric fit together to form a coherent picture of a personality disorder that involves both particular kinds of life stress in its development and a particular pattern of childhood experiences. Following Freud, we have to understand the hysterical patient's symptoms, then, not as the patient staging a dramatic form of faking but as the result of psychological conflict between potent and irreconcilable motives.

At the same time that he was studying the disorder of hysteria, Charcot became intrigued by the phenomenon of hypnosis. He thought—wrongly, as Freud would conclude and as we now know—that there was a significant resemblance between the neurosis of hysteria and hypnosis. He also believed that hypnosis held promise as a treatment for hysteria. How did he arrive at those conclusions? Here are a couple of telling observations. A person responsive to hypnotic suggestion is told by the hypnotist that she cannot move her right arm, as if she could no longer remember how to produce movement in it. In response to this suggestion, the arm hangs limply at her side, and try as she will she is unable to move it. The hypnotically induced paralysis is very convincing, and it appears compellingly similar to hysterical paralysis. It might be taken for a flaccid neurological paralysis except for the fact that its extent and boundary correspond to an untrained person's *idea* of a paralysis, not neurological innervation. Another example of a hypnotic phenomenon is the absence of sensation, including pain, in a part of the body, also very convincing, and we make use of the suggested disappearance of painful sensation when hypnosis is used as the anesthetic in obstetrics or dentistry. Now remember that we sometimes see hysteric patients who have lost or have altered sensation in part of the body. It seemed to Charcot that the same result occurred in the one case by the simple procedure of hypnotic induction and suggestion and in the second case as a part of a neurotic predisposition to hysteria. He concluded that the underlying processes must be identical.

As Pierre Janet, one of Charcot's former pupils and a distinguished colleague in his own right, was to explain, hysteria results from a hereditary neural weakness. Perhaps, thought Charcot, that neural weakness exists as a predisposition to hysteria before hysteria ever develops—a predisposition shown in a person's susceptibility to hypnosis. If so a psychiatrist could take advantage of the patient's own neurotic manifestation, 'hypnotizability', to treat the disorder, by suggesting to the patient under hypnosis that her symptoms would disappear.

Freud also learned of another view of hypnosis, one closer to our current understanding. This was the view of two French physicians, Ambroise Liébeault and Hippolyte Bernheim, who used hypnotic suggestion in the treatment of a variety of neurotic and other disorders. They were convinced that hypnosis did not represent pathological suggestibility but was simply a normal response to suggestion. On the way home from his sojourn with Charcot, Freud took the opportunity to observe their work in Nancy, France, and made a later visit as well.

After his brief study with Charcot, Freud returned to Vienna and set up what we would call a psychiatric practice together with an older friend and colleague, Josef Breuer. They saw patients with a variety of neurotic disorders, most frequently hysteria, but also other neuroses:

- chronic fatigue and generalized anxiety, which we now call generalized anxiety disorder
- attacks of exceptionally severe anxiety, now panic disorder
- severe phobias
- obsessive ideas—recurrent thoughts, disturbing to the person, that can't be controlled—and compulsive ritual acts such as the need to wash the hands repeatedly because of the obsessive idea that disease and contaminants are everywhere. This is obsessive-compulsive disorder.

The treatment techniques that Freud followed, like those of Breuer, were largely hypnotic suggestion, encouragement to rest, and reassurance. Before Freud and during the beginning years of his practice, the physician's armamentarium to make disturbed behaviour better was largely limited to prescriptions for bed rest, a trip to sunny Italy, drugs (such as laudanum, an opium solution), confinement in an asylum (or a sanitarium, if you were wealthy), or, in the extreme, a straitjacket for agitated patients. These hardly amounted to medical science. You can appreciate how little was understood of neurosis, its origins, and its treatment from reliance on such methods. Freud was not terribly successful, and his practice must have caused its share of frustration and disappointment. Not every patient could be hypnotized, and so hypnosis was not an effective technique for many. From modern research, we know that perhaps 20 to 25 per cent of people are capable of the depth of hypnosis that makes its clinical use feasible (Hilgard, 1965). Of those patients who could be hypnotized, some failed to lose their symptoms or suffered recurrences later. Hypnosis, however, did work sometimes, and Freud together with Breuer made some important discoveries about why it did work when it did, and about the processes underlying the cure of neurotic disorders.

Freud began to discover that when hypnosis was successful, patients often recalled specific traumatic episodes as a result of suggestions he made while they were under hypnosis. The recall of these terrible experiences (mostly of sexual seduction) was likely to be accompanied by a great outpouring of the feelings they engendered—shame and guilt, fear, desperate anguish. Freud called this emotional release *abreaction* (from German, meaning 'to work off, to get rid of'). He found that when it occurred the patient was often relieved of her symptoms. I say 'her' deliberately, for many of Freud's patients were women; hysteria is far more frequent in women, and these recollections of sexual seduction were made by female patients. The emotional outpouring of abreaction came to form a significant part, a kind of underpinning, of later developments in psychoanalysis.

One of Breuer's patients was a remarkable young woman to whom he and Freud gave the pseudonym Anna O. She was actually Bertha Pappenheim, a friend of Martha Bernays, Freud's fiancée. Later in her life, after a prolonged and difficult recovery from her neurosis, Anna (Bertha) distinguished herself for her work as a social worker and feminist. Anna developed a hysterical neurosis during and after a very traumatic period in which she nursed her father through his terminal illness until she was incapacitated by her symptoms. She developed painful contractures of the neck and shoulder and partial paralyses. Her vision became blurry and indistinct, and her consciousness was also affected. She lapsed into dreamy and abstracted states, and her whole personality changed. Sometimes she would speak only English, which she had not spoken since she was a small child, or French or Italian. She had outbursts of temper and would throw her pillows at visitors to her room. She had hallucinations of black snakes, skulls, and skeletons.

Breuer, who treated her at her bedside, was puzzled by this mystifying symptom picture, and the methods he was using to treat Anna (hypnosis and suggestion, reassurance, encouraging the patient to rest) were not working. He hit upon the idea of writing down the strange and incomprehensible things—the mutterings, the snatches of English, the angry outbursts and odd remarks—that greeted him when he found Anna in one of her 'states'. Then, he tried repeating them back or recalling them to her the next day, or when he found her to be lucid and reasonable, asking her to explain to him what they brought to mind.

Breuer's novel approach was initially successful. Anna was able to trace her associations to the traumatic period of her care for her father, and she could recall the specific origins of each of her symptoms. She embraced the sessions and even came up with names for Breuer's new method, calling it her 'talking cure', or sometimes, more playfully, 'chimney sweeping'. Things were going splendidly and then, suddenly, her treatment with Breuer came to a premature end. Anna showed many signs of a deep emotional attachment to Breuer (which Freud would later recognize by the term **transference★**, regarding it as the transfer of childlike feelings for a parent to the analyst and an essential part of the psychoanalytic process). Breuer had developed his own emotional attachment to Anna: his mother, who died when he was three, was named Bertha—Anna's real name—and his patient was bright, beautiful, and captivating. Breuer's feelings for Anna were inadmissible in an analyst, as Freud would later caution, labelling the analyst's attachment to his patient **countertransference★**.

Anna's feelings for Breuer, strongly sexualized, came to a dramatic climax in a last encounter with him in which she disclosed that she was pregnant—'Here comes Dr Breuer's child,' she cried, writhing with her labour pains. (This, as it turned out, was a false pregnancy, a striking example of Anna's transferance.) Breuer, frightened and uncomprehend-

Anna O. (Bertha Pappenheim), Breuer's patient. (Ullstein Bild/ The Granger Collection, New York)

ing, ran from the house, and turned his treatment of Anna over to a colleague. Many years later, writing to a young friend and devotee of psychoanalysis, Freud told of this episode. At that instant, he said, Breuer held 'the key in his hand but he dropped it' (E. Freud, 1961, p. 427–8).

Following this episode, Anna had rather a bad time of it for a while. Hospitalized in a sanitarium when her symptoms recurred, she was sedated with morphine and developed a drug dependency that she then had to conquer. Anna's unsuccessful treatment does not appear so in Breuer's account of it in *Studies on Hysteria*, the 1895 book of case studies he wrote with Freud. Anna's, he claimed, was a complete cure. Despite the exaggeration, this case turned out to be pivotal in the development of psychoanalysis, and we might think of Anna as the paradigm's founding patient. The technique of 'chimney sweeping' that Breuer and Anna hit upon led to a whole new method of treatment of neuroses in Freud's hands.

Another patient, one of Freud's, also contributed significantly to the new method. Frau Emmy von N. was being treated by the old methods, which included questioning to force disclosure of unmentionable, neurosis-inducing experiences. She became impatient with Freud's slow procedures and with his insistent questions, and she was 'pretty surly' in reproving him. She demanded, Freud wrote, that he cease 'asking her where this or that came from, but let her tell me what she had to say' (Breuer & Freud, 1955, p. 63). Freud consented, and though her analysis became long and tedious, it was effective. He concluded: 'Treatment by means of hypnosis is a senseless and worthless proceeding' (Andersson, 1979).

Freud, astute clinician that he was, saw the success of Anna's chimney sweeping and Frau Emmy's reproof and came to a momentous realization: that treatment proceeded more surely if patients were encouraged to speak of themselves freely. He saw that the associations of the patient were a significant source of knowledge about the events that lay buried in the background of a neurosis. Gradually, by means of the new talking cure, he was able to help patients to recover lost memories of the traumatic experiences he was sure had caused their neuroses. He was already well convinced that the traumata were sexual, and the new method, though difficult for the patient to carry out, seemed to confirm this belief. Freud termed it **free association**★—free because the patient was instructed to speak freely of whatever came to mind. It must have taken great courage to abandon the methods he had relied on and take up this new and unproved technique. But when he did, Freud began to make one significant discovery after another. Psychoanalysis as a method of treating neuroses started to take shape, and Freud began to formulate the first version of a theory of neurosis.

Perspective 2.1   Early Evidence: The Case of Elisabeth von R.

Breuer and Freud's *Studies on Hysteria* contains chapters on the nature of hysteria, with discussion of its treatment through psychotherapy and some speculative theory about the disorder. The most compelling part of the book is the presentation of five cases, those of Breuer's Anna and four of Freud's patients. One case stands out, marking the turning point in the treatment of neurosis. If Anna (via Breuer) and Frau Emmy taught Freud the value of listening to patients as they strove, free of the fetters of conventional inhibition and censorship, to speak their minds, Fräulein Elisabeth von R. gave him the opportunity to try it out.

Elisabeth von R. was born Ilona Weiss in Budapest, Hungary, in 1867. When Freud began to treat her in the late fall of 1892, she had been afflicted for more than two years by severe pain in the legs that caused her to walk with a peculiarly awkward and ungainly gait and fatigued her so much that she would have to sit down after the shortest interval to rest. She was not distressed, however, but rather oddly cheerful. Freud immediately thought of *la belle indifference* and hysteria. She had endured a number of difficult stresses over the period in which her leg cramps had appeared—the death of her father, a major operation on her mother's eyes, and an older sister's death from a chronic heart condition following the birth of her second child. She had coped with these terrible events reasonably well, taking care of the ill ones; sad though it was, family illness and tragedy could not be the true cause of her symptoms.

Freud had, of course, to rule out a physical basis, possibly a neurological disorder, and this meant (among many other things) testing her responsiveness to mildly painful stimulation of the affected part of her body. During his examination, Freud pressed and pinched the skin and muscles of her thighs. He must have been both astonished and triumphant at her response: 'Her face assumed a peculiar expression, one of pleasure rather than of pain; she cried out—somewhat, I could not help thinking, as with a voluptuous tickling—her face flushed, she threw back her head, closed her eyes, her trunk bent backward. None of this was very exaggerated but it was distinctly noticeable, and it could only be reconciled with the view that her disorder was hysterical. . . .' (Freud, 1955, p. 137).

This was not to be an easy neurosis to treat. Indeed, wrote Freud, it 'turned out to be one of the hardest that I had ever undertaken, and the difficulty of giving a report upon it is comparable, moreover, with the difficulties I had then to overcome. For a long time, . . . I was unable to grasp the connection between the events in her illness and her actual symptom. . . .' (p. 138). Elisabeth's long account of the distress of her family ordeal revealed nothing that Freud could identify as a probable cause of hysterical symptoms, nothing to link with the erotic pleasure that neurological testing for response to painful stimulation gave her, nothing to link with *la belle indifference*. Moreover, she was 'pert and disputatious', complaining that Freud's treatment was wholly unhelpful. When he sought to use the old standard, deep hypnosis, she was resistant, and Freud wrote that he was mightily relieved that she didn't taunt him with, 'I'm not asleep, you know. I can't be hypnotized' (p. 145).

Freud wasn't ready to abandon hypnosis and a hypnotic trick or two, however. He tried pressing on her head, requiring her to tell him 'whatever appeared before her inner eye or flashed through her memory at the moment of the pressure' (p. 145), and he would not accept the reply of 'Nothing'. The technique worked, and he was able to evoke recollections leading presently to the disclosure of a failed romantic attachment, a casualty of the unending demands of her nursing regimen. She was bereft, sad, and very lonely. She had cared a great deal for the young man, despite her protestation that she had no interest in marriage but wished instead for training in music and a career. So there *was* an erotic link! The leg pains did not begin immediately with the appearance of a conflict—irreconcilable to her—between her attachment to the young man and the self-imposed duty to care for her severely ill father. It took an attack of pain that was probably of muscular origin—due to jumping out of bed with bare feet on a cold floor to respond to her father's call. This was 'the model copied in her later hysteria' (p. 147).

Elisabeth and Freud achieved notable progress, and Freud made a striking observation:

As a rule the patient was free of pain when we started work. If, then, by a question or by pressure upon her head I called up a memory, a sensation of pain would make its first appearance, and this was usually so sharp that the patient would give a start and put her hand to the painful spot. The pain that was thus aroused would persist so long as she was under the influence of the memory; it would reach its climax when she was in the act of telling me the essential and decisive part of what she had to communicate, and with the last word of this it would disappear. I came in time to use such pains as a compass to guide me; if she stopped talking but admitted that she still had a pain, I knew that she had not told me everything and insisted on her continuing her story till the pain had been talked away. Not until then did I arouse a fresh memory (p. 148).

Freud had unmistakably embarked on the new method, free association, but with a gimmick he would soon completely abandon. Free association wasn't going to need a helping hand.

Despite her gains, and her greater freedom from pain, Elisabeth would still suffer relapses, and it was clear that the psychological core of her hysteria remained. Getting to that came with the recital of one of her two elder sisters' happy marriage to a wonderful man whom Elisabeth greatly admired. She saw their intimacy and yearned to enjoy their happiness herself. Her sister had one child and then soon after became pregnant again. The second pregnancy was a disaster, for she had a silent, undiagnosed congenital heart condition that soon manifested itself. Confined to bed, she became more and more ill. Elisabeth, accompanied by her mother, had journeyed to the Austrian Alps for hydrotherapy treatment; then, there was a sudden summons home with the grave news that Elisabeth's sister was dying. When they they arrived at her bedside, they found Elisabeth's sister already dead. Freud now received the answer, a stunning one: 'At that moment of dreadful certainty that her beloved sister was dead without bidding them farewell and without her having eased her last days with her care—at that very moment another thought had shot through Elisabeth's mind and now forced itself irresistibly upon her once more, like a flash of lightning in the dark: "Now he is free again and I can be his wife"' (p. 156). The thought was quickly banished but it had a lasting effect. The leg pains now began in earnest, and from this time on were extreme and unremitting.

They had proceeded through the critical events. Freud thought Elisabeth was ready and gave her his understanding—the interpretation of her hysterical leg pains.

The recovery of this repressed idea had a shattering effect on the poor girl. She cried aloud when I put the situation drily before her with the words: 'So for a long time you had been in love with your brother-in-law.' She complained at this moment of the most frightful pains, and made one last desperate effort to reject the explanation: it was not true, I had talked her into it, it *could* not be true, she was incapable of such wickedness, she could never forgive herself for it. It was easy to prove to her that what she herself had told me admitted of no other interpretation. But it was a long time before my two pieces of consolation—that we are not responsible for our feelings, and that her behaviour, the fact that she had fallen ill in these circumstances, was sufficient evidence of her moral character—it was a long time before these consolations of mine made any impression on her (p. 157).

Elisabeth, though shocked and anguished, was on the road to recovery, and Freud had a final, confirming observation to make. 'In the spring of 1894 I heard that she was going to a private ball for which I was able to get an invitation, and I did not allow the opportunity to escape me of seeing my former patient whirl past in a lively dance. Since then, by her own inclination, she has married someone unknown to me' (p. 160). Many years later, Elisabeth's daughter confirmed Freud's account of her mother's history and added that her mother had a happy marriage. Talk, the new therapeutic method, had done its job and done it well in the first complete analysis of a case of hysteria.

We have to yet to answer the question of how erotic longing in conflict with a sense of duty and later with Elisabeth's strong moral sense could turn into a hysterical neurosis, could become *converted* into a physical symptom. Freud pointed to an underlying **motive**★—defence against an intolerable realization—and a **mechanism**★ by which the physical symptom became the expression of a psychological conflict resolvable by no other means. He concluded that the mechanism was the process of conversion: 'in place of the mental pains which she avoided, physical pains made their appearance. In this way a transformation was effected which had the advantage that the patient escaped from an intolerable mental condition. . . .' (p. 166). The model, as we have seen, was the leg pain Elisabeth experienced during the nursing of her father. It was unconsciously adopted in the face of an immoral wish.

The First Discoveries

Resistance

You might think that a neurotic sufferer would try his or her level best to comply with the therapeutic requirement of free association, for Freud clearly indicated that this was the best method of achieving a cure. To a degree they did try. Patients worked at free association, unfamiliar and awkward as it is to say everything that comes to mind, and they did lead Freud backward in time to their childhoods. Of course, Freud must have shown his interest in early recollection. As a result, psychoanalysis quickly became a historical technique, one of excavating the past to find the damaging events. Freud came to understand that the critical period for the development of neurosis was childhood—much earlier than anyone might have supposed. It did not appear to be so in the case of Elisabeth, but Freud would find that most neuroses owed their existence to happenings in the youth of the patient.

Free association, as productive a therapeutic technique as it turned out to be, also served up a puzzle. In a very important sense, it wasn't free at all, meeting with stiff resistance in every patient. Elisabeth had taught Freud about resistance, with her silences and exacerbation of her symptoms just when their origin was close to disclosure. Freud must at first have been perplexed that patients would become hostile and battle with him, remain stubbornly silent, attempt to subvert talking on a particular topic by one or another stratagem (some female patients became openly seductive, for example). It became evident that resistance reared up whenever the patient was close to a very disturbing and anxiety-provoking revelation. With the analyst's gentle perseverance, recall would finally come, the traumatic remembrance tumbling out with strong abreaction, great relief following.

Resistance would appear, then, whenever disturbing material threatened to become conscious. Freud inferred from resistance that there must be a powerful force holding back awareness of the anxiety-evocative material and its expression. Why else would patients fight so? The phenomenon of resistance suggested to Freud that this powerful force was exercised by the ego (or 'ego instincts', as he termed it in these early days). The ego repressed awareness of wishes, feelings, and memories too painful to be dealt with openly, banishing them from consciousness in a desperate attempt to protect itself from unspeakable anxiety.

Repression

Resistance became one of the outstanding signs that repression—a process so important that Freud termed it the cornerstone of psychoanalysis—had occurred. Simply defined, repression is the process of turfing out ideas, memories, and feelings that could make one unendurably anxious, and rendering them unconscious. The banishment, at first a deliberate choice not to think, very quickly becomes automatic and unalterable.

I want to emphasize that we see in resistance a clear expression of a person at war within himself or herself, a person in conflict. Patients wish to comply with the analytic requirement but cannot in spite of themselves. They carry on self-destructive resistance, believing themselves to be fully justified and behaving appropriately in the circumstances. It is anxiety that makes them do that. Resistance is a most significant piece of evidence for repression, as it is evidence of psychological conflict.

Symptom Irrationality

Freud as a matter of course asked patients to explain their symptoms and was struck by another observation. Even though their symptoms were profoundly disturbing and often involved quite peculiar behaviour, patients could not provide a satisfactory and intelligible account of why they had them. They frequently felt as if they were going crazy, their symptoms imposed on them as if by some malevolent, unseen agent. Thus, it followed that neurotic symptoms are, from the standpoint of the awareness and consciousness of the patient, fundamentally irrational. This irrationality is another of Freud's beginning discoveries.

The Unconscious

Resistance, repression, and symptom irrationality all imply that there are aspects of experience of which people can be unaware. So, these early discoveries led Freud to a conclusion he saw as inescapable: there is an unconscious mental life, one that can lead us to do things we fully believe we don't want to do or to do things that we explain with exceptionally improbable justification. The concept of the unconscious was not Freud's creation. Age of Enlightenment and later romantic poets—Goethe, Schiller, Coleridge—had found poetic inspiration in the idea, and it appeared in the philosophies of Schopenhauer and Nietzsche. Freud knew their works intimately. His genius 'was to take a shadowy, as it were poetic, notion, lend it precision, and make it into the foundation of a psychology by specifying the origins and contents of the unconscious and its imperious ways of pressing toward expression' (Gay, 1988, p. 128). Whyte (1962) has given a detailed account of the history of thought about the unconscious in his book *The Unconscious Before Freud*.

Childhood Origins of Neurosis

We've already noted Freud's discovery of the importance of childhood in the development of neurosis and the eventual recovery by his patients of traumatic experiences in their upbringing. Moreover, when recall and abreaction were complete, patients were relieved of their symptoms. What kinds of childhood experiences did his patients recall? As I've already said, they were sexual, and this astounded Freud. Patients recalled sexual seduction by a parent or relative, and Freud found especially compelling the fact that these recollections occurred in every case. There was no choice but to conclude that early childhood was not a period of sexual innocence in his patients, and he greatly expanded that proposition when he came to argue that children have sexual motives and interests whose socialization is a critical element in personality development.

A Theory of Neurosis

Let me begin this section by noting that neurosis—a term first coined by an English physician in 1769 and the chosen diagnostic term from Freud's time to the late twentieth century for disorders of crippling anxiety, guilt, and anxiety-based symptoms—has been supplanted by more objective and reliable terms that do not depend so greatly on inference. These include *conversion disorder*, *anxiety disorder*, and *obsessive-compulsive disorder*, to name a few. The *Diagnostic and Statistical Manual* of the American Psychiatric Association abandoned neurosis as a diagnosis in 1980 (American Psychiatric Association, 1980, 1994). In theories of personality, however, neurosis retains its place to this day, largely, I suspect, out of tradition. So, I will continue to use it, since personality theories *do* make inferences about processes that are not directly observable.

Freud followed in the footsteps of Charcot, who was also struck by his observation of sexual factors in neurosis. Freud had heard him exclaim that the cause of neurosis was invariably sexual: '*Mais dans des cas pareils c'est toujours la chose génitale . . . toujours . . . toujours . . . toujours*' (Freud, 1957, p. 14). The origin of hysteria, Freud now believed, lay in traumatic sexual seduction. He was shocked by the disclosures of his patients and reproved by his medical colleagues when he reported what he had found, but he did not withdraw from a conclusion he felt he had to make. On the basis of his clinical evidence, Freud saw hysteria and other neuroses as the result of sexual seduction in childhood that was so horrific to the patient that awareness of it was repressed. The traumatic experiences producing hysteria, he wrote, 'must belong to early childhood (the time before puberty), and their content must consist of an actual irritation of the genitals (proceedings resembling coitus)' (Freud, 1962, p. 163).

Repression of traumatic experiences did not repair the damage these experiences had caused, however, for the patient was unable to develop a normal sexuality. Her sexuality was inhibited, dammed up by what Freud termed the 'strangulation of affect' associated with the repressed events. Neurotic symptoms developed out of dammed-up emotionality and inhibited sexuality. Freud extended the theory further on the basis of the histories of patients, reporting that there were two distinct patterns. Patients who had been passive victims of childhood sexual abuse later developed the symptoms of hysteria, as in the cases of *Studies on Hysteria*. Patients developing obsessive-compulsive neurosis had been more active participants. Freud found evidence that these patients had wished for, become excited by, and been emotionally involved in childhood seduction.

A New Theory of Neurosis

Freud held this theory for just a year. With great initial reluctance and disappointment, he decided he had to jettison it because it was simply wrong. He had followed where he believed the facts directed. Those facts as he had understood them dictated the sexual theory, which he steadfastly advanced in spite of the revulsion of the public and medical community alike. Now, because he became convinced that he had been misled in his conclusion, he gave it up.

What was the mistake? It was strongly hinted at by the fact that every neurotic patient had a revelation of sexual seduction. Freud began to think it very improbable that the incidence of sexual seduction in otherwise proper Viennese families could be that high. Surely, he thought, there must be other causes. Also causing him to doubt the plausibility of his earlier theory was the fact that one of his sisters had had a hysterical neurosis. That his gentle, devoted, affectionate father, Jacob, could have been responsible was absurd. He also began to uncover inconsistencies in the stories his patients related. He was thus led to conclude that the experiences were not experiences at all but fantasies. 'There are no indications of reality in the unconscious,' he said, and so there is no way to distinguish between something that happened and a fiction (Masson, 1985, p. 264). These accounts were expressions of *wishes*.

This was a momentous turn, for it meant that the patient was the victim not of the contemptible acts of family members necessarily, but of his or her own ideas and feelings, wishes expressed in fantasies. Freud did not, however, wholly abandon seduction in childhood as a cause of neurosis. Almost thirty years later he wrote in a footnote, 'Seduction has retained a certain significance for etiology [of hysteria]' (Freud, 1962, p. 168n). Masterful in distinguishing fact from fantasy, he recognized that sexual abuse did occur on occasion and could lead to the development of symptoms. But childhood seduction failed as an overall explanation of the cause of neurosis, while, in listening to his patients, he found that wish and fantasy had consistently significant consequences.

It is interesting to note that the theory of sexual seduction as a cause of personality disorder did not die when Freud abandoned it as the major explanation of neurotic disorder. It languished, dormant, for the better part of a century, to be revived in recent times by some psychotherapists who are convinced that the symptoms of troubled women can be traced directly to childhood sexual abuse. The modern version differs from Freud's first theory in two ways. First, the modern theory uses the concept of **denial**★ and not repression—Freud's more basic mechanism—to account for adult failure to remember. The reason is that repression, as the process of banishing intolerable ideas—wishes, fantasies, memories associated with them—from consciousness, is more closely tied to Freud's revised theory of neurosis, with its focus on wish fulfillment. Denial means the banishment of memory of an event and all its emotional and cognitive baggage. Second, while the early Freudian theory proposed a one-to-one relation between childhood sexual abuse and specific adult neurotic symptoms, modern seduction theory says that any of a large array of adult psychological symptoms may reflect such a history—anxiety, depression, phobic fears, drug indulgence or dependencies, dissociative identity disorder (two or more distinct personalities in the same person), and so on.

You can see that there may be a considerable clinical problem here. For example, is all adult depression the result of early abuse? If not, which is and which isn't, and how do we tell? It is also important to note the clinical problem of determining when patients are providing us a real story, when the idea may have been incautiously implanted by suggestion, and what all the links are between experiences in childhood and the development of neurotic symptoms in adulthood. It is clear that false memories of sexual abuse have been introduced to some distressed patients through the aggressive use of suggestion by psychotherapists convinced of a direct link between adult personality disorder and the traumatic childhood experience of sexual abuse. A number of tragedies have resulted from allegations of abuse that were in fact false memories, and patients themselves have been badly served by accepting memories of things that never happened. And as Loftus (2003b) observes, the experiences of true victims of childhood abuse are trivialized by crediting false memory. Loftus has written compellingly about false memory, its consequences and legal implications, and how psychotherapy and the law can better take memories that aren't real memories into account (see Loftus, 2002, 2003a; Loftus and Ketcham, 1991, 1994).

To conclude, let's consider the implications of Freud's new theory. It must be the case that there is strong conflict between internal forces—between forbidden wishes on the one hand and forcible ego restraint of them on the other. When Freud arrived at this conclusion—that his patients were afflicted by anxiety-inducing wishes and fantasies, *unconscious* wishes and fantasies—he laid the groundwork for two of the fundamental psychoanalytic components of personality. Where do the wishes originate? They must arise from a person's motivational life, from his or her urges, impulses, or **instincts** as we call them in translation from the German noun *trieb*. The psychological expression of an instinct is a wish. Instinctual wishes are both imperative and asocial, devoid of morality. The opposing force is the sense of propriety, the person's understanding of what is right and proper and what is unacceptable and wicked. Here was the ego's role in this early version of the new theory. Freud had now set down the basis for the psychoanalytic concepts of personality structure. Implicit in this nascent scheme was the idea of an unconscious mental life and a clear understanding of psychological conflict between wishes demanding to be acknowledged and indulged and the ego rejecting them.

The content of the unconscious is not passive. Once repressed, wishes and feelings continue to press for expression, like the prisoner behind bars who is forever seeking escape. These wishes and feelings manifest themselves in small irruptions that, when partially recognized, give the person exceedingly painful experiences of anxiety. Moreover, repression requires the continual expenditure of energy. We see here why many neurotic persons seem chronically fatigued: they are, for their energy resources are drained by the necessary job of keeping the unconscious unconscious.

Freud also began to see evidence that patients expressed their conflicts symbolically. A patient ridden by guilt might have repeated accidents and suffer painful injuries. Patients would sometimes say things they had not intended to say, slips of the tongue, that unintentionally gave evidence of an unconscious wish. Most of us have had the experience of the Freudian slip, the odd verbal blunder that we dismissed because it just popped out and was not what we were thinking at all. Freud wrote a marvellous book on slips of the tongue, accident-proneness, and other evidences of the unconscious, *The Psychopathology of Everyday Life* (Freud, 1971). A complete determinist, he did not think that these things were simply accidents. With some knowledge of the associations and experiences of the person, slips become meaningful expressions of hidden wishes.

At this point, with the notion that unconscious mental life betrays itself in indirect ways, Freud had the essentials to take the big, decisive step. He would not be limited to the distressed minds of neurotics any longer, but was ready to include the mental life of all people. A theory of *personality* was in the offing, one having its origin in a theory of neurosis.

SUMMARY

1. The scientific creations that are personality theories bear the stamp of the era and circumstances of their creation. Although they are embedded in that *Zeitgeist*, they may reflect the genius of their creators in going beyond contemporary knowledge and thought. We are better able to understand personality theories if we know something about the contemporary scientific concepts, beliefs about theory and theory construction, and ideas about personality that influenced their development.

2. Examining Freud's psychoanalysis gives us a view of a theory emerging from the science and culture of its time. By studying the beginnings of psychoanalysis, we can clearly see the database of the theory, the processes of hypothesis formation and test, the rejection of misleading hypotheses, and the gradual merging of fractional hypotheses into a complete theory of the human person.

3. Freud was born in 1856 in the small Moravian town of Freiburg (now the Czech town of Příbor). His family, then living in impoverished circumstances, moved when Freud was young to Vienna, where their fortunes improved somewhat. Freud excelled in school, gained admission to the University of Vienna, and was admitted to medical school, where he continued to perform brilliantly. He was taken on as a research assistant by physiologist Ernst Brücke, one of the foremost proponents of scientific positivism, which sought to apply the experimental standards of astronomy, physics, and chemistry to biology, physiology, and medicine. Freud admired Brücke and was greatly influenced by him. His own belief that human behaviour could be understood in physical terms, that bodily processes and the dynamic forces of energy systems could apply to personality, came from Brücke. As a young research scientist, Freud made a name for himself in physiology, neuroanatomy, and neurology.

4. Freud yearned for an academic career, but his path was blocked by a senior colleague who stood to be appointed the professor of physiology, and by anti-Semitism in Vienna. No Jew could hope for such a high position. Brücke advised him to take up medical practice and helped to get him a small travelling fellowship to study in Paris with the noted neurologist Jean Martin Charcot.

5. Charcot specialized in treating patients with neurotic symptoms, patients afflicted with the disorder known as *hysteria*. However, Charcot thought of hysteria as an illness, a neural weakness that also manifested itself in susceptibility to hypnosis. Cleverly, he proposed that a symptom of the hysteric patient, hypnotizability, could be used to treat the disorder by suggesting the patient's other hysterical symptoms away. Freud was much impressed by Charcot and by Charcot's ideas, although he soon doubted that hypnosis was pathological and in any way linked to the neurosis of hysteria. He did, however, take hypnosis back to Vienna to use as a major treatment technique, and he also absorbed Charcot's belief that hysteria inevitably had a sexual basis.

6. Freud joined an older colleague, Josef Breuer, in what would now be called a psychiatric practice, treating patients with a variety of neuroses, of which hysteria was the most frequent. Their treatment techniques were advanced for the time but achieved only limited success. Bed rest, trips to sunny climes, drugs such as laudanum (an opiate), and hypnosis used to try to suggest the disappearance of symptoms were as much as a physician could do to help a neurotic patient.

7. Breuer had a remarkable patient, identified in Breuer and Freud's *Studies on Hysteria* as 'Anna O.', a talented young woman afflicted with a variety of severe neurotic symptoms. Often unable to understand her strange mutterings, Breuer hit upon the idea of taking them down and later asking Anna to associate to them. Anna named the technique 'chimney sweeping', and it was successful in uncovering the origin of many of her symptoms and relieving them. Anna, however, had a powerful emotional attachment to Breuer (a *transference*, Freud would later call it), and when she confronted him with a false pregnancy, Breuer turned her case over to another physician. His treatment of Anna ended in failure, but Freud saw that Breuer had discovered a hugely important method, one that would transform the therapeutic approach to neurosis. We could think of Anna as the founding patient of psychoanalysis.

8. Freud began to hone this new approach in his treatment of other patients, and he abandoned the use of hypnosis (ineffective, because it was not possible with

every patient and did not in many cases lead to the causes of a neurosis) in favour of *free association*, Breuer's method.

9. Discoveries now seemed to come at every turn. This early period in the development of psychoanalysis was exceptionally fruitful, producing observations and sparking the formulation of concepts that would take psychoanalysis from a theory of neurosis and its treatment to the doorstep of a theory of personality. The first of these concepts was that neurosis had its basis in sexual trauma, specifically in experiences of sexual seduction. Disclosure of this buried secret was accompanied by an emotional outpouring from the patient (which Freud labelled *abreaction*) followed by great relief and the reduction of symptoms. Freud held this theory for just a year, abandoning it when he concluded that it wasn't believable. Replacing his seduction theory was the view that the neurotic patient was the victim of his or her own wishes and fantasies, which create unbearable anxiety and guilt. Banishing those forbidden ideas, the new theory argued, does not solve the problem. It inhibits normal development and expression of sexuality and creates the very conditions for a neurosis. This would become part of the theory of personality that was still on the horizon.

10. Free association brought new evidence that would form the cornerstone of psychoanalysis. Required to tell everything without censorship, patients balked, employing one stratagem after another to avoid having to face the hidden and horrible. Freud used the term *resistance* to describe this process whereby patients involuntarily block the path of their own cure, and inferred that resistance must be the result of an internal struggle to avert painful disclosures. This struggle pitted the forbidden wishes, striving to be expressed, against the ego instincts (as Freud then called what would become the ego), which stuggled fiercely to keep these wishes from view. Because of the psychoanalyst's insistence on the patient's talking freely, revealing the unthinkable became a terrifying risk and the analyst an enemy. Resistance, Freud now

understood, implied a process of denial to consciousness that he termed *repression*, the most basic of defences against the anxiety engendered by the internal danger of the unconscionable.

11. Implicit in the concepts of resistance and repression were two further discoveries. First was the head-to-head struggle between the ego instincts, striving for propriety and goodness, and the forbidden wishes. This was the first formulation of *psychological conflict*. Moreover, psychological conflict may be expressed symbolically by slips of the tongue and other accidents that are not really accidents. Second, resistance and repression clearly entailed the idea of a part of mental life beyond conscious access, an *unconscious*. Before Freud, poets and philosophers had seen into this dark part of the human mind, but Freud made the unconscious a psychological concept and cited evidence for it (i.e. resistance). The unconscious is not passive, not simply an inert store of things we cannot deal with. The contents of the unconscious push for expression, and the neurotic sufferer is constantly reminded by twinges of anxiety of their presence. Maintaining repressed material in the unconscious demands energy, so the neurotic person is chronically tired and drained.

12. Another consequence of rendering experience unconscious is that the neurotic person cannot provide an intelligent account of his or her symptoms. Freud repeatedly found that neurotic sufferers felt their symptoms were mysteriously imposed on them and could offer up as the only explanation the possibility they were going crazy. In this sense, he said, the symptoms of the neurotic are irrational. This, of course, was due to repression.

13. The origin of neurosis, Freud observed, lay in childhood experience. We may say that, psychologically, he discovered childhood. At first, according to the discarded seduction theory, neurosis occurred because of actual sexual trauma. According to the revised theory, it was wishes and fantasies growing out of the child's relation to his or her parents, and a severely punishing rejection of them.

TO TEST YOUR UNDERSTANDING

1. In what ways did Freud's scientific education and experience shape the development of psychoanalysis? How much is psychoanalysis the offspring of nineteenth-century science and medicine?

2. What was the influence of the database of psychoanalysis? How do you think Freud's source of observations contributed to the emerging theory?

3. How much influence do you think Freud's time and culture exercised on the developing theory of neurosis and personality? Were these influences on Freud the person, or did they mainly affect his thinking about how people become disturbed and his ideas about human personality? Can we separate the things that moulded Sigmund Freud, child and man, from the theory he developed, or are theory and theorist inseparable? Did he rise above his time in the development of psychoanalysis or reflect it?

4. What is your view of the seduction theory? Consider the evidence for it and against it. What are its weaknesses? Are they the ones Freud saw? What are its strengths? What does it have going for it as a theory of neurosis? Is its replacement a better theory? How?

CHAPTER THREE

Psychoanalysis: Sigmund Freud

Introduction

Who could have imagined as its early years were drawing to a close and psychoanalysis was hardly more than a fragmentary and radical theory of the cause and treatment of neurosis, rejected by most of the Vienna medical establishment, that it would become an incomparably grand, full-fledged theory of personality—a theory with a vision of human nature so compelling that no one in psychiatry, psychology, and the culture at large could ignore it or take it lightly? No one but Freud himself, for he had intimations of greatness almost from the start. His was to illuminate the world of the mind, until then cloaked in darkness and misunderstanding, and to make the 'demon' of irrationality 'a comprehensive object of science', as he wrote years later to a friend, the novelist Stefan Zweig (Freud, 1925). We shall see his entire picture, mind revealed for all to see, both fascinating and forbidding, one of the most renowned and far-reaching scientific creations of the twentieth century. We shall review it and then judge it by the modern standards of psychological science.

In this chapter, we'll take psychoanalysis from the beginning days of theory building to its complete account of thought, feeling, and behaviour. These are some of the topics we'll cover:

- The structure of personality as Freud finally developed it—the three concepts of id, ego, and superego. We'll consider what each means, what processes are involved, and how these three personality components interact in the ongoing activities of human personality.
- The scheme of personality development, or the theory of psychosexual stages, through which children become adult.
- Dreams and symbolism and their relation to id, ego, and processes of ego defence.
- Some important implications of psychoanalysis for both individual and group behaviour.
- A sample of the evidence from testing the theory, both clinical and experimental.
- How psychoanalysis measures up in the contemporary world of personality theory.

Emphases

Traumatic Events and the Symptoms of Neurosis

Freud had taken major steps toward a comprehensive theory of personality in the first theory of neurosis and its revision. At the centre was his recognition of the role of childhood trauma in causing psychological distress. Even though he rejected seduction as the principal traumatic source, there remained the essential idea that some disturbance in the course of a child's development could have serious neurotic consequences. The nature of that disturbance, as we have seen, is a conflict between, on the one hand, wishes and fantasies (and memories of experiences associated with them) and, on the other hand, the censorship of the ego, which does not allow them into consciousness. When the conflict becomes intense, neurotic symptoms are likely to follow. Those symptoms represent a terribly self-denying and unsuccessful compromise between instinct-based wishes and the role of a forbidding ego in rejecting them. Symptoms are a constant reminder of instinctual urgings (sexual wishes and fantasies) and their banishment. In this way they are a highly disguised and crippling expression of the forbidden. 'Symptoms', Freud observed, 'are the sexual activity of the patient' (1953a, p. 163). They afford some relief from the wish–denial conflict, but it is relief gained at great cost.

Instincts, the Unconscious, and Defences

Psychoanalysis reflects Freud's understanding that mind is both psychological and biological, and this is especially true of the theory of instincts. The elemental drives that motivate humans are internal bodily stimuli that compel the mind to work in order both to provide an acceptable measure of fulfillment and to discipline and regulate these drives, fending off by forceful defensive processes the constant pressure that instincts exert for full and immediate expression and gratification. Psychologically, biological urges become wishes of the most extreme sort. The conditions are thus laid for internal conflict. Freud's appreciation of psychological conflict in neurosis grew to the larger understanding that it is a human inevitability to be at war within oneself. A struggle between wishes for instinctual satisfaction and the imperatives of reality and moral teaching, one that begins to confront us in early childhood, cannot be avoided and is never-ending.

Since instinctual wishes cannot be allowed through the door to consciousness, it follows that a significant part of personality is unconscious. Indeed, conscious awareness—which we all think of as the essence of personality—is only the tip of a great iceberg. We are largely blind to the raw motives that impel us, the troublesome ones of sex and aggression. Moreover, the defensive efforts of the ego to keep instincts in their place are themselves unconscious. We know this is true because what we do in defence gives away what we are defending against; if we were aware of the battle raging within ourselves, we would be conscious of the impulses the ego fights to suppress. To make the case stronger, Freud pointed to the unconsciously driven defensive measures empirically shown in psychoanalysis. The ego undertakes the job of restraining instinctual demands by invoking a variety of defensive stratagems—ego defences we shall presently consider—that mainly but not completely succeed. Unconscious wishes have a way of getting through and will betray themselves in snippets of thought and behaviour that seem strange and inexplicable, and that may make us anxious. 'I must be going crazy,' we might think. We aren't; it's just that we cannot understand.

Three Parts of Personality

Psychoanalysis sees three agencies that determine thought, feeling, and action: the concepts of *id* (containing instincts, the motive forces of the id) and *ego*, and the moral agency of the *superego*. How they function and relate to each other are the basic stuff of personality.

Although we are engaged throughout life with the events of the external world, it is the world within that controls our engagement and makes us the individual persons we are. The internal world also shapes the happenings of the external world. Squabbles, wars, and great human achievements ultimately derive their impetus from instinctual life and the way it is socialized, and the ability of the ego to reach heights of creative accomplishment depends on harnessing the urgency of instincts, most especially the sexual instinct.

Personality Development

The life of the mind starts in earliest childhood, and its first expression is an instinctual wish. So the processes of development are, no less than the mind they produce, both biological and psychological, and they are processes that appear in stages. A course of personality development unfolding in stages derived from Freud's view, based on clinical discoveries, that children are sexual creatures from infancy—not sexual in a genital sense (until later), but involved nonetheless in an insistent, sexualized drive for pleasurable stimulation. Three sensitive bodily zones—mouth, anus, and genitals—become successively the foci of sexual pleasure. They are so significant that residues of pleasure and denial, sometimes highly peculiar, can be found in adults. Freud might also have pointed out that these are biological zones whose functions must be socialized in every human society and that they mature sequentially in childhood. No zone or the stage that reflects it can be omitted, and the consequences of improper socialization—too lax or too repressive—are vastly damaging to both growing children and fully developed adults.

The Broad Sweep of Psychoanalysis

Freud applied the principles of psychoanalysis to the whole canvas of human existence. All manner of conflict with others, individual and collective, came under his gaze, as did the sexualized aggression of sadism and masochism. Love, wit and humour, the creative expression of the artist, the personality of artists in history—each finds interpretation by the concepts of the theory. Freud would not have been at all surprised by the self-indulgent sexual peccadilloes of a recent president of the most powerful country on earth, the chicanery of industrial barons, or the proliferation of Internet porn. Psychoanalysis is infinitely more than a theory of personality disturbance. It is a portrait of human beings struggling to make their lives in society.

The Major Concepts of Psychoanalysis

The Structure of Personality

The child psychoanalyst and student of psychoanalysis Bruno Bettelheim observed that Freud sought through his choice of terms and use of language to bring the most intimate and personal parts of ourselves, the deepest elements of our personalities, into clear and understandable view. He tried, said Bettelheim, to describe personality for us in language that would genuinely help us to understand ourselves. His English translators made his intimate language objective, scientific, and medical, losing Freud's purpose in the process (Bettelheim, 1983, pp. 8–10; 52–60). Bettelheim has lost credibility with some members of the academic community, including me, since he was discovered to have misrepresented himself and his training and background. Here, though, he had a point.

The Id

The place to start is with the driving force, the id. Freud's term for the id★ was *das Es*, literally 'the it', which expresses what all German children know: the word for 'child' is neuter gender, *das Kind*, and every child is referred to by the pronoun *es*. No 'he' or 'she' for children. Freud felt that *das Es*, with its insistent nature, the motive force in personality, transcends even something so basic as sexual differentiation.

The id represents the biological stratum of personality, which intrudes psychologically, as we have seen, in the form of imperative wishes. The id, in its utter intolerance of frustration, seeks to discharge tension immediately, and it does so by two mechanisms at its command that constitute the **pleasure principle★**. One mechanism for pursuing pleasure and avoiding pain is **reflex action★**: sucking, sneezing, coughing, and other reflexes discharge uncomfortable intensities of tension automatically. By far the more important mechanism of the id is the **primary process★**. It discharges tension by means of hallucinations of objects that will satisfy an instinct. The infant hallucinates its mother's breast when it is hungry and she is absent, and the hallucinated image occurs wishfully. In the image, the wish is fulfilled, and so we refer to wish fulfillment as the expression of the primary process. Normal adults don't have access to primary process images directly; they are unconscious. We only come as close as the disguised and neutered content of dreams (discussed later in the chapter). However, the psychotic person who hallucinates is experiencing primary process content and thus seems strange and disturbing to us.

Instincts have four attributes: a source, an aim, an object, and impetus. The source of an instinct is a state of need—a nutritional deficiency, for example, or a state of sexual arousal. The aim of an instinct is the removal of tension. The object of an instinct refers both to the environmental object or person that will reduce the state of excitation *and* to all the things that must take place before the need is satisfied (the behaviour of the person in seeking and finding food, for example). So everything between wish and need satisfaction is the object. Impetus is the strength of an instinct. The greater the deprivation experienced, the greater is the impetus.

Instinctual life is cyclical and must be so. A need is aroused and excitation increases. With gratification of the instinct, its aim is fulfilled and the person is quiescent. This instinctual cycle is called the **repetition compulsion**. We are condemned by our nature to repeat throughout life the arousal of tension and its diminution. This is the ultimate compulsion of existence. Repetition compulsion also refers to the perseverative repetition of inadequate and unsuccessful attempts to gratify instincts. You're right on if you can see the repetition compulsion in neurotic symptoms.

Freud was not a biologist, and he left open the question of the number of instincts. However many, there are two broad classes of them: the life and the death instincts. Life instincts have individual survival and species preservation as their purpose; examples are hunger and sex. The motor of the life instincts is **libido★**; this is their form of energy. There is a strong connotation of the sexual in the term 'libido', and it is fully intended. The death instincts are responsible for destructive behaviour, to others and to ourselves. These instincts are responsible for the ending of life. The idea of self-destroying motivation came from mechanistic nineteenth-century biology, especially the constancy principle of Fechner, which held that inherent in all organisms is the descent to a stable inorganic state. Freud made it psychological: all of us have a wish to die, and it is normally unconscious. The death instincts may be displaced to other targets. Thus, aggressiveness is self-destructiveness directed toward others. That displacement comes about because the death instincts are opposed and redirected by the life instincts. When instincts are frustrated, we attack those we think are responsible. We lend ourselves to aggressive causes like war because of the thwarting of instincts that is an inescapable part of human social life. Displacement is rarely a rational process.

As we have seen, Freud was convinced by his clinical experience and the daily probing of his self-analysis that the cardinal instinct in personality development is sex. The great cataclysm of World War I persuaded him that aggression is also an instinct of epic significance in human behaviour. I'd like to note here the fact that in every human society children must acquire control and socialized expression of sex and aggression. These are imperious motives, and it is little wonder that they have such a central influence in personality.

Psychoanalysis fully recognizes the fundamental importance of socializing the drives of sex and aggression as well as the difficulty of doing so. In its account of sexual and aggressive deviations, it gives the most complete account of disorders of sex and aggression of all personality theories. No other theory, for example, provides the understanding of sadism and masochism—the perverse fusing of aggression and sexuality—that psychoanalysis does. Not that the Freudian account of sexual and aggressive disorders can't be questioned; four subsequent chapters present theories by the neo-Freudian and ego psychology theorists doing exactly that. And, by the evidence of modern research, psychoanalysis is wrong about sex and aggression in some major respects. The expression of aggression is one major instance (see Chapter 12; also Westen, 1998). On the grounds of comprehensiveness and sheer boldness, though, the theory stands above all the others.

The Ego

The id has only the most primitive mechanisms for instinctual gratification—reflex action and primary process. By themselves, these two mechanisms are inadequate to the task of instinctual gratification. Reflex sucking doesn't get nourishment in the absence of the instinctual object, and you can't eat wishes. Thus, the ego★ emerges in earliest infancy, endowed by the id with energy to carry out activities related to need reduction. The ego is the actor, the executor in personality. It is also profoundly personal, the 'I', for that is what Freud called it: *das Ich*. The ego has many functions. In carrying out the wishes of the id so far as is possible, the ego must plan, cope with delay, and restrain. It must also engage in defence, holding back those wishes of the id that cannot be gratified or whose gratification must be made to conform to social rules. The ego must remember past punishments and anticipate them again when forbidden wishes make their presence known.

In contrast to the id, which knows only the urge for immediate pleasure, the ego and its various activities are governed by a different, but no less imperative, rule. This is the **reality principle★**, and we see in its operation the **secondary process★**. By means of reality testing, the secondary process invokes realistic and appropriate means of attaining need satisfaction, and in this it is doing the job set by its master, the id. It is the id's energy that enables the ego to carry out its worldly and intrapersonal missions. The ego has a certain independence, but it owes its existence to the id. It makes its appearance with the infant's experience of brief periods of deprivation that occur because the mother cannot instantly sense and respond to the arousal of needs and tension in her baby. Deprivation, however brief, results in a primitive but significant awareness of 'me', who experiences tension, and 'not me', the object of gratification. On this fundamental distinction, the life of the ego begins.

As the ego matures, it increasingly has to cope with peril from outside and from within. The ego sees, then, that there is threat and is frightened. That experience of fright is anxiety. There are three kinds of anxiety. One is the fear of realistic danger in the environment. This is **reality anxiety★**, and it is anxiety's prototype. **Neurotic anxiety★** is the anxiety experienced by the ego when dangerous instincts of the id are poised to break through. It develops out of reality anxiety in that what we learn from reality anxiety is applied to internal dangers. The ego must now stand in the way of urges that are extreme or that have been punished by parents, and it erects barriers called **anti-cathexes★**. A **cathexis★** (an unfortunate substitution by a translator for Freud's *Besetzung,* a familiar word in German that can mean 'occupation by troops' or 'electrical charge') is an investment of energy in an object associated with instinctual gratification. So an anti-cathexis functions to prevent that investment of energy. Anti-cathexes, or **defence mechanisms★** as they are more commonly known, are unconscious in that the anxious person will not know that he or she is employing them to defend against anxiety. These defence mechanisms also distort reality—the reality of the dangerous instinct and external reality as well. This distortion may be in the form of denial or falsification. Adding to these two kinds of anxiety is a third, **moral anxiety★**, which we'll discuss when we consider the superego.

The ego has in its arsenal a number of specific defence mechanisms, including repression—the defence that first impressed itself on Freud—plus reaction formation, projection, fixation, regression, and several others elaborated by Freud's daughter, Anna, in an excellent book, *The Ego and Mechanisms of Defence* (1966). As we look over just a few of these fundamental defences it is important to remember that all defences are variations on the purpose of denying conscious access to intolerable ideas by banishment or by distortion.

We could not do better than to let Freud himself explain the nature of repression and other defences. Here he is in 1937, in the twilight of his career, with the clearest of all his statements on ego defence:

It was from one of those [defence] mechanisms, repression, that the study of neurotic processes took its whole start. There was never any doubt that repression was not the only procedure which the ego could employ for its purposes. Nevertheless, repression is something quite peculiar, more sharply differentiated from the other mechanisms than these are from one another. I should like to make this relation to the other mechanisms clear by an analogy, but I know that in these matters analogies never carry us very far. Let us imagine what might have happened to a book, at the time when books were not printed in editions but written out individually. We will suppose that a book of this kind contained statements which in later times were regarded as undesirable—as, for instance, . . . the writings of Flavius Josephus must have contained passages about Jesus Christ which were offensive to later Christendom. At the present day the only defensive mechanism to which the official censorship could resort would be to confiscate and destroy every copy of the whole edition. At that time, however, various methods were used for making the book innocuous. One way would be for the offending passages to be thickly crossed through so that they were illegible. In that case they could not be transcribed, and the next copyist of the book would produce a text which was unexceptionable but which had gaps in certain passages and so might be unintelligible in them. Another way, however, if the authorities were not satisfied with this, but wanted to conceal any indication that the text had been mutilated, would be for them to proceed to distort the text. Single words would be left out or replaced by others, and new sentences interpolated. Best of all, the whole passage would be erased and a new one which said exactly the opposite put in its place. The next transcriber could then produce a text that aroused no suspicion, but which was falsified. It no longer contained what the author wanted to say; and it is highly probable that the corrections had not been made in the direction of truth.

If the analogy is not pressed too strictly, we may say that repression has the same relation to the other methods of defence as omission has to distortion of the text, and we may discover in the different forms of this falsification parallels to the variety of ways in which the ego is altered (1964, pp 236–7).

Altering or falsifying the nature of threats to the ego is not as primitive as trying to erase them, and for this reason tampering defences may be both less demanding to maintain and tougher nuts to crack for the psychotherapist. Here we'll outline some of these tampering defences.

REACTION FORMATION

Reaction formation★ makes intolerable feelings harmless by turning them into their opposites. Sexual attraction is turned into renunciation and revulsion, hatred into love. A mother who resents the intrusion of her newborn infant into her life lavishes care and attention on the baby to an extravagant and less than credible degree. She has something to prove and can't relax for a moment in doing so. To understand how reaction formation comes about, we need to remember that in all of us associations to emotional opposites—bad–good, love–hate—are well learned and readily available for defences to call on. Parents may unwittingly teach this defence to their children when they demand that an angry child deny his or her anger and profess love. Sibling battles are sometimes handled in this way. A mother finds her two boys fighting and makes them renounce their angry feelings and say that they love each other. At the moment, of course, they don't. If this occurs in highly charged emotional situations in which the children are made to be fearful of the consequences of their anger (loss of parental love), a basis for reaction formation may be laid.

PROJECTION

Projection★ entails the attribution to others of wishes and feelings that are intolerable to our own egos, making them appear as external threats that can be defended against. We may see others as hostile to us, when it is really within us that the hostility lies. Freud saw projection as the basis of the psychosis of paranoia. For example, the paranoid person projects homosexual wishes, impossible to acknowledge, onto another person or persons; he contrives evidence that they have designs on him and now has a fight he can conduct in the open.

FIXATION AND REGRESSION

Fixation★ and **regression**★ are closely related. If children are anxious and fearful, progress from one developmental stage to the next stage may be interrupted. They remain fixated in a particular stage. A child who sucks his thumb at age four may be showing fixation of a characteristic of the earlier oral stage (we will be discussing developmental stages and their modes of expression a bit later on). Regression means the return to an earlier developmental level when a child (or adult) is traumatized by anxiety. A six-year-old, terrified by his first days in school, may regress by wetting himself or by crying and clinging to his mother when it is time to go. An adult may regress by overindulgence in alcohol when stressed. The specific forms of regression a person shows are likely to be related to earlier fixations. If we regress in adulthood, it is usually to a level at which we showed childhood fixation.

UNDOING

Undoing★ neutralizes an unconscionable idea or act by following it with another that negates the first, as if it had never happened. Angry thoughts or words are repeated, the anger replaced by a witty remark, as if to say (perhaps to others, but more importantly to oneself), 'See, this is what I mean; I couldn't have meant anything else because there wasn't anything else.' As Anna Freud wrote, '[Undoing] is a kind of negative magic in which the individual's second act abrogates or nullifies the first' (1966, p. 33).

Finally, in our portrayal of the ego, let's consider just a little more the cathexes of the ego, those instances of investing energy in an object to achieve instinctual gratification. People who live rich, complex lives have many object cathexes. Their libidinal energy is invested widely in a great variety of objects—activities, environmental objects, and persons. People who live narrow, constricted lives may be characterized by the poverty of their object cathexes. Freud regarded schizophrenia as a particular problem because it represents a vast withdrawal of energy investment in external object choices and a great preoccupation with the self, which he called narcissism. This is so much the case, he believed, that the schizophrenic person is untreatable by psychoanalysis.

The Superego

The third in the trio of personality is the voice of society, speaking through our parents to teach us what we must and must not do and demanding that we live up to an ideal. It is the moral element in personality, what we refer to as **conscience**, and it is also the self to which we aspire, the **ego ideal**★. We know it as the superego. Freud's original term was the *Über-Ich*, the 'above-I'. The above-I emerges much later in personality development than the 'it' and the 'I', and some critical experiences that we'll discuss in the next section are required for it to emerge successfully. When the superego★ does appear, it is expressed in two dramatic new developments in the child's behaviour. The capacity for internalized behaviour control is one of them. Conscience goads us into behaving decently and resisting temptation to act in ways we know are bad. When this capacity is achieved, the child does not require the surveillance of adults to ensure his or her good behaviour. The ego ideal is the other. Derived from parents, it is chiefly the model provided by the parent of the same sex.

I must point out that the superego is not fully conscious, nor is it fair and reasonable. It is typically too severe, too demanding of restraint, and too condemning. When the superego condemns, we experience moral anxiety or guilt, the third form of anxiety. The superego is a tyrant. We see its tyranny in the punishments children would mete out to each other

(Original drawing © Dr Sandra Crowne)

when we ask them how we should deal with miscreants. We see its fierce demands and accusations in the crippled lives of neurotic patients. And, we see it in the cruelties adults may inflict on others in the name of morality, when it is corrupted by instinct.

The Stages of Personality Development

There are, broadly, two ways by which we could think of the development of personality. To take the simpler first, we could view development as continuous, each new accomplishment building on and elaborating the previous ones. Maturation will set the timetable for the acquisition of new skills; it does so with walking, bowel and bladder control, and talking, and it does so with the increasing complexities of behaviour, thinking, and emotion through which mature personality emerges. Learning theories of personality, which we'll look at later in this book, exemplify this approach.

Psychoanalysis did not adopt the simpler view. As I pointed out in reviewing the emphases of the theory at the beginning of this chapter, psychoanalysis finds discontinuities in the developmental course, distinct stages that must be entered and completed, each in turn, before the formation of personality is complete. These stages correspond to the biological unfolding of instincts, and they represent the psychology of that unfolding.

In the developing infant and young child, three areas of the body emerge in sequence as **erogenous zones***, which when stimulated give a sexualized pleasure. We should understand that the sequence has adaptive significance: infants and young children need to find pleasure in certain kinds of activities to ensure their survival and growth into socialized human beings. The experience of pleasure also makes it probable that mature individuals will contribute to reproduction and the preservation of the species. Thus, the stages in this plan are psychosexual stages.

The Oral Stage

The procession of stages begins at birth with the newborn's need for food and the necessity that the infant be responsive to the source of food and to stimuli associated with food intake. The newborn has to experience nursing as rewarding, and so the process must give pleasurable sensation. In this way, a variety of stimuli become associated with the pleasure of suckling. This is part of the equipment a fragile and helpless infant requires. During this initial period of life, the primary erogenous zone is the mouth and neighboring tissues (tongue, lips, cheeks). Accordingly, this is the oral stage, and it takes up approximately the first year.

The oral stage is divided into two subperiods. The first six months constitute a period that Freud termed *incorporative*. Pleasure derives from sucking and nursing, and stimulation of the oral cavity produces an immediate response. Touched on the cheek, a new infant turns its head and begins to suck. Mother's dependable friend the pacifier works because it provides pleasurable stimulation. As the infant begins to develop teeth and is able to

Freud in 1909, about the time of the first statement of psychosexual theory. (© Bettmann/CORBIS)

take in solid food, there is a change in emphasis. The infant becomes much more active and derives oral pleasure from biting and from the beginning of chewing. Infants at this stage reject and spit out foods they don't like, and this is done with such vigour as to suggest that this new ability is highly pleasurable. This is the oral biting or *oral sadistic* period. Freud was not just thinking of devilish little infants terrorizing their mothers by refusing to ingest anything but mother's milk, ice cream, and chocolate doughnuts; his term recognizes the implications for later personality development of things that happen during this oral substage.

Here is a good place to elaborate Freud's view of how early development can have a lasting influence on personality. We have already encountered the concept of fixation as a defence mechanism. Fixation, however, has broader implications. In any stage of development, frustration and threat that flood the child's ego with anxiety, or excessive indulgence by a parent (usually the mother) so that the child is not motivated to progress to the next stage, may result in fixation. Thus, characteristics of a given psychosexual stage become a permanent part of personality and will leave their mark on adult personality. If severe enough, psychoanalysis says, the result may be neurosis or even psychosis in adulthood—the result of traumatic experience (overwhelming anxiety) in development—or perversion from inadequate socialization (that is, excessive indulgence).

The consequences for the adult of fixation in the oral sadistic period include using and exploiting people and a mode of expression that makes use of biting sarcasm, verbal abuse, and hostility. The mouth has become an instrument of aggression, and the person's relationships with others are marked by anger, resentment, and defiance. Those attitudes have their prototype in feelings that may be traced back to this oral substage. Fixation in the oral incorporative period is likely to result in dependency, gullibility, and passivity. Truly severe oral incorporative stage trauma may so damage the immature ego that schizophrenia is the eventual result.

The Anal Stage

During the second year of life, the oral stage gives way to a new stage corresponding to a different bodily zone. The infant is now less responsive to oral stimulation; instead, he or she derives pleasurable sensation from the ano-genital region. There are again two subperiods. In the first anal subperiod, the infant experiences pleasure from the expulsion of waste material, and it is accordingly called the *anal expulsive* period. During the second half of this stage, pleasure comes from the newly matured ability to control the musculature associated with urination and defecation. Pleasure is derived from being able to control and retain feces, and so this substage is called *anal retentive*.

The notion of an anal stage and ano-genital pleasure may seem grossly inappropriate, but I need to point out that in every human society children undergo the socialization of eliminative activity. No human society allows this behaviour to go unregulated, and no child develops without having this behaviour socialized. We need to appreciate that the anal stage confronts the infant with the demand that it give up an instinctual source of pleasure which will now be subject to control and discipline. This is the first of many impositions that socialization demands, and in European and North American cultures it comes early.

What kinds of problems may develop during this stage? They are very likely to revolve around defiance and submission, a power struggle between parents and child—a young child with new-found muscular abilities and an independence that arrives with walking and the beginnings of language, versus insistent and often angry parents disgusted by the messy and stinky contents of diapers. If the child is made to give in by an overbearing mother, it may withhold feces. Constipation results, as will unfortunate psychological developments. If the power struggle spreads to other parent–child interactions, the child may develop an anal retentive character. He or she is in danger of becoming miserly and obstinate, unable to love, and obsessed by a strong interest in amassing possessions. On the other hand, a child who does not submit and has temper tantrums in the anal power struggle may learn to defecate in anger at unacceptable times and places. As Hall, Lindzey, and Campbell (1998) say, 'This is the prototype for all kinds of expulsive traits—cruelty, wanton destructiveness, temper tantrums, and messy disorderliness . . .' (p. 54). A mother who encourages her child and gives praise for bowel movements teaches her child that this is a very important and praiseworthy activity. Freud believed that the idea that defecation is laudable could generalize and form the basis for the development of productive habits and creativity.

The Phallic Stage

From the anal stage, the child at about age three progresses to a new stage that lasts for perhaps two years and has, like its predecessors, profound consequences for personality development. In fact, the consequences of this new stage may be even more significant. Freud called it the *phallic stage*, because in his view the male sex organ is psychologically significant to both sexes. We'll consider the male child first, not because I'm sexist but because of what I've just said. Libidinal energy is localized in the genital region in the phallic stage. We see the appearance of distinct signs of pleasure from manipulation of the genitals, as when the child is bathed or plays with himself (autoerotic behaviour). It is at this time that the boy may discover masturbation, and there emerges a clear sexual interest in his mother. Freud was quite explicit about this. Little children are not the innocents we naively thought they were. The child has a developing sexual life a part of which is this very sexual interest.

Where did Freud get this idea? First, he got it from the wishes and fantasies symbolized in the retrospective accounts of his psychoanalytic patients. Then, there was mythology. Freud identified the small boy's sexual longing for his mother as the **Oedipus complex**★ after Sophocles' tragedy of King Oedipus, who unwittingly slew his father and married his mother. It is a theme that appears in myths as well as in Greek tragedy, and it shows up in dreams. A third source was Freud's self-analysis. Fourth was a slender but very significant body of evidence on young children, most particularly on a boy called Little Hans. Hans's father, an amateur psychoanalyst and member of Freud's weekly discussion group (the Wednesday Psychological Society), consulted Freud on the treatment of his son. Little Hans had developed a severe phobia—a fear of seeing horse-drawn wagons turn over with injury to the horses—that was so intense that he could not be prevailed upon to leave his house. Freud saw Hans only briefly but gave advice to Hans's father and received regular reports. From Little Hans's phobia and a remarkably symbolic fantasy, Freud found confirmation of the Oedipus complex. We need a little more of the theory of the Oedipus complex, and then we'll turn to Hans's phobia and fantasy in Perspective 3.1 to see how they might contribute.

So, the boy of three or four comes to desire his mother. But, we must not liken his sexual longing to a mature, adult sexual desire. It is a childish wish, inchoate and not well imagined. He does, however, have something of the idea of sexual possession and of displacing his father, toward whom he may show signs of resentment. At this point, another element is introduced, a theme of punishment. The little boy comes to fear that his yearning for his mother will result in castration by his powerful rival. Why castration? Well, the boy's genitals are the focus of his sexual arousal, and this is just the sort of primitive notion of punishment that could occur to a small boy. Of course, an insensitive and punitive father (not, though, Little Hans's) could contribute to a nascent idea by dealing thoughtlessly with his son's bid to replace him, or a parent could actually suggest the idea (when Little Hans was three-and-a-half, his mother caught him touching his penis and told him that she would call the doctor to cut off his 'wi-wi-maker'). This may seem a terribly severe scenario, one that no child ought to have to undergo, but it is absolutely essential that the boy renounce his incestuous wishes, and the threat of castration is the signal for him to do so. The boy's fear of such a punishment is no more a clear and articulate idea than his sexual desire for his mother. It is vague, existing half in the dark, and it is phrased as the idea of a young child.

Perspective 3.1   Little Hans and the Oedipus Complex

Little Hans provided the developmental theory of the Oedipus complex with a phobia and a fantasy that Freud saw as significant confirmation. First, three facts about Little Hans: (1) His sister was born when he was three-and-a-half. (2) His mother habitually allowed him in her bed when he awoke early in the morning. (3) His father would object.

Hans's phobia began when he was five. He developed a strong dread of large animals at the zoo and feared that horses pulling carts, wagons, and buses in the street would fall down. He was also terrorized by the thought that horses in the street might bite him, and he refused to leave the house. He was especially afraid that white horses with black around the mouths (their harnesses) and blinders would bite him (his father had a black mustache and wore glasses). We may note Freud's comment on the phobia: 'A little boy's foolish anxious idea, one may say. But a neurosis never says anything foolish, any more than a dream. We always scold when we don't understand. That is to make things easy for oneself' (1955, p. 27; this translation from the German by Gay, 1988, p. 257).

In the night, said Little Hans one morning, 'there was a big giraffe in the room and a crumpled one, and the big one called out because I took the crumpled one away from it. Then it stopped calling out, and then I sat down on top of the crumpled one.' Suppose we treat this fantasy as we would a dream. We can liken the fantasy to the remembered dream, the manifest content, and what we want is its meaning, the latent content (see the discussion of dreams and symbolic expression below). Before we go further, you might like to stop and work up an interpretation, find the latent content. And, you might like to try your hand at the phobia. Do that and then see what you think of the following. How does your interpretation compare?

The major elements in the manifest content of Hans's fantasy are the big giraffe, the crumpled giraffe, and taking away the crumpled giraffe and sitting down on it. The latent content? We might think of two possibilities. First, the big giraffe represents his father, the crumpled giraffe his mother (crumpled, maybe, in reference to his mother's pregnancy and giving birth to his sister Hanna). Taking away represents possession of his mother, and it is linked to 'coaxing', his term for his affectionate (and sensuous) play with his mother in bed in the morning. Is this a small boy's version of intercourse? His father vainly objects. Note that sitting on can mean possession to a child, as when a child protects a toy from other children by sitting on it. This is Little Hans's wish (fulfilled). A second possibility is that the big giraffe represents Little Hans's mother, the crumpled giraffe wrinkled newborn Hanna, whom Hans had seen shortly after her birth. Sitting on her means destruction (Hans had repeatedly said that he wished Hanna weren't alive). Sitting down hard on another, smaller child is an aggressive idea that does occur to children.

Are these two distinct interpretations, conflicting with each other? The psychologist Roger Brown (1965) thought they could be reconciled by recognizing that Hans harboured strong resentment of two rivals for his mother's affection, his father and Hanna, an example of the principle of dream interpretation known as *condensation*. We want to note the symbols in the dream, giraffes, which must represent people (both his parents or mother and Hanna). And if you favour the first interpretation, the giraffe's neck is clearly phallic.

Next, the phobia. Does the biting horse suggest Hans's fear of castration, carried out by his father, a half-formed, dark and shadowy fear? And does the fear of seeing horses falling down represent Hans's wish and fear that his father would die? With his father out of the way, the path to his wish would be open, but at a dreadful price because he also loved his father. Remember that ambivalence in our feelings for our parents is surely universal. Or, does the falling horse-and-cart phobia represent his mother's pregnancy and the birth of Hanna? Hans had commented on his mother's fullness during pregnancy and the full buses that might fall over. The fear in this case is the appearance of a rival. Again, we may wish to see the phobia, like the fantasy, as a condensed expression of a single theme—as Brown suggests, 'resentment of rivals who deflect a mother's attentions' (1965, p. 366).

You will want to reflect on Little Hans and this clinical evidence. How persuasive is it? Does the evidence converge convincingly on the Oedipus complex, or are there other possibilities? If you think there might be, see Brown's *Social Psychology* (pp. 368–72). It presents a classical conditioning account of Hans's phobia.

The resolution of the Oedipus complex entails two vital outcomes. First is the renunciation of incestuous wishes. Second, the young boy takes a momentous step in personality development by identifying with his father as an ego ideal and moral model, incorporating major aspects of his father's personality and making them his own. This is a critical step in his becoming a man. Thus, in the normal course of events, the boy 'identifies with the aggressor', as Anna Freud put it (1966). In so doing, his infantile sexuality is repressed, and he models himself after his father. The resolution of the Oedipus complex leads directly to the development of internalized behaviour control (conscience) and the child's ego ideal. The psychoanalytic concept is **identification**★. As Brown said, 'With the concept of identification, Freud sought to solve two great problems: (1) the continuity of conscience across generations, the appearance in children of the values of their parents; (2) the institution in children of biologically appropriate sexual identities causing them to have the values, desires, and manners of their own sex' (1965, p. 375). Brown also noted that sexual identity is not biologically inevitable. It derives from relations within the family. Note that in the psychoanalytic view, the essentials of manhood and morality are inextricably linked.

Serious difficulties during the Oedipal period are likely to impair a child's conscience development. Repressive parents who fail to understand their son's behaviour in this stage and threaten the loss of love may traumatize him and foster an overbearing and tyrannical superego that will not allow even normal and appropriate sexual urges. Such a child may later be subject to excessive anxiety and guilt, making him a potential victim of neurosis. The consequence of excessively indulgent parental practices (a mother who is seductive and encourages her son's 'cute' attraction to her, for example) may be too weak a superego, one that does not produce sufficient feelings of guilt to ensure moral choices. Such a person may act on impulse and experience little guilt when he does things that society condemns.

In boys, the threat of castration initiates the events that will end with identification and the formation of the superego. For the girl, however, it is not a threat but a *perceived fact*, and thus the whole course of this stage is different. The little girl discovers that she lacks a protruding genital organ and, comparing herself to her father and male siblings, is angry and disappointed. She sees that her mother also lacks this organ and holds her responsible for what she regards as a loss (again, a childish idea, not an adult one). This weakens her cathexis for her mother, and she turns to her father to possess vicariously what she does not have. For proper feminine identification and superego development, the girl will have to reestablish her cathexis for her mother and give up the yearning for her father. This process does not involve the intensity of anxiety and the repression of the instinctual wish as it does in the male child. Boys and girls are no more alike in conscience development than they are biologically, and the nature of feminine conscience will show it. The formation of the superego is more gradual in the girl, and as a result the woman's superego will be less severe than the man's. Freud regarded the girl's path to womanhood, the completion of her personality, and her adult sexual life as more fraught with potential difficulty than the boy's progression to manhood and his mature sexuality. This was as inevitable, he said, as the permanent legacy of her anatomy, **penis envy★**.

Now feminine psychosexual development is frankly problematical, as I'm sure you've already thought. Sexist and demeaning are stronger words that may have occurred to you. The whole idea is based on clinical evidence, and we've certainly talked about the difficulty of making a good scientific case from clinical data, especially reconstructions of childhood and, moreover, not just events but wishes and fantasies. Freud wasn't happy with it. Late in his career, he complained that despite his devoted effort to understand, the sexual life of women remained 'a "dark continent" for psychology' (Freud, 1959b, p. 212). And, in exasperation, he demanded of one of his favourites, Marie Bonaparte, a devotee and former analysand: '*Was will das Weib?*' (*What does woman want?*), and answered his own question with a shrug (Jones, p. 421). Freud had not created a theory of the female side of psychosexual development with anything like a good fit to the real world of personality development in women, and he knew it. But he also stubbornly refused to abandon one of the weakest parts of the psychoanalytic edifice. For critical views, see Chodorow (1978) and Gilligan (1982).

The Latency Period and the Genital Stage

Following the phallic period and its momentous episode of the Oedipus complex, we see, particularly in boys but also to some degree in girls, an interlude lasting until puberty that is characterized by the term **latency★**. During this period the sexual instinct is no longer expressed; it has been repressed in the boy and exists only in latent form. Behaviourally, we observe the absence of any sexual interest. In the boy, this is the consequence of the anxiety engendered by the threat of castration. With puberty comes the ability for mature sexuality, and the postpubescent adolescent enters the final stage of psychosexual development, the genital stage. He or she is not finished with the urges and cathexes of the three preceding stages, however. Oral, anal, and phallic themes will be incorporated into genital sexuality. As adults, we don't outgrow our pregenital impulses.

With the resolution of the Oedipus complex, the basic work of personality development is finished. By the time the superego is formed, children have all the components of personality, and the particulars of their own individual personalities are established. In this very important sense, the child of five or six is a small grown-up. This is a very complex view of personality development, even though it focuses on a single motive. Freud's evidence persuaded him that adult personality reveals the way in which each individual passed through the psychosexual stages. The way in which each stage was mastered will leave its mark in character structure. These childhood residues may be modified by later experience, they may be subtle, but they are indelibly there. The major question that you should ask yourself is this: where does the theory of psychosexual development touch base with reality, and where is the evidence for it weak? How adequately does Freud's evidence support the theory? How else could we go about determining the validity of psychosexual theory?

Adult Character Structure

If adulthood betrays a person's psychosexual history, how can we know? Psychoanalysis proposes that there are three avenues to follow in looking for the developmental origins of an adult's character structure.

1. The *libidinal origins of adult behaviour*, although sometimes not obvious, can be observed. An example: what is the psychosexual basis of smoking or of indulgence in alcohol? These are oral activities, and the persistence into adulthood of such dependency on oral gratification suggests this early origin. We have already noted the libidinal origin of stubbornness, stinginess, the compulsive need to surround oneself with possessions, and anal or toilet rituals. These are leftovers of the anal stage, its libidinal gratifications, and fixation. So adult behaviour may tell us something about the way sexual energy was socialized. When we see oral, anal, or phallic traits in adults, it's a pretty good hypothesis that the person has not grown out of pregenital libidinal habits.

2. Adult character structure may be characterized by the clinical picture we see in an adult person. This is the classification of adult character by the *behaviour* or *symptoms* displayed. As an instance, a person might manifest hysterical character structure without overt symptoms of conversion disorder. Such a person would be likely to show unstable, over-reactive emotionality; a tendency to swallow things said to him or her uncritically; narcissism and a preoccupation with self; an inclination to express anxiety and tension in bodily symptoms (the conversion symptoms we encountered in the last chapter are stronger and more explicitly neurotic). Psychoanalysis would see the adult displaying these attributes as an oral incorporative character. Another example is obsessive-compulsive behaviour: we may see a very obsessional way of thinking, with a lot of rumination, doubt, and pedantic picking

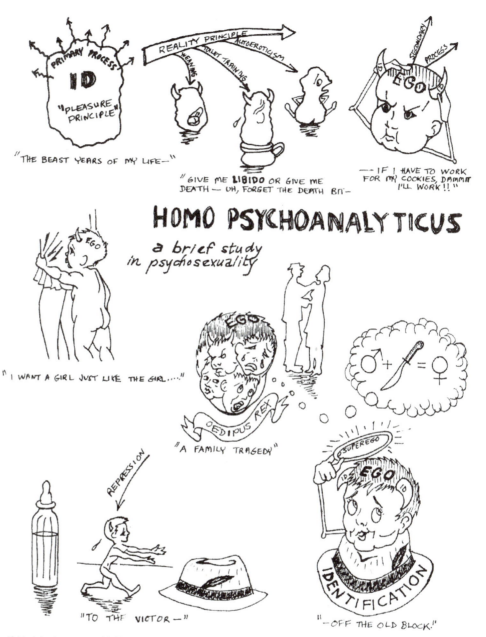

(Original drawing, courtesy of Dr William Perry)

over small points; compulsive rituals (a fetish about cleanliness, say); a rigid and stereotyped way of going about doing things; little ability to experience feeling, except perhaps some anxiety at times. This kind of obsessive-compulsive behaviour reflects anal eroticism.

3.   Third, we could try to classify adult character structure by the kinds of *fixations* that must have occurred. So, from angry and verbally abusive adult behaviour, cruelty, and messy and disorderly habits we may infer an anal fixation traceable, perhaps, to a parent–child struggle in which the mother could not control her child's rages over the demands of anal socialization.

Dreams and Symbolic Expression

Freud's masterwork, *The Interpretation of Dreams*, appeared in its first edition in 1900. He introduced it boldly:

> In the following pages, I shall furnish proof that there is a psychological technique which permits the interpreting of dreams, and that with the application of that procedure every dream reveals itself as a meaningful psychical structure, which can be inserted at an assignable point into the mental activities of waking life (1953b, p. xxiii).

It is an astonishing book, both rich in sweep and very complex. As Gay (1988) describes it,

> Freud's *Interpretation of Dreams* is about more than dreams. . . . [I]t offers a survey of fundamental psychoanalytic ideas—the Oedipus complex, the work of repression, the struggle between desire and defense—and a wealth of material from case histories. It provides, quite incidentally, sharply etched vignettes of the Viennese medical world, rife with rivalries and the hunt for status, and of Austrian society, infected with anti-Semitism and at the end of its liberal decades. It opens with an exhaustive bibliographical survey of the literature on dreams, and it concludes, in the difficult seventh chapter, with a comprehensive theory of the mind (p. 104).

What Is a Dream?

Let's begin with this elemental question. A dream is a hallucination in the sense that it represents perception in the absence of sensory input—the mind perceives something not actually present for the eyes to see, the ears to hear, and the body to feel. In dreams, there is vivid experience, usually visual but sometimes in other senses as well, that does not come directly from reality. Nor is the dream a transcription in memory, a replay of past events by the nervous system during sleep. We know that reality is often very distorted in dreams. Experiences are recombined in dreams in novel ways, and we do things in dreams—flying, for example—that are impossible in waking life. Sometimes dreams have a realistic aspect, but they are often highly altered.

Why Do We Dream?

What is the function of this curious aspect of mental life? Dreams must have a purpose, and Freud concluded that they occupy a central place in expressing the unconscious part of our minds and concealing it from us. He began his inqiry into the nature of dreams with an exploration of the significance that peoples from ancient times attributed to them. The ancients were right, he said, in believing that dreams are not mental nonsense, but wrong in their often superstitious interpretations. Dreams are not caused by the supernatural, and they don't predict the future. Their cause lies in ourselves, each and every one of us; in dreaming, which everyone does, we are doing something with fundamental adaptive importance.

Basically, the dream is like a relief valve to discharge tension and excitation that might otherwise disrupt sleep and cause anxious disturbance and awakening. We all know what happens when we have a bad dream or nightmare: we wake up, and often the residue of the nighttime disturbance lasts into the next day or even beyond. Why might tension be aroused during sleep, which is supposed to be restful? Tension is an inevitable consequence of sleep because our instinctual life is constantly pressing for expression and does not desist after we lose consciousness. The ego must not admit forbidden instincts, however, for they would arouse intolerable anxiety, and so even in sleep the ego must be watchful.

The Ego as Dream Censor

Though the ego is more relaxed during sleep it keeps up its vigilance, disguising the dangerous material by making it fanciful and innocuous. The ego, then, functions in sleep as a **dream censor★**. Freud proposed that in this role it works according to the following scheme. All dreams originate with an instinctual wish, one most often of a sexual nature. This wish is recognized by the ego and distorted. We call the instinctual wish the dream's **latent content★**, its real meaning. The instinctual wish is represented in the dream as being *fulfilled*, although the fulfillment, like the wish itself, is disguised. Why would the hidden wishes of dreams be fulfilled? For two reasons, Freud argued: because of their origin in instinctual life, and because of the imperative demands that instincts pose for immediate gratification.

The censorship carried out by the sleep-relaxed ego to make the expression of the instinctual urging harmless is called the **dream work★**. It relies on processes that are like those used by the waking ego in defence against anxiety-arousing impulses. The dream work transforms the latent content of the dream into a safer version—the dream as it is experienced and remembered (if it is) by the dreamer. This is the **manifest content★** of the dream, often curious, puzzling, and fanciful, but seldom frightening. Figure 3.1 gives us the dream schema.

Dream Symbolism

Since the unmasked latent content of dreams is quite elemental, consisting of instinctual wishes that are basic and primitive, we might expect a finite number of things to be represented in dreams. These are things like the human body, parents and siblings, birth, death, nakedness, and sexual life, and they are very likely to be represented *symbolically*. Freud was a student of mythology and found abundant evidence in myths of symbolic expression. Here are some examples of symbolism in dreams.

Figure 3.1 From latent to manifest content: The schema of the dream

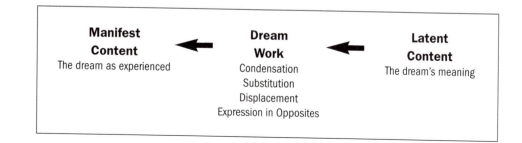

Manifest Content
The dream as experienced

Dream Work
Condensation
Substitution
Displacement
Expression in Opposites

Latent Content
The dream's meaning

- Male genitalia are generally represented by elongated objects capable of causing injury. Reptiles (remember Anna O.'s horrifying dreamlike experiences), knives, obelisks are examples of phallic objects. The sacred number 3 represents the male genitalia.
- Female genitalia are generally symbolized by receptacles—houses, rooms, enclosed spaces. Fruit is another symbol. The topography of the female body may be represented by dreams of landscapes.
- Parents may appear as figures of authority—kings and queens or others with commanding positions.
- Children are often dreamed of as princes and princesses or animals.
- Birth may be symbolized by water, death by going away on a journey.

This is only a small sample of Freud's more comprehensive view of symbols and their appearance in dreams. His list, however, was a basic one. He cautioned fellow analysts against adding new symbols to his library, insisting that the symbolic life of the unconscious mind is fundamentally simple, not a catalogue of all the things we can imagine. To follow his guidelines, we must also remember that we can't simply take the symbols that are found in dreams, apply their symbolic meaning to a dream, and immediately understand it. We need to be able to recognize the processes of the dream work that transform the latent content into the manifest content. We also need to know something of the experiences of the dreamer and the dreamer's associations to the dream. These things help us work backward from the manifest content, using our knowledge of symbolic expression and reconstructing the dream work, to arrive at an interpretation of the dream.

Dream Work and Ego Defences

As I mentioned earlier, the processes of the dream work are akin to the defences the ego uses in waking life to ward off anxious thoughts. First, **condensation★**. Can you remember having had a dream in which there was another person who seemed familiar yet whose face was unrecognizable? This was surely the work of condensation, putting two or more people together and having them represented by a single composite. Condensation may also be applied to time, to episodes, and to places.

A second dream work mechanism is **substitution★**. Potentially disturbing elements in the latent content of a dream may be substituted for by innocuous things. A patient of mine, a young woman in her early twenties then unhappily married for the second time and pregnant, presented the following dream. She returned to her apartment to find the body of a man under the bed, stabbed in the stomach with a knife. In the middle of the dream, there was a sudden transformation. She had not, it seemed, returned home to make the discovery; rather, she watched this unfold on a motion picture screen. Can you see the process of substitution here? It is the switch from a personal experience to something much more distant and safe—watching a movie scene. Something in the experience of this dream episode personally was dangerous. Freud says it would be reminiscent of an inadmissible wish.

What could this dream mean? You might like to put aside your text for a moment and jot down your ideas on its mean-

CAST OF DREAM

THE MONSTER . . . . . . YOUR FATHER
KIND WOMAN . . . . YOUR MOTHER
POLICEMAN . . . . YOUR ANALYST
FIRST STRANGER . . . . YOUR BROTHER
SECOND STRANGER . . YOUR SISTER
LITTLE BOY . . . . . YOU

ing. It is a very aggressive dream, and the instrument of aggression is phallic. Stabbing is an act of naked aggression, and it is typically masculine. It calls to mind particularly violent sexual intercourse. A relevant fact is that the man is stabbed in the stomach. Further, the body lies beneath the bed. Could the dream express the wish to injure her husband, the author of her pregnancy, in the same way she herself was injured? Could the real feeling of the dream be, 'I'd like to do to you what you did to me—put something hurtful into your body?' We would clearly like to know about this young woman's concept of feminine sexuality. The dream strongly suggests that she does not accept her own femininity and would instead be masculine, wielding a masculine instrument.

In **displacement**★, feelings, experiences, or the scenes in which things happen may be shifted or displaced. Displacement is closely related to substitution: it creates a safer distance. The scene of a dream, for example, may be displaced to a former time (for example, a period in history). Angry feelings may be displaced to another target, a person who doesn't arouse the anxiety that recognition of the real target would. **Expression in opposites**★ may also occur, as when positive, loving feelings replace hatred, or sexual attraction and arousal call forth disgust. This process is the dream equivalent of the ego defence of **reaction formation**★, which, as we saw, makes intolerable feelings harmless by turning them into their opposite.

A dream from the 1926 silent film *The Secrets of a Soul*, directed by Georg Pabst, which portrays psychoanalytically the case of a man afflicted with impotence (erectile dysfunction) who cannot make his wife pregnant. In this dream, he is seen planting a tree, accomplishing symbolically the fostering of life that he is unable to do in reality. (The Kobal Collection/Neumann-Film-Produktion)

The Sources of Dream Theory

In the construction of his dream theory, Freud drew on the dreams of his patients, his own dreams, and his extensive knowledge of mythology, in which dreams figure prominently. We know that in a number of preliterate societies dreams have special significance. It is quite striking that the meaning attributed to dreams in some preliterate societies has a close similarity to the meaning psychoanalysis gives to them. But I should say this the other way around. The Ashantis, a tribe in Africa, for example, believe that dreams have their basis in reality. A dream of adultery is sufficient to cause an Ashanti male to subject himself to a fine for adulterous behaviour. The Iroquois have long believed that dreams express secret wishes of the soul and should be reenacted when the dreamer is awake to arrive at the meaning, the secret desire. So, in these two societies we see the fundamental idea that the latent content of the dream is a wish. Freud's contribution was to formulate a theory about the source of those wishes, the danger they represent, and how wishes are made to seem more innocent than they are.

Freud dramatically called dreams the 'royal road to the unconscious'. If we are able to capture what dreams express, how symbols are used, how the ego does its essential work of transformation, and if we have particular knowledge of important and recent experiences of the individual dreamer and dreamer's associations to the dream, we can gain entry to the unconscious mental life of the person. A bold claim, this.

Perspective 3.2   The Dream of Mary Fields

Late in 1927, Mary Fields was twenty, working as a stenographer and living at home. Early one fall morning, she awakened from a dream that distressed her, and in the weeks that followed she couldn't get it out of her thoughts. Bright, well read, and bold, she determined to consult Freud, and thereupon wrote him a long, detailed account of her dream, asking him if he could interpret it and set her mind at ease. Though 'eternally ill and plagued with discomfort' as he wrote to a colleague (Jones, 1957, p. 136), he thoughtfully replied, giving her what he could of his understanding of the dream. Here is Mary Fields's dream, followed by Freud's interpretation. Read Mary Fields's letter and test yourself by applying the principles we have been considering to her dream. Then, go on to Freud's interpretation and see how yours fares. You can find more details about Mary Fields and Freud in 'Dream analysis by mail' (Benjamin & Dixon, 1996).

Professor Sigmund Freud,   *November 11, 1927*
Bertggasse 19,
Vienna Austria

Dear Professor Freud:

I am writing you because I have read a great many of your books and admire you immensely and also because I hope you can help me. In the event that you find yourself too busy to do so I hope that you can tell me who I can go to that will be able to overcome the difficulty.

My desired information is concerning dreams, or rather a dream. First I should like to know the meaning of the dream and secondly whether it will have any direct meaning or reference on my future. I must sound as if I wanted you to be a fortune teller or the like but this is not so because I realize that a man of your fame certainly would be anything but. You see among your books I have read your views on dreams and because of my great respect for you and because of my interest in your work I thought you might be able to help me. Now to go on with the dream and the series of events connected with it. I mention the events previously connected with the dream because if I remember your text on Dream Psychology rightly, you spoke many times of previous occurrences often times having a great deal of influence on dreams. Now for the basis of this letter.

But a short two months ago I met a young man who since has held a great facination for me. Not being of age as yet of course my parents tyranize over me in many respects and one of them happens to be the choosing of my friends. Possibly you may think me an ungrateful child but still it is only a few short months until I reach the age of independence. Perhaps also I ought to mention the fact that I am the only child in our family. In the case of this young gentleman there have been some very hard words spoken. The reason for this is that the young man in question is an Italian and of course is Catholic. My parents are thorough bred Americans and are also of a Protestant Religion and although they are not snobbish they feel that in going around with an Italian I am going around with some one who is not my equal. Of course the religious part of it comes in pretty strong as neither father or mother have a very strong love for the Catholic Religion. As for my self it does not bother me at all for I feel that because a person happened to be born into a family of the Catholic or Jewish Religion is nothing against them. In fact if I want to marry either a Jewish or Catholic fellow you may rest assured that I shall do so. But how well I shall accept that religion is another question.

The facination which this young man has for me has twice transported us into a forbidden paradise, it is also a fool's paradise, leaving us forgetful of every day morals and conventions. Before I met the young man in question he had been going steady with a girl of his own station in life and was going steadily enough with her so that she was wearing his ring, but since he has practically given her up entirely and devoted his time to me. These are the circumstances leading up to the dream. Now for the dream.

I saw myself sitting in a place that was unfamiliar to me still I seemed to be very much at home. It seemed to be a place poorly furnished so it could not have been home for our place is very beautifully furnished. My uncle, rather my mother's brother, and my father were sitting on the front porch talking and as it was a very hot day I was seated inside by an open window fanning my self, and while I was dreaming as I sat there the door bell rang. Upon answering the ring I found the brother of my young Italian friend. He was dressed very pecularily wearing the modern civilian clothes of the average American but with a large gaudy colored Mexican Sombrero on his head. We passed the time of day and for several minutes conversed politely on daily news topics of interest, the both of us standing up he on the porch and [me] in the house. He did not disclose the object of his visit until he was ready to depart when he handed me a letter saying that it was from his brother. As a parting remark he told me that he was coming into the city to see me next week and that probably there would be four or five other fellows along with him. In the meantime my father and uncle seemed to have disappeared when they went I have no recollection of but when I answered the door bell they were not upon the porch. The young man who called upon me lives in a small town not far from my summer home and that is why he told me he was coming in to see me.

Well I opened the letter and I can still see the expression of horror, dismay, and dispair which was shown on my face. The letter told me that this young Italian boy had been married on the afternoon of October 17th to a Miss Mildred Dowl. I cannot account for the girl's name because it is not the name of the girl to whom he was formerly engaged or even her initials. The name I cannot account for as I have never known any one by the whole name given above or even the last name.

Well in my dispair I happened to look down on a small table standing near me and saw a large brass paper knife with a sharp edge. Grabbing the thing up I struck myself a hard blow around the region of my heart (I must sound quite dramatic, but I assure that I was and am far from feeling that way). I remember the sensation distinctly of the knife passing into my body. The first was the somewhat like the eternal thrill and it passed into something more powerful, lasting and serious, which cannot possibly be explained. I distinctly remember dropping to the floor without the slightest cry or shudder. I saw myself laying on the floor on my right side with my legs drawn up and my left hand outstretched and my right hand still clutching the paper knife. At this time I awoke and I was somewhat startled to find myself lying in the same position in bed as I was when I last saw myself lying on the floor presumably dead. Upon awakening I found the tears coursing down my face and it took me some little time before I could control myself. The next day I found myself thrown into the worst case of blues or dejection or whatever you want to call it and it was an impossibility to pull myself out of it. This comes back to me after I have been thinking about the dream and trying to find a solution of it myself.

This dream occurred during the early morning of the 18th of October. I hope that you will not think me bold for telling you the things I have and also for writing you and asking the favour that I have. If I have annoyed you with my troubles please dear Professor Freud forgive me I really did not intend to. Please believe me when I say that. And also please won't you help me for there seems to have been nothing on my mind but this confounded dream and as I am a stenographer it does not pay to have your mind occupied with anything other than business during business hours. I feel perhaps that just writing you and waiting a reply will relieve the sense of something formidable hanging over me which was caused by the dream.

Awaiting your reply, I am thanking you now for whatever help you can be to me, and begging you to pardon me for bothering you with my troubles.

Sincerely yours,
Mary Fields

PROF. D^R. FREUD   *WIEN IX. BERGASSE 19*
                                                                    Dec. 2nd 1927.

Dear Miss Fields,
I found your letter charming and I am willing to give you as much help as I can. Unhappily it does not reach very far. Dream interpretation is a difficult affair. As long as you cannot explain the name Mildred Dowl in your dream, find out what the source of these two names is, where you got it, a trustworthy explanation of the dream is not possible. You must have heard or read this name somewhere, a dream never creates, it only repeats or

puts together. If you were here in Vienna and could talk to me in my study, we could detect where these names come from. But you are not here and the fact is, you have forgotten it and not yet remembered.

Now for the little I can grasp of the hidden meaning of your dream. I see your emotions towards the young Italian are not undivided, not free from conflict. Besides the love you feel for him there is a trend of perhaps distrust, perhaps remorse. This antagonistic feeling is covered up during your wake life by the love-attraction you undergo and by another motive, your resistance against your parents. Perhaps if your parents did not dislike the boy, it would be much easier for you to become aware of the splitting in your feelings. So you are in a conflict about him and the dream is a way out of the maze. To be sure, you will not leave him and fulfill your parents' request. But if he drops you this is a solution. I guess that is the meaning of the dream and your emotional reaction is produced by the intensity of your love while the content of the dream is the result of the repressed antagonism which is yet active in your soul.

Please write me another letter if after the receipt of mine you are able to explain the origin of the two names.

With best wishes
yours sincerely

Freud

From Benjamin, Jr, L.T., and Dixon, D.N. 1996. 'Dream analysis by mail: An American women seeks Freud's advice.' *American Psychologist*, 51, 461–8.

Some Extended Implications of Psychoanalysis

We've mapped out the theory, its developmental scheme, how it regards personality disorder, and some of the kinds of evidence of unconscious mental life and conflict that bear on it. Now, let's follow Freud as he applied the theory to a whole variety of social problems and questions about individual behaviour. In his hands, psychoanalysis offered answers to a number of human riddles, individual and social. Here are some of them.

Creative Expression

Where does human creativity come from? Because all ego activity derives from the id (remember how the ego emerges from the id to serve the id's purposes), everything we do has origins in the id's instinctual wishes. Creativity is no exception. It represents a particular way in which libidinal energy is expressed. The creative person, the artist, has an unusual access to instinctual life that most people do not have, and the artist is able to use his or her awareness—partial and veiled though it is likely to be—of those wishes, images, and fantasies to produce something new and beautiful. As psychoanalyst Ernst Kris observed, the creative person is capable of 'regression in the service of the ego' (Kris, 1964). This means turning back, regressing, to more primitive forms of instinctual expression, not just in immediate pleasure-seeking and not because the ego has broken down. Rather in these very special people the ego is able to make a disciplined, creative use of instinctual material.

Aggression

Freud had a curious view of aggression, as we've seen. It stems from a self-destructive instinct that represents an entropy principle, the end result of biological catabolic processes. All living things eventually die, and Freud believed that this biological principle was inherent in humans as an instinct of self-destruction. Aggression against other humans represents a displacement of the death instinct, a displacement that is most necessary from the point of view of human survival. The death instinct is opposed by the life instincts, but there is an inevitable cost in internal tension. Moreover, we cannot avoid frustration of our instincts: the ego is always offering delayed and expurgated opportunities for gratification. Human socialization exacts a severe price: for the privilege of being raised among and living with other humans, each of us must surrender the immediate gratification of instincts not easily turned down. In fact, Freud asserted that the more civilized the society, the greater are its demands for instinctual modification and delay, the more it expects its individual members to renounce direct instinctual pleasures in favour of 'civilized' ego pursuits.

The consequence of civilization, then, is frustration and tension. That contributes to the displacement of aggression by individuals, and by the recruitment of individuals to group causes such as war or participation in terrorism. Freud was very pessimistic about the possibility that humans could ever learn to control their aggressiveness. In a famous correspondence with Albert Einstein in 1933, he gave expression to his doubt that humans could ever discipline aggression. Humans, wrote Einstein to Freud, have a 'lust for hatred and destruction' (1933), and Freud agreed. His way of making the point was to claim the existence of an 'active instinct for hatred and destruction' (1959a).

Now, a question for you: can you apply Freud's concept of the death instinct and its displacement to sadism and masochism? What do these personality deviations represent in Freud's aggression theory? Try to explain in psychoanalytic terms the Australian composer Percy Grainger's pleasure in being whipped. How about the sadist's pleasure in inflicting pain and injury?

Transference

In Chapter 2 we considered the concept of transference, according to which the psychoanalytic patient comes to attach to the analyst attitudes and feelings that are truly retrospective, that really were acquired in and characterized the patient's childhood relationships with his or her parents. Freud believed that patients in psychoanalysis were not alone in the transference of childhood attitudes. Indeed, the model for many relationships of both children and adults is the relationship of child to parent. With their teachers, children betray their feelings toward and depend-

The Dream by Salvador Dali. © Salvador Dali. Fondation Gala-Salvador Dali/SODRAC (2006). (Photo credit: Erich Lessing/Art Resource, NY)

ence on their parents. A kindergarten or first-grade child raises her hand and when the teacher acknowledges says, 'Mummy, I . . .' and is, of course, painfully embarrassed. This is transference; for a moment, the teacher 'is' Mummy.

The relation of people to their leaders is another instance in which transference is unconsciously expressed. Attitudes and feelings toward leaders are often more emotional than the leader's public acts warrant—sometimes hostile, in other cases filled with adulation. We'll find, says Freud, strong residues of childhood feelings for parents (dependency, for example, or resentment and rebelliousness). In other words, we overreact to our leaders, endowing them with attributes that are not actually theirs. When we become disappointed in a leader, we attack and try to bring down that leader with much greater ferocity than the immediate circumstances usually warrant. Political life is not really understandable without recognition of the unconscious intrusion of transference.

Wit and Humour

Both internal and external cues can provoke bad impulses, which will arouse the anxiety that is the ego's signal to come to the rescue with mechanisms of defence to counter these impulses. But we also relieve anxiety aroused by the unthinkable and discharge excess tension in other ways. One of them is through wit and humour. When we laugh at a dirty joke or a hostile putdown, the laughter is a sudden discharge of energy. We laugh in relief because a dangerous idea has been expressed openly in a way that divests it of its danger. This relief by laughter is related to the process of abreaction—the sudden emotional outpouring that accompanies the lifting of repression.

Psychoanalysis in Literature

Psychoanalysis has attracted a large following in literature. Literary critics have applied a psychological and specifically psychoanalytic point of view to understanding literary creation. Novelists and poets delve into the world of psychoanalytic ideas to fashion characters and images, and they also acknowledge hidden depths of their personalities from which inspiration comes. In the *Collected Poems* of the noted poet W.H. Auden is 'In Memory of Sigmund Freud', with these lines:

> If often he was wrong and at times absurd,
> To us he is no more a person now
> But a whole climate of opinion
> Under whom we conduct our differing lives.

Consider Norman Mailer, a contemporary American icon. Mailer says of writing, 'If you tell yourself you are going to be at your desk tomorrow, you are by that declaration asking your unconscious to prepare the material. . . . Count on me, you are saying to a few forces below: I will be there to write' (Mailer, 2003, p. 142). In this he gives what many writers give—a Freudian credit.

Research

In Freud's view, and in the view of many psychoanalysts (there are some notable exceptions), the principal evidence for the theory is necessarily and appropriately clinical.

Only in the intimate and benign setting of an extended psychoanalytic session is it possible to discover the realities of instinctual life and what happens to instincts. Freud was adamant that no other investigative method could possibly provide such data. He was convinced that psychoanalysis represents both a method of treatment and a scientific method of validation of hypotheses derived from the theory. He thought the experimental laboratory inadequate to study human personality, and it remained for a few brave psychologists and research psychiatrists to take psychoanalytic hypotheses into the laboratory to test them.

Freud was a brilliant clinician. Not at first, when he was discovering technique, but over time he became supremely adept. One finds in reading Freud and reading about Freud that his clinical skill was exceptional. He once treated the Viennese composer Gustav Mahler for erectile dysfunction, a treatment that took place over about four hours on one afternoon, all the time that Mahler could bring himself to devote to his problem and all the time Freud could give after Mahler's considerable procrastination. In those brief four hours, a tiny fraction of the time a psychoanalysis requires, Mahler was astonished to discover how much Freud had penetrated the depths of his character. At one point, Freud expressed surprise that Mahler hadn't married someone named Marie, for that was the name of Mahler's mother who, as Freud observed to him, '. . . played such a dominating part in your life'. Mahler's wife was named Alma Maria. 'Ah,' said Mahler, 'but I call her Marie.' During that afternoon, Mahler came to recognize that his music, especially some of the complex, mocking, satirical, or despairing parts of it (in the Third Symphony, for example, or in one movement in particular of the First), had significant origins in childhood experience. Mahler acknowledged to Freud that he could never complete a beautiful and lyrical theme but always seemed compelled to destroy it, mock it, and spoil it (Jones, 1955). It was Freud's clinical genius that brought these things out.

But let's recall our discussion of scientific method and of the clinical method. The clinical method, although it represents a start, has serious scientific shortcomings. It is good at generating hypotheses but weak in testing them, weak in ruling out competing alternatives. What does the clinical method rely on to test the validity of a hypothesis? Basically, it is the internal consistency of the evidence provided by the patient's account, awareness of the patient's culture, knowledge of myths and dominant themes in many cultures (as in the interpretation of dreams), and fit with the evidence from other patients. Freud was exceptionally diligent in testing his ideas—about a single patient and about theoretical ideas applying to all patients and to all people—before coming to a conclusion. And he was honest in rejecting ideas—truly important, significant ones—when the evidence failed them. Rejection of the seduction theory is a good example. But we still have the problem of converging, without ambiguity, on a single hypothesis, confirming it positively so that other rival hypotheses cannot stand. From data input to filtering relevant from irrelevant, to fitting the pieces together, we have one individual using his observational powers and wits. A keen observer and a towering mind can produce a compelling theoretical account.

What we don't have, however, is assurance that another acute observer and astute mind would observe exactly the same things, would filter them in the same way and arrive at the same conclusions. It is a central feature of the experimental method to ensure that other investigators doing just what the reporting investigator does will reproduce his findings. Nor do we have **replication**★ of the observations. Individual patients who contribute essential evidence come by only once. Other patients may have important similarities, but their data are not reproductions of the original. Indeed, critical observations are often not repeated. So the task of the clinician/scientist is greatly complicated by the need to recognize the significant when it appears (it might not again in the same form), to recognize it in different form in other cases, and to find the consistency, internal and between-case, in the evidence. It's no wonder that we can have so many differing interpretations of similar clinical material. Thus, the experimental method.

Freud lectured on psychoanalysis at Clark University in Massachusetts in 1910, and a number of psychologists attended. At the time, though, there really wasn't much serious interest, and psychoanalytic hypotheses attracted little research. It wasn't until the late 1930s, at the Institute of Human Relations at Yale University, that experimentally trained psychologists began in earnest to study psychoanalytic propositions. Since then, research based in psychoanalysis has increased vastly. In the 1950s, there were dozens of experiments, hundreds by the end of the 1960s, and now thousands. Many psychologists identify themselves as psychoanalysts or at least as interested in and influenced by psychoanalysis.

Research on psychoanalytic ideas falls under a number of headings. Two of the most important are defence mechanisms, especially repression, and unconscious processes. These are cornerstones of psychoanalysis, and we'll consider research in these two areas. We'll look at repression first, then at the evidence for unconscious mental processes.

Repression

Repression—the selective forgetting of ideas, wishes, memories whose recall would lead to unendurable anxiety—is involuntary, and what is repressed does not simply vanish but remains, inaccessible to consciousness. It continues to exert a covert influence whenever there are associative or external reminders. Anxiety may be experienced when the repressed threatens to appear, and it requires constant energy to keep it from view. Unpleasant stuff, this. Psychologists studying repression have had their work cut out for them. It takes patient effort and lots of skill to create the clinical conditions to draw out the repressed (that is, to see repression through the return of the repressed). And if it's difficult clinically, how much harder must it be to set up the conditions to observe repression in the laboratory?

Oh, but we have a problem. We don't, as the great psychologist Kurt Lewin pointedly observed many years ago, investigate hydrodynamics by studying the biggest rivers in the world; we create the essential conditions of the phenomenon in the laboratory, in miniature and manageable (1935, p. 21). So, couldn't (and shouldn't) we do that in the experimental study of repression? Of course, and this is exactly what psychologists have done since the very first of the repression experiments early in the 1930s. What, though, are the essential conditions? Just how afraid do experimental participants have to be? How much threat do they have to experience to set the process off? Were the psychoanalysts—who from Freud on disdained the experimental study of repression and other psychoanalytic hypotheses—right in believing that repression could *only* be observed clinically and the hypothesis tested clinically? Likely not; this would be a serious violation of the principles of scientific investigation. The question, however, stands: what are the conditions for repression to occur, and can we create them in the laboratory?

So, how *have* psychologists tackled repression as an experimental problem? There are two basic approaches to studying repression experimentally. In one of them, we *arouse* anxiety in the form of fear of a frightening prospect like receiving electric shocks, or from threatening the ego (experimental participants are made to feel stupid, incompetent, unworthy of being at university). The test is to see if there is failure to remember critical stimuli closely associated with the threat. There are a number of these experiments, dating back to the 1930s. Because of equivocal findings, there are few of them undertaken now; enthusiasm for this experimental paradigm has waned.

In the second approach, we *select* experimental participants by personality tests that measure the tendency to repress uncomfortable ideas or feelings, then we look for behaviour that is consistent with a repressive personality. One thing we might do is expose these participants (and, of course, nonrepressing controls) to critical material (sexual and aggressive stimuli, as in the studies described below) and see if they are able to recognize them. If not, we infer that a disposition to repress is responsible. We'll consider an example of each approach.

The Experimental Induction of Anxiety

The very best of this type of experiment, I think, was one by Glucksberg and King, conducted in 1967. It is clever and subtle. The experiment relies on the phenomenon of **associative mediation**. Think of a word (any word will do) and then an association to that word and another association to the second word. Just before breakfast, I immediately came up with *bacon . . . egg . . . chicken . . . feathers . . . pillow . . . sleep*. There will be an association between feathers and bacon, an indirect one mediated by the two intervening words. We know that learning can be eased considerably by associative mediation. Here's how this works. Have experimental participants learn a list of items consisting of pairs such as *CEF* (a nonsense syllable)–*stem*. *Stem* strongly tends to elicit the association *flower*; *flower* thus acts as an inferred mediator. Let's call this group of inferred mediators the A–B list. Now, make up a set of words that are associations to the inferred mediators (the D list); as our D list word for *stem–flower* we'll use *smell*, a strong association to our inferred mediator, *flower*. Now have participants learn to pair the nonsense syllables with the D words. The result is the A–D list; in our example, the result would be *CEF–smell*. If participants learn the A–B list first, their learning of the A–D list is appreciably quicker.

Glucksberg and King turned this procedure on its head, associating certain of the D words with the expectation of strong electric shock. This should make the corresponding B words—each one associated indirectly with these D words through its inferred mediator—unpleasant to remember. They started by training their participants on the A–B list until it was learned. Now, they administered electric shock to a number of the D words (the remainder were control words to establish a baseline against which to compare the D-word effects). Now, in the critical part of the experiment, participants got a single trial on the A–B list. The question: how many of the B words (associatively linked to the D words by the mediator) would they fail to remember? They compared the forgetting of the B words linked associatively to shock to the forgetting of the control words. The results: significantly greater forgetting of the shock-linked words. Glucksberg and King concluded that this was due to repression.

The principal criticism of most of the experimental studies inducing anxiety has been that the experiments did not demonstrate a memory failure (i.e. motivated forgetting, repression) but rather the effects of interference with learning from anxiety and stress. That

Table 3.1	Word lists in the Glucksberg and King Experiment		
Glucksberg and King's Repression Experiment			
A	*A-B List* *B*	*C* *(Inferred Mediator)*	*Shock D Words* *D*
CEF	stem	flower	*smell
DAX	memory	mind	**brain
YOV	soldier	army	navy
VUX	trouble	bad	**good
WUB	wish	want	need
GEX	justice	peace	*war
JID	thief	steal	**take
ZIL	ocean	water	drink
LAJ	command	order	disorder
MYV	fruit	apple	*tree

*Words were shocked words for one group
**Words were shocked words for another group
Source: After Glucksberg & King, 1967.

criticism can't apply here because the A–B list was learned *before* shock was administered. This is an awfully good experiment, but it is really only one out of a considerable number to show convincing evidence of a repression-like process. It would have been even better if Glucksberg and King had tested one more group of participants in exactly the same way as the experimental group except for removal of the shock electrodes before the final A–B test. Now, with no expectation of shock, we might see what Freud termed the 'return of the repressed', a critical bit of evidence that repression has actually occurred.

Individual Differences

Now, the second approach. This method studies individual differences in motivated forgetting by selecting participants who on the basis of personality test scores are likely to repress, and comparing them to participants who are not potential repressors. Among the best of these experiments is a series by Weinberger and his associates (1995; Weinberger, Schwartz, & Davidson, 1979). They classify their subjects according to the results of two personality tests—one a measure of anxiety and the other a measure of defensiveness. They identify those who have low anxiety scores and high defensiveness scores as 'repressors' and compare them to participants who are truly 'low anxious' (those with low anxiety scores and low defensiveness scores). Compared to the truly low anxious, repressors show longer reaction times to sexual and aggressive verbal stimuli. They find it more difficult to remember unpleasant childhood experiences, and they have a higher risk to health due to their hyperreactivity to stressful events.

These are interesting findings, but they don't necessarily indicate repression—that is, an inaccessibility of memory for difficult events. So-called repressors could be more upset by distressing stimuli and memories and more reluctant to acknowledge their distress. We have no way of knowing whether repression or unacknowledged distress is the better interpretation.

Equivocal Findings

An experimental case for repression has not been made. As Holmes, a critic of repression research, has written,

> . . . despite over sixty years of research involving numerous approaches by many thoughtful and clever investigators, at the present time there is no controlled laboratory evidence supporting the concept of repression. It is interesting to note that even most of the proponents of repression agree with that conclusion. However, they attempt to salvage the concept of repression by derogating the laboratory research, arguing that it is contrived, artificial, sterile, and irrelevant to the 'dynamic processes' that occur in the 'real world' (Holmes, 1990, p. 97).

He recommends that requirements for 'truth in packaging' be extended to include the following: 'Warning: the concept of repression has not been validated with experimental research and its use may be hazardous to the accurate interpretation of clinical behaviour' (Holmes, 1990, p. 97). Other critics of the repression hypothesis (for example, Loftus, a noted memory investigator) point out that victims of horrific, unimaginable events like the Holocaust don't repress the memory of them. Instead, they are far more likely to be tormented by recollection. I think we have to conclude that repression is a genuinely problematical and uncertain hypothesis.

Unconscious Processes

If repression has not fared well in the laboratory, Freud's central proposition of an unconscious mental life has done better, and there is an abundance of evidence to support the idea that our cognitive processes are in part unconscious. First, let's note that the notion of unconscious mental processes had a life outside psychoanalysis. Charcot's pupil and later associate Pierre Janet proposed that aspects of consciousness could become split off—*dissociated*—and inaccessible to consciousness. Complex acts could be performed completely without awareness, although they would intrude disruptively on consciousness. The phenomena of hysteria exemplify dissociated ideas and affect. The great American psychologist William James recognized hysteria and multiple personality as instances of unconscious (he preferred the term *subconscious*) mental states, and he also believed that ideas and feelings could be unattended or unconscious mental states in their own right. It was Freud, though, who took the concept of unconscious mental life and made it a core feature of personality. Freud thought of the unconscious as the store of ideas, wishes, and feelings that could not be admitted to consciousness. The processes by which cognition and emotion are banished he also saw as unconscious; repression and other defences against anxiety are not under voluntary control. A psychology of consciousness, he argued, would be woefully inadequate to understand human motivation and cognition.

The American movement in psychology known as 'behaviourism' rejected the study of consciousness, since it regarded thought as an implicit, covert process inaccessible to observation. If you can't see it and measure it, behaviourists contended, it's not a fit subject for psychological inquiry. And if they wouldn't consider consciousness, you can imagine their attitude toward the study of mental life the person isn't even aware of! Behaviourism reigned for half a century, but then came a revolution in the 1970s—the cognitive revolution—that brought the study of processes like attention and information processing into the mainstream of psychology. And with them came the study of cognitive processes beyond awareness—unconscious processes. This has been an experimental inquiry broader and less constrained by issues of unconscious motivation and defence against anxiety than Freud's. But Freud indubitably provided a provocative stimulus to present research on what we may characterize by the umbrella term of the psychological unconscious. The literature is now vast, but we can touch on some major findings:

- Nisbett and Wilson (1977) presented a persuasive body of evidence that we can make judgements and decisions without knowing why we make them, including judgements about others that reflect attitudes of prejudice.

- We have memories we're not aware of that nevertheless influence conscious thought and action. This is *implicit memory*, and we can distinguish it from *explicit memory*, the kind of memory we understand and know, in which we can recall past events (Schacter, 1987). Implicit memories can influence our choices and preferences and our readiness to accept the persuasion of propaganda and politicians. How can we tell? Here's an example: we show experimental participants a number of sentences ('House mice can run an average of four miles per hour.' 'Crocodiles sleep with their eyes open.'), and (just for a plausible reason for the sentences) we ask the participants to rate how interesting each one is. Later, we present a new set of sentences, with some of the earlier ones repeated, asking our participants to judge their credibility on a scale from 'certainly true' to 'certainly false'. Although the participants do not recall having seen any of the new sentences before, they are more likely to accept as true the ones they had actually read previously (Begg, Armour, & Kerr, 1985; Brown & Halliday, 1990). This is an effect of implicit memory, one outside awareness. Can the familiar influence you, even though you're not conscious that it is familiar? Can subtleties of commercial advertising or propaganda or political claims affect, say, the choices you make even though you have no conscious memory of having paid any attention to previous exposures?

- Thought may also be unconscious, although that seems oxymoronic: how can we think if we are unaware of thinking? There are experiments, however, that establish thought beyond awareness. Among the best of them is a series of Canadian studies by Bowers and colleagues (Bowers, 1984, 1987; Bowers, Farvolden, & Marmigis, 1995; Bowers, Regehr, Balthazard, & Parker, 1990). The experimental procedure involved presenting subjects with word triplets and asking them to think of a word common to all three. Some triplets were soluble, but others could not be solved. The key finding is that subjects could identify which triplets were soluble and which insoluble even when they could not solve the potentially soluble ones. They knew but didn't know how they knew, a kind of 'feeling of knowing' as Kihlstrom (1999) observes or, as Bowers (1984, 1987) termed it, intuition. We may have, as Kihlstrom goes on to say, 'gut feelings that we are correct, without knowing why, or even whether, we are right' (1999, p. 429).

- A *motivational unconscious* comes closer to the psychoanalytic unconscious. McClelland, Koestner, and Weinberger (1989) have proposed the idea of *implicit motives*, which can be inferred from fantasy measures such as the Thematic Apperception Test. The TAT (as it's called) and related kinds of personality measures ask respondents to tell a story about a picture (or sometimes to develop one from a story stem) that is general enough that it could yield many different stories. The picture or stem thus draws out what is important to the person, and we can score the stories for the expression of needs such as achievement or affiliation or the need for power. Such tests are called *projective tests* because the person responding must project his or her own themes (motives) to create a story. We're mostly unaware of our implicit motives. We do, though, have *explicit motives* that we can identify and characterize to others.

- Now, say McClelland and colleagues, let's see what kinds of predictions can be made from implicit and explicit motives. So, we might try to predict motive-related

A Fresh Look: Research Today

Some research psychologists have followed psychoanalysis right into its lair to study psychoanalytic hypotheses in the place Freudians regard as critical to scientific tests of the theory, the place where therapeutic work gets done. There and nowhere else, Freud insisted, when patients have to talk about things that arouse anxiety, we have the opportunity to see the mechanisms they call up to ward anxiety off, to put the cause of it beyond danger, and then we may get to find out what it was that made them feel so threatened.

We have seen that experimental psychologists of personality brought psychoanalytic propositions into the laboratory to give them the rigorous look of a controlled experiment. Repression and unconscious processes are notable examples. But to take on the Freudian at home, inside his own doorstep, studying the behaviour of people under threat is to raise the challenge by several notches. This is just what contemporary investigators have done, creating a context analogous to the psychoanalytic hour, in which self-esteem can be assaulted and the person's habitual mode of defence observed. That context? The interview.

My colleague Geoff Fong joined Lisa Feldman Barrett and Nathan Williams to study defensive verbal behaviour— exactly what we have to observe in the psychoanalytic hour—evoked by stressful questions put to interview volunteers (Feldman Barrett, Williams, & Fong, 2002). Their participants weren't patients, you (and the doubting psychoanalyst) might object, but I think it's fair to say, close enough. Anxiety is anxiety, and Freud never claimed that the *only* place anxiety and the defences used to protect against it may be seen is behind the psychoanalyst's office door. Feldman et al. took the psychodynamic position that we can see in every person a characteristic repertoire of verbal behaviour to ward off the personally distressing. As they said, 'Defense mechanisms are active when the speaker uses speech primarily to influence himself or herself or to confirm a positive self-belief . . . a method of modifying, dissipating, or preventing the articulation of thoughts and feelings that will threaten the self, . . . designed to help the speaker try to think or feel something different from what he or she originally thought or felt' (p. 778). That defensive armament will be called out especially when there is threat—the probing nature of the psychoanalytic requirement or an interviewer's questions.

The interviews began innocently enough ('How do you feel about coming in for the interview today?' 'Tell me a little bit about your family.'), but then became intrusively personal, asking about violations of morality ('Describe a time when you've broken your own moral code.'), aggression to another ('Describe a time when you've deliberately said something to hurt someone's feelings.'), sexuality behaviour—for example the tendency to seek help from others—from an implicit-motive measure (the TAT) and from a self-report questionnaire that assesses explicit motives. Let's say the two motivational measures don't correlate with each other. Is this the fault of personality tests with weak validity, as we have conventionally thought? Not at all. A motive that is accessible for conscious report is not related to the same motive inferred and scored from imaginative stories. However, McClelland et al. find that implicit motives tell us about long-term goals and behaviour, while explicit-motive measures speak to immediate goals. Want to predict the goal of seeking help today for a difficult calculus test coming up? Respondents whose high dependency (help-seeking) scores on the explicit motive test show their motivation are likely to seek help. Want to predict a lifestyle of dependency on others? Try the implicit motive measure. Thus, these conscious and unconscious motive systems are *dissociable*. A given motive may have both implicit and explicit aspects affecting different behaviour and goals and different accessibility to awareness.

('How satisfied are you with your sex life?'), and negative self-image ('Tell me about a time when you felt that your parents were really disappointed in you.'). The interviewers pressed for more details if the participant wasn't forthcoming enough. Responses were coded on a four-point defensiveness scale (0 if none, 3 if there was no or hardly any awareness of threat, only positive self-references, or attribution of responsibility for harm or misbehavior to others). Thus, the criteria were awareness of potential threat to self and distortion if the threat was recognized.

Defensive verbal behaviour was clearly evoked, and it varied among individuals. Some denied that there was any threat at all, managing to deflect it by banishing awareness of potential danger to self-esteem or manipulating the threat to make it innocuous or a reflection on others. Others rolled with the questioning punches, readily handling personal exposure. A contrived experiment, then, made an essential Freudian point: defensiveness is a personal attribute to be seen in individual verbal behaviour. Moreover (no surprise), some people have greater need to be defensive than others.

A second experiment challenged the interview participants with questions to expose contradiction and self-deception more openly ('It sounds like you have two feelings. When you first responded, you said that you doubted your ability to succeed in school, but also said that you think you have a bright academic future.'), comparing this stronger threat condition to two neutral ones. It thus offered the possibility of examining both individual defensive response and variation induced by the situation. Both could be seen. The confrontational questions increased the self-protective efforts of most participants, but the vulnerable defensive person was threatened not only by the stressful questions but by the easy, non-invasive ones as well. As Feldman et al. noted, 'defensive behavior itself does not necessarily tell us anything about chronic motivations of the individual—it might tell us something about the situation, or a person's response to the situation' (p. 786).

Freud, we know, gave insufficient acknowledgement to the situation as a source of influence on individual personality. Investigations such as this (see also the work on self-deception as positive illusion: e.g. Shedler, Mayman, & Manis, 1993; Taylor, 1989) are an important corrective to the narrow focus of psychoanalysis on processes within the person. But they also emphasize, as the authors concluded, that 'Some individuals may be less able to adapt to the changing environmental conditions that they are faced with in their everyday lives, . . . and such inflexibility constitutes a vulnerability' (p. 786). Research today shows that psychoanalysis, taken out of its protected clinical domain into the tough realm of the experiment and tested by sophisticated modern methods, may well be confirmed (and usefully modified).

These are just a few examples from a now huge field of current research on a psychological unconscious. You can see that this modern cognitive research does not directly test hypotheses drawn from the *psychoanalytic* unconscious. Indeed, one authority on unconscious processes, John Kihlstrom of the University of California at Berkeley, says, 'Modern research on cognition and the cognitive unconscious owes nothing whatsoever to Freud, and that is also the case with modern research on emotion and the emotional unconscious' (1999, p. 430). He even titled a section of his chapter on the psychological unconscious in the *Handbook of Personality* 'This is not your psychoanalyst's unconscious'. He's a little too ungenerous in dismissing Freud's contribution. Even though modern research on the cognitive unconscious is not specifically in Freud's debt, it is hard to imagine that we would have gotten as far as we have had psychoanalysis simply not existed.

Psychoanalytic Research and Psychoanalysis

A full history of research on psychoanalytic hypotheses yields an unavoidable conclusion: there has not been repeated accomplishment and confirmation. Instead, we are left in doubt about many psychoanalytic propositions, including very basic ones like repression. And although the even more elemental idea of a complex motivational unconscious does have promising support in recent experimental studies, modern findings are yet scanty, and the contribution of psychoanalysis to them has been questioned.

Psychoanalysis in Perspective

How shall psychoanalysis be judged? Does it have its finger on the pulse of our cognitive and emotional life? Is its picture of the human and human nature one that leads to understanding? Or is it misleading, frankly wrong in some critical places? Think of feminine psychology and the psychology of aggression. What about the fact that psychoanalysis is full of propositions that resist operational definition and measurement? Consider the emergence of the superego out of a successfully resolved Oedipus complex, or what specific events in the course of development determine a successful or neurotic outcome. Freud's psychological tapestry is wonderful in its intricacy, and it challenges us in the range and depth of its ideas about humans and their psychological difficulties. Is it true? The answer is that psychoanalysis has been an exceptionally difficult theory to test, and there is a considerable record of failure.

Modern Revisions

Notwithstanding its flaws, psychoanalysis is very much alive and kicking, and it still has a strong clinical presence. We must also recognize that psychoanalysis from the late twentieth century on is no longer the classical theory of Freud. A number of changes reflect the theory's coming to grips with problem concepts and with trenchant criticism of its focus on the internal, interminable, battle between instinct and ego restraint. Under Freud's directing influence, psychoanalysis was a psychology of the id, its foremost concern always with the sexual instinct and secondarily with the instinct to aggress. Recent psychoanalytic theorists have brought a radically different emphasis, one on the ego and the ego's role in cognitive activity, social living, and adaptation to the environment. In Chapter 8, we shall see how far ego psychology has taken classical psychoanalysis.

Object Relations

While Freud was in thrall to—as he liked to say—the 'vicissitudes of instincts', there was even in his time a major question in the treatment of most patients surrounding their 'object relations', their relationships with others and their often-confused ways of thinking and fantasizing about others. 'Objects', as I said much earlier in this chapter, are all the things between instinct arousal and gratification, but most importantly they are people, as a group of psychoanalytic theorists began to appreciate. These theorists began to stress both relationships and the cognitive and emotional activity that is the personal side of relating to others, elevating object relations to a central role in the expression of personality and in personality disorder. Family, society, culture, and adaptive processes take the place of id–ego conflict, and one particularly radical object relations theorist, Heinz Kohut, replaced internal conflict with a concept of self that organizes relationships, thinking, goals, and abilities, integrating them in a personal sense of self. Id, ego, and superego are still there, joined by the self to form a ruling foursome. Personality disturbance, Kohut argued, reflects a defective self with a negative and destructive self-view (see Kohut, 1977; Kohut & Wolf, 1978).

Another object relations theorist of note is Kernberg (1975, 1984), who has proposed a multi-level model of personality organization. By personality organization Kernberg means the consistent and long-lasting ways in which we regard ourselves and others, how we conduct our relationships with others, follow paths to goals, and deal with distressing feelings. Levels of personality organization may be seen in the degree of pathology a person displays. Westen and Gabbard (1999) describe Kernberg's levels very clearly:

> Individuals whose personality is organized at a psychotic level have difficulty knowing what is inside or outside their heads and tend to be tremendously interpersonally alienated. Individuals with a borderline level of personality organization can clearly distinguish inner and outer (that is, they do not hallucinate), but they have difficulty maintaining consistent views of themselves and others over time, and they are prone to severe distortions in the way they perceive reality—particularly interpersonal reality—when the going gets tough. People at a neurotic to normal level of personality organization may have all kinds of conflicts, concerns, and problems (such as low self-esteem, anxiety, and so forth), but they are generally able to love and to work effectively (p. 64).

If the emergence of object relations theory is proof that psychoanalysis has willingly adapted to a view of people as social and cognitive beings, one more consistent with the rest of psychology, in other respects Freud's theory has changed only grudgingly. The psychology of women and their personality development is a case in point. Freud would not give up penis envy as anatomically destined; we'll see the extent to which he stuck to his Victorian prejudice in Chapter 6, when we examine the neo-Freudian theory of Karen Horney. Most contemporary psychoanalysts, however, have had to abandon Freud's indefensible ground and have come to regard the psychological development and motivation of women as the result of family, social, and cultural attitudes and influences. Psychoanalysis fought a losing battle over the hypothesis that a little vicarious aggression—children watching a schoolyard fight, TV violence—is good for people, draining off instinctual tension that could mount and result in explosions. A far better hypothesis comes from social cognitive learning theory, discussed in Chapter 15.

Still, a kind of reverence for the old psychoanalysis may be seen to creep into otherwise sophisticated research-based discourse on the place of the theory in the psychology of personality. As two of the most knowledgeable and persuasive of present-day psychoanalytic writers have said,

Psychoanalysis repeatedly leads one to think about what one does not wish to think about. It is an approach to personality that one does not care to discuss with one's mother. Motivation and fantasy are rich and sometimes aggressive, socially grossly inappropriate, or perverse, and any theory that is entirely comfortable to discuss is probably missing something very important about what it means to be human.

A good example is social learning research on the influence of television aggression on children's behaviour. This research is important and suggestive, but it fails to ask a crucial question: Why is it that aggressive television shows appeal to people so much? Would Freud be surprised to learn that the two variables that censors keep an eye on in television shows and movies are sex and aggression? One can read a thousand pages of the best social-cognitive work on personality and never know that people have genitals—or, for that matter, that they have bodies—let alone fantasies. . . . [I]f readers try generating for themselves a list of all the profanities they can call a person, they will notice an overrepresentation of Freud's erogenous zones. Indeed, the *worst* name a person in our culture can call another person has a distinctly Oedipal ring (Sophocles, circa 500 BCE), and we doubt this term came to the United States via the Viennese doctor (Westen & Gabbard, 1999, pp. 79–80).

What, then, do you believe about psychoanalysis? Does it deserve a place in our thinking about human behaviour? Does it generate a dependable body of scientific evidence? Should it continue as an important clinical theory in the treatment of psychologically disturbed persons?

SUMMARY

1. Freud's first theory of neurosis and its treatment represented a significant step toward a theory of personality in its recognition of the role of traumatic events in the cause of personality disorder. Even with the abandonment of the flawed seduction theory, Freud had hit upon the essential idea that problems in the development of the child could have neurotic consequences in the adult. In the revision of his early theory, Freud linked those problems to inadmissible wishes, fantasies, and memories, which are opposed by ego censorship. This formulation of psychological conflict became the basis of neurotic symptom formation. Symptoms represent an unsuccessful compromise between instinct-based wishes and the ego's denial of them, and they constantly remind the neurotic person of the conflict.

2. The psychoanalytic theory of instincts is both biological and psychological. Instinctual drives are internal bodily stimuli that compel the ego to work to both fulfill and control them. Psychologically, instincts are wishes, demanding immediate recognition and gratification. The wishes significant for personality, sex, and aggression are extreme and must be closely regulated. Thus, the concept of psychological conflict in

neurosis developed into the larger proposition that a chronic war within the person is part of the human condition and begins to appear in childhood.

3. A significant part of personality is unconscious. Instincts themselves and much of the ego's functions (the defensive actions taken by the ego to restrain instincts, for example) are not available to consciousness. Freud likened personality to a great iceberg, the bulk of which lies beneath the surface. Unconscious wishes, constantly pressing for expression, make themselves known in unwanted thoughts and behaviour, sometimes creating momentary anxiety.

4. In psychoanalytic theory, there are three agencies at work in determining thought, feeling, and behaviour. Freud called them the 'It', the 'I', and the 'over-I'; his translators gave them more scientific-sounding names: *Id*, *Ego*, and *Superego*. The id, with its psychological counterpart, wishes, is the instinctual basis of personality. The id demands complete and immediate reduction of tension, and it employs two mechanisms that constitute the *pleasure principle*. These are *reflex action* (sucking, for example) and the **primary process**, which involves the hallucination of objects that will provide instinctual satisfaction. The hallucinated image represents the wish as fulfilled. Normally, there is no access to primary process material except in disguised form. It appears directly only in the severely disturbed person. Instincts have four attributes: a *source* in a state of need; an *aim*, the removal of tension; an *object* that will reduce the state of tension; and *impetus*, the strength of an instinct. Instinctual activity is cyclical: needs are aroused, excitation increases, and then, as the need is satisfied, excitation diminishes. This cycle is called the *repetition compulsion*. The repetition compulsion is also seen in neurotic symptoms. Psychoanalysis does not specify the number of instincts. It does classify them, however, into the life instincts (such as hunger and sex) and the death instincts, responsible for the ending of life. The energy source of the life instincts is *libido*. The death instinct is an extension of the principle of conservation of energy. It is often displaced to other targets; thus, aggressiveness is self-destroying motivation directed toward others who frustrate the gratification of our instincts. Two instincts, sex and aggression, are decisive in personality, and every human society must subject them to socialization.

5. The ego is endowed by the id, which does not have the resources to achieve instinctual gratification, with the energy to fulfill the id's demands. The ego has many functions: it must carry out the id's wishes, restrain the id, plan, delay when necessary, and remember what led to past punishments. The ego acts on the *reality principle* and makes use of the *secondary process*, which involves reality testing to discover the most appropriate paths to instinct gratification. Because the ego functions on instinctual energy, all human activity will of necessity reflect instinctual life, although largely in very indirect, displaced form. The ego must cope with danger from outside and from within, the latter in the form of instinctual wishes that can't be admitted. When danger is recognized, anxiety is experienced. *Reality anxiety* is fear of environmental dangers. *Neurotic anxiety* results when forbidden instincts must be dealt with; it is the signal to do so, and the ego puts up barriers—ego defences that seek to block the investment of energy. An investment of energy in an object or activity is a *cathexis*; hence, defences are *anti-cathexes*. There are a number of ego defences that either banish the unacceptable (*repression*) or distort it. Distorting mechanisms include

   • **reaction formation**, which turns forbidden wishes and feelings into their opposite—sexual attraction into revulsion, hate into love;

   • **projection**, which involves attributing to others wishes and feelings we cannot stand in ourselves;

   • **fixation** and **regression**, each entailing failure to resolve developmental stages successfully. In fixation, a child does not conclude a developmental stage, and residues of it continue in later personality (oral or anal traits, as examples). Regression, is the return to a previous stage in the face of fear or frustration (a child of six, frightened by his first exposure to school, regresses by wetting himself; an adult under stress begins to drink heavily);

   • **undoing** neutralizes the unconscionable by the magical pretence that it never happened, replacing it by some act or thought that denies that the bad one ever occurred.

6. The superego is the moral voice of personality and also an *ego ideal*, the person—modelled on the parent of the same sex—that we aspire to be. It develops

only upon the resolution of the Oedipus complex, and when it does the capacity for internalized behaviour control appears. The superego is not entirely conscious, and it tends to be over-demanding and condemning. When we transgress or fail to behave morally, we experience moral anxiety or guilt. An oversevere superego plays a key role in neurosis. The superego is responsible for cruel treatment of transgressors in the name of morality when it is corrupted by instinct (displaced aggression).

7. In psychoanalysis, personality development proceeds through a series of **psychosexual stages** from birth to sexual maturity. These stages represent the biological unfolding of instincts, and in the developing infant and child, three bodily areas—*erogenous zones*—give sexualized pleasure as they appear.

8. The **oral stage** begins at birth and guides the infant's responsiveness to the source of nourishment and to stimuli associated with food intake. During the oral period, the primary erogenous zone is the mouth and neighbouring tissues. This stage is divided into two substages—the *incorporative*, in the first six months or so, during which pleasure derives from sucking and nursing; and the *oral biting* or *oral sadistic* substage, lasting to the end of the first year, in which pleasure comes from active chewing and rejecting disliked foods. Fixation in the early oral stage will likely leave its mark on personality in dependency, gullibility, passivity, and oral habits (chewing fingernails, for example). Later oral fixation will show that the mouth has become an instrument of aggression: the person's relationships with others will reflect resentment, expressed in sarcasm, verbal abuse, and hostility.

9. The **anal stage** starts in the second year, and its erogenous zone is the ano-genital region. There are again two substages. In the first, the infant derives pleasure from the simple expulsion of waste material; it is the *anal expulsive* period. During the second half of the anal stage, the infant has acquired control of the musculature of elimination and derives pleasure from the ability to retain as well as to expel feces. This is the *anal retentive* period. It is important to recognize two social features of this developmental stage. First, every human society requires strict socialization of eliminative behaviour. Second, this stage confronts each infant with the parental demand that it give up an instinctual source of pleasure that will now have to be disciplined and controlled. Problems, if they arise, are likely to involve a power struggle between infant and parents, expressed in defiance and an inevitable but grudging submission. Anal character traits may persist into adulthood, shown in obstinacy, selfishness, inability to love, and an obsession with possessions.

10. The period from about three to five years of age is the **phallic stage**. It is so named because Freud considered the male sex organ psychologically significant to both sexes. The genital region is the erogenous zone, giving pleasure when stimulated. At this time, the boy may discover masturbation, and he shows a distinct but clearly childish sexual interest in his mother that Freud termed the Oedipus complex. The boy's wish to possess his mother is supported by only a slim body of evidence—the free associations of psychoanalytic patients, a small boy whose father consulted Freud on a phobia and fantasy that implied Oedipal wishes, and Freud's own self-analysis and study of myths—but to Freud it met the test of consistency. The boy's desire for his mother must be seen as an immature and childish wish, not to be likened to adult sexual longing. He possessively seeks to displace his father in his mother's affection but comes to fear the punishment of castration for his rivalry. Note that the boy's genitals are the source of pleasure, and this primitive notion is the kind of punishment a child might imagine. It is no more a well-formed idea than his sexual desire but it creates anxiety, the signal for him to abandon his incestuous wish, and this is something he must do. The resolution of the Oedipus complex brings a highly significant outcome. First, the boy identifies with his father, who becomes his ego ideal and moral model, a large step in becoming a man. Second, the process of *identification* brings the morality and conscience of the father to the child, and creates in the boy a masculine sexual identity. Difficulty in working all of this out is likely to be shown in adult flaws in conscience. Repressive parents who don't understand their son's behaviour and threaten the loss of love will create undue anxiety and risk his development of a superego that is too severe and will not allow normal sexual urges. This is a prescription for neurosis in adulthood. Excessive indulgence by a seductive mother who thinks her son's attraction to her is 'cute'

can result in a weak superego and an experience of guilt that is insufficient for moral behaviour.

11. For the girl, the significant event of this stage is not the threat of castration and the arousal of anxiety but the perceived fact of castration. Discovering that she lacks a protruding genital organ like male members of her family, she is resentful and disappointed. She sees that her mother is just like herself and holds her responsible for the loss. This, like the boy's sexual ideas, is to be understood as the childish notion that it is. Her cathexis for her mother is weakened, and she turns to her father. Proper feminine identification and super-ego development will require that her attachment to her mother be restored. Since the girl does not experi-ence the anxiety that the boy does, her superego will not be as severe as the boy's, and Freud viewed this developmental stage as more difficult for the girl than the boy. She is left with a permanent psychological reminder of her anatomy, *penis envy*. This is a highly unsatisfactory and offensive theory of the develop-mental psychology of women, reflecting the attitudes of the Victorian era in which Freud was schooled. It has a very poor fit to the personality development of women, as many critics have pointed out.

12. Development is complete with the conclusion of the phallic stage, and the child's personality is basically all formed with the appearance of the superego. A **latency period** ensues until puberty announces the final **genital stage** of mature sexuality. It is important to keep in mind that pregenital oral, anal, and phallic residues will be incorporated into genital sexuality.

13. The character structure of the adult reveals his or her psychosexual history in three ways: the libidinal origins of adult behaviour, as in the persistence into adulthood of dependency on oral gratification; the behaviour or symptoms shown by the person, such as hysterical character traits without a hysterical neurosis; and the fixations that must have occurred to cause adult behav-iour with pregenital traces as, for example, abusive, cruel, and messy habits expressive of an anal fixation.

14. Dreams are a rich source of data to the psychoana-lyst, 'the royal road to the unconscious'. The dream is a relief valve to discharge tension that might result in anxiety and disrupt sleep. Even in sleep, instincts remain active, and the ego, although more relaxed, continues to be watchful. The ego continues to cen-sor dangerous material by transforming it into an innocuous, if fanciful, form. In this, the ego functions as a *dream censor*, and its censorship is the *dream work*. The basis of every dream is an instinctual wish, the latent content, most often of a sexual nature, and the wish is always represented in the dream as fulfilled. When the ego has done its work, the dangerous con-tent has been turned into the manifest content that the dreamer may remember and be puzzled by in the morning. Dreams use symbolism to express elemen-tal ideas such as the human body, nakedness, birth, sexual life, and death, and dream symbols are one source of evidence on the meaning of dreams. The dream work employs several processes that are related to ego defences. Among them are *condensation*, which can merge images of people, time, places, or episodes and make them unrecognizable; *substitution*, which replaces disturbing elements with innocuous or more remote ones; and *expression in opposites*, closely related to reaction formation. To find the latent content, knowledge of the life and recent and important experiences of the dreamer, as well as the associa-tions of the dreamer to the dream, are required.

15. Psychoanalytic theory has many implications for individual and social life. Creative expression derives from libidinal sources in the id, unconscious in most of us and unavailable. The creative person, however, has some access to wishes, images, and fantasies. Aggression represents a displacement—necessary for human survival—of the self-destructive instinct, a biological catabolic principle. Frustration of instincts is inevitable in social life, and there is thus abundant provocation to commit acts of aggression, individu-ally and collectively. The consequence of civilized societies is frustration and tension, which fuel the displacement of aggression. Sadism and masochism represent the fusing of sexuality and aggression, the latter turned against the self. The therapeutic concept of *transference*, which identifies childhood attitudes and feelings of patients toward parents that become attached to the psychoanalyst, is a model for other significant relationships. The relations of students to teachers and of people toward their leaders are important examples. Psychoanalysis has an account of wit and humor, explaining them as the discharge of uncomfortable tension by the relief of laughter. This

is related to the sudden emotional outpouring of abreaction. The influence of psychoanalytic ideas on literature has been extensive: Novelists, poets, and literary critics have applied a whole point of view to literary creation.

16. Despite Freud's insistence that only in psychoanalysis itself can the theory be properly tested, psychologists have conducted thousands of experimental studies of psychoanalytic hypotheses. They have recognized that the clinical study of patients, so fruitful as a source of hypotheses in the development of the theory, is fallible in hypothesis testing. In the experimental literature on psychoanalysis, two important areas are cornerstones of the theory—defence mechanisms, especially repression, and unconscious processes. The chapter reviews examples of repression experiments and studies of unconscious mental processes. Two basic experimental approaches have been followed in studying repression. In the first, anxiety is aroused by threat of something unpleasant (such as electric shock) or by ego threat (making participants feel stupid, incompetent), and the test of repression is to determine whether there is failure to remember critical stimuli associated with the threat. There are very few examples of these experiments that withstand scrutiny. Most of the results can be more plausibly explained by processes other than motivated forgetting. An experiment presented in the chapter, however, does appear to have elicited repression in its subjects. The second approach investigates individual differences in motivated forgetting. Experimental participants are selected by personality tests presumably measuring the tendency to repress uncomfortable ideas, and other behaviour consistent with a repressive personality disposition is examined. The response to sexual and aggressive stimuli is one example. A series of studies outlined in the chapter finds a number of characteristics that distinguish repressive subjects from those who are not repressors, but there are other possible interpretations of the results. One critic of repression research concludes that 'there is no controlled laboratory evidence supporting the concept of repression.'

17. Research on unconscious processes, especially modern work on a cognitive unconscious and a motivational unconscious, has clearly established that both cognitive and motivational processes can go on without consciousness of them. Studies of implicit memory show that recently encountered stimuli, not recalled by experimental participants, exert an influence on their attitudes and judgement, a finding significant for understanding the effects of commercial advertising and propaganda. Unconscious thought, or intuition as one investigator calls it, has also been demonstrated. Work on a motivational unconscious finds that self-reported motives and motives assessed by projective tests are dissociated, pointing to different behaviour and goals. A given motive may have both explicit (conscious) and implicit (unconscious) aspects; an explicit motive will govern short-term goals and behaviour, while implicit motives are related to consistent patterns of behaviour over a long period of time. Although some authorities in cognitive psychology deny the influence of psychoanalysis on the study of a psychological unconscious, it is hard to imagine that present research would have examined many facets of unconscious mental activity had psychoanalysis simply not existed.

18. Psychoanalysis is a difficult theory to evaluate. It is the most comprehensive of all personality theories, it can point to a wealth of clinical evidence, and it has had exceptional influence on clinical practice and on the culture at large. Examined closely, a number of its concepts are vaguely stated and untestable, and it is in places misleading or frankly mistaken. The record of the theory in experimental research reveals some confirmation but also a considerable history of failure. Psychoanalysis focuses on personality processes that are internal to the person, neglecting situation and social relationships. A number of recent psychoanalysts, recognizing this problem, have set out to address issues of family, society, culture, and social relationships. Object relations theory represents a notable modern revision of classical psychoanalysis in emphases on social relationships and the self.

TO TEST YOUR UNDERSTANDING

1. Why did Freud choose to represent the mind by the three agencies of id, ego, and superego? Does this scheme adequately account for human thought, feeling, and action? Can you think of an alternative way of viewing the fundamental nature of personality?

2. Do you agree that the cardinal motives in personality are sex and aggression? What other motives might qualify as equally significant?

3. Of the two alternative ways of viewing personality development—in stages or as a continuous process—which do you think is more persuasive? What does a theory of stages of development accomplish that a theory of continuous developmental cannot do or does less well? What do you think of Freud's argument for psychosexual stages?

4. How would you sum up the contemporary status of psychoanalysis as a theory of personality and psychotherapy? Is it still viable, or has it outlived its usefulness? What should we think about the difficulty of testing the theory experimentally?

CHAPTER FOUR

Analytic Psychology: Carl Jung

Introduction

Psychoanalysis had barely reached maturity when some objections to the theoretical system began to arise, objections of a rather profound sort. They resulted in deviations from Freudian orthodoxy first by Carl Gustav Jung and Alfred Adler, and later on by other psychoanalysts who sought to modify essential principles in ways that to Freud undercut the very foundation of the theory. Jung's analytic psychology, like the neo-Freudian theories we'll see beginning in the next chapter, was in this sense very much a child of dissent from psychoanalysis. Jung thought his mentor and erstwhile collaborator Freud greatly overstated the sexual instinct as the prime mover in personality, and at the time of their parting—a bitter one full of recrimination—he had the essential ideas of his own theory well in mind.

Many concepts in Jung's theory may at first seem familiar, concepts that reflect a disciple's early hero worship of Freud. There is an ego and an unconscious, instincts, psychic energy (libido), repression and projection, and stages of development. Beyond a surface similarity, however, these are definitely not Freudian; they bear Jung's distinctive imprint. A large part of the theory is unique, the result of Jung's experience, personal and clinical, and his wide reading and knowledge of history, philosophy, religion, mythology, and the mystical. The most startling to newcomers is the concept of a **collective unconscious**★, which is not the preserve of individual experience but a memory store of elemental human ideas and feelings. It is a psychological counterpart to biological evolution.

Psychoanalysis was born of nineteenth-century scientific **empiricism**★. Freud, as we know, was a resolute determinist, finding the cause of all human behaviour in the history of the individual and his or her struggles over the socialization and control of instincts. Jung, as Ellenberger (1970) has written, considered deterministic causality insufficient and held to a view of the mind as seeker of future aims (a **teleology**★) and a view of humanity midway between religion and psychology. Jung thought religion to be an inborn need. He said:

> Man positively needs general ideas and convictions that will give a meaning to his life and enable him to find a place for himself in the universe. He can stand the most incredible hardships when he is convinced that they make sense; he is crushed when, on top of all his misfortunes, he has to admit that he is taking part in a 'tale told by an idiot' (1964, p. 76).

Carl Jung: Personal History

Carl Gustav Jung was born in midsummer 1875, in the Swiss village of Kesswil on Lake Constance. He was the second child; the firstborn son had died in early infancy two

(© Bettmann/CORBIS)

years before. A sister, Johanna, arrived nine years later. Jung's father was a country pastor, a talented man who held a PhD in ancient languages. But without the income to support an academic career he studied for the ministry instead, forsaking intellectual pursuits for the quiet and unchallenging life of a village vicar. He was kindhearted, hardly sustained by his calling, and—some colleagues said—boring. He was not the father to whom a young man could turn for wise counsel, and so Jung and his father became alienated from each other. Jung remembered his father's 'sentimental idealism' along with a tendency to lose himself in pleasant reminiscence about the glory of his student years. These were aided by puffing on a relic of those days, a student's pipe. Disappointed in his marriage, Jung's father battled angrily with his wife, and at length, faith lost, simply parroted the teachings of his church (Jung, 1973, pp. 91–2).

A person who had known the Jungs told psychiatrist Henri Ellenberger many years later that Mrs Jung was 'fat, ugly, authoritarian, and haughty' (Ellenberger, 1970, p. 662). Jung himself seems to have in part agreed, characterizing his mother as a 'kindly, fat old woman' (1973, p. 48). This wasn't the whole story, however. She may have been, as he said, 'a very good mother to me' with 'a hearty animal warmth',

> . . . but then her unconscious personality would suddenly put in an appearance. That personality was unexpectedly powerful: a sombre, imposing figure possessed of unassailable authority—and no bones about it. I was sure she consisted of two personalities, one innocuous and human, the other uncanny. This other emerged only now and then, but each time it was unexpected and frightening. She would then speak as if talking to herself, but what she said was aimed at me and usually struck to the core of my being, so that I was stunned into silence (1973, pp. 48–9).

The Jung family remained in Kesswil for only a short time, moving to a village on the Rhine and later to another village across the Rhine from Basel. Here, Carl grew up and went to school with peasant children. He knew himself to be different, an introverted boy who would become an introverted man. 'Today as then I am a solitary, because I know things and must hint at things which other people do not know and usually do not even want to know' (1973, pp. 41–2).

As a preadolescent schoolboy, Jung began to believe that he, like his mother, had two personalities. An everyday personality, which he called 'No. 1', was that of a vicar's son and indifferent student, altogether uninteresting. 'No. 2' was an august and important person, elderly and respected, a 'wise old man', as, in his imagining, was old Dr Stückelberger, an eighteenth-century notable, a statuette of whom he had seen in the house of his aunt. In school, he frequently wrote the date not as 1886 but 1776 and thought that he lived, contemporaneously, in two times. His two personalities did not coexist comfortably. He had dreams that frightened him, and doubts about the church and God that he could not take to his father. Confirmation in the church was a disappointment, the preparation stultifying. Then, one day, he conceived a blasphemous scene, one that might have shocked him and consumed him with guilt:

> . . . the cathedral [in Basel, on a day in summer], the blue sky. God sits on His golden throne, high above the world—and from under the throne an enormous turd falls upon the sparkling new roof, shatters it, and breaks the walls of the cathedral asunder.
>
> So that was it! I felt an enormous, an indescribable relief. . . . Why did God befoul His cathedral? That, for me, was a terrible thought. But then came the dim understanding that God could be something terrible. I had experienced a dark and terrible secret. It overshadowed my whole life, and I became deeply pensive (1973, pp. 39–40).

There was no guilt but instead a great lightening, the sense that grace had descended on him, that God had accepted him.

> At that time, too, there arose in me profound doubts about everything my father said. When I heard him preaching about grace, I always thought of my own experience. What he said sounded stale and hollow, like a tale told by someone who knows it only by hearsay and cannot quite believe it himself (1973, pp. 42–3).

Jung was a poor student, bored and unhappy. Religious instruction was 'unspeakably dull' and mathematics gave him 'downright fear'. Then, one day, he was shoved by another boy and fell to the pavement, hitting his head. Dazed, he had a sudden thought: 'Now you won't have to go to school any more,' and he feigned unconsciousness. He began to have frequent fainting spells which produced a remarkable effect: his parents removed him from school. For six months he indulged himself in solitary games, fantasy, and reading in his father's library. His freedom, bought at the price of 'the obscure feeling that I was fleeing from myself' (1973, p. 31), came to an end when he overheard his worried father talking about him to a friend. What would become of him if these spells were epilepsy? How could he ever hope to lead an independent life?

> I was thunderstruck. This was the collision with reality. 'Why, then, I must get to work!' I thought suddenly.
>
> From that moment on I became a serious child. I crept away, went to my father's study, took out my Latin grammar, and began to cram with intense concentration. After ten minutes of this I had the finest of fainting fits. I almost fell off the chair, but after a few minutes I felt better and went on working. 'Devil take it, I'm not going to faint,' I told myself, and persisted in my purpose. This time it took about fifteen minutes before the second attack came. That, too, passed like the first. 'And now you must really get to work!' I stuck it out, and after an hour came the third attack. Still I did not give up, and worked for another hour, until I had the feeling that I had overcome the attacks. Suddenly I felt better than I had in all the months before. And in fact the attacks did not recur. From that day on I worked over my grammar and other schoolbooks every day. A few weeks later I returned to school, and never suffered another attack, even there. The whole bag of tricks was over and done with! That was when I learned what a neurosis is (1973, pp. 31–2).

This strange boy, who lived so much in a world of his own making, became overnight a hardworking and competent student, his behaviour largely the expression of No. 1 personality. He did well in his schoolwork, and even managed to get by in mathematics, with which he struggled manfully. Sitting the examinations for entrance to the University of Basel at nineteen, he passed. What would he study? There were biology and paleontology, but against these stood seemingly incompatible interests in comparative religion and archaeology. Factual science, firmly grounded in actuality, appealed to No. 1 personality; No. 2 yearned for meaning that philosophy and comparative religion could give, a choice that would deny the empirical bent of personality No. 1. For a long time, he couldn't decide (1973, pp. 72–3).

At last, he decided to pursue medicine and in the fall of 1895 began the five-year course of study for the MD at the University of Basel. He enjoyed his student life, which opened up 'treasures of knowledge', and even joined a student fraternity. He was outgoing and convivial, and he excelled in medicine. He was made junior assistant in anatomy and was given the course in histology to teach. But inclining toward surgery or internal medicine and about to take his final examinations, he encountered Krafft-Ebbing's psychiatry text. He was captured. In psychiatry, he saw the two streams of his interests coming together, biological science and a humanistic spirituality. 'Here at last', he recalled, 'was the place where the collision of nature and spirit became a reality' (1973, p. 109).

On graduation, Jung took a job as an assistant—what we would today call a resident—at the famous Burghölzli Psychiatric Hospital in Zürich. The director of the hospital was Eugen Bleuler, who had given schizophrenia its name and codified its symptoms. Bleuler was devoted to patient care and was a gentle but exacting taskmaster. The residents had to live in the hospital with the patients, and their daily hours ran from early morning to late at night. It was a hard and Spartan life, but Jung prospered, learning from Bleuler to listen to patients in order to gain a humane understanding of them. He published important work and conducted groundbreaking studies of word association as a technique to diagnose 'complexes'. He read Freud (*The Interpretation of Dreams*) and together with others at the Burghölzli began to apply psychoanalysis in his psychiatric practice. He spent a winter in Paris studying with Pierre Janet, a pioneer in dynamic psychiatry, and was presently appointed clinical director and head of the outpatient service at Burghölzli. He also gained a coveted appointment as a lecturer at the University of Zürich.

Jung now had an established reputation as a psychiatrist and scientist that extended far beyond the Burghölzli, and he was becoming known as an outstanding psychotherapist. Through Bleuler, he began to correspond with Freud, a mutually admiring correspondence:

> Freud was the first man of real importance I had encountered; in my experience up to that time, no one else could compare with him. There was nothing the least trivial in his attitude. I found him extremely intelligent, shrewd, and altogether remarkable. And yet my first impression of him remained somewhat tangled; I could not make him out (1973, p. 149).

He was truly impressed by psychoanalysis and gratified at Freud's recognition. From the outset, however, Jung had serious reservations about the role of sexuality in personality and in neurosis. He thought, however, that in adopting psychoanalysis he would be free to follow his own ideas, taking from Freud the large part of the theory he considered valid and modifying its objectionable aspects in his own way. This he did, presenting his altered version of psychoanalysis—with his far more general concept of libido and ideas derived from his growing mystical interest (see Jung, 1953, 1956)—in lectures, in articles, and in books. He was brash, an upstart, and he was aware that Freud would find his independent approach to psychoanalysis difficult to swallow. There is no doubt that he relished his effrontery.

Freud, who had small patience with disputatious followers, was blind to a potential conflict of ideas and will. He was delighted to have the Swiss join the psychoanalytic movement, bringing it international stature and a buffer against anti-Semitism, and he would soon begin to regard Jung as his 'crown prince' and successor. He could not altogether ignore the signs that his prized new recruit might step over the line, but he failed to appreciate the seriousness of their warning. Gently exacting a promise would surely do: 'My dear Jung,' he wrote, 'promise me never to abandon the sexual theory. That is the most essential thing of all. You see, we must make a dogma of it, an unshakable bulwark' (1973, p. 150). Jung was appalled. To be the crown prince of psychoanalysis, an Alexander conquering all of the unknown world in Freud's memorable image, was one thing, but to be enslaved by Freud's unbending demand for conformity to the principles of psychosexuality was quite another.

There were several years of warm and mutually admiring correspondence, and a memorable trip with Freud in 1909 to Clark University in Worcester, Massachusetts, to lecture and to receive an honorary degree. Jung became the first president of the International Psychoanalytic Association and the editor of its journal. The falling out, though, was inevitable, and by 1913 the two men had each had enough. The correspondence, increasingly filled with acrimony and mutual accusation, ended and Jung resigned his positions as president and editor.

In those early days, psychoanalysts couldn't leave the unconscious alone. They had to interpret everything, in themselves and in their colleagues—like the joke about the two analysts who meet in the elevator: 'How are you?' one asks; 'Now what does he really mean?' wonders the other. When divisions appeared, the interpretations were likely to get nasty, and between Freud and Jung—as with Freud and Adler—they did. If you should find in this story more than mere traces of No. 1 and No. 2 personalities as Jung first worshipped and then opposed Freud with his own theory, I should not object. Neither, I think, would Jung have resisted your interpretation.

The emerging difference between the two was distressing to both men. Freud suffered episodes of fainting during their growing antagonism, and in the aftermath of the split Jung, for a period of six years, underwent what Ellenberger (1970) characterized as a 'creative illness'. He had built a splendid house in Küsnacht on the shore of Lake Zürich and left the Burghölzli to open a private practice there and to write. He now resigned his university lectureship and, except for his family and patients, isolated himself. In a 'state of disorientation' and 'totally suspended in mid-air' (1973, p. 170), he undertook a lengthy experiment, exploring his own unconscious by immersing himself in understanding his dreams and fantasies. Mysterious ideas began to appear, and he recognized his dark exercise as exceptionally dangerous. He clung fiercely to the realities of his life—family and patients—to avert what one may guess might have become a psychotic episode. He emerged in 1919, unscathed and full of energy, with reams of material from his 'journey through the unconscious'—the **archetypes**★, symbols, and other concepts that would together form his model of analytic psychology.

Jung spent the rest of his long life, except for travels and lecture tours, in Küsnacht. His fame, now worldwide, brought him a wealthy international clientele, and he had his own psychological association. He wrote extensively, adding to the theory in book after book; his *Collected Works* number twenty volumes. He also led a complicated domestic life. Married in 1903, he and his wife, Emma, had five children. Beautiful, talented, and energetic, Emma was also his collaborator and a Jungian analyst in her own right. You would have thought it a perfect union, but Jung was obviously not content.

He had an affair with a former patient, Toni Wolff, and then brought her into his home for Sunday dinners and more. Emma was at first distraught, but the *ménage à trois* seems in the end to have worked, a relationship between Jung and his wife and mistress that was unusually loving and free of conflict. It lasted for forty years.

Honoured throughout the world as a scholar and theorist, Jung died at eighty-five, shortly after completing his autobiography in 1961. In that revealing account, which went back eighty years to his childhood, Jung clearly invited his readers to consider the intimate details as relevant to his theory and how he arrived at it. We don't have to feel that we are prying into matters that have nothing formally to do with analytic psychology, for Jung made them a part of theory formation. His growth and development and his personal life were significant sources of theoretical concepts. In effect, Jung tried to show that he did Freud's self-analysis one better.

Emphases

Teleology

In a very complex theory with many concepts, there are two features that stand out above everything else. The first, as we noted at the beginning of this chapter, is Jung's teleology—his decisive view that the events of the past are insufficient to explain present behaviour. Like Adler, the subject of our next chapter, whose concept of fictional finalism substituted the pursuit of future goals—often imaginary and unrealizable—for 'Causes, powers, instincts, impulses and the like' (Adler, 1930, p. 400), Jung insisted that personality has a basis in ongoing aims, a reach toward an ultimate self-realization. He did not reject causality as thoroughly as Adler did, putting instead the pursuit of individual destiny on an equal footing with **determinism★**. Indeed, he argued that to believe one is nothing more than the product of one's experiences is depressing, since the past has done its work and cannot be changed. Purpose and future orientation give hope and meaning to life. He said: 'Life has also a tomorrow, and today is only understood if we are able to add the indications of tomorrow to our knowledge of what was yesterday' (Jung, 1966a, p. 46).

The Collective Unconscious

The second outstanding feature of analytic psychology is the concept of a collective unconscious, an inheritance of the fundamental experience of our species. This is a store of memory traces, latent but capable of being revived, of ancestral wisdom accumulated over all the time of humans on earth. Primordial ideas—of motherhood, a deity, elemental fears, powerful forces of nature, masculinity and femininity, fundamental human types (the wise old man, the hero, the demon), the experience of self—are represented in racial memory, as Jung called it. According to his followers, Jung was sensitive to the implication that the collective unconscious is formed through the inheritance of acquired characteristics—Jean Baptiste Lamarck's thoroughly discredited notion of heritability—and denied it. Munroe (1955) noted that Jung came dangerously close to Lamarck's bad idea but gave him the benefit of the doubt: 'If . . . Jung's meaning is limited to the statement that evolutionary history has conditioned very deep reaction patterns implicit in man's biological make-up and infantile experience, then I see nothing to quarrel with in the concept of the collective unconscious' (p. 555). We shall have more on the content of the collective unconscious later in the chapter.

Psychic Energy

In addition to these two most remarkable features Jung's analytic psychology involves a number of concepts drawn from similar ideas in psychoanalysis. For one, there is a concept of psychic energy, which originates in bodily metabolism. Like Freud, Jung used the term *libido*, but he departed from the psychoanalytic interpretation that libido is sexual energy to argue that it is a far more generalized life force, an *élan vital*. Unlike physical energy, the expenditure of which can be measured, psychic energy is conceptual. It underlies and fuels psychological activities such as attention, feeling, goal-directed activity, wishing for something. There is a relation between psychic energy and physical energy, discussed below.

Ego and Self

In analytic psychology there are both ego and self. The ego is the core of the aware part of personality, responsible for conscious perception, thought, memory, and feeling. Personal identity and our experience of the continuity of time are also functions of the ego. The ego is opposed to the unconscious.

The self is a grander idea. If the ego is the centre of the conscious mind, the self is at the centre of the whole personality, at a midpoint between conscious (ego) and unconscious. The self drives behaviour, impelling a search for completeness. Religion affords the total experience of selfhood. The self does not appear until other aspects of personality develop fully and become individuated.

Religion

Freud dismissed religion as an illusion, a belief that is very unlikely to be true. It is a vestige of the helplessness and dependency of the human infant, a fearful attitude toward parents who hold a small life in their hands. It is an adult security blanket to which the grown-up person clings to make an unpredictable and threatening world understandable and safer. This was definitely not Jung's view. To him, religious belief was one of humankind's great forward-looking aspirations, a source of hope, completeness, and self-realization. It is a derivative not of childish terror and naive trust but of ages-long experience, 'a psychic function whose importance can hardly be imagined' (1929, p. 49).

The Principle of Synchronicity

To the great majority of personality theorists, behaviour and the events around us affecting our behaviour are the products of causality, even if we cannot at the moment identify the specific causes. Theorists like Jung—and Adler, as we'll see—did argue for a future orientation and striving for distant pursuits, but they preserved the scientific principle of causality. Jung, however, added to the complexity of personality and the relation of people to events around them by introducing the unknowable. He noted the long history of human fascination with the mysterious and the occult, conducted studies of parapsychology, and introduced a principle in his theory to deal with non-causal coincidences. The principle of synchronicity accounts for paranormal experiences such as mental telepathy and clairvoyance. A person prays for a special dispensation and it occurs, or one has a dream of the death of someone dear and learns that it happened, wholly unexpectedly, on the night of the dream. Events of this kind reflect a layer of order and relatedness beyond causality, and humans are right, Jung argued, to be impressed by them.

The Major Concepts of Analytic Psychology

Analytic psychology is a challenging theory that can be difficult to approach, and it will help if we sort its many concepts into some simplifying categories. We'll consider structural and dynamic concepts, process concepts, and Jung's typologies. First, the **structural** parts of the theory.

The Ego

The ego, as I noted above, is the conscious core of personality. Perceiving, thinking, feeling, and remembering are its principal functions. The sense of identity, without which we are less than human, is equally fundamental. People with damaged identities are inevitably severely disturbed, and no wonder—to lose a secure sense of self is to be cut off from one's being, lost in a personal sense, even more than the person who is badly disoriented and loses touch with his or her surroundings.

Personal identity is intimately related to the continuity of our experience. Humans are not moment-to-moment creatures; it is a significant property of consciousness to appreciate the sameness of ourselves as time passes. Thus, although Jung's ego is wholly conscious (unlike the Freudian ego, which carries on much of its work outside awareness), it cannot be thought of as a trivial part of personality (an accusation Freudians might make). Consciously accessible perception, thought, feeling, and memory, and the momentous awareness of self and of continuity in time, are profound human qualities.

The Personal Unconscious

The ego and the **personal unconscious**⋆ are adjoining, as we see in Figure 4.1, adapted from a drawing by Jacobi as a way to represent relations among the fundamental concepts of analytic psychology (Jacobi, 1942, p. 22). The two structures, however, are in opposition. They sometimes vie with each other for control, unconscious wishes and urges distressing our conscious selves because we (our egos) don't understand what possessed us. But they also communicate with each other, as when the ego represses painful experiences by ban-

Figure 4.1 An adaptation of Jacobi's diagram of the relations among the structural concepts of analytic psychology

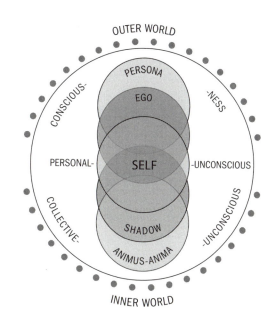

ishing them to the unconsciouss, or when the ego recalls a forgotten or repressed experience. The contents of the unconscious consist mostly of ideas, feelings, wishes, and experiences that were once conscious but have been denied awareness (by repression) or forgotten. Some experiences too insignificant to be noticed at the time and without the psychic energy to become conscious are also in the unconscious. Jung's unconscious and Freud's unconscious differ appreciably. The Freudian unconscious is a Stygian and forbidding repository of instinctual urges and their allied wishes and experiences, one that for most people is extremely difficult and painful to access. Not so, the Jungian unconscious. It may harbour extremely distressing thoughts and memories, but it may also be the source of creative imagination that can burst into consciousness and dramatically change our conceptions. In general, Jung's personal unconscious is not as walled off and impenetrable as the psychoanalytic unconscious.

Also in the personal unconscious are **complexes★**, emotionally significant and often disturbing constellations of ideas. Complexes dominate our actions and thoughts, though their influence on our behaviour goes unrecognized. One complex described by Jung is the **mother complex**, which derives both from the maternal experiences of the species (this is an archetype from the collective unconscious, described below) and from the individual's childhood experience with mother. Other complexes similarly represent elemental ideas from the human heritage: a father complex, a complex about power, or an urgent preoccupation with reducing things to their simplest, which powerfully affected Tolstoy. A complex has a nuclear idea that draws related ideas to it, and the stronger this core the more extensive and dominating will the complex become. Complexes can be very potent influences on behaviour, thinking, and feeling, uniting strong emotion with the central theme. In fact, a complex can become so strong as to control and seriously affect one's life, causing an abnormal pursuit of an idea. Jung developed a method to investigate complexes, the word association test introduced by Sir Francis Galton, which we shall take up later on in the chapter.

The Collective Unconscious

The personal unconscious is an individual's store of repressed, forgotten, and weakly registered experiences. More significantly, Jung, a student of other cultures, myths, human history and prehistory, and religion, proposed another unconscious, a far more powerful one whose contents are shared by all humans. This collective, universal unconscious is the 'deposit of ancestral experience from untold millions of years, the echo of prehistoric world events to which each century adds an infinitesimally small amount of variation and differentiation, (Jung, 1928, p. 162). Evolution gave us our human characteristics—the traits, abilities, and features that distinguish us as a species. Among evolution's contributions, Jung boldly asserted, are **ideas**, a psychic bequest of the memory of primitive ancestors for quintessential experiences.

We want to be clear that Jung did not claim that *specific* memories are inherited; rather, it is the *potential* for these memorable experiences to be revived in us and for them to influence our reactions to fundamental aspects of our contemporary world. What sort of ideas? Remember the preadolescent Jung's No. 2 personality, representing in him the wise old man. You might start by trying to imagine the lives of early humans and compelling experiences that would have awed, mystified, or terrified them—experiences crying out for explanation. Birth and death? Certainly. Mother and father, the sexes, great wisdom, the hero? Absolutely. Natural phenomena also: lightning bolts, claps of thunder, the sun and the moon. Here is Jung on the primordial ideas of sun and moon:

One of the commonest and at the same time most impressive experiences is the apparent movement of the sun every day. We certainly cannot discover anything of the kind in the unconscious, so far as the known physical process is concerned. What we do find, on the other hand, is the myth of the sun-hero in all its countless variations. It is this myth, and not the physical process, that forms the sun archetype. The same can be said of the phases of the moon. The archetype is a kind of readiness to produce over and over again the same or similar mythical ideas. Hence it seems as though what is impressed upon the unconscious were exclusively the subjective fantasy-ideas aroused by the physical process. We may therefore assume that the archetypes are recurrent impressions made by subjective reactions (1966a, p. 69).

These 'mythical ideas', archetypes, which Jung also called primordial images, mythological images, behaviour patterns, and some other names as well, exercise an inestimably potent and pervasive influence on every person. Archetypes appear, as we might expect, in religious symbolism, in the myths and fables of cultures, and in dreams. They are the substance of the collective unconscious, which is the basic structure, indeed the foundation, of personality. Ego, personal unconscious, and all the other parts of individual personality develop from this universal unconscious, and their functions are affected by archetypal myths throughout life, starting from birth. For every child, 'The form of the world into which he is born is already inborn in him as a virtual image' (Jung, 1966b, p. 190). The ego may try to ignore the intrusions of the collective unconscious, but it does so at its peril.

The dark side of the animus. This is Alberich, the ugly, power-crazed, violent, thieving dwarf in Richard Wagner's opera *Das Rheingold*. (Alberich and Neiblungs, © Arthur Rackham. Photo courtesy of Mary Evans Picture Library.)

The mythical wisdom of the ages cannot safely be dismissed; if it is, the result may be a twisted and distorted—and likely terrifying—version of archetypal ideas. This is how symptoms of neurosis and the delusions of psychosis originate.

It is not easy to imagine this universal unconscious and its constant but covert influence on our thought, feeling, and action. It is especially not easy to imagine it in scientific terms. What could archetypes be? One writer has proposed that archetypes are like feature detectors in nonhuman animals—movement detectors in the frog, for example (Berger, 1977). Seligman (1971) noted the readiness of animals to acquire associations between some types of stimuli and not others (taste with subsequent illness, for example, but not with bright lights and noises), a phenomenon called preparedness. Phobic fears, he pointed out, occur in response to stimuli (heights, snakes, small dark places) that may have been ancestrally frightening.

All of this makes for a fascinating part of personality, no doubt, but a scientifically problematical one, because Jung simply stepped too close to the Lamarckian edge in positing the inheritance of racial myths. I do not see how it is possible for analytic psychology to escape this taint, and I believe that Munroe was overgenerous in excusing Jung. Hall and Nordby (1973) proposed that archetypes could have arisen out of genetic mutations, but as we shall see in Chapter 16 on behaviour genetics, mutations are uncommon and usually unsuccessful. Could they have been naturally occurring variations that conferred a selective advantage? I believe this stretches the evolutionary process beyond the limit. Such variations would have had to appear spontaneously in widely different habitats, each resulting in the myth holders having a greater chance to survive and reproduce. The number of myths, moreover, that would have had to evolve in this way hugely increases the improbability. In the concept of the collective unconscious, this repository of archetypal great ideas, we are left with extreme doubt about its genetic basis. Without question, Jung found abiding human concerns across history and cultures, but whether we can unite them in all their various forms as universal archetypes in a grand unconscious collective is a huge question, a probably unanswerable one.

Four archetypes have become (through evolution?) so significant for personality that they are themselves personality structures representing timeless experiences and human attributes. They are the **persona**★, **animus**★ and **anima**★, the **shadow**★, and the **self**★.

The Persona

This is the public face in each of us, the mask of ourselves that we present to others. 'In essence', as Munroe wrote, 'the persona is a necessity for social living. Constant baring of the soul in everyday situations with all one's associates would be not only embarrassing but highly inefficient for most of the small transactions required in a complex society' (1955, p. 558). Everyone plays roles in social interaction. People always have, and it's something societies demand. People involved in business, sales representatives, and pro-

A Fresh Look: Application Today

Social life in much of the world is sexually inequitable. Even in the advanced and democratic West, women on average don't get anything like a fair shake. Their opportunities to participate fully in productive and creative work are far from realized. The place of women, say the dominant and privileged males in many parts of the world, is in the home, doing all the domestic work while bearing and caring for children. If work outside the home is allowed, it is mostly in support of male enterprise, and it pays badly. The men don't appeal to their convenience to justify the consigning of women to homekeeping and childrearing; God decrees it and/or it is woman's nature to do these things and not in woman's nature to try to do what the man does (and is adapted for and good at).

Freud took a strong position on womankind, as you remember, holding to a notion of biological inferiority and its psychological scar, penis envy. He accorded professional equity to females, welcoming his daughter and others to the psychoanalytic fraternity, but in his psychology woman is not the equal of man. Jung was more liberal and open-minded. Anima and animus have equivalent archetypal status, and both are essential to every person for balance in personality. To the male, he

said, neglect your feminine side and put at severe risk your serenity and the warmth and closeness of your personal relationships. A life of dependence and abject devotion to husband and children is the fate of the woman who fails to heed her animus. Jung, though, was not all that fair-minded. He wrote:

> But no one can get round the fact that by taking up a masculine profession, studying and working like a man, woman is doing something not wholly in accord with, if not directly injurious to, her feminine nature. It is a woman's outstanding characteristic that she can do anything for the love of a man. But those women who achieve something important for the love of a *thing* are exceptional, because this does not really agree with their nature (1978, p. 117).

This was not the sort of statement for someone interested in feminine equality to appeal to: the woman who enters the male preserve of accomplishment essentially denies her own archetype.

Feminists, you may well imagine, have taken umbrage over Victorianism imposed on fundamentals of personality fessors could not do without their public faces, and even intimate relationships need them on occasion.

Sometimes, however, the ego invests too heavily in the persona, and the person essentially becomes the mask. Said Munroe: 'The shell becomes too strong, smothering the life within, preventing genuine contact with people and with life itself. Too often the [ego] becomes almost exclusively identified with the persona. The individual becomes a fine lawyer, a gracious hostess, or whatever, and forgets how to be a human being' (1955, p. 558). A person who is introverted (see below) tends to adopt a single persona, which may fit some situations but is awkward and uncomfortable in many others. Thus, the introvert feels socially ill at ease and full of self-doubt. On the other hand, extraverts often readily change the persona to fit the situation and may do so quite unconsciously. An adroit extravert may not be a hypocrite but simply adept in meeting the demands of many different situations. Of course, taken too far, the hypocrisy is evident, and the person within may become lost.

Animus and Anima

There is an unconscious maleness in women and femaleness in men, which have grown out of the ages-old experience of the sexes with each other. No one, said Jung, can success-

and on culture (see, for example, Lauter & Rupprecht, 1985). In the modern study of the working world by organizational psychologists, however, some authorities think principles in Jung's theory fit. Lyons (1997) has reviewed the history of the feminine in organizational psychology from its first appearance with the human relations movement that may be dated to the period beginning just before and after World War II with the social research of Kurt Lewin (1947; Lewin, Lippett, & White, 1939) and the organizational experiments of Harvard Business School professor Elton Mayo at the Hawthorne Works of the Western Electric company in Chicago (see Rothlisberger & Dickson, 1939). This early research was instrumental in upstaging a tough-minded, hard-nosed, and task-driven organizational psychology of management that regarded the worker's only motivation as self-interest and the only motivator money—a bare-chested, muscular and masculine approach to getting the greatest productivity from workers. Lewin and others made clear that this was not always so. Democratic principles, the importance of the woman's role in family life (Lewin), and the striking demonstration of the Hawthorne experiments that when (as some wag put it) 'someone upstairs cares' and shows it, productivity goes up—these became a core of human relations. Elton Mayo himself saw that needs for recogni-tion and security and a sense of belonging are more important in worker morale (and effort) than even the nicest surroundings an employer could provide. Lyons notes that these needs are the recognizable, softer qualities of the anima, and an egalitarian application of them in organizations produces happier workers—females and males—and better work. She says:

> Jungian theory allows that each of us is capable of accessing and expressing the feminine archetype, even though there are psychic differences between men and women. Bringing an archetypal perspective to gender work in organizations can reinforce the idea that men are capable of developing the feminine aspects of themselves and contributing to the manifestation of the feminine in organizational life. Moreover, it suggests that women are also subject to social forces that undervalue the feminine; like men, women have internalized cultural messages that can cause them to devalue the feminine in themselves and others. . . . Each sex must not only develop its contrasexual aspects but also uncover those aspects related to its own identity that have been repressed by culture or personal experience (p. 24).

The dark side of the anima. In German legend and in Wagner's *Das Rheingold*, Rhine maidens, the Lorelei, sit on rocks in the river and sing beautiful songs that lure sailors to their deaths. (Rhinemaidens, the Lorelei, © Arthur Rackham. Photo courtesy of Mary Evans Picture Library.)

fully deny these psychological counterparts to his or her sex. The animus gives women an understanding of men and the possibility of taking on certain traditionally male attributes—independence, aggressiveness, competitiveness—that help to overcome passivity and submission. In the personality of the male, his anima gives him appreciation and understanding of women and some valuable feminine traits such as intuitiveness and tenderness.

However, the archetypes of animus and anima are not all good. Women can be deceitful and use their beauty and wiles to entrap men for their own purposes. Men can be violent and aggressive, using their masculine power to subjugate and destroy. The man who rejects his anima may develop, as Munroe said, 'a pervasive sense of coldness and aridity, or frustration or fear' (1955, p. 561). Similarly, the woman who denies her animus is in for helplessness and perhaps total absorption in motherhood and stereotypical feminine activities. On the other hand, too strong an identification can lead to feminized males and masculinized females, and very unsatisfactory relations with the opposite sex.

Animus and anima are idealized images that are unlikely to be found in real persons. A man who seeks a woman like his idealized version is bound to be disappointed; so, too, will the woman who has her heart set on the perfect male.

The Shadow

As Jacobi's diagram shows, the shadow archetype resides in the deepest and most remote part of the psyche. It is made up of surviving animal instincts that go back to our prehuman origins, and it personifies evil. It is the devil in Christian doctrine, once portrayed (in a wholly unacceptable, racist way) as a dark-skinned or mongoloid caricature. In order to be a complete person, one must acknowledge the impulses of the shadow as part of oneself. At the same time, these impulses must also be held in check. Socially unacceptable thoughts that intrude on our consciousness and impulsive behaviour we didn't intend are the shadow's work. Animal instincts, however, are not all evil. They are certainly fulsome and vital; like the Freudian instincts, they make us passionate, urge-driven creatures. So long as they're controlled, that's not such a bad thing.

The Self

The archetype of the self represents a deep and enduring quest for unity of experience and the integration of personality. In our diagram, it is at the very centre of personality, expressed by a universal symbol, the **mandala**. The self does not exist in individuals from the beginning; as Munroe said, 'it is an achievement rather than a biological given' (1955, p. 563). Only in the mature person is the self realized, and then only in a rare few is true selfhood accomplished. We see the ideal in great religious figures—in Christ and Buddha, for example. The self unites conscious and unconscious. The ego, at the centre of conscious experience, assimilates unconscious life, and a new centre of personality is formed, a new equilibrium halfway between conscious and unconscious. This is a balance, self at the fulcrum, bringing together all the parts of the mature personality. Only years of constant striving and contemplation can bring such a unifying wholeness (1966b, p. 221).

A Jungian mandala, 'an expression of the self'. (From Carl Jung, *Mandala Symbolism*, Trans. R.F.C. Hull, Princeton: Princeton UP, 1959. Image courtesy of Steve Bernard.)

Perspective 4.1   Two Archetypes

An immanent memory that begins to affect us as we enter the world is the mother archetype, an accumulation of the most significant human experience with being mothered. If infants could form the idea and could tell us about it, they might ask in wonder and in gratitude, 'How does she know how and when to nourish me, how and when to look after my every need, all through the day and night?' And then, answering their own question, they would say, 'Oh yes, of course, that's easy. I know, and I know why I know. She has the mother archetype to call on, and she doesn't even have to scratch her head and puzzle about what to do. And because that's built into me, it only took me a moment to understand.'

In his beautifully literate and informed *Oedipus: Myth and Complex*, Mullahy (1948) gives a compelling portrait of the mother archetype:

> The mother is the most immediate primordial image or 'archetypal experience'. Since the child is not yet an individual in the sense of being aware of himself as a unique, differentiated personality, he remains for some time a psychological appendage of his parents. His mother is not known as a definite, feminine, and unique personality, but as *the mother*, a warming, protecting, nourishing entity. She is an 'archetype', a composite image of all pre-existing mothers, a model or pattern of all the protecting, warming, nourishing influences which man has experienced or the child will experience. The protecting mother is also associated with the nourishing earth, the provident field, the warming hearth, the protecting cave, the surrounding vegetation, the milk-giving cow and the herd. The symbol of the mother refers to a place of origin such as nature, to that which passively creates, to matter, to the unconscious, natural and instinctive life. As traces of the experience of mankind lie dormant, in a potential form, in the brain of the child, they become activated and blend with the nearest and most powerful experience, the child's mother, producing the archetypal experience of the mother (pp. 149–50).

Mothering is the earliest of the ancestral experiences that children encounter, but on its heels is another, also powerful but in a very different way. Again, Mullahy:

> As the child develops, the father comes into the picture and activates an archetype which is said to be in many ways opposed to that of the mother. The archetype of the father signifies such things as strength, power, authority, the creative breath ('*pneuma spiritus*'), and all that is moving and 'dynamic' in the world. The father image is associated with rivers, winds, storms, lightning and thunder, battle and weapons, raging animals, like wild bulls, the violent and changeful phenomena of the world, as well as the cause of all change.
>
>   While the primordial image of the mother always remains, subtly, unconsciously, determining our relation to woman, society, and to the world of feeling and fact, the father archetype determines our relation to man, spirit, law and the state, and the *dynamics* of nature. [Quoting Jung, he continues:] 'As the growing consciousness becomes more capable of understanding, the importance of the parental personality diminishes. But in the place of the father there comes the society of men, and in place of the mother, family and clan. Finally, instead of the father, the image of God appears, and in the mother's place, the mysterious abyss of all-being' (pp. 151-2).

Libido

Jung's principal dynamic concept is the **libido**★, the energy in the human psychological system. Vigorously disagreeing with Freud, Jung saw the libido as the energy that drives all activity, sexual *and* nonsexual, arising from the metabolic processes of the body. Libido can be depleted by the expenditure of effort and must be replenished by nourishment. Thus, the psyche is a partially closed energy system—partially closed because energy can be added from external sources or subtracted.

All psychological activity depends on libidinal energy. However, psychic energy cannot be measured. There is no 'libidometer' we can hook up to record the flow of energy to this or that part of personality or activity. We can, nevertheless, get a relative idea of energy investment from a person's activities, choices, or indeed, neurotic symptoms. For instance, a powerful conscious determination to do something or an unconscious complex will require and attract considerable libido. Also, when we see a person dominated by an archetypal idea—a complex—we can gauge its power and significance by the number of ideas associated with the nuclear core. This is called the constellating power of a complex. We can as well determine the strength of a complex and the energy invested in it by observing the intensity of emotion the complex arouses and what Jung called complex indicators—signs of disturbance such as the inability to recall a name or an experience, and other signs revealed through word association testing, discussed below.

Two principles govern the psychodynamics of libidinal energy. They are the **principle of equivalence**★ and the **principle of entropy**★, and they are derived from the first and second laws of thermodynamics in physics. The first law of thermodynamics states the principle of conservation of energy: the energy in a physical system is constant, and if it is subtracted from one part of the system it will be taken up by another. Psychologically, according to the principle of equivalence, libido withdrawn from the conscious activities of the ego will reappear elsewhere, invested in the unconscious or in the persona. Thus, there is an ongoing flow of energy in the personality from one structure to another and from one activity or value to another; personality is a dynamic and changing system. In physics, we think of closed systems, but as we have just seen human personality is only partially closed. Accordingly, we can only approximately understand libidinal flow. Someone who is tired from heavy work will have less energy to invest, say, in the thought processes of the ego, and will be unable to draw on other psychic resources (the unconscious, for example) for creative ideas.

The psychological principle of entropy means that energy flow seeks a balance or equilibrium, just as in a physical system heat flows from a hotter body to a cooler one (the second law of thermodynamics). So, if we have two activities in which we're interested—a weak one (writing an essay for a personality theory course) and a strong one (going to the pub for a beer), libido will flow from strong to weak toward an equilibrium. Now the strong may still win out—the equilibrium isn't achieved—but the principle remains. Also, there may be external influences to affect the balance. Similarly, weak personality structures (a frail and dependent ego as an example) will benefit from the energy of stronger structures (perhaps a dominant archetype). Surely, Jung's schoolboy personality, No. 1, callow and with little strength of character, benefited from his No. 2 personality, the wise old man. Libidinal flow from strong to weak structures, however, causes tension; the very imbalance in the personality is disruptive. Contentment and serenity are more likely to prevail when libido is more evenly distributed among the various parts.

Four Functions

Jung ascribed four functions to the ego and to the personal unconscious. In today's psychology, we would call them modes of cognitive processing or cognitive styles. The functions are *sensing*, *thinking*, *feeling*, and *intuiting*, and there *are* only four. Jung was sure of this 'on purely empirical grounds':

> But as the following consideration will show, these four together produce a kind of totality. Sensation establishes what is actually present, thinking enables us to recognize its meaning, feeling tells us its true value, and intuition points to possibilities as to whence it came and whither it is going in a given situation. In this way we can orient ourselves with respect to the immediate world as completely as when we locate a place geographically by latitude and longitude (Jung, 1971, pp. 540–1).

Two of the functions, thinking and feeling, are rational★ in the sense that they call upon reasoning, judging and evaluating, abstracting, and generalizing. Jung considered sensation and intuition to be irrational★, since sensation is concrete and particular, without cognitive elaboration, and intuition involves unconscious inference.

These four functions exist in all humans (except those who are cognitively or emotionally disabled), but they are not equals in every person. One function typically stands out: it is better developed and differentiated, and it dominates consciousness. This is the *superior* function. An *inferior* function, the least developed of the four, is unconscious, and because it has been repressed it will make its appearance in dream and fantasy. The inferior function will invariably be the pair of the superior. So, if the superior is a rational function—thinking, let's say—the unconscious inferior function will be feeling. Why one function should dominate consciousness and its rational or irrational mate should be repressed was not clear to Jung. Perhaps, he thought, this might be some inherited characteristic, and if so it would be unwise of parents or teachers to try to change a child's dominant function—to turn a feeling child into a thinking one, for example.

Personality Typologies

The Discovery of Personality Types

In 1917, Jung presented the case of a young married woman afflicted by anxiety attacks at night. She required considerable reassurance from her husband that he loved her and wouldn't leave her. Soon, she developed a psychosomatic asthma. There was a telling precedent for her neurotic asthma in adolescent fits of weeping and choking after discovering that her adored father was something of a womanizer. As an exercise, Jung considered her symptoms from both the Freudian and Adlerian points of view. Jung and Adler shared an objection to Freud's emphasis on sexuality in personality development, though beyond this there was very little in common in their views. What, then, would each of these rivals have to say about the woman's case? Jung concluded that Freud would have placed the focus of her symptoms, erotically but unconsciously, on her father and on her suspicion that her husband, as she had observed of her father, hankered after another woman. To Adler, whose views we'll see in fuller detail in the next chapter, the young woman sought to be the central figure in her father's attention. She essentially repeated her childhood symptoms with her husband—the anxiety attacks and asthmatic 'sickness' are patent techniques to control others and make them do your bidding.

Jung wondered how two capable theorists could arrive at such divergent interpretations of the same evidence and concluded that it had to be a fundamental difference in their attitudes. Freud, the extravert, focused on the importance of an external love object to the woman. Her conscious ego and unconscious seized on any shred of evidence that the significant people in her life, father and husband, didn't care enough for her. Adler, the introvert, was struck by the subjective, her striving for security as a way to overcome pervasive feelings of inferiority. Here are pictures of the introvert (Adler) and the extravert (Freud) as Jung drew them:

> The first attitude [introversion] is normally characterized by a hesitant, reflective, retiring nature that keeps itself to itself, shrinks from objects, is always slightly on the defensive and prefers to hide behind mistrustful scrutiny. The second [extraversion] is normally characterized by an outgoing, candid, and accommodating nature that adapts easily to a given situation, quickly forms attachments, and, setting aside any possible misgivings, will often venture forth with careless confidence into unknown situations (1966a, p. 44).

Comparing the distinct approaches of Freud and Adler to the symptoms of a neurotic patient was a highly illuminating thought experiment shedding light on the core idea of personality types. His two notable personality theorists, serving as unbidden subjects, showed Jung that people must vary in their **attitudes★**, their orientations toward themselves and others. He saw that attitudes involve far more than the conduct of social relationships; they represent one's whole accommodation to the inside world and to the object world outside. None of us is a pure introvert or extravert—that would be highly pathological—but we are able to classify people as generally one or the other.

According to the **principle of opposites★**, an important feature of Jungian theory, processes and structures in personality have their opposites (consciousness vs the unconscious, for example. or rational vs irrational functions), and the big task for normal development is to achieve balances. So it is for introversion and extraversion. Each person has both attitudes, one more conscious and in the forefront than the other, which is unconscious. The predominant attitude is better differentiated by virtue of genetics and experience; its unconscious counterpart is relatively undifferentiated. The unconscious attitude will gain in strength (via the principle of entropy) and occasionally burst forth in behaviour, but when it does the expression is likely to be crude and not well modulated.

Eight Types

Jung took typology a step further by combining the attitudes of introversion/extraversion and the four functions of thinking, feeling, sensing, and intuition. The result was a classification of eight types into which most of us fit (Jung, 1971). Each one is determined by its dominant attitude and function. There are probably no pure types since no one is a complete introvert or extravert and no one can rely on a single dominant function, but Jung thought that examples of pure types would illuminate the classification. We can think of four types of extravert and four of introverts.

- **Extravert thinking**. People of this type are dominated by the external world, both of objects and ideas. They repress feeling and demand objectivity, and they may be morally rigid and intolerant. Others are likely to see them as cold and distant.
- **Extravert feeling**. For such persons also, the outer world dominates. Thinking is repressed, while sensation and intuition are auxiliary, providing contact with the world. These individuals make friends easily and appear to be sensitive to the emotional dynamics of social situations. Because of their social adaptiveness, others may see their emotional responsiveness as inauthentic and hypocritical. These are intense people, thought of by others as bubbly and highly sociable.
- **Extravert sensation**. Individuals of this personality type are captivated by sensory experiences. Attuned to sensation, they are not introspective and may be thought well of by others because they attend to people and their well-being. Think of them as sensual, realistic in their perceptions, and outgoing.
- **Extravert intuitive**. These are not individuals high in persistence. They tend to jump from one new idea to another, and they arrive at their decisions without much conscious and deliberate thought. In tune with the unconscious, however, their decisions often may turn out to be good ones. They are not much concerned with others. We are likely to see them as creative visionaries.
- **Introvert thinking**. Introverted thinkers are rational, preoccupied with abstractions, and not very practical. Of this type Jung said: 'His judgment appears cold, inflexible, arbitrary, and ruthless, because it relates far less to the [external] object than to the subject [the person himself]' (1971, p. 384). To others, they are impractical intellectuals, eggheads. Jung thought of himself as one.
- **Introvert feeling**. It's not difficult to imagine this personality as self-absorbed, often turned inward on intense emotional experience that may be troubling and distressing. Was the poet Sylvia Plath an introvert feeling type? Descriptively, they are not communicative, not very grown up, and not much concerned with others.
- **Introvert sensation**. Unlike the extravert sensation type, these persons are greatly affected by their subjective experience of sensory input. Because of their subjectivity, they may misinterpret ongoing events, but because they are not skilled at thinking or in tune with their feelings, they don't seem to be bothered when others call their misinterpretations to attention. Passive and not readily excited, they may have an artistic bent.

- **Introvert intuitive**. This is a very inner-dominated person, who tends to be seen by others as artistic but strange. He or she doesn't monitor the world very well, being preoccupied with inner experience. Mystics and dreamers, say others.

Now, two questions for you to consider: Are these just stereotypes, simply caricatures that would accurately characterize very few people? And, would many people be readily fooled and taken in by these personality descriptions, their seeming plausibility, accepting pictures of themselves that might be, at best, gross oversimplifications?

Personality Development

We can rightly think of Freud as a developmental psychologist for his portrayal of the psychosexual stages. So, too, were the ego psychologist Erikson, whom we'll meet in Chapter 8, and the neo-Freudian Sullivan, one of the subjects of Chapter 6. Jung, however, painted the lifetime developmental sequence with a broad brush, showing especially little interest in the early years.

Childhood

Childhood spans the period from birth to puberty. For the first three or four years, nutrition and growth are foremost, with the development of language and thinking becoming more and more important. Jung agreed with Freud that young children have incestuous wishes, but he did not consider children to be sexual by nature. Parents are protectors, comforters, nurturers, and of the two of them the mother is most important to children of both sexes.

Young Adulthood

Young adulthood is announced by the arrival of puberty and genital sexuality. To get here, we have glossed over some profound events of early and later childhood, but from

Table 4.1	A summary of Jung's Eight Psychological Types
Extravert Thinking	objective, repress feeling, cold, distant
Extravert Feeling	sensitive to emotional tone of social situations, socially adaptive, thinking repressed
Extravert Sensation	captivated by sensory experiences, not introspective, sensual, outgoing
Extravert Intuitive	jump from one new idea to another, decide on a hunch without deliberate thought, creative visionaries
Introvert Thinking	rational, preoccupied with abstractions, impractical, cold inflexible, arbitrary
Inrovert Feeling	self-absorbed, occupied with intense emotional experience, uncommunicative, childish
Introvert Sensation	strongly affected by sensory experience in a subjective way, passive, may be artistic
Introvert Intuitive	inner dominated, 'strange' dreamer

Jung's perspective, knowledge of these early milestones doesn't help much in psychotherapy, nor does it advance our understanding of mature development and how it can go wrong. The young adult is a person in his or her own right and faces the large problem of encountering the world outside and finding a place in it.

Middle Age

This—the period from the late thirties or so until old age sets in—is the epoch of greatest importance to Jung. The person has a vocation, marital partner, children; he or she is well established in life. Middle age is a much more contemplative period, one in which cultural and spiritual values come to predominate. Striving for meaning supplants striving to accomplish. Some adults stall and lose the sense of the importance of their lives (see Erikson's era of Generativity vs Stagnation in Chapter 8), and they need to discover that 'The afternoon of life is just as full of meaning as the morning; only, its meaning and purpose are different. . . . What youth found and must find outside, the man of life's afternoon must find within himself' (Jung, 1966a, p. 75). A Jungian analysis could help, and Jung was very adept in treating patients of middle age who had become lost.

Old Age

We all have to face it, but Jung thought the epoch at the end of life was hardly important, a slide toward unconsciousness. Unlike middle age, which can be a productive period of self-realization largely not possible before then, old age doesn't offer rich possibilities in finding meaning. That will happen in the middle years, at the pinnacle of personality development.

Research

Jung was prodigiously devoted to research throughout his long professional career, but most of it was not the kind of research to earn recognition and praise from scientific personality psychologists. He drew on a few case studies—nothing to equal Freud's six long, detailed ones—but mainly his was a comparative method that involved studying history, myths, religion, and the occult. He became an expert in comparative religion, studying Hindu, Taoist, Yoga, Confucian, and Christian beliefs, as well as those of preliterate societies. Alchemy fascinated him, and he immersed himself in it. 'The secret of alchemy', he wrote, 'was in fact the transcendent function, the transformation of personality through the blending and fusion of the noble with the base components, of the differentiated with the inferior functions, of the conscious with the unconscious' (Jung, 1966b, p. 220). He took the alchemist's quest to turn base metals into gold as a representation of the search for unity in the dreams and visions—more than a thousand of them—of a young man, finding the same elements in alchemy and dream (Jung, 1968). He went on in this book with a scholarly treatment of medieval alchemy and religious symbolism, concluding that the identity of alchemical symbols and the symbols in the dreams of his dreamer incontrovertibly gave evidence for archetypes. His forays into Africa, the Native territory of the American southwest, and India to study religion, ritual, myth, and symbols provided the same confirmation: the symbols, he determined, were the same and thus universal.

Jung's research began, however, with his development of the scientifically admissible and respected word association test. It was on this that he reported in his lecture at Clark

University in 1909. The basic technique is simple. Read a list of words to a person one by one to get the respondent's verbal response to each, at the same time noting other kinds of response, including certain diagnostic signs, the complex indicators. Examples:

- a reaction time longer than average
- the repetition of the stimulus word
- an apparent mishearing, or the hearing of some other word
- bodily movements such as twitching or leg jiggling
- a response longer than a single word
- superficial responses such as rhyming (frog . . . dog)
- a failure to give a response
- a meaningless response, a neologism (made-up word)
- the perseveration of responses (the same response repeated to a number of stimulus words)
- slips of the tongue

Bodily responses may also be measured: breathing rate, for example, and the electrical conductivity of the skin—the so-called galvanic skin response (GSR)—which are common measures in the polygraph or lie detection test.

I first learned of the word association test in the hot Indiana summer of 1956, when I diligently read Woodworth and Schlosberg's monumental *Experimental Psychology* (1954) cover to cover in preparation for graduate school in the fall. In summing up word association they said:

> The discovery of a complex is a kindred problem to the detection of a criminal. There is, however, one important difference. The detective knows the crime but not the culprit; the psychotherapist knows the culprit but not the 'crime'. The psychotherapist does not know in advance what stimulus words will suit the individual case, but he can set traps for the complexes commonly encountered in clinical practice, arising from the sex life and its frustrations, from discontent with one's personal appearance or abilities, from disappointed ambition, from economic stress. Stimulus words calculated to tap such complexes are therefore included in the list, along with a padding of presumably neutral words (pp. 67–8).

The word association test in its various forms and applications is not infallible. Emotional responses can be disguised, and a nervous, apprehensive person may display apparently emotional complex indicators just because he or she is a nervous, apprehensive person. The method, however, gained the approval of psychologists and found its way into the study of verbal learning and verbal behaviour, which anticipated the interest of cognitive psychology in processes of thought (association) and language (Jenkins & Russell, 1960; Palermo and Jenkins, 1963). Lie detection procedures probably owe their development to the technique. Rotter reviewed the use of word association in 1951; since that time, however, it has largely disappeared in personality assessment.

Beyond the word association test, Jung's research has largely been of interest to scholars exploring history, mysticism, religion, and the occult, and to clinicians who have adopted a Jungian approach. There are a number of Jungian institutes, and important intellects (historian Arnold Toynbee, writers Philip Wylie and Hermann Hesse, lit-

Table 4.2   The Word Association Test: Some Stimulus Words from Jung's List

1.	head	31.	tree	76.	to wash
2.	green	32.	to prick	77.	cow
3.	water	33.	pity	78.	friend
4.	to sing	34.	yellow	79.	happiness
5.	death	35.	mountain	80.	lie
6.	long	36.	to die	81.	department
7.	ship	37.	salt	82.	narrow
21.	ink	41.	money	94.	contented
22.	angry	42.	stupid	95.	ridicule
23.	needle	43.	exercise-book	96.	to sleep
24.	to swim	44.	to despise	97.	month
25.	journey	45.	finger	98.	nice
26.	blue	46.	dear	99.	women
27.	lamp	47.	bird	100.	to abuse

erary critic Lewis Mumford) have recognized the astonishing range and depth in the thought of a very wise old man.

Jung's categorization of attitudes has been warmly welcomed by psychologists. The typology of introversion/extraversion was adopted by the British psychologist Hans J. Eysenck as a fundamental dimension of personality. An extraordinary amount of research using personality questionnaires and the statistical technique of factor analysis has confirmed the usefulness of classifying people in this way. We shall review it in detail when we consider trait theory and see its influence in behaviour genetics (Chapter 16).

Perspective 4.2   A Test for Personality Types: The Myers-Briggs Type Indicator®

Isabel Briggs Myers and her mother, Katherine Briggs, were impressed by Jung's psychological types and saw in his taxonomy a way to assess personality and a basis for giving vocational advice. The questionnaire they developed, the Myers-Briggs Type Indicator®, or MBTI®, took Jung's eight types and added another dimension, judgement/perception, giving sixteen types. The MBTI® has captured a significant piece of the personality test market (its publishers claim that two million people a year take it). Some university counselling services give the test at a cut rate to students seeking career guidance. There is validity evidence, some of which also confirms Jungian typology. For example, Carlson (1980) studied memories for important emotional experiences, categorizing her research subjects by Myers-Briggs® type. Judges knowledgeable in type theory were given memories provided by the participants and asked to identify them as the memories of introverted thinking or feeling types. The judges were well beyond chance in their assignments. For the emotions of joy, excitement, and shame, the emotional memories of extraverts tended to be 'social', while the memories of introverts were 'individual' in nature. Carlson and Levy (1973) reported that people classified as the introverted thinking type excelled in short-term memory for emotionally neutral items (digits); the extraverted feeling type was better at recognition memory for emotional facial expressions and for names. Extravert intuitive types were more likely to volunteer for social service.

These are interesting findings, and they do imply the usefulness of Jung's typology. As Carlson said, they are consistent with 'two basic assumptions of Jungian type theory—the social connectedness of extraverts . . . and the "emotional" quality of feeling judgment, (1980, p. 807). Nonetheless, they are patchy, covering only fragments of this very complex taxonomy. The MBTI® is a very transparent test; it is easy to fool either with deliberate dis-simulation or with self-deception. (For a very skeptical, indeed extremely critical, view of the Myers-Briggs Type Indicator—and of Jung—go to The Skeptical Dictionary: http://skepdic.com/myersb.html.) The personality types, all sixteen of them, are given quite detailed characterizations in the manual of the test. Here, I have paraphrased four of them:

- Individuals of the **Introvert/Sensing/Thinking/Judging** type are quietly earnest people who concentrate on being careful and diligent. Some descriptive adjectives are sensible, down-to-earth, trustworthy, responsible, systematic. Determined individuals who make up their own minds, they can be counted on to decide on what is to be done and work on it deliberately with focused attention.
- Individuals of the **Introvert/Intuitive/Feeling/Perceiving** type are enthusiastic and loyal but somewhat restrained until they get to know another person well. Devoted to ideas, the careful use of language, and developing tasks on their own, their enthusiasms may lead them to try to do too much; they often succeed anyway. They are friendly but may put others off by their preoccupations. They are indifferent to having things or to the place they happen to be in.
- Individuals of the **Extravert/Sensing/Thinking/Judging** type are down-to-earth and closely tuned to reality, with no interest in tasks that don't seem to them to be practical. They enjoy organizing and running things and are well suited for business and administration. They may find it difficult to take the views of others into account.
- Members of the **Extravert/Intuitive/Feeling/Perceiving** type are warmer than the Introvert/Intuitives, characterized by their high spirits, enthusiasm, and inventive-ness. They have broad capabilities and can both see solutions to and solve problems quickly. Their solutions are often improvised on the spur of the moment. They tend to be glib in explaining why they do what they do. They are outgoing and helpful.

Now, imagine the amount of research that would be required to establish the validity of all sixteen, each with a number of complex attributes. Then, note that I have reproduced the descriptive tone of the four. Like the originals, they are not factual and objective but rather are designed to appeal to the persons so characterized. We don't want to unduly challenge test respondents with cold and formal analyses of their attributes, but neither do we wish to give them the kind of glowing, sugar-coated portraits that appear in newspaper horoscopes. On such a continuum, where does the Myers-Briggs Type Indicator® fall?

Analytic Psychology in Perspective

We have already addressed many of the issues that Jung's analytic psychology raises. Its scholarship is immense and has earned Jung wide respect among world authorities in the history of ideas, religion, and mythology. The credentials of analytic psychology as a scientific theory, however, are dubious at best and at worst virtually nonexistent. Its principal contributions to personality theory include the type concept of introversion/extraversion, which has become firmly established in the research literature of personality, and the experimental study of complexes via the word association test. Apart from these it has left psychologists cold. In the end, one can marvel at the depth of Jung's probing of the psyche, his determined and even audacious pursuit of things that give scientists the willies, and the complexity of his theory, but when it comes to using analytic psychology as the source of testable hypotheses, there isn't much to add.

SUMMARY

1. Carl Gustav Jung was born in 1875 in a village on the shore of Lake Constance, the son of a country pastor who had lost his faith, not a father to confide in. He was an awkward, introverted boy, and an indifferent student. As a pre-adolescent, he determined that he had two personalities: No. 1, the dull schoolboy, and No. 2, a 'wise old man'. He was admitted to the University of Basel, where he was awarded an MD at 25. He became an assistant (resident) at the Burghölzli Psychiatric Hospital in Zürich, headed by the famed psychiatrist Eugen Bleuler. He studied with a pioneer in dynamic psychiatry, Pierre Janet, and quickly became widely recognized as a psychiatrist, scientist, and psychotherapist. Impressed by Freud, he began to correspond with him, and the two hit it off. But after several years of close relationship, Jung and Freud broke off their friendship. Jung resolved as well to cut his professional ties to his mentor; he would have his own concepts and emphases and would be free to reject many of Freud's. He left the Burghölzli to establish a psychiatric practice and to write, moving to a village on the shores of Lake Zürich. The break with Freud was costly: He underwent several years of either a 'creative illness' or a psychosis, emerging fully intact in 1919. He studied, travelled, and wrote voluminously, achieving worldwide fame. His theory grew incrementally over his long life. He died at eighty-five, honored the world over.

2. Jung was a disciple of Freud in the early years of the twentieth century but broke with the master over the significance of the sexual instinct in personality. Analytic psychology reflects many concepts from psychoanalysis—the ego, the unconscious, instincts, psychic energy (libido), repression and projection, and stages of development—but in Jung's hands they became distinct, with only surface similarities to Freudian theory. As a result, much of analytic psychology is unique, deriving from Jung's clinical experience and his deep study of history, philosophy, religion, mythology, and the mystical. Central in the theory is the concept of a collective (transpersonal) unconscious, a store of potential ancestral memory of fundamental human experience. Jung believed that determinism anchored in past events is insufficient to explain human behaviour, thinking, and feeling. Humans are oriented toward the future, and the effects of the past cannot be understood without knowledge of hopes and goals. It may be said that analytic psychology is a theory partway between psychology and religion.

3. Among the emphases in analytic psychology, two in particular stand out. The first is the principle of teleology, which asserts that personality is oriented towards the future. To understand human action, psychology must recognize 'intrinsic striving towards a goal'. The pursuit of future aims informs the causal events of the past; determinism by itself can be of only partial interest. Analytic psychology recognizes humankind's universal devotion to religion, a forward-looking source of hope, completeness, and self-realization. The second emphasis that stands out is the startling concept

of the collective unconscious, shared by every individual, from which significant experiences in the history of the species can be revived to guide (or bedevil) the present. These experiences centre on phenomena puzzling to the ancients and to us: birth and death, motherhood, fatherhood, people of great wisdom, heroism, the sun, the moon . . . They are archetypes, subjects of myths in every time and culture. Archetypes exercise a lifelong influence over us and cannot be dismissed without risk to the integrity of personality. Four archetypes are so important that they have become structures of personality study:

- The **persona** is the mask that we present to others. If the ego invests too much in the mask, genuineness is lost.
- **Animus and anima** represent the unconscious male part of women and female part of men. Animus gives women understanding of men; anima gives men understanding of women. Animus and anima have their dark sides.
- The **shadow**, in the deepest part of personality, is made up of animal instincts, the majority of them bad, though some contribute to vitality. The shadow personifies evil.
- The **self**, representing the quest for unity and integration in personality, develops in midlife.

A major question may be raised about the collective unconscious: does it imply Lamarck's fallacious idea of the inheritance of acquired characteristics? Jung denied that it did.

4. There is a concept of psychic energy, libido, not specifically sexual, that is the energy source for all psychological activity. Energy is regulated according to two principles derived from the first and second laws of thermodynamics in physics: the **principle of equivalence** (energy withdrawn from an activity is not lost but will be expended elsewhere in personality), and the **principle of entropy** (energy use seeks a balance, flowing from strong structures, values, or activities to weaker ones).

5. Both ego and self are part of the theory. The ego is at the centre of consciousness. Its functions include perception, thinking, feeling, remembering, and also the sense of identity and experience of continuity. The self, developing later in life, drives the search for unity and completeness and is ultimately the centre of personality. An expression of self is the mandala symbol. The ego opposes the **personal unconscious**, the store of memories, ideas, and feelings that each individual has repressed or forgotten. In the personal unconscious are **complexes**, emotional constellations of ideas. Complexes have an unrecognized but powerful effect on behaviour. An example: the **mother** complex. The Jungian personal unconscious is not as inaccessible as Freud's model. Ego and personal unconscious are adjoining and communicate with each other.

6. Jung accounted for noncausal coincidences by the **principle of synchronicity**, which explains paranormal experiences and clairvoyant thoughts. These are causally unconnected events that reflect a layer of order beyond causality.

7. There are four functions in the ego and personal unconscious: thinking, feeling, sensation, and intuition. They are paired, thinking with feeling, sensation with intuition. Everyone is endowed with all four but in different proportions. One of the functions is dominant and conscious; this is the superior function. An inferior function, the pair of the superior function, is unconscious. It is less developed and differentiated but will have covert effects in personality and will appear in dreams and fantasy. Two of the functions, thinking and feeling, are **rational** in that they involve deliberate cognitive processes; two, sensation and intuition, are **irrational**, not cognitively elaborated. Sensation involves immediate and concrete experience, while intuition depends on unconscious inference.

8. People vary in their **attitudes**, their orientations toward the social world and the world of objects and toward themselves. Attitudes involve more than the conduct of social relationships: they represent one's whole approach to the inside world and the outside one. The **attitudes** are **introversion** and **extraversion**. Each person has both attitudes, one dominant and more conscious, the other unconscious. Jung combined the two attitudes with the four functions, yielding eight psychological types:

- **extravert thinking**—objective; represses feeling; cold, distant
- **extravert feeling**—sensitive to emotional tone of social situations; socially adaptive; represses thinking

- **extravert sensation**—captivated by sensory experiences; not introspective; sensual, outgoing
- **extravert intuitive**—jumps from one new idea to another; makes decisions on a hunch without deliberate thought; likely to be a creative visionary
- **introvert thinking**—rational; preoccupied with abstractions; impractical; cold, inflexible, arbitrary
- **introvert feeling**—self-absorbed; occupied with intense emotional experience; uncommunicative; childish
- **introvert sensation**—strongly affected by sensory experience in a subjective way; passive; may be artistic
- **introvert intuitive**—dominated by inner thoughts; 'strange' dreamer

9. Analytic psychology offers only a brief sketch of personality development. The early years, so important to Freud and the neo-Freudians, were of little interest to Jung, and young adulthood he thought relatively unimportant beyond the important task of moving from the protective confines of the family to find a place in the world. Analytic psychology's developmental sequence consists of four stages:
   - *childhood*—from birth to puberty
   - *young adulthood*—from puberty to the thirties
   - *middle age*—from late thirties to old age; this was, to Jung, the most important stage, characterized by the search for meaning and the development of the self
   - *old age*—a slide toward unconsciousness; not a creative period and not of interest to Jung

10. Jung was deeply involved in research throughout his long career. The greatest part of his work was not research as the science of psychology defines it but explorations in history, religion, mythology, and the occult. However, early in his career, he did undertake experimental studies of complexes using a word association test, a simple technique in which the investigator reads a list of words to a person one at a time, recording a number of diagnostic signs, called complex indicators. The word association test has had extensive use in personality and research, and it is the basis of lie detection. The attitudes of introversion and extraversion have also been the subject of research, with particular influence on modern personality trait theory. H.J. Eysenck brought this typology into trait theory research, and it is now one of the major personality dimensions in behaviour genetics. Jung's typology was adopted in a test of personality types, the Myers-Briggs Type Indicator, which introduces an additional function, judging/perceiving, to produce a total of sixteen unique types. This test, widely used, has some (but incomplete) evidence for its validity.

11. Analytic psychology reflects a monumental degree of scholarship that has earned Jung recognition and a place of honour in the disciplines of history, religion, mythology, and anthropology. As a scientific theory, however, analytic psychology has not commanded respect. Its many concepts are largely untestable, and they are loosely connected. It also features a questionable heredity theory to account for the collective unconscious.

TO TEST YOUR UNDERSTANDING

1. Do you agree that Jung's concept of the collective unconscious crosses the line into Lamarckian inheritance of acquired characteristics? Are the efforts to rescue it and give it scientific respectability credible?
2. Whose notion of the individual unconscious do you favour, Freud's dark and frightening one or Jung's personal unconscious, less terrifying and more accessible?
3. What do the concepts of animus and anima add to our understanding of sexual differentiation? Are the psychologies of men and women so significantly different that parts of personality are devoted to representing the other sex?
4. In your view, what are the genuine contributions of Jung's analytic psychology to the scientific psychology of personality? Do you see analytic psychology as having an important place as clinical theory in the treatment of people who are troubled by personality disorders?

CHAPTER FIVE

The Neo-Freudians: Alfred Adler

Introduction

While Jung was developing analytic psychology, a number of theorists, beginning with Alfred Adler, attempted to take what they could from Freud's psychoanalysis and shape it as they saw fit. Jung, showing the influence of Pierre Janet and his training under Bleuler on the schizophrenic, developed a theory that departed profoundly from psychoanalysis. Adler, though he, like Jung, felt uneasy with Freud's position in some rather fundamental ways, maintained ties to other key psychoanalytic principles. In fact, apart from their break with Freud, Adler and Jung shared not much more than an emphasis on the importance of future goals to complement the causality of the past. (Indeed, Jung did not even like Adler, contemptuously labelling him an 'impudent rascal'.) As a result, despite the common heritage of divorce from psychoanalysis, there is very little resemblance between Jung's theory and the theories of Adler and the neo-Freudians.

The critical assaults on psychoanalysis that emerged beginning shortly after the first decade of the twentieth century fall into three major groups. First, critics both within psychoanalysis and outside of it took issue with Freud's consuming interest in the fate of instincts in the chronic war among the three personality systems, and in particular his preoccupation with sexuality. 'Pansexualism', they said accusingly, as if spitting out an epithet. In stressing instinctual life, Freud badly underestimated the significant dynamics of parent–child relationships. Although he surely did understand that parents influence the psychological destiny of their children, he did not grasp the real importance of the family and the parents as socializing agents in the development of the child. If you can recall our discussion of the situation–person interaction from Chapter 1, you will see that Freud was entirely too focused on processes within the person and just did not give sufficient weight to the family and social interaction.

Freud's failure to appreciate the significance of familial and social factors in personality development places him squarely in the fold of nineteenth-century biology and medicine, which, as we saw in Chapter 2, held that human behaviour, no less than disease, could be understood in physical terms. Bodily processes and energy dynamics were the stuff of personality, and disturbances of them the source of neurosis. A number of Freud's contemporaries, including Alfred Adler, were not so strongly captive to such a view. Rebels, they rejected instinctual life as the fundamental source of personality and sex as the prime mover. We use the term 'neo-Freudian' to refer to this group that defaced but did not destroy the psychoanalytic monument.

The second of the objections to Freud's psychoanalysis had to do with the role of the ego. For Freud, all ego activity was derivative, ultimately stemming from energy derived from the id, in other words from instinctual energy. Recall that in the doctrine of orthodox psychoanalysis the ego has no independent energy of its own. Its energy is 'borrowed', if you will, to carry out instinctually determined tasks. A number of analysts found it unacceptable that the hand of instinct must be behind every single act; they argued that we see in the behaviour of both children and adults activity that has to reflect an autonomous or at least semi-autonomous ego. One of the most prominent of these dissenters was Heinz Hartmann, whose ideas we shall take up in Chapter 8. He proposed that the ego itself has an independent source of energy, an endowment serving adaptation to the environment, mastery, the development of confidence, and curiosity. The kinds of things that Hartmann and others called 'intrinsic ego satisfactions' reveal not activity derived from instincts but activity carried out for its own sake. Hartmann and his fellow ego-psychologists had another, related, concern: the importance of society and family for the development of the ego, for the context in which the ego grows and expresses itself.

The third objection to psychoanalysis concerned Freud's pessimistic and conservative outlook. Freud looked on the grey side of human nature and human prospects, and in reaction there emerged a kind of Freudian left, which asserted that Freud was wrong to view human life so darkly. The Freudian left tried to argue that human nature makes it possible for growth, for healthy ego development, and for social amity to occur. Adler was at the forefront, and he was later joined by the distinguished neo-Freudian Erich Fromm, whose theory, a remarkable blend of Marxist social thought and psychoanalysis, we shall consider in Chapter 7.

Let's turn now to Alfred Adler and to the personality theory that he developed, which he named 'individual psychology'. Adler was the first of the neo-Freudians and in an important way those who followed (Erich Fromm, Harry Stack Sullivan, Karen Horney) might rightly be called neo-Adlerians. First, we'll consider Adler's personal history. It is instructive.

Alfred Adler. (Ullstein Bild/The Granger Collection, New York)

Alfred Adler: Personal History

Alfred Adler was born in February 1870 in a small village suburb of Vienna. His father was a corn merchant, and the family was at the time well off. The second of six children—four boys and two girls—he was a sickly child who suffered from rickets, a disease caused by vitamin D deficiency that makes bones soft. Rickets is successfully treated with the administration of vitamin D and exposure to sunlight, but this was unknown then. Adler's early years were a painful trial of inactivity; everything had to be done for him.

One of my earliest recollections is of sitting on a bench, bandaged up on account of rickets, with my healthy elder brother sitting opposite me. He could run, jump, and move about quite effortlessly, while for me movement of any sort was a strain and an effort. Everyone went to great pains to help me, and my mother and father did all that was in their power to do. At the time of this recollection I must have been about two years old (Bottome, p. 9).

When he was five, Adler had a terrifying brush with death from pneumonia, 'and the doctor, who had suddenly been called in, told my father that there was no point in going to the trouble of looking after me, as there was no hope of my living. At once a frightful terror came over me, and a few days later, when I was well, I decided definitely to become a doctor so that I should have a better defense against the danger of death and weapons to combat it superior to my doctor's' (Bottome, p. 12). The family later moved farther out in the country, and young Alfred began to spend hours roaming the fields, gaining just the sort of exposure to sunlight's beneficent vitamin D that he needed. He grew up vigorous and adventuresome, a broad, stocky man with nothing to mark him in adulthood as the weak and ill-favoured child he had been.

School was a torment. Adler did badly and was especially poor in mathematics. But he conquered his difficulties—a triumphant solution of a math problem before a class that had ridiculed him seems to have been a key event—and on graduation gained admission to the University of Vienna to study medicine. He completed his degree in 1895, but he was not a top student. After briefly specializing in ophthalmology, he turned to general practice and finally to psychiatry. Soon, he met and married a Russian student, Raissa Epstein. She was a dedicated socialist, fiercely independent, and well educated. Adler had found Marxism appealing and shared Raissa's political leanings, but he ultimately came to disappoint her by devoting himself not to socialist causes but to the development and practice of individual psychology (Ellenberger, 1970).

In 1902, Freud sent postcards to four Viennese physicians inviting them to join a fledgling discussion group, the Wednesday Psychological Society. Why Freud included Adler is not known; one account has it that Adler had written a newspaper article vigorously defending *The Interpretation of Dreams* after it had been publicly ridiculed, and that Freud had issued the invitation out of gratitude (Bottome, p. 56). Meeting weekly, the Wednesday Society discussed the new theory and competing ideas brought by its few members over cakes, black coffee, and one cigar or cigarette after another. As the membership grew, so did dispute, and the evening discussions were often contentious. Adler, however, was loyal enough, though he exasperated Freud with his independent turn of mind, that Freud nominated him for the presidency of the Vienna Psychoanalytic Society, successor to the Wednesday group, in 1910. Not a year later, having presented in two papers a theory that starkly contradicted core psychoanalytic propositions (including the Oedipus complex, the unconscious, infantile sexuality, and the primacy of the sexual motive), Adler was forced out.

The parting was acrimonious and vituperative. Freud saw Adler as 'an abnormal individual driven mad by ambition', adding that he was, as well, paranoid (Gay, p. 223). Adler did think Freud was persecuting him, saying that that was 'in character'. At the end, Adler demanded of Freud, 'Why should I always do my work under your shadow?' (Gay, p. 224). Years later, he would charge 'the Freudian theory [with being] the consistent psychology of the pampered child, who feels that his instincts must never be denied, who looks on it as unfair that other people should exist, who asks always, "Why should I love my neighbour? Does my neighbour love me?"' (Adler, 1931, p. 97). Freud frankly hated Adler, regarding him as a pathological traitor, and he nourished his enmity for more than a quarter of a century. Hearing of Adler's death in 1937, Freud wrote a particularly nasty epitaph to a friend: 'For a Jewish boy from a Vienna suburb, a death in Aberdeen, Scotland is an unprecedented career and a proof of how far he had come. Truly, his contemporaries have richly rewarded him for his service in having contradicted psychoanalysis' (Gay, p. 615).

During World War I, Adler worked as psychiatrist serving soldiers of the Austrian army. After the war, he returned to his psychiatric practice, to the founding of child guidance clinics for both treatment and prevention of psychological problems in children, to nurturing his nascent Society for Individual Psychology, and to the development of his theory. The thirteen years between 1920 and 1933 were highly creative; he modified and extended individual psychology, writing a number of books. The most important of these was *Understanding Human Nature* (1927), which constitutes an explicit statement of the theory.

Adler had forsaken his Jewish faith in 1904 to become a Protestant. This was not to escape anti-Semitism but to join what he saw as a more inclusive religion. In 1934, with the Nazi rise to power in Germany, there were ominous signs of the coming menace; conversion to Christianity would afford no immunity. He immigrated to the United States, where he taught at the Long Island College of Medicine, lectured widely, and continued to develop individual psychology. He died while taking a walk at the end of lectures in Aberdeen, collapsing on the sidewalk with a massive heart attack. As he was being lifted on a stretcher, a bystander said, 'It looked as if he were trying to help them arrange him, so that it would be easier for them to carry him' (Bottome, p. 277).

Adler was a charming and witty man, although in his difficult period with Freud he was often seen as rancorous and disagreeable by faithful members of the Freudian circle. As we shall see, he held an optimistic view of humankind's prospects and strove devotedly to further them. He was a clever and strikingly intuitive psychotherapist, direct and sometimes blunt but with a twinkle in his eye. He inspired confidence and hope in his patients and was especially good with children. To a man who came to him with severe stage fright he said, 'You should not try to chase two rabbits. If you do you will not catch either. Now, you wish to give pleasure to your audience. This is quite a good rabbit. Follow it up. But you also wish to be an outstanding success while doing it. This rabbit you might very well leave to run off by itself' (Bottome, p. 86).

Perspective 5.1   Adler, Jung, and Freud in Popular Culture

In the first half of the twentieth century psychoanalysis and its offshoots captivated popular imagination and became staple fare in popular culture. There was a time when you could hardly leaf through an issue of *The New Yorker* magazine without finding an analyst cartoon, and they regularly appear to this day. Broadway theatre succumbed to the appeal, and the Broadway musical nearly did. In 1932, George and Ira Gershwin wrote 'Pardon My English', a zany spoof whose hero was afflicted by amnesia and two alternating egos. In it was the following song sequence, 'Freud and Jung and Adler' and 'He's Oversexed'. After tryouts in Philadelphia and Boston, the two songs were dropped before the 1933 New York opening. That was a pity, because 'The Viennese Sextet'—two Freuds, two Jungs, and two Adlers—was, if weak on theory, very funny.

Adlers, Jungs, & Freuds: 'The Viennese Sextet'. (Adler: ullstein bild/The Granger Collection, New York; Jung, Freud: Archives of the History of American Psychology—The University of Akron.)

'Freud and Jung and Adler'

VERSE

Two Doctors:

> *If a person starts to quiver*
> *Through cirrhosis of the liver,*
> *We can't be bothered by that sort of thing at all.*

Two Others:

> *But how eagerly do we go*
> *To an egg who has an ego*
> *Or a brain that's scrambled 'way beyond recall.*

Two Others:

> *We don't cure appendicitis*
> *Or the mumps or laryngitis –*
> *That's not the kind of service that we sell.*

All:

> *But we're always on location*
> *When it's mental aberration,*
> *For that pays twice as well!*

Nurses:

> *You must know that when a*
> *Doctor's from Vienna –*
> *That pays twice as well!*

REFRAIN 1

Doctors:

> *Doctor Freud and Jung and Adler,*
> *Adler and Jung and Freud—*
> *Six psychoanalysts, we!*
> *Just let us make one diagnosis—*
> *We'll know was loss is'!*
> *Doctor Freud and Jung*
> *and Adler,*
> *Adler and Jung and Freud.*
> *Visiting hours, nine to three.*
> *If you ever had the dream that Mrs Grundy's*
> *Always keeping her eye on you on Sund'ys,*

And you suddenly find you're standing in your undies—
We are positive that you had better see
Doctor Freud and Jung and Adler,
Adler and Jung and Freud—
Six sex psychos we!

REFRAIN 2
Doctors:

Doctor Freud and Jung and Adler,
Adler and Jung and Freud –
Six psychoanalysts we!
Just let us make one diagnosis—
We'll know was loss is'!
Doctor Freud and Jung and Adler,
Adler and Jung and Freud.
Visiting hours, nine to three.
If you've any mental problem that perplexes—
If there's anything that's wrong with your reflexes—
If you're really not certain as to which your sex is—
We are positive that you had better see
Doctor Freud and Jung and Adler,
Adler and Jung and Freud—
Six sex psychos we!

'He's Oversexed!'
A
Drs Adler:

He's oversexed!

Drs Jung:

He's undersexed!

Drs Freud:

He hasn't any sex at all!

All:

This sort of thing commences
When children scribble on fences!

Drs Adler:

He's oversexed!

Drs Jung:

He's undersexed!

Drs Freud:

It happened when he was that *small!*

All:

His mind is in confusion;
There's only one conclusion:
He's oversexed,
He's undersexed,
He hasn't any sex at all!

B

Drs Adler:

> *It's father love!*

Drs Jung:

> *It's mother love!*

Drs Freud:

> *We're sure it isn't love at all!*

All:

> *His thoughts they should be purty,*
> *But they are probably dirty!*

Drs Adler:

> *It's father love!*

Drs Jung:

> *It's mother love!*

Drs Freud:

> *It happened when he was that small!*

All:

> *His head so badly cracked is,*
> *The analytical fact is:*
> *He's oversexed,*
> *He's undersexed,*
> *He hasn't any sex at all!*

Emphases

Individual psychology stands out for a number of distinguishing features. Among them are the following.

Practicality

Individual psychology is a singularly practical theory, devoted to understanding the human situation and treating common human problems. In dealing with people in psychological difficulty, Adler stressed the need for courage and common sense—attributes to be expected in the healthy person but weak or missing in those who have been damaged by parents who failed to equip their children well. Adlerian treatment focuses on teaching adults, parents, and children how to better manage their lives and make their social relationships more co-operative and satisfying. The eminent practicality of the theory led some critics to dismiss it as too informal and insubstantial, but this was a serious mistake. Many concepts of this appealingly useful theory showed up in other theories, quite unacknowledged, and in popular culture (notable examples include the inferiority complex and the notion of lifestyle, a derivative of Adler's 'style of life'). The influence of Adlerian theory has been pervasive, finding its way into Freudian theory and laying the foundation for the whole neo-Freudian movement (Ellenberger, 1970, pp. 641–5; Rotter, 1962).

A Conscious Ego

Individual psychology is a forthright psychology of a **conscious ego★**. Thought, feeling, and behaviour stem not from hidden and inaccessible motives or from unconscious activities of the ego but from conscious processes. We may deceive ourselves, to be sure, claiming implausible reasons for our behaviour, but, said Adler, we really know and have not the courage to acknowledge that we do. We can hardly imagine how radical it was for Adler to reject the Freudian view of a mind hidden from itself and replace it with a conception of mind that is mainly aware of motives, the meaning of action, and purpose.

The Individual in Society

This is a theory that puts the individual's relations with society right at the centre. It is a person–society theory, and it emphasizes that humans, individually, are by their very nature social creatures, motivated by inborn **social interest★**. They are social because there is no other choice, since no one can escape the essential **inferiority★** that arises out of individual helplessness and dependence. Humans compensate for and overcome these feelings of inferiority with an innate striving for superiority, a striving to conquer life's challenges. The neurotic person may experience a false superiority, one that is frustrating and destructive, but the basic principle remains an 'impetus from minus to plus' (Adler, 1930, p. 398). We shall see that the fulfilling path to compensation for inferiority is social.

Freud was contemptuous of such a departure from the essentials of psychoanalysis. Alluding to Adler (and to Jung), he wrote in 1914, 'The truth is that these people have picked out a few cultural overtones from the symphony of life and have once more failed to hear the mighty and primordial melody of the instincts' (1957, p. 62).

Individual Uniqueness

Adler proposed that each person develops a distinctively individual approach to living and pursuing goals, the **style of life★**, which expresses the uniqueness of each personality. As Hall, Lindzey, and Campbell—authorities on personality theory—say, 'Style of life is *the* system principle by which the individual personality functions; it is the whole that commands the parts' (1998, p. 132). Adler was ahead of his time in his emphasis on the unique profile of each person; several other theorists stressing individual uniqueness really got the idea directly or indirectly from him.

Pursuing Future Goals

Adler, like Freud, believed in the causality of human nature, that behaviour is caused (as by childhood experience). But for Adler, just as important was the idea that behaviour is directed toward the future. Humans pursue goals, ends that determine their actions. He called this concept **fictional finalism★**—'fictional' because the goals people strive to achieve are not necessarily realistic or achievable.

The Family as a Social Group

Individual psychology is explicit on the family as a social group, the effects of childrearing practices, and the unique psychological situation of children in each birth position.

Adler astutely pointed to parenting practices that are especially damaging to children, emphatically showing the connection between the flawed development of children and how parents behave toward them. His view represents a model of the social psychology of the family.

How Personality is Expressed

We reveal our personalities not only in our efforts to compensate for inferiority and in the major goals we pursue but in less obvious ways as well. Earliest memories, like dreams, give much away, and the symptoms of neurosis reveal the nature of mistaken striving.

The Major Concepts of Individual Psychology

Organ Inferiority and Compensation

In 1907, while still a committed and active member of the Wednesday Society, Adler published a small book on organ inferiority, developing the idea of abnormalities or—using Adler's word—inferiorities in bodily organs. An organ inferiority might be betrayed by frequent illnesses, or a chronic condition such as intestinal distress. This was not new, but Adler's proposal that the body often compensates for the weakness of an organ was.

Also new was a psychological turn to the theory of organ inferiority to account for the underlying basis of neurosis. Adler believed that a weak, dysfunctional organ, especially in an erogenous zone, would compel the person's attention and become a focus, resulting in neurotic preoccupation. Thus, Adler accounted for the sexual aspect of neurosis. Freud was gratified to see neurosis given an essentially biological basis, but Adler was just beginning. Organ inferiority soon became too narrow and restrictive in his thinking. He did not abandon the idea but went beyond it by arguing for psychological processes as counterparts to the physical. Organ inferiority became a model for a larger concept of inferiority, a psychological model. Adler argued that there must be a psychological parallel to the physical principle of **compensation★** for weakness in bodily organs. He made psychological compensation a major determinant of personality.

As Adler's ideas developed, he began to stress the importance of universal feelings of inferiority stemming from the fundamental human condition of vulnerability and need for one another. He pointed to the human infant's long period of utter dependence and helplessness and to the unarguably social nature of individual beings. No solitary person is capable of survival. Yes, there is the odd hermit, but the odd hermit is a rare exception and indeed in indirect ways depends upon the rest of society for his survival. We are not the commanding creatures we think we are. Adler:

> . . . in some ways men are the weakest of all creatures. We have not the strength of the lion or the gorilla, and many animals are better fitted to meet the difficulties of life alone. . . . [H]uman beings have need of more varied and deeper cooperation than we can find anywhere else in the world. The human child is especially weak; it needs care and protection for many years. Since every human being has at one time been the youngest and weakest of mankind, and since mankind, without cooperation, would be completely at the mercy of its environment, we can understand how inescapably a child which has not trained itself in cooperation will be driven towards pessimism and a fixed inferiority complex. We can understand, too, that life

will continue to offer problems even to the most cooperative individual. No individual will find himself in the position of having reached his final goal of superiority, of being complete master of his environment (1931, p. 56).

Feelings of Inferiority

There is no escaping the feeling of inferiority; it is a part of life. Everyone feels inferior, Adler said, and the question is how we deal with it. Inferiority feelings may be thought of as a drive that promotes striving to overcome incompleteness. The goal is to be complete, to achieve perfection, but we must think of it not as an ultimate aim but a lifelong and never-ending pursuit. Feelings of inferiority, even sometimes painful ones, 'are not in themselves abnormal. They are the cause of all improvements in the position of mankind' (Adler, 1931, p. 55). Life would be very dull if we reached the exalted goal of complete perfection; there would be nothing else to do, no new challenges. It's the race, not having crossed the finish line, that matters.

Our lifelong efforts to overcome inferiority are governed by two things. First is the body—our constitutions, the kind of physical beings we are. Developmentally, a bright and active child will compensate for inferiority feelings in ways that are distinct from those of a child less intellectually and physically capable. A child with a chronic medical condition or disfigured appearance has an especially hard row to hoe in overcoming the disability and the inferiority feelings going with it. The second great influence is childhood experience. Adler, the first social psychologist among the personality theorists, saw the family, family interactions, and the child's situation within the family as the psychological source of the ways we deal with inferiority feelings.

It follows from these broad influences on striving to quell inferiority that inferiority feelings may be shown in many different ways. 'Perhaps I can illustrate this', wrote Adler,

> by an anecdote of three children who were taken to the zoo for the first time. As they stood before the lion's cage, one of them shrank behind his mother's skirts and said, 'I want to go home.' The second child stood where he was, very pale and trembling, and said, 'I'm not a bit frightened.' The third glared at the lion fiercely and asked his mother, 'Shall I spit at it?' All three children really felt inferior, but each expressed his feelings in his own way, consonant with his style of life (1931, p. 50).

As each of us distinctively compensates for feelings of inferiority, we will achieve the greatest success if we are co-operative with others and contribute to life, to 'a real improvement of our common situation' (1931, p. 51). Co-operation, courage, and hope are the true antidotes to becoming mired in inferiority and the striving for goals—neurotic ones—that are impossible to attain. Neurotic goals reflect an **inferiority complex**⋆, a term of Adler's we all intuitively understand.

Superiority Striving

Still in his days as a psychoanalytic disciple, Adler gave striving for superiority a primary importance. He thought it was aggressive in nature and far more important than the sexual instinct. An aggressive drive then became a will to power, and during this stage of his thinking, just before the break with Freud, he equated power with masculinity. Thus, anyone in a position of being or feeling powerless was likely to overcompensate by engaging in behaviour expressive of 'masculine protest'. Because of discrimination, women were (and still are, though to a lesser degree) particularly susceptible to these feelings of powerlessness, but as Adler wrote, 'It is not only girls who suffer from a "masculine protest", but all children who overvalue the importance of being masculine, see masculinity as an ideal, and are dubious whether they are strong enough to achieve it' (1931, p. 192). **Masculine protest★** might take a variety of forms—rebellion and defiance, extreme submission, failing to try—depending on circumstances and the person's history. Finally, masculine protest became one instance of compensation for inferiority.

In the evolving individual psychology, striving for superiority was exalted as the dominant goal in life, one that Adler believed is innate. We must be very clear that Adler did not mean striving to be better than others, to hold power, or to achieve distinction. If someone has these as superiority goals, we should have to say that he or she is chasing neurotic pursuits that cannot bring fulfillment. In individual psychology, superiority striving means the constant struggle to meet life's problems and to do one's part in making life better for everyone. As the Adlerian experts Heinz and Rowena Ansbacher observed, Adler wrote 'variously of a striving for perfection, superiority, overcoming, an upward striving, a coercion to carry out a better adaptation, "*innate as something which belongs to life*"' (Adler, 1979, p. 29).

The Style of Life

What we have to work with, in terms of our physical and intellectual makeup, and the kinds of experiences we have as young children direct our striving into a particular and individual form of expression that Adler called the style of life. The style of life is the unique way in which each person pursues the goals important to him or to her, including most importantly the overriding goal of superiority. It develops early in childhood, arising out of the child's physical traits and mental abilities, position in the family, and experience of the parents' childrearing practices, and is largely set by four or five. You may take note of Adler's adoption of Freud's claim about the age when personality is fixed.

One's style of life doesn't immediately impress itself on others, even experienced professionals. Adler wrote:

> The goal of superiority, with each individual, is personal and unique. It depends upon the meaning he gives to life; and this meaning is not a matter of words. It is built up in his style of life and runs through it like a strange melody of his own creation. In his style of life he does not express his goal so that we can formulate it once [and] for all. He expresses it vaguely, so that we must guess at it from the indications he gives. Understanding a style of life is similar to understanding the work of a poet. A poet must use words; but his meaning is more than the mere words he uses. The greatest part of his meaning must be guessed at; we must read between the lines. So, too, with that profoundest and most intricate creation, an individual style of life. The psychologist must learn to read between the lines; he must learn the art of appreciating life-meanings.
>
> It could not be otherwise. The meaning of life is arrived at in those first four or five years of life; and it is not arrived at by a mathematical process, but by dark gropings, by feelings not wholly understood, by catching at hints and fumbling for explanations. The goal of superiority, in a similar way, is fixed by groping and guesswork; it is a life-striving, a dynamic tendency, not a charted and geographically

determined point. Nobody knows his own goal of superiority so that he can describe it in full (1931, pp. 57–8).

Fictional Finalism

All humans have but one cardinal goal, as we have just seen, but there are ideas that dominate us in the process of its pursuit. In 1911, as Adler tossed the psychoanalytic bit, he read a book by noted German philosopher Hans Vaihinger called *The Philosophy of 'As If'* (Vaihinger, 1925). Vaihinger observed that people invent their own realities, creating 'fictions' to explain the world around them. This, a neo-Kantian notion (Vaihinger was an authority on Kant), greatly appealed to Adler, who saw that those fictions could explain much of human behaviour. We are forward-looking creatures, striving for ends that are in the future, looking toward the goals that we've set for ourselves. Those goals revolve around attaining superiority, but we have specific aims. Some of them are realistic and appropriate. We seek to make a living, to achieve comfortable situations for ourselves, to raise happy and healthy children, to have periods of enjoyment, to establish close and intimate relationships. We may also pursue goals that are not realistic, goals that are in fact fictions, and to that sort of goal pursuit Adler gave the name fictional finalism.

Subjective beliefs may exercise a strong influence on our actions, and some of those beliefs are not infrequently unnecessary and unattainable. Adler regarded the dominant male role and pursuit of it as a fictional goal, one that serves no real social purpose. We don't all have to be powerful, aggressive, and unassailable, commanding subordinates, driving great hulking impressive cars, and laying down the law to wives and children. It would be a dreadful world if we were. This is, though, a fiction that, taken as gospel, drives many of us. Women, reacting to lesser status and the masculine ideal, can develop a keen sense of inferiority and damaging feelings of worthlessness or an aggressiveness that destroys relationships—again, not socially useful and certainly unlikely to bring happiness. Fictional goals are not necessarily neurotic and destructive. A person who believes in an afterlife and is guided by religious precepts has a goal that determines his or her choices. It is an 'as if' goal—as if this were an aspect of reality—and in this sense is fictional; it is taken on faith and cannot be proved. The outcome for this person may be a lifetime of co-operation and helpfulness.

Thus, Adler said, 'Individual Psychology insists absolutely on the indispensability of finalism for the understanding of all psychological phenomena. Causes, powers, instincts, impulses and the like cannot serve as explanatory principles. The final goal alone can explain man's behaviour. Experiences, traumata, sexual development mechanisms cannot yield an explanation, but the perspective in which these are regarded, the individual way of seeing them, which subordinates all life to the final goal, can do so' (1930, p. 400).

Social Interest

Adler, the socialist, worked tirelessly for human betterment. His particular path was as a social psychological theorist and practising psychiatrist. He would conclude that 'Social interest is the true and inevitable compensation for all the natural weaknesses of individual human beings' (1929, p. 31). Social interest is an innate characteristic, but it is not shown by everyone in the same way. We can see in human life two broad kinds of compensation. Children fortunate in having parents who show them love and thoughtfulness and teach them co-operation and productive accomplishment are likely to develop 'social feeling' or 'social interest'. In the aftermath of World War I, Adler stressed the importance of social interest as a paramount characteristic of appropriate life goals. On the other hand, a less fortunate child may develop neurotic goals that set him or her apart. Neurotic goals are not social in purpose but have as their aim self-protection, rendering oneself invulnerable to threat, and making it possible for one to escape difficulty and pain. Goals such as these can never be fully satisfying and are likely to make the lives of people around the neurotic person miserable as well. True social interest lies in co-operation with others, and co-operation is learned—or fails to be learned—in the first few years of life. It comes from experiences with parents, siblings, and other children, and once learned becomes part of the style of life. Of course, if co-operation isn't well learned, that similarly becomes an enduring feature of personality, one impossible to erase entirely.

The Creative Self

This concept, which Adler articulated very late in the development of individual psychology, is the part of personality from which the style of compensation for inferiority and striving for superiority stem. In their review of Adlerian theory, Hall, Lindzey, and Campbell (1998) take special note of the creative self, calling it 'Adler's crowning achievement as a personality theorist. When he discovered the creative power of the self, all his other concepts were subordinated to it; here at last was the prime mover, the philosopher's stone, the elixir of life, the first cause of everything human for which Adler had been searching' (p. 135). It is an ego concept, not of an ego incessantly alert to keep wayward instincts under suppression, but of one whose primary task is to find the ways to pursue life's goals. The self creates the style of life, the distinctive features of each personality, out of experience (mostly from early childhood). What we strive for and the means by which we strive are the self's creations. A woman says, 'I wish to be thoughtful and to work for the good of others.' That is an expression of the creative self. A man says, 'I'll be damned if anyone ever gets the better of me. You've got to keep people at arm's length or they'll take advantage of you.' That, also, expresses a goal of the creative self.

Personality Development

The development of personality is shaped by three important variables that Adler saw as the defining characteristics of family life. First, there is the '**family constellation**', by which he meant the roles occupied by various members of the family. He was particularly concerned to see whether parents had a democratic arrangement or, to their detriment and their children's, a one-sided and inequitable one. A father might exercise a dominant, controlling, and distant role within the family or a mother might be chronically sick and helpless, requiring all the other family members to look after her. In stressing the family constellation, Adler really asked us to look at the kinds of models that parents provide for the behaviour and developing attitudes of a young child.

Second, Adler pointed to the critical importance of the relationship between parents and their children, and he particularly noted the damaging consequences of two extremes: on the one hand **pampering** or indulgence—'spoiling', as we used to call it—and on the other hand **rejection**. A pampered child, said Adler, can never be independent and becomes a tyrant, expecting others to look after him and indulge him. This is '. . . *a creation of the child himself*' (1979, p. 89), growing out of parental overindulgence. By contrast, a child who is rejected is in danger of concluding that everyone is hostile and is likely to develop the feeling that he or she must erect barricades against a world peopled by others who are cold, cruel, indifferent, and hurtful.

The third variable Adler emphasized is the psychological effects of ordinal or birth position. He did not mean the child's nominal position in the family (first child, second child, third child) but the situation into which each child is born. The situations of oldest child, middle child, youngest child, and only child are unique and will carry some regular and predictable characteristics, influencing the style of life. The oldest child in a family of two or more children has experiences in growing up that are not shared by the others. For a time, the oldest child is an only child. He or she is the first child of parents who typically will be keen and excited about their new offspring, apprehensive, and not very skilful in their childrearing. Doted on and worried over, the oldest child may develop the idea that it is his or her right to be the absolute centre of attention. The birth of a sibling, however, is a brand new (and often resented) development bringing a rival, and it occurs dramatically. The special problems of the oldest child derive both from having been the little lord or lady and from the child's eventual **dethronement★**, or ouster from an enviable position on the family stage to a new position where he or she must share and co-operate. Oldest children tend to express in their behaviour both a fear of competition from those younger than themselves and a conservatism and subservience to parental authority. If parents handle their tasks with skill and thoughtfulness, the orientation of the oldest child toward parents and parental authority may be turned to useful social advantage. The oldest child may develop a life style of helping and being concerned for others. If handled insensitively, the oldest child may feel perennially threatened and defensive, showing an authoritarianism based upon an unhappy misreading of his parents and their roles.

The middle child in a family of three or more children has the particular problem of competitiveness. It is true that the middle child is also dethroned, but the child in the middle position has already had the experience of co-operating with an older sibling, and thus dethronement is not so acute and painful. For children with older siblings, there is always the struggle to compete with an older and more accomplished brother or sister, and thus the goals of middle children are likely to express competitiveness in one form or another. 'A typical second child is very easy to recognize,' Adler wrote. 'He behaves as if he were in a race, as if some one were a step or two in front and he had to hurry to get ahead of him. . . . The second child is often more talented and successful than the first' (1931, p. 148). A competitive and ambitious style of life can be socially useful, but if accompanied by anticipations of failure and acute inferiority feelings it may lead the middle child to suffer constant pangs of defeat.

The youngest child is uniquely the baby of the family and is in danger of being spoiled. Among the ranks of problem children, said Adler, we will find oldest children leading the list: they're the most likely candidates for neurotic solutions. However, they are closely followed by youngest children. Spoiling, of course, means the child learns to expect to be indulged in every wish, to have special exceptions or provisions made for him or her, laying the groundwork for

"Only child."

expectations that the world outside the family simply will not fulfill. Thus the youngest child who develops unreal goals is doomed to a life of disappointing relationships with others, a life in which his or her demands on others cannot be met. If the help of other members of the family leaves the youngest child room to grow independently, however, an ambitious and cooperative person may emerge.

A Fresh Look: Practice Today

There are dozens of Adlerian institutes all over the world, in places in which you might expect them (Vienna, New York, London, Munich, San Francisco), and places where you wouldn't (Japan, West Texas, South Carolina). There are several across Canada (Vancouver, Saskatoon, Toronto, and Montreal). All of them are imbued with Adler's dream to advance individual psychology and to help individuals and families stricken by neurotic troubles and the effects of poor parenting. In many, the primary mission is to train professionals in the principles and practices of Adlerian psychotherapy. Some specialize in therapy for families and couples. A few offer treatment to distressed individuals and families through affiliated clinics, and a number offer programs to educate parents.

The problem child was of special interest to Adler, and his founding of child guidance clinics to treat problem children and their helpless and distraught parents was the expression of a great aim to better humankind by helping its troubled new members. What does the Adlerian therapist actually *do*? What does he or she have to offer to children whose styles of life reflect a bad beginning and to their clueless parents? The following, in modern form, are guidelines for therapists to diagnose the difficulty—what the child's behaviour means, how parents mistakenly respond, and the reaction they are likely to elicit—and to teach parents a more intelligent and helpful approach. Parents may profit from them as well, but they are likely to need the gentle guidance of a therapist. The guidelines are adapted from course handouts from the Distance Training Program of the Alfred Adler Institute of San Francisco (Stein, 2000).

The Problem Child's Goal	Typical Behaviour	How Parents Feel and Respond	Frequent Child Reaction	How Parents Can Do It Better
Constantly Demanding Attention	Interrupts adults, too cute, showing off, issues challenges, mischievous and naughty.	Annoyance and impatience. May try to meet child's demands but can't keep it up.	May desist temporarily, but attention demands are insatiable.	Don't respond to attention-seeking. Make sure not to reward the problem behaviour. Reward positive acts (e.g., politeness, considerateness).
Demands for Sympathy and Help	A whiny, tearful, fearful child who feels picked on by siblings. Exaggerates sickness.	Parent tries but cannot meet constant demand. Resentment is likely to be shown.	Feels hurt and neglected. Crying and whining may increase.	Sympathetic approach, but focus on what can be done for the child to feel better. Increased emphasis on self-reliance.

You will have anticipated that the problem of the only child is also one of being spoiled, of developing the idea of an absolute right to attention. There is a critical difference between the only child and the youngest child in that the only child is not the baby of the family and isn't spoiled in that particular way. A male child, if pampered by his mother, can develop a strong rivalry with his father. Such a boy 'develops what is

The Problem Child's Goal	Typical Behaviour	How Parents Feel and Respond	Frequent Child Reaction	How Parents Can Do It Better
Power and Rebellion	Refuses to accept parental authority. Insolence, rebellion and outright disobedience. Pouting and temper tantrums.	Anger toward child is understandable but unhelpful. Attempts to assert parental authority without success.	A power struggle. Child fights back.	Don't engage in the battle. Set reasonable limits without anger. Don't surrender responsibility to a wilful child.
Seeking Revenge	This is an angry child who tries to hurt parents and siblings verbally or physically. May take it out on a family pet.	Such behaviour is likely to make parents feel abused and want to retaliate.	Striking back at the child risks escalating the conflict. A vengeful child and vengeful parents means serious family discord.	Parents mustn't let the revenge-seeking child get under their skin. Respond to verbal hostility with reason and calm. Try to show child that home is a safe place. Families with such children will need professional help.
Withdrawal	Isolated child who gives up on almost everything. Wants to be left alone.	Parents will be extremely worried over a child difficult to make emotional contact with whom they are at a loss to help. Sometimes they may give up on a 'stupid' or 'out-of-it' child.	Such a child is unresponsive to parents' concern and efforts to communicate love.	It's important not to fail the child by doing nothing. Small successes by the child are much better than none. If parents see no improvement, therapeutic help will be needed.
Escaping Reality	This is a profoundly unresponsive, depressed child. Escapes by sleeping; behaviour may be gravely inappropriate: irrational fears, self-injury, alcohol or drug abuse in an adolescent.	Parents are truly afraid for a child who is manifestly seriously disturbed, a child who is out of contact with them and with the realities of life.	This child doesn't respond to parents' efforts or is irrational and strange.	Parents must seek professional attention for such a child.

called a "mother complex"; he is tied to his mother's apron strings and wishes to push his father out of the family picture' (1931, p. 152). This is Adler's analysis of the Oedipus complex. It may be sexual because young children are developing sexually, but it is not based on an erotic longing for the mother.

Expressions of Personality

Dreams

The style of life is seen in the goals that we pursue and in the actions in which we engage; it is also behind the fantasies and the dreams we have. Adler absorbed a lot from Freud, but most of it did not turn up in individual psychology in a form recognizable as psychoanalysis. So it was with dreams. Adler agreed with Freud that dreams are significant and express important themes in life. He did not agree that those themes represent sexual wishes, and he did not agree that they are invariably disguised. Rather, said Adler, the dream is an instrument for struggling with the problems that our particular life situations confront us with. We strive in dreams to overcome the difficulties that we see before us, but seldom in a realistic way. We can quail before problems that seem insurmountable. We can make them loom and seem fantastically difficult. We can butt our heads against stone walls. We can sometimes, though rarely, arrive at more realistic and insightful solutions. In dreams we often fool ourselves, so dreams give us an indication of shakiness in the style of life. Adler wrote:

> If, during the day, we are occupied with striving towards the goal of superiority, we must be occupied with the same problem at night. Every one must dream as if he had a task to fulfill in dreaming, as if he had to strive towards superiority also in his dreams. The dream must be a product of the style of life, and it must help to build up and enforce the style of life. . . . We can conclude that we dream only if we are not sure of the solution of our problems, only if reality is pressing in on us even in our sleep and offering us difficulties. This is the task of the dream: to meet the difficulties with which we are confronted and to provide a solution. Now we can begin to see in what way our minds will attack problems in our sleep. Since we are not dealing with the whole situation, the problems will appear easier, and the solution offered will demand as little as possible adaptation from our own side. The purpose of the dream will be to support and back the style of life, to arouse the feelings suited to it. But why does the style of life need support? What can attack it? It can only be attacked by reality and common sense. The purpose of dreams, therefore, is to support the style of life against the demands of common sense. This gives us an interesting insight. If an individual is confronted by a problem which he does not wish to solve along the lines of common sense, he can confirm his attitude by the feelings which are aroused in his dreams (1931, pp. 98–100).

In our dreams we give expression to the childhood experiences that shaped our personalities, our styles of life. The dreams of oldest, middle, youngest, and only children will differ in important ways. The oldest child is likely to be preoccupied by themes that stem from the problem of dethronement and also themes that reflect the struggle and difficulties in keeping up the pace of life. I am an oldest child and I can vividly recall dreaming as a youngster of running through sand on a beach—dry, deep sand that denies the feet their freedom—running and being pursued. I never saw the pursuer in the dream but since I've studied Adler I'm pretty sure I know who he was. The dreams of middle and of youngest children often involve competitiveness. The dreamers battle to catch up and overcome, or else they despair at falling by the wayside. Adler made important use of dreams as an avenue to understanding the style of life, a person's distinctive ways of pursuing goals and avoiding defeat.

Perspective 5.2 Adler on Dreams and the Style of Life

'A girl of twenty-four years old, living alone and doing secretarial work, complains that her boss makes life intolerable for her by his bullying manner. She feels that she is not able to make friends and keep them. Experience would lead us to believe that if an individual cannot keep friends it is because he wishes to dominate others; he is really interested only in himself and his goal is to show his personal superiority. Probably her boss is the same sort of person. They both wish to rule others. When two such people meet, there are bound to be difficulties. The girl is the youngest of seven children, the pet of the family. She was nicknamed "Tom" because she always wanted to be a boy. This increases our suspicion that she has identified her goal of superiority with personal domination; to be masculine, she thinks, is to be the master, to control others and not to be controlled herself. She is pretty, but she thinks that people only like her because of her pleasant face and she is afraid of being disfigured or hurt. Pretty girls find it easier in our time to impress and control others; and this fact she understands quite well. She wants to be a boy, however, and to dominate in a masculine way: in consequence she is not elated by her prettiness.

'Her earliest memory is of being frightened by a man; and she confesses that she is still frightened of being attacked by burglars and maniacs. It might appear odd that a girl who wanted to be masculine should be afraid of burglars and maniacs; but it is not really so strange. It is her feeling of weakness which dictates her goal. She wants to be in circumstances where she can rule and subjugate and she would like to exclude all other situations. Burglars and maniacs cannot be controlled and she would like to extinguish them all. She wishes to be masculine in an easy way and to keep extenuating circumstances for herself if she fails. With this very wide-spread dissatisfaction with the feminine rôle, the "masculine protest", as I have called it, there always go feelings of tension—"I am a man fighting against the disadvantage of being a woman."

'Let us see whether we can trace the same feelings in her dreams. Frequently she dreams of being left alone. She was a spoiled child: her dream means, "I must be watched. It isn't safe to leave me alone. Others could attack and subjugate me." Another dream she frequently experiences is that she has lost her purse. "Take care," she is saying, "you are in danger of losing something." She does not want to lose anything at all; . . . [especially] she does not want to lose power of controlling others; but she chooses one thing in life, the loss of a purse, to stand for the whole. We have another illustration of how dreams reinforce the style of life by creating feelings. She has not lost her purse, but she dreams she has lost it, and the feeling remains behind. A longer dream helps us still more to see her attitude. "I had gone to a swimming pool where there were a lot of people," she says. "Somebody noticed that I was standing on the heads of the people there. I felt that some one screamed to see me and I was in great danger of falling down." If I were a sculptor, I should carve her in just this way, standing on the heads of others, using others as her pedestal. This is her style of life; these are the feelings she likes to arouse. She sees her position, however, as precarious, and she thinks that others should realize her danger too. Others should watch her and be careful, so that she can continue to stand on their heads. Swimming in the water she is not safe. This is the whole story of her life. She has fixed as her goal, "To be a man in spite of being a girl." She is very ambitious, as most youngest children are; but she wants to seem superior, rather than to achieve adequacy to her situation, and she is pursued all the time by the fear of defeat. If we are to help her, we must find the way to reconcile her to her feminine rôle, to take away her fear and over-valuation of the other sex, and to make her feel friendly and equal among her fellow beings.'

From *What Life Should Mean to You* by A. Adler, 1931. Reprinted by permission of Sanford J. Greenburger Associates. Inc.

Earliest Memories

We might expect the very earliest event we can remember to say something about us. Adler did. He believed that earliest memories, by taking us back to the time when personality was being formed, give an especially telling view of the style of life. They also confirm the beliefs that are part of our life styles. Adler would never, he said, interview someone without asking for the very first recollection, and from it he could glean an astonishing amount of detail about a person. Earliest memories are not necessarily true; they serve lifelong strivings and may be fictions, but they are still helpful. Munroe (1955) gives this example:

> The earliest memory of a woman who appears somewhat excessively poised, assured, and rather cold concerns her first day in a new neighborhood at about the age of four. There are two pretty little girls with a big dog. One of them says 'You don't have to be afraid of Shep. He won't hurt you.' The woman remembers being surprised at this remark because she had not thought of being afraid of the *dog*. She had wanted to be friends with the children, had not known how to go about it, and had felt shy because she thought they might not want to be friends. The Adlerian is not surprised to discover in further conversation that this woman's poise is a cover for shyness; that social relations are very important to her and that she typically anticipates rejection. The dog is important too. At forty, as at four, she is courageous in situations which do not involve people (p. 429).

The Meaning of Symptoms

Neurotic symptoms reflect a mistaken style of life. We can see them as purposive attempts at self-protection, attempts to achieve invulnerability; they are poor compensations for inferiority feelings and, despite the neurotic person's wish to conceal his or her inferiorities behind a barrier, they betray the style of life just like dreams and earliest memories. Symptoms, said Adler, 'are a big heap of rubbish on which the patient builds in order to hide himself' (1979, p. 198). The edifice, though, is not at all as successful as the patient thinks it is; careful study and some informed guesses will reveal the purposes behind it.

Research

Adler's research method was clinical. He focused on studying neurotic adults but also pioneered the investigation of the young and how they become problem children. He was, arguably, Freud's equal as a clinician, able to arrive at complex interpretations of behaviour from the incomplete and confusing data provided by patients, especially children. Here is where the understanding of family dynamics came from—parental interaction and childrearing practices, the child's situation in the family—and these data showed him how psychological damage comes about. But his discoveries, like Freud's, arose from the clinical method with its significant vulnerabilities.

Psychologists were attracted by Adler's emphasis on family interaction, one congenial to the behaviourist movement that began to arise in the United States in the first quarter of the twentieth century, and they recognized the possibility of testing certain propositions of individual psychology in a controlled way. The most readily accessible of these was the situational hypothesis on the effects of birth order. The 1920s and early 1930s saw a spate of birth order studies that were reviewed in a chapter by Jones in *The Handbook of Child Psychology* (1933). There were studies comparing the intelligence of children in the various birth positions, their language development, school achievement, personality characteristics, and delinquency. These were not, by and large, well designed and controlled investigations, and the personality measures used (teachers' ratings, for example) were crude and surely questionable in their reliability and validity. They turned up little, if anything.

Affiliation When Afraid

Here matters stood for a quarter of a century. Then, in the late 1950s, a social psychologist at the University of Minnesota published in a small book a series of experiments on a powerful motive for affiliation with others (Schachter, 1959). He had begun with experiments to see if anxiety made people wish to be with each other. When introductory psychology students showed up individually for an experimental appointment, they were met by an imperious and formal experimenter, more than a little menacing, in a white doctor's coat, stethoscope hanging out of a pocket. He introduced himself as a medical investigator studying the effects of electric shock on bodily processes. There were two conditions in the experiment, high and low anxiety. In the high anxiety condition, the shocks would be intense and painful, quite necessary, the experimenter said, to be able to draw conclusions about electroshock therapy and other electrical insults to the body. In the low anxiety condition, the shocks would be mild, more like a tickle. There would be a brief interval, he said, to set up the equipment, during which the participant could wait alone in a small, comfortable room or with others also waiting for the experiment to start. High anxiety made many participants want the company of others.

But what was it about waiting in a group that made affiliation appealing? Schachter's experiments established that the presence of others reduced anxiety by offering experimental participants the opportunity (even when talking was not permitted) to see how others were coping, to look to them for a reassuring evaluation of a frightening situation. Now, Schachter made a big jump. He was quite unaware of Adler, and formulated a birth-order hypothesis on his own (Crowne, 1962). It was, in fact, as Adlerian as can be in proposing that first-born children and only children are more likely to be comforted by the presence of others when frightened than later-borns. The reason? First-time parents, nervous and less adept in child care, will be more worried about their children and more attentive to hurts and fears. The later-born child won't get such nurturance from a now experienced and probably overworked parent (likely the mother). Accordingly, the early-born learn from parental solicitude to be dependent and to generalize it.

This is exactly how Schachter's studies turned out. To a striking degree, participants in the high-anxiety condition who were first-born and only children more often chose to wait with others than the later-born. Schachter's book also presented a number of related findings. In a sample of patients applying for treatment at a mental health centre, those who were first-born and only children more frequently accepted the offer of psychotherapy and remained in treatment longer. Among a group of Korean War fighter pilots, a significantly higher proportion of aces were later-born, presumably because they were less fearful and hence less cautious.

There are many other studies of personality and birth order, but it is fair to say that most of them are accompanied by one or more failures to replicate. An example is an exceptional historical study by Sulloway (1996), who examined the acceptance of new scientific, religious, and social ideas by contemporaries who were first-born or later-born. As he reported, 'For the 28 [scientific] innovations included in my survey, the odds are 2.0 to 1 in favor of laterborn adoption. The likelihood of this difference arising by chance is substantially less than one in a billion' (p. 42). His conclusion: 'For the past five centuries, the most consistent predictor of revolutionary allegiances turns out to be *birth order*. Compared with firstborns, laterborns are more likely to identify with the underdog and to challenge the established order. Because they identify with parents and authority, firstborns are more likely to defend the status quo. The effects of birth order transcend gender, social class, nationality, and—for the last five centuries—time' (p. 356). Clearly physicists who claimed at the end of the nineteenth century that there were no new discoveries to be made in physics must have been first-born children! In a large survey of adults, Freese, Powell, and Steelman (1999) could not confirm Sulloway on the conservatism of first-born children and greater independence of later-borns. 'We find no support for these claims,' they wrote (p. 207).

Why should these findings on birth order and personality relations be so fleeting and difficult to substantiate? Better dependent measures closer to the ideal set by Schachter would certainly help establish the personality effects of birth order. More radically, though, Harris (1998), whom we shall encounter again in Chapter 16, contends that birth-order effects on personality may well appear *within* the family and may well exist in the perceptions of family members of each other. But outside the family, in school or playing with their own friends, children don't carry their first- or later-born family attributes with them like the contents of their schoolbags. They develop whole new personality repertoires based on their out-of-home interactions, and these continue into adulthood. This, she says, is the result of *context-specific learning*, adapting behaviour to new situations and only generalizing from one context (family) to another (schoolyard) when the transfer of experience is discovered to be appropriate (Harris, 1995).

Intelligence

Adler did not advance a specific claim that intelligence would be affected by a child's position in the order of birth. We could contrive an approximate Adlerian interpretation based on differences in intellectual stimulation. The oldest child gets more parental time, is talked to and read to and generally given an intellectual head start. Later-borns have to compete for attention from a tired mother and get less of it; their vocabularies and intellectual striving suffer. Or, perhaps, the later-born child receives not only intellectual stimulation from parents but from his or her older sibling and is thus advantaged. These are not uniquely Adlerian, but you can see how we might adapt the situational concept of birth order to the task.

Generations of psychologists have supposed that birth order *might* affect intelligence, and they have produced a huge number of studies to see if this is so. Each new cohort proceeds apparently undaunted by the failures of the preceding ones to find durable effects. The most promising studies have been conducted in recent years by Zajonc, summarized in a 2001 article. Zajonc is well aware that for any study showing that firstborns have an IQ advantage, we can find one with the opposite result; he proposes a model to show why and provides supporting data. He calls it the ' "*confluence model*" (Zajonc, 1976), so named because the mental maturities of children growing up in the same families flow together over time in their influence on each other, changing constantly over time and changing most profoundly when new offspring join the sibship or some family members leave' (2001, p. 491). It focuses on two influences affecting intellectual development: the intellectual environment of the family and the tutoring that older children provide to their younger siblings. In the early years, younger children benefit from exposure not only to the words and ideas of the parents but to the speech, however immature, of an older child. 'This differential exposure', says Zajonc, 'may well manifest itself later in younger children's performance on tests of verbal fluency, vocabulary, and comprehension' (p. 491). At a later point, the older child's contribution is greater, answering the endless questions of the younger and giving direction and advice. There is real benefit to the firstborn in doing so: he or she learns by teaching. Now the intellectual advantage shifts to the first-born child, and, mathematically, the model predicts that the crossover from later-born IQ superiority to first-born will occur at the approximate age of eleven. Reanalyzing the data of fifty studies from the 1920s into the 1980s, Zajonc showed exactly this pattern. In research samples younger than eleven, later-borns had an IQ advantage; in samples of children tested after eleven, the first-borns performed better.

The confluence model has had its critics, notably Rodgers (2001), who sees it as an artifact. His argument is that sampling first-born and later-born children from different families opens up the possibility that other happenstance variables (social class, for instance) could account for the results; he would prefer to see within-family samples instead. Zajonc rightly points out that comparing children of different birth order in the same family confounds birth order and age. I am persuaded that the confluence model has made a useful contribution to our understanding of environmental influences on intelligence and is not bad as Adlerian research. It is important, however, to recognize that what the order of birth contributes is not large.

To summarize the most active area of research on Adlerian concepts, we shouldn't be surprised when a more complete story is written to discover that the effects of birth order on personality are smaller and more limited than Adler's clinical observations led him to claim. Dunn and Plomin (1990) conclude that the order of birth 'plays only a bit-part in the drama of sibling differences' (p. 85).

Adler in Perspective

Let's review Adler's emphases, and then we shall conclude by contrasting individual psychology with psychoanalysis. Looking back with our twenty-first century insight, it seems clear that Adler's outstanding contribution was to cast the role of the family and of childhood experience as critical factors in personality development. He drew a strikingly insightful picture of the social psychology of the family. While that picture emphasized the errors that parents could make and the difficulties that could block the progress of children toward successful lives—understandable in a clinical theory— individual psychology was ahead of its time in singling out specific psychological events in the family and their specific effects on children. Adler himself surely would have thought that our all-too-human inferiority feelings, striving for superiority, social interest, and the creative self were incomparably greater than individual psychology's empirical emphasis, but times and psychology have changed.

Adler laid little store by the unconscious. Yes, he did think there were things of which we are unaware, but he largely stressed that we are conscious beings. We may take wrongheaded perspectives on our own behaviour and on the actions and motives of others, but that's not an affirmation of unconsciousness. It simply means that we fail to see, fail to grasp correctly, the significance of our own feelings or of the situations in which we act. His view on consciousness, of course, stemmed from the importance he gave to ego functions. He was hardly concerned at all with instinctual life and did not hold with Freud's conception of socially destructive motives underlying human behaviour that must be disciplined and regulated to achieve a precarious kind of socialization.

There is a dramatic emphasis in individual psychology on the goal-directedness or purposiveness of behaviour. On this matter Adler was in agreement with Jung, who likewise rejected Freud's deterministic views and saw personality as directed toward the future. Humans are not just creatures of hedonism, seeking to find those objects to quell—or at least to appease, temporarily—the needs of an imperative id. Rather, human behaviour looks to the future, to great life goals. I have noted Adler's insistence that causes in the past do not determine behaviour; it is what we make of them in our striving that shapes action, thought, and feeling.

Table 5.1   Freud and Adler Contrasted

Freud	Adler
Philosophical pessimism	Philosophical optimism
Cause orientation	Teleological orientation
Importance of libido	Sexuality, love and marriage involve social interest and require the preparation of two equals
Family sexuality: the Oedipus Complex and its feminine counterpart	The family situation and the child's situation in the family, parent-child and sibling relationships
'Penis envy' in women	Feeling of inferiority and the 'masculine protest'
Neurosis inherent in civilized human condition	Neurosis a 'trick' of the individual to escape duty
Post WWI: the death instinct	Post-WWI: social interest
Psychoanalytic patient lies on couch	Patient faces therapist

Adler and Freud stand in stark contrast. Freud's essential philosophical position was darkly pessimistic. Adler's was profoundly optimistic. Following from his social and familial orientation, Adler, like Jung, saw hope for mankind. For Freud, every person is constantly engaged in internal struggle, a war among the powers of personality. Adler saw the essential indivisibility of human personality, expressed in a coherent style of life that cannot be carved into contesting factions.

Neurosis occurs, said Freud, because the ego is tyrannized by the superego. Indeed, civilization and its demands for the renunciation of instincts pose a threat to individual personality. For Adler, the neurotic person sets himself or herself against others and acts aggressively toward them in pursuit of a false goal of superiority. Neurosis, said Freud, is an inescapable burden imposed on unfortunate victims by civilization, part of the human condition. The more civilized the society, the greater its prevalence. For Adler, neurosis is a trick to escape fulfilling duties a person doesn't want to be confronted by or feels he or she can't master. It's a way of ducking one's contribution to the community.

Within the family, Freud emphasized the male child's relationship to his father, the development of the Oedipus complex, and the incorporation of the attributes of the same-sexed parent in the completion of personality development. Adler looked at the roles played by parents, the child's situation in the family, and the child's relationships to parents and siblings. We might call his a social psychology of expectation, in which the child has to learn what others may give and how he or she can co-operate in return. As we examine other theorists in the neo-Freudian group, you will see an essential core of ideas introduced by Adler that appear in each of their theories.

SUMMARY

1. Early in the development of psychoanalysis, dissident psychoanalysts and critics outside the psychoanalytic group entered three significant objections to issues that were central to the theory. First was Freud's insistence on the dominance of the sexual motive in personality and his strongly held belief that instinctual forces are behind behaviour, thought, and feeling. Freud, they said, badly neglected the importance of the family, society, and culture in personality development and in the expression of personality. Second, the psychoanalytic critics rejected the subordinate role of the ego, required to do the id's bidding and with no energy source of its own. They argued that the ego is at least partly autonomous and has the energy to fuel its own activities (including environmental adaptation, mastery, confidence, and curiosity). A consequence of this view is an emphasis on a conscious ego, not a largely unconscious one. The third objection took on the dark and pessimistic world view of psychoanalysis, opposing it with an optimistic outlook on the possibilities for human growth, healthy ego development, and the prospect of peaceful societies devoted to human welfare. Adler was at the forefront of these critics.

2. Alfred Adler was born in 1870, the second of six children. He started life with a lot to conquer. He was a sickly child—he nearly died from pneumonia at the age of five, and developed rickets, a disease caused by a vitamin D deficiency that makes bones soft. His activity was severely curtailed until the family moved into the country. He was a poor student, especially in math, but mastered his difficulty and gained admission to the University of Vienna and to medical school. Graduating in 1895, he took up the practice of ophthalmology, switched to general medicine, then entered psychiatry. He married a dedicated socialist who strongly influenced his social leanings. Devoting himself to his psychiatric practice, he soon came to Freud's attention and was invited to join his fledgling group of psychoanalysts. A valued member,

he was elected to the presidency of the Vienna Psychoanalytic Society but began to diverge, rejecting fundamentals of the theory (among them the importance of the sexual instinct, the Oedipus complex) and offering his own independent views. After resigning he formed his own society and began to develop the theory that became individual psychology. He engaged in clinical practice, founded child guidance clinics, lectured widely, and wrote a number of influential books (the most important being *Understanding Human Nature*). In 1934 he immigrated to the United States, where he taught, lectured, and further developed individual psychology. He died in 1937 of a heart attack, leaving a thriving movement that is active and influential to this day.

3. Individual psychology is a practical theory aimed at understanding the human situation and the problems that we all have to face. In treating people in psychological difficulty, Adler emphasized the importance of common sense and courage, and sought to convey hope and optimism in his patients. To some critics, individual psychology was too down-to-earth, too practical to be a serious psychological theory, but they were wrong to dismiss it. Adler was a pioneer in the psychology of family and social relationships, and many of his concepts (inferiority complex, the style of life) influenced other personality theorists and found their way into popular culture. It could fairly be said that he is the intellectual father of the neo-Freudian movement.

4. Individual psychology got its start with the concepts of organ inferiority and compensation. Adler noted that a defective organ system resulting in frequent illnesses or a chronic condition could be seen to lead to compensatory bodily processes. He gave this a psychological turn by proposing that weakness in an organ system could produce persistent overstimulation. He especially called attention to erogenous zones, where bodily problems might cause preoccupation and eventual neurosis. This was his early answer to the sexual in neurosis. Organ inferiority and compensation became the psychological principle of **inferiority feelings**, universal in humans, and compensation for them. The helplessness and dependence of the infant became the model for human inferiority, and the striving to overcome it a major determinant of personality. Co-operation and

helpfulness are the best compensations; neurotic compensation reflects an *inferiority complex*.

5. Individual psychology is a theory of a *conscious ego*. Adler rejected the largely unconscious psychoanalytic ego in favour of conscious ego, one accessible to thought. He recognized that at times we may not understand why we do things and may deceive ourselves. The problem, though, is not in the unconscious but in a lack of courage to face what we don't wish to acknowledge.

6. The relation of the individual to society is central in individual psychology. Human beings are innately social creatures, and they are motivated by an inborn social interest. Individual humans are dependent and weak; they start life that way and remain dependent on their societies for social relationships and for co-operation in solving the common problems of all. Individual helplessness and dependence create inferiority feelings, experienced by everyone, that impel compensation to overcome them and to achieve a true superiority in coping with life problems. The only satisfactory path to compensation for inferiority is a social one.

7. Adler strongly held to a view of individual uniqueness. Although there are fundamental motives in personality (inferiority feelings, striving for superiority) common to everyone, each person fashions his or her own way of expressing them in a **style of life**.

8. How personality develops from early childhood to adulthood is the result of both causative events in each person's history and the future goals that he or she pursues. Thus, to think of behaviour as caused just by prior determining events is to see only a small part of the story. The goals that people pursue, fashioned out of early experience, are far more significant determinants. Adler referred to this future orientation as **fictional finalism** to emphasize that our aims are not always realistic or attainable. They may sometimes be neurotic fictions and unrealizable.

9. Experience in the family is the principal shaper of personality. Adler stressed family relationships, the childrearing practices of the parents, and the special situations of children in each birth position. He pointed to particularly harmful parental behaviour that leads to the development of faulty styles of life in children. Individual psychology is a model for the social psychology of the family.

10. Like Freud, Adler saw that personality is expressed both directly and indirectly. Personality is revealed in the ways each person compensates for inferiority and strives to achieve superiority, but more subtle evidence is also seen in dreams, earliest memories, and the specific features of neurotic symptoms.

11. All humans aim toward achieving superiority—that is, as Adler put it, 'an impetus from minus to plus'. Striving for superiority means an innate striving for completion, a better adaptation to life, improvement of the human condition, perfection. These goals are never attained, but in everyone there is a drive toward superiority. The neurotic person may strive to be superior over others, but this is mistaken and doomed to failure. Inferiority and superiority striving are two faces of the motivational principle in individual psychology.

12. The style of life is each person's unique way of compensating for inferiority and striving for superiority and of pursuing individual goals. It develops in early childhood from the child's physical traits and experience in the family and is largely fixed by the age of four or five. The style of life is subtle, not fully understood by anyone (although it is not unconscious in the Freudian sense). This is not surprising since it represents the meaning of life to each individual, expressed in behaviour, thought, feeling, and goal striving.

13. Finalism is the pursuit of ultimate goals. Adler observed that while many of the goals people strive for are realistic (making a living, for example, or marrying and raising a family), others are fictional—unrealistic and unattainable. Adler saw the goal of male dominance as a fictional goal, serving no social purpose; he also viewed attempts to struggle against it—which he termed **masculine protest**—as a similarly fictional goal. Feelings of inferiority and worthlessness because one isn't a dominant male, feelings of rebelliousness and aggression are unlikely to bring satisfaction. Fictional goals are not inevitably neurotic. A person who is religious pursues an 'as if' goal, taken on faith, that may be part of an exemplary style of life.

14. Another innate characteristic is **social interest**, 'the true and inevitable compensation for all the natural weaknesses of human beings,' as Adler wrote. He pointed to two broad kinds of compensation for inferiority. Co-operation with others and helpfulness in working for the betterment of others is one of them.

This represents social interest. The other is the useless side of life, as Adler called it—the selfish pursuit of neurotic goals such as self-protection, trying to make oneself invulnerable, or seeking to be superior to one's fellows.

15. The ego concept of the **creative self** was a late addition to individual psychology. It is responsible for the style of life, and it is created out of early experience and one's physical endowment. All striving—to overcome inferiority, to achieve superiority—is an expression of the creative self. So, what humans strive for and the means by which they strive are its creations.

16. Personality development is shaped by three significant variables in family life. First is the family constellation, which refers to the roles of family members—both parents and children. The roles taken on by parents set models for their children, as do those of older siblings for younger ones. Second is the way parents rear their children, which, Adler stressed, could have damaging consequences if it involved pampering or rejecting children. An indulged or pampered child learns to expect others to meet his or her every wish; unhappy social relationships with a person who is really a kind of tyrant result. The lesson learned by the child who is rejected is likely to be that the world is hostile, cold, and cruel. This is acquired through the indifference and anger of the parents. The third variable is the psychological effects of ordinal or birth position, which Adler viewed as having a major influence on the developing personalities of children. Oldest children have a favoured period in which they are the centre of attention before being dethroned by a new sibling. If this situation is badly handled by parents, oldest children may become both authoritarian and fearful of competition. Middle children have the special problem of competitiveness, struggling to keep up with someone who is older, quicker, and more accomplished. Youngest children risk being the babies of their families and are in danger of being spoiled by the indulgence of others. The problem of only children is also one of indulgence, of expecting as a right to have anything and everything done for them. Knowledgeably and sensitively handled by parents, these birth order situations can produce favourable attributes in their children leading to useful styles of life. The ambition and competitiveness of a middle

child, for example, can be an advantage in an adult life devoted to leading others.

17. The style of life is vividly expressed in the goals that people pursue, but it also appears less distinctly in dreams and in earliest memories. Dreams represent our struggles with problems and are usually oversimplified versions of them. Some dreams are about failed striving, problems looming impossibly large; others present solutions that are too easy, confirming what we wish to be true, not what common sense would tell us must be the case. Sometimes, but not often, a dream will give us a realistic answer to a life problem. Earliest memories also give away something about our styles of life, since they come from a time when personality was being formed. They are not necessarily true; they may reflect beliefs about childhood experiences that dominate the style of life. The particular form that neurotic symptoms take will also be informative about the style of life, since they are compensations—inadequate and defensive ones—for inferiority.

18. Adler's research method was clinical. The principles of individual psychology were formed through the study and treatment of neurotic adults and problem children. We have to note again the scientific vulnerabilities of the clinical method. Many psychologists were attracted by Adler's ideas, particularly those on family interaction and the influence of birth order. A large number of studies on the psychological effects of birth order yielded inconsistent and inconclusive findings, due in part to personality measures with weak reliability and validity. Then in the late 1950s, social psychologist Stanley Schachter published a series of studies in a small book, *The Psychology of Affiliation*, showing that when made anxious, subjects who were first-born and only children preferred to be with others; later-born subjects did not care. These careful experiments clearly established a link between anxiety arousal and the reassuring presence of others in the same boat among the first-born. There were other findings confirming the relationship between anxiety and birth order. Among recent birth order research is a historical study showing that over a period of five centuries acceptance of new scientific, religious, and social ideas was preponderantly by later-born contemporaries. This finding has not been replicated, however. Although Adler did not specifically propose that intelligence might be affected by birth order, it is possible to contrive a hypothesis consistent with the theory. Zajonc has developed a hypothesis on birth order effects, the *confluence model*, which predicts that before the age of eleven later-born children will show an IQ advantage from teaching by parents and older siblings; after the age of eleven, the advantage shifts to the first-born because they learn from their informal tutoring of their younger siblings. Reanalyzing the data of fifty IQ–birth order studies, Zajonc found confirmation of the model. Critics of birth order influences argue that despite findings such as these the effects of order of birth on personality are small. It does seem clear from well-done research, however, that Adler's hypothesis about this family variable is in important respects correct.

19. Individual psychology has had a considerable influence on other personality theories, especially those we call neo-Freudian, and on popular culture. Adler's emphases on family life, childrearing, and the situations of children in the family focused attention on the social psychology of the family and away from unconscious instinctual forces. Other significant Adlerian emphases with major influence on other theories include the goal-directedness of behaviour and a largely conscious ego. This practical and down-to-earth theory has left a large imprint on the psychology of personality.

TO TEST YOUR UNDERSTANDING

1. Trace the development of Adler's thinking from organ inferiority to inferiority feelings and superiority striving. How do feelings of inferiority and striving for superiority get derailed and become serious problems for a person? How does he or she get back on track?

2. Give an Adlerian interpretation of the cartoon on page 127. Try to provide as much detail as you can.

3. Judith Rich Harris thinks that the effects of birth order reflect learning that takes place and is expressed within the family and not outside it. This would explain the often weak and inconsistent birth order results of research in which birth order is the independent variable. There are, however, some powerful and replicable findings, notable among them Schachter's on affiliation when afraid. Can these be accounted for by Harris's hypothesis? What is your view of birth order as a personality variable?

4. Look at Table 5.1. Where would Jung fit into this comparison. Try placing him in relation to Alder and Freud on each point.

5. Is Adler's theory of personality, neurosis, and psychological treatment just watered-down Freud, stripped of the explanatory power of psychoanalysis? Or, does it represent a genuine advance over psychoanalytic theory and a model for other personality theories? If so, in what ways?

CHAPTER SIX

The Neo-Freudians: Harry Stack Sullivan and Karen Horney

Introduction

The neo-Freudians began with Freudian psychology, adopted its fundamental stance on dynamic processes within the individual, accepted the basic idea that personality is shaped in early childhood, and had no quarrel with the remarkable picture Freud drew of motivated distortions in thinking and remembering, the defence mechanisms. They appreciated that people may not understand the internal forces that drive their behaviour and, except for Adler, recognized the importance of the unconscious.

But they rebelled over Freud's all-determining view of infantile sexuality and the primacy of the sexual motive. It is not, they insisted, the 'vicissitudes of instincts', as Freud said, that determine personality and can by an unfortunate turn make one sick with neurosis, but happenings in the family, in social relationships, and in culture. Out of social interactions, intimate or broadly drawn, does personality develop, and out of them neurotically false solutions emerge. Adler, as we have seen, was the pioneering rebel, the others coming later. In a sense, though, all four of our neo-Freudians were pioneers in a social psychological view of personality and personality development, each one with an individual stamp.

Harry Stack Sullivan: Introduction

The theorist we take up first in this chapter, Harry Stack Sullivan, stands in sharp contrast to Freud, Adler, and the subject of our next chapter, Erich Fromm, all of whom were European, raised in a persecuted minority group, and exposed in their training to some of the best minds in medicine. Even the Swiss-born Gentile Jung shares much in common with these three. Sullivan, was dramatically different—an American who grew up poor on a remote farm in rural New York, was isolated and looked down on for his Irish Catholicism, and received an adequate but undistinguished medical education. Sullivan's biographer, Helen Swick Perry, compared his upbringing and the influences on him to Freud's experience:

> Freud came from a middle-class, Viennese, Jewish background; Sullivan came from a Catholic, Irish-American family. Freud had the orientation of the typical middle-class neurotic of his day and time. Sullivan had first-hand information on the pecu-

liarly isolating experience of a young Irish Catholic boy . . . growing up in a farming area where all the other families were Protestant and mostly old Yankee. Freud's thinking reflects a Talmudic background, scholarly, thoughtful, and deep; Sullivan's thinking is almost Joycean in its intricate processes, rich and varied, occasionally almost poetic, but difficult and complex (Perry, 1962, pp. xi–xii).

They could hardly have been more different, yet Sullivan was to join the ranks of the neo-Freudian movement and become its outstanding American exponent. The path is not an obvious one.

Harry Stack Sullivan: Personal History

Harry Stack Sullivan was born in the winter of 1892 to an unskilled workman, Timothy Sullivan, thirty-four, and his wife Ella, thirty-nine, in the small upstate New York town of Norwich. He was the third and only surviving child, his siblings dying in infancy. When Harry was three, his father took over his grandmother Stack's farm, on a dirt road outside the village of Smyrna twelve miles distant. Even many years later, when rural electrification was well advanced, the house had no electricity. The circumstances of his childhood are well described by the phrase 'dirt poor'.

Sullivan's father was a withdrawn, taciturn, inarticulate man with whom Harry's relationship was, he wrote in adulthood, 'morbidly distant'. His mother seems to have had a depressive episode before Harry was three, and he was entrusted to the repressive care of his grandmother. Later, his mother protected and watched closely over her son, whose ear she bent with her unhappiness over her lot—impoverished and married to a man she regarded as her social inferior. He would say to his analyst and devoted friend Clara Thompson that his mother was a 'complaining semi-invalid with chronic resentment at the humble family' (Perry, 1982, p. 107). Young Harry was set apart by the remoteness of

his family's farm, by the majority Protestant rejection of Catholics, and by his own awkwardness. With the single exception of a boy five years older who became a preadolescent chum (Sullivan's choice of word), he was the loneliest of children. Clara Thompson wrote, 'The close friends of his childhood were the livestock on the farm. With them he felt comfortable and less lonely' (Thompson, 1962, p. xxxii).

Sullivan was a loner in school, painfully eager for recognition from his teachers, and bright. He won a New York State scholarship to Cornell University but was suspended at end of his second semester with failing grades when, having been set up by his co-conspirators, he was charged with attempting to obtain 'chemicals' illegally from the town drugstore through the mail. It was a minor prank and the suspension was only for a term, but he was humiliated and never returned to Cornell. He dropped out of sight for the next two years and seems to have had a schizophrenic episode for which he may have been hospitalized briefly in New York City's Bellevue Hospital and treated by the noted psychoanalyst A.A. Brill.

At nineteen and with a goal, he set off for the Midwest and the Chicago College of Medicine and Surgery, medical school of

Harry Stack Sullivan (© Bettmann/CORBIS)

Valparaiso University in Indiana, at best average in quality for the time. Far better—and absolutely critical for Sullivan—it was both forgiving of students' deficiencies and affordable. He had to work to support himself, compromising his studies, and earned very indifferent grades. In 1917, at the age of twenty-five, he was awarded the MD.

He would later say of the next period, before he landed the job that started him in his professional career, that he had had seventy-five hours of psychoanalysis, but beyond the likely short treatment by Brill, there is no record of it. He practised general medicine in Chicago and applied to the Army Medical Reserve Corps, serving as a lieutenant for seven months. His history during this period is replete with fabrications—or, more charitably, inventions—of his qualifications. They were Irish inventions all, not credible achievements but poetic fantasies.

Three years later, Sullivan, not yet a psychiatrist, arrived in Washington, DC, to take up duties as liaison officer for the Veterans Bureau at the renowned St Elizabeth's Hospital. The atmosphere was stimulating, and he was befriended by St Elizabeth's superintendent, the dean of American psychiatry, William Alanson White. White introduced him to a number of distinguished social scientists, the most important among them to Sullivan being the Chicago (and later Yale) cultural anthropologist Edward Sapir. Sullivan learned rapidly, but White had private doubts and felt there was no place for him as a psychiatrist in the hospital.

After remaining at St Elizabeth's for just more than a year, Sullivan found a place as an assistant psychiatrist at Sheppard and Enoch Pratt Hospital in Towson, Maryland. Here, over a period of eight years, came an astonishing transformation for Sullivan: he was hardly to be called a psychiatrist at the beginning, but when he left he was 'a legend in both the clinical world and the world of the social sciences' (Perry, 1982, p. 190). Almost wholly self-taught out of his own experience, observation, and voracious reading, he established an experimental ward for young male schizophrenic patients and introduced a radical therapeutic regimen. Violating established precept and practice, he accepted the schizophrenic as a respected person, rejecting the common view of an 'insane' patient incapable of responding to psychoanalysis. On his ward, he attempted to create the preadolescent reciprocal trust he believed his schizophrenic charges had never had, and he developed psychotherapeutic procedures in which the therapist became a 'participant observer', an expert but warm and tender and far from authoritarian.

He soon began to write a series of papers that had increasing impact. He met Clara Thompson and their relationship blossomed, first as analysand and analyst, then as close friends, and finally as teacher (Sullivan) and disciple. In 1927 he took in a fifteen-year-old boy, James Inscoe, who may have been a patient; 'Jimmie' lived with him for Sullivan's remaining twenty-two years as secretary, cook, keeper of the house and office, and devoted companion.

By the end of the Sheppard period, Sullivan's ideas were taking shape, ideas that would form the Interpersonal Theory of Psychiatry, first presented in 1932 in a privately circulated book, *Personal Psychopathology*, published posthumously (Sullivan, 1972). The subsequent publication of a series of five lectures given in 1939 became an updated statement of the theory in 1947 (Sullivan, 1953a).

Leaving the Sheppard Hospital in 1930, Sullivan opened a Park Avenue practice in New York City, having 'decided that I could not find the dividing line between obsessional neurosis and schizophrenia, and that obviously they were so closely related that I would have to overcome my hesitancy about obsessionals and do my bit with them, which I did, by God, for six years. . . .' (Perry 1982, p. 350). Now famous, he soon became president of the William Alanson White Foundation. By the middle of the 1930s, he was a co-founder and later director of the Washington School of Psychiatry and not long after a supervising analyst and regular lecturer at Chestnut Lodge, the school's psychiatric hospital. In 1938 he was the founding inspiration for the interdisciplinary journal *Psychiatry*, which stood for psychiatry as a social science, an idea dear to Sullivan's heart.

Sullivan returned to Maryland in 1939 and remained there until his death, writing, teaching, consulting, supervising, and lecturing. Among later achievements, he participated in a study of race relations in the South (see Johnson, 1941) and was a consultant to the White House during World War II, a participant in the 1948 UNESCO [War] Tensions Project, and one of the founding lights of the World Foundation for Mental Health.

About to return home from a meeting of the World Foundation in January 1949, Sullivan died in a Paris hotel room of a brain hemorrhage. He was fifty-seven. In the months after he died, the emotional level at Chestnut Lodge, always bordering on high in those days before antischizophrenic drugs eased the turmoil of patients, became palpably higher. The psychiatrists at the Lodge were stricken at the loss of a colleague, a friend, and a brilliant teacher and theorist, and they showed their hurt. Otto Will, a cadaverous giant of a man, looked even more sad than he usually did, which was pretty sad. Herbert Staveren threw his dinner across the doctors' dining room in a hardly characteristic outburst of uncontrolled feeling. Staff, too, loyal and devoted to a man, showed their suffering. I know about that, about Will and Staveren, because I was there, a young Antioch College student on a co-operative job placement.

Sullivan was not an easy person to know. Throughout his life, he was an anxious, lonely, eccentric, financially improvident, and very complicated man, at once witty and warm, aloof, and capable of biting criticism. He was fascinating and appealing in his complexity. He would inexplicably put on an Irish brogue, although he had grown out of that grandmotherly influence in adolescence. Clara Thompson wrote of him in a memorial address, 'He had a characteristic phrase when parting from a friend—'Gods keep you'. This phrase always seemed to me to roll back a curtain and one got a glimpse of the Irish lad with the tradition of pagan gods. One could have no doubt that he meant, May good forces in your world protect you' (in Sullivan, 1962, p. xxxiv).

Emphases

Sullivan, like Freud and Adler, was a clinician. His observations, which influenced the development of the Interpersonal Theory of Psychiatry, were made on patients in treatment. He was also a psychoanalyst, and early in his career he gave recognition and even paid homage to Freud. Here, however, some differences become as important as the similarities.

American Psychiatry and Sociology

Sullivan was strongly influenced by Adolph Meyer, whose psychobiology was an independent and pragmatic American parallel in psychiatry to Freud's psychoanalysis, and he owed a significant intellectual debt to William Alanson White, whose interest in the social sciences Sullivan emulated. In the development of his theory, we see Sullivan's attraction to the ideas of the Chicago school of sociology, particularly those of the sociologists George Herbert Mead, W.I. Thomas, and Charles H. Cooley (University of Michigan) and of the anthropologist Edward Sapir, close friend and collaborator. Mead's influence appears distinctly in Sullivan's concept of the self-dynamism, which adopts and extends Mead's theory of the self as the reflected appraisals of others. We see an American pragmatism and empiricism, most certainly evident in his attempt to treat schizophrenic patients at a time when psychoanalysts, following Freud, asserted that because of withdrawal and autistic preoccupation with self (secondary narcissism), the schizophrenic was incapable of forming a transference relationship and could not be analyzed.

An Interpersonal View of Personality

Sullivan could have concluded that personality inheres in the person; he had, after all, adopted psychoanalysis early in his career. But he didn't. He had listened well to the Chicago sociologists and understood their message. We cannot, he decided, imagine personality outside interpersonal interaction. It is *only* in interaction with others that we can find individual personality. Thus, a definition: 'Personality is the relatively enduring pattern of recurrent interpersonal situations which characterize a human life' (Sullivan, 1953a, p. 10). Sullivan was explicit and emphatic about this. Personality is 'an illusion', as he put it, an abstraction from the commonalities observed in repeated interpersonal relations. Going on, he pointed out that 'Psychiatry is the study of phenomena that occur in interpersonal situations, in configurations made up of two or more people all but one of whom may be more or less completely illusory' (Sullivan, 1964, p. 33).

It follows that one cannot study the personality traits of individuals; instead, we must study individuals in the course of their interaction with others. However, as he said, others don't have to be real persons and physically present. Interactions may be remembered or fantasized, with real people or fantasy people. The dealings of a schizophrenic patient absorbed by hallucinated voices qualifies; so, too, would a recalled exchange with someone, or a fantasy about a real or imagined person. Sullivan was thus a true situation–person interactionist. But personality doesn't exist somewhere out there between the interacting participants; it is a set of attributes of a person to be seen when that person is engaged with others, and it derives from processes that begin early in life and form the basis of interacting with others. More about them later.

Parataxic Thinking and Distortion

An important implication of this view of the person is the very different nature of the doctor–patient relationship in psychotherapy. To Freud transference was the key, the unconscious and irrational repetition in the presence of the analyst of feelings acquired in early childhood, one manifestation of the repetition compulsion we saw in Chapter 3. Sullivan introduced a new term and a whole new way of thinking about doctor and patient, derivatives of his conception of personality. The term is **parataxic** (from the Greek for *a placing beside*) **distortion**★, an extreme version of the cognitive mode of early childhood, **parataxic thinking**★ (in which adults also commonly engage).

Parataxic thinking means the assumption of a causal connection between events that is not rationally examined or confirmed by others. For instance, a small child notices that his mother is tense and seems uncomfortable when she holds him; he parataxically thinks this is due to something bad in himself—his own feeling of discomfort or an urge to wiggle. He connects the two because they co-occur. Parataxic distortion occurs when a patient attaches to his analyst attitudes and feelings based on an erroneous identification of the analyst with significant others in his experience. A patient who is hostile and critical from the first meeting is making an untested and unshared assumption about his analyst. If it could be stated, the parataxic idea might be: 'He is a person in authority, and people in positions of authority—just like my old man—are demanding and demeaning, and always try to put me in my place.' The therapist, though, is not just a 'screen' on which this distortion is played out. As a participant observer, he himself influences what the patient does. He has his own personality attributes as seen by others and does not confirm the patient's mistaken thinking in his behaviour. These elements in this interpersonal situation—patient interacting with a real but fantasized person who does not conform to the patient's assumption—are the basis on which a new understanding can ultimately develop. To remember: the personalities of patient and doctor are visible only in their interaction, and the behaviour of neither can be understood without reference to the other.

The Self

A central feature of interpersonal theory is an ego concept of self similar to those of the other neo-Freudian theories, with the self developing in infancy and early childhood out of the child's experience with his or her parents. The outstanding task of the **self dynamism**★, as Sullivan called it, is the pursuit of **security**★—the attaining of comfort and relief from the disapproval of others. Thus, the processes of the self dynamism are empirical, not structural, coming from experience, and the concept incorporates the conscience and ego ideal of the superego. The self dynamism is involved in the organization of all interpersonal behaviour in the pursuit of security.

Needs

Security is one of two categories of needs that humans are motivated by. The other is satisfactions, by which Sullivan meant bodily needs, including sex, for which his term was lust. The pursuit of security is psychological and interpersonal: how we succeed in its quest determines how we feel about ourselves, the tension and anxiety we experience, and the ways in which we relate to others. Sullivan did not want to distinguish too sharply between the two pursuits. 'Always', wrote Munroe, they 'interact to the point of being dynamically merged' (1955, p. 359).

The Major Concepts of the Interpersonal Theory of Psychiatry

Tension

Sullivan, like Freud, adopted a tension-reduction model but rejected out of hand the implications of Freudian libido—the idea of psychic energy and the dominance of sexual energy. The human being is a physical energy system—'the only kind of energy I know' (Sullivan, 1953a, pp. 101–2)—that engages in work to reduce tension. The goal, as Munroe captured it, is 'a state of *euphoria*, of tensionless bliss, an end state best approximated in deep, dreamless sleep' (1955, p. 358). We spend our lives between the extremes of euphoria and the outer limit of tension, absolute terror, either from exceptional bodily danger or from a catastrophic threat to security. This terror is so great that it engenders unendurable anxiety. People suffering from disorders like schizophrenia experience anxiety of that magnitude, although a badly mothered infant would also know such a level of anxiety. For the great majority of us, we come close to a tension-free state in deep sleep and succeed in reducing the tension of bodily states and threats to our security before they become severe and beyond endurance.

Tensions are aroused when bodily needs must be met—'physicochemical' needs for sustenance, including oxygen, warmth, sleep, and sex. 'Tensions can be regarded as needs for particular energy transformations that will dissipate the tension, often with an accompanying change of 'mental' state, a change of awareness, to which we can apply the general term *satisfaction*' (Sullivan, 1950, p. 85). There are two sources of tension: the needs of the body, rooted in biology, as we've just considered; and anxiety, aroused by endangered security. 'Of the very unpleasant experiences which the infant can have we may say that there are generically two, pain and fear. Now comes the third. . . . It is anxiety which is responsible for a great part of the inadequate, inefficient, unduly rigid, or otherwise unfortunate performances of people' (Sullivan, 1953a, p. 19; 1953b, p. 160). Anxiety is a universal interpersonal experience that none of us entirely escapes. It confounds our relationships with others and impairs our thinking and attention. Anxiety can interfere with bodily processes, making sleep impossible and swallowing difficult.

Anxiety, said Sullivan, is the fear of disapproval, and its prototype is the experience of the infant whose mother conveys her own anxiety and tension. If the mother is stiff, tense, and anxious or angry when her infant cries, for example, the feeling of disapproval is bound to be communicated, and the infant cannot know what he or she did to provoke it. There is no remedy, no action to restore approval and relieve anxiety. Infantile anxiety will create an infant view of self as 'the bad me' to which certain behaviour and feelings become adventitiously attached. The extreme tension of prototypical anxiety always and inevitably involves the child's experience with significant adults, most often the mother, and is not to be thought of as the vague overwhelming of the nervous system envisioned by Freud. Beyond early infancy, the imperative experience of anxiety mobilizes efforts to reduce it, to regain security, and a system of personality, the self system, develops to accomplish that essential task.

To recapitulate, tension is aroused by bodily states of need and by the interpersonal experience of anxiety, and in both cases motivates efforts to reduce it. Humans pursue satisfactions and experience pain and fear just as animals do, but only the human is faced with the problem of anxiety.

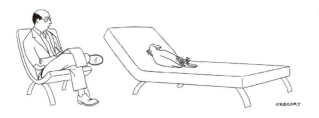

"I think what Polly really want is approval."

Dynamisms

The concept of dynamism★ is the most difficult in Sullivan's theory to understand. It is a process of energy transformation, of turning physical energy into thought, feeling, and behaviour, and it is the basic unit of personality. The dynamism shares some of the attributes of the everyday concept of habits, but it is more complex by far. Unlike the habit, dynamisms are responsible for the organization and channelling of energy into behaviour.

Here is the formal definition: a dynamism is 'a relatively enduring configuration of energy which manifests itself in characterizable processes in interpersonal relations' (Sullivan, 1953b, p. 103). In other words, dynamisms are, first, recurrent transformations of energy into particular aspects of behaviour. They are not, however, static bodily mechanisms—'peculiar more or less physiological apparatus about which our present knowledge is nil' (Sullivan, 1938, p. 123n). They are dynamic and may undergo change. A second thing to note about dynamisms is that they emerge only out of interactions between one person and another or others, through various interpersonal situations; they are made evident in interpersonal relations. As Munroe said, 'They do not properly belong to the organism itself in any ultimate fashion, contrary to the theoretical implications of all schools that point to "instincts", no matter how "basic", or to an inborn "self" . . .' (Munroe, 1955, p. 357). Munroe made a good point in characterizing Sullivan's use of the concept:

> He applies it mainly to the emergent 'self', which takes on enduring contours in infancy and early childhood. . . . But he also applies it to part-systems *within* the developing *self dynamism*. Thus, instead of presenting 'orality' as a psychological need, stage, or whatever, he speaks of an 'oral dynamism', compounded of hunger and oral pleasure, which is very likely to function as a relatively enduring configuration; indeed, it becomes linked with language and organizes very substantial sub-aspects of the self dynamism (Munroe, 1955, p. 357).

Many dynamisms serve the pursuit of satisfactions, but one is at the absolute centre of personality organization and interpersonal relations. It is the **self dynamism**, and it protects the person from threat to security. The self dynamism (Sullivan sometimes referred to it as the **self system★**) begins to develop in infancy with the first awareness of approval and disapproval. Sullivan thought of it as the product of an irrational society in the sense that no rational parent in a rational society would think of making an infant or small child anxious. As the child develops, the self dynamism becomes more and more adept at forestalling and deflecting anxiety. At first, the infant becomes capable of differentiating a 'good mother', who makes him or her feel secure, and a 'bad mother', who arouses anxiety. Out of that readily develops in the emerging self dynamism a differentiation between 'good me' and 'bad me', and this self-referring distinction between imagined attributes that result in comfort or anxiety will likely last for life.

The self dynamism becomes capable of two processes to contend with anxiety—**dissociation★** and **selective inattention★**. The latter is the easier to define. It is the directing of attention away from experiences—sounds, sights, words, and ideas—that carry an anxious meaning. We might hear the words of someone who says something that threatens our security, but we do not attend to the meaning. In dissociation, anxiety-laden experiences (and thoughts as well as behaviour) are denied, excluded from awareness. Dissociated experience is not necessarily bad (as Freud thought), except from the point of view of the parent who enforces a child's self-conception by approving some behaviours and disapproving others. The dissociated thoughts and behaviours may be expressed in dreams, fantasies, and actions that other people notice but that are unnoticed by the person dissociating them (a characteristic tendency to apologize, for example). Another device in the face of anxiety is regression.

There are many sub-dynamisms: the hate dynamism, organizing hatred and targeting it, is one; the paranoid dynamism is another. Of this Sullivan wrote: 'The paranoid dynamism is rooted in (1) an awareness of inferiority of some kind, which then necessitates (2) a transfer of blame onto others' (Sullivan, 1956, p. 145). We have already spoken of the oral dynamism. Another that is particularly vital is the imperative genital lust dynamism, 'which can be dissociated only at grave risk to effective living, and . . . in most people . . . cannot be dissociated at all' (Sullivan, 1947/1953, p. 63).

Cognitive Processes

Sullivan approached the way humans think, all the way from infancy to the cognitive achievements of adulthood, at a time when behaviourism held sway and cognitive psychology was not even a gleam in the eye of its founders. This was a developmental psychology of thought that came from close study of the pathology of thought in schizophrenia. He identified three cognitive modes, beginning in earliest infancy.

Prototaxic★ (from the Greek *proto* meaning 'first') thought is a kind of undifferentiated stream of consciousness, an extreme version of the stream of thought sketched by William James (1890, p. 239). It is simply raw, moment-by-moment sensation, without organization or connection. The infant is not yet capable of the fundamental distinction between me and not-me, and thus experience consists of the momentary noticing of ongoing stimulation. The prototaxic may sometimes occur in the most profoundly disturbed schizophrenic.

When infants first cry as a signal and, without awareness of what they are doing, summon their mothers, **parataxic** experience has begun. That cry, the most primitive form of language, signifies that self exists apart from non-self and that there is a connection between events. In the parataxic mode it is as if associations were conditioned without the intervention of mind. Associations are not linked logically and are likely to be perceived causal connections between events that have simply occurred sequentially and have no real relationship.

It is not difficult to think of the small child's mental activity in this way; it is less easy to appreciate that in all of us there is parataxic thought. Our existence is too complex and our cognitive resources are too often challenged to allow rational thinking all the time. The person who automatically reacts with fear and distrust of people whose skin colour or national origin are different is thinking parataxically. Many emotionally charged responses are similarly parataxic, and all superstition is. Anxiety situations will tend to make cognition parataxic since anxiety constricts attention and impairs the ability to think. People who are prone to anxiety—those who are neurotic, for example—will have plenty of parataxic experience. We want to take note of the highly personal, autistic nature of parataxic thinking: there is no testing of reality, no comparison with the experience of others, for these are features of the highest cognitive level.

The **syntaxic**★ (from Greek, meaning 'orderly arrangement') mode is logical, operational, and confirmable by the experience of others. It is, in a favourite phrase of Sullivan's, consensually validated. Syntaxic thought is eminently verbal: we use words and symbols to communicate with others. Sullivan emphasized that knowledge is acquired interpersonally. Would that we could be consistently syntaxic in our thinking; our lives and world would be much the better for it.

There is another very important aspect of cognitive processes: the images, pictures, attitudes, and interpretations of others and of ourselves that occupy much of our thought. These are **personifications★**, and they reflect our experience in satisfying needs and guarding our security. If experiences in need satisfaction have been positive and rewarding, so too will be personifications associated with them. That is not to say, however, that favourable personifications are necessarily accurate; more often, they are oversimplifications and may have a wishful aspect. Personifications of ourselves and others will involve the pursuit of security and may entail distorted representations. Good-me and bad-me are personifications that begin in infancy with experiences of comfort and of anxiety irrationally associated with the self. Personifications may be fantasized—a perfect mate who does not (and could not) correspond to a real person—or may represent a belief about what certain kinds of people are like. Think of a personification of authority, stemming perhaps from a demanding and overbearing father and generalized to others in positions of authority.

Dreams are a part of our cognitive life, and they are interpersonal phenomena no less than waking cognition. But in dreams, as Sullivan explains, 'the other fellow is wholly illusory, wholly fantastic, a projection, if you please, of certain constructive impulses, or of certain destructiveness, or of certain genital motivations, or something of that kind. . . . Dreams, we have to assume, are for the purpose of maintaining sleep, and the fact that they fail now and then is not any reflection on the utility and efficacy of dreams, but is an index to the gravity of the situation with which the person is confronted' (1953a, p. 69). The self dynamism is not as watchful in sleep, allowing the tensions of the day to be partially discharged. The dream, however, is not particularly revealing of latent meaning since the self dynamism reasserts itself when the sleeper awakens. 'There is a real barrier in this very transition of consciousness that makes us somewhat obscure in our relation to that which went on when we were asleep' (1953, p. 70).

Communication

Sullivan was an expert in communication. He had to be to treat schizophrenic patients. From his dealings with schizophrenics he understood that by no means is all communication verbal, nor is all verbal communication consensual. While syntaxic verbal communication is the basis of social thought and a necessary process in individual socialization and acculturation, we do sometimes communicate obscurely, with wholly personal, idiosyncratic meanings and usages of words; in extreme form, this is the hallmark of schizophrenia. Parataxic thinking and communication are part and parcel of development, but we learn in growing out of childhood to discipline them so that they are occasional and not habitual. The task of translating private meaning, cryptically expressed, into something we can understand—as in trying to understand a schizophrenic patient—is formidable and may take great patience and a long time.

Another form of communication predates the development of language. It is non-verbal, in Sullivan's words a 'peculiar emotional linkage that subtends the relationship of the infant with other significant people—the mother or the nurse. Long before there are signs of any understanding of emotional expression, there is evidence of this emotional contagion or communion' (1953, p. 17). **Empathy★** is the process by which the mother conveys comfort and security or tension and anxiety, and her feelings will take root in the infant's emerging concept of self. It is not clear how empathy works, but Sullivan was convinced that it is a profoundly important mode of communication in infancy. Adults—at least some of them—have an empathic capacity; I believe Sullivan did, to the enormous benefit of his schizophrenic patients.

Personality Development

For a man who never married, had no children to raise, didn't treat children, and had no formal exposure to child psychiatry (then, at any event, an infant discipline), Sullivan knew a very great deal about infancy and childhood. His language was awkward—he referred to mom as 'the mothering one'—but his psychological grasp of what she had to give and what she could inflict was both intuitive and incisive. His data source was the schizophrenic patient—mostly young schizophrenic males under his care and analytic treatment—from whose experiences he formulated much of his developmental theory. He had to reconstruct mother–child interactions to do this, an incredible imaginative feat, recapitulating Freud's method—the more astonishing since he had patients who couldn't free-associate and whose speech and cognition could be virtually incomprehensible. This was a data source that psychiatry and psychology had largely eschewed.

Sullivan's is a theory of development in stages, like Freud's, but there are few similarities. Psychoanalysis is a theory of libidinal development, a theory of the psychosexual path of an internal instinct and its ultimate socialization. Sullivan rejected this. His stages reflect the interpersonal situations and experiences of the child. Of course, he said, they are based on biology, on neuromuscular maturation, but the significant events are the relationships of the child to parents and significant others and the way the self dynamism develops in the pursuit of security. The stages are not stages in interpersonal theory; they are **epochs** or **eras**, his preferred terms, that continue well after the formative psychosexual stages and might be different in non-Western cultures because of differences in childrearing practices and childhood social experiences.

Sullivan's stages were captured by his friend and disciple the philosopher Patrick Mullahy, in a book about psychoanalytic theories, *Oedipus: Myth and Complex* (1953). Following that brief outline, let's review them in detail.

Infancy

Infancy begins with the birth of the infant who, though more helpless and dependent than the young of any other species, has critical competencies. Suckling is one of them, and the ability to notice movement and objects of importance another. 'There is no room for doubt', Sullivan wrote, 'as to the significance attached to the object which satisfies the hunger and thirst of the infant, and we may safely infer that the *mothering one is*

Table 6.1   Sullivan's Epochs of Personality Development
1. *Infancy* to the maturation of the capacity for language behaviour.
2. *Childhood* to the maturation of the capacity for living with compeers.
3. *Juvenile Era* to the maturation of the capacity for isophilic intimacy.
4. *Preadolescence* to the maturation of the genital lust dynamism.
5. *Early Adolescence* to the patterning of lustful behaviour.
6. *Late Adolescence* to maturity.
Source: From Mullahy, 1953.

the first vivid perception of a person relatively independent of the infant's own vague entity' (1953, p. 33). One part of that object, the mothering one's nipple, is the first 'meaningful symbol', a 'protoconcept'. By its association with comfort or anxiety, the nipple takes on a far greater significance than the source of nourishment. A tense and anxious mother may destroy the infant's euphoria and lead to the development of the pathological dynamism of apathy and somnolent detachment.

The primary mode of communication in this epoch is empathy, the emotional apprehension of the mother's state (giving comfort, approving; tense, anxious, hostile, disapproving). Empathy takes some time to develop fully and is at its height from the sixth to the twenty-sixth month. Research on attachment—so-called maternal bonding—confirms the responsiveness of infants to mothers, beginning very early, and the ability of mothers to recognize their own infants by nothing more than smell (Bushnell, Sai, & Mullin, 1989; Kaitz, Good, A., Rokem, & Eidelman, 1987). Attachment soon becomes more discriminating as infants start to form representations of their mothers (in Sullivan's terms, a good mother, a bad mother) (Bretherton, 1993).

Cognitively, the infant will make the transition from prototaxic to parataxic thought and develop personifications that will have enduring significance: good, approving, calm, comforting mother or bad, disapproving, anxious, rejecting mother; good-me and bad-me. The self dynamism appears, organizing the infant's self-perceptions and coping with disapproval and anxiety. The self dynamism will in later development come to dominate interpersonal relationships, self-awareness, and openness to experiences implicating security.

Paramount in infancy is the oral dynamism, which begins with the channelling of energy into the action of drinking milk from the mother. It includes the infant's own efforts to reduce tension through thumbsucking and will, quite early, acquire a new feature—the cry, which is actually language, calling for need satisfaction or security. The oral dynamism will form the basis of language using words. The development of talking in babyish ways marks the end of this era. It is a profoundly important period for personality and will leave a lifetime imprint on the pursuit of security as it well may in smaller oral habits.

Childhood

Parents know that the child of two, walking, talking, inquisitive and into everything, is no longer an infant. Infants are to be nurtured and cared for; children need to be socialized in the ways of the human. The epoch of childhood, from approximately two to six, entails the child's exposure to the basic requirements of the culture that, through the parents, he or she must learn. Inculcating the culture starts with toilet training but includes far more: teaching the elemental rules of social interaction (how to ask for things; being patient; manners; minimizing outbursts of temper). This period is the making of a socialized person.

Language learning proceeds from the very simple and only primitively articulate to an advanced verbal level, and from the communication with parents of thoughts, feelings, as well as facts the child starts to develop syntaxic thought, consensually validating his or her own experience. Thus, the parataxic mode, never actually outgrown, is partly supplanted by the syntaxic. The self dynamism becomes more coherent and organized, and it incorporates a concept of gender and gender-appropriate roles. Children play at being adults, trying on what they see in their parents and significant others for size. These are *dramatizations*, enabled by new symbolic ability, and they are an important way of stepping into adult shoes. The children of anxious or harsh parents may also develop *preoccupations* with ways to forestall disapproval and anxiety.

Children learn to **sublimate★**—in Sullivan's use of the term, to combine anxiety-inducing thoughts and behaviour (bad things they think of doing, say) with thoughts and acts that gain approval, a sort of double-talk all of us probably acquire. They also learn to manipulate their parents—and will extend this to others—in pursuit of security. A particularly dire development is the *malevolent transformation*, in which a child whose security is badly threatened retreats from affectionate contact with the attitude that he or she lives among hateful enemies. Maybe, such a child thinks, things were nice when I was a baby, but now I have to contend with people.

Juvenile Era

Childhood ends with the first emergence of the ability to co-operate with other children—'compeers' as Sullivan called them. He wrote: 'Childhood . . . is marked off from the juvenile era by the appearance of an urgent need for compeers with whom to have one's existence. By "compeers" I mean people who are on our level, and have generically similar attitudes toward authoritative figures, activities, and the like. This marks the beginning of the juvenile era, the great developments in which are the talents for cooperation, competition and compromise' (1953, pp. 37–8).

The self dynamism is now the self-view of an independent person, one who has a recognizable conception of self. Juveniles compare themselves to others and feel a need to belong; they may fortify their appraisals of themselves if they feel threatened by ostracism. Juveniles can discipline their own impulses and separate fantasy from reality. They are also more adept in the interpersonal strategies of manipulating others, and they begin, from parents, other significant adults, and compeers, to form stereotypes. There are derogatory ones—'crybaby', 'teacher's pet', as well as disparaging ethnic attitudes—and ones that amount to hero worship. Stereotypes may be simple at this age, but they are formative and may develop into something stronger and more embellished. Such personifications, as we have noted, are parataxic.

Not everyone successfully graduates to the next stage. Many adults do not grow beyond the juvenile era. They do pass through the remaining epochs but remain juveniles in the complexity of their self systems, in their interpersonal interactions, and in the parataxic level of their thinking.

Preadolescence

Sullivan caught the essence of the transition to preadolescence in calling it 'miraculous', not in a celebratory way but softly and quietly:

> Around the age of eight and one-half, nine and one-half to twelve, in this culture, there comes what I once called the quiet miracle of preadolescence. Quiet because there is nothing dramatic or exciting about its appearance; there is no sudden change by which one has ceased to be a juvenile and has become a preadolescent. In fact, everything is rather gradual, flows out of the past through the present into the future in personality performance, however dramatic somebody else's story of it may sound. I say 'miracle' of preadolescence because now for the first time from birth, we might say even from conception, there is a movement from what we might, after traditional usage, call egocentricity, toward a fully social state (1953, p. 41).

It is the first manifestation of the capacity to love, awkward and fumbling though it may be, that introduces preadolescence. We tend to like and love those who are similar to us, and so boys are comfortable with boys and girls with girls. Boys find 'chums' among other boys; girls among other girls. These chumships become the interpersonal situations for sharing experiences, thoughts, and feelings in a true equality. Reaching out with affection and sharing is made possible by the protected life of preadolescents—secure boundaries of home and school, parents they understand better and more realistically, and responsibilities commensurate with their immaturity.

Early Adolescence

Early adolescence is announced by the onset of puberty and the appearance of genital lust, which Sullivan called 'the most spectacular maturation of all' (1953, p. 57). The postpubescent adolescent experiences clear sexual impulses, masturbates and has orgasms, and encounters—sometimes painfully—western culture's ambivalent attitudes toward sex. 'Ridicule from parents and other elders is among the worst tools that are used on early adolescents. Sometimes a modification of ridicule is used by parents . . . and this modification takes the form of interfering with, objecting to, criticizing and otherwise getting in the way of any detectable movement of their child toward a member of the other sex' (1953b, p. 268). If awkwardness and clumsiness (perfectly natural for a novice) and ridicule from parents and others (especially peers) too strongly threaten security, the adolescent may retreat—a truly damaging developmental setback.

Late Adolescence

Late adolescence brings pattern and organization to the lust dynamism and brings lust together—sometimes in collision—with intimacy. There is now the question of meeting not just the challenge of genuine intimacy but also the challenge to competence—to the adolescent's readiness to become a full-fledged adult. Late adolescents have to confront their abilities and measure them against the opportunities and barriers before them. Further schooling? Taking on a job, and if so, at what level? Continuing to live with parents, or setting out on a new, independent existence? Living with a partner? Some, threatened and anxious, regress to become juveniles with vastly diminished life possibilities.

Adulthood

Hall, Lindzey, and Campbell (1998) put very well the outcome of this long developmental sequence from infancy through adolescence: 'When the individual has ascended all of these steps and reached the final stage of adulthood, he or she has been transformed largely by means of interpersonal relations from an animal organism into a human person. One is not an animal, coated by civilization and humanity, but an animal that has been so drastically altered that one is no longer an animal but a human being—or, if one prefers, a human animal' (p. 166).

Research

Sullivan was engaged in research almost from the start of his career, beginning with his creation of the experimental ward at the Sheppard Hospital. It was, very largely, social research in a psychiatric setting. With the encouragement of William Alanson White, Sullivan established his small ward of six young male schizophrenic patients. The ward was set apart from other wards and services and staffed only by male 'assistants', whom Sullivan particularly chose because they were 'sensitive, shy, and ordinarily considered handicapped employees' (Perry, 1982, p. 195). His principle was *similia similibus curantur*, 'like cures like'. He believed that female nurses were irremediably indoctrinated in professional officiousness and would be too threatening to his badly damaged charges. Sullivan's goal was to create an interpersonal environment that would give his patients the kind of preadolescent trust and intimacy—that chumship—they had missed out on.

Over the several years of the project, Sullivan tried a number of treatment procedures (including hypnosis, for a time, dropped because of the implied submission of patient to doctor). His practice was not without controversy: his special status and hospital ward set the teeth of envious colleagues on edge, which led in part to some restrictions on his freedom to experiment. Over time the essence of his treatment distilled more and more into the fostering of benign interpersonal relationships and a focus on understanding the nature of schizophrenia—its onset, its precipitating factors, and the peculiarity of thought and behaviour that are its hallmarks. Out of that distillate would come the Interpersonal Theory of Psychiatry.

Sullivan's observations and treatment were reported on in a series of articles that had great impact. More, perhaps, than the work of anyone else, Sullivan's clinical research changed the prevailing view of schizophrenia and its treatment, bringing to psychiatry the recognition of interpersonal factors in its appearance and betterment.

What he was able to elicit from schizophrenic patients—the basis of his extraordinary understanding—came in part from the trust he established on the ward, but it grew more directly out of his skill as an observer and interviewer. In a posthumously published book, Sullivan defined the interview, characterized its basic elements, and laid out prescriptions for the role of the interviewer (Sullivan, 1954). The interviewer—or therapist, since the interview may extend over a long course that involves the goal of helping the other person, the patient—is an expert in interpersonal relations and must not forget that his task is to provide benefit to that person. The interviewer does not brandish his or her role as expert in the patient's face but does control the interview, deciding as it goes along what to ask, what to comment on, when to intervene to interrupt the trivial and tangential, and just how to leave the patient with the sense that something important has been accomplished.

Sullivan characterized the interview—one, or many in a therapeutic sequence—as a process consisting of four stages:

1. a beginning, the *formal inception*;
2. a discovery stage, the *reconnaissance*;
3. a more *detailed inquiry*, the real business of finding out, forming hypotheses, and testing them; and
4. the *termination*.

In concluding his contact with a patient, Sullivan said, 'I try never to close all doors to a person; the person should go away with hope and with an improved grasp on what has been the trouble' (1954, p. 211). *The Psychiatric Interview* was widely influential and provided a model even for those who were themselves expert in the process.

Perspective 6.1   Sullivan on Anxiety in the Psychiatric Interview

'The concept of anxiety is central to this whole system of approach [to the psychiatric interview]. In other words, one might say that anxiety is the general explanatory concept for the interviewee's trying to create a favorable impression. More important, it is this concept which gives the psychiatrist the most general grasp possible on those movements of the patient which mislead him, whether those movements are found in the statements of the informant or in the psychiatrist's interpretation of what he hears. The use of abrupt and accented transitions in the interview becomes understandable in terms of this same concept, for the transitions make it possible for the psychiatrist to alter communicative sets, or to restrain or increase the development of anxiety in the interviewee. And this concept of anxiety can be understood in terms of what everyone of us has known most intimately and continuously from the beginning of our available memory.

'An important part of a reasonable grasp on the concept of anxiety might be stated quite simply as: *The presence of anxiety is much worse than its absence*—which is in essence what I have said previously at great length. Under no conceivable circumstance that has ever occurred to me has anyone sought and valued as desirable the experience of anxiety. No series of "useful" attacks of anxiety in therapy will make it something to be sought after. This is, in a good many ways, rather startling, particularly when one compares anxiety with fear. While fear has many of the same characteristics, it may actually be sought out as an experience occasionally, particularly if the fear is expected or anticipated. For instance, people who ride on roller coasters pay money for being afraid. But no one will ever pay money for anxiety in its own right. No one wants to experience it. Only one other experience—that of loneliness—is in the special class of being totally unwanted.

'Not only does no one want anxiety, but if it is present, the lessening of it is always desirable, except under the most extraordinary circumstances. Anxiety is to an incredible degree a sign that something ought to be different at once. As the interviewer studies the circumstances of his contact in the interview situation with any stranger, he will observe that those times when the stranger is clearly at a loss to know what the interviewer thinks of him are occasions on which the stranger is suffering considerable anxiety. And anxiety is such a distressing condition to be in that it is often easier for the interviewee to think privately that he is reading the interviewer's mind than to evaluate a situation more realistically. If the interviewer is to have any skill at the work of interrogating, he must realize that he doesn't know what the other fellow is thinking. Yet it is so much more comfortable, even for a psychiatrist, to be carried away by the hope that one does know, that sometimes one acts just as if he did. The only conceivable explanation of this singular travesty of human ability is that it is better than feeling more anxious.

'How in the world does it come to be that anxiety exerts such a powerful influence in interpersonal relations? Why does it have this ubiquitous effect of making people act, you might say, like asses? People act so in the exceedingly dubious hope of not being uncomfortable. They may still be terribly uncomfortable when the events are finished, but they haven't suffered as much anxiety as they might have without the use of defensive behaviour. Quite often in the therapy situation, if the patient suffered more anxiety, the returns might be highly desirable. He might not need to experience further anxiety about that particular problem. But that fact makes little difference to the patient. Anxiety rules.'

From *The Psychiatric Interview* by Henry Stack Sullivan. Copyright 1954 by the William Alanson White Psychiatric Foundation. Used by permission of W.W. Norton & Company, Inc.

Sullivan was instrumental in bringing a sociologist to join one of the psychiatrists at Chestnut Lodge in a 'socio-psychiatric study of a ward in a psychiatric hospital' (Stanton & Schwartz, 1954). This three-year research was prompted by Sullivan's own inquiry into '*personality functioning* as a part of *institutional functioning*' (p. 13), and it set out to examine in detail one ward, the most disturbed ward, in the context of the whole hospi-

---

A Fresh Look: Practice Today

Like generations of psychologists, psychiatrists, and other mental health workers, I cut my teeth on Sullivan's *The Psychiatric Interview*. From it, we all learned how to structure a clinical interview, shape it according to Sullivan's stages, ask questions that would be probing but not intimidating, search for hypotheses we could subject to test, manage the patient's inevitable anxiety, and conclude—patient and ourselves alike—feeling that this demanding and sometimes fearsome process had been worth it. In the years since Sullivan set forth the principles, a great many psychodynamic authorities have, in book and article, applied them, adapted them, or reset them in an updated format. This is a tribute to Sullivan's own seminal authority. Just as he trained novices of his generation in the delicate art, he left instructions for us to follow and might well have been pleased to see how those succeeding him took in his ideas and made them their own.

Significant in the large post-Sullivan literature on the interview is the work of two J. Christophers, Fowler and Perry, who have studied its processes in depth to illuminate the things clinicians may do to enhance (or thwart) the expression of emotion, conflict, defences, and the details of close relationships (for example, Perry, 1989; Perry, Fowler, & Semeniuk, 2005). In a recent article (published, appropriately, in the journal Sullivan helped to found), they report research identifying the tasks of the dynamic interview and illustrating success and failure in accomplishing them (Fowler & Perry, 2005). They analyzed a large number of interviews conducted with an appreciable sample of patients, setting their findings in a context closely reminiscent of Sullivan's stages and presenting verbatim interview excerpts to show how the good interviewer does it and where the bad one misses the boat. Here are examples from the final phase (the 'Termination' stage to Sullivan, 'Dynamic Formulation and Feedback' to Fowler and Perry). One is an example of an excellent interview, the other of an inadequate one. Can you see places in which the accomplished interviewer succeeded in conveying his astute understanding of Star's troubled feelings and what the weak interviewer failed to recognize in his interview with patient Bev?

Interview with Star

I: We started out with this complaint about the cheat sheet [the typed prompts before the interviewer, reminders of the areas to be explored] and the . . .

Star: I'm impressed.

I: . . . dread of this interview, you know, whether it would be the 'same old, same old', or is this going to be special.

Star: Right.

I: And, um, later I learn that what's important to you now, uh, is that Dr Z. holds you in special regard so that you can conquer the world of relationships, and, you know, the kind of things that are on this cheat sheet.

Star: Right.

I: All right. And the question is, what does having someone shine on you do for you?

Star: Um, I don't know, it makes me stronger, um, I don't know, it's more of a feeling and not something I can ever describe into words, um, it's just I don't have to look inside anymore, it's like I'm pretty confident about what's in there that I don't have to constantly be like sort of opening myself up and looking inside so I have all this time and energy and space to look outside, um, for once, and it's like I get to see all these things that I've been to busy to see.

I: And when you were busy looking inside, what were you looking for?

Star: Um, probably a way out [chuckles], um, I was looking for somebody to love me out of my, sort of out of my madness or out of my depression, it would take somebody to sort of love me really completely and that would make it better, and I think to a certain extent I was right even though everyone said, oh, you have to love yourself, um, I think I was right that I did that.

tal. The intent was to fuse a sociological level of analysis and sociological method with psychiatric description and analysis. Most of the things that those familiar with mental hospitals would think of were put under this combined lens: the needs of the institution, the roles of the staff (doctors, nurses, aides), the roles given to patients in the hospital environment, communication and miscommunication, patient upset and its

I: Hm. This may be in agreement with what you're saying, but I wonder if having someone shine on you helps you avoid feeling evil, like there's something bad inside you.

Star: I think so, I don't, um, I guess I feel like if I was evil then she [her mother] couldn't love me and if she does then I must not be evil, um, I mean like all of the bad things that I do, like she gets mad at them but she never stops loving me regardless in her own way, um, and so, I don't know.

I: Hm. Last question, anything you feel like is important that we haven't covered that just absolutely demands that we speak about?

Star: Um, I think we covered most of it, I'm sure I'll think of something as I'm walking out, but, um, I'm haven't . . . I think that's all I can interrogate you. So I'm actually kind of impressed that you kept me going enough that I never turned it around, like I always try and turn it around, but I kind of liked this, this was fun.

Interview with Bev

Bev: I think about if . . . I think if I wasn't . . . I . . . I think it . . . I would be more naturally be like . . . caring for my body in a different way; like I haven't been eating well [pause] and I . . . you know, I started smoking . . . [sigh]. Which is like so against everything I believe in [short sigh] and . . . you know . . . [whispering] and I've been cutting [myself] and . . . but I just . . . I . . . I just think that if I'm . . . you know, when I'm happier that those things will naturally . . . go away.

I: Is there anything else about how your life is going now, or . . . or it has . . . how it has gone or anything . . . you wanna bring us up to date on, or . . .

Bev: [pause]

I: Anything important in your life that I haven't asked you about?

Bev: [pause] Um, [sigh] well [sigh] you know I [sigh] was having troubles with drinking when I came in, and I haven't had a drink this year. And that . . . and

that's not even . . . like that's one area that I feel much better . . . you know like it's just . . . I don't want to. And . . . you know but . . . I guess that's why I trust that the other things will just drop by the wayside as I get better.

I: What do you think led into your being able to not drink?

Bev: Knowing that lands me in a worse place than I am to start off with.

I: Um-hm.

Bev: You know, like [sigh] know that . . . um . . . for . . . for whatever reason when I . . . when I've . . . um . . . had a drink instead of . . . I mean it relaxes me, but it relaxes me [sigh] into thinking about doing something like right away to kill myself; you know, like I know it's really suicidal to drink, for me. So . . . um . . . and . . . and like . . . [pause] that was really a problem last Christmas with my sisters, because like [pause] you know I was at parties with them, or drinks were put in my hand and . . . you know, and then they had to deal with me . . . and my cutting and stuff, like right in their face—you know. 'Cuz I . . . I . . . ah . . . I dunno how to explain it. But anyways, I . . . I get it and my family gets it that I can't do that, and . . .

I: You attribute your really . . . your . . . choice to cut to being related to the fact that you drank, or . . .

Did you catch the first interviewer's appreciation of Star's parataxic distortion, and his sensitivity to her need to be a special person to the interviewer? He enables Star to reflect on her feelings about herself and the fear that she is evil, and to deal, at least for the moment, with the big issue of whether her mother hates or loves her. The second interviewer is preoccupied with his own questions, which don't relate to the intensity of Bev's conflict and self-destructiveness and reveal his lack of understanding of them. His final question about the serious matter of Bev's cutting herself is superficial and ignores the significant leads she gives about anger toward her sisters and the wish for revenge ['like right in their face . . .'].

ramifications, staff morale, and even how the incontinence of patients affected everyone. The probing was intense, and within the limits faced by the investigators (limits of time, of co-operation from staff, of opportunities to observe) a remarkable social picture of an institution traditionally dominated by administration and psychiatric practice emerged that gave confirmation to 'the reasonable hypothesis that at least some aspects of the disturbances of the patients are a part of the functioning of the institution' (Stanton & Schwartz, 1954, p. 12).

Interpersonal theory did not contribute directly to research in child development, but it did anticipate findings in the study of attachment and maternal bonding (e.g., Bushnell et al, 1989; Kaitz et al, 1987) and in the preadolescent development of intimacy (Berndt, 1986; Youniss, 1980).

Sullivan in Perspective

In a period of twenty-five years, Harry Stack Sullivan had an enormous and transforming influence on psychiatry. Adopting the pragmatic views of Meyer and White, he convinced many in his discipline that the schizophrenic patient was a person who could be treated psychologically (or perhaps I should say, sociopsychologically), and that crude neurological interventions (lobotomy, shock therapy) and 'back ward' institutionalization should be struck from the list of acceptable techniques. His understanding of the interpersonal effects of the hospital milieu and the developments in psychoanalytic methods he introduced had lasting effects on the profession. We still have trouble sitting down face-to-face with a schizophrenic person and understanding him or her—indeed, even dealing with such a person without strong discomfort and the need to retreat behind a professional mask. Sullivan showed, for those able to listen, how it could be done and what the dividends could be.

In the days before behaviour genetics established the risk of heritability and before antischizophrenic drugs came along to provide relief from the crippling symptoms of schizophrenia, Sullivan's approaches to treatment were humane and as effective as any psychological methods could be. But they were not efficient in ridding patients of disabling thought disorder and other schizophrenic symptoms, and they took an endless amount of time. When they succeeded, they did so probably because they relieved the one component leading to the descent into schizophrenia that they could deal with: stress and stress magnified by incessantly crazy and frightening thinking.

The Interpersonal Theory of Psychiatry, never fully developed by Sullivan, took a commanding place of importance in the neo-Freudian group. Its interpersonal emphasis, though delivered in language and concepts difficult to understand, is in many ways more sophisticated, detailed, and inclusive than the social theories of Adler, Horney, and Fromm. It showed persuasively that personality develops and is expressed in interpersonal contexts. In many respects, it is a theory about the damaging effects of anxiety— surely understandable since its database was the schizophrenic patient—but it is also a theory with much to say about normal development and functioning.

The outstanding strengths of interpersonal theory lie in the theory of personality development, normal and abnormal, and in its treatment of cognitive processes and their sequential appearance. Sullivan traced the ontogenesis of the self, beginning with experiences of need satisfaction and security in early infancy. Although the debt to Freud is considerable, his analysis is original and has great plausibility, anchored as it is in interpersonal acts of mothering. Development is set out in a sequence of sensible and identifiable stages extending right up to adulthood. The important interpersonal events of each, within the family and with peers, are characterized, and their implications, favourable and destructive alike, are drawn clearly. We see mother and infant as an interpersonal unit, a compelling way of looking at early development. Concepts referring to processes within the person and the outcomes for which they are responsible are effectively portrayed, although the language can be obscure. The self dynamism is an especially creative synthesis of ego and self-related processes in the developing child.

These are the strong points. There are not many negatives. The theory does fall short in its specification of the ways in which processes occur—how the self dynamism carries out its many tasks, how to operationalize the sometimes loose concept of dynamisms, for example—which Sullivan might have dealt with if he had lived and remained active for another fifteen years or so. He could well have interested social and developmental psychologists in the theory, and they would then have pursued its implications in controlled studies. As it was, said Ernest Hilgard, 'With the deaths of Horney and Sullivan, and Fromm's move to Mexico, the period of excitement generated by these neo-Freudians was over by the 1950s although residual influences persisted' (Hilgard, 1987, p. 503). This is, perhaps, a little strong, but it makes the point.

Karen Horney: Introduction

Karen Horney was at an early stage in her career a respected teacher and supervisor of psychoanalysis. After her immigration to the United States in 1932 she became increasingly involved with a group of analysts critical of Freudian libido theory, the group whose nuclear members became the neo-Freudians. Her stature increased, especially with her forceful, counter-Freudian position on feminine psychology, and with the publication of five books—*The Neurotic Personality of Our Time, New Ways in Psychoanalysis, Self-Analysis, Our Inner Conflicts*, and *Neurosis and Human Growth*—between 1937 and 1950, her place among the neo-Freudians was assured. Those books also gave her a large popular following. She was, like Freud, Adler, and Fromm, a student of neurosis; neurotic sufferers were the patients who made up her analytic practice and on whom her theoretical ideas were based. Horney never presented a full-grown theory, but that is not to diminish her substantive contributions, especially her development of a cultural and social feminine psychology; it is simply to recognize that her presentation of neurotic trends and their origins falls short of an inclusive theory of personality.

Karen Horney: Personal History

Karen Danielsen Horney was born in September 1885 in the German village of Blankenese on the river Elbe, a short distance from Hamburg. Her father, Berndt Wackels Danielsen, was a sea captain, a Norwegian émigré, gruff, authoritarian, excessively pious, and not supportive of his daughter. Horney's mother, of Dutch-German background, was nearly twenty years younger

(© Bettmann/CORBIS)

than her husband and dominated by him. She left Wackels (as he preferred to be called) in 1904, taking Karen and her older brother with her.

After what was clearly an emotionally difficult childhood, Horney entered medical school at Freiburg in 1906 before moving two years later to Berlin to complete her studies and to marry a young lawyer and businessman, Oskar Horney. She trained in psychiatry and later as a psychoanalyst at the Berlin Psychoanalytic Institute where, from 1918 to 1932, she taught.

Her personal and marital lives were difficult and unsatisfying. Early in her marriage, she began the first of the many affairs she would have for the rest of her life. She and Oskar separated in 1926. Before she completed her medical education, struggling with depression, she underwent analysis, first (and disappointingly) with Karl Abraham and later with the nonmedical analyst Hanns Sachs.

Despite the disappointments of her personal life, Horney was becoming increasingly well regarded at the Berlin Institute, presenting papers and formulating her ideas on feminine sexuality. But the the late 1920s and early 1930s brought anxious portents with the rise of Nazi anti-Semitism, street violence, and anti-intellectualism. In 1932, she accepted an invitation from Franz Alexander, a pioneer in the effort to make psychoanalysis briefer and more efficient, to join the Chicago Psychoanalytic Institute as assistant director. Disagreement with Alexander led her to move to New York two years later. There, at the New York Psychoanalytic Institute, she became increasingly embroiled in dispute with her more orthodox analytic colleagues over what they considered to be her radical and non-Freudian ideas (her replacement of penis envy with an egalitarian feminine psychology, her rejection of infantile sexuality and the Oedipus Complex, and her significant revisions of therapeutic technique). In 1941, she was voted out as a training analyst and left, defiantly, to form new organizations, the Association for the Advancement of Psychoanalysis and the American Institute for Psychoanalysis. She was dean of the Institute until her death in 1952 of liver cancer.

There is material aplenty to psychoanalyze Horney's theory—to find its roots in an unhappy childhood, experiences of depression, libertine sexual behaviour, and the like, and her biographers have done just that (Paris, 1994; Rubins, 1978). Real danger lurks in this, however. First, she was an exceptionally complicated and very private woman, and the evidence about her is fragmentary, often coming from conflicting sources. Second, and of perhaps greater importance, Horney had extensive experience in psychoanalysis as a patient and practising analyst, she had exposure to the keen psychoanalytic minds of people with like ideas in Berlin, Chicago, and New York, and she taught alongside eminent social scientists at the New School for Social Research. We badly overlook the intellectual roots of her theory in trying to find psychological ones. Then, we must note that once a theory has been advanced, it is a scientific creation to be judged on its merits as a theory. We do theories no service by digging in the garden for buried neurotic treasure.

Emphases

Clinical Evidence

As we've just seen, Horney's training was in medicine and in psychoanalysis, and the clinical practice of psychoanalysis was her professional career. Her patients were neurotics, and when she addressed the intelligent lay audience for whom she wrote (in *The Neurotic Personality of Our Time*, for example) she largely dealt with neurotic solutions to life and their origin.

The Psychology of Women

The outstanding feature of Horney's approach to personality is her utter rejection of the inadequate and demeaning Freudian psychology of women as disappointed males. The teaching of the family, instructed by culture and society, shapes women's psychosexual development and feelings about themselves. Her alternative was a positive theory of femininity.

Personality Development

Horney's developmental psychology focused, like those of Adler, Sullivan, and Fromm, on the triad of culture, society, and family. She brooked no Freudian argument: it is the way in which parents rear their children that channels the growing child's needs. Horney echoed the message of the other neo-Freudians that children come into the world utterly dependent on their parents for both physical and psychological nurturance. Parents who fail them arouse anxiety—her term was *basic anxiety*—by endangering their security. Basic anxiety is responsible for neurotic developments and for the Oedipus complex, which only masquerades as a sexual phenomenon.

The Self

There is an ego-as-self concept in the theory, incorporating features of the psychoanalytic ego and superego. Horney wrote of three selves, one healthy and two the outcomes of an insecure childhood: a **real self★**, which may be overshadowed by an **idealized self★**, and a **despised self★**. Alienation from the real self, self-hatred, and an unrealizable version of oneself do not live together harmoniously. This 'war among the selves' represents the principal internal conflict to Horney. She did not accept Freud's three-party battling among the intrapsychic factions of id, ego, and superego.

The Analytic Situation

Horney held a revisionist view of the analytic situation. She contended that psychoanalysis proceeds best with a greater focus on the immediate—on opening up the patient's attitude toward self, and on the intrinsic, habitual character defences of the patient. She also viewed analysis as a power struggle between patient and analyst in which the patient fights the analyst to hang on to his or her neurotic defences. It is basically a hostile situation (not from the analyst's but from the patient's perspective), a resistant battle by the patient to cling to and gain satisfaction of neurotic needs.

Perspective 6.2   Horney on What the Analyst Does

'It is the analyst's consistent focus on the patient's best interest that eventually helps him to gain the latter's confidence. Of course, the patient would never have decided to work with the analyst if he had not had some confidence in him to begin with. But his initial confidence, though based on a good intuitive feeling, is not built on especially solid ground. After all, most of us are aware of the difference between an intuitive trusting of another person and the repeated, concrete evidence of his reliability. For the neurotic, however, this difference is considerably greater. With all his anxieties, suspicions, and defensive hostilities—conscious or unconscious—he needs proof after proof before he can dare to take the risk of really trusting someone.

'As for the analyst's nonauthoritative attitude, I prefer to define it in positive terms as an endeavour to place the patient under his own jurisdiction. The analyst firmly believes in the desirability of every person taking his life into his own hands, as far as possible, and assuming responsibility for himself. He respects individual differences and knows that each person can ultimately decide only in accordance with his own wishes and his own ideals. Hence he sees his main task as helping the patient to recognize his own wishes and find his own set of values.

'This attitude is responsible to a large degree for the analyst's reluctance to give advice. Another perfectly good and simple reason for his reluctance on this score is that in most cases he feels incapable of giving advice. Being more aware of the complexities of the human mind than most people, he has developed an attitude of realistic humility that allows him to be fully aware of his own limitations. Naturally he will express his opinion whenever it is clear to him that the patient is about to act against his own interest. Furthermore, if certain of the patient's symptoms point to the possibility of an organic disorder, he will suggest a physical examination. He may definitely advise against a major decision if he is convinced that the patient is acting under the pressure of irrational emotional factors. . . .

'Another way in which the analyst helps the patient is his attitude of accepting him as he is. What does this mean and why is it important? It may mean scientific objectivity. Freud expected the analyst to look at the patient with the eyes of a scientist and to eliminate value judgements. This, however, necessarily creates an artificial situation because no one can exclude his set of values when human behaviour and motivations are involved. Actually, the patient himself does not believe in such objectivity but assumes that it is adopted for the sake of therapy.

'It may mean tolerance. Tolerance is, of course, important in view of the self-condemning attitude harboured by most patients. Although the patient may distrust this attitude, too, it is actually genuine by virtue of the analyst's understanding.

'It means, finally, that the analyst is interested in the patient as a human being who is engaged in the process of development and that he appreciates the patient's every move ahead. In order to help you to understand the value of such an attitude I must tell you something that may surprise you. When he begins analysis, the patient as a rule is not interested in himself as he *is*. He is constantly concerned with what he *should* be and blames himself for his shortcomings instead of tackling them realistically. Naturally this has to be analyzed. But it is also the analyst's consistent interest in him as he is and as he could be that helps the patient to develop a constructive interest in his real self.

'The analyst can have this positive attitude because he believes in the constructive forces within the patient which will eventually enable him to resolve his neurotic conflicts. Is this a blind optimism on the part of the analyst, or is it a realistic faith in the existence of such forces or at least in existing potentialities? On the basis of our experience, it is a most realistic faith. Initially, the patient's constructive, forward-moving forces may lie buried under illusions, hopelessness, *and* destructiveness. But with rare exceptions we see them come to life during analysis.

'As he gains insight into the workings of his mind, the patient gradually comes to feel: '*I* can do something; *I* can have feelings other than mere irritation and fear; *I* can like somebody; *I* can enjoy things; *I* can want.' And with each taste of freedom and of strength his incentive to gain more of it grows. The analyst's belief in and clear recognition of the patient's potentialities helps the patient to regain his faith in himself. This is particularly important at those periods in analysis when the patient loses faith in himself or when it dawns upon him how little of it he has ever had.

Neurotic Needs

We find in the theory a very complex characterization of neurotic needs, well beyond the other neo-Freudians in inclusiveness and specificity. It is a descriptive list but one that captures some essential features of neurotic pursuits.

The Major Concepts of Horney's Theory

Basic Anxiety

The core organizing concept in Horney's theory is basic anxiety. It stems from a **basic evil** that pervades parental treatment of a child:

> The basic evil is invariably a lack of genuine warmth and affection. A child can stand a great deal of what is often regarded as traumatic—such as sudden weaning, occasional beating, sex experiences—as long as inwardly he feels wanted and loved. . . . The main reason why a child does not receive enough warmth and affection lies in the parents' incapacity to give it on account of their own neuroses. . . . [V]arious actions or attitudes on the part of the parents . . . cannot but arouse hostility, such as preference for other children, unjust reproaches, unpredictable changes between overindulgence and scornful rejection, unfulfilled promises, and not least important, an attitude toward the child's needs which goes through all gradations from temporary inconsideration to a consistent interfering with the most legitimate wishes of the child, such as disturbing friendships, ridiculing independent thinking, spoiling its interest in its own pursuits . . . altogether an attitude of the parents which if not in intention nevertheless in effect means breaking the child's will (Horney, 1937, pp. 80–1).

Basic evil is the condition for basic anxiety, 'the feeling the child has of being isolated and helpless in a potentially hostile world. . . . This attitude as such does not constitute a neurosis but it is the nutritive soil out of which a definite neurosis may develop at any time' (1937, p. 89). She adds, 'It may be roughly described as a feeling of being small, insignificant, helpless, deserted, endangered, in a world that is out to abuse, cheat, attack, humiliate, betray, envy' (1937, p. 92). Basic anxiety, 'the most painful experience man can experience', is created by severe threats to the child's psychological well-being, and it arouses—understandably but dangerously—*basic hostility*. The child is trapped in an impossible situation. Anxious, insecure, and resentful, he or she cannot make evident feelings as close to the brink as these nor even acknowledge them. They are denied access to awareness—repressed—but this hardly solves an intractable problem.

The Vicious Circle

Evil, anxiety, and hostility set up a vicious circle, a self-defeating sequence of distress, followed by an insatiable need for reassurance and love, hostility when these are not forthcoming, even greater anxiety, and an intensified need for love. Unhelpful and unproductive strategies only make things worse. This self-generating circle may begin quite early on in childhood, and it becomes a practised neurotic approach to others. If not impossibly severe, vicious circles can sometimes be interrupted by a 'lucky circle' of favourable events. The child who begins life confronted by evil parenting, however, has been dealt a truly bad hand and has a crushingly difficult task ahead to overcome it. That, Horney thought, is the job of psychoanalysis.

The Basic Nature of Human Needs

Horney rejected the instinctual basis of personality to focus on one paramount need, the need for security. Unlike Adler's superiority striving, which is a constant drive, the need for security comes into play only when security is threatened. **Safety devices** are developed in childhood as coping strategies to contend with chronic and severe threat. They are neurotic, impelling the search for security in a way determined by a child's particular circumstances and the way parents undermined security.

She elaborated the idea of safety devices into a set of ten neurotic needs that represent unproductive and alienating strategies to achieve security. They may become permanent features of personality that characterize interactions with others.

- **A need for affection and approval.** The person is driven by an insatiable need to gain love and approval. Indiscriminately striving to please others, he or she is exceptionally sensitive to any hint of rejection or dismissal, and will go to any lengths to avoid displeasure.
- **A need for a 'partner' to take over one's life.** A parasitic version of the need for affection, this condition drives the person to extreme dependency on the partner. It is a need to be needed and to be taken care of, and it engenders fear of desertion.

Figure 6.1 The vicious circle (Diagram based on Horney, 1937)

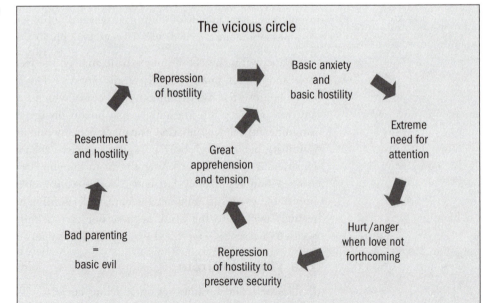

- **A need to restrict life within narrow borders.** A person dominated by this need is resigned to an unfulfilling, joyless, and lonely existence, to living a life of passive resistance to challenge and accomplishment. Self-belittlement is a notable sign.
- **A need for power.** The person who needs power over others has a 'need to pile up personal insurance against the danger of being overwhelmed' (Munroe, 1955, p. 345). An individual with this tendency believes that the world is a competitive jungle. Everyone has hostile designs, and the only way to compete is to control and dominate. Such a person often demands recognition of his or her power as a way to ensure invulnerability. This individual fears helplessness.
- **A need to exploit others.** This is the least admirable need. Others are judged by the likelihood that they can be used or exploited for personal gain. The exploiter fears being exploited him- or herself and acts first to avoid appearing to be stupid.
- **A need for prestige.** An individual with this need derives self-worth from the recognition of others. 'All things—inanimate objects, money, persons, one's own qualities, activities, and feelings—[are] evaluated only according to their prestige value' (Horney, 1942, p. 54).
- **A need for personal admiration.** The person who must be admired has an idealized and very inflated self-image and lives to have it validated. Recognition and admiration are all.
- **A need for personal achievement.** Horney's version of the achievement need is a neurotic quest to 'surpass others' and be 'the very best'. It is, like all the other needs, driven by insecurity.
- **A need for self-sufficiency and independence.** Fearing rejection, a person so driven cannot ever be dependent on or obligated to anyone. Closeness is danger, and so being tied down is a trap to be avoided. This is a loner.
- **A need for perfection and unassailability.** An inordinate fear of making mistakes and being criticized or reproached is behind this need. The only answer is to be perfect. There is an obsessive dread of finding flaws in oneself, and a compensatory feeling of superiority over others. 'After all,' says this individual, 'no one is as good as I am.'

In a later book, Horney (1945) classified these neurotic needs under the three categories 'moving toward people', 'moving against people', and 'moving away from people'. This classification helps us to see the basic orientation of the neurotic person toward others through helplessness, aggression, or detachment. We want to remember that trying to find security in these neurotic ways is not consciously determined and is compulsive and rigid.

The Ego as Self

The sense of self is a powerful attribute of human cognition and emotion, and disturbances of it are extremely distressing and sometimes unendurable. Horney's self is, as we have seen, a tripartite concept. The image we have of ourselves emerges out of our childhood experience of security or the lack of it. If we are fortunate to grow up in warm and protective homes, the self that develops is the *real self*, healthy, robust, and with an aim toward self-realization. Horney thought of this self as 'that central inner force, common to all human beings and yet unique in each, which is the deep source of growth' (1950, p. 17). Anxious upbringing results in a defensive, *idealized* image of self that exaggerates

Table 6.2 Horney's Classification of Needs

Moving Toward People	Moving Against People	Moving Away from People
Need	*Need*	*Need*
Affection and approval	Power	Self-sufficiency
Partner to take one's life over	Exploiting others	Perfection, unassailability
Restriction of life within narrow borders	Prestige	Also, restriction of life within narrow borders
	Personal admiration	

good, ideal (and unattainable) attributes. We all have idealized versions of ourselves to a degree, but in the neurotic person the idealized self is impossibly demanding and submerges the real self. Horney also described a *despised self*, an image made up of the failures and shortcomings, real and imagined, for which one berates oneself. The idealized and despised images of self are in sharp conflict—a conflict at the core of all neuroses:

> A person builds up an idealized image of himself because he cannot tolerate himself as he actually is. The image apparently counteracts this calamity; but having placed himself on a pedestal, he can tolerate his . . . [actual] self still less and starts to rage against it, to despise himself and to chafe under the yoke of his own unattainable demands upon himself. He wavers then between self-adoration and self-contempt, between his idealized image and his despised image, with no middle ground to fall back on (Horney, 1945, p. 112).

There is a clear link between despised and idealized selves and the various strategies that the neurotic needs represent. Children who feel unloved, even hated, and who lack the opportunity to express their resentment, begin to think of themselves as bad, the 'bad' attributes resembling (in a child's way of thinking) the unlikeable things about them that their parents have conveyed. The child who feels unloved has, of course, an exaggerated, indeed desperate, need for affection; unmet, it leads her to adopt one strategy or another—expressed in the neurotic needs—to either gain affection or show that she doesn't care. The idealized image incorporates the essential features of the particular need (examples: 'I don't need anyone. Everything I need I can get for myself'; 'Eat or be eaten—it's a dog-eat-dog world.').

None of us has wholly escaped childhood insecurity, and no one will be entirely free of self-idealization and neurotic-like needs. These will be moderate, not insatiable, and not alienating to others. The hope for the severely neurotic person, however, lies in successful psychotherapy, which will demand hard and painful work and a good psychotherapist.

An idealized self-image leads to tyrannical self-imposed demands to live up impossible standards, which Horney called the '**tyranny of the shoulds**' (1950). They could never be achieved—being invariably good and thoughtful, productive, beyond criticism—and failure to meet them makes one hate oneself, which reinforces dependence on the idealized self. This is a recognizable version of the vicious circle.

Horney recognized other defensive manoeuvres. **Externalization★** is a tactic whereby one attributes to others thoughts or feelings one cannot accept in oneself, and it may also involve blaming an unfriendly environment or bad luck for one's failures. The **pride system★** falsely gives one status, prestige, or recognition for accomplishments that are not genuine, such as being smarter than everyone else or prettier or physically stronger. **Self-effacement★** is the process of seeking affection with behaviour that is endlessly good, loving, and undemanding. Suffering for the good of others is an excellent self-effacement strategy. Of course, it is all too much and puts the others off, and so the effort has to be redoubled; needless to say, that doesn't work either.

Personality Development

We see no formal scheme of development in Horney's personality theory. Instead, she points to the dangers of thoughtless, self-indulgent, neglectful, unloving childrearing and the enormous dividend in healthy growth paid by warmth and love. She considered herself a psychoanalyst and regarded her revisions, so radical to the orthodox, as necessary alterations to a theory that had outgrown its time and place. She was adamant in rejecting the Oedipus complex as a developmental fact of life. She did begin her own theoretical analysis by acknowledging the contribution of Freud to the understanding of sexuality. However, she dismissed the psychoanalytic interpretation of such adult behaviour as, for example, the sexual advances of a patient toward the analyst as the repetition of a fixation on the parent of the opposite sex. It is, rather, a misguided bid for reassurance.

The Oedipus complex in the child grows out of family situations, sometimes sexually tinged, but more often 'brought about by the child clinging to one parent for the sake of reassurance. In fact,' she explained, 'a fully developed Oedipus complex, as Freud has described it, shows all the trends—such as excessive demands for unconditional love, jealousy, possessiveness, hatred because of rejection—that are characteristic of the neurotic need for affection. The Oedipus complex in these cases is not then the origin of the neurosis, but is itself a neurotic formation' (Horney, 1937, p. 161). Clinging to one parent by an insecure, anxious (and also angry) child and harbouring hostile wishes toward the other is certainly one strategy to seek love from the parent who seems most willing to give it. It is, though, a doomed one.

Feminine Psychology

Over a period of thirteen years, Horney evolved a new view on feminine psychosexual development and its consequences for personality. Freud had arrived at the position, as his biographer Peter Gay writes, 'that the little girl is a failed boy, the grown woman a kind of castrated man. . . . Man, then, the male, was Freud's measure. . . . Varying Napoleon's famous saying about politics, he offered a provocative aphorism: "Anatomy is destiny"' (Gay, 1988, p. 515). Women could not help being envious of the male sex organ; penis envy occupied a significant place in the psychoanalytic picture of the psychology of women.

This was arrogant and offensive theory, and Horney began to question it, though at first only in part. She had herself seen clinical evidence in neurotic women of sexual identity problems, but she disputed their claimed origin. In an extended set of articles, she set forth the view that it is masculine prerogatives that are enviable, not penises. Indeed, she argued, it is the female whose anatomy is to be prized. Woman, after all, is primarily responsible for bringing new life; the male's role is necessary but no more than momentary. Moreover, she pointed out, there is abundant evidence of male fear of women and their defensive need to derogate them and deny them their rightful place. Men often choose less capable women as partners and indulge their masculinity in visits to prostitutes.

No, she said, it is male-dominated culture and societies that give women an inferior role and make them feel cheated. 'The conclusion that half the human race is discontented with the sex assigned to it and can overcome this discontent only in favourable circumstances . . . is decidedly unsatisfying, not only to feminine narcissism but also to biological science' (Horney, 1924, p. 50).

Research

Horney was not a research psychiatrist, although she would have thought of her clinical studies of neurotic patients as scientific investigation. Without controlled studies, her theory found no favour in the research community, and we have to judge its adequacy as theory on the basis of clinical evidence. The more we can take hypotheses out of an immediate, ongoing, and vastly complicated social setting (the psychoanalytic hour) to test them in controlled situations, the more confidence we have in them. Interesting without a doubt but unproved and uncertain is the view of Horney's work we are left with. That judgement is not to demean this neo-Freudian but simply to recognize the problems of the clinical method we discussed in Chapter 1.

Horney in Perspective

Karen Horney's incomplete theory of personality is deservedly recognized for its many contributions to the understanding of neurosis and the origins of neurotic personality development in the family, influenced in turn by culture and society. She bravely contested psychoanalysis on the Oedipus complex, on infantile sexuality, on the instinctual determination of behaviour—indeed, she contested Freud himself on the psychology of women. Hers was a necessary—if ill received—message, a corrective that psychoanalysis needed like a good swat on the behind. It was unconscionable of Freud to dismiss Horney with the spiteful comment, 'We shall not be very greatly surprised if a woman analyst who has not been sufficiently convinced of the intensity of her own wish for a penis also fails to assign proper importance to that factor in her patients' (Freud, 1964, p. 197).

The social psychological understanding of personality development, especially that of women, received a great contribution from Horney. She carried her part of the load in bringing psychoanalysis to its modern view. Her characterization of the features of neurosis and how it develops in loveless and rejecting families enriched our understanding, and she advanced our appreciation of the roles of the self, healthy and disturbed. Psychotherapists worth their salt do not fail to look for neurotic needs in their patients and how the self copes with anticipated rejection. How these expressions of disturbed personalities are dealt with will differ according to the theoretical persuasion of the therapist, but recognition of them is, thanks to Horney, widespread.

Horney also taught us to look at ourselves and advocated self-analysis for those serious and motivated enough and not too neurotically crippled to undertake it. Freud and virtually no one else could carry out such an arduous task, said the classical analysts.

Not so, said Horney. Many of us can profit from the exercise. It is one that affirms the possibilities for human growth. The rest of the neo-Freudians thought so too, and this is one of the admirable traits in the movement.

SUMMARY

1. Harry Stack Sullivan's origins and training were very different from those of European psychoanalysts and neo-Freudians. He was raised as an Irish Catholic, grew up poor and isolated, and managed by being bright and resourceful to get a medical education, albeit a very average one. He was exposed early in his career to the pragmatic ideas of American leaders in psychiatry, William Alanson White and Adolph Meyer, as well as to psychoanalysis. His theory reflects both influences.

2. His early work was with young hospitalized male schizophrenics. They were a primary data source for his understanding of this most devastating personality disorder, and they provided him with the opportunity to experiment with then unorthodox methods of treatment. His insight into schizophrenia and the treatment techniques he developed had a profound influence in psychiatry.

3. There is a strong emphasis in the Interpersonal Theory of Psychiatry on sociological concepts of the Chicago school. The origin of the self in social interaction is one of them, and it appears in Sullivan's view of the *self dynamism*. Social scientists also influenced Sullivan's approach to schizophrenia, which he came to see as a social psychological disorder reflecting a history of severely damaged interpersonal interaction.

4. Personality is uniquely defined in interpersonal theory, revealing again the influence of sociology. Sullivan noted that personality can be observed only in social interactions and is thus not a fixed, inherent property of the person. It is an abstraction from consistencies that appear in repeated social interactions. This view makes Sullivan an advocate of **situation–person interaction★**, in clear contrast to Freud.

5. Among the implications of such a definition of personality is a significantly different approach to the doctor–patient relationship in psychotherapy. Freud saw this relationship as one of transference, as the playing out of attitudes and feelings acquired in early childhood on the 'screen' of the objective and largely impersonal analyst. '*Parataxic distortion*', Sullivan's term, is seen in the patient's approach to the analyst, which may reflect private and unverified assumptions that the analyst doesn't confirm. The psychoanalytic situation is an interpersonal encounter in which two people interact; the analyst has his or her own personality, which is bound to have an influence. Thus, the psychoanalyst is a 'participant observer'.

6. The ego in interpersonal theory is a concept of self with important similarities to the selves of other neo-Freudians. Sullivan's self is the **self dynamism**, whose fundamental task is to protect the psychological security of the person, to achieve comfort by warding off threat and anxiety. The self dynamism develops out of experience, beginning in early infancy, and it comes to organize the individual's approach to all interpersonal interaction.

7. Human needs are divided in Sullivan's theory into two major categories. One is the pursuit of **satisfactions**, which are bodily needs (including sex, referred to as lust). The other is the pursuit of **security**, which determines how we relate to others, feel about ourselves, and cope with experiences of tension and anxiety. The two types of needs are not independent of each other; they dynamically interact because pursuing satisfactions occurs in an interpersonal context, and the way we satisfy bodily needs has significant implications for our view of ourselves.

8. Interpersonal theory recognizes the human organism as a physical energy system that operates on a *tension reduction principle*. The extremes of tension range from the tensionless state of dreamless sleep to high terror resulting from grave bodily danger or the most severe threat to security. Unpleasant experiences of tension come from pain, fear, and anxiety. The last of these is the fear of disapproval, first encountered in the infant's experience of careless or bad mothering, and it will in time motivate efforts to reduce it and to restore security. A system of personality, the **self**

system, emerges to accomplish exactly this. When tension is aroused, both bodily systems and psychological processes (for example, attention, thought, or defensive cognitive activities to ward off anxiety) are mobilized to reduce it. The pursuit of satisfactions is likewise directed toward tension reduction.

9. The central concept in interpersonal theory is the **dynamism**, a process of energy transformation that turns physical energy into the psychological processes of thought, feeling, and behaviour. The dynamism is the basic unit of personality. It resembles the everyday concept of habit, but it is far more complex. Unlike habit, dynamisms organize and channel energy into behaviour. Dynamisms are not simply biological mechanisms of need satisfaction, however. They are just as much interpersonal, growing out of interactions and expressed in interpersonal relations. There are many dynamisms serving the pursuit of satisfactions (the oral dynamism, for example, and the lust dynamism), but there are others that involve the all-important pursuit of security. One of these is at the centre of personality: it is the self dynamism, which emerges to protect against anxiety and to preserve security. The self dynamism makes use of the processes of *dissociation* (excluding anxious experiences and thoughts from awareness) and *selective inattention* (diverting attention away from experiences and events that are associated with anxiety). Sub-dynamisms are part of larger dynamisms. Sullivan spoke of the hate dynamism and the paranoid dynamism, both of which derive from the self dynamism.

10. Sullivan dealt more explicitly than Freud, or the other members of the neo-Freudian group, with cognitive processes, casting human thought in a developmental framework. There are three cognitive modes, beginning in earliest infancy:

    - The **prototaxic** mode is the cognitive life of infancy. This is moment-by-moment experience of the sensory world, entirely undifferentiated. We know nothing of prototaxic cognition in adulthood, though the thinking of the severely disturbed schizophrenic perhaps comes close.
    - **Parataxic** cognition recognizes connections between events that may be causal or only apparently so. It is as if the association of events were conditioned through their sequential appearance in time. Parataxic thinking is characteristic of

early childhood, and it diminishes with cognitive development. We never outgrow it, however, and we succumb to this primitive mode when anxious or challenged beyond our capacities. Superstition and prejudice are outstanding examples.

    - **Syntaxic** thought is logical and confirmable by observation and by the experience of others. It is, in a favourite phrase of Sullivan's, consensually validated. The acquisition of knowledge comes from shared experience; thus, syntaxic thinking is verbal. We use words to frame ideas and to communicate them.

11. Images, attitudes, and interpretations of others and of ourselves form another part of human cognitive life. Sullivan termed these *personifications*. They are often irrational, acquired parataxically, and they reflect experience in satisfying needs and maintaining security. Warmth and nurturance in early childhood will result in favourable images of mother and self—'good mother' and 'good me'. Anxious experiences will promote opposite images and may lead to aspects of the self that are dissociated. Personifications may be fantasized, as in an imagined perfect mate who does not represent a real person, and they are likely to be an important part of the prejudiced picture of other peoples.

12. Dreams are both cognitive and interpersonal. They reflect our struggles and fantasies and occur because the self dynamism is not as watchful during sleep and permits a degree of tension reduction. Upon awakening, however, the self dynamism is immediately on the job again, distorting the residues of dreams to suit its security needs. Sullivan accordingly thought that dreams are not very useful as pointers to dissociated mental life.

13. Sullivan was an authority on communication—verbal, implied, and emotional—deriving his expertise from his experience with schizophrenic patients. He clearly understood that at times we communicate irrationally, parataxically, much as we might wish to be rational and to seek consensus. Emotional communication between mother and infant appears before language. This is the process of *empathy*, by which comfort and security, or anxiety, are conveyed by the mother to her infant. The self dynamism, with its images of mother and self, develops through empathic communication. Most adults lose the

capacity for empathy, although a few remarkable ones retain it. Sullivan was surely one.

14. Interpersonal theory contains a very complete and persuasive map of personality development. There are six *epochs*, beginning in infancy and ending with the conclusion of late adolescence.

- *Infancy*. The newborn brings to life outside the womb a number of essential competencies. Suckling and the ability to attend to the varied stimuli that impinge on sensory receptors are two significant ones. Infants also notice and respond to the mother's emotional communication by the process of empathy, feeling comfort and security from a 'good mother' or anxiety conveyed by an indifferent or tense 'bad mother'. Psychological research on attachment confirms the empathic connectedness of infants and mothers. The earliest cognitive mode of the infant is *prototaxic*. Soon, however, *parataxic* cognition begins to develop, and the first personifications will appear ('good mother' for comfort and security, 'good me' for doing things that gain approval; 'bad mother' for anxiety and tension, 'bad me' for behaving in ways that produce disapproval). These primitive self-perceptions that arise out of empathic communication will form the basis of the self dynamism, which organizes them into a view of self that maximizes security. The oral dynamism is responsible not only for suckling but for other oral activities such as crying when hungry and thumbsucking. Infancy will come to an end with the beginnings of language.

- *Childhood* introduces the young to the first serious socialization demands that society and the parents impose. In the years from two to six, children are made aware of the social rules that govern elimination, social interaction, and self-control. Language learning develops to a considerably advanced level, and parataxic thinking is partly supplanted by the syntaxic mode. Children play at being adults, adopting grown-up roles in an experience Sullivan called *dramatization*.

- The *juvenile era* is distinguished by the development of co-operation with other children—*compeers*, in Sullivan's vocabulary. The self dynamism is now that of an independent person, and there is a definite concept of self. Juveniles compare themselves to others and have a strong need to belong. They discipline their impulses, distinguish fantasy and reality, and are capable of manipulating others. They also begin to form stereotypes.

- *Preadolescence*, between roughly eight and twelve, brings the capacity to love, first experienced with others of the same sex ('chums'). In these relationships preadolescents share experiences, feelings, and ideas. The boundaries of their lives are still protected, making affection toward and sharing with chums possible.

- *Early adolescence* begins with the onset of puberty. The postpubescent adolescent experiments with his or her sexuality and encounters the difficult world of adult sexuality. Parental ridicule or excessive control may cause a damaging retreat in regression to juvenile feeling and behaviour.

- *Late adolescence* sees the maturing of the *lust dynamism* and the coming together of lust and intimacy. Late adolescents also face the task of assessing their competence and readiness to become full-fledged adults. They have critical decisions to make about further education, a job, living with parents or independently, living with an intimate partner. Some adolescents fail and regress to become lifelong juveniles.

15. Sullivan was a research psychiatrist, studying serious personality disorder (mainly schizophrenia), the therapeutic milieu of the hospital ward, the process of psychotherapy, and interpersonal communication. His work revolutionized American psychiatric practice with schizophrenic patients, and his book on the interview provided a model for mental health professionals. Following his interest, a major sociopsychiatric study of a small psychiatric hospital established how significantly hospital practice and staff behaviour affect patients and the course of their recovery. Sullivan's views on early personality development anticipated some of the findings of developmental psychologists on maternal attachment and bonding.

16. The Interpersonal Theory of Psychiatry made major contributions in its analysis of personality development, both normal and abnormal, and in its sophisticated approach to cognitive processes. Many of its concepts are original and creative, and the theory reflects an exceptional sensitivity to the developing

person. However, interpersonal theory does not clearly specify a number of important processes—for example, how to operationalize the concept of the dynamism, and how the self dynamism carries out its tasks.

17. Karen Horney was a highly respected member of the neo-Freudian group—psychoanalyst, teacher, and author of significant modifications to psychoanalysis. Her views on society, culture, and the family in the shaping of personality, on feminine psychology, and on neurotic needs were closely in tune with other neo-Freudians and had a major influence on psycho-analytic theory. She did not, though, present the systematic analysis of personality that Adler, Sullivan, and Fromm did, so it cannot be said that she produced a personality theory.

18. Horney's principal contribution was her rejection of the Freudian psychology of women, which argued that women are, in a most significant sense, incomplete males driven by 'penis envy'. She noted instead that cultures put women in subservient roles, and families raise girls to conform to the cultural prescription. It is, she said, the position of the male that is enviable.

19. Personality development is decisively influenced by family practices in childrearing. Parents can fail their children by creating a condition Horney referred to as **basic evil**; such parents are insensitive to the needs of their children, neglectful, often hostile and rejecting, and above all lacking in warmth and affection. Basic evil engenders **basic anxiety**, '. . . a feeling of being small, insignificant, helpless, deserted, endangered, in a world that is out to abuse, cheat, attack, humiliate, betray, envy'. Basic anxiety lays the basis for a **vicious circle**, a self-defeating cycle of anxiety, an insatiable need for warmth and reassurance, hostility when rebuffed, and an intensified need for affection. The Oedipus complex is not a developmental fact of life, emerging only under special family circumstances. As an example, a child may cling to the one parent he or she sees as more likely to give love, and turn on the other parent.

20. Children who grow up insecure develop **safety devices** to cope with lack of love. Safety devices become **neurotic needs** which, because they alienate others, are doomed to failure and only make the person more alone and anxious. There are ten neurotic needs:

- a need for affection and approval
- a need for a 'partner' to take over one's life
- a need to restrict life within narrow borders
- a need for power
- a need to exploit others
- a need for prestige
- a need for personal admiration
- a need for personal achievement
- a need for self-sufficiency and independence
- a need for perfection and unassailability

These needs may be classified as moving toward people, moving against people, or moving away from people. Whatever their orientation toward others, however, they are self-destructive and alienating.

21. Horney saw the ego as a self—a **real self**, growing out of a nurturant upbringing, or either of two damaged selves resulting from anxiety and insecurity. The real self is a healthy, realistic view and its aim is self-realization. The damaged selves are an **idealized self**, which exaggerates idealized and unattainable attributes, and a **despised self**, consisting of personal qualities that one bewails and condemns. The idealized self leads to what Horney called the '**tyranny of the shoulds**', which are all the perceived things one hates oneself for not accomplishing. She characterized other defensive devices such as *externalization*, the *pride system*, and *self-effacement*.

22. Karen Horney did not develop a personality theory as such nor did she contribute research on personality. She is deservedly recognized, however, for her social psychological modifications to psychoanalytic theory—her recognition of the role of the family in personality development, her keen appreciation of the social nature of neurotic symptoms and defenses, and her forthright rejection of the offensive Freudian concept of penis envy.

TO TEST YOUR UNDERSTANDING

1. It's not easy to imagine Sullivan's view that individual personality can be seen only in a person's interactions with others. Explain how this can be and how it contrasts with more traditional conceptions. Where do you think it came from?

2. What is it that makes the schizophrenic person so difficult to understand and to treat? How does Sullivan's approach help?

3. Contrast Sullivan's stages of personality development with Freud's. Does Sullivan's conception of developmental stages represent an advance over the psychosexual stages? In what way? If you don't think it does, how does Freud's psychosexual scheme better describe personality development?

4. Of Karen Horney's contributions to the understanding of personality and personality disturbance, which do you think are the most outstanding? Defend your selection.

5. How does Horney's classification of neurotic needs help us better to understand neurosis? How does this approach to neurotic solutions differ from the psychoanalytic picture of neurosis?

6. What do these two theories do to give a picture of normal personality and its development? Do you see them as theories of personality or as theories of personality disturbance?

CHAPTER SEVEN

The Neo-Freudians:
Erich Fromm

Introduction

The theorist we now take up brought society and culture to personality formation and expression. Like Sullivan and Horney he gave psychoanalysis high marks for its extraordinary insightfulness into the vast complexities of human motivation. He may even have gone further than his neo-Freudian contemporaries in crediting Freud for his account of instincts, though he differed with Freud in the role instincts play in human behaviour. Yes, he said, there are the 'viscissitudes of instincts', but there are also intrinsic human needs that societies must meet, and families that raise children according to their society's general plan, and these things trump instincts. It was his belief that Freudian theory was unable to cope successfully with the personality–family–society relation that led him to construct a theoretical view of humankind recognizing the human situation and social context in shaping behaviour, thought, feeling, and personality deviation.

(Ullstein Bild/ The Granger Collection, New York)

Erich Fromm: Personal History

Erich Fromm was born into the family of a wine merchant in Frankfurt am Main in March 1900. His parents were orthodox Jews, practising a faith he dutifully subscribed to until he broke with formal religion at the age of twenty-six. Fromm's father was a moody man, and his mother suffered frequently from depression. Of his family and himself he said, 'I was an only child, and I had very neurotic parents. I was probably a rather unbearably neurotic child' (in Evans, 1966, p. 56). Fromm was exceptionally bright, entering the University of Heidelberg at eighteen and receiving the PhD in sociology at twenty-two. His interests were wide and varied; among his intellectual explorations, he delved into Karl Marx and was profoundly influenced. He turned to psychoanalysis, undergoing a training analysis in Munich and then becoming an analyst himself. (Psychoanalysts have long been required to undergo psychoanalysis with a senior analyst, a personal immersion in the theory.) He underwent his first analysis in 1926, after being accepted by the Berlin Psychoanalytic Institute, with Frieda Reichmann, a distinguished psychoanalyst ten years his senior; soon afterwards they were married. They separated amicably four years later.

There were two further training analyses in the late 1920s with distinguished analysts Theodore Reik and Hanns Sachs. Shortly thereafter, Fromm was invited to join the Institute for Social Research at the University of Frankfurt, where he taught psychoanalysis. He embarked with other members of the Institute on the study of authoritarianism, investigating authoritarian attitudes and personality characteristics in pre-Hitler German workers. He also helped to found the Frankfurt Psychoanalytic Institute. In 1933, in the wake of the Nazi rise to power, the entire faculty of the Institute for Social Research—Fromm included—fled Germany, moving first to Geneva and a year later to New York. After teaching briefly at the Chicago Psychoanalytic Institute, Fromm returned to New York, where he rejoined the reconstituted Institute and took up a post as visiting professor at Columbia University.

Fromm soon became part of a circle of accomplished young neo-Freudian psychiatrists living and working in New York in the 1930s and early 1940s. Among them were Clara Thompson, Harry Stack Sullivan, and Karen Horney. Fromm became associated with Horney's American Institute for Psychoanalysis and was involved in the founding of a New York branch of the Washington School of Psychiatry. His involvement with Horney became personal when the two had an affair that ended badly after Horney's institute terminated Fromm's training privileges because he did not have an MD. It is grist for your interpretative mill that Fromm's two youthful romantic dalliances were with psychoanalysts older than he (Horney by fifteen years). He did learn a lesson, evidently, since neither of his two following wives (wife number three died) was trained psychoanalytically nor much his senior.

During the 1940s Fromm taught at a number of universities and colleges, among them Michigan State University, Yale University, Bennington College, and New York University. He moved to Mexico for the health of his wife, writing, teaching, and conducting the research described later in this chapter, and he spent his last years in Switzerland, where he died in 1980. Fromm was a prolific writer. Among the most important of his more than twenty books are *Escape from Freedom* (1941), *Man for Himself* (1947), and *The Sane Society* (1955). The principal ideas we'll consider come from them.

Emphases

The Personality–Society–Culture Relation

In 1969, Philip Roth's novel *Portnoy's Complaint* appeared. The entirety of the novel takes place on a psychoanalyst's couch. Alex Portnoy, the hero (or, I should say, antihero) is guilt-ridden and as completely narcissistic as we could imagine someone to be. His free associations *are* the novel, a truly clever adaptation of the stream of consciousness. In a review of the novel for the 'New York Times Book Review', Josh Greenfield, the reviewer, was struck by the way Roth captured the western European and especially North American experience of guilt. Yes, he agreed, Freud had made a monumental contribution to our understanding of guilt, but he had also left us with a great problem: what is it about European and North American culture that exerts such a self-accusing influence on the shaping of individual personality?

It is this very problem, noted by Greenfield, that also puzzled Fromm and led him to an important cultural question: how did Western culture come to be the way it is?

How did it acquire the oddly mixed features of contemporary mass technological and industrial society—alienation, conformity, the politicization of violence, the turning of guilt into self-indulgence, and the wanton, wholly undisciplined pursuit of materialism?

Fromm did not stop there. His quest for greater understanding of personality and its deviations led him to ask how modern humankind got from the state of primitive humanity, intimately tied to nature and closely identified with natural forces, to an almost unimaginably creative society whose members have lost their relatedness to nature and to one another. In essence, these were Erich Fromm's deepest concerns. To frame them as questions about personality, we can say that he struggled to understand human character orientation, how it has evolved, and the relation of character development to society and to social change. He charged psychoanalysis, in which he was schooled and expert, with failing to meet the challenge of those questions. Psychoanalysis gives insight into individual motives and their development but deals conservatively and pessimistically with the trinity of person–family–society. Fromm rejected Freud's view that humans are inextricably trapped in a frustrating, sacrificing, denying relation to their societies, doomed in society's interest—the maintenance and preservation of the species—to subordinate their most insistent instincts (sex and aggression). You cannot, in Freud's conception of the person–society relation, become a socialized being without surrendering the immediacy of instinctual gratification.

Instead, Fromm argued, the essential issue is not the perversity of the instinct-driven individual but fallible human societies, incompletely designed, that fall far short in fulfilling intrinsic human needs, notably a need for **relatedness★**. In psychoanalysis, the instincts that must be subjugated and disciplined in the process of socialization—sacrifices to civilization, we may call them—are *bad*, morally wrong. So, what is repressed is the immoral, the wicked side of personality. Fromm contended that what is repressed and rendered unconscious in the process of individual socialization is not necessarily evil. Parents (and society as a whole acting through parents) may demand the repression or denial of innocent, nondestructive characteristics through the exercise of irrational authority. Here's Fromm on this point:

> Freud accepted the traditional belief in a basic dichotomy between man and society, as well as the traditional doctrine of the evilness of human nature. Man, to him, is fundamentally antisocial. Society must domesticate him, must allow some direct satisfaction of biological—and hence, ineradicable—drives; but for the most part society must refine and adroitly check man's basic impulses. In consequence of this suppression of natural impulses by society something miraculous happens: the suppressed drives turn into strivings that are culturally valuable and thus become the basis for culture. Freud chose the word sublimation for this strange transformation from suppression into civilized behaviour. If the amount of suppression is greater than the capacity for sublimation, individuals become neurotic and it is necessary to allow the lessening of suppression. Generally, however, there is a reverse relation between satisfaction of man's drives and culture: the more suppression the more culture (and the more danger of neurotic disturbances). The relation of the individual to society in Freud's theory is essentially a static one: the individual remains virtually the same and becomes changed only in so far as society exercises greater pressure on his natural drives (and thus enforces more sublimation) or allows more satisfaction (and thus sacrifices culture) (Fromm, 1969, pp. 24–5).

Moreover, he continued,

> It is not as if we had on the one hand an individual equipped by nature with certain drives and on the other, society as something apart from him, either satisfying or frustrating these innate propensities. Although there are certain needs, such as hunger, thirst, sex, which are common to man, those drives which make for the *differences* in men's characters, like love and hatred, the lust for power, and the yearning for submission, the enjoyment of sensuous pleasure and the fear of it, are all products of the social process. The most beautiful as well as the most ugly inclinations of man are not a part of a fixed and biologically given human nature, but result from the social process which creates man. In other words, society has not only a suppressing function—although it has that too—but it has also a creative function. Man's nature, his passions, and anxieties are a cultural product; as a matter of fact, man himself is the most important creation and achievement of the continuous human effort, the record of which we call history (1969, p. 27).

The Emphases and Major Concepts of Fromm's Theory

In Fromm's writings, what we see is less a formal theory of personality than a persuasive and often moving portrait of human societies and how they have failed, in each era of history and now, to meet what he regarded as the special, intrinsic needs of humans. We also see a picture of individual struggle to cope in unfulfilling societies.

Humans, individually, are alone and insignificant, and the awareness of that condition is terrifying. Human existence, then, is nothing less than a lifelong search to find a secure relatedness to others and to grasp the significance of life. Personality is expressed in the ways each of us conducts that pursuit. Fromm emphasized the self and its relations to society, and he portrayed the ways in which many people try to escape the awful loneliness and isolation with which we all have to contend. He described a number of character orientations, productive and unproductive, by which we are taught in families and in our societies to cope with the human condition.

With his emphasis on self and character orientation, Fromm was clearly an ego theorist. Yet he only grudgingly accepted Freud's basic formulation of personality structure. We won't see in his writings much at all of the antisocial urges that drive humans but get them into trouble with themselves and others. We will see major stress on ego and on defences, though he preferred to talk about how we escape from aloneness. He accepted the unconscious, repression, and intrapersonal conflict, but without Freud's insistence that these always involve defence against instincts.

The essential concept of the superego, or the simple term **conscience★**, which he liked better, was agreeable to Fromm, and the ego's relations to conscience were critical for him. Conscience can be subverted by some character orientations, as we'll see. He did say, however, that psychology is fettered by 'the restrictive influence of the libido theory, and particularly the concepts of *id, ego, and superego*' and would do well to get rid of them (Fromm, 1973, p. 84).

Fromm's Basic Propositions

Humans are, wrote Fromm, 'an anomaly . . . the freak of the universe' (1955, p. 55). Freaky in what way? Intellect, reason, self-awareness, and reflectiveness are attributes to marvel over, but they are also responsible for experiences of boredom, restlessness, and discontent with the lot one is dealt, and they carry with them, inevitably, awareness of ultimate death. The human's 'tragic fate' is to die before reaching his or her true potential. In *Man for Himself* he said of the human:

> He is part of nature, subject to her physical laws and unable to change them, yet he transcends the rest of nature. He is set apart while being a part; he is homeless, yet chained to the home he shares with all creatures. Cast into this world at an accidental place and time, he is forced out of it, again accidentally. Being aware of himself, he realizes his powerlessness and the limitations of his existence. He visualizes his own end: death. Never is he free from the dichotomy of his existence: he cannot rid himself of his mind, even if he should want to; he cannot rid himself of his body as long as he is alive—and his body makes him want to be alive (1947, p. 40).

Dichotomies

Human life entails some inescapable and potentially very painful confrontations, **dichotomies★** that Fromm labelled **existential** and **historical**. The most basic and difficult of existential dichotomies is 'life versus death'. Our lives are finite and are bound by a brief interval in the historical period in which we happen to live. These conditions of existence are immutable. Another existential dichotomy: how you made out in the genetic lottery. Are you endowed with genes that will make for a long, disease-free life, or have you been unlucky in inheriting genes for a life-damaging disorder like schizophrenia, say, or a susceptibility to heart disease?

Then, there are historical dichotomies. Peace versus war is one of them. In modern society, we seem unable to use our vast intellectual and technological resources for peace, nor do we well apply them to feed, clothe, and minister to less fortunate peoples. Conservation versus wastefulness is another. We are heedless of the long-term consequences of our inability to discipline the use of our diminishing natural resources. There are many historical dichotomies in our present age; you will be able to think of a great number of them.

Existential and historical dichotomies do change in the course of history. For instance, over the last hundred years, the average lifespan of humans in the Western world has increased from less than forty years to eighty. As changes occur to the conditions of human life, our relations to nature, and our relations with other humans, new dichotomies emerge. A major point of Fromm's, then, is that history is a dynamic flow, bringing new issues to the fore in the personality–family–society relation. This isn't a pessimistic view but rather a profoundly hopeful one. Marxist social theory leavens the darkly irreversible situation of humans envisioned by psychoanalysis. Fromm believed that with a better understanding of human needs societies might be shaped deliberately to create peace and fulfillment. As he said, 'The dynamism of history is intrinsic to the existence of reason which causes [the human] to develop and, through it, to create a world of his own in which he can feel at home with himself and his fellow men. Every stage he reaches leaves him discontented and perplexed, and this very perplexity urges him to move toward new solutions' (1947, p. 41).

The Special Needs of Humans

Humans, having the capacity to think, are distanced from nature by their cognitive gifts, and they are motivated by unique needs that set them apart from other animals. Nonhuman animals don't reason or contemplate a finite existence; they don't create or evolve an enduring culture. The relation of animal to nature is based on the instinctive equipment each animal species possesses. There is struggle for survival, but no deep worry, no lasting fear, no sense of triumph when a great problem is solved. Fromm did agree with Freud about elemental instincts: hunger, thirst, sex, and the self-protective fear that results in fight or flight. Instincts, though, regulate only the most primitive human behaviour.

Thus, in Fromm's view, psychoanalysis seriously confused instincts (sex and aggression) and their mode of expression. How instincts appear in thought, feeling, and action is culturally and socially determined and will differ from one culture, one society, to another. Humans are social creatures, the most helpless at birth and the most dependent on each other of all animals. They are individually alone and know it shortly after leaving the security of family and childhood. They experience boredom and can't help being anxious over what the future may bring. They are made unhappy by failure to accomplish what their minds tell them they can.

Said Fromm, '*The understanding of man's psyche must be based on the analysis of man's needs stemming from the conditions of his existence*' (1955, p. 25). In the human endowment are noninstinctual needs that derive from aloneness and isolation from nature. We may think of them as innate, as arising phylogenetically out of human liberation from instinctive action patterns, because they are universal, appearing in every culture and throughout history. Fromm listed five of these needs, though in his later writings he collapsed two of them into one.

- The first need is for **relatedness★**, a need for others and for close relationships. It is possible to escape from the loneliness and isolation of the human condition—or, at least, to try—and we'll consider escape mechanisms shortly. But the only real way to cope, the only way that has any prospect of security and comfort, is through loving relationships with others. In every one of us there is an imperative need for relatedness. As Fromm wrote, 'Love is not primarily a relationship to a specific person; it is . . . an *orientation of character* which determines the relatedness of a person to the world as a whole. . . . If I truly love one person I love all persons, I love the world, I love life' (1956, pp. 38–9). It is a given that to fulfill the need for relatedness we must find a *productive* (Fromm's term) way to relate to others; the alternatives are personally unfulfilling or socially destructive.

- In earlier writings, Fromm proposed a need for **rootedness★**, for an enduring sense of place and relationships within that place. This need is perhaps best revealed by social conditions that frustrate it. As an instance, in modern society, most of us don't live in the same place we were born in; we migrate. We go off to university, find jobs far from home, get different jobs in different places, marry people who are not from our hometowns, and raise children who will follow in our peripatetic footsteps. The need for rootedness is not well served in contemporary life. It has a close affinity with the need for relatedness, and Fromm came to collapse the two into a single, relationship-based need.

- A need for **transcendence★** recognizes the human necessity to rise above an animal level of existence and to change and improve our lives and environment. Frustration of this need may result in destructive, malignant aggression. As Fromm wrote in *Escape from Freedom*, 'The more the drive toward life is thwarted, the stronger is the drive toward destruction; the more life is realized, the less is the strength of destructiveness. *Destructiveness is the outcome of the unlived life*' (1969, p. 207).

- Even the highest of the nonhuman primates does not have, and is incapable of achieving, a **sense of identity**★. As humans, we all require a strong sense of self, a sense of personal being, a sense of personal independence that emerges (if not blocked by a denying society) as we gain freedom from our families in the process of growing up. Personal independence is frightening, though, and this fear can drive us to become dependent on, say, an all-powerful leader.

- We find meaning and purpose in our lives by satisfying the need for a *frame of orientation*, a belief system that makes our relationships, our efforts, and our place in society valuable and worthwhile. A belief system that prizes loving relationships, productive endeavour, reasoned thinking, and enjoyment is our great goal, but we would rather have a destructive frame of orientation than none at all. Submission to a tyrant, the cultivation of power and wealth for their own sakes, or narcissistic preoccupation are personally and socially unhealthy. They are irrational solutions to the problem of finding meaning.

A calendar illustration for the month of September from the illuminated *Très Riche Heures*, a fifteenth-century book of liturgical text, prayers, masses, psalms, and calendars. It shows grapes being harvested by peasants and carried into the Château de Saumur. In feudal society, peasants were tied to the estate of a nobleman such as the Duc de Berry, who commissioned the *Très Riche Heures*, and owed absolute fealty to him. For the serf, feudal society fulfilled needs for relatedness and place but offered only a hard, stultified life and nothing to satisfy needs for personal independence and transcendence (living beyond an animal level of existence). A receptive and passive-dependent character orientation was the likely result. (Réunion des Musées Nationaux/Art Resource NY [ART 152723])

The Role of Society

Human societies are created to fulfill these needs. That is the function of societies. On the heels of this proposition, however, Fromm said that no human society has yet existed that fulfills all them. Every society through history has failed to provide the conditions for the fulfillment of some or several needs. We can understand history and historical change by examining cultures and historical periods to see which needs were fulfilled and which stifled, and this will give us insight into character structure and the way it is related to society.

In *Escape from Freedom*, written when Nazi Germany was ascendant in its drive to conquer Europe, Fromm analyzed the sweep of Western history from medieval times to the middle of the twentieth century. His thesis was that the gaining of individual freedom after the long medieval era of absolute, monarchic control over the lives of the many by the very few, and the chaining of each person to a prescribed place in the social order had together created great fear and apprehension. 'The *abolition of external domination* seemed to be not only a necessary but also a sufficient condition to attain the cherished goal: freedom of the individual,' he said (1969, p. 18). But it wasn't. Freedom sounds unarguably wonderful, but it turned out to be double-edged, not wholly positive at all. Instead, with freedom had come the looming threat of aloneness, isolation, and vulnerability, a nightmare mobilizing efforts to escape. In the end, it had led to submission to authority and recruitment to the inhuman causes of totalitarian regimes.

The great tragedy of modern times began with a government so malevolently authoritarian that we still have trouble understanding it and how it could have risen. Fromm understood and said so in *Escape from Freedom*. Appealing to a people disillusioned and frightened by the loss of the First World War and the dreadful economic toll of the Depression, the Nazi government had made submission to absolute authority seem perfectly right by offering the prospect

A city street scene. What needs does this picture suggest modern mass society meets and fails to meet?(Alan Schein Photography/CORBIS)

of German ascendancy in perpetuity. They had held out the consummate method of escape from the awful uncertainties of the human condition that Germany's desperate post–World War I war situation had unmasked. What could be seen on the level of a whole society had to be true of a majority of its citizens. Fromm saw in Nazi Germany a prototype of mechanisms of escape from the terrors of freedom.

A Sane Society

We have a big question to confront in this: is there any possibility of inoculation against such mechanisms, on the level of a society or individually? Yes, said Fromm, there is. We can't, as we would with a communicable disease, inoculate every citizen against the disease of escape, and there certainly aren't enough psychotherapists to treat all the infected. But, with time and forethought, we could take an approach to rid humankind in succeeding generations of the most virulent escape mechanisms. To do so would be to create a sane society.

In *The Sane Society* (1955), From drew a blueprint of the kind of society that would nurture humans, make the transition from childhood to adulthood and independence a welcomed challenge to productivity and not a threat, a society that would foster co-operation and not competitiveness, a society that would foster free expression and not demand subjugation. Social sanity would meet each human need. He called his social design *humanistic communitarian socialism*. Its values would be humanistic ones, its social structure based on communities bringing people together, and its economics—in significant departure from competitive, exploitative capitalism—socialistic. Fromm, then, envisioned a society

Crowds of Hitler youth salute during a rally in Nuremberg, 1937. (© Hulton-Deutsch Collection/CORBIS)

...in which man relates to man lovingly, in which he is rooted in bonds of broth-erliness and solidarity...; a society which gives him the possibility of transcending nature by creating rather than by destroying, in which everyone gains a sense of self by experiencing himself as the subject of his powers rather than by conformity, in which a system of orientation and devotion exists without man's needing to distort reality and to worship idols (p. 362).

Impossible, you say. So have some critics (for example, Schaar, 1961). But Fromm didn't think so, and he believed that our modern technological culture could be transformed to fit (Fromm, 1968).

Character Orientations

How do we link society and culture with the individual? Fromm began with a distinctly Freudian idea, the concept of character structure, which we considered in Chapter 3. He accepted much of Freud's descriptive analysis of character structure but departed from it in his insistence that it is the family and how it exercises authority that shapes character, not the happenings of instinctual life and the attachments of libido. Families produce character orientations in children, and they get the specifications from their societies. Character orientations are the various ways in which people relate to each other and to their societies, and how they assimilate and acquire things—as well as intangibles like ideas and feelings—from others and produce things and intangibles themselves. Relating to others particularly expresses character orientation. Primarily loving relationships or sadistic, masochistic, destructive ones reveal character orientation and give strong clues about its family origin.

We can roughly divide Fromm's character orientations into two basic types: productive and nonproductive. The **productive character**★ is loving, committed, ethical, striving, and unwilling to surrender to mechanisms of escape. The productive character is **biophilous**★, a term Fromm invented to denote those having a love of life.

There are five **nonproductive character**★ orientations, three of which resemble Freudian character types.

- The **receptive character**★, like Freud's oral character, is a person who takes from and depends on others, a person who must be loved and cannot give love. Unlike the Freudian character, however, there is no implication of a failure to outgrow pre-genital sexuality; rather, this is a way of adapting to society that is learned in early family life. The same can be said of each of the other nonproductive orientations.
- The **exploitative character**★ orientation (corresponding to Freud's oral sadistic character) involves taking from others, by force if necessary, deceit, and an attitude that others are there to be used, manipulated, and capitalized on.
- To be a **hoarding character**★ (Freud's anal retentive character) is to find one's security in saving, keeping, and amassing, not in productive work and love. The hoarding character is orderly, a pedant, and can't stand disorder. He or she is an anal person, but anality does not cause the character orientation; it is just one more manifestation of a pervasive character expression.
- The **marketing orientation**★ is a modern character type without precedent in Freudian typology. It is the expression of automaton conformity, signified by the person as commodity: 'I am as the social exchange wants me to be.' The marketing

character has no stable, enduring values but is instead the personality counterpart of the economic marketplace. For such people, it is how they are packaged and labelled that counts, not what they are, believe in, and stand up for.

- The most socially disordered and malign of the nonproductive character orientations is the **necrophilous character★**, which fosters love of or attraction to death. Narcissism and malignant aggression are often associated features in people of this orientation. Hitler was unquestionably necrophilous in his character orientation.

Fromm believed that all the character orientations—productive and non-productive—are found in everyone, with one or two being dominant. A person may be fundamentally productive but show attributes of hoarding. In such a productive-hoarding individual, the drive to acquire capital and goods might stimulate productivity, making the person especially welcome in, say, the business world. You can see how various aspects of society, affecting the beliefs and childrearing of parents, might appear in the character orientations of children.

Devices to escape—unconsciously motivated mechanisms of self-protection from isolation and fear—are embedded in nonproductive character orientations. An orientation toward authority that may involve submission to a powerful leader (or a marital partner), masochism, or sadism toward those who are weaker (one's partner, or minority groups) is one common mechanism. Another is malignant aggression, aggression that serves no rational purpose. Aiming to strike out destructively at threats rather than to master them, it is ugly, and its escape motivation is beyond the conscious understanding of the person. In contemporary times, automaton conformity is the most prevalent of the escape mechanisms. 'It must be OK because that's what society wants' is the conformer's watchword.

Perspective 7.1   The Profile of a Marketing Character from Arthur Miller's Play *Death of a Salesman*

Willy Loman's world is closing in on him. Despite his efforts to keep the Great American Dream of success alive, he is failing, and all the wishful thinking and denial he can muster aren't helping. Past sixty and tired, he barely manages to make the mortgage payments on his house and the instalments on household appliances and his car. He regularly hits up his neighbour Charley for a loan to meet his insurance premium and to keep up the pretence that he has a decently paying job; the ledger is long on unkept promises to pay him back. His sons, now in their early thirties and home for a visit, bitterly disappoint him. Biff, the elder, who as a boy was doted on by his father, is a farmhand with no prospects, making thirty-five dollars a week. He is a petty thief, lost, a failure. Happy has a better job, a car, and an apartment but is committed to nothing but the pursuit of women and the least difficult choice possible. His mother calls him a 'philandering bum'.

Willy is a salesman and has worked for the same company for thirty-six years. He lives on the fiction that he has always been at the top of the ladder, but the truth is that he has never been more than average and is declining. He daydreams, talking loudly to himself about past glories. In his daydreams, his sons, especially Biff, a high school football hero, were 'magnificent'. In the following passage, he excuses Biff's theft of a football from school:

A scene from the 1958 CBC production of *Death of a Salesman*. In this daydream sequence, it is seventeen years ago. Willy imagines how close to his sons he was and what splendid boys they were, especially seventeen-year-old Biff, a high school football hero. (Courtesy of the CBC Still Photo Collection)

WILLY, *examining the ball*: Where'd you get a new ball?
BIFF: The coach told me to practice my passing.
WILLY: That so? And he gave you the ball, heh?
BIFF: Well, I borrowed it from the locker room. *He laughs confidentially*.
WILLY, *laughing with him at the theft*: I want you to return that.
HAPPY: I told you he wouldn't like it!
BIFF, *angrily*: Well, I'm bringing it back!
WILLY, *stopping the incipient argument, to Happy*: Sure, he's gotta practice with a regulation ball, doesn't he? *To Biff*: Coach'll probably congratulate you on your initiative!
BIFF: Oh, he keeps congratulating my initiative all the time, Pop.
WILLY: That's because he likes you. If somebody else took that ball, there'd be an uproar . . . (p. 31).

In Willy's fantasy, he is admired throughout his territory, 'well-liked':

WILLY: And they know me, boys, they know me up and down New England. The finest people. And when I bring you fellas up, there'll be open sesame for all of us, 'cause one thing, boys: I have friends. I can park my car in any street in New England, and the cops protect it like their own' (p. 31).

He has 'the greatest career a man could want': selling. He tells his sons, 'the man who makes an appearance in the business world, the man who creates personal interest, is the man who gets ahead. Be liked and you will never want. You take me, for instance. I never have to wait in line to see a buyer. "Willy Loman is here!" That's all they have to know, and I go right through' (p. 33).

It's personality, he says, that does it. To his daydreaming self he is Willy the great salesman, Willy the fond, indulgent father, Willy the family breadwinner, Willy the devoted husband.

But there's the reality. They've taken his salary away from him and for a while now he has been on commission only, just like a naive, untried beginner:

LINDA, *Willy's wife, to Biff and Happy*: When he brought them business, when he was young, they were glad to see him. But now his old friends, the old buyers that loved him so and always found some order to hand him in a pinch—they're all dead, retired. He used to be able to make six, seven calls a day in Boston. Now he takes his valises out of the car and puts them back and takes them out again and he's exhausted. Instead of walking he talks now. He drives seven hundred miles, and when he gets there no one knows him any more, no one welcomes him. And what goes through a man's mind, driving seven hundred miles home without having earned a cent? Why? When he has to go to Charley and borrow fifty dollars a week and pretend to me that it's his pay? How long can that go on? (p. 57)

Then, he's fired, no longer of any use to his company. His sons are ne'er-do-wells, and Willy has nothing to fall back on. His conformity to a shallow version of the Great American Dream has caught up with him. He has no answer to being fired, to this final assault on his self-esteem, no excuses he can make for the bums his sons turned out to be. Willy can't get beyond his conforming image of the good life. He cannot appreciate that he has no sustaining values that could see him through his adversity; he doesn't see that he has failed his sons, giving them neither a moral compass nor an enduring belief system to guide them and make their lives meaningful. Daydreams of a false past don't do it, and he has no defence against the attacks on him. The only thing he can think of is to kill himself so that Biff and Happy can make a new beginning with his insurance.

As the play moves to a close, there is the sound of a car speeding off. We have no doubt what it means. Willy's funeral is attended only by Linda, Biff, Happy, and friend Charley. At graveside, each struggles to explain why he destroyed himself:

BIFF: He had the wrong dreams. All, all, wrong.

HAPPY, *almost ready to fight Biff*: Don't say that!

CHARLEY, *stopping Happy's movement and reply, to Biff*: Nobody dast blame this man. You don't understand: Willy was a salesman. And for a salesman, there is no rock bottom to the life. He don't put a bolt to a nut, he don't tell you the law or give you medicine. He's a man way out there in the blue, riding on a smile and a shoeshine. And when they start not smiling back—that's an earthquake. And then you get yourself a couple of spots on your hat, and you're finished. Nobody dast blame this man. A salesman is got to dream, boy. It comes with the territory.

BIFF: Charley, the man didn't know who he was . . .

LINDA: Forgive me, dear. I can't cry. I don't know what it is but I can't cry. I don't understand it. Why did you ever do that? Help me, Willy, I can't cry. It seems to me that you're just on another trip. I keep expecting you. Willy, dear, I can't cry. Why did you do it? I search and search and I search, and I can't understand it, Willy. I made the last payment on the house today. Today, dear. And there'll be nobody home. *A sob rises in her throat*. We're free and clear. *Sobbing more fully, released*: We're free. *Biff comes slowly toward her*. We're free . . . We're free . . . (pp. 138–9)

Expressions of Personality: The Dream

Fromm *was* a Freudian, if a restive and sometimes recalcitrant one. He thought Freud's discovery of coherent and recognizable patterns of behaviour, *syndromes* of character structure and their reflection of childhood experience, was—his word—'brilliant', though he repudiated Freud on their origins and nature. He was a Freudian in his view of dreams, great avenues to unconscious mental life. Secular though he was, he wrote: 'the Talmud says, "dreams which are not interpreted are like letters which have not been opened."...' (1951, p. 10). In other words, they speak to us and are intended to be noticed.

As a Freudian, Fromm accepted the proposition that unconscious meaning in dreams is disguised and requires decoding of the manifest content to find its latent sense. He departed from Freud in noting that not all dreams are reflections of the unconscious. Like Adler, he thought dreams could represent struggles with seemingly intractable life problems, and he agreed with Jung that some dreams are not unconsciously based and do not come from deeply rooted sources. A young man, struggling to free himself from what he sees as his parents' insistence on determining his life, dreams of singing in a choir, which is seated. He suddenly stands up. The choir is gone, and he has a startling realization: I don't *have* to sing their song. On awakening, he understands the dream immediately. He sees its message as the beginning of a transformation: it's *my* future; I don't have to do what they want. Yes, there is both manifest and latent content, but the latent content does not contain a disturbing wish. It is, rather, what must have been germinating for some time.

Personality Development: How We Get to Be the Way We Are

Fromm dismissed the classical psychoanalytic picture of staged libidinal development, but he did agree with much of Freud's description of the stages, the difficulties that could follow from them, and processes such as fixation and the appearance of unconscious motives and repression. In Fromm's view, the outcome of development turns on how parents treat their children, not on how libidinal development is fostered or arrested. He regarded parents as teachers of their children, not as libido police enforcing demands for renunciation of certain expressions of instincts (the Oedipal wish is a prime example) and for delay of gratification and the strict discipline of others. While he departed from Freud on psychosexual stages, we must note that he recognized oral and anal character traits, and he did accept Freud's fundamental emphasis on childhood sexuality.

Children adapt to the situations their families create for them, with significant implications for the development of their personalities. Fromm called this **dynamic adaptation**, a process

> ...that occurs, for example, when a boy submits to the commands of his strict and threatening father—being too much afraid of him to do otherwise—and becomes a 'good' boy. While he adapts himself to the necessities of the situation, something happens in him. He may develop an intense hostility against his father, which he represses, since it would be too dangerous to express it or even to be aware of it. This repressed hostility, however, though not manifest, is a dynamic factor in his character structure. It may create new anxiety and thus lead to still deeper submis-

sion; it may set up a vague defiance, directed against no one in particular but rather toward life in general (1969, p. 30).

To highlight Fromm's developmental emphasis, we'll look at the Oedipus complex. Fromm agreed with Freud on three points:

- There is, undeniably, sexual interest in young children.
- Children can remain tied to their parents psychologically long after they should have attained independence. This, he acknowledged, is an irrational fixation.
- Father–son conflict can result from the son's unsuccessful rebellion against his father and his fears after his defeat. Here is a prescription for neurosis.

However, Fromm insisted, the Oedipal complex and the myth from which it takes its name are not, by definition, sexual. In the myth (Sophocles' tragedy), Oedipus's unwitting marriage to his mother is but one minor theme in the Oedipus trilogy. As Fromm contended, the dominant theme is not incest but the rebellion of the son (who kills his father); his marriage to his mother is '. . . *only one of the symbols of the son's victory, who takes over his father's place and with it all his privileges*' (quoted in Mullahy, 1953, p. 271). The Oedipus complex is not universal in human societies but appears only in societies that are patriarchal (Fromm, 1970). Only when fathers treat their sons as chattel, as possessions they own, are sons motivated to rivalry and rebellion. The son's battle may be irrational and one he cannot win, but it is very likely to occur when fathers fail to temper their exercise of authority.

In authoritarian families, parents may make demands on their children to accomplish what they themselves could not, living out their own unrealized ambitions through their children. This is an indirect but nonetheless real encroachment on a child's independence. In asserting their authority, authoritarian parents may resort to physical methods of control that we call abuse. There are other ways in which parents can damage their offspring: pessimism and lack of joy in life, narcissistic self-preoccupation, and—most damaging— necrophilia. Sadly, said Fromm, bad parenting is so common that 'one must believe that loving parents are the exception, rather than the rule' (1976, p. 45). Psychological damage inflicted in childrearing does not have to happen. If societies were to influence parents to raise their children gently and lovingly, helping them toward independence and fostering courage and enjoyment of life, neurosis and destructive social behaviour would diminish, productive character orientations would flourish, and societies themselves would change. We would see marked progress toward a sane society.

Research

In the early 1930s, Fromm began an unprecedented investigation of attitudes and character in German workers, antedating by twenty years the monumental post-war study of authoritarianism, *The Authoritarian Personality* (Adorno, Frenkel-Brunswik, Levinson, & Sanford, 1950). For this research, Fromm and colleagues at the Frankfurt Institute developed a massive open-ended questionnaire of 271 items that asked for written responses to questions on politics, leadership, powers of the state, the use of corporal punishment, the role and place of women, abortion, and many other issues. Some of the responses gave 'a simple, descriptive account' of the respondent; others were interpreted psychoanalytically to probe beyond the conscious, deliberate, and possibly deceptive replies. Fromm would have none of yes–no or true–false questions that must give, he thought, only a superficial picture of what respondents believed and felt. The investigators of *The Authoritarian Personality* would later take a huge step by developing a truly penetrating objective measure of authoritarian attitudes and prejudice; in the 1920s and 1930s, however, assessing attributes of personality was in its infancy.

Fromm uncovered startling evidence of authoritarianism in this sample of blue-collar workers. One might have expected a more productive character structure (early on, Fromm used the Freudian term 'genital') and more socially conscious (indeed, socialistic) attitudes among industrial, working-class men, but instead there was weak social concern and lukewarm support for the socialist cause. In fact, 10 per cent of the respondents emerged as sadomasochistic, potential recruits for a totalitarian regime. On the basis of these data, Fromm unhappily predicted that the Nazis would take over Germany (1984, 1986).

This truly provocative research was actually not fully published until after Fromm's death. It was derailed by the forced emigration of the Institute members in 1933, and it received severe criticism from within the Institute on both methodological and political grounds. Fromm withdrew the data in 1939. Methodologically, the clinical interpretation of questionnaire responses aroused worries about whether the study's findings could be reproduced by other investigators—that is, whether they were reliable. Politically, some thought that the findings could be misinterpreted to show that German workers were vulnerable to Nazism *because* of their socialism (Bonss, 1984).

Late in his career, Fromm came back to empirical research. In 1957, together with both Mexican and American collaborators, he undertook an extraordinarily detailed study of a small Mexican village (Fromm & Maccoby, 1970). The object was to investigate character orientation in peasant villagers, who make up more than half of the world's population. The research was addressed to

> those who are not dogmatically sealed off from at least being interested in a new venture: the application of psychoanalytic categories to the study of social groups, by the minute examination of the personality of each member of the group, by the simultaneous and equally minute observation of all socioeconomic data and cultural patterns, and eventually, by the attempt to use refined statistical methods for the analysis of the data (1970, p. 8).

Fromm had learned a painful lesson from the reception of his research on authoritarianism nearly thirty years before. He did revive the old questionnaire with modifications but added depth interviews, questions aimed at gathering detailed demographic and anthropological data, and projective tests (the Rorschach and Thematic Apperception tests). This time, there was careful attention to the question of reliability in the scoring of the questionnaire and the projective measures; Fromm spent a year training his raters in how to judge character orientation from the questionnaire and tests. Test interpretation was not helped by the fact that the villagers found the tests strange and worried that they were betraying things about themselves (seeing things in the Rorschach that no one else might see, for example). They didn't like it that the tests made them '"heat up their heads" (*me calienta la cabeza*) for no good purpose' (p. 275), and they tended to hold back.

Out of this great mass of data, Fromm and Maccoby found three major character types and located them in the social structure of the village.

- A nonproductive-receptive character orientation was the most prevalent, and it appeared in the lowest and most disadvantaged stratum. These were submissive and passive labourers, dependent on their employers; the men tended to feel insecure, were afraid of their wives, and often abandoned their families to become drifters and alcoholics.
- Nearly a third of the villagers were characterized by a productive-hoarding orientation. They farmed small plots of land, hoarding a portion of their crops and seed against the unforeseen—drought, insects, plant diseases. They were independent, suspicious, slow and methodical in their farming. With few pleasures in life, they would say things like, 'Love is to respect all that is human. It is a sentiment one can have even toward a plant. I work my land with love because my children and I live from the plants' (p. 121).
- The members of the smallest group were exploitative in character. Nonproductive men were frequently aggressive and destructive, not uncommonly fighting among themselves with knives or pistols. Women expressed their aggression in gossip mongering. A few of the exploitative were productive; these were villagers who as entrepreneurs and capitalists held the power and were the richest. They dominated other villagers, especially the nonproductive-receptive, taking advantage of them. Their large farms made dependent labourers of the landless.

Despite the vast collection of data and more sophisticated application of psychoanalytic principles and techniques, Fromm and Maccoby's sociopsychoanalytic study was largely met with indifference. Personality psychology in the 1970s had moved away from psychoanalytic concepts and their application to social psychological field studies. Concepts like character orientation were now seen as too encompassing and general to be useful, as too difficult to define and measure. A reviewer of *Social Character in a Mexican Village* wrote, 'The trouble is that since the entire process of clinical inference remains covert, undocumented, unanalyzed, there is no way to correct, refine, or revise . . . [the theory] on the basis of their findings' (Smith, 1971, p. 636). Had the Mexican research appeared in the late 1950s, when it was begun, its shortcomings may not have been detected and its influence would have been substantial. This wasn't due to a waning interest in Fromm's ideas but to changing research emphases in personality psychology and greater methodological sophistication. In 1970, interpretive clinical ratings just wouldn't do, even if they were made by the most qualified interpreters possible.

Fromm in Perspective

Erich Fromm's personality theory does not, in an important sense, stand on its own two feet. It has an indubitable Freudian stamp. We've reviewed his denial of psychoanalytic instinct theory, with its primacy of the sexual instinct in the development of personality, and his rejection of psychosexual stages, although with an acceptance of Freudian character structures derived from those stages. Fromm remains, though, a psychoanalytic theorist in his recognition of the early childhood origins of personality (and of neurosis), the unconscious, and mechanisms of defence. Fromm's psychology is an intimate derivative of the ego psychology of Freud.

One of his major contributions was to make the teachings of the family central. The ways in which we relate to others and to the societies we live in come from our parents' treatment of us, in large part how they exerted authority. Our parents, in turn, absorbed from their parents and their society the beliefs and feelings that governed their child-rearing practices. Childrearing creates character orientations, delineated by Freud but considerably modified and extended by Fromm. He invented names for them that capture their social nature—how character orientation determines our relationships with others and the social usefulness and satisfaction of our lives.

From a societal and cultural point of view, character orientation is the expression of the fulfillment or frustration of basic human needs. Fromm was very persuasive here in his analysis of needs arising from human intelligence and self-awareness and in his condemnation of society—his own as well as society throughout history—for letting human beings

A Fresh Look: Research Today

Fromm and Maccoby's probing field study into the character orientations of peasant villagers and farmers in rural Mexico got a cool reception, as we saw, and it might simply have been interred in the musty archives of dead and gone psychological research. But that hasn't been its fate, thanks to Fromm's co-author, Michael Maccoby, who has had the 1970 book reprinted (Fromm & Maccoby, 1996) and has carried on with the concepts and methods of the Mexican study and Fromm's earlier work. He applies the core ideas of character and character types to contemporary life in social organizations. A 'science of social character,' he calls it.

Social Character in a Mexican Village took as fundamental the principle that the ways in which social life is organized in every society define and shape the character of its people. Fromm had set out to show precisely that in his study of post-World War I German workers, and he applied the principle to the relation of individual personality to social organization in every society throughout human history. The authors of *Social Character* introduced a concept with visible roots in Darwinian natural selection, the concept of *social selection*. In any society, they argued, a few people with specifically adapted character types will rise to controlling positions at the top and modify the existing institutions of government, business enterprise, and group life to their

own benefit. In the process, the social character of all is changed. The small group of exploitative entrepreneurs in the Mexican village used their money, land, and power to further secure their wealth, making the nonproductive and the peasant farmers dependent on them. The nonproductive (peons) became, as Maccoby (2002) says, 'unhappy cultural misfits', passive, imbued with fatalism, chronically alcoholic. The small farmers (free campesinos), although traditional, conservative, and independent in their orientation, had little choice but to conform. The fabric of this village society, imposed by the dominance of the few, came to shape social character in the many.

So it is with life in the modern technological and industrial world. Maccoby has spent much of a career as a tireless advocate of Fromm's views and the confirmation of them that—as he is convinced—he and Fromm accomplished (see, for example, Maccoby, 1976, 1981, 1988). Extrapolated and speculative as the application of social character and social selection may be, he makes a case that contemporary business and industry, no less than the peasant village, exemplify the ways in which social character defines roles. Social character, as he says, is 'internalized culture', which 'provides not only ideals but also meanings of behaviour' (2002, p. 34). The great capitalist barons of the nineteenth and early twentieth centuries down. We want to take human societies and shake them severely for being so obtuse and self-serving as to starve us of need fulfillment. It doesn't have to be that way, he insisted; we could redesign the social world to meet our uniquely human requirements. If we only had enough people with productive and socially committed character orientations . . .

Fromm's views, then, are partly theory, a greatly revised, extended, and socialized psychoanalytic ego psychology. Beyond that, they represent the statement of a social philosophy, powerful and moving and eminently sensible—but not formal psychological theory. It is understandable that Fromm had a large popular audience and a strong clinical presence yet only a small influence on personality research. From theory, after all, we expect to derive propositions that we can test, but much of the body of ideas in Fromm's writings doesn't allow it. But this may not be the standard against which to measure the value of his contributions.

shaped not only their industries but the culture, the working life of everyone, and family living in North America. Men the likes of Andrew Carnegie, Henry Ford, Thomas Edison, and John D. Rockefeller were exploitative character types (productive narcissists, as Maccoby names them) who gained power by force of social character and used it to build huge industrial empires that controlled their workers, dominated governments, and became the model for the culture to emulate. Their personalities—exploitative, productive, and power-seeking—found opportunity aplenty in the emerging industrialization of the mid-nineteenth century. As they built and drove out competitors, they dictated the lives of their workers, social life in communities, states, and nations, and politics. How did they do it? By forceful personality at a time ready to adapt to them.

The last years of the twentieth century and the start of our own are not like that freebooting industrial capitalist era. The barons went too far. Their exploitativeness invited government intervention, and the nature of business and industry changed. Technology and the growth of a 'service society' intruded on factory and assembly line to alter work, family organization and the rearing of children, and education. Present-day productive narcissists—the Silicon Valley giants like Bill Gates and Steve Jobs, CEOs of such vast corporations as Ford, General Motors, or General Electric—are not different in social character from their baron forebears. Technology has transformed work and the organizations in which work is performed. The productive narcissist has not diminished in aim, social importance, and influence, but he—even she—now does it differently. More efficient incorporation of technical creations has replaced dependence on the unskilled worker, and downsizing—the replacement of human by robotic effort—is a watchword. Working men and women, perforce, adapt to the new organizational design. Some, however, the receptive-passive ones, can't, and become 'cultural misfits'. As Maccoby writes,

> Impatient with bureaucracies, the new productive narcissists downsized organizations and automated work to cut costs, maximize flexibility, and institutionalize continuous change in order to improve profits. Loyalty and years of service no longer guaranteed life-time employment. It was also more cost-effective to contract out services, sometimes to small entrepreneurial firms or reduce labor costs by exporting work to Asia and Latin America (pp. 35–6).

For Maccoby, however, the principles underlying social character and social explanation, seen clearly in the microcosm of the Mexican village, can be readily extended, without strain, to our modern lives. His research with Fromm, he has forcefully argued, forms the empirical basis of a science of social character with the widest of applications.

SUMMARY

1 Although they began with Freudian psychology and accepted its propositions of dynamic processes within the individual, the role of early experience in determining personality, and motivated cognitive distortions, the neo-Freudians would not accept Freud's emphasis on the sexual motive and his view of infantile sexuality. The fate of instincts is not decisive in forming personality, they insisted; personality is shaped by the family, which represents the beliefs, attitudes, and practices of society and culture.

2. Erich Fromm was born in 1900 in Frankfurt am Main, Germany. He entered the University of Heidelberg at eighteen, studying sociology, psychology, and philosophy, receiving the PhD in sociology at twenty-two. He turned to psychoanalysis, undergoing a training analysis in Munich, and was accepted as a student by the Berlin Psychoanalytic Institute, where he met Frieda Fromm-Reichmann, one of his training analysts, whom he later married. Two further training analyses followed. Joining the University of Frankfurt Institute for Social Research, he carried out research on authoritarianism in German workers. When the Nazis came to power, he fled the country, winding up in New York, where he became involved with a group of young neo-Freudians while teaching and practising psychoanalysis. He taught at a number of universities and colleges and over a period of forty years produced more than twenty books; the most significant of them is *Escape from Freedom*, published in 1941. He spent several years in Mexico teaching, writing, and doing research, and toward the end of his life moved to Switzerland.

3. Fromm's interest in Marxism led him away from classical psychoanalysis to study the relation of person to society and culture. He saw personality and personality deviations as profoundly influenced by society, reflecting social and cultural evolution. The great human problem, he said, lies not in the difficulty of controlling instinctual life but rather with inadequate societies that fall short in fulfilling intrinsic needs. Social processes, not instincts, shape personality.

4. The major concepts of Fromm's theory stem from the propositions that human existence is actually an unending search for secure relatedness to others and for meaning to life, and that personality is expressed in the way each person carries out that quest. He emphasized character orientations, which represent individual approaches to the problems brought about by social living and by the struggle to find meaning.

5. Humans, said Fromm, are 'an anomaly . . . the freak of the universe'. They are so because intellect, reason, self-awareness, and reflectiveness set them apart from all other creatures. They bring vast creativity but also the distress of boredom and discontent, and the frightening awareness of a finite life. Thus, human life entails inescapable confrontations with conditions of existence that Fromm called **existential dichotomies** and **historical dichotomies**. Life versus death is the prime example of an existential dichotomy. Historical dichotomies are opposing choices that characterize the era in which we happen to live; peace versus war and conservation versus wastefulness are examples. Fromm noted that while existential and historical dichotomies cannot be escaped, they undergo change (the human lifespan in North America, for example, has increased from forty to eighty years over the last century).

6. Human beings are distinctively endowed with five unique needs that stem from their individual helplessness, dependence on each other, and their social nature. They are universal and innate, having emerged in the long course of history as humans grew away from the instinctive action patterns that govern animal behaviour. The five needs are

   • **relatedness**—a need for others and for close relationships

   • **rootedness**—a sense of place and of relationships to others that accompany it

   • **transcendence**—to rise above an animal level of existence and to improve the conditions of human life

   • a **sense of identity**—a sense of self, personal being, and personal independence

   • a **frame of orientation**—a belief system that makes life understandable and meaningful.

7. The entire purpose of human societies is to fulfill these needs. However, Fromm observed that no society has ever fulfilled all of them; he pointed out that history and historical change become clear through the examination of cultures and historical periods to see which needs were met and which frustrated. Such

an analysis reveals character orientation and the way character orientation is related to society. His book *Escape from Freedom* analyzed Western history from the medieval period right up to the time he wrote it (1941). Its thesis is that liberation from feudal life and the individual freedom it conferred brought great fear of aloneness, isolation, and vulnerability, seen most clearly in the rise to power of the Nazis and their appeal to a disillusioned and frightened German public. With an understanding of human needs, Fromm proposed that it is possible to design a rational society that would foster growth, productivity, and fulfilment, a sane society he called *humanistic communitarian socialism*.

9. The concept of **character orientation** links personality and society. Fromm accepted much of Freud's analysis of character structure but rejected the instinctual emphasis. Instead, families create character orientations in children, the specifications coming from society. By character orientation, Fromm meant the ways people relate to each other and to society, how they assimilate things and intangibles, and how they produce things and intangibles. Character orientations may be divided into two broad types—*productive* and *nonproductive*. The productive character is *biophilous*—loving, ethical, striving, and not dependent on mechanisms of escape. There are five nonproductive orientations, three of which are derived from Freudian character types:

   - The **receptive character**, resembling the oral character, is dependent on others, a taker and not a giver, a person who is incapable of love.
   - The **exploitative character** uses and manipulates others for his or her own ends without regard for their welfare. This is an oral sadistic orientation without the pregenital instinctual implications.
   - Like the Freudian anal retentive person, the **hoarding character** seeks security through amassing possessions and an orderly existence.
   - Fromm identified a modern character orientation, the **marketing character**, seen in people who are automaton conformers, whose beliefs, values, and behaviour are shaped by the economic marketplace.
   - The most socially disordered and malign of the character orientations is the **necrophilous character**, a person who is attracted to death and destruction.

   Everyone will have some features of all the character orientations, productive and nonproductive, with one or two dominating. Escape mechanisms, such as submission to a powerful leader, sadism, masochism, or automaton conformity, are intrinsic to nonproductive character orientations.

10. Fromm accepted the Freudian approach to the dream as a road to unconscious mental life, but he observed that not all dreams have an unconscious meaning. He agreed with Adler that dreams may represent efforts to contend with life problems.

11. There is no developmental progression through libidinal stages in Fromm's theory, but the outcomes in character structure, fixation, and unconscious motivation do appear. Personality is determined by the way parents treat their children, especially how they exercise authority. Fromm's treatment of the Oedipus complex is illustrative of his approach to personality development. He agreed with Freud that we find signs of sexual interest in young children, that some children do not attain independence from their parents, and that father–son conflict is a fact in some families. However, he argued that the Oedipus complex is not principally sexual: it is an expression of the son's rebellion against an authoritarian father who treats him as a possession. Damaging family influence on children also comes from parental pessimism, narcissistic preoccupation, and pleasure in destruction. Bad parenting, although common, is not inevitable. If societies took a greater interest in how children are raised, Fromm argued, many of the social ills of life would diminish, and there would be progress toward a sane society.

12. Although Fromm was a clinical psychoanalyst, a critic of society, and a social philosopher, he also pursued empirical research. He studied the attitudes and personality attributes of workers in pre-Hitler Germany, applying a psychoanalytic interpretation to their responses to an extensive questionnaire. This provocative and controversial investigation foreshadowed the more sophisticated study of authoritarianism twenty years later. In the 1950s, Fromm and colleagues examined character orientation in a peasant village in Mexico, using anthropological data, questionnaires, interviews, and personality tests. They found three prevalent character orientations and

identified them with positions in the social structure of the village—nonproductive-receptive, productive-hoarding, and exploitative. While this research gives a close view of the relation of personality to peasant society, it is flawed by its reliance on clinical interpretation and its conceptual basis in a concept (character orientation) difficult to define and measure.

13. Fromm, a rebel psychoanalyst, turned from instinct theory and psychosexual development to fashion a sociocultural neo-analytic approach emphasizing unique human needs and the way societies meet or frustrate them. He saw the family, influenced by society, as the agent of personality development, creating character orientations in children and perpetuating both the good and bad in society. He was hopeful that societies could be reshaped to become sane societies that would fulfill every human need. In large part, Fromm presented a social philosophy, an analysis of the person–society–culture relation based on a greatly modified and socialized psychoanalytic ego psychology. It is not formal personality theory, but it is nonetheless admirable for what it is.

TO TEST YOUR UNDERSTANDING

1. Defend the proposition that Fromm is to the individual in society, culture, and history as Adler is to the child in the family.

2. What could Fromm have meant by the title of his 1941 book, *Escape from Freedom*? How can freedom be a negative condition?

3. What are the dangers to the individual of automaton conformity? What are the dangers to societies that encourage or even demand conformity?

4. Fromm was severely criticized for relying on psychoanalytic interpretation of questionnaire responses in his early research on authoritarianism in German workers. Many years later, when he studied character orientation in Mexican villagers, he again used principles and interpretation drawn from psychoanalysis. As a psychological scientist, was he captivated too much by the idea of taking his guiding ideas and procedures from the psychoanalyst's bag of tricks? Was his research justly criticized for not being reproducible by other investigators? Can you think of ways in which his studies of authoritarianism and character orientation could have been improved?

CHAPTER EIGHT

Ego Psychology: Anna Freud, Heinz Hartmann, and Erik Erikson

Introduction

Psychoanalysis did not remain static over the fifty years from Freud's first uncertainly formed ideas to the end of his life. It grew from a theory of neurosis, soon discarded, to a full-fledged theory of personality, a complete view of the nature of human nature. Freud was willing to introduce changes, even radical ones, when he concluded that the weight of evidence required them, and he developed and elaborated the major concepts of psychoanalysis as new clinical experience and his self-analysis demanded.

On a number of questions, however, Freud adamantly refused to recognize the infusion of ideas that departed from his conception, nor would he consider the data put forward in their support. He would not accept the deviations of Adler and Jung—extreme to be sure—and there were difficult and unpleasant confrontations with other members of the analytic circle.

One of those questions concerned the role of the ego. As Freud, late in life, reminded his readers, 'id and ego are originally one' (1964, p. 240). Although the ego is commissioned by the id as the executive of personality, responsible for choosing behaviour, selecting and attending to stimuli in the environment, fulfilling instinctual demands of the id and restraining others (the dangerous ones), defending against anxiety, and coping with the superego's moral strictures, it does so under exceptional handicap. Having no energy of its own, the ego is permanently indentured to the id. Freud recognized the difficulty besetting the ego, 'a poor creature owing service to three masters and consequently menaced by three dangers: from the external world, from the libido of the id, and from the severity of the super-ego' (1961, p. 56). He didn't blink at the implications of the ego's subservience—the perpetual conflict in which the ego has to hold its ground internally and with reality demands and proscriptions, and the stamp of the id, however masked, on every human activity. Although there was little hope for redemption offered in this picture of individual psychological war, Freud was unwilling to modify it. If that's the tough life of the ego, so be it.

A group of psychoanalysts, however, begged to differ. They have come to be known as ego psychologists. The first of them to be heard—and it was only a murmur, not unwelcome dissent and ideas foreign to the theory—was Freud's daughter Anna.

Anna Freud

The youngest of Freud's six children, Anna, was born in 1895. Her relationship with her father was special indeed. He was protective, indulgent, and analytic with her from child-

Anna Freud in 1925. (© Bettmann/CORBIS)

hood; she was 'the most gifted and accomplished of my children', as he wrote to a colleague (Gay, p. 434), and until she was well into adulthood it was clear that he had difficulty letting 'the little one' grow up. She trained as a teacher, but became captivated by her father's theory and determined to become a psychoanalyst. Freud encouraged her, having no reservations about lay analysis—the non-medical practice of psycho-analysis—and he psychoanalyzed her for several years while she was in her twenties. This breached a rule that Freud had laid down, one that would become in time a firm prohibition: do not analyze those close to you, for the complications of transference and countertransference are simply too great. When Freud was afflicted in 1923 by the cancer of the jaw that would torment him for the rest of his life, Anna took over his care. She became, increasingly, nurse, companion, confidante, secretary, and professional colleague. She was, in a word, indispensable.

Anna was soon a well-respected member of the psychoanalytic community, treating patients, writing scientific papers, and training new analysts (Erik Erikson, who appears later in this chapter, was her analysand). She specialized in the treatment of children, con-tributing both technique and a psychoanalytic understanding of child development and childrearing over the course of a long career that continued more than forty years after her father's death (she died at 87 in 1982). Her developmental contributions gave an expanded importance to the ego and to ego mastery of critical steps in the process of growing up. She added to the picture of ego defences, extending the list and portraying more clearly how defences develop and how the choice of a particular defence is related to the child's level of development. As she pointed out, free association is of very limited use in child psychoanalysis, but it is effectively replaced in the diagnosis of child neurosis by the analy-sis of defences (A. Freud, 1946).

One of her major contributions to child psychology was the concept of **devel-opmental lines**★ (A. Freud, 1965). Developmental lines plot the sequence of a child's growth from helpless dependence and a total absorption in self to greater maturity and independence. Among the six developmental lines she proposed is the oral pro-gression from nursing infant to a child who has mastered the choosing of food and eating independently. Others are the anal line, in which the child matures from dia-per-clad infant to child with self-control of elimination, and a sociability line of growth from complete egocentricity to the capacity for companionable relationships. We can see the implications for the developing ego in the way that developmental lines broaden the approach to personality growth well beyond the classical scheme of instinctual socialization.

Important to the psychology of the ego as these (and other) contributions were, we must remind ourselves that they were made by a fiercely loyal disciple. Anna Freud accepted all the fundamental elements of psychoanalysis—the dominant place of the instincts, infantile sexuality and the superordinate role of the sexual motive in personal-ity, the Oedipus complex, and the rest—that more severe critics and modifiers of the theory turned on and set out to change.

Heinz Hartmann

Modern ego psychology owes a great debt and perhaps its very existence to Heinz Hartmann. He is universally recognized as the father of the ego movement in psycho-

> **Table 8.1**   From Egocentricity to Companionship:
> One Example of a Developmental Line
>
> · The child begins with a selfish outlook on the world in which other children either do not
>   figure at all or are seen only as disturbers of the mother–child relationship and rivals for
>   the parents' love.
>
> · Other children are objects, like toys to be handled, pushed, sought out, and discarded
>   on the wish of the moment, with no positive or negative response expected from them.
>
> · Other children are helpmates in carrying out a desired task such as playing a game,
>   building with blocks and tearing down, getting into mischief. The relationship is
>   determined by the task and last as long as the task does.
>
> · Other children can be partners and are related to as distinct individuals whom the child
>   can admire, fear, or complete with, whom he loves or hates, with whose feeling he can
>   identify, whose wishes he recognizes and often respects, and with whom he can share
>   possessions on an equal basis.
>
> Source: Reprinted from *The Writings of Anna Freud*, Vol. 6, by Anna Freud. By permission of
> International Universities Press, Inc. Copyright 1965 by International Universities Press, Inc.

analysis. Viennese, Hartmann was born in 1894 to well-off and cultured parents. Like Freud and Adler before him, he attended the University of Vienna, receiving his MD in 1920. It did not take him long to gravitate to psychoanalysis, and he undertook the first of two training analyses with a distinguished member of the Berlin Psychoanalytic Institute, Sándor Radó. In the 1930s, he was a teacher and training analyst at the Vienna Psychoanalytic Institute and was signally recognized by Freud's invitation to continue his didactic analysis with him. Hartmann became one of Freud's favourite analytic pupils. Forced to flee Austria in 1938, he wound up in New York, where he opened

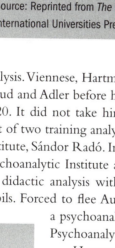

a psychoanalytic practice and became a faculty member of the New York Psychoanalytic Institute. He died in 1970.

Hartmann was not at all charismatic; his was a quiet, highly intellectual influence that began to make itself felt early in his psychoanalytic career. In 1939, he published *Ego Psychology and the Problem of Adaptation*, the book that set ego psychology on its course (Hartmann, 1958). In it he redefined the ego in both origin and function, but not rebelliously. Munroe made very clear that 'Hartmann and his associates in no slightest sense repudiate either Freud's instinct theory or his elaboration of the defence mechanisms of the ego. Rather, they *add* the concept of the primary autonomy of the ego functions (apparatuses) as operating to organize important aspects of the personality. To some extent, such organization occurs independently of the major instinctual drama . . .' (1955, p. 107).

The ego begins together with the id; as Freud said, they are not differentiated from each other. 'Strictly speaking,' Hartmann wrote, 'there is no ego before the differentiation of ego and id, but there is no id either, since both are products of differentiation' (1958, pp. 102–3). That may not seem to be a momentous idea, but it was. It partially frees the ego from the dominance of the id and gives it a degree of autonomy, a 'conflict-free sphere'

Heinz Hartmann (Duschnitz, Archives, New York Psychoanalytic Society and Institute Archive.)

in which the ego is free to act. The ego still serves instinctual purposes, must still serve its three taskmasters, and indeed matures because of conflict and mastery of it. But there are significant aspects of experience in which the ego is independent.

> We must recognize that though the ego certainly does grow on conflicts, these are not the only roots of ego development. . . . Not every adaptation to the environment, or every learning and maturation process, is a conflict. I refer to the development *outside of conflict* of perception, object comprehension, thinking, language, recall-phenomena, grasping, crawling, walking, and to the maturation and learning processes implicit in all these and many others (Hartmann, 1958, p. 8).

In loosening the instinctual bonds of the ego, Hartmann brought the ego closer to reality and gave it a self-directing role in adapting to and coping with the endless challenges that life brings. This was an ego of the normal person as well as the conflict-ridden neurotic, and it caught the imagination of psychologists interested in child development, perception, language, and thinking. The evidence was clinical, of course, an intuitive and imaginative reconstruction of infant and child development, but Hartmann also drew importantly on developmental psychology, reaching beyond the analytic situation in a way that many psychoanalysts were unwilling to do (see A. Freud, 1966, p. 22).

The major developments to come in ego psychology would build on Hartmann's contributions, placing the ego decisively in the social world. The next theorist we consider gave the ego new stature in the internal rivalry of personality structures, responsible for 'man's capacity to unify his experience and his action in an adaptive manner' (Erikson, 1963, p. 15).

Erik Erikson

Erik Erikson: Personal History

Erik Homburger Erikson was born in June 1902 near the industrial, intellectual, and scientific centre of Frankfurt am Main, Germany. He was the child of an extramarital liaison of his Danish mother and an unknown father. His mother moved to Germany shortly before her son was born, and settled, when Erik was three, in the German industrial port of Karlsruhe. Erik was ill, and was taken to a pediatrician, Dr Theodore Homburger, who treated him and promptly fell in love with and married his mother. Erik was raised as a Jewish child, following the religion of his stepfather, in the most comfortable of circumstances. He did not learn that Dr Homburger was not his real father until adolescence, and kept his mother's indiscretion and his unknown parentage a strict secret until he was sixty-eight.

He went to the Gymnasium in Karlsruhe, where he managed to graduate, although with poor marks. This high school education, a classical one with eight years of Latin, six of Greek, would give Erikson the only diploma he ever earned. He was through with school, quite unready for college; says his biographer, 'he felt at a loss, out of place and out of joint' (Coles, 1970, p. 14). And so he wandered

Erik Erikson (Courtesy of Jon Erikson)

through Europe off and on for several years, briefly attending art school, observing, recording in his notebook, sketching, and struggling with the great problem of the young—alienation—that he would capture in a compelling psychoanalytic portrait of identity a quarter of a century later in *Childhood and Society*.

Erikson was invited by a friend to join him as a teacher of art in a small Viennese private school founded by Dorothy Burlingham, a wealthy American patient of Freud and later a colleague of Anna, with four children to be educated. The other children were English and American, many in psychoanalysis. Erikson and his friend made the school a progressive jewel, a sweet, gentle, liberating oasis of learning and exploring in troubled and menacing late-1920s Austria. Here, for a close observer, the world of children opened up—their excitement in discovery and creation, and their psychosexual development. Erikson met the Freuds and many others in the Vienna psychoanalytic circle, and was in very short order invited by Anna to undertake a training analysis with her. He also studied psychoanalysis with a distinguished group of Viennese analysts. Concluding his analytic training in 1933, he was signally honoured by being made a full member of the Vienna Psychoanalytic Society, which conferred universally recognized membership in the International Psychoanalytic Association.

With the Nazis at the doorstep and anti-Semitism festering in Austria, Erikson decided that it was time to leave Vienna. On the eve of his departure, he gave himself a new identity. He had been Erik Homburger, having adopted his stepfather's surname; he now became Erik Homburger Erikson. With his American wife, Joan, Erikson left Germany first for Denmark and then, after failing to obtain Danish citizenship, for the United States. Hanns Sachs, Karen Horney's analyst, helped him to open a practice as the only child analyst in Boston. Within a decade, he had been appointed to positions at Harvard, Yale, and the University of California at Berkeley. His appreciation of personality development, the identity crisis of adolescence, and the role of society and culture in personality formation and neurosis was greatly enhanced by studies of undergraduate students at Harvard through the Harvard Psychological Clinic, field research on two Native American societies, and research on infant and child development; Yale and Berkeley abetted the latter two.

The year 1950 saw the publication of *Childhood and Society*, a remarkable book that had a profound influence on psychoanalysis, in psychology, and in popular culture, particularly among youth. It is, like all of Erikson's work, exquisitely written, 'Freud in sonnet form', as one of his colleagues said. Before it, personality theory had hardly attended to ego psychology, but that now changed.

And, in 1950, when McCarthyism gripped America and the University of California required the signing of a loyalty oath, Erikson resigned his professorship in protest. He returned to Massachusetts, mainly to clinical practice with deeply troubled adolescents, and to the study of identity. Ten years later, Harvard invited him to return as professor of human development. He retired in 1970, dividing his time between California and Massachusetts, in Cape Cod and Cambridge. Erikson died in Harwich, Massachusetts, in 1994.

Beyond *Childhood and Society*, his books include *Identity: Youth and Crisis*, *Insight and Responsibility*, *Toys and Reasons*, *The Life Cycle Completed: A Review*, and two psychohistories, *Young Man Luther* and *Gandhi's Truth*. His study of Gandhi was awarded both a Pulitzer Prize and a National Book Award. His last book was a collaborative effort with his wife and a third author: *Vital Involvement in Old Age*.

Emphases

Erikson himself, in the prefatory comments to the first edition of *Childhood and Society,* offers the best introduction to the influences on his ego-psychoanalytic theory:

> I came to psychology from art, which may explain, if not justify, the fact that at times the reader will find me painting contexts and backgrounds where he would rather have me point to facts and concepts.... I began my career as a child analyst. In this I was guided by Anna Freud and August Aichhorn. I graduated from the Vienna Psychoanalytic Institute.... Henry A. Murray and his co-workers at the Harvard Psychological Clinic gave me my first intellectual home in this country. Over the years I had the privilege of long talks with anthropologists, primarily Gregory Bateson, Ruth Benedict, Martin Loeb, and Margaret Mead. Scudder Mekeel and Alfred Kroeber introduced me to the field (1963, p. 17).

The Ego and Ego Development

Erikson was a dedicated psychoanalyst, accepting Freud's views on personality structure, the ultimate dependence of ego on id, infantile sexuality, and the vicissitudes of the instincts in the course of their socialization. However, like Hartmann, who was one of his teachers, he saw the ego in relation to society, or as he put it, 'the ego's roots in social organization' (Erikson, 1963, pp. 15–16). To Freud, as we know, personality development comes to an end with the last decisive psychosexual stage. With the Oedipus complex resolved and the superego formed, with all the constituents of personality in place and their relations in each individual person basically determined, there is nothing further to be done; the picture of the person for the rest of his or her life can be drawn from this childhood outline. Erikson, on the other hand, saw that societies exercise a great influence on how the heritage of infancy is expressed. Societies shape the ego, not only in its earliest developments but in the course of the lifespan. We humans cannot be rid of infancy and childhood's instinctual demons but, Erikson said, 'societies lighten the inescapable conflicts of childhood with a promise of some security, identity, and integrity. In thus reinforcing the values by which the ego exists, societies create the only condition under which human growth is possible' (1963, p. 277).

We thereby derive one of the most significant features of Erikson's ego psychology: there is ego development throughout life, from infancy to old age, as critical events (crises) of each life stage present themselves. These he identifies as **psychosocial★** crises to emphasize that they originate in psychological (ego) processes and in the social environment.

Epigenetic Development

How do we characterize the psychological development of infant and child from birth, from the point at which there is an independent organism that must rely on its own native equipment (reflexes, for example) to survive? Do we require a whole new set of principles that begin at birth, principles that supersede those that apply to understanding embryological development? Not at all. Erikson turned to embryology for a model of the way human infants, children, and, indeed, adults grow. This was **epigenesis★**, which describes the emergence of an embryonic organism from unorganized, undifferentiated protoplasm, and a regular, sequenced programming of organ development.

Epigenetic psychological development tells us 'How the maturing organism continues to unfold by developing not new organs, but a prescribed sequence of locomotor, sensory, and social capacities . . . by which an individual becomes a distinct person' (Erikson, 1963, p. 66). The psychosexual stages exemplify this process, but Erikson thought particularly of the ego, id's child, evolving according to a 'ground plan'. If we restrain the hand of an infant in the first, oral-sensory stage of development, she struggles 'angrily' to free it, a kind of elemental expression of autonomy. We won't, however, see autonomy appear full-grown until the second, muscular-anal stage a year and more later. Each stage in the life cycle presents its own special challenges for the ego to struggle with and master. Epigenesis is not a psychosexual view, then, but a way to cast life-long ego development.

Zones, Modes, and Modalities

Psychosexuality unfolds in its succession of erogenous zones—oral, anal, and phallic-genital—and each bodily zone has its own **mode★** of expression. In very earliest infancy, the mode of the oral zone is incorporative; by the second year, the dominant mode is eliminative, then retentive, accompanying the newly matured control of the musculature of elimination. Developmentally, Erikson considered five modes:

- *incorporative*—taking in both nourishment and sensation
- *incorporative*—the active, biting, teething oral mode
- *retentive*—the ability to hold in, as with feces
- *eliminative*—the mode of letting go
- *intrusive*—the aggressively exploratory moving-in on adults' and other children's space, activity, bodies (as with physical attack); active locomotion

We understand these to be the primary modes of the psychosexual stages, but Erikson pointed out that they can appear as auxiliary modes at any stage. They are available nearly from the beginning, but each one becomes preeminent only at its appointed time. He wrote of the first oral stage:

> But while the mode of incorporation dominates this stage, it is well to get acquainted with the fact that the functioning of any . . . body zone requires the presence of all modes as auxiliary modes. Thus, there is in the first incorporative stage a clamping down with jaws and gums (second incorporative mode); there is spitting up and out (eliminative mode); and there is a closing up of the lips (retentive mode). In vigorous babies even a general intrusive tendency of the whole head and neck can be noticed, a tendency to fasten itself upon the nipple and, as it were, into the breast (oral-intrusive) (Erikson, 1963, p. 73).

Modalities★ are the ways in which societies and cultures deal with zone-mode features of the psychosexual stages. Every human society must bring the powerful, sexualized instincts behind ingestion, elimination, and sexual yearning under control, each subjecting behaviour to its own form of discipline. Social modalities generalize modes to many interactions in the social environment. The social modality of the oral-sensory period, which will have its own expression in different cultures, is captured by the verb 'to get'—that is, to receive (maternal nurture and nurturance). 'One may say . . . that in thus *getting what is given*, and in learning to *get somebody to do* for him what he wishes to have done, the baby also develops the necessary ego groundwork to *get to be a giver*' (Erikson, 1963, p. 76). How this reciprocity with the mother works out is socially determined by the feeding and weaning practices of individual mothers and of the cultures in which they themselves were nourished. Social responsiveness at each stage is similarly shaped by the way mothers and societies cope with zone-mode imperatives.

In the course of psychosocial development, one stage stands out. It is adolescence, and its crisis has to do with the end of protected childhood and entry into the adult world. As adolescents pass through this stage they gain a sense of identity—of who they are, of the beliefs they have arrived at and made their own, and of the commitments they must make to a role in society, especially the demanding choice of an occupation. Adolescents may stumble in this stage, with identity confusion and alienation as the result. In the view of many, this is the outstanding emphasis in Erikson's ego psychology.

The Major Concepts of Erikson's Ego Psychology

The Eight Ages of Man

Erikson saw human life in stages—the 'eight ages of man' he called them—appearing successively in response to biological developments, the emerging qualities of the ego, and social institutions. As we review the eight ages, beginning at birth and concluding with the end of life, we shall see the nuclear crisis at each age, how it challenges the ego, and how success or failure affects ego development and coping. Although in Erikson's presentation these are stages, it is important to appreciate that they are not sharply delineated, each emerging at a specific time. Instead, they are nodes, concentration points, whose appearance is not exact and may vary from one individual to another. The order, however, is invariant. In the nodes of infancy and early childhood, there is a coming together of zone, mode, and modality to shape the developing ego.

Table 8.2	Zones, Modes, and Psychosocial Crises		
Age	Psychosexual Stage	Mode	Psychosocial Nuclear Crisis
Infancy (to 1 year)	Oral-Sensory	Incorporative (first passive, then active)	Basic Trust vs Mistrust
Early Childhood (1–3)	Muscular-Anal	Eliminative-Retentive	Autonomy vs Shame and Doubt
Play Age (4–5)	Locomotor-Genital (Phallic)	Intrusive/Feminine Inception	Initiative vs Guilt
School Age (6–12)	Latency		Industry vs Inferiority
Adolescence (12–20)	Puberty and Genital Maturity		Identity vs Identity Confusion
Young Adulthood (20–30)			Intimacy vs Isolation
Adulthood (30–65)			Generativity vs Stagnation
Maturity (65+)			Ego Integrity vs Despair

1. Trust versus Mistrust

It is curious to identify the very first crisis in life as one of establishing in the infant a sense of basic trust or its cataclysmic opposite, basic mistrust. Trust and mistrust seem to us to be mature attitudes, products of observation and judgement. Erikson, however, used these terms to mean an elemental experience of comfort and security provided by the mother, or else uncertainty and anxiety over the mother's unpredictability and too much unrelieved discomfort—the first discovery of an immature ego. This is a sense that everything is (or is not) 'all right', the reassurance of the medley of sights, sounds, and bodily sensations that come together with 'a feeling of inner goodness' (or its opposite) that the mother brings. So, it is trust or mistrust of the mother that the infant learns, and it is also the baby's trust that he or she can let mother out of sight and not be overwhelmed by anxiety. Erikson reminded us that the quality of maternal care is decisive in establishing the baby's trust, not how often she appears, the amount of milk the baby ingests, or how demonstrative she is. To be sure, the quality of mothering is not easy to define; we will look for a 'sensitive care of the baby's individual needs and a firm sense of personal trustworthiness' (1963, p. 249).

As the baby learns to trust, he or she takes the first step toward a sense of ego identity, simple and basic, but one on which all later ego development depends. There is an inevitable experience of loss and abandonment when babies are left alone to sleep, when mothers don't arrive at the moment they awake, or when mothers don't know what to do to soothe their crying infants. This is a part of life, this 'universal nostalgia for a paradise forfeited' (1963, p. 250). Basic trust gives the infant the ego strength to endure deprivation, and it is the foundation for acquiring the virtue, as Erikson called it, of *hope*—'the enduring belief in the attainability of fervent wishes, in spite of the dark urges and rages which mark the beginning of existence' (1964, p. 118). Basic mistrust is a poor and sad preparation for social life, meaning as it does that no one can be depended on and that the fulfillment of one's needs is forever in danger.

2. Autonomy versus Shame and Doubt

In the second year, there are new muscular capacities and cognitive abilities, and the young child has to acquire self-control. The prototypical conflict between child and parents is toilet training, which requires the child to give up a stubborn insistence on eliminating when he or she feels like it and to accept the rituals of elimination. Toilet training has the potential in Western society to become a confrontation, a power struggle, between parents and child because of the disgust we feel over excretory products. Messy children often make angry parents, and it is angry parents who create and fuel the battle. The small child cannot win, and wilfulness, a hollow victory, is more likely to result in feeling shameful and self-doubtful (because parents are accusing and damage the child's self-esteem) than in achieving genuine autonomy. There are many other faces to growing autonomy—mobility, getting into things, and testing the limits of naptime and bedtime are just a few for harried parents to cope with.

The parental task is to impose socialization demands (toilet training, for example) and set limits in a firm, reasonable, and reassuring way, so that children experience pride in being able to control themselves. That's the sense of autonomy of which Erikson spoke. Shame and doubt leave children feeling exposed, 'caught with their pants down' as our saying goes, and unsure of their abilities and independence. Erikson summed it up well in saying, 'From a sense of self-control without loss of self-esteem comes a last-ing sense of good will and pride; from a sense of loss of self-control and of foreign over-control comes a lasting propensity for doubt and shame' (1963, p 254). The virtue associated with this stage is *will*★, a self-determination and understanding that one can make choices, including the choice to refrain, the choice to obey rule and social ritual.

3. Initiative versus Guilt

Children between three and six, approximately, have grown beyond autonomy. They are more active and verbal, taking on new things, planning and anticipating in their play and interactions. Their initiative is accompanied by a new genital sexuality that is sex-typed—in Erikson's terms, **phallic intrusiveness**★ in boys and a feminine mode of **inception**★, by which he means a softer, less aggressive way of relating. 'For the girl at this stage matches the boy's potentially more vigorous muscular life with the potentiality of richer sensory discrimination and with the perceptive and acceptant traits of future mother-hood' (1963, pp. 88–90). He affirms, then, that anatomy destines. Both sexes have to come to terms with their newfound urges, immature and inchoate as they are. There are, after all, wishes—'so simply and trustingly expressed in the boy's assurance that he will marry his mother and make her proud of him and in the girl's that she will marry her father and take much better care of him' (1963, p. 90)—that have to be disciplined and put away. Parents can deal with this infantile genital stage and with the exuberance that accompa-nies it in a gentle and reassuring but also decisive way, rewarding initiative, pride in self, and sense of purpose. But, if they become overbearing, condemning, or ridiculing, they may inculcate the crippling experience of guilt, which children sometimes try to deflect by aggressiveness and resentment of their parents. Erikson rightly labelled this the 'play age', for it is in play that children explore reality and try on new roles by their imitation of adults. *Purpose* is the virtue that successful navigation of this stage confers.

4. Industry versus Inferiority

The play age gives way at age six to the school age, Freud's latency period. It is a 'lull before the storm of puberty' (Erikson, 1963, p. 260), but its significance is far greater than the temporary submergence of sexuality. Before entering on a productive life as a worker and parent, the child must first pass through a school life, acquiring skills and learning that being recognized and rewarded depend on being productive. Even chil-dren who come from cultures with little formal education will undergo a period of instruction in the knowledge necessary to become full-fledged members of society. Learning to put effort into tasks, to follow the formalities of learning, and to co-operate with others—these are the critical elements in developing industry and acquiring the virtue of *competence*. The child who fails here loses faith in his or her own abilities and loses status among peers. These are devastating discouragements, and they lead to an encompassing sense of inferiority. Parents have the necessary task of preparing their children for school, and schools must not let children down by giving up on those who learn slowly or whose families have sent them off with a bad start.

5. Identity versus Identity Confusion

If all stages have to be lived through and their nuclear crises resolved in one way or another, then no stage can be more important than another. However, apart from the first, whose lifetime significance is profound and enduring, there is one stage that deserves serious consideration, the stage that stands at the threshold of adulthood. It is adolescence, whose turbulence everyone knows of. But commonplace or not, the transition to adult responsibilities and life comes at a time of rapid physical growth and sexual maturity. 'Genital puberty floods body and imagination with all manner of impulses, . . . intimacy with the other sex approaches and is, on occasion, forced on the young person, and . . . the immediate future confronts one with too many conflicting possibilities and choices' (Erikson, 1968, pp. 132–3).

No wonder it can be stormy. The years from twelve to twenty seem like a generous interval in which to get ready, but the tasks loom very large and the consequences are momentous. Erikson summed up what must be achieved in one word: **identity★**. Ego identity means making decisions about who one is and what one will become; these decisions result in commitments, and there are three of them. The most difficult is the commitment to an occupation and to the preparation for it; let it slip and the cost in missed opportunities may be enormous. Not much easier is the approach to intimacy with a life partner. There is no formal preparation in this case, but the consequences of a poor choice (or no choice at all) can be severe. Then, there is a belief system, an ideology to guide one's life. Religion, politics, morality in daily living, which authorities to believe and what one owes to them in the way of allegiance and conformity—these are some but hardly all of the ideological commitments that adolescents will need to make before they are fully adult.

The basics of ego identity are established in all the preceding stages by the resolution of their respective nuclear crises. The commitments that signify the achievement of ego identity begin with parents, the models they provide and the urgings they press on their children. Simply to accept what parents have to pass on, however, is not enough. Wiser and more experienced they may be, but parents cannot give their own commitments to their adolescent children. Some do, of course, and some adolescents accept their parents' teachings, a too-ready acceptance called *foreclosure*. The problem, though, is that they are unexamined and unchallenged, and Erikson maintained that the commitments of youth have to undergo the scrutiny and questioning that is at the heart of this stage's nuclear crisis. Many teenagers postpone the necessary struggle over choice and belief, paying a price in prolonged anxiety and doubt. This is a *moratorium*, 'a psychosocial stage [in itself] between childhood and adulthood, and between the morality learned by the child and the ethics to be developed by the adult' (Erikson, 1963, p. 263).

At some point in the crisis period, many adolescents experience identity confusion (or sometimes, in Erikson's terminology, role confusion). The decisions seem too awesome to make, giving in to sexual urges too frightening, actively confronting what one believes too confusing. Afraid of making mistakes and not certain whom to believe, the adolescent can be wildly variable—self-conscious and withdrawing, exuberant and full of abandon, captivated by one cause or another. Identity confusion is painful, and in some it endures for a long time—into the twenties and beyond. We may guess that dropping out of school, drug use, indiscriminate sexual behaviour, and confrontational and rebellious relationships with parents and teachers are signs of identity confusion.

Most distressing to parents, perhaps, is a teenager's development of a negative identity, 'an identity perversely based on all those identifications and roles which, at critical

I'M A LITTLE TEAPOT, SHORT AND STOUT...

MANKOFF

| THE LITTLE ENGINE THAT HAD AN IDENTITY CRISIS |

stages of development, had been presented to them as most undesirable or dangerous and yet also as most real' (Erikson, 1968, p. 197). A negative identity may say to parents, to authority, to adult society in general, 'Anything you're for, I'm against,' or it may project the source of a troubled parent–child relationship on the parents themselves as in the claim, 'You're the problem, not me.'

We know that many adolescents can be thoughtless and hurtful in their exploration and testing of relationships. As Erikson wrote,

> Young people can also be remarkably clannish, and cruel in their exclusion of all those who are 'different', in skin colour or cultural background, in tastes and gifts, and often in such petty aspects of dress and gesture as have been temporarily selected as *the* signs of an in-grouper or out-grouper. It is important to understand (which does not mean condone or participate in) such intolerance as a defense against a sense of identity confusion. For adolescents not only help one another temporarily through much discomfort by forming cliques and by stereotyping themselves, their ideals, and their enemies; they also perversely test each other's capacity to pledge fidelity (1963, p. 262).

The virtue to emerge from the identity crisis is *fidelity*, meaning the readiness to be faithful to commitments, ideals and values, and other people. Fidelity emerges in part from the group identifications of the adolescent and the proving ground of loyalty tests. Its appearance is another important sign of identity achievement.

6. Intimacy versus Isolation

The decade from twenty to thirty, approximately, brings the end of preparation and the formal beginning of a career, a settled way of life, and, most important, the establishment of both close and intimate relationships. The pattern of friendships is laid down and, for most, an intimate partner is chosen. Thus, the virtue of this stage is *love*, and the fateful alternative is isolation. Emerging from the preceding stage with a weak identity, the young person may be incapable of intimacy and unable to form meaningful relationships with others. Isolation in this stage does not bode well for friendships and closeness with a partner in the future.

Erikson issued a reminder that the stage of intimacy versus isolation is decisive in achieving Freud's formula for a successful life: '*Lieben und arbeiten*', love and work. Each must have its place; work cannot encroach on a loving relationship, and an enduring relationship depends in part on productive and satisfying work. Parasites and slackers don't make good marriage partners. As Erikson said,

> the utopia of genitality should include:
> 1. mutuality of orgasm
> 2. with a loved partner
> 3. of the other sex

4. with whom one is able and willing to share a mutual trust
5. and with whom one is able and willing to regulate the cycles of
   a. work
   b. procreation
   c. recreation
6. so as to secure to the offspring, too, all the stages of a satisfactory development (1963, p. 266).

7. Generativity versus Stagnation

This stage encompasses the years of maturity, from thirty to the typical retirement age of sixty-five, and it demands sustained productivity and accomplishment. Generativity also means 'concern for establishing and guiding the next generation' (Erikson, 1968, p. 138). It is not only work, then; being a model for one's children and teaching them (or finding a generative substitute) is an integral part. To do that requires *care*, the virtue of the stage.

Opposed to generating and caring is stagnation—slouching in front of the television set, beer in hand, life going by in an unending succession of mindless sitcoms and football games, brushing the children off, putting in time on a dead-end job. That's a stereotype, of course, but it is one that does fit a number of people who haven't done the homework for a mature and contributing life.

8. Integrity versus Despair

Integrity sustains the last years of life with the knowledge that one has done one's part, held on to a standard of accomplishment and loving, and will leave—to one's children and to others—a world that is as much better as one could help to make it. A tall order this, to believe in the face of the end of life that the style of living one chose was right and good and possessed of meaning. A sense of completion and the virtue of *wisdom* give dignity to old age. The terrible alternative is despair, which says that there is no longer time to go back and do it again, to make the missed choices, to act—as one failed to do—with courage. Cultures make different provisions for the aged. There are some that revere the wisdom of the aged and honour them. North America, sadly, isn't one of these. If anything, old people are patronized because of their loss of mental quickness, putting integrity, except for the hardiest, beyond reach.

Ritualization, Ritual, and Ritualism

Irrespective of the cultures in which we live, we humans are creatures of **ritual★**. Erikson added a layer to the scheme of life cycle development when he proposed that processes of cultural and social ritual add to and influence each stage. Rituals reveal a cultural identity in the way that social interactions are conducted at each developmental stage, from mothering and the baby's response to the treatment of the elderly and the acceptance in old people of their life contributions.

There are three faces to ritual. **Ritualizations★** characterize significant interactions at each stage. They often have a playful aspect in the sense of exploring the new and untried. Formal rituals of adulthood are exemplified by such social occasions as weddings, christenings, funerals, and graduations. **Ritualism★** is a pathological excess of ritualization

Table 8.3   Ritualization, Ritual, and Ritualism

Stage	Ritualization	Ritual	Ritualism
Infancy	Numinous	Moving experience with others	Idolism
Childhood	Judicious	Judging others (e.g., court of law)	Legalism
Play Age	Authenticity	The dramatic in adult life	Impersonation
School Age	Formal	Work and accomplishment	Formalism
Adolescence	Ideology		Totalism
Young Adulthood	Affiliation		Elitism
Adulthood	Generational		Authoritism
Maturity	Integral		Sapientism

that is not mutual and serves only the needs of the individual. Adulation of a cult figure is one example. Let's now examine the ritualizations of each stage.

Infancy

Here is how Erikson envisages the first ritualization:

> The awakening infant conveys to his mother the fact that he is awake and (as if with the signal of an alarm clock) awakens in her a whole repertoire of emotive, verbal, and manipulative behaviour. She approaches him with smiling or worried concern, brightly or anxiously rendering a name, and goes into action: looking, feeling, sniffing, she ascertains possible sources of discomfort and initiates services to be rendered by rearranging the infant's condition, by picking him up, etc. If observed for several days it becomes clear that this daily event is highly ritualized, in that the mother seems to feel obliged, and not a little pleased, to repeat a performance which arouses in the infant predictable responses, encouraging her, in turn, to proceed. . . . The whole procedure is superimposed on the periodicity of physical needs close to the requirements of survival, but is an *emotional* as well as a *practical* necessity for both mother and infant. And . . . this enhanced routine can be properly evaluated only as a small but tough link in the whole formidable sequence of generations (1966, p. 338).

Erikson calls the experience of mother and baby *numinous* (from the Latin *numen*, meaning divine, awe-inspiring). To the baby, the mother is a 'hallowed presence', her face and smile, talk, cooing, smell all evoking a kind of breathless sense of warmth and closeness. This is the prototypical numinous experience, the model for experiences we will have in later life with lovers and close friends. Great personages—an admirable leader, for example—evoke them as well.

Mothers who do not give their infants this experience may produce a kind of blind and helpless devotion, the ritualism of idolism. Mistrustful and anxious, the baby clings worshipfully as if to allay doubt and may learn to idolize himself or significant others when he is grown.

Childhood

In the struggle over autonomy and the discovery of rules and limits, two key words are 'right' and 'wrong', and very small children do learn to judge themselves and their parents, trying on their judgements for size. Respectfully treated, they begin to learn the *judicious* ritualization. The small child's acceptance of what he or she sees as fair and indignation at the unfair will foster beliefs about adult rituals in which people and events are judged—the courtroom, for example, and sporting events with offside and penalty calls. Judging people is the element behind prejudice, or *pseudospeciation* as Erikson calls it, and the basis for the inclusion and exclusion of others is laid here. The excessive ritualism of childhood is *legalism*, which we see in a stubborn insistence on rule (or legal precept) with little understanding of morality and social conscience. The punishment's the thing, says the legalist.

The Play Age

In imaginative play, children invent roles, pretending to be animals, heroic figures from books and television, 'mommies' and 'daddies'. These are often morality plays in which good conquers evil, but sometimes children dare to be bad, testing their own limits and flirting with guilt. The ritualization is *authenticity*, the discovery of character and role that suits and compliments each child. There is a danger, one of getting lost in a role, in which the child begins to think that he or she *is* the fantasy person. This is the ritualism of *impersonation*. Exposure to the uglier qualities of people—for instance, in TV antiheroes who are violent—may fuel role taking that is less than social.

School Age

Children in school, as we've seen, must acquire the formal discipline of learning and be able to match their effort to standards of accomplishment. They must participate effectively in the *formal* ritualization and not become excessively perfectionistic, preoccupied in the ritualism of *formalism*. Obsession over good grades leads a child to lose sight of the real purpose of education and is bound to create disappointment.

Adolescence

Ritualization and ritual begin to coalesce in adolescence, and Erikson cites only the ritualization and its extremity for this and the remaining stages.

One of the developmental tasks of adolescence is to arrive at the beliefs and values that will guide a lifetime of choices and one's relation to society. 'Solidarity of conviction' is the necessary achievement, and the ritualization is one of *ideology*★, assembling and synthesizing the contributions of earlier stages to ego identity. A belief system may be affirmed by ceremony, such as high school graduation. Look what you've achieved, this says, and what you're now ready to do. *Totalism* is going too far, a blind submission to a system of belief or, say, to a popular figure and the lifestyle he or she represents. Fixed and simplistic beliefs are unlikely to be of much help with difficult life choices.

Young Adulthood

Love is the young adulthood virtue, and the ritualization is *affiliation*. The outstanding ritual of this stage is marriage; it is especially significant because it brings together earlier ritualizations—the numinous (adoration of each other) and judicious (exchanging of vows). Other important rituals involve work and recreational activities that bind one to social groups. The ritualism of *elitism* is indulged in by those whose relationships to others are not close. Becoming a member of an elite group gives a spurious sense of comradeship and identity.

Adulthood

It is the adult's task to mind the generational store, passing along beliefs, values, and skills to the young. Thus, the ritualization is *generational*. Family rituals and the rituals of teachers mark occasions when we teach children and young people. Those who have nothing to teach or do not think they do may simply become authoritarian, demanding conformity. We see in them the ritualism of *authoritism*.

Maturity

An affirmation of 'the meaning of the life cycle' is the *integral* ritualization. Said Erikson,

> We can see now what rituals must accomplish: by combining and renewing the ritu-
> alizations of childhood and affirming generative sanction, they help to consolidate
> adult life once its commitments and investments have led to the creation of new per-
> sons and to the production of new things and ideas. And, of course, by tying life cycle
> and institutions into a meaningful whole, they create a sense of immortality not only
> for the leaders and the elite but also for every participant (1977, pp. 112–13).

The pretense of wisdom tries to conceal its lack by the ritualism of *sapientism*.

Research

Erikson's research was strikingly diversified, ranging across a wide map of method and subject. There were psychoanalytically based studies of children's play using play therapy techniques, anthropological studies of Sioux and Yurok Indian tribes, and psychoanalytic investigations of historical figures. Following Erikson, psychologists have taken up the question of adolescent identity, devising measures and experimental procedures to examine identity achievement and identity confusion and their consequences. We'll review each of these.

Children's Play

Erikson had learned his craft as a child analyst from the early experts, Anna Freud and August Aichhorn, and went on to make significant contributions of his own. Children cannot be analyzed by the techniques of adult analysis. Their egos are not mature enough for free association and the interpretation of dreams, and so something different is required. For Erikson, a major alternative was play. In his therapy he used toys—a variety of small figures, doll furniture, blocks—to explore the world of a child's fears, insecurities, and fantasies, and to allow the child to 'associate freely'. He applied the play therapy method to study child personality. Open at first to anything he might find, this soon became research into the differentiation in fantasy of boys and girls.

The method was quite simple, as Erikson explained: 'I set up a play table and a ran-dom selection of toys and invited the boys and girls of the study, one at a time, to come in and to imagine that the table was a movie studio and the toys, actors and sets. I then asked them to "construct on the table an exciting scene out of an imaginary moving picture'" (Erikson, 1963, p. 98). His children were the subjects of a longitudinal study at the University of California at Berkeley, between ten and twelve years old, 150 or so of them.

The findings astonished him. The productions of boys and girls barely resembled each other. The girls largely built enclosures of furniture surrounding people; the boys constructed buildings, towers, street scenes full of activity. Figure 8.1 shows two examples from *Childhood and Society*. Erikson was careful to obtain ratings of photographs of the play constructions from independent observers, who were in substantial agreement on the configurations of boys and girls. The facts themselves are clear: the play constructions of preadolescent boys and girls were quite unalike, and the question is why. Erikson proposed that the spatial organization of the play constructions was strongly influenced by biology, deriving from genital morphology and affecting social roles. 'We may accept, then,' he wrote, 'the evidence of organ-modes in these constructions as a reminder of the fact that experience is anchored in the ground plan of the body' (1963, p. 108).

His interpretation was sharply rejected by critics, who pointed out the obvious differences in the socialization of boys and girls. What kinds of toys, they asked, do parents buy for their children, and how would the choice of toys affect children's play (Caplan, 1979)? Society and culture created the differences, not the form of the genitals. Erikson acknowledged the point, but insisted that effects of biology on psychological processes and social roles are inescapable (1975).

Anthropological Studies of American Indians

With anthropologists Scudder Mekeel and Alfred Kroeber, Erikson made field trips to two American Indian tribes to study childrearing, its tribal roots, and the effects of the clash of white and Indian cultures. Mekeel introduced him to friendly and trusted informants among the Oglala Sioux in South Dakota. Kroeber took him to coastal Oregon to study the Yurok. Interviews with informants and 'seminars' with groups provided the data. Erikson then combined history, the anthropological accounts of the two societies, and his own observational data in a psychoanalytic account relating childrearing

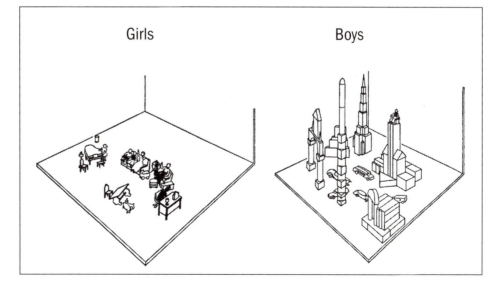

Figure 8.1 Representative play constructions of girls and boys (From *Childhood and Society* by Erik H. Erikson. Copyright 1950, © 1963 by W.W. Norton & Company, Inc., renewed © 1978, 1991 by Erik H. Erikson. Used by permission of W.W. Norton & Company, Inc.; Published by The Hogarth Press. Reprinted by permission of The Random House Group, Ltd.)

practices to adult behaviour and—among the Sioux—to the alienation of child and adult resulting from the imposition of an incompatible white culture on the dying culture of the Plains Indian. This research did not generate the degree of resistance that had met his work on play, perhaps because of the fascination psychoanalysis held for distinguished anthropologists like Mekeel and Kroeber (see, for example, Erikson, 1949).

The Psychoanalytic Study of Historical Figures

This field of inquiry, known as *psychohistory*, was begun by Freud, though Erikson became its acknowledged master. Before Erikson, it could hardly be said that there were any rules for the psychoanalytic investigation of figures in history; he formulated rules (Erikson, 1975) and then applied them in studies of Martin Luther (Erikson, 1958) and Gandhi (Erikson, 1969). *Childhood and Society* contains psychohistorical chapters on Hitler and on the Russian writer Maxim Gorky.

How *do* you approach the psychoanalysis of someone who is not there, who cannot provide a personal history, free-associate, and develop a transference betraying his relationship to his parents? For a start, we know that everyone must contend throughout life with conflict and crisis, and that patients in analysis are there because one crisis or another got the better of them. Great historical figures managed to conquer their crises or put their peculiarities of struggle with crises to powerful social use. Attempts to 'psychoanalyze' historical persons, however, are all too easy and likely to be glib. Erikson was aware of this and issued a strong warning about diminishing the psyches of important historical figures to psychoanalytic simplicities: 'I consider any attempt to reduce a leader of Gandhi's stature to earlier as well as bigger and better childhood traumata both wrong in method and evil in influence' (1969, p. 99).

Another requirement is that the psychohistorian be knowledgeable in history and not tempted to gloss over the relevant historical period and its developments. Needless to say, intimate experience with psychoanalysis is also a clear requirement. Erikson thought that a personal analysis would help the investigator to avoid imputing his own sensitivities to the subject and missing aspects encroaching on his defences. Freud's biographer, Peter Gay, is an exemplar of these last two points. He is both a historian *and* a trained psychoanalyst.

Perspective 8.1   Erikson's Psychohistorical Portrait of Mahatma Gandhi

Mohandas K. Gandhi was a study in contradiction. He began his professional life as an Anglicized dandy but became an extreme ascetic, renouncing all the trappings of a comfortable life to live as an Indian villager. He was brilliant and literate, the author of many books, and politically powerful, but he dressed in the simple draped *dhoti* of the village Indian. (So garbed, he met King George at Buckingham Palace in 1931. Asked by incredulous reporters if he was actually going to wear the *dhoti* to his audience with the King, he said, 'Some go in plus-fours, I will go in minus-fours.' Afterward, he would acknowledge no embarrassment over his peasant dress. 'The King', he told his questioners, 'wore enough clothes for the both of us.') He was small and frail, but he walked all over the vastness of India. He was sophisticated but simple; his economic dream was that India should become a nation of cottage industry, village-based, each family producing its own food

© Mahatma Gandhi Foundation, India.

and clothes. He was spiritual, playful and a great tease, loving, phenomenally magnetic, calculating and at times deceptive, and determined beyond all imagining.

He was the youngest of six sons of the chief minister of Gujarat state. His childhood circumstances were comfortable though crowded; the household included his brothers and their families. He was a precocious and wilful youngest child, a tease from the beginning, but he was devoted to his father and even more deeply attached to his mother. He was married at age thirteen, an arranged marriage which neither he nor his wife found comfortable or easy. His father died when Gandhi was in his late teens; he was filled with self-reproach for 'failing to preside mercifully over his father's death'. Shortly thereafter, he set sail for England, where he became a barrister and a cultured English gentleman. He went to South Africa to practise law, but quickly ran afoul of cruel racial customs. Thrown off a train for having the temerity to sit in a whites-only compartment, he was angered by the humiliation and became almost immediately an advocate, an organizer for the cause of 'coolies', as natives of India were called. He became, in a word, a revolutionary, but one of a very special kind, a nonviolent revolutionary. He was at times fitful and indecisive, his methods and purpose obscure. From this time on, however, to his death by an assassin's bullet in 1948, he never wavered from *satyagraha*, which means both the force of truth and the fullest dedication to passive resistance to injustice and intolerance. Gandhi's struggle for his people in South Africa lasted more than twenty years, a period that established militant nonviolence and his own leadership, with significant but far from complete success. The white racism of South Africa would endure for another seventy-five years.

Gandhi returned to India a 'Mahatma', a wise, 'great-souled' person, but not yet *the* Mahatma. The critical 'Event', as Erikson referred to it, was a huge step in making Gandhi a spiritual and political leader of his people, a truth force for India. In 1918, Gandhi began to campaign on behalf of textile workers in the city of Ahmedabad, who were underpaid and terribly impoverished. This was the first appearance of *satyagraha* in India, and it was the occasion for Gandhi's first public fast. It also seems to have marked the final resolution of a crisis of identity which had begun with his bad treatment in South Africa. Had there been any doubt, he was now a totally committed nonviolent revolutionary.

Erikson saw in this 'the difference between a case history and a life-history: patients, great or small, are increasingly debilitated by their inner conflicts, but in historical actuality inner conflict only adds an indispensable momentum to all superhuman effort' (1969, p. 363). Of the problem of understanding posed by Gandhi, Erikson said, 'what a man adds up to must develop in stages, but no stage explains the man' (1969, p. 98). A key point: It would be demeaning, he thought, to reduce the superhuman effort of a supreme human being to a psychosocial catch phrase—identity crisis.

The Adolescent Crisis of Identity

At the absolute centre of Erikson's ego psychology is the concept of identity. It was a dominant idea from his first major work, *Childhood and Society*, and can be seen throughout his research and writings. He himself, however, was not the one to turn the lens of research on the adolescent identity crisis; this was a contribution made by psychologists of personality. In a series of studies going back to 1964, Marcia and colleagues have formulated an approach to the measurement of ego identity and investigated the outcomes of identity crises. There are two extensive summaries of this work (Marcia, 1980; Marcia, Waterman, Matteson, Archer, & Orlofsky, 1993).

Studying the adolescent crisis of identity requires that we overcome a very large problem at the outset. Ego identity is subjective and private, an experience of self and of commitment or wavering that is shared—if it is at all—only with intimates. How, then, will entry to this most personal of ego attributes be gained? How can ego identity be made objective and its behavioural expression observable? Identity cannot be represented by a continuous distribution of scores from 'little' or 'none' to 'high', as we might do with a questionnaire measure of anxiety. The four possibilities of which Erikson spoke—identity achievement, foreclosure, moratorium, and role confusion—are discontinuous, each a distinct phase.

Marcia's strategy was to regard each of Erikson's possibilities as an identity status, and to develop measures to show in which category each individual can be placed. He devised semi-structured interviews to probe two critical aspects of identity—crisis, and commitment to an occupation and a political and religious ideology. Later, because women seemed less engaged by the occupational issue, he included an additional interpersonal-sexual area to explore feminine identity status. The final form of the interview, for both males and females, includes the three identity areas—occupation, belief system, and questions of interpersonal and sexual commitment. A companion measure, a sentence completion test, was also developed to establish that independent methods of assessing identity status could yield the same findings. Other measures have since appeared, including an identity status questionnaire (see, for example, Craig-Bray & Adams, 1986). The best of the techniques, Marcia believes, remains the interview (Marcia et al., 1993).

In the 1993 book, Marcia noted that more than 300 studies had been reported, a number that will have increased greatly in the time since. The original research investigated the ego-controlled process of cognitive activity, stressing the experimental partici-

Table 8.4 Criteria for Identity Status in Marcia's Studies of Ego Identity		
Identity	*Exploration of Alternatives?*	*Commitment?*
Identity Achievement	Present	Present
Moratorium	In Process	Present but vague and uncertain
Foreclosure	Absent	Present
Identity Confusion	May be present or absent	Absent

Source: From Marcia, 1980. Reprinted with permission of John Wiley & Sons, Inc.

pants by making them feel doubtful about themselves in order to reveal differences among the identity status groups more clearly. On a difficult concept-formation task, subjects whose identities had been achieved showed the best performance of the identity status groups. Foreclosure subjects set high goals on the concept-formation task and did not adjust their goals downward after failure. Efforts to manipulate self-esteem were better resisted by achieved-identity and moratorium subjects than by those classified as foreclosure or confused-identity. Subjects in the middle of identity crisis, the moratorium group, were more anxious than the members of the other groups, as measured by a well-known anxiety questionnaire. And, on a measure of authoritarian attitudes, the foreclosure group had the most authoritarian scores. Each of these findings is consistent with the identity concept.

Many other variables, all theoretically related to identity achievement, foreclosure, and crisis, have been studied. Among them are conformity (identity-achievement subjects conformed less and were less distressed by social pressure); drug use (foreclosure subjects were unlikely to use drugs; those in moratorium and identity confusion were likely to do so); and autonomy and independence from family (foreclosure and identity-confusion were associated with less autonomy and more dependence on family, identity-achievement with greater self-reliance). Studies of moral development showed the expected: a higher level of moral reasoning in subjects with secure identities.

Family relationships have also been examined. Foreclosure subjects described their families as close and encouraging, and those in identity confusion saw their parents as distant and less accepting of them. Subjects in moratorium were ambivalent in their feelings about their families. The family studies were based on reports of the subjects themselves and reflect perceptions of families, not necessarily the realities of family interaction. There have been observational studies of family relationships, however, and these tend to bear out the self-report research.

In a literature this large, we might expect inconsistencies, and they do appear. Investigators have used measures with weakly established validity, and we need to note the difficulty in obtaining distinct differences among identity status groups that will share at least some attributes. There is much to commend in this identity research, however. It does, in the main, support identity theory predictions, and it has become impressively cross-cultural. Late adolescents in more than twenty cultures have been studied in investigations that both confirm basic predictions and reveal cultural differences in adolescent ego development.

Table 8.5   A Summary of Some Ego Identity Findings

Concept formation under stress (experimental task)	Identity Achievement had best performance & self-esteem didn't change; Foreclosure set high goals
Anxiety (questionnaire)	Moratorium most anxious
Authoritarianism (questionnaire)	Foreclosure had highest scores
Conformity (experimental task)	Identity Achievement conformed least
Drug use	Moratorium and Identity Confusion had higher use; Foreclosure low
Moral development	Identity Achievement showed higher level of moral development
Relationship to family	Identity Achievement independent; Foreclosure more dependent; Moratorium ambivalent about family; Identity Confusion thought parents distant and less accepting

Ego Psychology in Perspective

The appearance of ego psychology came like a breath of spring to psychoanalysis, giving freshness and light to the theory and its wearying emphasis on irremediable instinctual struggle. Ego psychology showed the ego in the social world to psychoanalysts and followers of the theory, plotting out—even dramatizing—its psychosocial development. It did so, moreover, without arousing antagonism and stubborn rejection. Psychoanalysis could remain psychoanalysis with all the concepts that for Freud were indispensable. All the classical theory had to do was to acknowledge that biology has handmaidens—

A Fresh Look: Research Today

Achieving the sense of identity that will—except in unusual circumstances—last one for a lifetime is no mean accomplishment. It isn't done easily, nor does it involve completing a defined set of tasks like those required for a scout badge. There is no patch to stitch on our shirts certifying that we have passed the identity trial. Moreover, surviving the critical developmental stage and coming out secure in our beliefs about ourselves doesn't mean the end of identity issues. Identity will be challenged, often when we don't expect and wouldn't choose to be confronted, and our sense of self and meaning needs to be maintained and nourished. That comes from the stories we tell, both for our own benefit and to explain ourselves to others, narratives that account for our behaviour, thought, feelings, and purpose in life, tales in which we have the hero's role.

Erikson introduced psychology to the stormy interval in which identity is—or is not—forged. Crisis, from which, chrysalis-like, commitments will emerge, is the developmental forebear. Its signature, identity, will take shape and become a dominant individual feature. Contemporary theorists propose that personal identity takes form in a story of self, 'an internalized and evolving narrative . . . that incorporates the reconstructed past and the imagined future into a more or less coherent whole in order to provide the person's life with some degree of unity, purpose, and meaning' (McAdams & Pals, 2006, pp. 209–10). It is this story of self that gives individual existence its sense, aim, and place in society (McAdams & Pals; Sarbin, 1986; Singer, 2004). McAdams (1987) has a compelling aphorism: 'Identity is a life story,' one that contains the recognition that life society and culture, with family acting as their agent—in the development of personality. There *were* a few other concessions to be made. For instance, ego autonomy does mean that there will be many human activities in which the id does not have a hidden hand. And, a psychosocial ego emphasis implies that personality will not be set with the final instinctual moments of the psychosexual stages, the resolution of the Oedipus complex, and the formation of the superego. Personalities may change in later years as events intrude and the crises of ages beyond childhood appear. We may think of Gandhi and of our own experience.

Many of the ideas that appear in ego psychology are found as well in the neo-Freudian theories, and for that reason it is difficult to keep these two branches of Freudian derivation entirely distinct. But ego psychologists phrased their demands for revision more loyally and gracefully than the neo-Freudians and kept more of the classical theory intact.

Ego psychology has not gone without criticism, and most of it has been directed at Erikson. This is surprising, because of the high regard in which he is held by psychologists, by psychiatrists, and in informed popular culture. Erikson, however, stretched psychoanalysis farther than any of his contemporaries, probing society and culture and history more deeply and extending the theory well beyond clinical concerns; big targets are vulnerable and attract more attention. The most serious of the criticisms is that Erikson diluted psychoanalysis, watering down a complex theory to social simplicities. This is, without doubt, a mistaken view. A close reading of Erikson's writings, especially *Childhood and Society*, makes clear how much of psychoanalysis his theorizing preserves and honours. It is not Freud diluted but Freud extended and elaborated. True, there is little precedent in the classical theory for the ego developments of adolescence and adulthood that Erikson proposed, but this does not represent the weakening of psychoanalysis. Life-cycle ego psychology will stand or fall as it makes—or fails to make—

narratives have an identity core and evolve as our experience elaborates them.

Here is Kristin, age twenty-two, her identity story cloaked in uncertainty:

When our mothers were our age, they were engaged. . . . They at least had some idea what they were going to do with their lives. . . . I, on the other hand will have a dual degree in majors that are ambiguous at best and impractical at worst (English and political science), no ring on my finger, and no idea who I am, much less what I want to do. . . . Under duress, I will admit that this is a pretty exciting time. Sometimes, when I look out across the wide expanse that is my future, I can see beyond the void. I realize that having nothing ahead to count on means I now have to count on myself; that having no direction means forging one of my own (Page, 1999, pp. 18, 20).

We have no idea what experience will have brought to Kristin nor how her vague and unformed sense of identity will have incorporated it, shaped it, and given it a place in her personal life narrative. We can be sure that Kristin's identity story, even when its contours of self-definition are filled out, will not remain static. Neither Kristin nor we will be able to put the stamp of completion on identity formation. There will be no 'Done; now on to the next stage'. Will there be a recognizable centre, though, a Kristin or you or me, that makes the tale a unique narrative of an individual personality? Without doubt. We will have to be good enough as psychologists to see it, but an identity—a vague and undefined one, a secure and committed one, one built on episodes of failure and excuses, one that becomes despairing as the end of life approaches—will be the narrative's nucleus. Narrative theorists focus personality study on exactly this: each individual's story of his or her experience, relationships, and future hopes and fears, all built around a person, an identity.

useful contributions to clinical practice and generates, like the concept of identity, testable and confirmed predictions.

Erikson has also been upbraided for too conservative a view of society—'throwing a mantle of morality over the preexisting world and endorsing everything that already "is" with an ethical sanction' (Roazen, 1980, p. 339). Roazen accuses Erikson of excessive conventionality in the endorsement of heterosexuality, marriage, and the raising of children—'*Lieben und arbeiten*' taken beyond Freud (Roazen, 1976). In view of Erikson's strong cultural emphasis—his studies of American Indian societies, for example—this seems an overstated criticism. In a very important sense, Erikson was as much concerned with the preservation of human society as he was with healthy human growth. As long as societies make a place for individual expression and variation—and Erikson surely advocated that—there seems little wrong in recognizing the things that keep the human species going.

SUMMARY

1. Freud gave the ego a subservient role, servant of the id, dominated by the severity of the superego, and responsible for meeting reality demands. Since the ego has no energy of its own, he said, it is dependent on the id. Thus, in every activity the instincts will be present even though they will almost always be heavily disguised.

2. One group of psychoanalysts saw the role of the ego differently. While they were loyal to the theory and accepted its fundamental propositions, they gave the ego an independence that Freud had not. The ego, they argued, is strong, resilient, and creative; some of them even claimed that the ego did not emerge *from* the id but along *with* the id. Three of the most influential of these theorists were Anna Freud, Heinz Hartmann, and Erik Erikson.

3. Anna Freud, trained and analyzed by her father, became a child psychoanalyst. She made notable contributions to the treatment of children, to the psychoanalytic theory of child development and childrearing, and to the understanding of ego defences.

4. An important concept of Anna Freud's was the developmental line, which represents the course of a child's growth from helpless infant to competent child. Among the six developmental lines she proposed is a line from egocentricity to companionship—from total self-centeredness to the ability to relate companionably with other children and to share with them feelings, wishes, and possessions.

5. Credit for introducing the essential concepts of ego psychology is deservedly given to Heinz Hartmann, who proposed that both id and ego emerge through differentiation, and that the ego is at least partly autonomous. Important ego functions (apparatuses, he called them) develop independent of conflict with id, superego, and reality; they include perception, thinking, language, memory, and elemental motor skills. Hartmann's ego is the ego of the normal person as well as the person in neurotic conflict. His conception of a 'conflict-free sphere' of ego function brought psychoanalysis much closer to developmental psychology and influenced the study of personality development in children.

6. The outstanding figure in ego psychology was Erik Homburger Erikson, an artist and teacher, trained in psychoanalysis by Anna Freud and taught by other distinguished analysts, including Hartmann. He became a child analyst, a pioneer in technique and in the ego psychological development of children. His first book, *Childhood and Society*, published in 1950, presented a lifetime view of ego—a series of eight stages from birth to the end of life, each consisting of a nuclear crisis with significant implications for personality development.

7. Erikson began his analysis of personality growth with a model from embryology, *epigenesis*. Epigenesis is the process by which an embryonic organism develops from unorganized and undifferentiated protoplasm, with organs developing in an orderly sequence. Epi-

genetic psychological development refers to a sequence of motor, sensory, cognitive, and social abilities. The psychosexual stages exemplify the process, but the epigenetic view is not limited to the early socialization of the instincts; it extends to the development of the ego throughout life.

8. Freud had localized the infantile appearance of instincts in three erogenous zones. Erikson added to classical psychosexuality by describing the modes of expression of each bodily zone. Starting in the earliest, oral period, they are incorporative (taking in), incorporative (active), retentive, eliminative, and intrusive. These are the primary modes of the first three stages of development, but they can also appear as auxiliary modes at any later stage. Associated with zones and modes are *modalities*, which are the ways in which societies and cultures bring instincts under social control. The feeding and weaning practices of societies and of individual mothers exemplify the social modality of the oral-sensory period.

9. The eight stages of personality development represent distinctive periods in the growth of the ego in response to emerging biological changes, qualities of the ego, and social institutions (for example, how societies socialize childhood sexual behaviour, or their treatment of the elderly). The exact ages at which they appear may vary from person to person, but the order in which they appear does not vary. They are better thought of as nodes or concentration points in which there is a decisive psychosocial crisis to be met.

10. The first three stages correspond to the psychosexual stages, but the psychosocial aspect, the crises confronting the infant and young child, are the distinctive view of Erikson's ego psychology. The psychosocial crisis of the first stage is one of acquiring a basic sense of trust or of mistrust, and it is the comfort and security provided by the mother that will determine which occurs. With basic trust comes the ego strength to endure the inevitable deprivations of early life, a virtue that Erikson identifies as *hope*. In the second year, with growing muscular and cognitive capacities, the very young child must begin to acquire self-control. The crisis is one of autonomy versus shame and doubt. Parents face the task of imposing socialization demands (toilet training, setting limits) without crippling the child's sense of autonomy. Harsh and angry parents are likely to cre-

ate shame and doubt, which may be lasting. The virtue to be acquired at this stage is *will*, the child's understanding that he or she can decide to obey rule and social ritual. The third early childhood stage brings the psychosocial crisis of initiative versus guilt. There is a new sex-typed genital sexuality—phallic intrusiveness in boys and a feminine mode Erikson called inception. He clearly agreed with Freud that anatomy influences psychological development. Children do have to learn to adopt appropriate roles and to accept reasonable limits on their exuberance and aggressiveness. If they do, they acquire initiative and the virtue of *purpose*; if they are condemned or ridiculed, guilt may immobilize them. This is an age in which children explore reality through play, exploring and inventing roles.

11. Freud termed the years from six to twelve the latency period; for Erikson, they constitute the school age, and they are significant for more than the temporary suppression of the sexual instinct. This is the period in which children learn the requirements of productive endeavour, a stage in which the crisis is industry versus inferiority. School-age children must put effort into the tasks assigned to them, learn how to conduct themselves and co-operate with others. Along with these accomplishments comes *competence*; falling by the wayside means a loss of confidence in oneself and diminished status among peers.

12. A critical stage for future development is adolescence, with its nuclear crisis of identity versus identity confusion. Late in adolescence, young people are faced with the large task of developing a sense of identity, which entails commitments to an occupation, to a sexual identity, and to an ideology. All this must be accomplished with the maturing of genital sexuality in the background. These commitments must be struggled over and made by each person; they cannot be handed down by parents, even wise and devoted ones. During this long stage, many adolescents will find themselves in an anxious interval called *moratorium*, where they are temporarily unable to make the essential decisions. Others fail for a longer period, called *identity confusion*, and there are those who continue to depend on their parents, a resolution labelled *foreclosure*. The virtue that accompanies identity achievement is *fidelity*, signifying that one is ready to be faithful to one's commitments.

13. There are three stages to adult life. The early years of adulthood entail entry into productive life and the establishment of an intimate relationship and close friendships. This is the stage of intimacy versus isolation. The virtue of this stage is *love*; to let these years slide by without loving commitment is to risk becoming isolated. The mature years, typically from 30 to 65, require productive accomplishment and concern for the young; generativity versus stagnation is the psychosocial crisis. A mature and contributing lifestyle expresses the virtue of *care*; the alternative, stagnation, implies going through the motions, living from one moment, from one day, to the next. The last years of life bring the elderly into the crisis of integrity versus despair. Integrity means a deep sense that one has lived one's life to the best of one's abilities. The virtue of *wisdom* confers dignity; despair is the sad alternative. The choices one has made or failed to make cannot be revisited; an indifferent life cannot be redone.

14. Individuals are bound to their societies by cultural and social rituals. Some stand out as highly significant (marriage, for example), while others are small, daily observances (how to behave in the classroom; how to greet others). Erikson added to his scheme of life cycle development in proposing that at each stage social interactions are conducted according to significant rituals. Rituals are the adult form of social practices. They have a more elemental basis in ritualizations, which are ritual aspects of interactions in each developmental stage. There are also exaggerated and pathological forms of ritualization that are named ritualisms. These are the ritualizations and rituals of each stage:
    - In *infancy* the ritualization is *numinous* (awe-inspiring), experienced by both baby and mother. The ritualism is *idolism*, a blind and helpless worship.
    - In *childhood* the ritualization is called *judicious*. It is the prototype of judging people and events to be fair or unfair. Judging people is the basis of prejudice (*pseudospeciation*). The ritualism is a stubborn insistence on rules, called *legalism*.
    - During the *play age*, children begin to imagine roles, testing their own limits and, sometimes, flirting with feelings of guilt. The ritualization is *authenticity*, finding suitable roles, and its extreme is the ritualism of *impersonation*.
    - During the *school age*, children have to learn to meet standards of achievement and learn proper ways of doing things. This requires mastering the *formal* ritualization and avoiding the perfectionistic ritualism of *formalism*.
    - In *adolescence* comes a major task in the achievement of a sense of identity, the commitment to a set of beliefs to guide one's choices and relation to society. Thus, the ritualization: *ideology*. Its extreme form is the ritualism of *totalism*.
    - The psychosocial challenge of *young adulthood* is intimacy. The ritualization is one of *affiliation*, concerned with establishing close relationships. *Elitism* is the ritualism of those who are not close to others and gain a sense of comradeship through elite associations.
    - The ritualization of the mature adult in *adulthood* involves the care and teaching of the young; it is called *generational*. Adults who have little to teach may become demanding and authoritarian; this ritualism is *authoritism*.
    - Old age is sustained by wisdom and integrity; the ritualization is *integral*. A pretense of wisdom is seen in the ritualism of *sapientism*.

15. Erikson was far more than a clinical psychoanalyst. He investigated personality development seriously in several very different areas. He studied the play of school-age children using play therapy techniques, undertook anthropological investigations of two American Indian tribes, and used psychoanalytic methods to develop psychological portraits of historical figures, notably Martin Luther and Mahatma Gandhi. Personality psychologists have taken up his concept of identity, developing measures of adolescent identity status and testing implications of ego identity theory. Erikson's ego psychoanalytic interpretation of his own research, particularly the work on play, is subject to the criticism that there are other possible interpretations, a risk facing research without adequate controls. The studies of ego identity, however, have been well conducted and have an established place in the literature on adolescent development.

16. Ego psychology brought significant changes to psychoanalysis in establishing what may be called the social psychology of ego development, a develop-

ment that received its greatest contributions from Erik Erikson. While Heinz Hartmann's concept of the autonomous ego gave ego psychology its start, Erikson extended the approach to include ego developments throughout the life cycle. His developmental scheme has earned wide interest and respect, particularly the core concept of ego identity. Some critics have alleged that Erikson's ego psychology is just simplified Freud, but such a view does not recognize the major point that ego psychology as clinical and scientific theory will succeed or fail on its contributions to practice and research. Another criticism is that Erikson was too socially conservative in endorsing the social institutions of marriage and family. This, too, may be undeserved. Erikson was certainly not illiberal, accepting variation in the roles and sexual preferences of women and men. He was properly concerned with the preservation of the human species no less than with fostering healthy human development.

TO TEST YOUR UNDERSTANDING

1. Explain how the epigenetic principle helps us to understand personality formation and development. When does epigenetic development end—or is it lifelong? Defend your view.
2. Do you agree with Erikson's 'utopia of genitality' (pp. 208–9) or disagree? Explain your agreement or disagreement.
3. To Freud and to Erikson, 'anatomy is destiny'. Explain what this aphorism means. Do you agree? If so, defend it as Erikson might have. If not, what is the alternative?
4. How do ritualization and ritualism differ? Use one of the eight ages to define these terms and illustrate them.
5. Caplan, among others, sharply criticized Erikson's interpretation of his play construction research. Did the children's constructions reflect 'experience anchored in the ground plan of the body'? Defend Erikson's point of view or Caplan's.

CHAPTER NINE

Trait Theory: Gordon Allport, Raymond Cattell, Hans Eysenck, and the Big Five

Introduction

Traits have a long history in psychology, one that reaches back to antiquity. The Athenian philosophers were well aware of basic differences in character among people. Theophrastus, pupil of Plato and Aristotle and Aristotle's successor at the Lyceum, depicted more than two dozen character types, among them the 'offensive', the 'surly', the 'arrogant', and the 'late learning'. In Figure 9.1 is his portrait of the arrogant person and a caricature by an artist of the nineteenth century. Aristotle himself had written of types of human being, and Theophrastus may have been expanding on the work of his mentor and predecessor.

Before we embark on our discussion of trait theory, let's clarify two essential terms. There are—in ancient Greek philosophy and in the lifespan of personality theory—both personality **types★** and **traits★**; the distinction between them is more often than not blurred. Jung, as you remember, worked out a theory of eight psychological types—eight *categories* into which we could place people, combining the two attitudes of introversion and extraversion and four functions. With types, like introversion and extraversion, we can say that everyone is either one or the other. Traits, however, are continuous measuring sticks along which people may be ordered on the extent to which they possess a certain trait. On a trait of inquisitiveness, for example, we will find that a few people are not inquisitive at all, many are in the middle of the distribution, moderately inquisitive, and a few are highly so.

Jung believed there were varying degrees of types, treating them in effect as attitude–function distributions. So did our major type-trait theorist, Hans Eysenck. He set out to study personality types, beginning with Jung's typology of introversion–extraversion, but he regarded these types as superordinate traits. Gordon Allport, who may be said to be the father of modern trait theory, did observe that traits and types are different and laid it down strongly: 'A man can be said to *have* a trait; but he cannot be said to *have* a type. Rather, he *fits* a type' (Allport, 1937, p. 295). Types, he insisted, are in the mind of the observer, traits in the personality organization of the person. We're not going to be strict about it, as Allport was. This chapter is about trait theory—dimensional human

Theophrastus on the arrogant person (From Theophrastus, 1831)

Figure 9.1 The arrogant man is the sort of person who stops a man hurrying along to tell him he will see him after dinner while he is taking his stroll. When he does you a good turn he tells you to remember it. Meeting those who have asked him to decide a quarrel, he declares he will just do so here in the street. If elected to some office he calls off, saying he has no time. He is never the first to greet if he meets a friend, and is fond of telling his tenants, or people who have anything to sell, to come and see him at daybreak. While walking in the streets he does not speak to those he meets, but keeps his head down, or, if the fancy takes him, high in the air. If he gives some friends a dinner he will not sit down with them, but will send some one under him to preside. Whenever he goes out he sends on a messenger to say he is coming. He will not allow anyone to enter while he is anointing himself or bathing or at a meal. If he is settling with anyone he usually tells his servant to add up the account and set down the amount to him. When writing a letter he does not say 'I should be obliged' but 'I desire', and is fond of the phrases 'I have sent to you for', 'Obey my orders to the letter', 'Without losing a moment'.

attributes—but it is also about the types that were central to Eysenck. We shall follow what the modern trait-type theorist and investigator does and not worry much about a distinction that few observe, and we shall simply accept that the outstanding type theorist, Eysenck, is, to be accurate, a trait theorist.

Where could we get traits from? How could we learn about them? Well, we might start by observing people over time and in different situations, recording shared consistencies in their behaviour. This would be very time-consuming and labour-intensive, and it would undoubtedly be extremely difficult and expensive to find willing participants for observation. But have you considered that this is something people everywhere have always done—taking note of the behaviour of their fellows—and that trait description is enshrined in language? Aristotle and Theophrastus and all the citizenry of Athens relied on just such a data source for their understanding of the behaviour to be seen around them. Theophrastus drew on the Greek language and the people concepts represented by it for his character portraits. Galton, student of intelligence and vastly more in the human mosaic, who might have had to read his Plato and Aristotle in the original Greek and would have known about Theophrastus, was captivated by individual variety. He pored over the dictionary to find words denoting personal attributes, finding many with similar meaning (Galton, 1884).

Gordon Allport did it more systematically. In a personality study of the dictionary that is unmatched for its thoroughness, he and a colleague, H.S. Odbert, turned up 17,953 terms descriptive of people and behaviour (Allport & Odbert, 1936). There is a contemporary name for this trait-description-from-language idea. It is the **lexical hypothesis★**, and its claim is that the folk wisdom of languages tells everything we could want to know about personality dimensions (Goldberg, 1981, 1993). How convenient for the personality investigator: we have no end of observers and subjects of observation, and when new trait-like words appear—'dork', 'geek', 'dweeb'; then, there are 'ditz' and the somewhat dated 'jerk'—we are on the spot to witness their use and to see how they fit.

Traits have an intuitive appeal. They seem to explain differences among persons, the things that make individuals recognizably unique. Everyone uses them to describe others. All those people to observe, all those observers. Could we possibly go wrong? Certainly not, said Raymond Cattell, one of our trait theorists, putting the case about as strongly as it could be put: '[A]ll aspects of human personality which are or have been of importance, interest, or utility have already become recorded in the substance of language' (Cattell, 1943, p. 483). There's no denying that trait terms can begin—and likely most often do—as lexical descriptions. But do they *explain*? In a personal, subjective sense—the sense in which we use them every day—of course they do. To us. But they are not *scientific* explanations; they are circular, explaining by recourse to the very behaviour they address. Traits are only explanatory as scientific concepts if we can predict subsequent behaviour from them, behaviour not yet observed and independent of the situations in which the particular trait dimension was formulated. They are also scientifically useful when we can discover their **antecedents**★, as behaviour geneticists have begun to do with a few of them.

So what *is* a trait? We have begun to answer the question, but there is great depth in trait theory as modern trait theorists have developed it. The next step is to take up the story with the trait psychology of an American pioneer, Gordon Allport. Traits had centre stage in Allport's theory of personality, and his conception of them will be our initial focus.

The Trait Theory of Gordon Allport

Gordon Allport: Personal History

Gordon Willard Allport was born in the small western Indiana town of Montezuma in November 1897. When he was young the family moved to Glenville, Ohio, a Cleveland suburb, where he grew up in an environment 'marked by plain Protestant piety and hard work'. His father was a physician, and in the small towns in which the Allports lived, his father's medical practice was at home. Allport would later recall that 'Tending office, washing bottles, and dealing with patients were important aspects of my early training' (Allport, 1967, pp. 4–5). He was the youngest of four boys; an elder brother, Floyd, also became a psychologist, in fact a social psychologist of considerable distinction. On his graduation from high school, he was persuaded by Floyd to apply to Harvard. He did and was admitted, passing the entrance examination by the skin of his teeth. Very quickly, however, he did much better. Majoring in economics and philosophy, he graduated in 1919. He took courses in psychology, though, with notable professors Hugo Münsterberg, Edwin Holt, and Herbert Langfeld. Three years later, Langfeld would be his PhD adviser. He then spent a year teaching English and sociology at Robert College in Istanbul. On his return home, the brash young Allport, BA Harvard, wrote to Freud asking if Freud would see him. Freud would.

Gordon Allport (© Bettmann/CORBIS)

> Soon after I had entered the famous red burlap room with pictures of dreams on the wall, he summoned me to his inner office. He did not speak to me but sat in expectant silence for me to state my mission. I was not prepared for silence and had to think fast to find

a suitable conversational gambit. I told him of an episode on the tram car on my way to his office. A small boy about four years of age had displayed a conspicuous dirt phobia. He kept saying to his mother, 'I don't want to sit there . . . don't let that dirty man sit beside me.' To him everything was *schmutzig* [filthy]. His mother was a well-starched *Hausfrau*, so dominant and purposive looking that I thought the cause and effect apparent.

When I finished my story Freud fixed his kindly therapeutic eyes upon me and said, 'And was that little boy you?' Flabbergasted and feeling a bit guilty, I contrived to change the subject. While Freud's misunderstanding of my motivation was amusing, it also started a deep train of thought. I realized that he was accustomed to neurotic defenses and that my manifest motivation (a sort of rude curiosity and youthful ambition) escaped him. . . . This experience taught me that depth psychology, for all its merits, may plunge too deep, and that psychologists would do well to give full recognition to manifest motives before probing the unconscious (1967, pp. 7–8).

Admitted to the PhD program in psychology, he completed his studies in 1922 with a dissertation on 'An experimental study of the traits of personality: With special reference to the problem of social diagnosis'. In 1922, a PhD dissertation on personality traits—and in the staunchly experimental department of psychology at Harvard—was certainly unusual. While writing his thesis, he was invited to attend a conference convened by Edward Bradford Titchener, the leader of the now long dead school of structuralism, to review developments and issues in the psychology of sensation.

After two days of discussing problems in sensory psychology Titchener allotted three minutes to each visiting graduate to describe his own investigations. I reported on traits of personality and was punished by the rebuke of total silence from the group, punctuated by a glare of disapproval from Titchener. Later Titchener demanded of Langfeld, 'Why did you let him work on that problem?' Back in Cambridge Langfeld . . . consoled me with the laconic remark, 'You don't care what Titchener thinks.' . . . The whole experience was a turning point. Never since that time have I been troubled by rebukes or professional slights directed at my maverick interests (1967, p. 9).

He shouldn't have been troubled. Langfeld had a substantial reputation, and one of his thesis readers was the great psychological generalist William McDougall. They wouldn't have let him get away with anything nonsensical.

On a travelling fellowship, Allport spent two years in Germany and England, working with distinguished psychologists, among them the fathers of Gestalt psychology Max Wertheimer and Wolfgang Köhler, and William Stern, who conceived the IQ. They disabused him, he said, of his youthful faith in behaviourism. Back at Harvard, he taught social ethics and then, in 1926, moved to Dartmouth College to teach psychology. Four years later, Harvard asked him to return, and he stayed for the rest of his career.

Allport wrote extensively—*Personality: A Psychological Interpretation* (1937), *The Nature of Prejudice* (1954), *Becoming: Basic Considerations for a Psychology of Personality* (1955), *Personality and Social Encounter* (1960), *Pattern and Growth in Personality* (1961), and *Letters from Jenny* (1965). He did research on expressive movement with Philip Vernon, developed personality tests, and gave signal emphasis to the importance of studying individual persons (in, for instance, *Letters from Jenny*). Despite the influence of his study in Germany and England, Gordon Allport was as American as apple pie. He embodied the national virtue of eclecticism, of willingness to recognize a breadth of ideas. He was generously inclusive in his theory of personality, accepting a variety of concepts as long as they weren't too Freudian, based on a psychology of disturbed persons, behaviouristic, statistical, or founded in animal research. He was a genuine iconoclast in the personality field, but an influential one, highly respected and revered by his students, many of whom became prominent. He was honoured by the presidency of the American Psychological Association in 1939, receiving its Distinguished Scientific Contribution Award (1964), and in 1966, a year before his death, he was named the first Richard Clark Cabot Professor of Social Ethics at Harvard.

Personality and the Trait

Allport's theory of personality, although it survives in many a textbook of personality theories, no longer has advocates—it never had a great many—but the influence of his ideas lives on. His concept of the trait is one of them. It was very sophisticated in its recognition of both cross-situational consistency, which traits require, and individual variability in the expression of traits. Allport didn't deny the role of situations in controlling behaviour or insist that traits are all; on the contrary, his concept makes room for variability because traits do not mechanically cause behaviour irrespective of 'determining conditions' in situations.

The Reality of Personality

Most personality psychologists consider that the concepts of personality are fictions, invented to account for individual consistency. We infer them because they help us to make sense of our observations, because they are economical bridges between antecedents and consequent behaviour. You'll remember this from the first chapter. Not Allport, though. For him, personality was *real*. 'Personality *is* something and *does* something. . . . It is what lies *behind* specific acts and *within* the individual' (Allport, 1937, p. 48). The reality of personality is evident in his definition: 'Personality is the dynamic organization within the individual of those psychophysical systems that determine his unique adjustments to his environment' (1937, p. 48). Let me emphasize the triad: first, personality is '*within the individual*'; second, it is '*psychophysical*', thus consisting of both mental (I should say cognitive, shouldn't I?) and physiological components; and, third, it is *dynamically organized*—not static but developing and changing, and more than a collection of attributes.

In *Pattern and Growth in Personality* (1961), Allport slightly modified the last part of the definition to replace 'unique adjustments to his environment' with 'characteristic behaviour and thought' (1961, p. 28). His intent was to 'designate whatsoever an individual may do' (p. 28) instead of a more narrow emphasis on adjustment. In summing up his definition, Allport made perfectly clear what he meant: 'Personality is what a person "really is", regardless of the way other people perceive his qualities or the methods by which we study them. Our perceptions and our methods may be in error, just as an astronomer may fall short in studying the constitution of a star. But the star is still there, a challenging object for study' (1961, p. 35).

Idiographic and Nomothetic Approaches

An individual is 'a system of patterned uniqueness', and to study a single person we look to see *how* his or her individuality is patterned. This is, as Allport referred to it, an

idiographic★ approach (from the Greek, meaning 'one's own'). We narrow our focus to the constellation of traits that makes one person different from all other persons. As scientists of behaviour, however, we wish to find *general laws* applying to all (or, in a probabilistic sense, most) individuals. We want the *universal law*, and this is **nomothetic★** (from the Greek for 'the giving or enacting of laws'). Is, then, the study of individual uniqueness, idiographic study, not science but something else—biography, say, or art? Allport, who came down on the side of idiography, studying individuals in depth, saw no fundamental conflict with the investigation of many individuals to arrive at general laws. In fact, most of his research was nomothetic, although he noted that nomothetic laws would inevitably result in oversimplification and rough approximation when applied to individuals.

Real People, Real Traits

If personality is real, then so are its constituents. That means that traits are also 'real', within the person, determining 'characteristic behaviour and thought'. Exactly. A trait, in Allport's definition, is a *'neuropsychic structure having the capacity to render many stimuli functionally equivalent, and to initiate and guide equivalent (meaningfully consistent) forms of adaptive and expressive behaviour'* (1961, p. 347). His language, unnecessarily complicated, means that a trait causes a person to treat the stimuli of different situations as equivalent, alike. We may see traits in action by the *frequency* of behaviour (*Hermione is frequently petty and mean*), by the *range of situations* in which the behaviour appears (*She is petty and mean to her roommates, to her sister, to her boyfriend, and to new people she meets*), and by the *intensity* of the behaviour (*Hermione's pettiness and meanness stand out strongly*). Make no mistake about it, traits are built-in elements of personality, being both cognitive and physiological. Like habits, perhaps, with a structural basis? No, Allport distinguished between traits and habits:

> The young child learns (with difficulty) to brush his teeth night and morning. For some years this habit stands alone, aroused only by appropriate commands from the parent as an item in the chain of acts he performs night and morning. With the passing of years, however, brushing the teeth becomes not only automatic (as is the way with habits) but it is woven into a wider system of habits, viz., a trait of *personal cleanliness*. Many adults have a generalized habit of removing all manner of dirt from their persons. If someone omits to brush his teeth, he is uncomfortable, not only because a habit is frustrated, but because the omission violates a more general trait of cleanliness (1961, p. 345).

Types of Traits

Allport distinguished between types of traits: *common traits*, characteristic of *people*, and *individual traits* (called *personal dispositions*) that are attributes of *individual persons*. Both are generalized determiners of behaviour.

Common traits tell us about consistency across situations in many persons, although each individual with a given trait will not express it in the same specific ways as others. That variability is the cost of comparing people to one another, each with his or her own signature. Personal dispositions 'reflect the structure of a given personality' and reflect it accurately (1961, p. 359). Some personal dispositions are more important than others. The most striking are *cardinal dispositions*, by which a person is distinctly recognizable. In someone with such a dominant disposition 'Almost every act seems traceable to its influence' (1961, p. 365). Pierre Trudeau's dramatic, commanding, incisive intellectual style and his unswerving devotion to the intelligent and right course could be seen in virtually everything he did as prime minister, husband, lover, father, private citizen. Few people, though, seem to be characterized by a single, cardinal disposition. More commonly, individuals will have several *central dispositions*—distinguishing traits that determine behaviour in different kinds of situations. How many central dispositions will we find in most people? Allport thought that five to ten would be a likely number (1961, p. 367). William James's biographer, Ralph Barton Perry, characterized him by eight central dispositions, four 'morbid' and four 'benign': '(1) hypochondria, (2) preoccupation with exceptional mental states, (3) marked oscillations of mood, . . . (4) repugnance to the processes of exact thought, . . . (5) sensibility, (6) vivacity, (7) humanity, (8) sociability' (1961, p. 366). Perry's set of James's dispositions found Allport's approval.

After central dispositions, there are *secondary dispositions*, and there will be many in everyone. You might think of them as minor individual traits like preference for dress or foods, frivolity at parties, and so on. They are not linked to more general consistencies of behaviour. The number of secondary dispositions Allport saw as an empirical problem to be addressed by such research methods as personality tests—or the dictionary, as he did in his landmark research with Odbert, extracting trait names from the words we typically use to describe people.

Readers of Allport saw a sophisticated view of the way traits determine behaviour. The trait is not absolute in its influence; situations will cause variations in whether and how the trait is expressed. 'Perfect consistency [in behaviour] will never be found and must not be expected.' This was in 1937 (p. 330). In 1961, he tried to make it clearer: 'The young teacher is not always "friendly"; he is not uniformly "ambitious" in every direction; his "enthusiasm" surely depends on what and whom he is teaching' (p. 333). Characteristics of the person (traits) and the attributes of situations *interact* in determining behaviour. He would certainly have agreed with Lewin's formulation, Behaviour = f(Person, Environment), or $\mathbf{B} = f(\mathbf{P}, \mathbf{E})$, and we might see his interactionist view of traits as an expression of partially bidirectional influence of person and environment discussed in Chapter 15. His thinking was probably not sufficiently advanced to recognize reciprocal determinism proposed by Albert Bandura (also in Chapter 15).

Allport in Perspective

The trait was indisputable to Gordon Allport and the study of traits indispensable to personality. Although the modern trait theories we take up next—the theories of Cattell and Eysenck, and Big Five theory—do not owe a specific debt to Allport, they are obliged to him in more general (but not less important) ways. At Harvard, he had an extraordinary influence on a large number of graduate students who went on to important careers. Cattell, at Harvard for a period of three years in the early 1940s, profited from his exposure to Allport's thinking. You couldn't be a trait psychologist without intersecting in your views with the trait contributions of Gordon Allport.

There is no question that Allport's trait research was a way of showing personality psychologists how to go about trait study. They could develop personality tests to study common traits, as he did, with questionnaires on ascendance–submission (Allport, 1928), values (Allport, Vernon, & Lindzey, 1960), and religious orientation (Allport &

Ross, 1967). His idiographic study of Jenny was intended as a model for psychologists to follow in using personal documents (her letters) to arrive at an understanding of traits dominating personality (Allport, 1965).

Raymond Cattell and Factor-Analytic Trait Theory

Introduction

Factor Analysis

Raymond Cattell's trait theory is rigorously quantitative, and in that respect would not have pleased Allport. It depends on the statistical technique of factor analysis, by which we can find order and system in sets (matrices) of correlations far too large to make sense of otherwise. The factor analyst begins with a number of measures taken on a large number of subjects—the more the better. The measures might be scores on personality tests or ratings on a large set of traits. In a moment we'll follow Cattell as he obtains ratings on sixty traits, made on a sizeable sample of subjects by raters who know them well. But first let's review briefly what correlation is, as it figures prominently in the discussion.

Correlation is a statistic that tells us about the relationship between two sets, or *arrays*, of numbers—scores on a personality test, IQs, heights, weights. The two arrays might be the scores of identical twin pairs on such measures. The index of correlation, r, varies between $+1.0$, a perfect positive correlation, and -1.0, a perfect negative correlation. Zero means no relationship at all. What, then, does a correlation coefficient of, say, .60 signify about the relationship between two variables? A property of r is that its square tells us about the amount of variance, the variability around the mean, that can be predicted in one array by the other. That is, r^2 tells us how precisely we can predict the order of scores in one array from the other. Our correlation of .60, squared, tells us that 36 per cent of the variance in one array is accounted for by the other. Practically, it will be the case that with a correlation of such magnitude there will be a fair number of scores in the predicted array that will not match up with scores on the predictor array, but very few of these will be major discrepancies—a score at the high end of the predictor array and a score at the very low end of the predicted array.

Back to Cattell and his ratings. The first thing he does is to correlate each one of the sixty trait ratings with each of the others to produce a huge correlation matrix. Factor analysis reduces the number of correlations by extracting commonalities—in other words, factors—that represent the shared variance among groups of correlations. Each of the sixty trait ratings will correlate with each of the factors. Some of these correlations will be substantial—far closer to the limiting 1.0 of perfect correlation than to 0— at least, we hope they will, and these substantial correlations will be with single factors. They are called factor loadings, and they define the factors. How many factors and the size of the factor loadings will depend on the structure of the original data. There are actually two major factor analytic procedures, one of which (generally preferred because it is simpler and more straightforward) produces factors that are not correlated with each other. If you think of factors as axes in space (beyond three factors, we have to stretch our minds to imagine in hyperspace), the first procedure makes them *orthogonal*, right-angled to each other. Another procedure, favoured by Cattell, is to allow the factors to be correlated, so the axes will be *oblique* to each other. Cattell thought this to be more realistic in the personality domain, since traits may well be correlated with each other. One more thing: having arrived at a set of factors, we can determine each individual's scores on each of the factors—his or her position on the factor dimension.

This is exactly what Cattell did. He began with Allport and Odbert's reduced list of 4,500 trait names and distilled it by eliminating those that were simply synonyms of others. That left him with 171 trait names, on which he obtained ratings by people familiar with individual members of a large group. These ratings were intercorrelated and factor-analyzed to produce a list of thirty-five factors called *surface traits* (which are discussed below). Following a number of factor analyses of different types of data, Cattell arrived at sixteen factors representing the basic traits of personality (see Cattell, 1957). These factors became the basis of a personality test, the 16 Personality Factor (16PF) Questionnaire (Cattell, Eber, & Tatsuoka, 1977).

Types of Data

There is one more question to answer before we look at Cattell himself and the theory he developed. What kinds of data do we subject to factor analysis? First, there are the data from 'the actual, everyday-life situation' (Cattell, 1965, p. 61). These would include the second-hand ratings we touched on above—Cattell began with these. But these 'everyday-life' data also include information taken from the life record. The frequency of automobile accidents, health, school, and police records—these are examples of what he called **L-data★**. The second-hand ratings were the data with which Cattell started. Next, there are responses to personality questionnaires designed to measure all manner of personality attributes, attitudes, and interests. These are **Q-data★**. Personality and measurement psychologists have known for a very long time that Q-data are vulnerable to distortion, because respondents may not understand themselves well, may portray themselves in a socially desirable way (Crowne, 2000), or may otherwise bend self-description to suit their motives. Objective tests that are less affected by the inaccuracies that afflict Q-data are called **T-data★**. T-data are gathered from tests that do not make evident what is being measured; it is in this sense that Cattell calls them 'objective'. Personality tests of this kind might feature questions with hidden aims that respondents won't be able to detect and shape their answers accordingly. They might also have special scales to detect improbable self-report (the Minnesota Multiphasic Personality Inventory, or MMPI, is a good example). Projective tests that require telling stories to pictures (the Thematic Apperception Test) or interpreting inkblots (the Rorschach) are sources of T-data, as are covert behavioural observation, measures of neural processes (the electroencephalogram, EEG), or physiological activity (heart rate, blood pressure, changes in skin conductance, GSR).

The most common research approach in multi-trait personality assessment is to measure people on many variables and then follow the steps to trait definition by factor analysis or trait confirmation by other methods (experimental tests of trait hypotheses, for example). This is **R-technique★**. But we could also be idiographic, as Allport urged on Cattell. Suppose we collected trait data from an individual through a diary kept over a long period of time—eighty entries over a forty-four day period in one study of a single person, a procedure called **P-technique★**. Plotting the variation in strength of eight traits over daily entries in the diary will show how traits vary with changes in the person's circumstances. Figure 9.2 shows an example of this technique, in which the individual had rehearsals for a play, developed a cold, appeared in the play, had to cope with

Raymond Cattell (© Devon Cattell. Reprinted by permission.)

an accident his father had, was reproached by his aunt for not being helpful, and worried that his adviser held a hostile attitude toward him.

Raymond Cattell: Personal History

Raymond Bernard Cattell was born in March 1905 in the midland county of Staffordshire, England, and grew up in a town on the Devonshire coast. His father was an inventive mechanical engineer who applied his talents to improving military equipment, the steam engine, and the internal combustion engine. The young Cattell enjoyed a happy and active childhood, but that changed when, during the First World War, he saw gravely wounded soldiers being treated at a nearby hospital. This was a sobering exposure to the fragility of life, and out of it came a lifelong sense of urgency to accomplish as much as he could.

Cattell entered the University of London at sixteen as a chemistry major, taking first-class honours on graduation in 1924. He was strongly influenced by reading provocative British writers—Bertrand Russell, George Bernard Shaw, H.G. Wells, Aldous Huxley—and immersed himself in psychology, which he soon came to see would give greater opportunity to make a difference in helping to solve the social problems he saw around him. He worked in social service and then entered graduate school at the University of London. Charles Spearman, successor to Galton in the study of intelligence and the creator of factor analysis, was his PhD adviser. After a period of 'fringe jobs' (which included, however, some clinical experience), he was invited to Columbia University, joining E.L. Thorndike as a research associate, and was then appointed to a chair in psychology at Clark University. The interlude at Harvard came next, 1941 to

Figure 9.2 An example of P-technique—the same person over 44 days and 80 measurements (From *Personality and Motivation Structure and Measurement* by Raymond Cattell. © 1957. Reprinted with permission of Harcourt Inc., a division of Thomson Learning: www.thomsonrights.com. Fax 800-730-2215.)

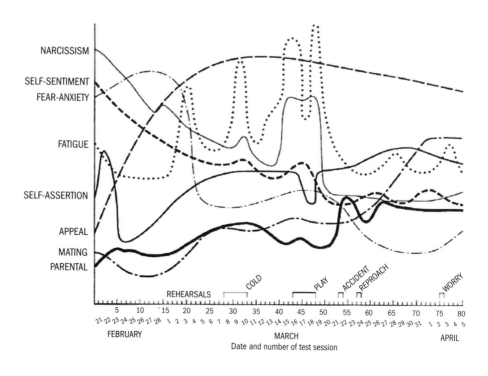

1944, and in the last of the war years he was a civilian consultant on officer selection to the US Army. He accepted a research professorship at the University of Illinois in 1945, founding the Laboratory of Personality Assessment and Group Behaviour and further developing factor analysis and applying it to the study of personality. He retired in 1973, moving first to Colorado to pursue his research and then to the University of Hawaii and the Hawaii School of Professional Psychology.

Cattell was widely recognized and highly regarded for his prodigious accomplishments—more than 450 scientific articles, forty-plus books, and several personality tests. Among his books, the following are especially noteworthy: *The Description and Measurement of Personality* (1946), *An Introduction to Personality Study* (1949), *Personality: A Systematic Theoretical and Factual Study* (1950), *Personality and Motivation Structure and Measurement* (1957), *The Scientific Analysis of Personality* (1965), and a two-volume work on learning (Cattell, 1979, 1980). He developed the principal research instrument of factor-analytic trait theory, the 16PF (Personality Factor) Questionnaire.

At the age of ninety-two, Cattell was nominated for the American Psychological Foundation's Gold Medal Award for lifetime achievement in psychological science. The award was announced in the *American Psychologist* and the presentation ceremony was all set, when two non-psychologists and a psychologist launched scathing attacks on him, accusing Cattell of racism for his advocacy of eugenics and his support of research on group ('racial') differences in intelligence (Hunt, 1998; Hilts, 1997; Mehler, 1997). He had clearly been immoderate in his youth but corrected himself to urge voluntary—not coerced—selective breeding of humans. Hilts and Mehler, however, found the eugenics policies and condemnation of mixed marriages ('race mixing') in his later writings disturbing. (Mehler, I might note, promotes himself on a website of the 'Institute for the Study of Academic Racism'.) Cattell's support of intelligence research showing heritable differences in intelligence between blacks and whites also made him, like the researchers themselves, a racist in the eyes of the critics. We must note that his conclusion on black–white intellectual differences was that differences *within* groups were far more significant than the difference in mean IQs.

The American Psychological Foundation postponed the award to consider the charges. Cattell published a strong rebuttal and removed his name from consideration. Then, sadly, without resolution of a tawdry affair, he died in February 1998. His children staunchly defend him on a Cattell family website (http://www.cattell.net/devon/rbcmain.htm).

Emphases and Major Concepts

Cattell had a statistician's—a factor analyst's—definition of personality:

> *Personality is that which permits a prediction of what a person will do in a given situation.* The goal of psychological research in personality is thus to establish laws about what different people will do in all kinds of social and general environmental situations. . . . Personality is concerned with all the behaviour of the individual, both overt and under the skin (1950, pp. 2–3).

Personality is made up of traits, the core concept in the theory. You can see that the research method Cattell adopted and developed would produce a set of traits, so the theory rests on some initial assumptions about how to proceed and the method to follow. Cattell's empirical procedure indicated that there are two kinds of traits: surface traits and source traits.

Surface Traits and Source Traits

Observations that go together, that are correlated, make up **surface traits**. We collect some L-data and find that people who are judged honest are also self-controlled, self-denying, loyal, fair-minded, and reliable. Cattell suggested that we might call this surface trait 'sound character' versus 'psychopathic personality' (1950, p. 37). Not very profound, these correlations, although they may seem more basic than they are if personality theory is unfamiliar to you. They are descriptive, and they will stem from a number of determinants, likely two or more source traits. A behavioural syndrome of neurosis—the symptoms displayed by patients—represents a surface trait.

Source traits are far more than correlated observations and can be discovered only by the factor analysis of trait-like data. They are the real stuff of personality. As we've seen, Cattell found sixteen source traits, personality in its underwear, its absolute essence, so to speak. Since the factors he extracted were correlated, he could look for 'second-order factors', finding eight. He regarded the sixteen 'first-order' factors, however, as the structure of personality. What is the source of source traits? It should not be a surprise, given Cattell's heritage (study with Spearman, the lingering influence of Galton), that he thought some source traits must be genetic in origin. He called them *constitutional* source traits, 'springing from *internal* conditions' (1950, p. 34). There are, as well, source traits that come from environmental influences, *environmental-mould* traits. Since source traits reflect 'pure, independent influences, as present evidence suggests', said Cattell (1950, p. 33), they cannot represent the combined influence of hereditary and environmental influences but must come from one or the other. He gave as an example the source traits behind the surface trait of schizophrenia:

> It has long been known . . . that both hereditary predisposition and environmental stress are usually needed to produce [schizophenia]. . . . [F]actor analysis *has* revealed two source traits in this area, one influencing a pattern of traits including obstructive, secretive, hostile, withdrawn—which may be the pattern produced by a frustrating environment—and one loading such indicators as timid, aloof, conscientious, languid, uninterested in the opposite sex—which seems to be the pattern of prepsychotic behaviour found in those constitutionally prone to schizophrenia. Certainly we see here two distinct source traits which, if they are both present in sufficient endowment in the same positive direction, will account for the surface-trait pattern of schizophrenia (1950, p. 34).

How can we be sure that factor-analytic procedures have reliably converged on traits? After all, factor analysis can only give us a factor structure of the data we put through it. Cattell argued that if analysis of all three types of data—'L', 'Q', and 'T'—each produce the identical pattern of source traits, we can be confident that the source trait solution is 'real'. Also, if we find the same source traits in different countries and cultures, as Cattell reported, we are likely to have discovered 'real' traits (Cattell, 1965). Factor analyses of L- and Q-data tend to yield the same factors; T-data factor analyses result in somewhat different traits (Cattell, 1959).

Modalities of Source Traits

Source and surface traits reflect different kinds of attributes. They may be based on the modalities of ability, temperament, or dynamic aspects of personality. Except for ability, factors don't necessarily represent a single modality. A given factor (source trait) might involve both temperament and dynamic modalities. As Cattell acknowledged, 'complete modality separation and clarity has not yet been reached, either theoretically or in the findings' (1959, p. 276). **Ability traits** determine how well we are able to accomplish things. Intelligence is the prime example. Cattell proposed that there are two independent 'intelligences'—*fluid intelligence*, our problem-solving ability, mostly independent of specific previous experience; and *crystallized intelligence*, 'a general factor, largely in a type of ability learned at school, representing the effect of past application of fluid intelligence, and amount and intensity of schooling' (1965, p. 369).

You might think that fluid intelligence would be genetic in origin, crystallized intelligence environmental, but Cattell concluded that the evidence favoured a substantial heritable component to both: by his reckoning, 65 per cent of the variance in fluid intelligence is genetic in origin, 60 per cent of crystallized intelligence (Cattell, 1980). Why would the effects of learning be influenced by heredity? This must be because of differences in the ability to profit from experience. To identify two distinct intelligences and to examine their heritability, we must have measures of each. The conventional intelligence tests—Stanford–Binet, the Wechsler tests, and others—are good measures of crystallized intelligence, with subtests measuring vocabulary, simple numerical ability, comprehension of common problems and situations, verbal analogies. But how do we get away from assessing the accretions of experience and the influence of culture to reveal fluid intelligence? Cattell, confronting that problem years earlier, had developed a culture-free intelligence test (Cattell, 1944); he later called the test 'culture-fair', recognizing that freedom from cultural influence in the requirements of testing and in test items is impossible. Culture-fair tests present analytic and reasoning problems that don't require the use of language, depending only on pictures.

Temperament traits are constitutional in origin and are the basis of emotionality. How quick, full of energy, emotionally responsive versus slow, energy-less, and generally devoid of emotion you are will be determined by temperament traits. Then, there are **dynamic traits**, which consist of **attitudes**, **sentiments**, and **ergs**. *Attitudes* are surface traits, dynamic because they express a disposition to respond to persons or objects. Attitudes come from a more basic level, environmental-mould source traits, that Cattell called *sentiments*. They are 'major acquired dynamic trait structures which cause their possessors to pay attention to certain objects or classes of object, and to feel and react in a certain way with regard to them' (1950, p. 161). Ergs are dynamic constitutional source traits. *Ergs* (from the Greek for 'work, energy') motivate or drive behaviour and, as constitutional traits, they are innate. They determine our perception of objects, our emotional responses to them, our instrumental behaviour to achieve goals related to the object, and the satisfaction we experience on goal attainment. Cattell claimed that ten ergs had been well identified in factor-analytic studies: hunger, sex, gregariousness, parental protectiveness, curiosity, escape (fear), pugnacity, acquisitiveness, self-assertion, and narcissistic sex. The tenth erg might be named self-indulgence, including sexual pleasure in the self, smoking, drinking, and drug use.

There is a definite relation among attitudes, sentiments, and ergs: attitudes are subsidiary, secondary to and expressive of sentiments; sentiments, in turn, are derived from ergs, the elemental motives. The most important of the sentiments is the **self★**, which will derive from many ergs and appear in many of our attitudes. It is the 'master senti-ment'. We can see how attitudes, sentiments, and ergs are organized and related to each other by constructing a dynamic lattice, a kind of path analysis from ergs to attitudes. Figure 9.3 shows us the complex picture, and Cattell complicated it still further by rec-ognizing **metaergs**, dynamic environmental-mould traits. A man driven to earn money is motivated by metaergic tension.

The Specification Equation

We now have the trait organization of personality. How can we take this personality scheme and turn it to the predictive task that personality theory is all about? We do this by entering an individual's factor scores into a **specification equation★** and weighting the traits by their significance to the situation we are trying to predict behaviour in:

$$R = s_1T_1 + s_2T_2 + s_3T_3 + \cdots + s_nT_n$$

R is the response to be predicted. The s's refer to the *relevance* of the trait to the situation (the greater the relevance, the bigger the value of s). If a trait is relevant but inhibitory—that is, it makes the predicted response less likely to occur—s will have a negative sign. T's are traits. The equation assumes that traits are independent and additive in their effects. Suppose we want to predict performance in an achievement situation, a psychol-ogy midterm, say. We have measures on four traits, two we think will have positive effects, one inhibitory, and one irrelevant. Source trait B, intelligence, should make a strong positive contribution to our prediction (the higher a student's intelligence, the

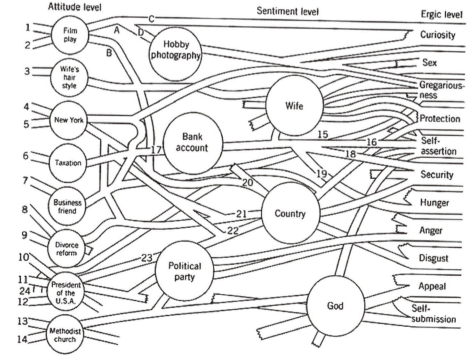

Figure 9.2 Attitudes, sentiments, and ergs in a portion of the dynamic lattice of a single individual (From Cattell, 1950, p. 158. Reprinted by permission of Raymond B. Cattell.)

better his or her midterm). This will also be the case with source trait C (high ego strength confers emotional stability, resistance to stress, and the ability to deal with distraction). The values of the s's for these two traits will be positive and high. Factor O is the trait insecurity (outstanding attributes are apprehensivness, self-reproach, insecurity, worry, being troubled). The s for this trait will be given a negative weight. Our fourth trait, factor I, sensitivity, is irrelevant to achievement, so it receives a weight of 0.

This method is simple but effective. It's effective because as a linear model it's a good first approximation and predicts successfully. The specification equation is *multidimensional* in representing both person and situation by a number of variables, and by including both traits of the person and situational characteristics it is a mathematical approach to the **person–situation interaction**. The specification equation enables us to quantify conflict, by summing the weights determined for ergs and sentiments. If there are both positive and negative weights whose sums equal each other, conflict will be maximal.

Personality Development

Changes in personality, including developmental changes, can be approached by assessing the same traits in an individual at different ages. Cattell developed child measures of the 16PF traits for four age ranges, making it possible for trait measurement to be carried out on children ranging from as young as four to high-school age. There is a problem, however: do the trait tests of children measure the same factors as the adult 16PF? Cattell was aware of this problem and applied a bridging strategy, giving the test for eight- to twelve-year-old children and the adult 16PF to sixteen-year-old high-school students. The personality pictures of the sixteen-year-olds from the two tests were not exactly comparable, but Cattell was persuaded that there were enough trait similarities to suggest that cross-age measurement of personality factors was perfectly feasible. He had established to his satisfaction that with some traits, at least, assessment could begin in very young children, continuing with the full list throughout the lifespan. He proceeded to plot curves of increases and decreases in each trait at intervals into old age (Cattell, 1965). We might, for instance, expect the youthful quality of high surgency (bubbling enthusiasm, acting on impulse) to decline with age, and it does. Between eight and sixteen, acceptance of authority is replaced by greater independence.

A technique called Multiple Abstract Variance Analysis (MAVA), developed by Cattell, has been applied to the study of heritable and environmental influences on traits and their interactions (Cattell, Blewett, & Beloff, 1955). It involves the study of twins and siblings reared together or apart, estimating the amount of variance on each trait attributable to heredity, environment, and heredity–environment interactions. It was curious that heredity–environment correlations were largely *negative*, suggesting to Cattell that environmental determinants oppose heredity. Parents and teachers, for example, want the behaviour of children to be more like the average. They encourage the shy and inhibited ones to be more outgoing and try to restrain the boisterous and overactive. With the strong influence shown by heredity on personality traits, it would be easy to conclude that learning in the family environment does not play much of a role. But Cattell thought it did. For some traits, he found, parent child-rearing practices have highly significant effects. To take one instance, socially adjusted, easygoing, warmhearted, and outgoing adults are likely to have come from families typified by a cheerful father, calm mother, and the exercise of discipline by reasoning instead of punishment (Cattell, 1973).

Cattell even took his large-scale factor-analytic approach to the societal level, proposing that dimensions analogous to traits could be derived for social groups. So, instead of the personality sphere of the individual, such an analysis would give the **syntality★** of social group, society, or nation. He and students did some early exploratory work on this bold question (Cattell & Wispé, 1948; Cattell, Saunders, & Stice, 1953), laying the groundwork for later study of groups—the neighbourhood and larger society that surround families, for example—that would greatly enhance understanding of personality development. Cattell was nothing if not daring and inclusive in his vision.

Perspective 9.1   The Factor Profile of the University Professor

Factor-analytic trait theory can claim a huge body of evidence on matters like the validity of the trait conception of personality, the number of traits necessary to represent the 'personality sphere', the appearance of the same traits in L-data and Q-data, the behavioural and surface trait expression of the fundamental (source) traits, trait heritability, personality development, psychopathology, and traits as attributes of societies.

This isn't an exhaustive list. Among other issues that Cattell, colleagues, and students investigated was the following: do members of recognizable occupational groups have common personality attributes, common trait profiles? Might personality traits incline people toward their occupational choices and enable them to fit more comfortably and effectively into their jobs? It would be a big validity bonus if the 16PF were able to identify trait differences from occupation to occupation. As a practical, applied bonus, distinctive profiles could be useful in the selection of job applicants and in vocational counselling, as Cattell pointed out (Cattell, et al., 1970). Indeed, there's a very substantial industry devoted to doing just that, as a trip to the Internet and a search for organizational consultants and vocational counsellors will quickly disclose. (We'll see in the heritability evidence presented in Chapter 16 that there is a sizeable genetic coefficient for vocational interests, so 'occupational personalities' is not a surprise.)

Cattell and collaborators collected 16PF data on a large number of occupations, reporting their personality profiles in the 16PF handbook. This isn't difficult research to do: we find the mean scores on each trait and the variability around the means, and use standard statistical techniques to determine the profile uniqueness of the occupations we've sampled. Then, individuals can be matched to profiles.

Here's the trait profile for a sample of university professors reported by Cattell et al. (1970). Take a moment to study it and then read on. The professor's profile is 'a very unusual one' (p. 186), compared to the general population and to many other occupations. It is distinguished by high intelligence, soberness, sensitivity and tender-mindedness, radicalism (free-thinking, liberalism), self-sufficiency, rejection of conventional morality, and an absent-minded imaginativeness. Professors are prone to neuroticism and not very good leaders. Cattell et al. drew on Rudyard Kipling's lines in the 1917 poem 'The Holy War' to caricature professors as 'brittle intellectuals who crack beneath a strain' (p. 186).

Did you find these attributes in the 16PF profile? And do they capture the professors you know? As the chair of a department of psychology, would you want to know whether a job candidate was a good personality match to the picture given by the 16PF? If so, would that influence you to hire the candidate? Now, a larger question: assuming that the 16PF accurately characterizes the typical professor, do we really want to pack the university with professors who fit a type? Do we really want that kind of uniformity? I don't think we need

Figure 9.4 The 16PF profile
of the university professor
(Adapted from Cattell, et al.,
1970, p. 184.)

CHARACTERISTICS OF LOW SCORE	STEN SCORES										CHARACTERISTICS OF HIGH SCORE
	1	2	3	4	5	6	7	8	9	10	
Reserved, detached, critical, aloof, stiff	.	.	.	.	A	.	.	.	.	.	Outgoing, warmhearted, easygoing, participating
Less intelligent (fluid + crystallized intelligence)	.	.	.	.	B	.	.	.	.	.	High intelligence (fluid + crystallized intelligence)
Affected by feelings, emotionally less stable, easily upset, changeable (low ego strength)	.	.	.	.	C	.	.	.	.	.	Emotionally stable, mature, faces reality, calm (high ego strength)
Humble, mild, easily led, docile, accommodating	.	.	.	.	E	.	.	.	.	.	Assertive, aggressive, competitive, stubborn
Sober, taciturn, serious	.	.	.	.	F	.	.	.	.	.	Happy-go-lucky, enthusiastic
Expedient, disregards rules (weak superego strength)	.	.	.	.	G	.	.	.	.	.	Conscientious, persistent, moralistic, staid (strong superego)
Shy, timid, threat-sensitive	.	.	.	.	H	.	.	.	.	.	Venturesome, uninhibited, socially bold
Tough-minded, self-reliant, realistic	.	.	.	.	I	.	.	.	.	.	Tender-minded, sensitive, clinging, overprotected
Trusting, accepting conditions	.	.	.	.	L	.	.	.	.	.	Suspicious, hard to fool
Practical, 'down-to-earth' concerns	.	.	.	.	M	.	.	.	.	.	Imaginative, bohemian, absent-minded
Forthright, unpretentious, genuine but socially clumsy	.	.	.	.	N	.	.	.	.	.	Astute, polished, socially aware
Self-assured, placid, secure, complacent, serene	.	.	.	.	O	.	.	.	.	.	Apprehensive, self-reproaching, insecure, worrying, troubled
Conservative, respecting traditional ideas (conservatism)	.	.	.	.	Q_1	.	.	.	.	.	Experimenting, liberal, free-thinking (radicalism)
Group dependent, a 'joiner' and sound follower	.	.	.	.	Q_2	.	.	.	.	.	Self-sufficient, resourceful, prefers own decisions
Undisciplined, self-conflict, lax, follows own urges, careless of social rules	.	.	.	.	Q_3	.	.	.	.	.	Controlled, exacting will power, socially precise, compulsive, following self-image
Relaxed, tranquil, torpid, unfrustrated, composed	.	.	.	.	Q_4	.	.	.	.	.	Tense, frustrated, driven, overwrought

Sten is a contraction of 'standard ten'. Stens are standard scores with a mean of 5.5 and a standard deviation of 2. The 16 factors are source traits. Factors A–O were found in L- and Q-data; Q1–Q4 only in Q-data analyses. They are listed in order of factor 'size'—that is, their contribution to the total measured variance.

to worry about it. The 16PF just isn't sufficiently reliable or valid to yield sharply drawn pro-files. It can give some guidelines to help people make career choices, but it isn't a person-ality mould, a cutter for the gingerbread man professor (or anything else). Nor could the professors who made up this 16PF occupational sample all (or mostly all) have been absent-minded, 'brittle intellectuals'.

Research

The whole of Cattell's factor theory of personality is research-based, right from the initial use of trait names in the language to establish the database. Moreover, this was a particu-lar kind of research, on a gargantuan scale in the vastness of its probing and its use of big samples of subjects, and almost exclusively statistical in its reliance on the correlation coefficient and the technique of factor analysis to discover common elements. Every-thing that we have discussed stems from this approach. That traits turned out to be the essence of personality was no empirical accident; it was foreordained by Cattell's method.

Implications

Traits were as real to Cattell as they were to Allport, and he believed without an iota of doubt that factor analysis was the perfect method to reveal the inner workings of the human being. Even though factor analysis can only simplify and group what has gone in (as, you might say, the output of the sewer pipe is simply a different form of what entered it at the other end), Cattell would have argued that he began with data repre-senting how people characterize each other. What could be more basic than that? Moreover, behaviour genetics research by Cattell and others has established that many of the traits that emerged from Cattell's research and the similar studies of a number of investigators show strong genetic influence. What could be more basic than that? If a trait (reactive versus emotionally stable, for example) has a substantial heritability coef-ficient, doesn't this lend strong credence to the validity of the empirical and statistical methodology? And, if we find similar trait structures in appreciably different cultures (Japan, India), does this not as well imply that factor analysis is the way to define what personality is? Finally, since personality was, to Cattell, that which enables us to predict the behaviour of persons, and since traits do enable us to do just that, although in a lim-ited way, does it not follow that the research path was correct?

Cattell's Factor-Analytic Theory in Perspective

Factor-analytic theory is demanding of the student of personality. To understand and apply it requires exhaustive knowledge; to gather the data required for trait–situation weights and the calculation of specification equations is beyond the resources of most psychologists. It is, for most, an impractical theory, a demonstration of what might be, a pipe dream to take your imagination into the beyond. The sheer amount of research that Raymond Cattell did over the course of a long career is staggering. His work spanned seventy years, but ninety per cent of us could not have approached his output in a hundred and forty. One person who knew him well quipped, 'Raymond Cattell can write faster than I can read.' Among his books were several that had wide influence. They integrated and applied the evidence from his factor studies, making what might have seemed piecemeal organized and comprehensive. Factor analysis met the high demands of trait extraction and identification, and Cattell's scheme appears to make a great deal of sense. But are we just traits, heritable or learned; is that what personality is? Gordon Allport accused factor theorists of perpetrating 'a complete abstraction'. 'An entire population (the larger the better) is put into the grinder, and the mixing is so expert that what comes through is a link of factors in which every individual has lost his identity. His dispositions are mixed with everyone else's dispositions' (Allport, 1937, p. 244). Sounds rather like the sewer analogy, doesn't it? We may note that factor theory is in a sense not a theory at all but more a catalogue of abstract attributes distilled from surface attributes. To Cattell's credit, he attempted to deal with (predict) individual behaviour through specification equations, and he did apply factor concepts to personality development, occupational choice, and the larger social context.

Cattell was captive to his heritage. In his research method and in his beliefs about personality, society, and how to improve the human condition, we see his PhD adviser, Charles Spearman, creator of the method of factor analysis and firm advocate of the role of heredity in intelligence, and in the shadow behind Spearman, Sir Francis Galton, measurer of mind, arch hereditarian, and eugenicist. Spearman was a member of Galton's Eugenics Society, and in 1912 advocated that people in positions of authority (parliamentarians, for example) should have to meet a minimum intellectual standard (not a bad idea that, when you think of the political spectrum).

The Type-Trait Theory of Hans Eysenck

Introduction

Hans Eysenck was another student of a statistician, authority on intelligence, factor analyst, and devoted admirer of Galton, and like Cattell he went to the University of London. His adviser was Cyril Burt—Sir Cyril, actually, knighted for reforming the British educational system in the 1940s, and the same Burt we met in Chapter 1, who later perpetrated the twin data fraud. Unlike Cattell, Eysenck went well beyond factor analysis in his research and theory. Perhaps this was because of his strange and distant adviser, with whom he was never close. Factor analysis, however, was the starting point in defining the variables of his theory.

Eysenck thought cultural ideas had important contributions to make to personality theory, and he went back 2,400 years to Hippocrates for 'the three main notions that characterize modern work in personality' (Eysenck & Eysenck, 1985, p. 42). In our world, the Hippocratic doctrine that four humours (blood, phlegm, black bile, and yellow bile) variously combine to determine character is scientific nonsense, but Eysenck saw behind Hippocrates' conception three ideas that make perfect sense. The first of them is that traits determine behaviour. The second is that traits derive from types, which form a higher order in the synthesis of personality. Third, types represent constitutional differences among people, based on heredity and neurology. Eysenck built his theory on these three ancient principles.

He began with two types that had been proposed by Immanual Kant and elaborated as dimensions by Wilhelm Wundt: stable (weak emotions) versus unstable (strong emotions), and unchangeable (slow to change) versus changeable (quick to change). Four temperaments (sanguine, choleric, melancholic, and phlegmatic) could be arrayed

Figure 9.5 Wundt's two-dimensional view of the four temperaments (Reprinted from *Personality and Individual Differences, 12*, Stelmack & Stalikas, Galen and the Humor Theory of Temperment, pp. 255-63. Copyright (1991). with permission from Elsevier.)

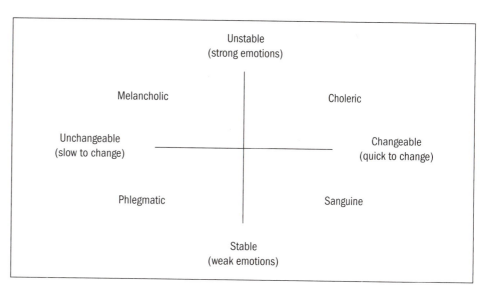

in these two dimensions. The melancholic person would be found in the unstable-unchangeable quadrant, the choleric person in the unstable-changeable quadrant; the sanguine individual was changeable-stable, and the phlegmatic individual stable-unchangeable.

Then, Eysenck read Jung's *Psychological Types* and saw that Jung's scheme closely resembled Wundt's and was better: *introversion–extraversion* perfectly covered the changeable–unchangeable dimension and entailed, as Jung said, different forms of psychopathology (introversion associated with anxiety disorders and extraversion with hysteria). *Neuroticism–normality* gave a fuller account of the other dimension, stable–unstable, and was implicit in Jung's type theory (see Figure 9.6).

Figure 9.6 The temperaments and the dimensions of introversion–extraversion and unstable–stable (neuroticism–normal) (From Eysenck and Eysenck (1985), *Personality and Individual Differences*. New York: Plenum, page 50. Reprinted with kind permission from Springer Science and Business Media.)

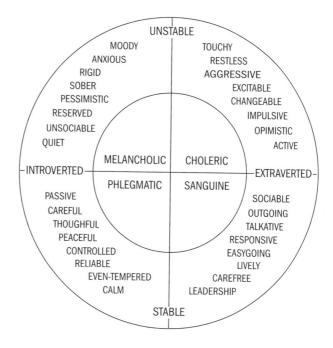

So here it was, a scheme for representing the principal variations in personality in two dimensions, and Eysenck set about testing its validity and implications, as we shall see. He would come to view *E* (introversion–extraversion) and *N* (neuroticism–normality) as more significant than any other descriptive factors in personality (Eysenck & Eysenck, 1975). There turned out to be three dimensions, however, not two. Factor-analytic research established a dimension of **psychoticism★**, ranging from normality at one pole to schizophrenia and other psychoses at the other. Criminality and psychopathic behaviour appear on this dimension.

Subordinate to the three types are traits, which could be uncovered through factor analysis and which are closer to behaviour. Eysenck thus pictured the organization of personality as hierarchical, with the three dimensionalized types at the top, the traits as closely interrelated 'habitual responses' of the person (Eysenck & Eysenck, 1969, p. 41), and observable behaviour on specific occasions (gossiping about an acquaintance before class) at the base (see Figure 9.7). Now came the question of how these phenotypic dimensions occurred—the **genotypes★** underlying them. Eysenck turned to biology—neural events—and to behaviour genetics for these underlying processes. From factor analysis to the activity of neurons and to genetics is a big leap. We shall see how far Eysenck got in his attempt.

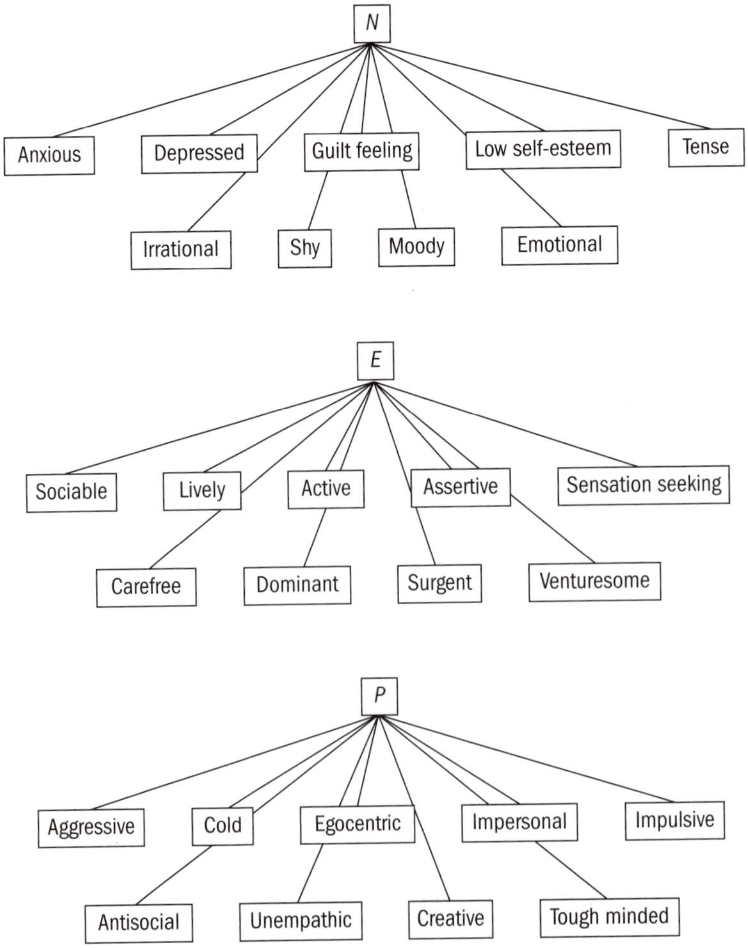

Figure 9.7 The hierarchical structure of type and trait. Types are neuroticism (*N*), extraversion (*E*), and psychoticism (*P*). The traits of each type are arrayed beneath. (From Eysenck & Eysenck (1985), *Personality and Individual Differences*. New York: Plenum, pages 14–15. Reprinted with kind permission from Springer Science and Business Media.)

Hans Eysenck (Ullstein Bild/The Granger Collection, New York)

Hans Eysenck: Personal History

Hans Jurgen Eysenck was born in wartime Berlin in March 1916. His father was an actor and singer; his mother appeared in silent films. They divorced when he was two, and he was raised by his maternal grandmother. Eysenck was introduced by his father to the stage when he was still a small child, and he had a small part in a film, starring his mother, about estranged parents who become reconciled. Art did not imitate life, however. His mother remarried, to a Jewish filmmaker, and in the 1930s fled to Paris to escape the fate of Jews under the Nazis. In late adolescence, Eysenck came to despise the 'murderous regime' of Hitler and, in an autobiographical account, recalls that 'very early on all my sympathy went to the persecuted Jews, and all my hatred to their persecutors (Eysenck, 1982, p. 287). He made no secret of his beliefs and was branded as a 'white Jew'. Refusing to join the Nazi party and enroll in the military, he was denied university admission. Outstanding athletic ability—he was ranked second in Germany as a junior tennis player—spared him worse things.

This was the time to leave for good, and Eysenck did, in 1934, at the age of eighteen. He went to France for a year before taking up his lifetime residence in Britain. He was not prepared to devote his life to tennis or the arts, however. Instead he applied to the University of London to study physics but was turned down because he had 'taken the "wrong" subjects'. He was determined on science and asked if there was another scientific subject he could study. 'Yes, I was told, there was always psychology. "What on earth is that?" I inquired in my ignorance. "You'll like it," they said. And so I enrolled in a subject whose scientific status was perhaps a little more questionable than my advisers realized' (Eysenck, 1980, p. 156). 'Thus is one's fate decided by bureaucratic stupidity,' he added. Whether he would have made a great physicist is unanswerable, but he became one of the most distinguished of contemporary psychologists.

Eysenck completed his baccalaureate degree in 1938 and the PhD two years later under Burt, studying individual variation in aesthetic judgement. Burt was difficult and odd, both in his capacity as professor and psychologist and personally. Said Eysenck, 'Burt was probably the most gifted psychologist of his generation, but he was seriously disturbed psychiatrically' (1982, p. 290). As a German émigré in 1940, Eysenck was going to have a difficult time finding a job, but as luck would have it he was offered a position as research psychologist at Mill Hill Emergency Hospital, a psychiatric facility. Never one to accept the conventional way of looking at things, he disdained categorical psychiatric diagnosis (schizophrenia, depressive psychosis, the various neuroses) and began to study patients dimensionally. Here was the birth of Eysenck's types—introversion–extraversion and neuroticism–normality—and the subject of his first book, *Dimensions of Personality*, in 1947. He had begun to make his mark and was appointed both director of the psychology department in the just-opened Institute of Psychiatry at Maudsley Hospital in London and professor of psychology.

Diplomacy not one of his strong traits, Eysenck lost no time in laying the groundwork for a 'great battle' with psychiatry, particularly psychoanalysis. He set to work on behaviour therapy and enraged psychoanalysts by telling them that their craft was a long, tedious, painful, and useless fraud. He was prolific in research and writing. If Cattell was prodigious, what do we say of Eysenck, who outdid him with 1,097 articles and 79 books? We're already at Super Deluxe, Giant Size, and there's no category bigger. His major works include *The Scientific Study of Personality* (1952), *The Structure of Human Personality* (1953/1970), *The Biological Basis of Personality* (1967/1977), and *A Model for Personality* (1981). He also wrote books for a popular audience: *Uses and Abuses of Psychology* (1953), *Sense and Nonsense in Psychology* (1957), and *Mindwatching: Why People Behave the Way They Do* (with his son, M.W. Eysenck, 1983). These are just a few of many. He wrote about smoking, psychoanalysis, behaviour therapy, sexual and marital behaviour, sports psychology. He even delved into astrology and parapsychology. He founded two influential journals, *Behaviour Research and Therapy* and *Personality and Individual Differences*, and developed personality questionnaires—the Maudsley Personality Inventory, supplanted by the Eysenck Personality Inventory, and the Eysenck Personality Questionnaire—to measure the dimensions of personality. He was fearsome in debate and did not suffer fools gladly. He was also a gentle and likeable man and a devoted husband. Eysenck died in September 1997 after a long struggle with cancer.

Type-Trait Theory: Emphases and Major Concepts

Three Personality Types

For Eysenck, formulating his type-trait theory, a test of Jung's types was the place to start. He reviewed the case files of 700 neurotic patients at the Mill Hill Hospital, extracting 39 behavioural and historical details common to the records. These were factor-analyzed, producing two factors. One of them appeared to be neuroticism versus normality; the second factor placed patients with anxiety symptoms at one pole and those with hysteria at the other. He gave the name *dysthymia* to the anxiety disorders and kept Jung's hysteria label for the other pole. This was the introversion–extraversion dimension (Eysenck, 1947). The two type dimensions could be thought of as *superfactors*, not a bad way to characterize them.

What characterizes these elemental types? In the manual of the Eysenck Personality Questionnaire, we find extraverts depicted as affable and sociable, seeking out others; in the extreme, they are party animals. Reading or studying alone is not for them. They seek change and excitement and take chances; venturesome is an apt description. They laugh readily, and find practical jokes irresistible. Although easygoing and friendly, they don't control their feelings well and can quickly become angry. They tend to be unreliable and are not to be counted on. Introverts, on the other hand, are typically quiet, reserved, and introspective. Given a choice of reading or socializing, they would choose to read. They don't leap into things, and they shy away from impulses of the moment. Excitement is to be avoided, and feelings are well controlled. They don't lose their tempers. Their emotional tone inclines to pessimism. The ideal for the introvert is a regular and well-ordered life. These are ethical, reliable people, placing high value on morality (Eysenck & Eysenck, 1975, p. 5).

Persons at the neurotic end of the neuroticism–normality dimension are chronically anxious worriers, often suffering bouts of depression. They are highly emotional, easily aroused, and slow to regain composure. Tendencies to rigidity and irrationality are brought out by their emotionality. The key to understanding the neurotic is worry—a never-ending preoccupation with all the things that could go wrong. People who are stable (normal) maintain an even disposition and do not readily become emotional. When they do, their arousal doesn't last long. They are calm, controlled, and not disposed to worry about things that might very well not happen (1975, p. 5).

Psychoticism was a late addition to the personality profile, meriting its own book, *Psychoticism as a Dimension of Personality* (1976). It is the result of polygenic inheritance, a number of 'small-effect' genes working in combination, together with exposure to environmental stress. Sometimes, one or a very few large-effect genes may produce psychosis, giving a full-blown clinical picture (Eysenck & Eysenck, 1976). Psychosis-prone individuals are loners. They don't like people and don't fit in with others—not surprising given their insensitivity, lack of feeling, and inability to empathize. They tend to cause trouble, to be cruel and indifferent, and they can be quite hostile. Making others look like fools and upsetting others provide an odd enjoyment. They are attracted to the unusual and strange. They tend to be impulsive sensation-seekers with little regard for dangerous consequences. High-scoring children are isolated trouble-makers, cold and without feeling for others. 'Poorly socialized' is a fitting way to see the person high on this dimension. Close to the psychotic will be found criminals, psychopaths, and drug addicts. At the pole opposite to psychoticism we find people whose test scores show them to be well socialized and capable of impulse control (Eysenck & Eysenck, 1975, pp. 5–6).

These personality type pictures flesh out the trait terms seen in Figure 9.7. They represent people at the extremes. Accordingly, a caution: we must remember that these are dimensions, so don't expect to find the spitting image of yourself in one type or another. Most people will be toward the middle of the distribution on each of the types.

Discovery of Traits versus Hypothesis Testing

We don't have the lexical origin of trait ideas in Eysenck's research and theory, but he and Cattell were not so terribly different. Cattell's traits came from common wisdom in the language, Eysenck's from classical notions of character (personality) organization. Where, empirically, did Eysenck's types and traits come from? Well, from factor analysis of data sources like the symptoms of neurotic patients in the beginning research, and personality questionnaire items derived from *hypotheses* about personality types and traits. So, we do have a difference: Cattell used factor analysis to *discover* the base traits of personality in a kind of grand fishing expedition; Eysenck employed factor analysis to *test hypotheses* about personality dimensions. The lexical hypothesis said to Cattell, 'Look at language. It will tell you everything there is to know about personality. Just write words about personality in the form of questionnaire items, throw the responses of a large number of people into a factor analysis, and see what structure falls out.' It was the theoretical model that spoke to Eysenck. It said, 'Take the sensible part of those ancient ideas of Hippocrates, formulate hypotheses from them, and use factor analysis to test them.'

What Causes Personality Types?

How do we get from phenotypic types/traits to the genes and neural processes that underlie them—the genotypes? Eysenck's views evolved in two stages: a *learning* conception based on Pavlovian conditioning and Hullian learning theory, and an *arousal* conception based on brain structures and processes.

LEARNING

Reading Pavlov, Eysenck found a neural theory of excitation and inhibition that caught his eye. He also found it applied to a curious problem. Pavlov's canine subjects in salivary conditioning experiments were strikingly unequal in their learning. Some acquired the conditioned salivary response readily: they were attentive in the conditioning appara-tus—the harness that restrained them during conditioning—and took fewer trials to pro-duce strong conditioned responses. Other dogs were poor subjects: they were lethargic in the apparatus and often fell asleep. These two 'conditioning types' differed outside the laboratory. The bad conditioners were sociable and friendly dogs—tail waggers—and they were active. Good conditioners were 'stolid' or extremely inhibited, cringing and avoiding their caretakers (Pavlov, 1927, 1928). Sounds rather like extraverts and intro-verts, doesn't it, except that we might expect the active and responsive extravert to be the more easily conditioned, the introverted dog a conditioning dummy. Pavlov had an answer to the apparent conundrum, and it relied on assumed processes of excitation and inhibition in the cerebral cortex. If excitation were to build up and then dissipate in the repetitive conditioning task (weak excitation), while inhibition, an incremental tendency not to respond, increased (strong inhibition), the dog would condition poorly. A dog with strong excitation and a slower accretion of inhibition would be a good subject.

Eysenck took these Pavlovian notions and turned them to the explanation of intro-version–extraversion and neuroticism–normality. But first, he had to have a better understanding of the role of inhibition, and for this he turned to Clark Hull. Hull, as we'll see later when we review Dollard and Miller's S-R theory, had proposed that the probability of a response (Dollard and Miller called it R, Hull called it E) is a function of drive times habit; this can be represented in the form of an equation, $\boldsymbol{R = f(D \times H)}$, where the strength of a habit (H), a learned association between stimulus and response, is energized by relevant primary and secondary drives (D). But Hull also found that in the course of learning, an inhibitory tendency (I) *not* to respond grows, a tendency that decreases the probability that responses will occur. Not responding gives inhibition the time to dissipate, and learning to continue. The reduction of inhibition is just like the reduction of a drive, so the behaviour of not responding is, in fact, reinforced. We have to modify our version of Hull's formula to include inhibition:

$$R = f(D \times H) - I.$$

Hull called this inhibitory process *reactive inhibition*. Eysenck's version of Pavlov's excita-tion–inhibition theory and Hull's reactive inhibition was expressed in two postulates. Here is the first, a postulate of *individual differences*: excitation and inhibition do not develop, dissipate, or reach the same strength in every person. Different rates of growth and dissipation and different strengths of these processes result from the physiological structures involved in linking stimuli and responses (Eysenck, 1957, p. 114).

The second postulate set forth a typology linking excitation–inhibition with extra-version and introversion. It is in two parts, on excitation and on inhibition:

1. *Excitation*. Persons who develop excitation slowly and at weak intensity are predis-posed to extraversion and, if they become neurotic, to hysterical-psychopathic symptoms. Persons who develop excitation rapidly and in strength are predisposed to introversion and to dysthymic symptoms if they become neurotic.

2. *Inhibition.* Persons in whom reactive inhibition grows rapidly to a high level and dissipates slowly are predisposed to extraversion and to hysterical-psychopathic symptoms in the case of neurosis. Those developing inhibition weakly and slowly and dissipating it rapidly are predisposed to introversion and in the case of neurosis to dysthymic symptoms (Eysenck, 1957, p. 114).

Table 9.1 shows how excitation, inhibition, and the rate of buildup differ in extraverts and introverts, and what their neuroses would be if they developed them.

Can you see how we might test some implications of the postulates? With introverts and extraverts as experimental subjects, we could examine the consequences of the assumed build-up of excitation and inhibition. Let's consider three types of experiment. In one, we require participants, extreme introverts and extraverts selected by personality questionnaire, to tap rapidly with a metal stylus on a metal plate. Contact interval and time are recorded. It's boring and monotonous; extraverts, with lower cortical excitation and higher, more slowly reduced, inhibition, should be found to take involuntary time-outs or 'rest periods'. Introverts, higher in excitation and lower in inhibition, should have fewer interruptions by far. This is just what Spielmann found in his PhD research (Spielmann, 1963). In the second test, neurotic introverts and extraverts perform a vigilance task: they must monitor the appearance of three consecutive odd digits, a monotonous auditory watch-keeping. Introverts were more vigilant, and measures of autonomic responses showed them to be more aroused than extraverts (Claridge, 1967).

As for the third, an even more direct kind of test, we study the classical conditioning of the eyeblink to a puff of air in dysthymics, hysterics, and normals. In two experiments, Franks found dysthymics to produce more conditioned eyeblinks than either normals or hysterics, confirming the Eysenck hypothesis (Franks, 1956, 1957). But tried a third time, he couldn't replicate the results, and neither could others (Franks, 1963). Eysenck (1967) concluded that some details of the experiments varied and must have been responsible for the replication failures. The critical features—ones that were not followed in the attempted replications—were the use of nonreinforced trials (i.e. trials based on the conditioned stimulus alone, showing better conditioning by introverts), weaker intensity of the unconditioned stimulus (which favours introverts), and the short interval between the unconditioned and unconditioned stimulus (which is likewise better for introverts). In his view, the hypothesis remained intact.

AROUSAL

In 1967 Eysenck modified the learning model by proposing that introverts and extraverts differ in level of *arousal*, providing an explicit neural account of the basis of

Table 9.1	The Typological Postulate of the Relation Between Extraversion and Introversion and the Processes of Excitation and Inhibition		
	Excitation	Inhibition	Form of Neurosis if developed
Extraverts	Low (slow build-up)	High (rapid build-up)	Hysteria-Psychopathy
Introverts	High (rapid build-up)	Low (slow build-up)	Dysthymia
Source: After Eysenck, 1957.			

excitation–inhibition. Introverts, his new model held, have a higher level of arousal than extraverts. He next gave a neural explanation of the difference between neurotics and normals. And third, he proposed that the relation between external stimulus intensity and cortical arousal is *curvilinear*, introverts and extraverts showing different functions.

The new model was influenced by the then conventional idea that arousal is the province of the *ascending reticular activating system* (ARAS), which, through ascending pathways, arouses the cerebral cortex. This, we now know, is too simple a version of the activities of the nuclei of the reticular formation; it is involved in a number of things, including sleep, attention, movement, muscle tone, and cardiac, circulatory, and respiratory reflexes. Eysenck's revision held that differences in ARAS-mediated arousal are responsible for the differential excitation and inhibition in introverts and extraverts. To account for the excessive emotionality in neuroticism, he implicated the visceral brain, better known as the **limbic system★**. Here, too, the view was oversimplified. In such limbic structures as hypothalamus and amygdala, neurotics and normals were presumed to differ in the level of neural activity.

The last proposition combined the arousal level hypothesis with the classic Yerkes-Dodson law, which specifies that the relation between motivation and performance is in the form of an inverted U. As motivation increases, performance rises to a peak and then declines. If arousal means motivation, then introverts reach maximum arousal more quickly than extraverts. But with arousal increasing beyond the level at which it produces effective performance, the introvert begins to perform poorly. On an easy task, the introvert, over-aroused, doesn't perform well and is especially bad on a difficult one. On the other hand, the extravert's low arousal is increased by the task to a close-to-optimum level, and her performance exceeds the introvert's. Among neurotic extraverts, the high demands of a difficult task should cause a kind of 'spill-over' from visceral brain activation, resulting in a decrease in effective performance—one that is, however, not as great as the introvert's. McLaughlin and Eysenck (1967) reported an experiment in the learn-

Figure 9.7 The ascending and descending connections of the reticular activating system. ARAS = ascending reticular activating system, VB = visceral brain (limbic system), AAP= ascending afferent pathways. (From H.J. Eysenck, *The Biological Basis of Personality*, 1967. Courtesy of Charles C. Thomas Publisher, Ltd., Springfield, Illinois.)

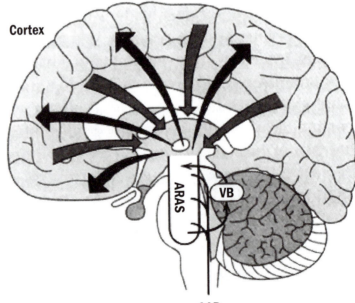

ing of nonsense syllables with nearly these results (Figure 9.9).The only deviation was in the reversed performance of the neurotic and normal introverts on the difficult task: the neurotic introverts should have been worse but performed at a slightly (but not significantly) higher level (Figure 9.10). Even better experiments by Geen (1984), which *measured* arousal instead of *assuming* it from the theory, confirmed McLaughlin and Eysenck and the arousal model of extraversion–introversion.

Research

From the development of type and trait measures and factor-analytic derivation of types and traits to experimental tests of hypotheses, Eysenck followed the research trail. It is

Figure 9.9 Learning on an easy verbal learning task, normal and neurotic extraverts and introverts plotted as points on the Yerkes-Dodson motivation-arousal curve (Adapted from Eysenck, 1967, p. 131.)

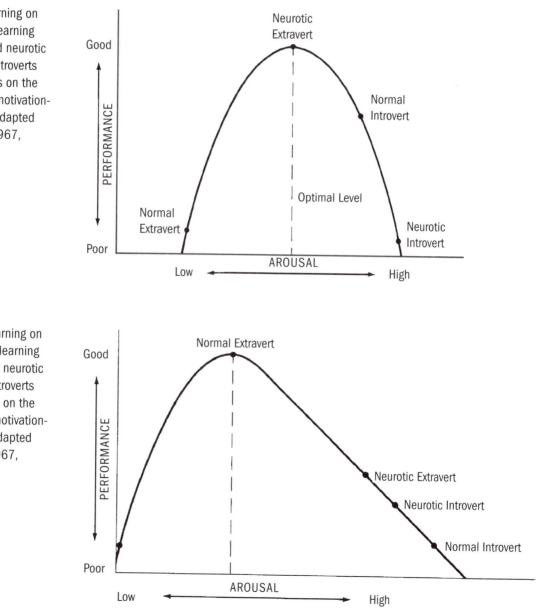

Figure 9.10 Learning on a difficult verbal learning task, normal and neurotic extraverts and introverts plotted as points on the Yerkes-Dodson motivation-arousal curve (Adapted from Eysenck, 1967, p. 131.)

like Cattell's factor theory in this exceptional foundation, but Eysenck went further. His is a true hypothetico-deductive theory: hypotheses were formally derived from theory and tested in experimental situations. You have to credit his theory formulation and utter devotion to experimental confirmation.

Implications

The big implication of Eysenck's work is that personality is best conceived dimensionally. Language contains trait wisdom, characterizations of people that represent behavioural consistency across situations. And if not the language itself, the wisdom of the ages, passed down to us, distills lexical intelligence about human traits. That's where trait theorists start. Develop measures of these lexical (or the ancients') traits, reduce them to a manageable number or make modern sense of them, apply them to subject populations in the form of self-ratings or personality questionnaires, intercorrelate them, and then factor-analyze the correlation matrix. Hypothesis testing may enter in all of this (as Eysenck pursued it), but what we get *is* the face of personality. We may go beyond, as Eysenck did, to formulate a theory relating this phenotypical level to neural processes and genotype. Personality *structure* and *processes* are now far from behaviour and organization by tests.

Eysenck laid out a stiff set of requirements for type-trait theory to meet in order to demonstrate the biological basis of personality convincingly:

- Research has to show that the major superfactors (E, N, and P, more commonly referred to by the easily-remembered acronym P-E-N) show significant heritability. Reviewing twin-study evidence of the kind we'll see in Chapter 16, Eysenck and Eysenck concluded that 'for practically all traits and dimensions of personality there is a considerable degree of genetic determination of individuals. . . . No serious worker in this field denies that genetic factors account for something like half the variance, and equally none would deny the importance of environmental variables' (1985, p. 96).
- Traits analogous to P-E-N must be found in nonhuman animals. This is a very tough demand indeed. Studies of rhesus monkeys and chimpanzees have unearthed three temperament dimensions that might resemble P-E-N (Chamove, Eysenck, & Harlow, 1972; Van Hooff, 1971).
- P-E-N traits must be truly cross-cultural and appear in non-English-speaking cultures.
- The basic superfactor dimensions of personality must be stable over time.

Type-Trait Theory in Perspective

We have taken note of Eysenck's vast and scarcely imaginable productivity in conceiving and investigating a theory of personality. His construction is highly believable, with abundant empirical support. Having said that, type-trait theory is not beyond question. Eysenck had a huge ego. To him, the personality business was all figured out—by him. Other theories didn't have much going for them. Witness the following:

> As an example, I would class among the inadmissible theories those of Freud, Adler, Jung, Binswanger, Horney, Sullivan, Fromm, Erikson, and Maslow. They fail essentially because for the most part they do not generate testable deductions; because where they do so the deductions have most frequently been falsified; and

because they fail to include practically all the experimental and empirical studies which have been done over the last 50 years. Historically, these theorists have had some influence, but their theorizing and their mode of working has not been in the tradition of natural science, and they have not been found responsive to adverse criticism or empirical disproof (Eysenck, 1991, p. 774).

Freud, 'a great story teller', or Jung, 'a great myth-creator', would excite people more than Cattell or himself, who demanded that they learn matrix algebra and the physiology of the nervous system (Eysenck, 1972, p. 24). Did he really have personality all figured out? Many critics have noted that the research was not all confirmatory, and Eysenck had to make *ad hoc* assumptions to rescue the theory (his explanation for the failure to replicate the Franks experiments, for example). His neural model was 1960s-style physiological psychology, far too neurologically simple for our contemporary understanding. The complexities of personality and its neurological bases extend well beyond mechanisms of arousal and activation. By comparison, Zuckerman's modern neurochemical theory of sensation seeking, based on the neurotransmitter dopamine (see Chapter 17), shows how far behind Eysenck's theory is (Zuckerman, 1994a).

Type-trait theory does little or nothing to help resolve the person–situation interaction question. Surely, contemporary personality theory has advanced beyond person explanations of behaviour. Eysenck did not deal well with situational variation, although the precedent was there for him to take advantage of.

It is perfectly possible and wholly appropriate, as we have seen, to develop a *psychological* theory of personality. It is not necessary to try to base the elemental psychological attributes of personality on biological processes or genetic endowment. That is not to diminish neurological models or genetic investigations—some of them (Zuckerman's for example) are powerful and provocative. But there *is* a legitimate place for the psychological.

Put it all together and what do we have? Psychologist Nathan Brody well summed up the status of type-trait theory when he wrote in 1988, 'in the past fifteen years the empirical inadequacies of Eysenck's biological theory have become more manifest, but it is still the case that there are virtually no competing theories of comparable scope' (p. 158). Agree?

Big Five Theory

How many traits are there? This was a rhetorical question posed by Eysenck in a 1991 article. Are there sixteen? Five? Three? He already knew the answer. It wasn't, however, so obvious an answer to others. In 1949, Donald Fiske, at the University of Chicago, tested research participants using rating scales from Cattell's work. He found five factors, subsequently replicated by other investigators: social adaptability, conformity, will to achieve, emotional control, and inquiring intellect (Fiske, 1949). This was the first 'Big Five'. Other investigators, typically beginning with lexical trait names and winnowing them down, have found five factors, and some, repeating Cattell's factor analyses, also wound up with five. In 1993, Goldberg commented that Cattell might have been the intellectual father of the Big Five, but he 'has consistently denied his paternity and has yet to embrace the model' (p. 27).

Of the numerous five-factor researchers, we shall concentrate on two, a team consisting of Robert McCrae and Paul T. Costa, Jr, of the National Institute on Aging of the National Institutes of Health. Their work has been exemplary, and they stand at the

Robert McCrae (Courtesy Robert R. McCrae)   Paul T. Costa, Jr (Courtesy Paul T. Costa)

front of the Big Five line. McCrae and Costa did not begin directly with lexical trait descriptions but with personality measures and trait ratings derived from the language source. They respect the source, however, and think it is definitive.

> All human languages . . . contain terms to characterize personality traits—relatively enduring styles of thinking, feeling, and acting. By *personality structure*, . . . psychologists mean the pattern of covariation among these traits, usually summarized in terms of a relatively small number of factors that represent the basic dimensions of personality. For example, in English-speaking cultures, people who are sociable are generally also energetic and cheerful, and these traits together define a dimension usually called *extraversion*. . . . If . . . personality traits represent variations in basic ways of acting and experience, the structure might be universal. Universality might be attributed to specieswide biological bases of traits, or it might represent a purely psychological consequence of the shared human experience of living in groups, using abstract thought, or being conscious of our own mortality (McCrae & Costa, 1997, p. 509).

Big Five Measurement

To measure these 'big five' traits Costa and McCrae (1992) developed a personality questionnaire, the NEO Personality Inventory, or NEO-PI-R (*N* for *neuroticism*, *E* for *extraversion*, *O* for *openness to experience*; *agreeableness* and *conscientiousness* became separate factors after the name was coined; *PI* stands for *personality inventory*; *R* is for *revised*). John (1990) coined an acronym, OCEAN, to help with the trait names. Six lower-level traits (called **facets**★) are assessed for each of the five 'superfactors'. The traits, attributes of high and low scorers, and the scales to measure them are in Table 9.2.

In the questionnaire, NEO-PI trait items are phrased in the first person (third person when they are to be applied to a target person by someone else), and they are to be answered on a five-point scale from 'strongly agree' to 'strongly disagree'; at the middle

Table 9.2   The Big Five Traits, their Attributes, and What the Trait Scales Assess

Characteristics of the High Scorer	Trait Scales	Characteristics of the Low Scorer
Neuroticism (N) Worrying, nervous, emotional, insecure, inadequate, hypochondriacal	Assesses adjustment vs emotional instability. Identifies individuals prone to psychological distress, unrealistic ideas, excessive cravings or urges, and maladaptive coping responses.	Calm, relaxed, unemotional, hardy, secure, self-satisfied
Extraversion (E) Sociable, active, talkative, person-oriented, optimistic, fun-loving, affectionate	Assesses quantity and intensity of interpersonal interaction; activity level; need for stimulation; and capacity for joy.	Reserved, sober, unexuberant, aloof, task-oriented, retiring, quiet
Openness to Experience (O) Curious, broad interests, creative, original, imaginative, untraditional	Assesses proactive seeking and appreciation of experience for its own sake; toleration for and exploration of the unfamiliar.	Conventional, down-to-earth, narrow interests, unartistic, unanalytical
Agreeableness (A) Soft-hearted, good-natured, trusting, helpful, forgiving, gullible, straightforward	Assesses the quality of one's interpersonal orientation along a continuum from compassion to antagonism in thoughts, feelings, and actions.	Cynical, rude, suspicious, uncooperative, vengeful, ruthless, irritable, manipulative
Conscientiousness (C) Organized, reliable, hard-working, self-disciplined, punctual, scrupulous, neat, ambitious, persevering	Assesses the individual's degree of organization, persistence, and motivation in goal-directed behavior. Contrasts dependable, fastidious people with those who are lackadaisical and sloppy.	Aimless, unreliable, lazy, careless, lax, negligent, weak-willed, hedonistic

is 'neutral'. These are examples: on habits—'I keep my belongings neat and clean'; on attitudes—'We can never do too much for the poor and elderly'; on relationships—'Most people I know like me'; on preferences—'I find philosophical arguments boring'; on social skills—'I don't find it easy to take charge of a situation'.

Validity of Measurement and Theory

Wholly without modesty, trait theories claim that their taxonomies *are* the fundamental dimensions of personality. A large and growing literature attests to the Big Five's right to say that its dimensions are the basic ones. First, we can point to the several investigators who have reduced the complexity of personality to five factors. They name them differently, a virtually inescapable problem in factoring personality measures when the interpretations of the factors, tests, samples of participants, and sometimes factor-analytic techniques vary, but they *do* find five and the five they find resemble each other. Table 9.3 lists five-factor discoverers, starting with Fiske in 1949. As McCrae and Costa (2003) said of their work on the Big Five, 'we now know the scope of personality traits', adding that five traits 'endure through adulthood and help to shape emerging lives' (p. 3).

More important is a literature putting hypotheses to test. A very large question confronting the Big Five is whether five factors (*just* five and in particular *the* big five) are found in different cultures. If so, it could well be that they are universal in humans, and if that were to be the case, personality psychologists would find encouragement to look for 'a common genetic basis for personality' (McCrae & Costa, 1997, p. 515; Loehlin, 1992). To this end, the NEO-PI was translated into a number of languages and administered to samples in the following language groups: German, Portuguese, Hebrew, Chinese, Korean, and Japanese. Then, a very complicated factor comparison was made to the American factor data, taking the American factor structure as a target to be matched. The mean congruence coefficients for *N, E, O, A*, and *C* were all above .90, and there were no anomalous findings. As McCrae and Costa noted, 'The structure found in adult American volunteers was replicated in Japanese undergraduates and Israeli job applicants. A model of personality rooted in English-language trait adjectives could be meaningfully applied not only in a closely related language like German but also in such utterly distinct languages as Chinese and Korean' (1997, p. 514).

There is a host of other findings, sampled in the following. The conscientiousness trait predicts the practice of safe sex (Trobst, Herbst, Masters, & Costa, 2002), a smaller arrest record in prisoners (Clower & Bothwell, 2001), child-oriented parenting (Clark, Kochanska, & Ready, 2000), and the use of negotiation in conflict resolution (Jensen-Campbell & Graziano, 2001). Persons scoring high in openness to experience strive for artistic expression, think less of traditional marriage, and disparage an indolent lifestyle (Roberts & Robins, 2000); they are more likely to have changed careers (Costa & McCrae, 1978; McCrae & Costa, 1985). People who are closed to experience tend to hold traditional family beliefs (Costa & McCrae, 1978). Extraversion predicts social recognition in fraternities and sororities (Anderson, John, Keltner, & Kring, 2001), and agreeableness better social relationships (Jensen-Campbell & Graziano, 2001). Extraverts want careers with status, influence in politics, excitement in their lives, and children; the first three goals are not valued by people with high agreeableness scores. Instead, they are more concerned with social good and concord within the family (Roberts & Robins, 2000). High scores on Neuroticism predict dissatisfaction with life (Costa & McCrae, 1986) and maladaptive coping that may fea-

Table 9.3   Some Trait Investigators Who have Found Five Factors

Investigator	Factor 1	Factor 2	Factor 3	Factor 4	Factor 5
Fiske (1949)	Social Adaptability	Conformity	Will to achieve	Emotional control	Inquiring intellect
Norman (1963)	Surgency	Agreeableness	Conscientiousness	Emotionality	Culture
Borgatta (1964)	Assertiveness	Likeability	Responsibility	Emotionality	Intelligence
Digman (1990)	Extraversion	Friendly compliance	Will to achieve	Neuroticism	Intellect
McCrae and Costa (2003)	Extraversion	Agreeableness	Conscientiousness	Neuroticism	Openness to experience

ture hostility, passivity, unrealistic thinking, or self-directed blame (McCrae & Costa, 1986). Despite significant stability, traits may mirror important life and cultural change. As a result of exposure to Canadian life and values, openness and agreeableness trait scores increased in Hong Kong Chinese university undergraduates who moved to British Columbia (McCrae, Yik, Trapnell, Bond, & Paulhus, 1998). Then there is the behaviour genetics research, which we will review in chapter 16. That heritability evidence is highly credible.

A Causal Five-Factor Model

McCrae and Costa have taken steps toward a theory embracing five-factor trait research (McCrae & Costa, 1996, 2003). It is called the Five-Factor Model (FFM), (or Theory—FFT—in their later writing), a way of viewing personality structure, personality processes, and the influence of external events (situations). Their diagram of the model is shown in Figure 9.11. The theory consists of six postulates:

- *basic tendencies*, covering individual differences on traits, the trait as the elemental disposition in personality, trait development from childhood to stability in adulthood, and the hierarchical organization of traits and facets
- *characteristic adaptations* of individuals to their environments, adaptive change, and maladjustment
- *objective biography*, by which McCrae and Costa mean a 'cumulative record' of behaviour containing every reaction, everything the person does
- *self-concept*, the conscious view of oneself, and the perceptions of self, consistent with dominant traits
- *external influences*, which include interactions with the environment, interpretations of environmental events, reciprocal influences of person and environment
- *dynamic processes*, the cognitive and emotional activity linking the personality structures and influences on the person

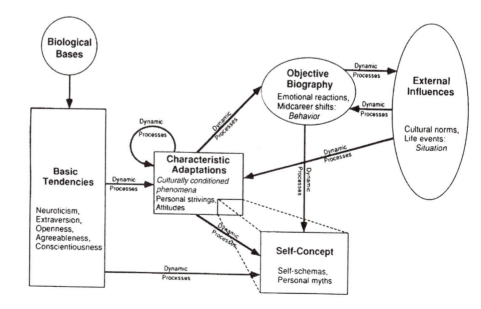

Figure 9.11 The Five-Factor Model of Personality. Core elements of personality are shown by rectangles and squares, behaviour and environment by ellipses. Arrows show the direction of dynamic influences. (From McCrae & Costa, *Personality in Adulthood* (New York: Guilford Press, 2003), page 192. Reprinted by permission of the publisher.)

The FFM is not quite bare bones, because a great deal of the trait structure of personality has been filled in, but it is far from a complete statement of a functional theory, as McCrae and Costa (2003) freely admit. Dynamic processes and their relation to traits and environment, the development and maturing of traits, and how traits and situations interact are only sketched in. Is the Big Five impressive as a representation of traits in personality and as a source of hypotheses to investigate? Surely, indeed emphatically. What can we say of the FFM as a theory based on five-trait factor structure? It organizes the evidence on personality traits in a factor-based system, relates traits to a variety of individual attributes, choices, and social behaviour, and acknowledges (if it doesn't actually account for) such dynamic processes as learning, defences, and the future orientation represented in anticipation and planning. There are, however, critics, one of the most informed and influential of whom said this:

A Fresh Look: Research Today

Among the nightly reveries of every personality theorist must be a dream of having in hand the data to establish with certainty the credibility of his or her theory—not just bits and pieces but the *whole thing*. For the Big Five theorists, reality may be close to coming within their grasp. In an important way, attainment of the dream may be easier for them. They do have to confirm a whole set of interlinked hypotheses, which has to be done in independent tests, but there is a way to provide evidence to give the theory an instant believability. If traits can be shown to be human universals, there would be strong reason to consider them as fundamental elements in personality. And, if a group of traits similar to the human set could be seen in an animal with which we share a common (though remote) evolutionary heritage, the persuasion would be truly compelling. Let's look at some extensive cross-cultural data and a counterpart on the chimpanzee.

None of the cross-cultural studies of Big Five traits has approached the comprehensiveness of one carried out by McCrae, Terracciano, and 78 members of the Personality Profiles of Cultures Project (2005). Their sample included participants from 50 cultures, many not previously investigated. African (Botswanan, Burkinan, Ethiopian, Nigerian, Ugandan) and Arabic (Kuwaiti, Moroccan, Turkish) cultures were far better represented than

heretofore. The trait measure was the FFM's NEO-PI-R, translated for the most part into the dominant language of each culture. It wasn't, however, administered in the usual way as a self-report questionnaire. Instead, research participants, largely college students, were asked to serve as trait observers. Each student rated another person (in two conditions it was someone of comparable age, in two others an adult over 40), using the form of the questionnaire designed for observer ratings. As McCrae et al. point out, observer ratings have an edge over self-report in that the target person and respondent are different people; when people describe themselves, 'it is impossible to know whether the ratings are a function of the person being rated or the person making the ratings' (p. 548). The number of observers, and hence targets, was huge, ranging from 106 (Northern Ireland) to 919 (United States).

The research hypothesis was simply that 'despite differences in language, history, religion, and culture . . . personality traits are basic features of the human species' (pp. 547-8). Are there universally observed features of personality? The answer is an unequivocal yes. A five-factor solution clearly appeared and was almost perfectly congruent with the FFM. Almost 95 per cent of the factors found in the analyses of the facet scales replicated the results of American samples used in the norms of the self-

The Big Five are often called 'the five-factor model of personality' and are referred to as providing an understanding of the 'structure of personality'. As the term 'model' is used in conventional parlance among psychologists, it means a theoretically based, logically coherent, working representation or simulation that, in operation, attempts to generate psychological phenomena of interest. However, no identifiable hypotheses, theories, or models guided the emergence of or decision on this five-fold space. . . . Because the Big Five formulation was entirely atheoretical, usage of the term 'model' may be premature (Block, p. 188).

Another critic, putting the five factors in their place even more sharply, said that 'they are to personality what the categories "plant" and "animal" are to the world of biological objects—extremely useful for some initial rough distinctions, but of less value for predicting specific behaviours of a particular object' (John, 1990, p. 93).

report version of the questionnaire, and in only one culture (Botswana) did a trait (openness to experience) fail to reproduce the consistency of other traits and other cultures. McCrae et al. conclude that these data powerfully confirm earlier and more limited evidence that five specific personality traits are universal in the human, and may be interpreted to support their biological basis.

Now, a twist on the question in the biblical story of Cain and Abel, 'Am I my brother's keeper?' It is one the chimpanzee might well ask: 'Am I my keeper's brother?' There are marked genetic resemblances between the chimpanzee and the human (see Waddell & Penney, 1996), and students of primate behaviour have noted a number of psychological similarities in language (Rumbaugh & Savage-Rumbaugh, 1994), theory of mind (Premack, 1988), politics and morality (deWaal, 1996), and psychopathic deviance (Lilienfeld, Gershon, Duke, Marino, & deWaal, 1999). Moreover, we and the chimpanzee share a common ancestor, a being (I hesitate to call him a creature) that existed somewhere between five and seven million years ago.

Several students of chimpanzee behaviour have used observers to rate the personality of these great apes. They find suggestive correspondences to the FFM and a chimpanzee-specific factor of dominance. King, Weiss, and Farmer (2005) undertook a small-scale chimpanzee version of FFM cross-cultural research, studying the residents

of nine zoos in the US and Australia, and chimpanzees in an island sanctuary and a re-introduction centre in the Republic of the Congo. The personality ratings were made by a number of raters who selected adjectives from a list of Big Five adjective descriptions.

Factor analyses extracted six factors, five humanoid and the chimpanzee dominance attribute. These factors largely replicated from zoo to the natural environment, so we cannot attribute the human resemblance to possible humanization by zoos. The human-like factors were remarkably similar to those of the FFM. Chimpanzees have distinct personalities, and they have trait attributes shared with us. King et al. think that the human and animal studies of personality traits carry two hugely important implications. First, neuroticism, extraversion, and agreeableness appear as factors in a number of species; they are not specific to us and to the chimpanzee. Second, conscientiousness (called dependability in the primate) is found specifically in the human and chimpanzee, suggesting a common heritage—perhaps, they propose, a phylogenetic beginning in our common ancestor five to seven million years in the dim past.

I have two questions to ask. Do the cross-cultural studies speak as forcefully as the Big Five theorists believe to the universality and probable biological basis of personality traits? And (I have to ask it), how shall we answer the chimpanzee's question?

A Final Perspective on Trait Theories

The nature of personality, say trait theorists, can be found in little bits and pieces, in the words that have evolved to portray the attributes and variations of human character. Discovering personality in this way is like poring over the shards of an ancestral culture that, pieced together, could tell us about its people and their lives. Do we have all the pieces? How do they fit? What *is* the final picture, anyway? The coiners of words had no intent to represent facets of a larger human image. They were (and are) fully content with the aptness of a word to convey a specific impression. So, too, with the long-vanished artisan, who could never have imagined that fragments of his clay pot or figure would in some distant time tell a small part of the story of his civilization. I mustn't press the analogy too far, but you see what I mean. Word and shard have their places in much grander endeavours, and the job of the personality psychologist and the archaeologist is to find what those places are and what they tell us about personality and ancient life.

The tools of the trait psychologist are the statistical techniques of factor analysis that can disclose order in the covariation of individual observations so numerous that we couldn't make sense of them otherwise. The order, though, depends on what is entered. Bias the data sample in some way—with a greater number of words about the outgoing and shy, for example, or about peculiarities of nervousness—and the factor structure, the putative structure of personality, will be bound to reflect it. Vary the procedures of factor extraction or alter the form of the questions asked, and a different factor solution may result. Trait psychologists know that fully representative samples of trait-relevant words, large samples of respondents, use of agreed-upon factoring techniques, and carefully constructed test items afford significant protection, but the problem of factor inconsistency lurks for the unwary and overconfident. Then, we might ask, whose dictionary do we use? Do all languages and cultures equally represent personality attributes? If trait words were chosen from languages other than English, could the English factor structure be reproduced? Although the factor solutions to personality structure of Cattell's theory and the Big Five have appeared in many cultures, far more have yet to be tested. Trait theories, as research-intensive and persuasive as they are, do leave us with unanswered questions.

Trait and Situation

No modern personality theory can be indifferent to the influence of situations on behaviour. Many theories, as we have seen, were slow to get the point, and their theoretical adequacy and scientific reputations have rightly suffered. Trait theories got off on the wrong foot in proposing a stable disposition of the individual as the essence of personality. Thus, from the start, trait and situation made uncomfortable bedfellows. Trait occupied his side of the bed, sure and stolid, never a thought of reaching out to his bedmate. Situation, neglected, squirmed. Yes, there were gestures. Early on, Allport saw that the expression of traits could be modified by the 'determining conditions' of situations. Cattell boldly tried with the simple, linear specification equation to bring trait and situation together. Other personality psychologists, however, haven't been impressed by s_n's weighting the effects of traits on behaviour; whether the specification equation answers the trait–situation issue is an open question. The FFM is just beginning to approach it.

SUMMARY

1. Traits have a long history not just in psychology but in culture and language. There is an important distinction between **traits** and **types**. Traits are *continuous dimensions*, types are *categorical*. Jung didn't observe the distinction; neither did Eysenck, who adopted Jung's typology. It is not necessary to make a strict distinction.

2. Trait names exist in language in every culture and time. This is the **lexical hypothesis**, that the folk wisdom of language fully describes traits. Traits are intuitively appealing, but are they scientifically explanatory, beyond the subjective? We must be able to predict and to find antecedents.

3. Gordon Allport was a twentieth-century trait theory pioneer. His background was midwestern, his father a country doctor. He was educated at Harvard University, where he majored in economics and philosophy. On graduation, he taught briefly in Turkey, then on the way home met Freud and was disappointed by psychoanalysis. He returned to Harvard, completing the PhD in 1922. Shortly, he was given a permanent appointment at Harvard, where he remained for his whole career. He created an eclectic and uniquely American theory of personality. Esteemed by his students, he became a significant and influential figure. His research and writing were extensive. His books include *Personality: A Psychological Interpretation* (1937), *The Nature of Prejudice* (1954), *Pattern and Growth in Personality* (1961) and *Letters from Jenny* (1965), which embodied his emphasis on study of the individual person. He conducted studies of expressive movement and devised personality tests. Allport was honoured with the presidency of American Psychological Association and its Distinguished Scientific Contribution award. He died in 1967.

4. To Allport, personality and its constituents were real: 'Personality is what a person "really is".' He held that personality is 'within the individual', 'psychophysical' (consisting of both mental and physiological components), and dynamically organized (developing and changing, being more than a collection of attributes). The 'patterned uniqueness' of individual personality requires an *idiographic* approach, not one that is *nomothetic* (based on general laws).

5. Allport identified different types of traits. *Common traits* are characteristic of people. How many common

traits are there? Allport saw this as simply an empirical problem. *Personal dispositions* are characteristic of individuals and represent the 'structure of a given personality'. *Cardinal dispositions* dominate a personality and make a person clearly recognizable. *Central dispositions* are distinguishing traits that determine behaviour. How many central dispositions are there in an individual? Five to ten, said Allport. *Secondary dispositions* are minor traits (preferences such as foods and dress), and there are many in every individual. Allport thought that language was a good place to begin the identification of traits. The four to five thousand trait names in the language could be reduced and systematized.

8. Allport had a sophisticated view of the way in which traits influence behaviour, arguing that traits interact with situations. This was an idea ahead of its time. He showed personality psychologists how to go about the study of traits and how to study people individually. His idiographic study of Jenny was a model. Every modern trait theorist and investigator owes a large debt to Allport.

9. Raymond Cattell was born in 1905 in England. His father was a mechanical engineer. He entered the University of London at sixteen, majoring in chemistry; he turned to psychology after reading British philosophers, completing the PhD under the creator of factor analysis, Charles Spearman. Immigrating to the US, he taught at Columbia, Harvard, and finally the University of Illinois, where he was research professor. Cattell was a prodigious researcher and writer and a major influence on the factor study of personality. His major books include *The Description and Measurement of Personality* (1946), *Personality: A Systematic Theoretical and Factual Study* (1950), *Personality and Motivation Structure and Measurement* (1957), *The Scientific Analysis of Personality* (1965), and a two volume work on learning (1979, 1980). He developed the principal research instrument of factor-analytic trait theory, the 16PF. Charged (perhaps unjustly) for racist and eugenic views, he died in 1998 at the age of 92 before he could clear his name.

10. It was Cattell who brought factor analysis to the study of personality traits. Factor analysis is a statistical technique for reducing large matrices of correlation coefficients to a small number of factors. There

are two major procedures. The standard is *orthogonal*, yielding independent (uncorrelated) factors. *Oblique* factor solutions yield correlated factors. Cattell thought the oblique analysis was appropriate to personality, since many traits are likely to be correlated with each other. Once factors have been obtained, individual scores on factors can be readily derived.

11. Cattell began with a list of 4,500 trait names, which he then reduced to 171. He obtained ratings on a large sample and intercorrelated them. After factor analysis of different types of data, he arrived at 16 factors, representing the basic traits of personality. This work led to the development of a personality test, the 16PF questionnaire.

12. Cattell used three sources of data: the life record (comprising factual data and observations of others) yields *L-data*. Personality questionnaires contribute *Q-data*, and 'objective' measures (based on the use of questions whose aim isn't apparent to the respondents) produce *T-data*. Two approaches may be followed: in *R-technique*, many subjects are measured on many variables, and the results are then correlated and factor-analyzed; in *P-technique*, a single individual is tested or observed on many occasions.

13. In factor-analytic trait theory, personality is what enables us to predict behaviour. Personality is made up of traits—*surface traits*, close to behaviour, and *source traits*, discovered only by factor analysis, which represent the basic dimensions of personality. Source traits number 16. *Constitutional source traits* are inherited. Other traits are influenced by environment (*environmental-mould traits*). There are three modalities of source traits. *Ability traits* are responsible for accomplishment; the most important ability trait is intelligence, composed of *fluid intelligence* (problem-solving) and *crystallized intelligence* (the accretions of experience). Cattell argued that both have significant genetic influence. There are *temperament traits* reflecting emotionality, and *dynamic traits*, which include attitudes, sentiments, and motivational source traits (ergs). Attitudes are subsidiary to sentiments, which in turn derive from ergs. Motivational metaergs are dynamic environmental-mould traits.

14. An individual's scores on the measure of source traits, the 16PF questionnaire, can be entered into a *specification equation*, which weights the traits by their significance to the situation in which behaviour is to be predicted. The specification equation is multidimensional, representing both person and situation by a number of variables. By including traits and situational characteristics, it is a mathematical approach to the person–situation interaction. Conflict is shown by positive and negative weights for erg and sentiment traits that equal each other.

15. Cattell studied personality change, including development, by first assessing traits at different ages. He addressed the issue of comparable trait measurement at different ages with a bridging strategy, testing adolescents with a 16PF form developed for younger children. He then tested people at various stages of the life span to study changes in the strength of traits with maturing and aging. Multiple Abstract Variance Analysis (MAVA) involves the study of twins and estimates of heritability and environmental influence. MAVA studies show heredity's influence but also an important role of learning in personality development. Cattell also applied the factor-analytic approach to society, proposing that dimensions analogous to traits could be found in social groups and societies. He termed this *syntality*.

16. The entirety of Cattell's theory was research-based, starting with the search for trait names in the language. In hundreds of factor-analytic studies, traits have been identified, reduced to a small number defining the structure of personality (16), and applied to empirical, theoretical, and practical questions. There are four basic implications following from factor-analytic trait theory: (1) Traits are built in to the person; (2) the data establishing personality traits originate in an unimpeachable source, everyone's language; (3) similar trait structures are found in other societies; and (4) since we can predict from traits, the theory must be on the right track.

17. In final perspective, Cattell's theory deserves recognition for the massive amount of research from which it is derived. Factor analysis works in extracting basic personality dimensions from trait names. However, it is necessary to ask whether the theory is not a theory at all but a catalogue of abstract attributes. In its defence, it may be noted that Cattell did attempt to predict individual behaviour through the specification equation, taking account of persons in situations. Finally, in important senses, in method and theoretical application, Cattell was a prisoner of his psychological heritage from Spearman and Galton.

18. Hans Eysenck was born in Berlin, Germany, in 1916 and raised from the age of two by his grandmother. He left Germany in 1934 for France, then England, where he attended the University of London, taking up psychology. He completed the PhD in 1938 under Cyril Burt. In 1947, Eysenck became director of the psychology department at the Institute of Psychiatry. He was incredibly productive in research and writing. His 79 books include *Dimensions of Personality* (1947), *The Scientific Study of Personality* (1952), *The Biological Basis of Personality* (1967), *A Model for Personality* (1981), and a number written for a popular audience. Eysenck died in 1997.

19. As the author of type-trait theory, Eysenck was influenced by factor analysis and by the lasting heritage of Galton. Like Cattell, he saw cultural and historical ideas as important in identifying traits. In Hippocrates' notion of bodily humours determining character—to the modern scientist a foolish belief—he saw three sound ideas: traits determine behaviour; traits derive from types; and types are constitutional in origin and are dimensional.

20. Wilhelm Wundt had already proposed a two-dimensional model of Hippocrates' four temperaments: stable vs unstable and changeable vs unchangeable. From Jung, Eysenck adopted introversion–extraversion, which replaced changeable vs unchangeable; neuroticism closely fit the stable vs unstable dimension. These are *phenotypes*; Eysenck thought the underlying *genotypes* were inherited and would be found in neural processes. Factor-analytic research made clear that a third dimension, psychoticism, was necessary. In Eysenck's theory, traits are at a level subordinate to these types; at the behavioural level of this personality structure hierarchy are specific responses.

21. An early test of the dimensions of psychiatric disorders found Jung's dimensions, introversion vs extraversion and neuroticism vs normality. These type dimensions are *superfactors*. Extraverts are sociable and venturesome, introverts quiet and retiring. The neurotic is a worrier. The person high on the third dimension, psychoticism, is poorly socialized and hostile. Eysenck identified neurotic introverts as *dysthymic*, neurotic extraverts as *hysteric*.

22. Experimental tests of learning and attention differences between introverts and extraverts confirmed hypotheses derived from the typological postulate (dysthymics acquire a conditioned response more rapidly and introverts sustain attention better), but there were critical failures to replicate these results.

23. In type-trait theory, arousal of the ascending reticular activating system (ARAS) is responsible for excitation–inhibition differences between introverts and extraverts. Neuroticism–normality involves the visceral brain (limbic system). The theory makes a third proposal: equating arousal to motivation, introverts, more aroused, will reach a level interfering with performance more quickly than extraverts. Experimental tests confirmed this hypothesis: overaroused introverts performed badly on easy tasks and worse on difficult ones. Task demands increased the low arousal of extraverts, whose performance was therefore better than the introverts'.

24. Like Cattell's theory, Eysenck's is based on factor-analytic research, but it goes beyond in its emphasis on the experimental test of hypotheses. It is also a better formal theory, with explicit statement of underlying processes and derivation of specific hypotheses. Eysenck made a strong (but not airtight) case that personality is best conceived dimensionally and that elemental personality processes can be accounted for by neural mechanisms of excitation and inhibition.

25. Eysenck set out four stiff requirements to show the biological basis of personality: (1) superfactors must show heritability; (2) the same factors must be found in nonhuman animals; (3) superfactors must be cross-cultural; and (4) superfactors have to be stable over time. There is some evidence to support each of these.

26. Type-trait theory and research are impressive and believable. However, critics have noted that the research was not all confirmatory. The theory is vulnerable on the person–situation interaction. It is a theory that could be a successful account of personality without invoking neural processes. Psychological processes don't have to be anchored in neurophysiology. Despite empirical inadequacies, it may be asked whether there are other theories of personality with as secure a base in theoretical statement, hypothesis derivation, and experimental evidence.

27. Big Five Theory begins with the question, how many traits are there? A number of factor researchers have not found sixteen or three. Two trait psychologists, McCrae and Costa, accepting the lexical hypothesis,

developed a personality questionnaire to measure traits, factor-analyzed scores, and came up with five.

28. The factors named by McCrae and Costa are extraversion, agreeableness, conscientiousness, neuroticism, and openness to experience. They argue that these five are the fundamental dimensions of personality, and they have presented a large body of evidence, factor-analytic and experimental, in support. Cross-cultural studies in a number of non-English-speaking societies replicate the five traits. There are many confirmed trait predictions (for example, con-scientiousness predicts safe sex and responsive parenting; extraversion predicts social prominence). The Big Five traits show strong heritability.

29. The Big Five investigators have proposed a theory, the Five-Factor Model. It casts personality structure, personality processes, and external events (situations) in a theoretical formulation that organizes the present data and may provide a basis for hypothesis formation and test. The development and maturing of traits and the interaction of traits and situations are major areas to study.

TO TEST YOUR UNDERSTANDING

1. The lexical hypothesis proposes that everyday language is the best source from which to obtain the descriptive terms for personality. What do you think of it? What are its strengths? Its possible weaknesses?

2. Is personality 'real', as Allport insisted? Agree or disagree with him and give your reasons.

3. How many traits are necessary for a full description of personality? Sixteen? Three? Five? Why do trait theorists disagree on the essential number of traits? Does their disagreement reflect a fundamental problem with trait theory?

4. Cattell presented a whole theory of personality, one that is complex and with many potential applications (to the organization of societies, for example). It is to a great degree based on measurement by questionnaires, and the reduction of a large number of scores to an irreducible number (as he claimed) that fully describe individual personality. Do you think his approach is on the right track? Why or why not? What, if anything, could throw a monkey wrench into the works?

5. Eysenck went back to ancient Greece for the ideas of traits, types, and the heritability of personality types. Borrowing again, he adopted Jung's introversion–extraversion typology and added to it. Factor analysis confirmed a simple three-dimension structure, and experimental studies provided significant evidence for his conception. Further studies established a neural and hereditary basis. Are you convinced that this is good theory with a firm experimental basis? Yes? Why? No? Where does it fall down?

6. McCrae and Costa adopt the same lexical hypothesis as other trait theorists, the use of personality questionnaires, and the technique of factor analysis to determine the trait dimensions that fully describe personality. Their experimental evidence and cross-cultural confirmation are persuasive. Are the Big Five 'it', the final story of trait theory? Have they succeeded beyond other trait theorists and, if so, what have they done that represents a big theoretical and methodological advance over the work of other trait theorists?

CHAPTER TEN

Existentialism: R.D. Laing

Introduction

Personality psychologists and psychiatrists come to existentialism from personal experiences that vary widely. So do patients. There is, however, a common denominator, and it is encounters with crises and events that make one feel profoundly vulnerable, threatened to the very core. This was so for the American existentialist Rollo May, whose mother—the 'bitch-kitty on wheels'—and a close call from tuberculosis as a young man deeply undermined his beliefs and goals. It was so for Viktor Frankl, Holocaust survivor, who developed logotherapy, an existential approach to finding meaning and purpose. It is so for anyone who has to try to fathom the unfathomable, like Samuel Bak, renowned painter and Holocaust survivor, whose art is a memoir of the 'miraculous fact of my survival' and an

'*The Family* is a painting that I have dedicated to the memory of the perished members of my family.' (Courtesy of Samuel Bak.)

appeasement of 'a sad sense of bewilderment' (Bak, 2002). And it was so for Ronald Laing, whose approach to existentialism we'll shortly take up. As a schoolboy, Laing, reading voraciously and with a keen eye for the poverty of the Glasgow slum he grew up in, arrived at the angry, bitter, disgusted realization that 'God suddenly seemed to be just the biggest collective put-on, the opium of the people and the unemployment and slums, factories, things that I didn't know anything about but I lived around where people who worked and lived in these things' (Mullan, 1995, p. 87).

There is a powerful inducement that existentialism holds out, to patients, to victims of appalling life experience, and to philosophers and theorists. I must say next, however, that—compelling though it may be as both a therapy and philosophy—I don't believe existentialism qualifies as a personality theory. It lacks process concepts by which to understand development and change, and it proposes no structural concepts within which processes take place. Even more critically, existentialists think it is totally wrong-headed to bring causality from the natural sciences into psychology as the principle by which sequential events are accounted for. *A* may be the clearly identifiable cause of *B* in physics, but human existence is different. There are no causes and effects to be found in the apparent sequences of human behaviour. It is fatuous to think that what happens to the child is the source of personality in the adult. The existential meaning of childhood events and evidently similar occurrences in adult life may be the same, but that similarity does not reflect the causal influence of the earlier on the later. Psychologists should never have modelled their quest on the natural sciences, thinking that a psychological science would be a quantum leap toward human understanding. The study of existence has its own rules, method (phenomenology), and concepts—being-in-the-world, freedom, responsibility, aloneness, transcendence are a few of them. It doesn't need the false path of science, and it doesn't need theory.

Ludwig Binswanger, one of the major European existentialists, saw theory as prejudiced against experience, against the phenomenology of reality. Existentialism instead 'places in the psychiatrist's hands a key by means of which he can, free of the prejudice of any scientific *theory*, ascertain and describe the *phenomena* he investigates in their full phenomenal content and intrinsic context' (1963, p. 206). Binswanger was right: an anti-deterministic, anti-scientific view should not be cast in the mould of a scientific theory and stand on the same ground as scientific theories. It is not good for personality theory as a whole to be encumbered by a philosophy masquerading as a *scientific* alternative, and existentialism is itself not well served by pretending to be something it isn't.

Existentialism represents a *radical* alternative to a science of human behaviour in its concern for the human's possibilities in the world, for the significance of phenomenal experience as the mode of understanding, and for ethics and responsibility, and it is a radical alternative in its belief that humans can *choose* what they want to be. Not that we will choose wisely, but choice is ours. While existentialism cannot and does not wish to claim to be a scientific theory, this body of thought has stood for some ideas and ideals that have had an important corrective influence on personality psychology and psychiatry, most particularly on clinical practice. Existentialism respects the person; it emphasizes personal choice and personal responsibility; it does not shy away from questions of value and ethics; and it shows a concern for the kind of world in which one must live.

Among existentialism's intellectual architects we must place the nineteenth-century Danish philosopher Søren Kierkegaard, a strange and tormented figure, at the head. Kierkegaard brought doubt and dread (anxiety) to philosophy as the ineluctable consequents of the question, 'What ought I to do?' The human situation, ethical life, and Christian belief were his targets. Being free, having to choose, and being faced with despair formed a triad that was hugely attractive to the post–World War II existentialist movement. The French existentialists Albert Camus and Jean-Paul Sartre gave nothingness equal stature with being. To Camus, life was absurd and irrational; said Sartre, 'nothingness haunts being' (1956, p. 16). Moreover, there is no escape from the burden of human destiny: 'man being condemned to be free carries the whole weight of the world on his shoulders; he is responsible for the world and for himself as a way of being' (p. 555). Poor humans: abandoned, alone, and helpless in a world for which each bears responsibility, they must also contend with the inevitable anguish of nothingness that 'lies coiled in the heart of being—like a worm' (p. 21). Martin Heidegger, pupil of Edmund Husserl (principal founder of phenomenology, whom we shall meet again in Chapter 11), also gave existentialism a dark view. His ontology, that each human is a being-in-the-world, is not bright and hopeful; being is a grave problem, we face an inevitable death, and modern society is tormented and dehumanizing. To American theologian and existentialist Paul Tillich, no human truth is ultimate. The great questions for humankind, as he saw them, are being, existence, and life. Demanding to confront? Yes. Hopeful for human serenity, which can only be achieved with great struggle? No (Tillich, 1952).

I have chosen to present some of the existentialist ideas of the British (actually, Scottish) psychiatrist R.D. Laing, whose central premise was that the experience of self and of one's world are the essence of psychology. He treated and tried to understand the schizophrenic person. The experience of schizophrenia, he said, can help us to come to grips with the nature of being. Laing's is an exceptional and illuminating application of existential psychology to the most frightening and destructive of psychological disorders. It will serve us well as a window to existential psychological thought.

R.D. Laing: Personal History

Ronald David Laing was born in October 1927 in southside Glasgow, a working-class district called the Gorbals. Laing called it 'a very heavy slum area' (Mullan, 1995, p. 14). He was an only child. His father was an electrical engineer for the City of Glasgow, his mother a beautiful

R.D. Laing (Stefan Tyszko/Hulton Archive/Getty Images)

but embittered woman who had married my father who could have but *didn't* earn enough money to get her and us out of this hell that she was living in, where a guy upstairs went to work in the shipyards. This was a disgrace as far as my mother was concerned, that she had to live in a block of flats, that even if it had a banister, even if it had a wooden railing, it hadn't any stained glass windows on the first landing, that she had to live under these circumstances. My father wouldn't address himself to earning money that at least would take us to a decent flat in Moss Park, a quarter of a mile further away from the Gorbals. So I was brought up in this family tension (Mullan, 1995, p. 20).

His upbringing was strict but comfortable and largely contented, not really unusual for southside Glasgow, he thought.

> I was taught not to pick my nose; not to slouch in a chair; not to put a finger in my ear; not, of course, to put a finger in my mouth; not to keep my mouth open; not to hum and haw; not to make a noise when eating; not drink out of a saucer, let alone to slop anything on it in the first place; to lift a teacup up to my lips, not my lips down to it, with two fingers; to blow my nose properly; how to brush my teeth, comb my hair, tie my shoelaces, do my tie, always to have my socks pulled . . . ; not to turn up my eyes; how to speak properly; when and to whom to speak, with proper diction—for instance not 'sing-song' or some of the at least half-dozen forbidden accents, and a considerable amount of vulgar vocabulary (Laing, 1985, pp. 36–7).

Later, though, he would see his parents as impossibly strict and harsh. He broke with them and never fully reconciled.

This young Gorbals lad had playmates at school and was well regarded by his fellows, two things that definitely did not mark him as unusual. But he had an exceptional musical talent, he was uncommonly curious, and then there was that omnivorous reading. He read Plato, Karl Marx, Adam Smith, and 'a completely other world—Kierkegaard, Freud and Nietzsche' (Mullan, 1995, p. 93). When his interviewer, Bob Mullan, expressed surprise at Kierkegaard ('*Why Kierkegaard? I mean how on earth did you come across him?*'), Laing replied:

> Because he was K in the reference library that was just across the back green from where we lived. The Govan Hill Public Library. I made my way through the library. From about the sixth form at school I was eating my way through the library, I mean I was looking at all the books and I was looking up the card index and I was working my way from A to Z. That was my idea of continuing to educate myself (Mullan, 1995, p. 93).

He was a good enough student to earn a free scholarship to Glasgow University (finishing twenty-fifth out of the first hundred; his parents, though, felt disgraced that he hadn't placed first). There he began medical studies as a first-year university student (this is the way it's done in the UK), only to fail all his final exams the first time and spend six months 'as a full-time, half-paid, unqualified internist, living in at the Psychiatric Unit at Stobhill Hospital in Glasgow' (Laing, 1985, p. 87). He passed them on the second try and took up an internship in a neurosurgical unit at Killearn, near Loch Lomond.

In 1951, Laing was conscripted into the British Army and chose to specialize in psychiatry. Two years later he left the army and returned to Glasgow, to the Royal Gartnavel Mental Hospital. His experience was disturbing.

> As a young psychiatrist in general hospitals and psychiatric hospitals, I administered locked wards and ordered drugs, injections, padded cells and straitjackets, electric shocks, deep insulin comas and the rest. I was uneasy about lobotomies but not sure why. Usually, all this treatment was against the will of its recipients. I went around in a white coat, with stethoscope, tendon hammer and ophthalmoscope sticking out of my pockets, like any other doctor. Like them, I examined patients clinically.

I had samples of blood, urine, spinal fluid sent for laboratory analysis, ordered electroencephalograms and so on.

It looked the same as the rest of medicine, but it was different. I was puzzled, and uneasy. Hardly any of my psychiatric colleagues seemed puzzled or uneasy. This made me even more puzzled and uneasy (Laing, 1985, p. xvi).

Laing was further disquieted by the thought that 'If I were being driven frantic by mental and emotional torment that nothing I or anyone or any drug could stop I might beg for electric shocks. Other people might beg to have electric shocks. The critical issue is the politics of the matter. Who has the power to do what to whom against whose will?' (Laing, 1985, p. 25).

Shortly thereafter he was appointed senior registrar in the Department of Psychological Medicine at another Glasgow hospital. It was during this time that he began to write his first—and most influential—book, *The Divided Self.* In 1956, he moved again, to the Tavistock Clinic in London, where he saw outpatients and began four years of training in psychoanalysis. He did not adopt it, though, becoming instead more and more committed to existential psychiatry. This was, in a way, an announcement to the profession (and to the world) of the position at which he had arrived—a position based on the deep belief that traditional psychiatry is inhumane.

The profession was antagonized, and they were to regard Laing as a troublemaking rebel even more with his subsequent publications. *The Divided Self* (1960) was followed by *Self and Others* a year later and then, three years after that, *Sanity, Madness and the Family* (with Aaron Esterson). In 1967, he published *The Politics of Experience and the Bird of Paradise*, which gave him the status of a prophet on university campuses and brought him international renown. This was 'psycho-politics', damning society:

A child born today in the UK stands a ten times greater chance of being admitted to a mental hospital than to a University, and about one fifth of mental hospital admissions are diagnosed schizophrenic. This can be taken as an indication that we are driving our children mad more effectively than we are genuinely educating them. Perhaps it is our very way of educating them that is driving them mad (Laing, 1967, p. 87).

He attacked science, which turns its back on 'love and hate, joy and sorrow, misery and happiness, pleasure and pain, right and wrong, purpose, meaning, hope, courage, despair, God, heaven and hell, grace, sin, salvation, damnation. . . .' (1985, p. xi).

For five years, beginning in 1965, Laing played an innovative part in an extraordinary experiment, one in which he expressed his commitments to the fullest. He, colleagues, and schizophrenic patients lived together in a therapeutic community with no distinctions drawn between doctor and patient. There were no drugs, no ordinary psychiatric interventions; patients lived and were helped to live through their schizophrenia. The experiment collapsed in 1971 (perhaps because Laing left, unable to write in this most demanding environment), and he suddenly departed for Ceylon and India to increase his knowledge of yoga and Buddhist meditation. He had published *Knots*, a small poetic book about interpersonal relations, in 1970, and he returned to private practice and lecturing. *Knots* achieved such popularity that it was performed on stage. Laing had become psychiatry's Harold Pinter. Laing himself acknowledged that he had turned into a biopolitician. His last book was a memoir in 1985, *Wisdom, Madness, and Folly: The Making of a Psychiatrist*, in which he set forth 'the sorts of things that "struck" me on the road to seeing and responding to the suffering with which psychiatry is involved in a different way from the usual' (Laing, 1985, p. xvi). He died in the south of France while playing tennis in August 1989, a youthful sixty-two.

Emphases and Major Concepts

The central premise in Laing's position is clearly laid out in *The Divided Self*: 'Existential phenomenology attempts to characterize the nature of a person's experience of the world and himself. It is not so much an attempt to describe particular objects of his experience as to set all particular experiences within the context of his whole being-in-the-world. The mad things said and done by the schizophrenic will remain essentially a closed book if one does not understand their existential context' (1969, p. 15). We have to recognize this essential contextual given from the outset: humans in relation to other humans and human *experience* of other humans. The schizophrenic person has horrifying experiences in his or her world; we shall never understand them if we take a clinical, outsider's perspective, thinking of the person in abstract clinical or physiological language. These are *it-terms*, said Laing:

> There is a common illusion that one somehow increases one's understanding of a person if one can translate a personal understanding of him into the impersonal terms of a sequence of *it*-processes. . . . [T]here remains a tendency to translate our personal experience of the other person into an account of him that is depersonalized. We do this in some measure whether we use a machine analogy or a biological analogy in our 'explanation'. . . . My thesis is . . . the contention that the theory of man as person loses its way if it falls into an account of man as a machine or as an organismic system of it-processes (1969, p. 21).

It will not help us to understand terrifying personal experiences of loss of identity—of experiencing oneself as an automaton, as a robot, as a piece of machinery, as an animal—to use clinical concepts and terms, objective as they may seem to be. We have to see the person's (the schizophrenic's) world as he or she experiences it, as he or she *is* in it. The great German psychiatrist Emil Kraepelin, who brought order and system to the understanding of psychosis, presented to a lecture hall full of students the case seen in Perspective 10.1. This was an object lesson to Laing in dehumanizing—in the failure to give credence to the world of someone else.

Perspective 10.1 The Schizophrenic Person to Classical Psychiatry

'The patient I will show you today has almost to be carried into the room, as he walks in a straddling fashion on the outside of his feet. On coming in, he throws off his slippers, sings a hymn loudly, and then cries twice (in English), "My father, my real father!" He is eighteen years old, and a pupil of the Oberrealschule (higher-grade modern-side school), tall, and rather strongly built, but with a pale complexion, on which there is very often a transient flush. The patient sits with his eyes shut, and pays no attention to his surroundings. He does not look up even when he is spoken to, but he answers beginning in a low voice and gradually screaming louder and louder. When asked where he is, he says, "You want to know that too? I tell you who is being measured and is measured and shall be measured. I know all that, and could tell you, but I do not want to." When asked his name, he screams, "What is your name? What does he shut? He shuts his eyes. What does he hear? He does not understand; he understands not. How? Who? Where? When? What does he mean? When I tell him to look, he does not look properly. You there, just look! What is it? What is the matter? Attend; he attends not. I say, what is it, then? Why do you give me no answer? Are you getting impudent again? How can you be so impudent? I'm coming! I'll show you! You don't whore for me. You mustn't be smart either; you're an impudent, lousy fellow, such an impudent, lousy fellow I've never met with. Is he beginning again? You understand nothing at all, nothing at all; nothing at all does he understand. If you follow now, he won't follow, will not follow. Are you getting still more impudent? Are you getting impudent still more? How they attend, they do attend," and so on. At the end, he scolds in quite inarticulate sounds.

'Although he undoubtedly understood all the questions, he has not given us a single useful piece of information. His talk was . . . only a series of disconnected sentences having no relation whatever to the general situation' (1905, pp. 79–80).

This is a deeply troubled—yes, schizophrenic—person. Laing suggested that he was parodying Kraepelin in a dialogue with himself, a very defiant and rebellious self. Laing went on:

> Now, it seems clear that this patient's behaviour can be seen in at least two ways. . . . One may see his behaviour as 'signs' of a 'disease'; one may see his behaviour as expressive of his existence. The existential-phenomenological construction is an inference about the way the other is feeling and acting. What is the boy's experience of Kraepelin? He seems to be tormented and desperate. What is he 'about' in speaking and acting in this way? He is objecting to being measured and tested. He wants to be heard (1969, p. 31).

From R.D. Laing, *The Divided Self*, Copyright © 1960 Pantheon Books. Reproduced by permission of Taylor and Francis Books, UK.

This brief glimpse of schizophrenic experience in Perspective 10.1 is foreign to us, and we have a hard time understanding it. The reason is that we and the schizophrenic boy are very different in our **ontological security**★. We are fortunate in our *sense of being* (for that is the meaning Laing gives the word **ontology**, not the formal usage in existential philosophy). We do not doubt the reality of our experience; we feel alive and complete, we have a comforting appreciation of the continuity of our lives from earliest memory to anticipation of the future. We can encounter difficulties, even great ones, in relationships, morality, health, all of which may challenge us but do not undermine our ontological security. Please extend yourself, however, to try to imagine what it might be like to have to fight to maintain the sense of self, living, reality, personal continuity, to preserve existence. If you can put yourself in the phenomenal world of such a person, you have joined him (if only for a moment and in imagination) in ontological insecurity.

Ontological Insecurity and Schizophrenia

What happens when a person becomes schizophrenic? This is the question of what happens when a person experiences not primary ontological security but primary **ontological insecurity**★. Terrible encounters with unreality are the forerunner of—and in a more extensive way, *are*—the disorder. Laing didn't want us to look for the cause or causes of schizophrenia, which would violate the terms of the existential position. Rather, he invited us to accompany him in trying to uncover what being-in-the-world might be like for a person sentenced to schizophrenic experience, and to trace existential continuities back to childhood. The schizophrenic world often began, he thought, in a sequence (not causal, mind you) of good–bad–mad, in which we could find the collective existence of the whole family of the schizophrenic person. It is a sequence that may begin with an apparently normal and good baby, undemanding and, in the view of the parents, taking easily the first developmental steps of life—nursing, weaning, walking, toilet training, talking.

Such was the early history of Julie, whom Laing encountered in her mid-twenties, a severely disturbed chronic schizophrenic with nine years of hospitalization under her belt. As she learned to walk, this 'perfect' infant could not let her mother out of her sight without screaming in terror. It wasn't until the age of three that the fright ceased. It had pleased Julie's mother to think that Julie couldn't stand to be alone because she loved her so much. Julie was exceptionally compliant, with no independence whatsoever. Indeed, as a ten-year-old, she demanded that her mother make every single decision for her for the entirety of every day. She did pick at her fingernails and often inverted words, but her family didn't find anything truly worrisome about such a good and obedient child. No one saw in her dependence on her mother and in her excessive compliance Julie's failure to develop any autonomy, any sense of self at all capable of choice. As Laing would write of her, 'In Julie's case, her actions appear to have been trained by her mother, but "she" was not "in" them. This must have been what [Julie] meant by saying that she had never become a person and in her constant reiteration as a chronic schizophrenic that she was a "tolled bell" (or "told belle"). In other words, she was only what she was told to do' (Laing, 1969, p. 203). Nothing in Julie's behaviour impressed anyone as a fateful sign, but there were a number of them, all pointing to an 'existentially dead' child in whose experience being was a source of terror, kept at bay by utter obedience.

The 'bad' of the good–bad–mad sequence emerged when Julie was fourteen or fifteen, and it consisted of furious verbal attacks on her mother, 'ranting and raving' as she described them to Laing. They were angry enough on the outside; on the inside, they were murderous—an incomprehensibly (to us) desperate expression of hatred toward her mother for denying her an existence. The madness, schizophrenia, came at seventeen, after a doll to which Julie was greatly attached disappeared. Julie accused her mother of killing her doll, but it may have been Julie herself, acting out as the 'bad mother', who destroyed it. In psychosis, Laing thought, 'Julie's self-being had become so fragmented that she could best be described as living *a death-in-life existence in a state approaching chaotic nonentity*' (1969, p. 212). Her speech was cryptic and so odd in its expression as to test severely the understanding of the most able of psychotherapists. To her, in 'chaotic nonentity', it made sense.

Was Julie's upbringing a kind of existential conspiracy, a 'schizophrenogenic family' creating her schizophrenic disorder? Laing was often misunderstood to be saying that schizophrenia is caused by families. He had, after all, written the book titled *Sanity, Madness and the Family*, and he did say in *The Divided Self* that if we had to point the finger, schizophrenogenic families would be better targets than schizophrenogenic mothers. But those who saw him as laying a guilty burden on the parents of schizophrenics—and there were many—made a mistake. By way of correction, he said, 'I'm not talking about the *aetiology* of schizophrenia. I've always said that. I'm talking about the experience and behaviour that leads someone to be diagnosed as schizophrenic is more socially intelligible than has come to be supposed by most psychiatrists and most people' (Mullan, 1995, p. 379). Are we in the end, however, left with a puzzle? Were the parents themselves schizophrenic or schizoid, on the edge? Laing did not picture them so, but he did believe they were insecure people with conventional but marginal relations to others, people who could not supply understanding and early guidance in the world to a vulnerable and easily overwhelmed child. But this is to focus on cause, not Julie's experience, and Laing, trying to teach us existentialism, didn't want us to do that.

Ontological Insecurity and Anxiety

The ontologically insecure person is exposed to anxiety in three dreadful forms. First is the experience of **engulfment**★—the fear that in any relationship one will lose one's autonomy and thus one's individual identity. To relate comfortably to others requires a strong and stable sense of identity, a sense of being an autonomous person. Grave self-doubt may rob one of belief in the autonomy of one's existence, and then relationships with others become a threat to personal identity. Engulfment is one form the threat can take, the fear that in any relationship (including one's relatedness to oneself) autonomy and identity will be destroyed. That someone else might show understanding or love is an unendurable incursion, an invasion of a self so shaky that it could simply be swallowed, engulfed. Better to be misunderstood or even hated. The most likely course is retreat and *isolation*, either physically or by closing others out, walling oneself off. Laing described some of the images of patients experiencing engulfment: 'being buried, being drowned, being caught and dragged down into quicksand. . . . Some psychotics say in the acute phase that they are on fire, that their bodies are being burned up' (1969, p. 47).

A second form that extreme anxiety over insecurity may take is **implosion**★. The person feels *empty* and in addition experiences an ominous threat that reality will overwhelm him or her at any moment, explode inward on him or her. To feel emptiness, to feel that being empty *is* you, invites the analogy of a vacuum into which the menacing world—the 'persecutor'—will rush. And, Laing cautioned, let's not congratulate ourselves that implosion or engulfment is someone else's problem, nothing to do with us: 'In fact, we are only two or three degrees Fahrenheit from experiences of this order. Even a slight fever, and the whole world can begin to take on a persecutory, impinging aspect' (1969, p. 48).

The third form of anxiety is **petrification**★ and **depersonalization**★. Petrification is the awful fear of being turned into something dead or just robotic, a thing, an 'it' that, although capable of action, has no being. 'I am stone,' such a terrorized person might say, recalling the biblical fate of Lot's wife. Depersonalization is a common practice in social life, although hardly a healthy and desirable one. We depersonalize others when we treat them as *things*, as mere occupiers of a role. Bored with another, we become totally indifferent to that individual's existence as a sentient, feeling person. Worse would be to treat everyone in this way. This sort of behaviour is pretty cold and unfeeling to the one who is depersonalized. The threatened, ontologically insecure individual may depersonalize others because she can't help herself, because humanized relationships with others are too fraught with anxiety. Laing illustrated a severe depersonalization with the case of a man who

could not become a 'person'. He had 'no self'. 'I am only a response to other people, I have no identity of my own. . . .' He felt he was becoming more and more 'a mythical person'. He felt he had no weight, no substance of his own. 'I am only a cork floating on the ocean. . . .' With his outer behaviour he forestalled the danger to which he was perpetually subject, namely that of becoming someone else's *thing*, by pretending to be no more than a cork. (After all, what safer thing to be in an ocean?) At the same time, however, he turned the other person into a thing in his own eyes, thus magically nullifying any danger to himself by secretly totally disarming the enemy. By destroying, in his own eyes, the other person as a person, he robbed the other of his power to crush him (1969, p. 50).

One may even feel oneself to be depersonalized, not by others but as a self-directed belief. No longer a person, one becomes an 'unembodied self', an object in the population of objects with core of self. The body is felt as the place of a false self.

To be schizophrenic is to live in a world that in essential personal senses cannot be lived in. The person being-in-that-world is exposed to one or more of these three terrors and retreats from the outer world into an inner life—mad though it seems from the outside, from our experience—that is an imperative act of defence that calls for every creative personal resource. In a simple diagram, Laing portrayed the relations to others of the person who is embodied and the person who is unembodied (Figure 10.1). We who are ontologically secure have the essential identity of self and feel ourselves to be real, whole, genuine, alive. We experience estrangement from our bodies, if we ever do, only in moments of intense stress, and we muster our resources to feel embodied again. But what does the ontologically insecure person, frightened in his or her relationships with others, have to trust, what reality to fall back on? Not being, not security in relationships with others, not even the body he or she lives in to be reassured by. Existence for such a person can hardly fail to be experienced as false and without meaning or hope of change.

Self-Consciousness

We are conscious of ourselves in two possible ways. One is to be self-aware, and this is simply part of the sense of our being. The other is self-awareness '*as an object of someone else's observation*' (1969, 113), and this is often a source of discomfort and, in the extreme, severe anxiety. The sense of being looked at by others and of others guessing intimate details about us is an adolescent experience that many of us (probably most) have lived through. Our shyness and awkwardness spoke reams about our vulnerability in being observed. To the ontologically insecure person, however, someone who lives in a schizophrenic or near schizophrenic world, it may be the sense that other people can look right into the self, the 'plate glass' feeling of complete and unpreventable exposure of every thought. Retreating, somehow, into the landscape, achieving invisibility, becomes an imperative. Wrote Laing: 'Being like everyone else, being someone other than oneself, playing a part, being incognito, anonymous, being nobody (psychotically, pretending to have no body), are defenses that are carried through with great thoroughness in certain schizoid and schizophrenic conditions' (p. 118).

For some, the dread of non-being is so awful that to be the object of scrutiny (or to think that one is) affords a great reassurance that one does in fact exist, and this person seeks out the danger of others and their ability to look within. Laing reported the words of one patient who felt that 'other people provide me with my existence. I can't feel real unless there is someone there . . .' (1969, p. 121).

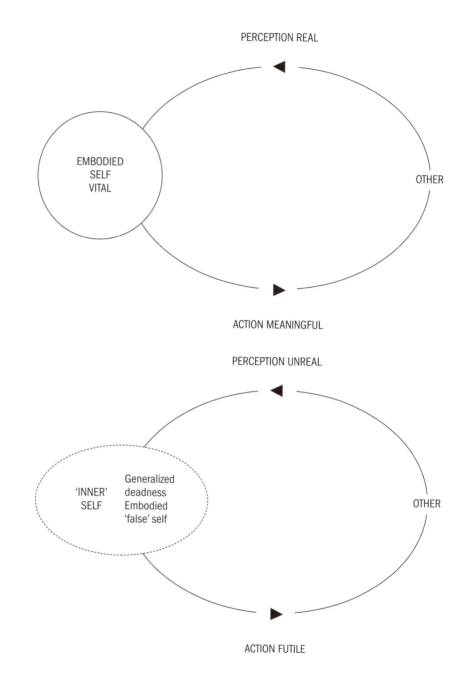

Figure 10.1 Embodied and unembodied selves as Laing diagrammed them (adapted from Laing, 1969)

Implications

For Laing, schizophrenia was *the* model for the distortion of experience—or better, I should say, experience that has become unlivable. We need to be very sure that we acknowledge the distinction between experience and cause. You may know, as Chapter 16 will document and Laing may have known, that schizophrenia is very largely a genetic disorder, afflicting those who have inherited a disabling set of genes. But that wasn't what Laing was talking about. Schizophrenia might just as well be due to a high trans-fat diet of Twinkies as far as he was concerned; that would have been no more irrelevant to his message. He meant *what it's like to be schizophrenic, what it's like to inhabit that world, what it's like to try to deal with it.* He saw schizophrenia as a creative solution to a problem of unendurable experience. Madness is not a very good solution, but we have to respect the person and the experience from which it comes. He tried to create a therapeutic environment in which schizophrenic persons could live through the affliction of their existence and perhaps arrive at a better creative solution. We don't have to search far in Laing's existentialism for the therapeutic core. This is it.

A Fresh Look: Research Today

The classical European existentialists saw life darkly, any solace in it hard won. Existentialism in North America acknowledges the confrontations to comfort and serenity—the uncertainty, the angst, the insecurity, the certain knowledge of an end—but has rewritten the script to give the alternative of a brighter, more hopeful outlook. Existence on this side of the Atlantic can be positive, affirming life and self, if one is not defeated by the challenges. It is as if French wines were intercepted at entry, the bottles opened and diluted with a native extract. We might call it an elixir of meaning.

Reared in a scientific culture, North American existentialists have also taken an accepting view of research in personality, studying questions of existential importance. Clearly, one of those has to be the meaning that we find or fail to find in life. A European existential analyst, Viktor Frankl, a Nazi death camp survivor, wrote movingly about the search for meaning in a book that commanded widespread interest (Frankl, 1963). He himself discovered out of the most ominous, brutal, and tragic circumstances that could befall a person that when everything possible was taken away in the concentration camp, one vital affirmation of life remained: 'the last of the human freedoms, to choose one's attitude in any given set of circumstances, to choose one's own way'. Out of that freedom to choose could come meaning, and the North American existentialists decided that it could be treated as an attribute of personality and measured.

Several meaning-in-life tests have been developed over the last forty years, including a recent one that seeks to improve on its predecessors in item content and a factor structure reflecting the presence of meaning or purpose and the search for meaning (Steger, Frazier, Oishi, & Kaler, 2006). It seems odd to speak of the most sophisticated techniques to select test items and factor analysis to explore the dimensionality of a questionnaire measuring a core existential con-

cept, but if you're going to swim in waters with dangers lurking at every stroke, this is the sort of gear you need. Steger et al. observed all the essentials, replicated the factor structure in the initial test-construction sample, and established both the convergent and discriminant validity of their Meaning in Life scale. Two dominant factors appeared: 'Presence of Meaning' and 'Search for Meaning'. The two subscales were found to correlate substantially with other meaning-in-life measures and, to an appropriately lesser degree, with scales measuring related but different concepts (well-being, long-term emotional state, self-reported psychological distress, and religiosity). Two forms of the Meaning in Life scale, one for self-report and the other to be completed by a knowledgeable friend or family member, correlated significantly but not as highly as we might like different measures of the same concept to relate to each other. Note, though, that to demand methodologically independent tests of the identical concept to correlate substantially is a stringent requirement, one that often failed. What we have here is a Pass, but not Pass with Distinction.

The Meaning in Life questionnaire is straigtforward and direct. It asks ten questions, each to be answered on a seven-point scale. The questionnaire follows, and you can complete it for yourself.

The Meaning in Life scale is in its infancy. Its relationships to similar scales suggest that it will likely be successful in predicting the variables they are reported to predict—examples: the need for psychotherapy (Battista & Almond, 1973), anxiety and depression (Debats, van der Lubbe, & Wezeman, 1993), and suicidal thoughts and substance abuse (Harlow, Newcomb, & Bentler, 1986) in those distressed by meaninglessness, and the enjoyment of work (Bonebright, Clay, & Ankenmann, 2000), feelings of satisfaction with life (Chamberlain & Zika, 1988), and

It may well have occurred to you that existentialism and phenomenology are, if not as alike as peas in a pod, at least members of the pea family. You would be right to think so. Beyond two familial characteristics, however, they are really quite different. Both owe their conceptual lives to the word experience. Both existentialism and phenomenology hold that experience *is* reality; this is similarity number one. Second, because reality is what each person experiences, existentialism and phenomenology see every person in a

general happiness (Debats et al., 1993) among persons who believe their lives are meaningful.

The existentialists are right in giving great weight to our human experience of meaning and its devastating converse. The optimistic and science-oriented investigators who have tried to measure the quest and attainment of life meaning may be right as well to try to do so. They have tried to apply measurement theory and practice with due diligence and in many respects have succeeded. The difficulty is that meaning and search for meaning as they have defined and assessed them are patently obvious; there is no distinction between the concept and its measured expression. Each refers to an avowed view. Do you get the feeling that two questions, asked straight out, would just as well get at the same thing—'Is your life is rich with meaning?' (or, 'Does it seem meaningless?') and 'Are you trying to find meaning in your life? 'If so, why are the rigmarole of test construction, development, and validation, and the time demanded of the respondent necessary? This is what I thought. If the question of meaning in life is as important as it surely is, perhaps it can stand on its own without the elaborate justification of a test. We depend on personality tests to tell us about attributes of people that we would otherwise find it difficult to discover. In the right circumstances to ask the questions about life's meaning to them, could and would people tell us?

Please take a moment to think about what makes your life feel important to you. Please respond to the following statements as truthfully and accurately as you can, and also please remember that these are very subjective questions and that there are no right or wrong answers. Please answer according to the scale below:

Absolutely Untrue	Mostly Untrue	Somewhat Untrue	Can't Say True or False	Somewhat True	Mostly True	Absolutely True
1	2	3	4	5	6	7

1. _____ I understand life's meaning.
2. _____ I am always looking for something that makes my life meaningful.
3. _____ I am always looking to find my life's purpose.
4. _____ My life has a clear sense of purpose.
5. _____ I have a good sense of what makes my life meaningful.
6. _____ I have discovered a satisfying life purpose.
7. _____ I am always searching for something that makes my life feel significant.
8. _____ I am seeking a purpose or mission for my life.
9. _____ My life has no clear purpose.
10. _____ I am searching for meaning in my life.

The Presence scale is scored from items 1,4,5,6, and 9 (reverse the numerical code).
The Search scale is scored from items 2,3,7,8, & 10.

respectful light. 'Who are we', they say, 'to argue with what you see, believe, and feel, or to impose our experience on yours?'

There, however, we come to the end of the common ground. Phenomenology of the North American kind has a hopeful and optimistic outlook on human possibilities, as we will see in the next chapter's discussion of Rogers. Create the fostering environment for personality growth, preach these phenomenologists, and people *will* grow; the potential is within everyone and just needs to be released. How different is the existentialist view! Everyone must contend with the forbidding conditions of human existence: meaning and purpose are elusive and uncertain, not given; nothingness, doubt, anguish, and despair lie in wait for us all; and death is there at the end. The exisistentialist says, 'Make peace with that if you can and try to make life choices responsibly. There are no guarantees that choice and responsibility will bring serenity, but there is nothing else. Courage helps.' How could such a message (and therapy based on it) be a comfort to people damaged by traumatic circumstances or catastrophic personality disorders such as schizophrenia? To the existentialist—and to those who accept its teaching—the answer is that it is better to see existence for what it is than to try to live with papered-over human ugliness and broken dreams. Experiencing and living fully are monumentally challenging, as other theorists we are familiar with have pointed out. Erich Fromm is one of them. To the existentialist, there is no straight path to being-in-the-world; unannounced twists, turns, and bumpy hazards await, and existentialists don't want to fool you about that. But it's the path of choice, as Laing and other notable existentialists made clear.

Research

True existentialists do no research; it is against their religion. As one existential psychologist has said, 'Experiences such as responsibility, dread, anxiety, despair, freedom, love, wonder or decision cannot be measured or experimented with. . . . They are simply there and can only be explicated in their givenness' (Van Kaam, 1966, p. 187). There have been some attempts to measure existential concepts. However, experiencing scales (Gendlin & Tomlinson, 1967) and similar approaches (such as the Meaning-in-Life test) can hardly represent the profound, the phenomenal experience of the individual person.

Existentialism in Perspective

Laing had no apology to make for the difficulty his books present. *The Divided Self* is full of strange terms and unfamiliar usages of words in everyday vocabulary; it delves into grotesque inner experiences beyond ordinary comprehension; and it is unflinching in its detail of the anguish and despair felt by the schizophrenic person, the existential model for Laing of everything ontologically wrong. Some of his later books are even more obscure. He had totally immersed himself in nightmares of being, and they had become a phenomenal reality for him. Understanding terrors of existence so well, I'm sure he thought he could make it all sensible to the existential outsider. Many a reader, though, has surely struggled mightily to grasp his meaning. I certainly did, and in trying to set his views before you I have feared that I might be doing no more than parroting the words, the real substance escaping me. Time after time, I have gone back to his writings to check my understanding and to seek assurance that my exposition brings Laing to you fairly and clearly. I can only hope so.

A humanistic emphasis, a concern for finding meaning in the unfriendly landscape that is human experience, and a stress on personal responsibility are—especially in modern times—vital and commendable. I grant also that a phenomenological approach can bring forth some compelling features of the inner life of the individual, and it has undoubtedly given us a glimpse of the dragons that breathe the fire of destruction on the cosmos of the schizophrenic person. It is an avenue to the world of people who have survived the unimaginably horrific (the Holocaust) and managed in some way to find sustaining meaning and purpose. But these are not enough to earn a seat at personality theory's table. Existentialism, as I said at the beginning of this chapter, is *not* theory. It generates no testable propositions and disdains personality theories that do. But that's all right: existentialists don't want to sit down with us anyway.

SUMMARY

1. European existentialism arose after World War II out of experiences of terrible threat to life and the meaning of life. Existentialists developed views that represent a radical alternative to a science of personality. What's important is phenomenal experience and the belief that humans can choose what they wish to be. Existentialism rejects the very idea of psychological determinism.

2. Major European existentialists include Ludwig Binswanger, Medard Boss, and Viktor Frankl. Foremost among their philosophical 'fathers' are Søren Kierkegaard, Jean-Paul Sartre, Albert Camus, and Martin Heidegger. The American theologian Paul Tillich has been a major influence on the unfolding of modern existential thought.

3. Born in 1927, Ronald D. Laing was the only child of a working-class Glasgow family. He had a 'contented' childhood that, upon later examination, was excessively strict. He was a voracious reader of philosophy and psychology even as a young boy. Admitted to Glasgow University, he took up medicine and after graduation saw Army service as a psychiatrist. Following a succession of hospital psychiatrist positions, he joined the Tavistock Clinic in London and then was a participant in a failed therapeutic community experiment with schizophrenics. Attacking conventional psychiatry, he was a 'biopolitician' for much of his career. He wrote extensively. The most important of his books are *The Divided Self, Sanity, Madness and the Family*, and *The Politics of Experience and the Bird of Paradise*. Laing died in 1989.

4. Existential phenomenology characterizes people's experience of their worlds and of themselves in the context of 'being-in-the-world'. In the study of people, we can't use abstract, objective, clinical terms; these are *it-terms*, and they are disdained by existentialists. Terrifying personal experiences such as schizophrenia cannot be understood outside the person's experience.

5. Laing distinguished between *ontological security* and *ontological insecurity*. The ontologically secure individual has a firm sense of self and being and of autonomy. The ontologically insecure person is exposed to extreme anxiety that can take three forms: *engulfment*, which is a fear of loss of autonomy leading to isolation; *implosion*, which is a feeling of emptiness and dread of reality 'exploding inward'; and *petrification* and *depersonalization*, the experience of emptiness, being turned to stone, not feeling oneself a person.

6. Ontological security and insecurity can be further differentiated. The person secure in the sense of self and being is also at one with his or her body. It is an extension of self. This is the experience of an *embodied self*. One who is ontologically insecure experiences a degree of detachment from the body, as if he or she were not a wholly unified person. The body is more like an object and the self more like an onlooker on it. This is the false and *unembodied self*. Bodily functions and desires are not self-originated and determined.

7. There are two expressions of self-consciousness. One is part of the sense of being, awareness of self as an independent, embodied being. The other is to be the object of others' observation, which engenders

discomfort or, more seriously, severe anxiety. Adolescents commonly worry about being scrutinized and as a result are shy. The person who is ontologically insecure may experience a far more intrusive version, thinking that others know his or her most intimate thoughts. Sometimes, dreading the loss of identity and self, the insecure person seeks others and their imputed probing as reassurance of the reality of self and personhood.

8. Laing did *not* seek the cause of schizophrenia. His concern was the *experience* of the schizophrenic person. He saw schizophrenia as a model for the distortion of experience. The disorder is a creative solution to unendurable experience. Though it might not be a good solution, we must respect the schizophrenic person and his or her experience. After all, achieving full-fledged being-in-the-world is a big challenge; existentialists don't want to fool you.

9. Existentialism's humanistic perspective, concern for meaning, and stress on personal responsibility are admirable. Phenomenology does give an important perspective on individual experience. But it is *not* personality theory. Existentialists disdain psychological causality and science and consider psychological research on personality and personality disorders irrelevant to the true concerns of human experience.

TO TEST YOUR UNDERSTANDING

1. What were the events of the first half of the twentieth century, particularly in Europe, that made existential philosophy appealing? To whom did it appeal and why? Existentialism has become a significant psychotherapeutic movement. Who is attracted to it and why?

2. What would Laing have thought about the strong evidence that schizophrenia is a heritable disorder? Would he have been disbelieving or distressed? Hint: Would he have distinguished between etiology and the experience of the disorder?

3. Think about Laing's meaning when he wrote that all of us 'are only two or three degrees Fahrenheit from experiences of [implosion and engulfment]. Even a slight fever, and the whole world can begin to take on a persecutory, impinging aspect.' Are all of us that close to ontological disaster?

4. Some existential psychologists have developed personality questionnaires to study existential concepts. One of them, for example, is an Experiencing Scale assessing the degree of self-awareness; another is a Meaning-in-Life test. What do you think of such research efforts? What do they add to existentialism? Are they consistent with existential philosophy and psychology, or do they violate basic principles of existentialism?

CHAPTER ELEVEN

Phenomenology: Carl Rogers' Theory of the Person and George Kelly's Personal Construct Theory

Introduction

The phenomenologists we take up in this chapter were not in the mould of great European phenomenologists like Edmund Husserl. Early in the twentieth century, Husserl formulated a philosophy of mind and of consciousness holding that objects in our experience *are* reality and are not defined by the assumptions, deductions, or theory of any other discipline, the natural sciences included. Husserl's formulations of consciousness, experience, and the perception of reality had a large influence on European philosophers, Martin Heidegger and Jean-Paul Sartre notable among them.

In North America, phenomenology had a distinct imprint that did not derive formally from the European philosophical movement, and a course that developed more on its own. A significant contribution to the North American movement came from the psychoanalyst Otto Rank, a troubled and troubling breakaway member of the Freudian circle. Rank turned his back on psychoanalysis as a historical therapy to advocate a focus on the present and the abbreviation of an overlong and exacting treatment. Carl Rogers, then a young child clinical psychologist, heard Rank present his ideas—only briefly—but this exposure strongly affected him. In particular he was struck by Rank's concept of **will**★, with which we are all endowed, expressed as a will to be ourselves and to free ourselves of the domination of others.

American phenomenology came of age in the years immediately before and after World War II. It appeared in such books as *Individual Behavior* by Snygg and Combs, published in 1949, which began with the statement that 'all behaviour, without exception, is completely determined by and pertinent to the phenomenal field of the behaving organism' (Snygg & Combs, 1949, p. 15). Keep this premise in mind, for we shall see that Carl Rogers enthusiastically adopted it. I wouldn't want you to think that Snygg and Combs wrote a particularly good book. It wasn't. The illustration of the phenomenal field idea was a long, trite, and tendentious passage about Snygg's banging up the fenders of his car (twice) in trying to sort out the figure and ground of an unfamiliar driveway. If you can't make a better case for a core concept of individual phenomenal experience and figure–ground relationships within it than that, perhaps you haven't thought it through very well. The time was ripe for the notion, though, and no one, Rogers included, seemed to notice. The phenomenal field—since it can't be known by another person—is a particularly elusive concept, one that invites foolish things to be said about it. Be alert to that as we continue.

Phenomenology—the American version—became in the next decades part of a larger humanistic and existential movement that one of its outstanding proponents, Abraham Maslow, called a 'third force' in psychology (Maslow, 1970). Maslow and the existentialist Rollo May were significant figures in the movement—Maslow especially for his view that human needs are ordered in a hierarchy, from physiological and other deficiency needs (safety, belongingness and love, esteem) to a growth need at the highest level, self-actualization, the pinnacle of human motivation pursued when deficiencies have been met (Maslow, 1970). The third force took aim at deterministic, scientific psychology, especially in its approach to personality, attacking the imposition of analysis, concepts, and methods foreign to the person. In one way or another, third force psychologists said, 'You can't do that. You are violating the human organism by imposing something wholly alien to the experience of the person.'

Rogers fell in love with the word *organism* to designate 'persons' or 'individuals', as we had customarily called them. This was a borrowed term, used most explicitly by the neuropsychiatrist Kurt Goldstein in trying to convey the unity of the perceiving and behaving person (Goldstein, 1939). Rogers and other phenomenologists (including Goldstein in his later years) didn't extend an all-embracing welcome to rats, pigeons, or other creatures studied by psychologists. Many of them used 'organism' because it sounds great. It implies 'whole', 'complete', 'self-contained'; it sounds, somehow, healthy and good, like the word 'organic' that we find in the supermarket applied to heads of lettuce, apples, or loaves of bread.

Carl Rogers (© Rogers Ressmeyer/CORBIS)

George Kelly, our second phenomenologist, came to the movement quite independently, and only much later would he consider himself part of it. He was an iconoclast, and he had none of the credentials that usually bring people to personality theory. He shared with Rogers a distaste for depth psychology, in his case one that was highly contemptuous, and he did have years of clinical experience, like Rogers, that lured him to a psychology of individual phenomenal experience. You can imagine Carl Rogers, Abraham Maslow, and Rollo May hugging each other, for they shared the deep conviction of a Rouseauian vision of humankind's essential goodness, but they wouldn't have hugged Kelly gladly. He was too cognitive, too abstract, and hardly Rousseauian at all.

Carl Rogers' Person-Centred Theory

Carl Rogers: Personal History

Rogers gave autobiographical accounts of his upbringing and the turns of his career in the belief that the facts of his life and his own view of them would help others to understand the roots of his theory (Rogers, 1959, 1967). However, this is not well-charted ground, as I've said, from which to explore a theory. It lures us to see a theory as a personal thing, more an expression of the personality attributes of the theorist than a statement of the-oretical principles. In this case, though, Rogers was indubitably right.

Carl Ransom Rogers was born in January 1902 in Oak Park, Illinois, a wealthy western suburb of Chicago. He was the fourth of six children 'in a large, closeknit family, where hard work and a highly conservative (almost fundamentalist) Protestant Christianity were about equally revered' (1959, p. 186). His father was a civil engineer who turned farmer when Rogers was twelve. 'It is widely known', wrote a biographer, 'that Carl Rogers grew up on a farm, but not so widely known that the farm house had a slate roof, tile floors, eight bedrooms and five baths, and a clay tennis court behind the house' (Kirschenbaum, 1979). The child of privilege, his early years in Oak Park were spent in a comfortable upper-middle-class neighbourhood; elementary school class-mates included Ernest Hemingway and the children of Frank Lloyd Wright.

Rogers' parents imposed an extremely strict and morally rigid religious training. It saw innocent things tainted by evil and the morality of neighbours as doubtful. Two illustrations:

> I have a hard time convincing my children that even carbonated beverages had a faintly sinful aroma, and I remember my slight feeling of wickedness when I had my first bottle of 'pop' (Rogers, 1961, p. 5).

> [Of his family's stance toward others, he said,] I think the attitudes toward persons outside our large family can be summed up schematically in this way: Other persons behave in dubious ways which we do not approve in our family. Many of them play cards, go to movies, smoke, drink, and engage in other activities—some unmentionable. So the best thing to do is to be tolerant of them, since they may not know better, and to keep away from any close communication with them and live your life within the family (1973, p. 3).

Such attitudes isolated him and made him an outsider among his peers; he turned to an immersion in reading, even the dictionary. He liked the farm, run scientifically by his father, and science became a lifelong absorption. He was fully explicit in identifying his theories of psychotherapy and of the person as scientific (Rogers, 1959).

At seventeen, he followed family tradition to enter the University of Wisconsin. His major was agriculture. Active in the church and church work, he was chosen as a dele-gate to the World Student Christian Federation Conference, meeting in Beijing (then Peking), China. Perhaps it was the exposure to other cultures and religions, perhaps a newfound freedom, that turned him from fundamentalism. Six months later, on board ship returning home, he had a liberating insight: 'It struck me one night in my cabin that perhaps Jesus was a man like other men—not divine! As this idea formed and took root, it became obvious to me that I could never in any emotional sense return home. This proved to be true' (1961, p. 351). No question about it—this revelation meant a sea change in his beliefs. Back in university, he abandoned agriculture for history. He also wrote his parents to say that he could no longer accept their constricting religious out-look. On graduation, he married (over his parents' objections) and carried out the first terms of his avowal of independence. He wasn't so much turned off religion as liberal-ized in his view. He enrolled at Union Theological Seminary in New York City, 'which at that time was deeply committed to a freedom of philosophical thought which respected any honest attempt to resolve significant problems, whether this led into or away from the church' (1959, p. 186).

Rogers' own attempt led away, and he left the seminary and religion for Teachers College, Columbia University, to study psychology. Here, he encountered the philosophy of John Dewey through a professor of education, William H. Kilpatrick, as well as a sensible and humanistic approach to clinical problems, a great deal of statistics, and Edward L. Thorndike's psychology of learning. This was a mix, especially the statistics and the no-nonsense associationism of Thorndike, that would have conflicted sharply with the Freudian orientation at the Institute of Child Guidance, where he spent a year of pre-doctoral internship. Treating patients for the first time, his head must have been buzzing.

Rogers received the PhD in 1931 and took a position at the Rochester, New York Guidance Center—officially the Child Study Department of the Society for the Prevention of Cruelty to Children—where he remained for twelve years. He took his Freudian learning with him but discovered that it was unhelpful. A diverse and eclectic staff and everyday clinical experience were far more important to his development. It was that practical exposure that opened his ears to patients—excuse me, 'clients' is what we call them in this approach—and taught him that a therapist's insight into a client's difficulty often didn't accomplish what it was supposed to. Here he is trying to tell the mother of a delinquent adolescent that her rejection of her son is the cause of his bad behaviour:

> Finally I gave up. I told her that it seemed we had both tried, but we had failed. . . . She agreed. So we concluded the interview, shook hands, and she walked to the door of the office. Then she turned and asked, 'Do you ever take adults for counselling here?' When I replied in the affirmative, she said, 'Well then, I would like some help.' She came to the chair she had left, and began to pour out her despair about her marriage, her troubled relationship with her husband, her sense of failure and confusion, all very different from the sterile 'case history' she had given before. Real therapy began then. . . .
>
> This incident was one of a number which helped me to experience that fact—only fully realized later—that it is the *client* who knows what hurts, what directions to go, what problems are crucial, what experiences have been deeply buried. It began to occur to me that unless I had a need to demonstrate my own cleverness and learning, I would do better to rely upon the client for the direction of movement in the process (1961, pp. 11–12).

His first book, *The Clinical Treatment of the Problem Child* (1938), came from the struggle to make sense of his experience in treating distressed parents and their children. In 1940, he was invited to join the Ohio State University Department of Psychology as professor. It was at first a jarring and exacting test to explain his immanent principles of psychotherapy to bright, psychologically sophisticated, and critical graduate students. He was forced to develop his ideas, 'more of a new pathway', he said, 'than I had recognized' (p. 187); the result was *Counseling and Psychotherapy* (1942), a book that eclipsed all expectation.

Rogers left Ohio State for war work, and in 1945 moved to the University of Chicago as professor and executive secretary of the Counseling Center. Here, over twelve years, he wrote a major exposition of client-centred therapy, developed the theory of personality that is the therapy's offspring, and with colleagues carried out research on psychotherapy in the Counseling Center that fully established client-centred therapy and gave it a research base to stand on (Rogers & Dymond, 1954).

In 1957 he moved on, giving up what seemed to outsiders (including me) the perfect academic position for a personality psychologist, psychotherapist, and psychotherapy investigator, to go the University of Wisconsin as professor of psychology and professor of psychiatry (on which he insisted). The psychiatric appointment, he felt, would give him the chance to apply client-centred therapy to schizophrenics, a challenge indeed. This was to be a big mistake. He found himself in a hornets' nest; as he saw them, his psychology colleagues were unsupportive, ruthlessly competitive, and harsh in their treatment of (his) graduate students. This was an anguished time, marked by ugly conflict with the Department of Psychology and discomfiture in the Department of Psychiatry over a nonmedical colleague who was rocking the boat (Kirschenbaum, 1979). And schizophrenics as client-centred clients did not work out. A preliminary report on the project was disappointing and inconclusive (Rogers, Gendlin, Kiesler, & Truax, 1967). Perspective 11.1 suggests the reason why.

Perspective 11.1   Client-Centred Therapy with a Schizophrenic Man

THERAPIST: And I guess your silence is saying to me that either you don't wish to or can't come out right now and that's ok. So I won't pester you but I just want you to know, I'm here.
> *A very long silence of seventeen minutes.*

T: I see I'm going to have to stop in a few minutes.
> *Brief silence.*

T: It's hard for me to know how you've been feeling, but it looks as though part of the time maybe you'd rather I didn't know how you were feeling. Anyway, it looks as though part of the time it just feels very good to let down and . . . relax the tension. But as I say I don't really know . . . how you feel. It's just the way it looks to me. Have things been pretty bad lately?
> *Brief silence.*

T: Maybe this morning you just wish I'd shut up . . . and maybe I should but I just keep feeling I'd like to, I don't know, be in touch with you in some way.
> *Silence of two minutes. Mr Vac yawns.*

T: Sound discouraged or tired.

CLIENT: No, just lousy.

T: Everything's lousy, huh? You feel lousy?
> *Silence of forty seconds.*

T: Want to come in Friday at twelve at the usual time?

C: *Yawns and mutters something unintelligible.*
> *Silence of forty-eight seconds.*

T: Just kind of feel sunk way down deep in these lousy, lousy feelings, huh? Is that something like it?

C: No.

T: No?
> *Silence of twenty seconds.*

C: No. I just ain't no good to nobody, never was, and never will be.

T: Feeling that now, huh? That you're just no good to yourself, no good to anybody. Never will be any good to anybody. Just that you're completely worthless, huh? . . . . These are really lousy feelings. Just feel that you're no good at *all*, huh?

C: Yeah. That's what this guy I went to town with just the other day told me.

T: This guy that you went to town with really told you that you were no good? Is that what you're saying? Did I hear that right?

C: Uh, hum.

T: I guess the meaning of that, if I get it right, is that here's somebody that meant something to you and what does he think of you? Why, he's told you that he thinks you're no good at all. And that just really knocks the props out from you. (*Vac just weeps quietly.*) It just brings the tears.

> *Silence of twenty seconds.*

C: I don't care though.

T: You tell yourself that you don't care at all, but somehow I guess some part of you cares because some part of you weeps over it (Rogers, 1966, pp. 189–90).

This, with its excruciatingly long silences and some significant insensitivities of the therapist in capturing and reflecting the feelings of a deeply disturbed client, was not very good therapy. Perhaps it couldn't have been. We know that the schizophrenic person is a tough therapeutic nut to crack, and client-centred procedures may not have been up to the job.

Rogers quit his positions to join the Western Behavioral Sciences Institute in La Jolla, California. This didn't last either, and he left the Institute to form the Center for Studies of the Person, also in La Jolla, with humanistically inclined colleagues. In his later years, he became more and more of a humanist and more and more devoted to discovering the conditions that enable people to become (his term) 'fully functioning'. Encounter groups and sensitivity training were keen interests. He was honoured by the presidency of the American Psychological Association (1947) and received its Distinguished Scientific Contribution Award (1956) and Distinguished Professional Contribution Award (1972). He died in 1987 at the age of 85.

Emphases

Let's start with an attitude, one that is central to Rogers' theory. A phenomenologist is bound to view humans as subjective creatures, every moment of whose lives is experienced as immediate and personal. Scientists are not exempted: everything they do stems from choices and purposes that cannot be anything but the expressions of a wholly individual view of the world. Rogers believed in the scientific prescription—all of it— as the avenue to travel, the one with the fewest potholes of self-deception. But, he said, there isn't any 'objective truth' at the end; there are only claims that appeared to him to qualify as objective and true. The knowledge base of science exists only in the perceptions of individual scientists (Rogers, 1959).

We can state the emphases in the theory succinctly; there are four of them.

1. First, there is the theory of psychotherapy and personality change, with which Rogers began. Far bolder than other personality theorists, he claimed to have identified the conditions necessary and sufficient for personality change. I refer to psy-

chotherapy—the theory and its body of research—as 'client-centred'; this was the term that Rogers mainly used.

2. Deriving from the theory of psychotherapy is a theory of personality. As Rogers said in his major statement, psychotherapy provided the model of the person in the form of hypotheses about personality dynamics, growth and development, and impediments to growth that therapy could remove (1959). Instead of designating the personality theory as client-centred, it seems more appropriate to free it from the context of client and therapist and recognize it as a theory of the person, person-centred theory.

3. The personality theory has an unusual extension, a theory of the fully functioning person.

4. Then, there are implications of the theory. Rogers listed interpersonal relations, family life, education, group leadership, and group conflict. We'll touch on them.

The Major Concepts of Person-Centred Theory

The Phenomenal Field

To be a phenomenologist is to give the greatest importance to immediate experience, the experience of the 'given moment'. By 'experience', Rogers meant

> all that is going on within the envelope of the organism which is potentially available to awareness. It includes events of which the individual is unaware, as well as all the phenomena which are in consciousness. Thus it includes the psychological aspects of hunger, even though the individual may be so fascinated by his work or play that he is completely unaware of the hunger; it includes the impact of sights and sounds and smells on the organism, even though these are not in the focus of attention. It includes the influence of memory and past experience, as these are active in the moment, in restricting or broadening the meaning given to various stimuli. It also includes all that is present in immediate awareness or consciousness. It does not include such events as neuron discharges or changes in blood sugar, because these are not directly available to awareness. It is thus a psychological, not a physiological definition (1959, p. 197).

You can't be a phenomenologist without accepting that one can never completely know the experience of another person. Appreciating another's experience can be approximated only by a process called '*empathic understanding*', which means perceiving his or her internal frame of reference and recognizing its significance and emotional meaning as if one *were* that person, never losing sight of the 'as if'. Truly knowing the experience of someone else can't be done, but it must be tried. Empathic understanding brings us as close as we can get.

Self and Self-concept

The phenomenal field is differentiated. Experiences of self (self-experience) form the **self-concept★**. 'Self, Concept of self, Self-structure . . . refer to the organized, consistent conceptual gestalt composed of perceptions of the characteristics of the "I" or "me" to others and to various aspects of life, together with the values attached to these perceptions. It is a gestalt which is available to awareness though not necessarily in awareness' (1959, p. 200). An **ideal self** is a further differentiation. This is the 'self-concept which the individual would most like to possess, upon which he places the highest value for himself' (1959, p. 200).

One's concept of oneself and the feelings that make up a significant part of that concept would seem to be so private as to forbid measurement. Rogers, though, saw in a technique developed by an English psychologist, William Stephenson, then at the University of Chicago, a way of penetrating private experience to gain access to the self-concept. This was **Q-technique★**, which Stephenson advocated as part of a larger, sophisticated Q-methodology to study the individual (Stephenson, 1953). Hypotheses developed out of Q-methodology would be tested by Q-technique, using a variety of procedures including factor analysis. Rogers and his associates dismissed Q-methodology and adopted only the method of measurement, Q-technique.

Measurement of the Self-concept

Q-technique's measure, the **Q-sort★**, became one of the standard procedures in research at the Chicago Counseling Center. A therapy client was given a set of 100 cards, each containing a self-descriptive statement. Here are some examples: 'I am a submissive person'; 'I am a hard worker'; 'I really am disturbed'; 'I feel insecure within myself'; 'I am likeable'; 'I have few values and standards of my own'; 'I feel emotionally mature'. The client was asked to sort the cards into (typically) nine or eleven piles, with the most accurate (to the client) statements going into piles at one end and the least accurate going into piles at the opposite end; the middle piles were reserved for those statements the client thought were neither like nor unlike himself or herself. A normal distribution was forced by requiring a large number of cards in the middle piles and few in the outer piles. The client was asked to carry out two sorts: one of the self as seen ('experienced' is the word we want) at the time, and the other of the self as he or she would like to be, an ideal self. With two sorts of the same 100 statements, both normally distributed, a correlation coefficient could readily be computed to express the correspondence of, or distance between, self-concept and ideal concept. We'll review some of the Counseling Center research with Q-sort measures of self—ideal-self discrepancies before, during, and after therapy.

Self-experience

Awareness of self becomes differentiated out of experience early in the course of development; this is self-experience. With the emergence of self-experience develops a need, one that every single person is endowed with; this is the need for **positive regard**. We infer the positive (or negative) regard of another person, and thus its satisfaction is frequently ambiguous. We can live without the positive regard of at least some others as long as we have a strong self-concept. Positive regard is reciprocal: when we satisfy another's need for positive regard, we ourselves satisfy our own need. Sullivan's concepts of needs for approval and security anticipated this Rogerian motive.

Following from the need for positive regard is a need for **positive self-regard**. We become for ourselves a 'significant social other'. Self-regard is itself a need, learned from selfexperiences of fulfillment or thwarting of the need for positive regard. We view ourselves and our experiences of positive regard (or its negative) quite independently of anyone else.

Conditions of Worth

These needs—for positive regard and for positive self-regard—may lead us to judge our self-experience. As Rogers explains, 'When a *self-experience* is avoided (or sought) solely because it is less (or more) worthy of *self-regard*, the individual is said to have acquired a condition of worth' (1959, p. 224). **Conditions of worth** say that you are more (or less) positively regarded because of what you have done, said, stood for. A mother who becomes angry at her child and communicates her feeling—or who says, explicitly, something to the effect of 'I don't like you when you do that'—is setting conditions of worth.

We tend to avoid or distort experiences associated with negative conditions of worth because they threaten the self. At the same time, pursuit of positive regard from others because of perceived conditions of worth is psychologically destructive. The person who does this is not 'true to himself, to his own natural organismic valuing of experience, but for the sake of preserving the positive regard of others has now come to falsify some of the values he experiences and to perceive them only in terms based upon their value to others' (1959, p. 226). We all experience conditions of worth. We all undergo the criticism of others and extend ourselves for the positive regard of others, and to that degree our evaluations of ourselves are bent and not organismic. We are, to that degree, less well psychologically adjusted and not fully functioning.

Congruence and Incongruence

Congruence and **incongruence** refer to the relation between self-experiences and the self-concept. 'When self-experiences are accurately symbolized and are included in the self-concept in this accurately symbolized form, the state is one of congruence of self and experience' (1959, p. 206). To be in a state of congruence in most relationships is to be a fully functioning person, but one could be congruent in one or a few relationships or only at some times. Adjectives to describe congruence are *integrated, whole, genuine.*

Incongruence arises when experiences conflict with the self. Conditions of worth will do it: 'I am a bad person for doing that, thinking that, not being liked or respected by this person,' one says to oneself. So, one now has a painful discrepancy between self and the experiences that led to those conditions of worth. Experiences must now be perceived selectively; they are distorted to agree with the conditions of worth, or will be partly or wholly denied awareness. The self-concept is compromised by inaccurate perceptions that represent neither the experiences nor the regard for oneself. This is distressing territory indeed and, under attack, we are likely to seek defences to protect the self. Mr Smith cannot bear to be badly thought of by his wife, who is often critical of him, and he will do almost anything to keep himself in her good graces. He unfailingly abides by her conditions of worth, to the point of altering his perception of their interactions and his role in them to preserve self-regard.

IT'S ALWAYS 'GOOD DOG'—NEVER 'GREAT DOG.'

GREGORY

Threat and Anxiety

Experiences that are incongruent with the self create **threat★**. If the threat is perceived and symbolized, the result is **anxiety★**. Defence occurs to protect the self from violation of conditions of worth, in this way serving as a last-ditch effort to preserve the need for positive self-regard. The basic defensive processes are very much akin to Sullivan's concepts of selective inattention and dissociation: they are perceptual defence and denial to awareness. In person-centred theory, the individual resorting to these defensive processes is said to be psychologically maladjusted. If the incongruence is severe and the defences cannot function successfully, the individual suffers breakdown and disorganization.

Perceptual defence seemed to fit right in with a term introduced in an experiment conducted by McCleary and Lazarus—*subception*, meaning perception below the threshold of awareness (McCleary & Lazarus, 1949). In the experiment, participants were exposed to ten nonsense syllables, five of which were conditioned to electric shock. The dependent variable was a classical measure of emotional arousal, change in skin conductance on the surface of the palm, the so-called galvanic skin response. After conditioning, the syllables, shocked and nonshocked, were shown in a projection device (tachistoscope—*tach* from the Greek for fast + scope) at varying exposure speeds. On presentations too fast for correct (verbal) identification of the shocked syllables, there was still a skin conductance response. McCleary and Lazarus called this galvanic skin response discrimination without awareness.

This was just what Rogers needed: experimental evidence of perceptual defence and denial to awareness. Was it, though? The experiment had a critical flaw, one centring on the fact that a 'language' of ten nonsense syllables was too inexact to reveal the discriminations the participants were capable of making. What very likely occurred was that the participants perceived partial cues—informative parts of the nonsense syllables—that correlated with the skin conductance discrimination. They knew more than the 'language' they had to use enabled them to say. Perceptual defence *might* be a useful concept to understand what happens when a person is threatened and incongruent, but the subception experiment was not a good demonstration of unperceived perception.

Motivation

The motivational principle is simplicity itself. There is only one motivation★. It is **self-actualization**★, the inborn drive (Rogers preferred 'tendency', a word much too weak for such an all-powerful motive) toward growth and self-enhancement. Self-actualization includes the meeting of physiological needs and beyond them the whole world of self-expressiveness and self-development. It means seeking autonomy, getting out from under the dominating thumb of others, even benign parents. It can be held back but cannot be conquered or truly surrendered. There are no personality structures dividing up motivational responsibilities—no id, no ego, no superego, no dynamisms. Humans are only motivated by this one tendency to grow, to self-actualize. What happens when self-actualization is stepped on by others? Rogers had an analogy from his youth on the farm:

> The actualizing tendency can, of course, be thwarted or warped, but it cannot be destroyed without destroying the organism. I remember that in my boyhood, the bin in which we stored our winter's supply of potatoes was in the basement, several feet below a small window. The conditions were unfavourable, but the potatoes would begin to sprout—pale white sprouts, so unlike the healthy green shoots they sent up when planted in the soil in the spring. But these sad, spindly sprouts would grow 2 or 3 feet in length as they reached toward the distant light of the window. The sprouts were, in their bizarre, futile growth, a sort of desperate expression of the directional tendency I have been describing. They would never become plants,

never mature, never fulfill their real potential. But under the most adverse circumstances, they were striving to become. . . . In dealing with clients whose lives have been terribly warped . . . I often think of those potato sprouts. So unfavourable have been the conditions in which these people have developed that their lives often seem abnormal, twisted, scarcely human. Yet, the directional tendency in them can be trusted (1980, pp. 118–19).

There is in this a rather naive optimism, the belief that inherent in every person is the tendency to growth. It appears in the theory of therapy and how therapy works, and in the way Rogers deals with child development, and it is apparent in his approach to education, which reflects his view that children (or adults) possess the necessary capacities for learning and growth. By directing learning, we only get in the way of something that is inborn. But since every behaviour stems from this self-actualizing motivational principle, we have to answer a large question: in explaining everything, does the principle explain nothing?

A Theory of Therapy and Personality Change

With growing confidence in person-centred psychotherapy, Rogers proposed that it conformed to the basic scientific paradigm of antecedent conditions, their consequents, and a set of processes in the middle (see Figure 11.1).

There are no intervening variables in this scheme, he claimed. Conditions, processes, and outcomes are all operationally definable, so we don't have to infer mediating variables. A bold claim.

Here are the necessary and sufficient conditions for inaugurating person-centred psychotherapy:

1. We need two persons in at least a minimal relationship ('contact' is the word). Not infrequently, the contact will have to continue for some time before the psychotherapeutic process can begin.
2. One person, the client, is in a state of incongruence. Depending on the magnitude of the incongruence, he or she is vulnerable, anxious, or both, threatened and disorganized (if aware), or describes himself or herself as adjusted if defences are functioning.
3. The other person, the therapist, is congruent *in this relationship*. (The therapist's incongruence in other relationships is not relevant to the therapeutic relationship unless he or she lets it spill over and affect the therapy.)
4. The therapist holds *unconditional positive regard* for the client. Whatever the client is like, none of the client's experiences is discriminated as being less worthy of positive regard than any other.
5. The therapist experiences an *empathic understanding* of the client's internal frame of reference (the phenomenal field). The therapist perceives the client's internal frame of reference with an 'as if I were he or she' reservation. The therapist recognizes that it's impossible to get inside someone else's skin.

Figure 11.1 The scientific paradigm of psychotherapy according to Rogers

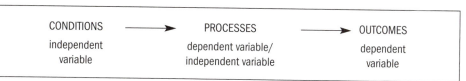

CONDITIONS ⟶ PROCESSES ⟶ OUTCOMES
independent   dependent variable/   dependent
variable   independent variable   variable

6. The client perceives—at least minimally—the therapist's unconditional positive regard and empathic understanding.

It does some violence to person-centred therapy to talk about techniques, which could be seen as manipulative. We must take note that Rogers was firmly against any manipulation of the client. The therapist reflects and shows his or her empathic understanding of the client's experience. For the therapist to repeat what the client has said in his or her own words is a very good technique. So is Mmm-hmm. There's an obvious potential problem here. Does the therapist subtly and without intent shape the client's verbal behaviour, his Mmm-hmms and reflection selectively rewarding good Rogerian things the client may say (for example, about self, self-doubt, positive regard, conditions of worth) via operant conditioning (see Chapter 12)? Later in this chapter we'll review a famous study by Raimy, who studied changes in self-reference by clients in therapy. Was Raimy's real finding that self-references were subtly shaped?

Now the processes:

1. The client experiences freedom to express feelings that may be shown in facial and body language as well as words.
2. The expressed feelings are about the self.
3. There is increasing differentiation and discrimination of the objects of feelings and perceptions (external environment, self, experience). Experiences are increasingly symbolized accurately.
4. The expressed feelings deal with incongruence.
5. The client now experiences threat—the awareness of incongruence. He or she is able to do that because of the unconditional positive regard of the therapist.
6. The client fully experiences in awareness.
7. The self-concept is reorganized to assimilate experiences that up to now have been distorted or defended against.
8. There is increasing congruence of self with experience. The self can incorporate formerly threatening and excluded experiences. There is less perceptual distortion and less defensiveness.
9. The client experiences without threat the therapist's unconditional positive regard.
10. The client comes to feel unconditional positive self-regard.
11. More and more, the client experiences him- or herself as the locus of evaluation.
12. He or she reacts to experience more in accord with an **organismic valuing process**, less to conditions of worth. (Is this nothing more than tossing nice, value-laden terms into the discourse? What could it mean?)

From setting in motion the conditions and processes of psychotherapy, we now see a number of outcomes, which will appear in therapy and without:

1. Clients are congruent and open to experience.
2. They perceive objectively.
3. Their problem-solving is more effective.
4. Their psychological adjustment is improved.
5. The vulnerability hitherto experienced by the client is decreased.
6. The ideal self-concept is more realistic and attainable.
7. The self-concept is more congruent with the ideal self.
8. Psychological and physiological tension and anxiety are reduced.

9. Positive self-regard increases.

10. The locus of evaluation and choice is more and more in the self.

11. Values are determined by an organismic valuing process. (We've just met this and wondered what it might mean.)

12. Others are more realistically perceived.

13. Behaviour is perceived and experienced as being more under self-control (one doesn't feel the victim of feelings and actions one can't control).

14. We have a more social, mature, creative, adaptive person, using the proper underarm deodorant and not saying rude words he can't spell.

Perspective 11.2   Fifteen Minutes in the Therapy of Mrs Oak

Mrs Oak has just upbraided the therapist, expressing strong resentment that she is being pressured to change, to abandon her old defensive self. She has said to him, 'You don't add a damn thing to my status' [to my getting better, I think she means].

CLIENT: And I have the feeling that it isn't guilt. (*Pause.*) (*Weeps.*) So . . . course I mean I can't verbalize it yet. It's just being *terribly hurt!*

THERAPIST: M-hm. It isn't guilt except in the sense of being very much wounded somehow.

C: (*Weeping.*) It's . . . you know, often I've been guilty of it myself, but in later years when I've heard parents . . . say to their children, 'Stop crying', I've had a feeling, instead I've thought it through, so that . . . I mean . . . a hurt as though, well, why should they tell them to stop crying? They feel sorry for themselves, and who can feel more adequate-a-a-adequately sorry for himself than a child. Well, that is sort of what . . . I mean, as–as though I mean, I–I thought that they should let him cry. And . . . feel sorry for him too, maybe. In a . . . rather objective kind of way. Well, that's . . . that's something of the kind of thing I've been experiencing. I mean, now . . . just right now. And in–in . . .

T: That catches a little more of the flavor of the feeling, that it's almost as if you're really weeping for yourself. . . .

C: And then of course, I've come to . . . to see and to feel that over this . . . see, I've covered it up. (*Weeps.*) But . . . and . . . I've covered it up with so much *bitterness*, which in turn I had to cover up. (*Weeps.*) *That's* what I want to get rid of! I almost don't *care* if I hurt.

T: (*Gently.*) You feel that here at the basis of it, as you experienced it, is a feeling of real tears for yourself. But that you *can't*, mustn't show, so that's been covered by bitterness that you don't like, that you'd like to be rid of. You almost feel you'd rather absorb the hurt than to . . . than to feel the bitterness. (*Pause.*) And what you seem to be saying quite strongly is, 'I do *hurt*, and I've tried to cover it up.'

C: I didn't *know* it.

T: M-hm. Like a new discovery really.

C: (*Speaking at the same time.*) I never really did know. But it's . . . you know, it's almost a physical thing. It's . . . it's sort of as though I–I–I were looking within myself at all kinds of . . . nerve endings and–and bits of–of . . . things that have been sort of mashed. (*Weeping.*)

T: As though some of the most delicate aspects of you—physically almost—have been crushed or hurt.

C: Yes. And you know, I do get the feeling, oh, you poor thing. (*Pause.*)

T: Just can't help but feel very deeply sorry for the person that is you (Rogers & Dymond, 1954, pp. 326-7).

In this brief therapy segment, we see the strong feelings about herself and the growing (and not at this point entirely welcome) self-awareness that Mrs. Oak is struggling with, and the therapist's difficult task in trying to understand and reflect his understanding.

From C.R. Rogers and R.F. Dymond, eds (1954). *Psychotheraphy and personality change: coordinated studies in the client-centered approach*. © 1954 by The University of Chicago Press. Reprinted by Permission.

Personality Development

Preparing children to lead happy and productive lives is very simply a matter of providing the conditions for inherent self-actualization. Parents need to give unconditional positive regard to their children. With positive regard, children experience positive self-regard; their evaluations of themselves are organismic; they are free to choose their own behaviour. Remember that conditions of worth imply that some behaviour is acceptable and valued, while other acts and thoughts (they can be hard to separate for a child) receive disapproval and criticism. Subjected to conditional positive regard, children feel themselves worthy only when they comply, are well behaved, and inhibit the bad. Whether or not living up to parent-imposed conditions of worth is actually good for a child's development, he or she can't help trying—or, in some cases, rebelling and making things worse.

Rogers laid out an extremely demanding program of childrearing for parents. Here is the essence of it:

> If the infant always felt prized, if his own feelings were always accepted even though some behaviours were inhibited, then no conditions of worth would develop. This could at least theoretically be achieved if the parental attitude was genuinely of this sort: 'I can understand how satisfying it feels to you to hit your baby brother (or to defecate when and where you please, or to destroy things) and I love you and am quite willing for you to have those feelings. But I am quite willing for me to have my feelings, too, and I feel very distressed when your brother is hurt (or annoyed or sad at other behaviours) and so I do not let you hit him. Both your feelings and my feelings are important, and each of us can freely have his own (1959, p. 225).

This is a truly idealistic developmental scene, an idealism like that of the therapist gently fostering 'the dissolving of conditions of worth, the achievement of a self which is congruent with experience, and the restoration of a unified organismic valuing process as the regulator of behaviour' (1959, pp. 226–7). There is some evidence that rearing children in such an undemanding, loving, and encouraging way works. In an important longitudinal study, Rogerian childrearing practices resulted in enhanced creative potential in young children that was maintained in adolescence (more details are given in the section on research, below). Just how parents are to do it, though, is not well specified. We can certainly advise laying off the obvious—creating conditions of worth, pushing children for accomplishment, and teaching them instead of allowing them to learn. And, as the therapy model implies, giving unconditional positive regard—love without strings—is the most important ingredient. It would be splendid if parents could be like therapists (and if children could respond like unconditionally regarded clients), but in contending daily with the impulses of small children whose socialization is incomplete, most parents will find the challenge great. My guess is that in the world of parenting, small and occasional deviations from this course are not going to have serious and lasting consequences.

Implications

The Fully Functioning Person

It isn't much of a surprise that a psychotherapist convinced that he had found the conditions to enable damaged people to get on the track of self-actualization would venture to define the ultimate aim. So what are the features of the ideal personality?

1. The fully functioning person is open to experience (there's no defensiveness).
2. All experiences are symbolized accurately in awareness.
3. The self-structure will be congruent with experience.
4. The self-structure is fluid and changing as new experiences are assimilated. (Rogers professed an unswerving scientific attitude, but then breached it in this attribute of the fully functioning person. If the self-structure at this high level of personality accomplishment is a changeling, incorporating modifications in the view of self as new events are taken in, then behaviour may be predictable only up to a point. Feel differently about yourself and your relation to the things you've just experienced? In this regard, you're a somewhat different person and may act in ways we—and maybe you—couldn't have anticipated. Of course there is an ebb and flow of our self-perception as the happenings of our lives affect us, but I think Rogers meant more than that. In other words, he seems to have asserted a *qualified* determinism: if we are fully functioning, the world of our past that shaped us has taken a back seat. Well, as scientists we know that opening the door to a denial of determinism, even if only by a crack, endangers any theory and may cause doubt about the theory's propositions.)
5. The fully functioning person experiences himself or herself as the locus of evaluation.
6. The valuing of other persons, other experiences, and the self will accord with the totality of the person—that is, will be organismic.
7. There are no conditions of worth. The fully functioning person won't say things like 'I'm a bad person when I do (think) that.'
8. Unconditional self-regard is experienced.
9. Creativity, adaptiveness, and a unique approach to new situations are characteristic.
10. The fully functioning person experiences harmonious relations with others because of the mutuality of positive regard.

Interpersonal Relations

The personality theory specifies the conditions for successful interpersonal relations:

1. To establish a relationship, we need two people in contact.
2. For the relationship to develop positively, there must be congruence (in this relationship specifically).
3. For the relationship to develop positively, there must be mutuality of positive regard.
4. Tension and discord are likely to come from failures of contact, incongruence in one or both parties, and increased defensiveness. Communication degenerates to superficiality, and a cycle of personal distortion and miscommunication ensues. The

reduction of group tension and conflict can be facilitated by increasing contact. Rogers recommended a 'facilitator', a go-between for the people in discordant groups. The facilitator is congruent in his relations with the warring parties, has an empathic understanding of their respective experiences, and the antagonists perceive his unconditional positive regard and empathy. Their openness to experience expands, and the basis is laid to understand each other.

Education and Family Life

Education can be enhanced by following the specifications of the theory. The role of education is to release the inborn tendency toward growth and development. Learning, like therapeutic personality change, is best achieved when the innate potential of the individual is allowed to express itself. If children are *taught*, their creativity is likely to be blunted and their potential stifled. Yes, children will learn, but the learning is at risk of becoming mechanical and not of intrinsic interest. These principles are mainly those of person-centred psychotherapy.

Improved family life is another consequence of following the principles of therapy, especially the provision of unconditional positive regard and the avoidance of conditions of worth. We need communication of experience, empathic understanding of the internal frame of reference of other family members, and openness to their experience. Rogers was not against freedom for marital partners to explore other relationships. Each allows the other room.

Research

An appreciable amount of research has grown out of person-centred theory, conducted by Rogers himself and his group of colleagues and students and by others. At the core are studies of psychotherapy, especially the work reported in Rogers and Dymond's *Psychotherapy and Personality Change* (1954), conducted in the University of Chicago Counseling Center, but there is as well a large body of applications of the theory. Rogers was a pioneer in opening the study of psychotherapy to investigation untrammeled by established conventions. The Chicago Counseling Center research was the first to use an untreated control group against which to measure treatment effects. Rogers introduced the practice of recording psychotherapy sessions, invading what most psychotherapists had regarded as a sanctuary, an inviolably private place where patients could speak with utter freedom in total security. Recording the sessions did no damage, and it gave researchers and clinicians an unprecedented body of data on psychotherapy process to study. We'll consider two outstanding examples of person-centred psychotherapy research and a Rogers-inspired study of childrearing contributions to childhood and adolescent creativity.

Self-reference in Client-Centred Therapy

Raimy (1948) studied expressed attitudes toward the self in counselling clients. He saw that self-referring statements in therapy could be classified as positive ('I'm intelligent.'), negative ('I am worthless.') or ambivalent ('I just don't know about myself—sometimes I feel so good about me, and sometimes I truly hate myself.'). Judges used this threefold classification to categorize every self-reference statement in transcripts of therapy hours of fourteen clients. Independently, the clients were rated on the outcome of their treat-

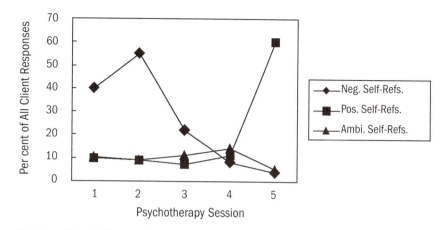

Figure 11.2 Raimy's study of changes in self-reference in client-centered therapy: A successful case

Neg. is negative self-references, Pos. is positive self-references, Ambi. is ambivalent self-references (adapted from Raimy, 1948)

ment. We can look at the results of two clients, one whose treatment was successful and one whose treatment was unsuccessful. Raimy reported: 'At the beginning of counseling the clients disapproved of and had ambivalent attitudes toward themselves. As counseling progressed fluctuations in approval occurred with mounting ambivalence. At the conclusion of counseling the *successful* cases showed a vast predominance of self-approval; the *unsuccessful* cases showed a predominance of self-disapproval and ambivalence' (p. 161). These changes mirror Rogers' description of process and outcome and, indeed, Rogers' analysis followed Raimy's findings. We must note, though, that this was extremely brief therapy, and the clients could not have had major distress to deal with. The processes of therapy would have been muted and much abbreviated.

Self-esteem Change in Client-Centred Therapy

One of the eleven studies in the 1954 Rogers and Dymond book was by Butler and Haigh, an exceptionally ambitious examination of change in self-esteem in the course of psychotherapy. All of the studies were based on data from three groups: a treated

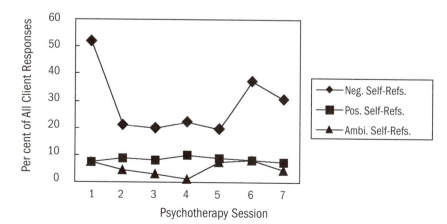

Figure 11.3 Raimy's study of changes in self-reference in client-centered therapy: An unsuccessful case

Neg. is negative self-references, Pos. is positive self-references, Ambi. is ambivalent self-references (adapted from Raimy, 1948)

group, a matched control group of non-client volunteers (tested before, during, and after the therapy of the treated group, and after the follow-up interval of six to twelve months), and a group of clients awaiting treatment (the 'wait group' or 'own-control group') delayed for sixty days before beginning their therapy. In the program of research, there were also clinical analyses of selected successful and unsuccessful cases. These were done by Rogers.

Butler and Haigh's self-esteem measure was the Q-sort correlation of self and ideal self. In the client group, the mean correlation before therapy was −.01, showing no relation at all between the Q-sort of the statements to describe the self and the ideal-self sort. Immediately following therapy, the average self-sort–ideal-sort correlation was .34, a significant increase, and one reflecting marked improvement. This was maintained at the follow-up: the correlation six months to a year later was .31. Among the non-client controls, tested twice at an interval equal to the duration of therapy for the clients, the correlations were .58 and .59, showing substantial and consistent agreement in their self and ideal sorts. With no intervention, the wait group showed self–ideal-self correlations of approximately zero at the beginning of their interval and again at the end. We need to take note that after therapy the clients weren't as happy with themselves as members of the control group were, but their view of themselves had moved closer to their ideal image.

Or did it? There's another possibility—that the ideal self-concept moved in the direction of the self-concept rather than the other way around. In other words, the increased congruence could mean not a happier image of self but instead a less idealized image of the person one would like to be. Indeed, both kinds of changes might have occurred. In another investigation in the series, Rudikoff did find just this, noting that in the wait group, 'The self-concept disclosed somewhat decreased adjustment over the control period [the sixty-day period before their therapy began], a very significant improvement over therapy, and a slight loss over follow-up. . . . The ideal was raised somewhat over the control period, but during the therapy and follow-up period it was somewhat lowered in the direction of the self, thus becoming a more achievable type of goal' (1954, p. 98). Well, perhaps. There are other possibilities these data don't rule out that you might like to puzzle over.

We can ask as well whether the changes found in the therapy group came as a result of therapy alone. Butler and Haigh did not find any relation between increase in the self-ideal correlation and therapeutic success, a finding—one I'm sure they weren't pleased to see—that they attributed to defensive sorting by some clients, making themselves appear to be happier and better adjusted than therapists might judge them. Defensive sorting does occur: Friedman (1955) found paranoid schizophrenics (who are diagnosed by extreme external attribution of the source of personal difficulty) to have self-ideal correlations that did not differ much from normals. Others have confirmed defensive sorting.

The pre-therapy, post-therapy, and follow-up data were reported for each individual client. Of the two cases studied clinically by Rogers, Mrs Oak, whose therapy excerpt we saw in Perspective 11.2, was rated as successful. Her Q-sorts showed the following self-ideal correlations: before therapy, .21; post-therapy, .69; follow-up, .71. Mr Bebb was judged a failure case. His correlations were, respectively, .06, .26, and .21.

Creative Effects of a Creativity-fostering Environment

Person-centred theory proposes that creativity is encouraged by the conditions that contribute to full functioning. Among them are openness to experience, an internal locus of evaluation, and the ability to explore things and ideas without giving in to inhibition. Harrington, Block, and Block (1987) studied childrearing practices in 106 families with children then four-and-a-half years old, measuring how well parents met these three conditions. The children—preschoolers—were tested for creative potential and were tested again years later in adolescence. The childrearing measures correlated significantly with both preschool and adolescent creative potential. Even when intelligence and creativity in preschool were held constant, the adolescent correlations remained. Childrearing–child behaviour relationships are not easily established, and longitudinal ones are yet more difficult. Harrington et al.'s findings are impressively consistent with the specifications of the theory for fostering a creative environment.

Person-Centred Theory in Perspective

Rogerian theory and therapy have had a dramatic influence and, by the measure of wide acceptance, have been hugely successful. The emphasis in Rogers' writings and in the theory on humanistic values and respect for the view of each person are welcome and much to be lauded. The world of psychotherapy needed to be reminded that the perspective and experience of the patient (better, here, to follow Rogers and say 'client') must be honoured. It was a signal achievement to launch and carry out the studies of psychotherapy process. Introducing the untreated control group and using measures of personality change that went well beyond therapists' ratings of improvement made this research more remarkable still.

Having said those things, however, it must be pointed out that person-centred theory presents us with a number of critical issues. First, this is a very naive phenomenology, its concepts stated in vague, imprecise, value-laden terms. We should commend a personality theory for concerning itself with values, but the theoretical concepts must be phrased in an objective, precise, operational way that leaves no room for unintended meaning to be surmised by the reader. Unfortunately, despite Rogers' ambitious claims for the theory and his formal presentation of it, complete with definitions of many concepts and their interrelations, it *is* vague and imprecise.

Person-centred theory is basically anti-intellectual, appealing to those who don't want to work or think to understand behaviour. As a Rogerian clinician, you don't have to *do* or *think* anything; you have to be warm, empathic (a lot of *Mmm-hmm*s help), and full of unconditional positive regard. You don't get to be a clinician by being a Rogerian; you start by learning Freud or some other personality system, become a convert, and then explain your therapeutic behaviour in Rogerian terms. The same criticism can be made of the applications of the theory to education.

Pioneering as it was, much of the research has raised questions, one of the most significant of which surrounds its apparent disregard for factors that we know can influence personality assessment techniques and self-description generally (Crowne, 2000). Phenomenologists are stuck with reliance on self-report; after all, what one says represents the phenomenal field of the moment. There is later research on psychotherapy using the Q-sort that appears to confirm the earlier findings (Deal, 1996; Du Caju, Fraile, Gonzales de Chavez, & Gutierrez, 2000), but the problem won't go away. Q-sorts themselves and the correlation between self and ideal-self sorts are ultimately dependent on the image the responding person is motivated to convey. Research not dependent on self-report— like the compelling longitudinal study of Harrington et al.—would help to dispel the doubt. A better version of the Chicago Q-sort items has been developed, the California

Q-set (Block, 1978). The selection of items by clinical and research investigators is a significant improvement, and an impressive body of evidence entirely independent of person-centred theory has accumulated, including the study of delay of gratification (Funder, Block, & Block, 1983), adolescent drug abuse (Block, Block, & Keyes, 1988; Shedler & Block, 1990), and depression in young adults (Block, Gjerde, & Block, 1991).

George Kelly's Personal Construct Theory

George Kelly bent phenomenology to suit his concern with the unique ways individuals construct their reality. His emphasis, true to orthodox phenomenology, was on the present, not a determining past, consisting of a personal world of concepts (he liked the word 'constructs') by which each person anticipates and organizes his or her relation to others and to the happenings of life. Because he dealt with anticipations and with the ways people think about their situations and their lives, he is sometimes thought of as a cognitive personality theorist, and in some quarters of cognitive psychology he attained a considerable reputation. Kelly didn't like that. He was insistent that he would not be classified, and he laid claim to his own ground, tossing out much of the psychology we know. 'It is only fair to warn the reader about what may be in store for him,' he wrote in the preface to *The Psychology of Personality Constructs.*

> In the first place, he is likely to find missing most of the familiar landmarks of psychology books. For example, the *learning,* so honorably embedded in most psychology texts, scarcely appears at all. That is wholly intentional; we are for throwing it overboard altogether. There is no *ego,* no *emotion,* no *motivation,* no *reinforcement,* no *drive,* no *unconscious,* no *need.* There are some words with brand-new psychological definitions. . . . *Anxiety* is defined in a special systematic way. *Role, guilt,* and *hostility* carry definitions altogether unexpected by many; and to make heresy complete, there is no extensive bibliography (1955, pp. x–xi).

George Kelly: Personal History

Among our personality theorists, George Alexander Kelly was another son of religious parents, an only child whose father had been a Presbyterian minister but turned to farming when ill health made it impossible for him to fulfill his calling. He was born in April 1905 in Kansas, on a farm near the small town of Perth. Kelly's father was a resourceful and pioneering spirit, taking his family to Colorado in a home-built covered wagon to work a land-grant plot. He could find no water, however, and the family had to make the long, wearying trek back to Kansas. Taking after his father, Kelly himself was a practical man, no task beyond him, designing and building his own house in Columbus, Ohio. He took considerable pride in the applications of his knowledge and ability. Like many a Kansas farm boy, he was taught in a one-room schoolhouse and then sent away to the big city, Wichita, for high school.

Kelly's higher education began at Friends University in Wichita, a Quaker school; he transferred to Park College in Missouri for his last year, earning a BA in physics and mathematics in 1926. Strong social

George Kelly (National Library of Medicine/Science Photo Library)

interest led him to pursue educational sociology at the University of Kansas, where he took his MA. His minor field was labour relations. He taught for a while—labour relations, speech, a class for new immigrants, dramatics—and tried working as an aeronautical engineer. An exchange scholarship enabled him to spend a year at the University of Edinburgh, where he earned a BA in education. Sir Godfrey Thompson seems to have turned him in the direction of psychology. Returning home, he entered the PhD program at the State University of Iowa; it took him a year to complete the requirements and write his thesis on speech and reading disabilities.

Academic jobs were scarce in the grim Depression years, and Kelly took what he could get: an appointment at Fort Hays Kansas State College, where he found that what was needed was not what he had been trained in, but instead clinical psychology. He became, on the spot, a clinical psychologist, entirely self-taught. Within the Kansas public school system, he established travelling psychological clinics, adapting his new specialty to school psychology. The needs of his clients, children and parents, were great; to cope at first, he adopted a Freudian approach complete with psychoanalytic interpretations. He didn't believe a word of it but, as he wrote many years later, 'a good many unfortunate persons seemed to be profoundly helped' (Kelly, 1963, p. 51). He expressed astonishment that his clients would accept what he regarded as impossible nonsense. To test the limits, he explained,

> I began fabricating 'insights'. I deliberately offered 'preposterous interpretations' to my clients. Some of them were about as un-Freudian as I could make them—first proposed somewhat cautiously, of course, and then, as I began to see what was happening, more boldly. My only criteria were that the explanation account for the crucial facts as the client saw them, and that it carry implications for approaching the future in a different way (Kelly, 1969, p. 52).

That was not a benign thing to do—to toy with clients desperate for an understanding of psychological troubles they felt helpless to solve. Kelly, though, had a mean streak, well known to graduate students and to his colleagues. If I may be permitted a clinical interpretation, I think his concern for the people he treated was not high. Psychotherapy to him was a practical and an intellectual problem, and therein lay its satisfaction.

He remained at Fort Hays for thirteen years, leaving for service in World War II. He was commissioned in the Navy and assigned to the Aviation Branch of the Navy Bureau of Medicine and Surgery. On his discharge in 1945, he received an appointment as associate professor at the University of Maryland. A year later, he was professor of psychology and director of the graduate program in clinical psychology at Ohio State University. It was there that I came to know him. In nineteen years at Ohio State, he contributed to the development of its superb clinical program, and in 1955 he published his two-volume *Psychology of Personal Constructs*. Following a year-long lecture tour in Europe, South America, and the Caribbean he had a sudden and severe heart attack. Along with his recovery came a remarkable transformation: the cruelties to graduate students, little and big, ended, and he became an easier-to-be-with and more friendly colleague. He was now warm, accepting, avuncular, taking on a brand-new role. As he would say a few years later,

> A good deal is said these days about being oneself. It is supposed to be healthy to be oneself. While it is a little hard for me to understand how one could be anything

else, I suppose what is meant is that one should not strive to become anything other that what he is. This strikes me as a very dull way of living; in fact, I would be inclined to argue that all of us would be better off if we set out to be something other that what we are (1964, pp. 157–8).

We *are* the way we construe ourselves, our relations to others, and to the world. Don't like the way you are? Change your constructs. Kelly was a walking, talking advertisement for *The Psychology of Personal Constructs*.

The clinical program at Ohio State changed markedly in 1963 when a number of us left, and Kelly departed two years later to accept the Riklis Chair of Behavioral Science at Brandeis University. A massive heart attack felled him in 1967, shortly before his sixty-second birthday.

Emphases and Major Concepts

Postulate and Corollaries

The Psychology of Personal Constructs begins with an assumption—'*that all of our present interpretations of the universe are subject to revision or replacement. . . . there are always some alternative constructions available to choose among in dealing with the world. No one needs to paint himself into a corner; no one needs to be completely hemmed in by circumstances; no one needs to be the victim of his biography. We call this philosophical position constructive alternativism*' (1955, p. 15).

It doesn't always work well to exemplify a theory metaphorically by a model of behaviour and mind that represents it. It really does, though, in the case of personal construct theory. Kelly saw the human as a scientist—often not a good one, but a scientist nevertheless. All of us hold theories about ourselves, other people, and the events and things in our lives. These personal theories are for the purpose of *predicting* what will happen, anticipating the forthcoming. 'Man looks at his world through transparent patterns or templets which he creates and then attempts to fit over the realities of which the world is composed. . . . Let us give the name *constructs* to these patterns that are tentatively tried on for size. They are ways of construing the world' (1955, pp. 8–9). With many of the constructs we hold we are flexible, and we abandon them when events prove them wrong. Sometimes, however, we cling to them as if they represented the only way one could possibly think about something or someone. Then, we are bad scientists unable to use the data before us to decide how the world is. All of this may be compressed into Kelly's single postulate: 'A person's processes are psychologically channelized by the ways in which he anticipates events' (Kelly, 1955, p. 46).

The construct postulate is elaborated by eleven corollaries. Essentially, the corollaries define personality—the attributes of this scientific person. Personality is the constellation of constructs—the construct system—a person holds. Change the constructs in an important way and there is a different personality.

1. CONSTRUCTION

'A person anticipates events by construing their replications' (1955, p. 50). Construing the world means predicting it, predicting how people will act, what's going to occur. People and the things that happen are largely predicable; Kelly prefers the term 'replicable'. An abusive boss's behaviour toward his secretary basically replicates today what it was yesterday. Small details may differ, but a construct of abusiveness will cover it. This is the way we make sense of life.

2. INDIVIDUALITY

'Persons differ from each other in their construction of events' (1955, p. 55). Personality, as we have seen from the very beginning, is intimately concerned with the attributes that make each person different. The individuality corollary is Kelly's answer.

3. ORGANIZATION

Construct systems are organized hierarchically, with some concepts subsuming others. There are *superordinate* and *subordinate* constructs.

4. DICHOTOMY

'A person's construction system is composed of a finite number of dichotomous constructs' (1955, p. 59). A construct is defined by a bipolar contrast characterizing experiences by the way they differ from other experiences. Kelly tells us that we can understand a construct by having a person tell us how two things (people, types of people, objects, events) are similar and how they differ from a third thing. Someone might tell us that mother and father are similar and differ from others—outsiders. We have a construct, then, of family. All constructs are like this.

5. CHOICE

'A person chooses for himself that alternative in a dichotomized construct through which he anticipates the greater possibility for extension and definition of his system' (1955, p. 64). We may choose in approaching a new situation to use existing constructs (this is *definition*, a low-risk choice), or we may elect a more risky alternative, trying out a new construct and elaborating our system by *extension*. Kelly: 'One may anticipate events by trying to become more and more certain about fewer and fewer things or by trying to become vaguely aware of more and more things on the misty horizon' (1955, p. 67). If we stuck with the old and well used, our construct systems would not be adaptable to new circumstances; we need to elaborate them to enhance prediction. It is meeting the challenge of prediction that goads us; this is Kelly's answer to the question of motivation.

6. RANGE

'A construct is convenient for the anticipation of a finite range of events only' (Kelly, 1955, p. 68). No construct is infinitely useful; all have their boundaries, which define their range of convenience. Sex is okay as a construct within which to place men and women. It won't do to extend it to the time of day.

7. EXPERIENCE

'A person's construction system varies as he successively construes the replication of events' (1955, p. 72). As we anticipate events, our construct systems will change with new experience. 'It is not what happens around him that makes a man experienced; it is the successive construing and reconstruing of what happens, as it happens, that enriches the experience of his life' (1955, p. 73). Experience can be a good teacher or can fail us. How we construe it as we adapt our construct systems is the heart of the matter. You will search in vain for any mention of learning in the theory, as Kelly warned us at the beginning. Here is where it belongs and what Kelly does with it.

8. MODULATION

Experience may or may not lead us to modify our constructs. Consider a narrow, constricted person whose construct system is rigid and unbending. His outlook on others and the world is fixed; new experience will have a tough time challenging his beliefs. His constructs are not **permeable**★, accessible to change when experience shows the way. Permeable constructs can be extended to adapt to and incorporate new evidence.

9. FRAGMENTATION

People can and do hold subordinate constructs that are incompatible with each other. Because our constructs change over time, we're bound to make modifications that don't fit. Our behaviour will then seem inconsistent, but that is because others haven't kept up with the changes.

10. COMMONALITY

Our common ground with others lies not in shared experiences but in shared constructs. With our fellow students we go to class, drink beer in the pub, and talk about issues in our lives late into the night, but our 'psychological processes', as this corollary says, will not be similar unless we construe those experiences in much the same way.

11. SOCIALITY

If we understand the construct system of another person, we may play a role *vis à vis* that person. Husbands and wives will not have roles to play with each other unless there is some understanding of each other's construct systems. That understanding is a *role construct*, and acting on the basis of a role construct *is* a role. This corollary is the underpinning for psychotherapy and for any mutual interaction with others.

It would seem that personal construct theory is entirely a psychology of consciousness, but Kelly did make room for a 'continuum of cognitive awareness'. Constructs may be acquired before language development is complete and so, in their primitive form, cannot be thought about. Patterns of trust and anxiety in infants are the typical grist of **preverbal** constructs. Constructs may also be **submerged**. This occurs when one pole of a construct cannot be accessed, so that aspect of the construct is, as we would say (but not Kelly), unconscious. Finally, experiences may be **suspended**. If there are no constructs by which to represent ideas or memories or feelings, we have no way to get at them. We can remember only what we can represent: 'one remembers what is structured and forgets what is unstructured. In contrast with some notions of repression, suspension implies that the idea or element of experience is forgotten simply because the person can, at the moment, tolerate no structure within which the idea would have meaning' (1955, p. 473).

Personal Construct Theory and the Rest of Psychology

Kelly took a strong and frequently contrary position on familiar psychological and personality concepts. He threw out *motivation* as wholly unnecessary to a psychology of already acting and construing beings. He dismissed *learning* with no little sarcasm:

> Salivation . . . takes place in a manner that suggests the anticipation of food, or perhaps hunger—I am not sure which. Perhaps what is anticipated is an activity we call eating. Whatever it indicates, Pavlov seems to have demonstrated it and there is

Table 11.1   Rep Test Instructions

1. Write your name in the first blank at the upper left.

2. Write your mother's first name (or stepmother).

3. Write your father's first name (or stepfather).

4. Write the name of the brother nearest to your own age (or a boy most like a brother to you in your early teens).

5. Do the same thing for the sister nearest your own age.

6. The name of your wife (husband). If not married, your closest present boy- or girlfriend.

7. The name of the closest boy- or girlfriend immediately preceding the above.

8. Your closest present friend of the same sex as yourself.

9. A person of the same sex as yourself whom you once thought was a close friend but in whom you were badly disappointed later.

10. The minister, priest, or rabbi with whom you would be most willing to talk over your personal feelings about religion.

11. Your physician.

12. The present neighbour whom you know best.

13. A person with whom you have been associated who, for some unexplained reason, appeared to dislike you.

14. A person whom you would most like to help or for whom you feel sorry.

15. A person with whom you usually feel most uncomfortable.

16. A person whom you have recently met and would like to know better.

17. The teacher who influenced you most when you were in your teens.

18. The teacher whose point of view you found most objectionable.

19. An employer, supervisor, or officer under whom you served during a period of great stress.

20. The most successful person you know personally.

21. The happiest person you know personally.

22. The person known to you personally who appears to meet the highest ethical standards.

After you have written the names in the space above the columns, look at the first row. There are circles under three persons' names (20, 21, 22). Decide how two of them are alike in an important way and how they differ from the third person. Put an X in each of the two circles under the names of the persons who are alike. Then write on the line under the column headed 'Construct' a word or phrase that identifies the likeness. Write the opposite of this characteristic under the heading 'Contrast'. Now go back and consider all the other people you listed on your grid. If any of them also share the same characteristic, put a check mark under their name. Repeat this procedure until you have completed every row on the form.

Source: Adapted from Kelly, 1955.

no reason we should not be grateful even though we are not quite sure what it was he demonstrated (Kelly, 1980, p. 29).

There is no *reinforcement*; instead, there is **validation★** when predictions of events, even unpleasant ones, are confirmed. You can probably guess what he did with anxiety: it occurs when our construct systems fail to account for events. There can, of course, be little anxieties and big ones, as when we have a superordinate construct that falls down. *Hostility★* is a kind of extortion—an attempt to wring evidence of validation of a construct that is a failure. Hostility reflects our refusal to accept the facts, like the man who resorted to violence when his wife demanded a divorce. We *aggress* not when we attack another person out of frustration but when we expand our construct system to test its validity. Aggression★ is exploration, even though the aggressed-against person doesn't at all appreciate it. *Guilt★* is aroused when we violate the terms of constructs that define our relationships—roles—with others. A man who construes his relationship with his wife as loving and trusting feels guilty when he has a surreptitious affair.

Implications

Personality Assessment

To know someone, we must understand his or her construct system; to know a client, we have to uncover—diagnose—that client's constructs. Kelly devised a unique way of doing that, a complex chart to represent the way significant people in a person's life are construed. He called it the Role Construct Repertory Test, and almost immediately it became the 'Rep Test'. It is *the* measure of personal constructs in the theory.

Kelly also thought that clients (and people generally) could provide useful and trustworthy data about themselves. '*If you don't know what's wrong with a client, ask him; he may tell you*' (1955, p. 201). Such personal evidence can be trusted in the sense that it is what the person *believes*. It could be an utter fabrication, but it comes from his or her experience. Such is a phenomenology.

Psychotherapy

The approach to psychotherapy in personal construct theory follows directly from the theory's view of the person as construer. People in psychological trouble are people whose constructs lead them astray, who are failures in a predictive sense. The problem, then, is not to extinguish their anxiety or to deal with destructive feelings; it is to change the ways in which they conceive of personal distress, problem relationships, or seemingly overwhelming events. There is a specific therapeutic procedure to do just this; Kelly called it **fixed-role therapy★**. It gives a client a new role, and the client is set the task of trying it out. The prescribed role, carefully scripted by the therapist and complete with a personality portrait of the client playing it, is based on constructs very different from the ones getting the client in difficulty. He or she must play the role in therapy *and* in daily life. A period of two weeks is common.

Handed such a fixed role, clients are awkward and embarrassed, and the therapist must take the stage—'play in strong support of an actor—the client—who is continually fumbling his lines and contaminating his role' (1955, p. 399). Fixed-role therapy, 'By providing validating data in the form of responses to a wide variety of constructions on the part of the client, some of them quite loose, fanciful, or naughty, . . . gives the client an opportunity to validate constructs, an opportunity which is not normally available to him' (1955, p. 165). Perhaps the greatest benefit occurs as the client discovers that there are alternative ways to construe experiences he or she thought utterly intractable. So, fixed-role therapy really *is* a therapy of constructive alternativism.

Research

Kelly himself did no research. (A young psychologist who did—like me, when we were both at Ohio State—was dismissed as a 'flash in the pan'.) Nearly all the work on the theory by Kelly's students and by a small but devoted and enthusiastic group of Kelly's followers has used the Rep Test. Limiting investigation of personal construct theory to a single measure, particularly one that doesn't lend itself to quantification, has unquestionably hindered testing of the theory. Psychologists not schooled in personal construct

Figure 11.4 The Rep Test grid

Name____________________

Date____________________

1	2	3	4	5	6	7	8	9	10	11	12	13	14	15	16	17	18	19	20	21	22		CONSTRUCT	CONTRAST
																			○	○	○	1		
																○	○	○				2		
												○	○		○							3		
					○	○	○															4		
	○	○	○																			5		
				○												○				○		6		
	○							○								○						7		
		○																○	○			8		
			○									○					○					9		
				○								○					○					10		
				○									○								○	11		
			○					○						○								12		
					○									○						○		13		
	○				○	○																14		
		○			○	○																15		
							○	○							○							16		
○			○	○																		17		
																		○	○		○	18		
	○	○												○								19		
○													○		○							20		
						○						○	○									21		
○					○		○															22		

(From *The Psychology of Personal Constructs, Volume One: A Theory of Personality* by George A. Kelly, PhD. Copyright © 1955 by George A. Kelly. Used by permission of W.W. Norton & Company, Inc.)

theory would have been put off by the need to rely on this strange (to them) test, tied intimately to a novel and foreign theory. So, there have been relatively few recruits to take up the task of theory testing.

Personal Construct Theory in Perspective

Personal construct theory gives us a view of the person that is unique in personality study. Yes, it's phenomenological, and yes, despite Kelly's protestation, it's cognitive, but it certainly does not lie in personality theory's mainstream. Kelly was cavalier toward concepts familiar to us, as we have seen, making the prediction of events the absolutely central goal of human thought and action.

'Is that all there is?' is the title of a famous Peggy Lee song, and we can ask that here. Is that all that human striving is about? When we know the extremes of emotionality that can torment people, the exceptional struggles to achieve, to avoid failure, to find

---

Table 11.2   Assessing Yourself: Interpretation of the Rep Test

When you have completed the form, take a close look at your results. First, consider the nature of the constructs you listed. How many different constructs did you list? What kind of constructs were they? Did you tend to make comparisons on the basis of appearance (skinny versus fat) or personality characteristics (thoughtful versus unthoughtful; honest versus dishonest)? Do any of the constructs overlap? You can discover this by examining the pattern of checks and X's in the various rows. If the pattern for one construct (such as honest versus dishonest) is identical to that of another construct (such as sincere versus insincere), you can suspect that these two constructs may really be one and the same for you. To how many different people did you apply each of the constructs? A construct that is applied to a large number of people may be more permeable than one that is restricted to only one person. Are the constructs divided in terms of their application to persons of the same age or sex? This may give you some idea of the limits on the range of your constructs. Now, take a look at your list of contrasting constructs. Are there any constructs that you list only as a difference and never as a similarity? If so, you may be reluctant to use that construct. If you list a contrasting pole for one person only, perhaps that construct is impermeable and limited to that person. Are any names associated only with contrasting poles? If so, your relationship to those persons may be rigid and unchanging even though you get along with them. Finally, compare your own column with those of the other people on the list. Which of the three people are you most like?

This analysis will not give you definitive answers; it will simply provide a starting point for further questions. Rather than consider the results on the grid as final, use your findings as the basis for additional study of yourself. For example, if you discover identical patterns for two constructs, such as honest versus dishonest and sincere versus insincere, you might ask yourself, 'Do I believe that all honest people are sincere?' In other words, use your findings for further questions. Numerous possibilities for self-exploration are initiated by the Rep Test. To take another version of the Rep Test, see this website: http://tiger.cpsc.ucalgary.ca:1500/WebGrid/WebGrid.html

love and security, that can dominate lives, can we fully accept a psychology *entirely* about personality constructs—a psychology claiming a unique grasp and representation of such powerful expressions of personality? I think that strains belief. We don't know how personal constructs develop; we find no details on personality development in the theory. And it is difficult to believe from all that we know about personality that we can simply change our behaviour by changing our constructs. Kelly thought so, and I'm sure he believed that was fully possible. 'If I can do it,' he might have said, 'anyone can do it'. But I saw the same person through the construct change, and our colleagues—his and mine—did also. People are not so malleable, even in the most optimistic theories.

Was it all a cognitive game, played seriously to be sure, but a game nonetheless, a way of moving the pieces on the chessboard of the mind? Perhaps not. Kelly gave us a provocative way of considering the behaviour and thinking of the human, one we can profit from studying. We cannot fail to ask, however, if personal construct theory is a viable theory with prospects for validation through research and continued clinical testing. That's a question you may think about.

Positive Psychology

The humanists, most particularly Rogers and Maslow, made many psychologists feel good. The hopeful humanist outlook on the possibility for close and abiding relations among people, its promise that the troubled could be freed of their distress, that marriages could be loving, that group relations could be amicable, that in education the young could be liberated to learn, just warmed the hearts of many psychologists and made a positive psychology of the person—of people—seem possible. This is one of the legacies of Rogers, Maslow, and others of like mind. The humanists have tended to think of personality psychology as obsessed with neurotic (or worse) disorder and treatment, a depressing and (as they have said) negative model of the person, of society, and of human potential. The positive, optimistic side appealed to them. What they could see, however, was a vast, intimidating task. How should psychologists begin to approach filling it? A modern movement with roots in psychological humanism is not daunted and proposes a whole new orientation in the science of psychology to carry it out.

An entire issue of the *American Psychologist* in 2000 brought fifteen positive psychologists together, each to consider how a positive psychology might alter traditional psychology's 'study of pathology, weakness, and damage' (Seligman & Csikszentmihalyi, 2000, p. 5). The editors of this series of articles pointed to the humanistic origin of positive psychology, and the unfortunate detour that humanism took:

> . . . Abraham Maslow, Carl Rogers, and other humanistic psychologists promised to add a new perspective to the entrenched clinical and behaviourist approaches. The generous humanistic vision had a strong effect on the culture at large and held enormous promise. Unfortunately, humanistic psychology did not attract much of a cumulative empirical base, and it spawned myriad therapeutic self-help movements. In some of its incarnations, it emphasized the self and encouraged a self-centredness that played down concerns for collective well-being. Future debate will determine whether this came about because Maslow and Rogers were ahead of their times, because these flaws were inherent in their original vision, or because of overly enthusiastic followers. However, one legacy of the humanism of the 1960s

is prominently displayed in any large bookstore: The 'psychology' section contains at least 10 shelves on crystal healing, aromatherapy, and reaching the inner child for every shelf of books that tries to uphold some scholarly standard (Seligman & Csikszentmihalyi, 2000, p. 7).

Emphases

Positive psychology thinks of prevention, not treatment after the fact, of the disorders, the traumas, the social ills brought to us to try to remedy. It also looks to discover the strengths in people that enable them to overcome truly malign circumstances and to encourage the great capabilities and resilience of people at their best. There are a number of perspectives that characterize this new vision of the 'third force'.

A personality-centred perspective focuses on the subjective, on positive personality traits that make for well-being, an optimistic outlook, happiness, and the belief that we

---

A Fresh Look: Research Today

The phenomenologists, especially Carl Rogers, and humanists left a rich endowment of concepts to positive psychology, sending their grandchild off on the right foot to turn personality psychology from its negative view of a troubled humankind to a positive one. 'Man,' they should have sung,

> You've got to accentuate the positive
> Eliminate the negative
> Latch on to the affirmative
> Don't mess with Mr In-Between

The lines penned by Johnny Mercer and Harold Arlen in the 1940s had it just right. Pity they didn't put their message to music. Maybe they did, but in any case, that was the message.

Prominent among the gifts Rogers bestowed on his heirs was the concept of the innate motivation to self-actualize, the fundamental principle behind all human striving. In the hands of two positive psychology theorists, Edward Deci and Richard Ryan of the University of Rochester, this has become a more fully specified view of 'the energizing basis for natural organismic activity', self-determination theory (Deci & Ryan, 1991, p. 244; see also Deci & Ryan, 2000). Behaviour that is self-determined is intrinsically motivated—perceived by the person and engaged in with 'a full sense of choice, with the experience of doing what one wants, and without the feeling of coer-

cion or compulsion' (1991, p. 253). A sense of personal autonomy is part and parcel of self-determination: I own my choices of thinking and behaviour and freely choose them. Contrast autonomy with the control of behaviour by others: this is something I *have* to do because my job, my professor, my parents demand it. The world is often grudging in recognizing personal autonomy, which makes it something we have to struggle to achieve. Consider the university student and his or her parents. Which of them, do you think, generally feels more autonomous, more in control of choice and action and less dominated by external motives, those imposed in common life situations?

Sheldon, Houser-Marko, and Kasser (2006) set out to explore just this question. They asked who has the greater experience of personal autonomy, students in university or their middle-aged parents. Now, we might think that the students would win this contest of self-determination and independence of choice hands down. They have youth, ability, bubbling self-confidence, a yellow brick road with opportunities opening at every turn. Their parents, in their fifties and sixties, are edging toward the physical decline of old age, their cognitive and motor abilities lessened, and they are in the danger age for serious illness and debility. They have seen how life can constrain and inhibit autonomy; they know that many choices simply have to be made, like it or not, because jobs, marriages, children, governments demand them. Let us see what Sheldon et al. found.

have a decisive influence on the things that happen to us. This last is *self-determination*, which may have its destructive downside when personal responsibility for choice becomes an oppressive burden. There is a now abundant and scholarly literature of research on optimism (Peterson, 2000), happiness—what makes us happy and an evolutionary perspective on happiness (Myers, 2000; Buss, 2000), subjective well-being (Diener, 2000), and self-determination (Ryan & Deci, 2000; Schwarz, 2000).

The positive psychology of personality has also addressed mental health (emphatically *not* mental illness). Life-span studies of adults over several decades have illuminated 'mature defences' that contribute to joyous and productive living, such as sublimation, suppression, and the use of humour. Note, though, how difficult it is to abandon old mental illness terms; could positive investigators not speak of 'cognitive strategies' (Vaillant, 2000)? Positive mental health investigators have shown that over-optimism is far from being unhealthy and can protect against illness (Taylor, Kemeny, Reed, Bower, & Gruenewald, 2000).

Their sample was drawn from undergraduate psychology students at the University of Missouri and their parents, whose participation was volunteered by their children. The students completed a set of questionnaires on subjective well-being and goal autonomy for bonus course credit. Their parents received a questionnaire packet in the mail and were asked to complete and return it (51 per cent of the mothers did, 41 per cent of the fathers). The subjective well-being measures assessed positive and negative mood and life satisfaction in the present and again in the past. Then, each respondent wrote down six personal goals, one in each of these categories: self-acceptance/personal growth, financial/material, intimacy/friendship, contribution to society, recognition/popularity, and physical appearance. They were asked to rate each goal on four possible reasons for striving to attain it: 'because somebody else wants you to or because the situation seems to compel it', an external motivation; 'because you would feel ashamed, guilty, or anxious if you didn't', an imposed and introjected motivation; and two autonomous motives, 'because you really believe that it's an important goal to have, and 'because of the enjoyment or stimulation which that goal provides you'.

To see whose experience of autonomy was greater, the investigators used regression analysis to find the relation between chronological age and the autonomy and goal measures. The parents reported greater subjective well-being and more autonomous reasons for striving to attain each goal than their offspring. Moreover, when the parents identified goals and rated reasons for pursuing them when they were their children's age, their present feelings of well-being and goal autonomy were higher. What do we conclude from that? Sheldon et al. believe that self-determined goal striving profits from experience and is accompanied by a sense of fulfillment and well-being. Life isn't an endless succession of knuckling under to serve the goals that others define for us. It can present opportunities to strive for goals that we set for ourselves, from which we learn about autonomy and take pleasure in it. For young people, there is the uncertainty that goes with inexperience and untested possibility. Their feelings of well-being and autonomy in the pursuit of goals they set for themselves will come—with age.

These are plausible and not unexpected findings, anticipated in fact in hypotheses that directed the research. There is a caution, however: the group that Sheldon et al. studied was largely educated and successful, favoured by probable good fortune. What might we find among working-class parents who have undergone adversity, struggle, and disappointment? Are they likely to feel autonomy in their choices and actions and an abiding sense of well-being in their middle age? And what of their children, having left home for jobs that will not feature autonomy and choice? Then there is also the larger situation to think about: how does autonomy influence the experience of self-determination?

Other perspectives in positive psychology include biology and culture, especially positive processes (optimal experience is one) that may influence cultural selection and evolution (Massimini & Delle Fave, 2000) and a perspective on emotion, long dominated by an emphasis on negative affect. There is a now an increasing body of evidence on the effects of positive emotions on both the physiology of bodily systems and health (Salovey, Rothman, Detweiler, & Steward, 2000).

Positive psychologists acknowledge that serious research on the perspectives of this humanist-derived approach to human development, well-being, health, and prospects (including evolution!) is just past the threshold of beginning. There are great gaps to be filled, research paradigms to be developed, and fuzzy concepts to be clarified. What has appeared so far, however, represents significant accomplishment. It puts the intent of the humanist movement back on track.

SUMMARY

1. American phenomenology did not derive from formal European philosophy (for example, the phenomenology of Husserl), which held that objects in experience *are* reality. Instead, it was largely a homegrown version, influenced by breakaway psychoanalyst Otto Rank's focus on the present and his concept of will.

2. Phenomenology in North America emerged in the years just before and after World War II. Among the first proponents were Snygg and Combs, who argued in *Individual Behavior* that 'All behaviour is completely determined . . . by the phenomenal field of the behaving organism.' This became a central proposition for Carl Rogers. The two theorists of this chapter, Rogers and George Kelly, arrived at phenomenological positions independently. Phenomenology became part of a larger humanistic and existential movement, a 'third force' in psychology.

3. Carl Rogers was born in 1902 to well-to-do, extremely religious parents. The family moved to a farm when Carl was twelve. He liked farming, which he viewed with a scientific perspective. He entered the University of Wisconsin to study agriculture but switched to history. A church conference in China turned him away from his parents' fundamentalism. On graduation, he enrolled at the liberal Union Theological Seminary, moving to Teachers College, Columbia University, for his PhD in psychology. He spent twelve years as a clinical psychologist, treating children and parents and writing his first book, *The Clinical Treatment of the Prob-*

lem Child. After a five-year stint as professor of psychology at Ohio State University, he joined the faculty of the University of Chicago, where he undertook pioneering studies of psychotherapy. A disappointing period as professor of psychology and psychiatry at the University of Wisconsin followed. Studies of person-centred therapy with schizophrenics didn't work out, and the atmosphere was unfriendly to his theoretical orientation. He concluded his career at a humanistic institute. He was president of the American Psychological Association (1947) and received its Distinguished Scientific Contribution award. Among his influential books are *Counseling and Psychotherapy* (1942), *Client-Centerd Therapy* (1951), *Psychotherapy and Personality Change* (1954, with Dymond), *On Becoming a Person* (1961), and *A Way of Being* (1980). He died at eighty-five in 1987.

4. Person-centred theory may be characterized by four principal emphases: (1) an attitude expressed by Rogers as 'belief in the fundamental predominance of the subjective'; (2) the theory of personality; (3) a theory of psychotherapy and personality change; and (4) several extensions—the fully-functioning person, interpersonal relations, family life, education, group leadership, and conflict.

5. This phenomenological theory focuses on the immediate experience of the person. It holds that we can only approximate understanding of another's experience. We can do that best through 'empathic under-

standing'. There is only one motive, *self-actualization*, which is the motivation for growth; it underlies all human behaviour, personality development, education, and therapeutic change. It can be inhibited by others.

6. The phenomenal field is differentiated into the *self-concept* and the *ideal self-concept*. They are not totally private and can be assessed by a measure called the Chicago Q-sort. The respondent sorts statements about self (and ideal self) in a normal distribution from 'most like me' to 'most unlike me'. Correlation of the two sorts tells us about self-esteem.

7. *Self-experience* is awareness of self differentiated out of experience. Each person has needs for *positive regard* and for *positive self-regard*. Judging of people (by others, by ourselves) leads to *conditions of worth*, which tell us we're more (or less) positively regarded because of our behaviour. We experience *congruence* when our self-experiences are accurately symbolized and represented in our self-concept. *Incongruence* is a discrepancy between self and the experience of conditions of worth. *Threat* occurs when experiences are incongruent with the self; if it is perceived, we experience *anxiety*. Defences attempt to protect us against threat; among them, perceptual defence denies threatening experiences to awareness. The threatened and defensive person is said to be maladjusted.

8. In addition to the personality theory, there is also a theory of psychotherapy and personality change that sets out the therapeutic conditions, processes, and outcomes necessary and sufficient for personality change. The most important conditions are *unconditional positive regard* and *empathic understanding*. The therapist doesn't interpret but seeks to reflect understanding of the client's frame of reference. Processes of personality change include freedom to express feelings, experiencing fully in awareness, and reorganization of self-concept, the experience of unconditional positive self-regard, and the initiation of an organismic valuing process. The significant outcomes of psychotherapy are congruence, openness to experience, decreased vulnerability, more effective problem solving, locus of evaluation and choice in the self, realistic perception of others, and the experience of self-control.

9. The theory spells out implications for the full development of the individual (the fully functioning person), successful interpersonal relationships, reducing group tension and conflict, education, and family life. They derive from the principles of the personality theory and the theory of psychotherapy and personality change.

10. Healthy personality development is the result of providing the conditions for the child's innate self-actualization. The child then experiences positive regard and positive self-regard; self evaluations are organismic. Subjected to conditions of worth, a child feels worthy only when he or she complies. Person-centred childrearing is extremely demanding on parents, who will struggle to refrain from imposing conditions of worth. Rogers' program for raising children is an ideal toward which to strive, but some conditional regard is realistic and not likely to be damaging.

11. Person-centred theory has been responsible for a considerable volume of research. At the core are studies of psychotherapy, especially the extensive investigations in the University of Chicago Counseling Center in late 1940s and early 1950s. This work is notable for the introduction of control groups, the recording of therapy sessions, and the use of objective measures of personality (the Q-sort, which provided a correlational index of the agreement of self-concept and ideal self-concept). Among the body of non-psychotherapy research is an especially significant longitudinal study of the childrearing antecedents of creative potential in children that bears out person-centred theory hypotheses.

12. Person-centred theory has had a major influence. Its emphases on humanistic values and respect for the person are laudable, and the research it has generated is significant and influential. It does, however, leave some serious concerns. This is a naive phenomenology, its concepts and language vague and value-laden. The theory is basically anti-intellectual in its approach to therapy and to education. There's an unwarranted trust in self-report, seen in reliance on self-report measures in psychotherapy studies.

13. George Kelly was a phenomenologist concerned with the ways humans construct their reality. His was an emphasis on the present and on the personal world of constructs by which each person organizes relations to others and to events. We may think of him as a cognitive personality psychologist (though he himself didn't want to be thought of as one). He rejected many common psychological concepts (motivation, learning, emotion, reinforcement) and gave unique definitions to others (anxiety, guilt, hostility, aggression).

14. Kelly was born in 1905 on a Kansas farm. Both parents were highly religious. His early education in a one-room school was followed by high school in Wichita. He studied physics and math in college, took an MA in educational sociology, and received the PhD in psychology from the State University of Iowa (1931). He taught in a small Kansas college for twelve years, gaining experience as a clinical and school psychologist. After serving in World War II, he taught briefly in Maryland, then at Ohio State University (1946–65). There he wrote his major work, *The Psychology of Personal Constructs*, and helped develop one of the best clinical psychology programs in the US. He left to take up a chair in psychology at Brandeis University. He died in 1967 at the age of 61.

15. Personal construct theory is built on one postulate ('A person's processes are psychologically channelized by the ways in which he anticipates events') and eleven corollaries that define personality. The corollaries:

    * *construction* (we anticipate events via constructs that enable us to predict them)
    * *individuality* (constructs differ from person to person)
    * *organization* (the construct system is hierarchically organized)
    * *dichotomy* (constructs are dichotomous in nature, bipolar contrasts of experiences)
    * *choice* (in new situations we must either choose established constructs [*definition*] or develop new ones [*elaboration*])
    * *range* (constructs have a finite ranges of events they can account for)
    * *experience* (construct systems change with experience)
    * *modulation* (experience may or may not lead to modification of constructs)
    * *fragmentation* (some constructs are incompatible with others, leading to inconsistent behaviour)
    * *commonality* (common ground with others lies in shared constructs, not experiences)
    * *sociality* (we develop *role constructs* that underlie relationships with others)

16. Personal construct theory recognizes that constructs can be inaccessible to awareness. They may have been acquired *preverbally*, they may be *submerged* (one pole of a construct is inaccessible), or they may be *suspended* (a construct may be intolerable to the person and hence unrecognized and unavailable to consciousness).

17. There are novel definitions of major concepts: there is no reinforcement but *validation* of constructs; *anxiety* develops when construct systems fail; *aggression* is brought on by the expansion of construct systems; *hostility* is the extortion of validation; and *guilt* results from any violation of role-defining constructs.

18. Personal construct theory has relied on a single measure, the Role Construct Repertory Test (Rep Test), based on a grid of similarities and contrasts describing important people in the respondent's life. It does give a picture of the construct system of a person and may be used in psychotherapy to understand the way a client makes sense of his or her world. Other possible applications include the assessment of managers in business and industry. The Rep Test, however, is suited to the discovery of the construct attributes of individuals, and not very much is known about its properties as a measure on which individuals may be differentiated. Thus, it has been infrequently applied in the test of the theory's hypotheses.

19. As a phenomenologist, Kelly proposed that people may reveal important aspects of their constructs by simply asking them. What they say may not be true, but it does represent their phenomenal experience.

20. Psychotherapy in this system employs a technique called *fixed-role therapy*, in which the therapist constructs a new role for the client to practise and play. The new role will be in contrast to constructs that make life difficult for the client.

21. Personal construct theory gives a unique view of the person as a scientist attempting to predict the events of his or her life. In this view of personality, Kelly dismissed accepted psychological concepts and redefined others. In its distinctive way, the theory's phenomenological interest in experience and its cognitive emphasis on the way people construe others and events takes personality into life as experienced by the person. It issues a salutary reminder to personality psychology that people do think and predict, that sometimes they do it badly, that individual differences in predictive systems make each person unique, and that successful prediction is rewarding and unsuccessful prediction is distressing. While prediction is the essence of person-

ality as the theory envisions it, we may ask if the human as amateur scientist adequately describes the complexities of thought, feeling, and behaviour that other theories attempt to deal with. There are other questionable features. Personal construct theory does not address the question of the development of personal construct systems, and it proposes a radical view of the consistency of personality. Change the construct system and change personality, Kelly argued. After all, an altered phenomenal field means altered behaviour. Finally, we must ask whether the theory is just too abstract, a cognitive game.

22. The hopeful humanist outlook of Carl Rogers, Abraham Maslow, and other humanistic-existential psychologists has been responsible for the development of a new focus in personality, positive psychology. It seeks to replace the conventional 'study of pathology, weakness, and damage' with new perspectives

- on prevention instead of remedial treatment;
- on positive personality traits that contribute to optimism, happiness, well-being, and self-determination;
- on mental *health*, not mental illness;
- on biological and cultural influences that might favour the selection of positive processes such as optimal experience; and
- on positive emotions as against negative ones (anxiety, for example).

Research programs in positive psychology are developing paradigms and are off to a sound beginning.

TO TEST YOUR UNDERSTANDING

1. How do we cross the bridge between our phenomenal experience and the phenomenal experience of another person? Indeed, is there a bridge and is it possible to understand how someone else thinks and feels? Or, are the major phenomenologists in psychology fooling themselves when they propose that an attitude of complete regard and some simple techniques can yield a degree of appreciation of the world of another?

2. Can a single motive—self-actualization—actually account for the whole range of human motivation? What about the fact that people seem to pursue a great variety of goals—achievement, affiliation, dependency, power, and so on? Does self actualization cover this broad ground?

3. If experience is truly private and unique, how can the person-centred psychologist even consider using tests to assess the self-concept and ideal self-concept of another person? Does the Q-sort, used to measure such central and sensitive individual attributes as these, violate the cardinal principle of phenomenology? Although the statements to be sorted come from clients in psychotherapy, they are someone else's statements about his or her experience of self. How can they apply to any other client?

4. What do you see as the principal contributions of Rogers' person-centred theory? What are its chief flaws? Do these cast serious doubt on the theory and its usefulness?

5. How can you be a personality psychologist concerned with the ways humans construct their reality and reject cognitive psychology and such basic processes as motivation, learning reinforcement, and emotion? Is the way we construe ourselves, our relationships, and the living of our lives so fundamental that only theoretical concepts concerned with the nature of personal constructs are required?

6. Why is it that experience is not necessarily the best teacher? What does personal construct theory have to offer that's better?

7. Mert Slocum and his wife just don't get along. Anything he likes or wants, it seems, she hates, and Mert can't find a good word to say about his wife's desires and point of view. Could fixed role therapy help? What are their problem constructs, and how might new roles help to change them?

8. Is personal construct theory a phenomenology? In what way?

9. What are the most important personal traits that foster psychological and physical well-being? Why might these traits head the list?

CHAPTER TWELVE

Learning Theories of Personality: The S-R Theory of John Dollard and Neal Miller

Introduction

We now consider four theories that differ in very significant ways from the psychoanalytically derived theories that have occupied us thus far. Their inspiration does not come directly from Freud and clinical psychiatry, although they owe (with the one notable exception of B.F. Skinner's radical behaviourism) an appreciable debt to Freud. Two of them in particular, Dollard and Miller's S-R theory and Rotter's social learning theory, explicitly seek to account for disturbed behaviour, and in this their debt extends to Freud's great clinical influence. These theories come from the laboratory—from the experimental study of learning—and they are built on principles derived from the systematic and controlled study of learning in humans and other animals. 'Uh, oh!' you say. 'This looks *bor-ing*. Experimental research on learning? Rats? Mazes and runways? I don't think my ego can stand it, and it's going to bring out the worst in my shadow!' Before you turn right off, though, I want to assure you that these theories are truly theories of personality, with the same grand aims as the theories we have just left. They are no less concerned with vital questions about human behaviour, motivation, thinking, feeling, and how conflict and misery occur and may be conquered.

Let's begin by anticipating one of the important differences we'll encounter between these learning theories and psychoanalytic theory and its offshoots. Psychoanalytic theory and the theories stemming from it may be characterized as **content theories★**. They each propose structural concepts such as ego, superego, and id that are hypothetical components of personality. These theories also have much to say about the content of mental life, conscious and unconscious. Think of Freud's treatment of instincts and their psychological representation—representations that can only be inferred in a very indirect way from behaviour. Here are some more examples: inferiority feelings (Adler); the self-dynamism (Sullivan); inborn needs arising from the human being's place in nature (Fromm). In these theories, there are dynamic processes that account for the relations among the structural concepts (remember primary process and secondary process; the way in which the ego invests energy in objects that will provide gratification of instincts—that is, object cathexes; or the processes by which the ego avoids anxiety through anti-cathexes—the defence mechanisms).

Learning theories do not propose such concepts. We will not encounter structural concepts in them, and these theories are by and large not concerned with mental content—that is, with an unconscious and the repressed material in it. Indeed, B.F. Skinner, whom we'll meet in the next chapter, insisted that psychology and the psychology of personality have no business trying to make scientific sense of covert, nonobservable events. Instead, the learning theories want to know about how behaviour (any behaviour) originates, what maintains it, and the factors responsible for behaviour change. So, these are **process theories***, and their concepts are process concepts. They provide theoretical accounts of the processes of behaviour acquisition, maintenance, and change. They are theories about *how* behaviour happens.

This is a major distinction, one that seems to imply that content and process theories are basically incompatible. One set of theories (the content theories) develops special concepts in personality that are not found elsewhere in psychology. The other set of theories (the learning theories) is based on established principles of the psychology of learning. However, the process theorists, most especially John Dollard and Neal Miller, sought to apply the rigour of learning theory to many of the questions taken up by the content theories, psychoanalysis in particular. So, despite the differences, content theories have significantly influenced process theories in the questions process theories have addressed. Some examples: the nature of personality disorder, especially neurosis; critical details of child development; processes of defence against anxiety; the displacement of aggression.

An Introduction to S-R Theory

Stimulus-response theory had its beginning in the 1930s in theory and research conducted at Yale University in the Institute of Human Relations. The Institute was founded in 1931 to bring scientists from many specialties together to collaborate in interdisciplinary research. By the middle of the decade, a distinguished core of scholars had been assembled, and their reluctance to take down the fences protecting their individual disciplines had begun to wane. Among them were experimental psychologists, social and personality psychologists, and a sociologist. They turned to a notable Yale learning theorist, Clark Hull, for the theory to guide their work, and they turned to great human issues and questions to try to illuminate them.

A young sociologist in this extraordinary group, John Dollard, carried out life history interviews with blacks in a small rural town in the southern United States, reporting his findings on the disgraceful treatment of black people, the aggression and privation to which they were subjected, in his book *Caste and Class in a Southern Town* (Dollard, 1957), first published in 1937. In that book, Dollard had written, 'The usual human response to frustration is aggression against the frustrating object' (p. 267). He was well aware of the personality device to deal with aggression that cannot be expressed toward the frustrating object—displacement—and he used this psychoanalytic concept in a broader sociological sense to understand the plight of black people, victimized and unable to fight back. *Caste and Class in a Southern Town* was banned in Georgia and in South Africa.

Perspective 12.1 The Uneven Playing Field: White versus Black in the South, 1930s

When John Dollard set out in the mid-1930s for Southerntown, a small rural centre in the Deep South, to spend five months studying personality in black people and the impact of their situation in this racially divided and intolerant land, he would have had an idea of what awaited him, but it would not have approached reality. The depth and intensity of prejudice toward blacks, the daily degradation to which they were subjected, he could not have anticipated, nor, certainly, could he have foreseen the extent of white suspicion and mistrust toward an inquisitive northerner, an academic, a scientist, whose avowed purpose was to study the lives of 'their' blacks. He would need courage, resourcefulness, and forthrightness to carry his research, every day, from the white part of town where he roomed and had his office to the low ground on the other side of the railroad tracks where the blacks lived. His study would not have been possible without these qualities in heroic measure.

What he did was to immerse himself in the ordinary life of the people, black and white:

> The basic method used in the study was that of participation in the social life of Southerntown. This social sharing was of two degrees and involved two rôles; there was first the casual participation possible as a 'Yankee down here studying Negroes', and second the more intensive participation and the more specific rôle of the life-history taker. . . . If the people in Southerntown watched me carefully, as they did, I also watched them, listened, thought about and participated in the common life then going on. The primary research instrument [was] the observing human intelligence trying to make sense out of the experience; and the experience was full of problems and uncertainty in fact. . . .
>
> In general, two kinds of observations were made, first as to what people said, and second as to what they did and seemed to feel. The first type is easily understood in terms of many conversations with Negro and white people about particular problems, conversations in parlors, loafing at the hotel, in automobiles, in business places, and the like. Observation without discussion was at least equally important. One could notice at what point in a conversation people became excited and what they did; one could see the sequence of behaviour at a Negro picnic or revival meeting, or note the reception of a Yankee in a social group of white people. In the struggle for clarity one should constantly record the material as it comes, make hypotheses, and reject or modify them; the observer must make active, formative use of his data (pp. 18–19).

White aggression toward blacks was freely expressed to Dollard but, notably, there was also defensiveness:

> The function of defensive beliefs is to make the actions of white-caste members toward Negroes seem expedient and in line with current ideals; if this cannot be done satisfactorily, then at least these acts can be made to seem inevitable. But what are the actions which must be barricaded behind distortions and excuses? It seems quite plain from the analysis . . . that they are, first, a method of justifying and perpetuating the gains of the white caste [at the expense of the black] . . . , and second, a technique for explaining the various types of aggression directed against Negroes. This aggression . . . is intended to paralyze pressure from the Negro's side which would tend to alter his fixed status in the lower caste (p. 365).

> Whites were defensive, too, because their raw and ugly aggression implied their own weakness. In terrible big ways and in the lesser ones of everyday humiliation, the attack of the white man on the black was the displaced answer to the frustrations of financial uncertainty in a rural cotton economy and his own perceived sexual inadequacy compared to black men. Keep the blacks in their place, Southerntown's whites endlessly said. They didn't give expression to the deep-down reason. 'What makes the belief defensive', Dollard concluded
>
> . . . is that there are concealed reasons for the act as well as ones that are alleged. The concealed reasons lying behind these defensive beliefs are the gains and the aggressions necessary to defend the gains. The defensive beliefs put the stress on partial and inadequate elements in the situation and obscure a clear vision of actual social forces. . . . In short, the function of the defense is to conceal the disparity between social justice according to our constitutional ideal and the actual caste treatment of the Negro (p. 366).

Two years later, the interdisciplinary collaborators in the Institute produced a larger, theory-based account of aggression. It was based on the principles of learning and the conditions under which learning takes place, a theoretical stance formulated by Dollard that he and Miller later elaborated in the S-R theory of personality. *Frustration and Aggression*, by Dollard, Doob, Miller, Mowrer, and Sears (1939), reported the results of research into aggression and what provokes it, and presented a theory that became hugely influential. Somewhat modified, the theory proposed that a significant antecedent of aggression is frustration (in its original statement in *Frustration and Aggression*, frustration was the *only* condition for aggression, a claim that was too strong and could not be supported). Among the findings in the book was an inverse relation between cotton prices in the southern US and lynching of blacks during a forty-two-year period from 1882 to 1930. The poorer the year's cotton prices, the greater the number of lynchings, a statistic that reflected a violent aggression displaced from a remote and untouchable target to a helpless and innocent minority.

Following this, Miller and Dollard took the basic principles–conditions formulation and Hull's learning theory to problems in social psychology, studying the role of imitation in the acquisition of social behaviour. Experiments with animals and children showed the learning of both imitative and nonimitative behaviour, which established the importance of models for the acts to be imitated. There were analyses of crowd behaviour and of training in cultural habits. 'No psychologist', they said,

> would venture to predict the behaviour of a rat without knowing on what arm of a T-maze the feed or the shock is placed. It is no easier to predict the behaviour of a human being without knowing the conditions of his 'maze', i.e., the structure of his social environment. Culture, as conceived by social scientists, is a statement of the design of the human maze, of the type of reward involved, and of what responses are to be rewarded. It is in this sense a recipe for learning. This contention is easily accepted when widely variant societies are compared. But even within the same society, the mazes which are run by two individuals may seem the same but actually be quite different. . . . No personality analysis of two . . . people can be accurate which does not take into account these cultural differences, that is, differences in the types of responses which have been rewarded (Miller & Dollard, 1941, pp. 5–6).

It is culture that makes the individual person, directly by reward, and no less powerfully by showing what behaviour will be successful and what will be punished.

With a well-practised approach, Dollard and Miller turned to personality, to the learning of neurotic symptoms, and to psychotherapy as a process of re-education, applying their 'liberalized' (as Miller called it) S-R theory to the very sorts of questions that had occupied Freud. This was some of the very best that psychology had to offer.

John Dollard & Neal Miller: Personal Histories

John Dollard and Neal Elgar Miller were both born in Wisconsin, Dollard in Menasha in 1900 and Miller in Milwaukee in 1909. When Dollard was in his teens, his father, a railroad engineer, was killed in a train wreck. His mother, a former schoolteacher, moved to Madison, where her children might attend the University of Wisconsin. John took the opportunity after brief service in the Army, graduating with Phi Beta Kappa honours in 1922. He remained at the university as a fundraiser for the Wisconsin Memorial Union and soon got to know the physicist Max Mason, who became, in effect, a surrogate father. When Mason was appointed to the presidency of the University of Chicago, he brought Dollard with him as an assistant. Dollard served him for three years before entering graduate studies in sociology, earning an MA in 1930 and the PhD in 1931. He was greatly influenced by notable Chicago sociologists, especially Edward Sapir, Sullivan's friend and inspiration.

Soon, he was awarded a Social Science Research Council fellowship to study psychoanalysis in Europe, and, in 1931–2 undertook a training analysis with Hanns Sachs and treated patients of his own under the supervision of Karen Horney and Abram Kardiner. He returned to the US a full-fledged psychoanalyst. Sapir, now at Yale, invited Dollard to join him in teaching a culture-personality seminar, and at the close of the semester the director of the Institute of Human Relations appointed Dollard as research associate in the Institute. Despite his growing stature, Dollard would remain in this anomalous position, not officially an academic, until he was fifty-two. Only then was he given a professorship in the Department of Psychology. As Miller said, he 'paid a price for his interdisciplinary work. One of the conditions that the traditional departments demanded in return for the consent to establish the Institute of Human Relations at Yale was that it should have no independent authority to make regular academic appointments. . . . [A]cademic departments tend to look askance at those who depart from the mold of their traditional discipline' (1982, p. 588).

Dollard's interests and achievements were extraordinary. He was accomplished at the highest level in sociology, anthropology, and psychology, and he was a practising psychoanalyst. During the war years he published two books on fear (Dollard, 1942, 1943). And in 1953, together with Auld and White, he wrote *Steps in Psychotherapy*, an extended analysis of the learning theory approach, containing a detailed case history. He was a hero to the younger Miller who, with his midwesterner's reserve, wrote in a 1982 obituary, 'If trying to bring together contributions from sociology, anthropology, psychology, and psychotherapy no longer seems so novel, it is because Dollard and

John Dollard (Courtesy Yale University Library Manuscripts and Archives)

Neal Miller (Courtesy of the Rockefeller University Archives)

other pioneers had the courage and tenacity to break through traditional barriers' (Miller, 1982, p. 588). Dollard died in 1980, honoured as a teacher and, as Miller said, a pioneer. He had a very large role in making sociology and anthropology more psychological and, with Miller, in bringing psychoanalysis into the mainstream of experimental psychology.

Neal Miller's family moved to Washington, where his father took up an appointment as professor of educational psychology at Western Washington State College. Irving Miller had studied with John Dewey and with psychologist James Rowland Angell, who became the president of Yale University. His son would become the James Rowland Angell professor of psychology in 1952. Miller graduated in 1931 from the University of Washington, where he was taught by the learning theorist Edwin R. Guthrie, and the following year received an MA from Stanford University. Lewis Terman, who developed the Stanford-Binet Intelligence Test, was one of his teachers. At Yale, where he went for doctoral study, he received the PhD under Clark Hull in 1935. Like Dollard, Miller was granted a Social Science Research Council travelling fellowship. He used the opportunity in 1935–6, to immerse himself in psychoanalysis in Vienna and to see if he could apply the roles of learning principles and conditions of learning to neurotic phenomena and analytic treatment. He gained admission to the Vienna Psychoanalytic Institute and received a didactic analysis from Heinz Hartmann, who was supervised by Anna Freud. He could have had a psychoanalytic hour with Freud himself but had to forgo it because he didn't think he could afford Freud's fee of $20.00!

Miller returned to Yale to accept a position in the Institute of Human Relations, where he conducted beautifully controlled animal experiments (on the nature of drives, on fear learning, and on conflict) in addition to his collaborative work with Dollard and other Institute members. He left Yale in 1966 to go to Rockefeller University as director of the Laboratory of Physiological Psychology. There, he undertook an extensive series of experiments on the physiological basis of drives, mainly using electrical and biochemical stimulation of the brain. His studies of the voluntary control of autonomic responses (altering blood pressure, for example), though at first convincing, were finally shown (in his lab) to be unlikely; he had had great hopes for biofeedback techniques to treat such disorders as chronic high blood pressure. Although his studies of the rat failed—by his own brave acknowledgement—to show voluntary autonomic control, the possibility remains in humans. He returned to Yale in 1985 as a research affiliate, remaining active well into the 1990s. He was a vigorous advocate of animal research and its great value in promoting health, both physical and psychological. He was president of the American Psychological Association in 1960–1, was elected to the National Academy of Sciences, and was awarded the National Medal of Science by President Lyndon Johnson in 1964. Miller was revered by his students as an experimentalist and as a teacher, and they warmly appreciated his keen sense of humour. Emerging from his office one day, he found some of his undergraduate students in heavy debate over the reality of the concept of insight. Quipped Miller, 'While we behaviourists don't believe in insight, we like to practice it.' He died in 2002 at the age of 92.

Emphases

The Principles and Conditions of Learning

'What, then, is learning theory?' asked Miller and Dollard in *Social Learning and Imitation*, as a way of introducing their summary of the theory:

> In its simplest form, it is the study of the circumstances under which a response and a cue stimulus become connected. After learning has been completed, response and cue are bound together in such a way that the appearance of the cue evokes the response. . . . Learning takes place according to definite psychological principles. Practice does not always make perfect. The connection between a cue and a response can be strengthened only under certain conditions. The learner must be driven to make the response and rewarded for having responded in the presence of the cue. This may be expressed in a homely way by saying that in order to learn one must want something, notice something, do something, and get something. Stated more exactly, these factors are drive, cue, response, and reward. These elements in the learning process have been carefully explored, and further complexities have been discovered. Learning theory has become a firmly knit body of principles which are useful in describing human relations (1941, pp. 1–2).

Drive, cue, response, and reward became an S-R theory mantra, a reminder of what goes into the formation of associations between stimuli and responses. For learning to occur, each of these must be present, and in order:

1. The arousal of a drive. We'll shortly take up the nature of the drive concept. Here, we want to note that learning requires a *motivated* human or animal.
2. Stimuli or cues that indicate the response to be made and where and when. Example: cross the street at the crosswalk when the walk sign is displayed.
3. The response has to occur when drive is aroused in the presence of the relevant cues.
4. The response must be rewarded. Unrewarded responses simply don't become part of the learned repertoire.

The Stimuli of Drives

Behaviour is driven by the potent stimuli of drives. Hunger, thirst, and sexual arousal produce strong drive stimuli, as we know intimately from experience. These are the stimuli of **primary drives★**. There are also a great many **secondary drives★**—for approval, for achievement, for affection—that are learned in the process of socialization. These secondary drives also entail the arousal of drive stimuli that may be very strong. Consider fear as an example of a significant secondary drive. The distinctly unpleasant state of being afraid is the result of powerful stimulation, both physiological (heart pounding, for example) and psychological (the awful feeling of dread). Many secondary drives will not involve intense physical stimuli, but psychological drive stimuli can certainly be intense enough to impel our behaviour. Responses that are successful in reducing drive stimuli are those that are strengthened by reward or, more properly, **reinforcement★**. This is the basis of reinforcement—the sudden reduction of drive stimuli. An affectionate reply from someone important to us, words of approval, a reduction in fear as we distance ourselves from a frightening situation, a beer on a hot day—these will all reduce their relevant drive stimuli, and the responses leading to them will become stronger.

The Concept of Habit

In Dollard and Miller's analysis—and in the theory of learning of Clark Hull, on which Dollard and Miller drew—the central concept is **habit★**, a learned association between a stimulus and a response. Responses strengthened by reinforcement become habits, so we may say that the habit is the product of learning. The relation between drive and habit is a simple one: drive multiplies habit strength. So, the probability that a given response will be made is a function of drive times habit:

$$R = f(D \times H)$$

We've already seen this formula in the context of Eysenck's theory of learning and inhibition. At the time, you very likely wondered why Hull and Dollard and Miller (and Eysenck) thought this relation between drive and habit was multiplicative. We can find the answer in the reason why hungry animals and people eat and sated ones don't. If the value of D is zero (or very low), relevant responses don't occur—in other words, the habit is not called up and expressed. It also follows that if a habit is weak or nonexistent, effective responses cannot occur even if D is very strong. I can wish with all my heart to be a championship tennis player, but without a whole repertoire of habits, a skilled performance just isn't going to occur. Said Hull and Dollard and Miller, no other mathematical relation satisfies the necessary requirement that D and H must have values greater than zero if behaviour is to occur.

Internal Responses

Strong stimulation arouses drive stimuli, but it will also produce internal responses—emotional responses, for example, such as increased heart rate and force of heartbeat that accompany emotional arousal. These emotional responses, which may also be psychological or have psychological counterparts (thoughts of failure, worry about dire consequences), produce stimuli that themselves can have the properties of a drive. Emotional responses can become conditioned to significant cues in the immediate situation, thus arousing fear whenever those cues are present. Just entering an examination room, for some, may produce emotional responses that intensify anxiety. Internal responses may also be cues as well as having drive properties. Sexual arousal, frustration, or hunger will produce patterns of internal responses that in turn have drive properties. The theory says that any drive state will produce distinctive patterns of internal responses and drive stimuli. Let me emphasize that internal responses are not necessarily physiological. They may be any responses that are known to be produced by a given stimulus, from implicit muscular contractions to thoughts.

The Major Concepts of S-R Theory

We can best see S-R theory in action by closely following Dollard and Miller's exposition in *Personality and Psychotherapy* (1950). They emulated Freud in using neurosis and its treatment as a model for personality processes in general—in their case, a model of maladaptive learning. As they argued (and as we saw in the first chapter), psychotherapy gives us the opportunity to look in on the intimate details of people's lives. Very few people, they pointed out, would voluntarily subject themselves to the long, taxing process of psychotherapy if they didn't need it. A few university institutes study normal individuals intensively, but there are not many of them, and they can put under the research lens only a small number of people. So, we look to psychotherapy with people suffering from neurotic disorders. Dollard and Miller wrote:

> If psychotherapy were used only as a way of curing neurotic persons, it would have a real but limited interest to students of human personality. The psychotherapeutic situation, however, provides a kind of window to mental life. Advanced research students in psychology are taught the rudiments of the therapist's art so that they may sit at this window. Learning something of the work of the therapist is a small price to pay for what the researcher sees.
>
> The elementary student similarly can profit by the reports on human personality which can be made only by the psychotherapist. As the therapist sees it, there is no artificial separation between intelligence, emotion, childhood, social influences, and behavior deviations. He must understand the patient's childhood, see him struggling in the grip of his social system, watch his intelligence contending with emotion, and identify behavior deviations. The mental-emotional life of man is seen the way it feels—as a single system.
>
> If normal people could be got to accept the conditions of psychotherapy, it would be possible to learn from them almost everything which has been discovered by studying neurotic persons. . . . The difficulty lies in the field of motivation. Normal people have low motivation to talk frankly and extensively about their most significant problems. Only neurotic misery seems to provide the strong drive required (1950, pp. 3–4).

What is a Neurosis?

The very best beginning is to consider what a neurosis is and how an approach to neurosis as learned behaviour can help us to understand the learning, maintenance, and change of any and all behaviour. One of Dollard and Miller's colleagues in the Institute of Human Relations, a co-author of *Frustration and Aggression*, was the psychologist O. Hobart Mowrer. In 1948, Mowrer proposed a solution to a well-recognized but unsolved problem in explaining neurotic behaviour. Mowrer called it the '**neurotic paradox**'. He said,

> . . . I invite you to consider what, in many respects, is the absolutely central problem in neurosis and therapy. Most simply formulated, it is a paradox—the paradox of behaviour which is at one and the same time self-perpetuating and self-defeating! . . . Common sense holds that a normal, sensible man, or even a beast to the limits of his intelligence, will weigh and balance the consequences of his acts: if the net effect is favorable, the action [producing] it will be perpetuated; and if the net effect is unfavorable, the action producing it will be inhibited, abandoned. In neurosis, however, one sees actions which have predominantly unfavorable consequences; yet they persist over a period of months, years, or a lifetime' (1950, pp. 486–7).

The paradox represents a considerable problem for any personality theory. Freud himself fully recognized it, acknowledging the difficulty of explaining behaviour that is repeated over and over despite the fact that it fails to solve any problem and actually creates lack of fulfillment and misery. The paradox is especially a problem for a learning theory. One of the concerns of learning theories is to account for the conditions under which behaviour changes. New behaviour that is not rewarded is unlikely to be repeated and undergoes extinction. We know that behaviour followed by negative consequences tends to be suppressed. Why, then, do self-defeating neurotic symptoms persist? Not only do they persist, they are, in fact, obstinately resistant to change, as any psychotherapist can tell you—resistant, as we say, to extinction. The neurotically troubled person has great difficulty in learning that conditions have changed—for example, that the anxiety-producing consequences of anger that characterized childhood no longer prevail in adulthood. He or she remains a victim of anxiety and of troublesome, crippling symptoms whenever anger is aroused.

There *is* an explanatory concept that will play a critical role in our S-R account of neurosis. It is the concept of **fear★** or anxiety. We'll presently take up the special features of fear as a **learned drive★**. In explaining neurosis, we also have to account for the characteristic indecision, vacillation, and conflict that so prominently appear. We'll explore the analysis of psychological conflict that Miller developed from the earlier work of another personality theorist, Kurt Lewin. Miller's experiments on conflict and his theoretical analysis help us to understand many details of neurotic behaviour—indeed, many details of quite ordinary behaviour that you and I may engage in from time to time when we are both attracted to some goal and also fearful of it.

I want to emphasize again how important it is to remember, as we delve into S-R theory (and the learning theories to follow), that in investigating neurotic behaviour in order to formulate and test theoretical principles, we are simply taking more extreme instances of behaviour that follow the same general laws of learning. I am reminding you of the **continuity assumption★**. What we are trying to understand is the learning of significant social behaviour—normal learning, maladaptive learning, and the unlearning of neurotic behaviour in psychotherapy. All follow from a common set of principles. Moreover, Dollard and Miller made a major point in noting that psychotherapy, the treatment of neurosis, is a process by which normality is created.

Any theory seeking to understand neurosis must deal with the following observations:

1. Neurotic behaviour is persistent, and we have to explain what maintains it, what reinforcing events are responsible for its unusual and paradoxical endurance.
2. Behaviour that habitually results in frustration, disappointment, dissatisfaction, impaired relationships with others, and just downright misery can continue to be repeated. It fails to extinguish.
3. Behaviour generalizes from the particular conditions under which it was learned to other situations that may seem, to the outside observer, to be very different. A neurotic adult fails to distinguish the consequences of anger or sexual expression for the grownup from the fearful consequences learned in childhood.
4. The neurotic person typically cannot provide an adequate and sensible account of the reasons for his or her symptomatic behaviour. Neurotic sufferers are unable to use their minds to think through the troubling behaviour.

Coming to terms with these observations is a very tall order. How does S-R theory fill it?

The Variables in S-R Theory

In S-R Theory, as we have seen, the acquisition of behaviour is a function of four variables.

1. Behaviour

Let's start here with the behaviour itself, the particular responses that we want to investigate. Dollard and Miller noted the essential requirement for careful description and analysis of actions. Their way of putting it was to say that we need to understand the *topography of responses*. Learning does not develop in a random, 'trial-and-error' way, as early theorists of learning (Edward L. Thorndike, for example) had proposed. Humans and nonhuman animals do not really learn by producing responses at random until some response or other is rewarded and gains strength over those that are not rewarded. Instead, the process of learning is much more systematic. Learners, human and nonhuman, will typically produce a limited repertoire of responses in a given learning situation. We see that some responses are very likely to be made (and repeated), while others are less so. Thus, learners show us an *initial hierarchy* of responses—a hierarchy that might consist of innate responses (a laboratory rat's rearing up to explore its surroundings; an infant's sucking or fear response to sudden loud noises or to loss of support) or responses that are strongly preferred. Learning *modifies* the initial hierarchy to produce a different set and ordering of responses, a *resultant hierarchy*. Some behaviour theorists thought of language development in this way—an innate hierarchy of sounds produced spontaneously by infants, which undergoes change with maturation and is modified over time by learning to result in intelligible speech.

2. Drive

Responses are driven by internal stimuli. To add to our earlier discussion, a drive is a strong stimulus that produces action. Any stimulus that is strong enough may become a drive, and the stronger the stimulus is, the more drive function it will have. We can classify drives. **Primary drives★** are based on the tissue needs of organisms and are built-in, biological equipment. Hunger, thirst, sex, and pain are examples. Other drives are acquired in the course of learning and are **acquired drives★**. Fear (or anxiety; we'll later distinguish between them) is one. The list of acquired drives is a long one; significant among them are love, approval, achievement, and dependency. These acquired drives are termed **secondary drives★**, and they develop, said Dollard and Miller, out of association with the reduction of primary drives early in life. A mother's social responses to her infant while she is feeding and cuddling her are cues that are regularly associated with primary drive reduction—the reduction of hunger drive stimuli. These cues can come to elicit internal responses linked with the drive and the reduction of drive stimuli. This is the fundamental way in which secondary drives are established. Dollard and Miller wrote:

> In the first year of its life the human infant has the cues from its mother associated with the primary reward of feeding on more than 2,000 occasions. Meanwhile the mother and other people are ministering to many other needs. In general there is a correlation between the absence of people and the prolongation of suffering from hunger, cold, pain, and other drives; the appearance of a person is associated with a

reinforcing reduction in the drive. Therefore the proper conditions are present for the infant to learn to attach strong reinforcement value to a variety of cues from the nearness of the mother and other adults. . . .

In the light of the fact that the required social conditions for learning exist in the family, it seems reasonable to advance the hypothesis that the related human motives of sociability, dependence, need to receive and show affection, and desire for approval from others are learned (1950, pp. 91–2).

We can state the basic motivational principle in S-R theory as follows: the sudden reduction of *any* strong stimulus reinforces behaviour associated with that stimulus reduction. That is, the abrupt loss of intensity of a strong stimulus strengthens an association between noticeable and noticed **cues**★ and the **responses**★ that led to drive stimulus reduction. There are two forms of this principle, one weak and one strong. Miller: 'In its weak form, the drive reduction hypothesis states that the sudden reduction in strength of any strong motivational stimulus always serves as a reward or in other words is a sufficient condition for reinforcement. In its strong form it states that all reward is produced in this way or in other words that drive reduction is not only a sufficient but also a necessary condition for reinforcement' (1959, p. 256). He was modest in his claims for the drive reduction hypothesis, particularly its strong form. He regarded it as the most appealing of all the alternative motivational hypotheses but conceded that it had in all probability less than a fifty per cent chance of being correct. He noted, however, that there is abundant evidence that the sudden reduction of motivational stimuli does indeed act as a reinforcement. It is important to remember that whether the reduction of drive stimuli is pleasurable (as in eating a tasty meal or sex), or simply involves the termination of painful or fearful stimuli, the same fundamental mechanism is at play.

3. Reinforcement

The formation of a learned association between a stimulus or cue and a response is determined by the consequences of the response. Responses that are reinforced (by causing a sudden reduction in drive stimuli) will tend to be repeated, and if the reinforcement is a frequent consequence, those responses become a permanent part of the person's repertoire. Sometimes, none of the responses a learner makes are reinforced; as a result, they drop out of the initial hierarchy to be replaced by other responses. This is, as Dollard and Miller termed it, a **learning dilemma**. Learning dilemmas cause unsuccessful, nonreinforced responses to extinguish and provide the opening for new responses to occur. Behaviour variability is the result—just what we want—and one response or another will finally be reinforced. If the learner were simply to stick with a response in the initial hierarchy, no learning could occur.

Reinforcement, then, is the critical event in determining which responses will drop out and which will be strengthened. Just as there are primary and secondary drives, there are primary and secondary reinforcements. Primary reinforcement is milk to a hungry infant, tasty pellets of lab chow to a hungry rat, a cold beer to a thirsty ballplayer after a game. Secondary reinforcements acquire their reinforcing ability through early association with primary reinforcement and primary drive reduction, as we just saw, and become powerful controllers of social behaviour. Once secondary reinforcements are established in infancy and early childhood, they require little further association with primary reinforcement to maintain their strength. In the laboratory, however, we find that when we establish a secondary reinforcement for an animal, responses rewarded by it will gradually extinguish if we do not occasionally pair it with a primary reinforcement. S-R theory does not fully help us to understand the exceptional persistence of secondary reinforcements in humans. This is a problem for the theory, but much of its account of personality, personality disorder, and treatment does not depend on coming up with a definitive solution. We'll have more to say about primary and secondary reinforcers in Chapter 13.

4. Cues

Drives motivate behaviour, and reinforcement selects those responses that are successful in reducing drive stimuli. Cues are the events (stimuli) that direct or guide behaviour. As Dollard and Miller said, 'Cues determine when [an individual] will respond, where he will respond, and which response he will make' (1950, p. 32). Cues enable *generalization*★ from one situation to another, helping us recognize some situations that are similar and call for the same response. *Discrimination* allows us to recognize situations that, having little in common, call for different responses. Cues may be distinctive aspects of situations or may be produced by the person herself. It is important to appreciate that what is an effective cue for one person in a particular situation is not necessarily a cue for someone else or may not be a cue for the same response. One person might respond readily to the slightest sign that her behaviour is considered inappropriate by others. Someone else whose learning history has been different might not respond to the social cue of disapproval in the same way. An example: a person who dominates a conversation with her bragging and doesn't respond to the signs of reproach—the smirking, eye rolling, yawning—given by others.

The very act of responding is a source of cues that guide subsequent responses. These are *response-produced cues*. Cue-producing responses direct much of our thinking and are the basis of 'higher mental processes'. We often rehearse in thought what we intend to say, providing the cues that shape our spoken ideas, and we do this formally when we outline the ideas for a paper. We instruct ourselves silently, and from that self-instruction come the cues that shape our performance. Cues are also produced by emotional states, by muscular tension—indeed, by any detectable and distinctive physical state or psychological process. Don't forget that strong stimuli can also function as drives. So, stimuli can both arouse (drive stimuli) and direct (cues) behaviour. Dollard and Miller took the position that all the laws we have discovered about external cues and their role in determining behaviour apply to response-produced cues.

Cues may vary in many dimensions. An obvious dimension is *intensity*. The same words spoken quietly and shouted do not have the same meaning because of the intensity difference. Another is the *pattern* of cues. We learn to respond to cues in combination with other cues. A wink accompanying a sexual innuendo distinguishes the nature of the remark and makes it sexual, a big effect for what might seem a small cue.

Let's pursue cue-producing responses just a little more. Much of our thought is determined by cues originating from preceding thoughts. Think of a word. Any word will do. Now, think of a word the one you just thought of brings to mind—an association to that word. Now, an association to the new word . . . and now another one to the word you just thought of. An association to that word . . . and one more. You probably got a long way, associatively, from the original word. You can see that each word provides the stimulus for a new word. This is the associative method with which Glucksberg and King began in the repression experiment we reviewed in Chapter 3. More basically, it is the process, said Dollard and Miller, by which our thinking is directed. Response-produced cues channel our thinking along associative lines—what is called the chaining of associations. Modern cognitive psychology has gone well beyond this behaviourist analysis of thinking, but no one doubts that our thoughts are linked by the strength of associations.

I want to remind you that the stimuli of acquired drives (fear, for example) can also be cues. A person may learn to identify response-produced stimuli in a given situation with the label 'afraid'. This label is now a cue that can cause responses learned in this situation to generalize to other situations. We call this **secondary generalization**. Differences in the intensity of drive stimuli can be discriminated, so that drive intensity can function as a cue. 'My, I really *am* hungry,' and 'Gee, I'm pretty sexually aroused' are examples.

S-R Theory Principles and the Explanation of Neurosis

These are the basic principles of the theory. We'll now take them and return to the problem of neurosis. The basis for the development of neurosis lies in the association of fear with cues significant to the neurotic person in specific situations. Not only will the reappearance of these cues arouse fear, but responses made to them may produce fear, also because of secondary generalization. So, fear may become attached to responses, including thoughts or the physiological responses of emotional arousal. The involuntary clenching of a fist might become a cue for fear in a person to whom anger arousal has become fearful because of early training.

We already know that responses leading to the reduction of fear are reinforced, and if the fear is sufficiently intense and if the situation and responses made to it are repeated, those responses will become habits that will resurface in similar situations. Indeed, because of secondary generalization, fear-reducing responses may be made even when the person *thinks* about the situation. Fear, thus, is averted or diminished before it has a chance to become intense. Responses that enabled escape from fear-producing cues in the original situation now result in the avoidance of fear. These responses anticipate and act to reduce fear before fear is fully aroused. As we shall see, avoidance responses are highly resistant to extinction.

An Experimental Model of Fear Arousal, Escape, and Avoidance Learning

Miller (1948a) tested rats in the apparatus you see in Figure 12.1. It consisted of two compartments, one painted white and the other black. Initially, the animals gave no evidence of fear—such as crouching, muscular tenseness, urination, and defecation—in either compartment. He then mildly shocked the animals in the white compartment through the electrified grid floor. They quickly learned to escape through an open door into the black compartment. When the escape had been well learned, the shock in the white compartment was discontinued. The rats, however, would immediately run through the door when placed in the white side of the apparatus, and they displayed the signs of fearfulness. Clearly, this was fear the rats had learned.

Next question: could this acquired fear motivate a new response, with escape from fear (not shock, now) reinforcing the new habit? The door was closed but could be opened by rotating a paddle wheel just above it. Placed in the white compartment, the animals, showing all the marks of fear, ran agitatedly in the compartment, bit the bars of the grid floor, and reared up in front of the door. The last bit of fear-motivated behaviour soon resulted in turning the wheel with the forepaws or nose, and the door opened, permitting escape. If

Figure 12.1 The compartments are distinctive. The left compartment has a grid floor to deliver shock and is painted white; the right compartment is painted black. A door separates the compartments, and a paddle wheel will open the door. (From Miller, 1948.)

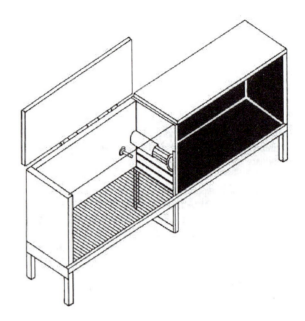

fear-reduction served as a reinforcement, wheel-turning should be readily adopted as a new response. This is just what happened. When wheel turning was well established and the animals were quickly escaping the fear-producing cues of the white compartment as soon as they were placed in it, Miller inactivated the wheel, eventually extinguishing this response. Depressing a bar became the new fear-reducing response, and it was easily mastered. An important point to remember: the wheel-turning and bar-pressing responses were acquired to the fear-producing cues of the white compartment, *not* to shock. The rats, anticipating shock and fearful, actively learned to avoid the dreaded compartment. We have an experiment that defines fear as a learned drive and fear-reduction as a learned reinforcement.

Passive Avoidance Learning

Animals or people (commonly, children) can also be taught what *not* to do—that is to say, to inhibit a response that will result in painful consequences. Suppose we train rats to run down an alley from a start box at one end to a goal box where food is obtained at the other. Once the animals are running reliably, quite fast and not dawdling, we introduce mild electric shock at the entry to the goal box. The rats very soon learn to avoid a now fearful place, approaching only part way and stopping. We call this inhibitory training **passive avoidance learning★**. It is a model for some very important learning situations in human childhood—learning situations in which we train children not to do things that could be dangerous to them (reaching for the top of the stove; running into the street) or that are socially unacceptable (hitting a sibling or playmate). These are examples of behaviour that parents frequently punish so that their children will be sure to inhibit them. Now if strong aversive stimuli are used, the inhibition of the punished response can become extremely persistent; a virtually permanent passive avoidance response can be established.

Avoidance Learning in Neurosis

How is it, then, that avoidance learning, especially passive avoidance, can come to be an enduring problem for the person subjected to severe avoidance training in childhood?

How is it that severe avoidance training can result in adult symptoms of neurosis? In neurosis, we find childhood histories of avoidance learning—fear attached to strongly motivated behaviour (often sexuality and aggression). Fear and the avoidance behaviour it motivates may, as a consequence, block the expression of normal sexual behaviour and assertiveness. The result is conflict and misery when sex or anger drives are aroused, conflict between a potent motive on the one hand and fear on the other, and a life of neurotic inhibition and misery.

We can now extend our analysis by examining the way in which defence mechanisms and symptoms are learned. If we understand the conditions responsible for the learning of neurotic behaviour, we can also answer the more general question of the relation between conditions of learning and behaviour that characterizes all of personality development. However, we must heed Dollard and Miller's caution: '*Behaviour* [is] *puzzling when conditions of learning are unknown*' (1950, p. 67). There is no problem in understanding the results of an experiment given the opportunity to observe a rat learning to associate a white compartment with the painful experience of shock, acquiring the motive of fear, and being reinforced for its escape habit. Suppose, though, we entered in the middle of the experiment and saw only turning the wheel to escape the white compartment. We would not have the full story of the conditions of learning, and the animal's behaviour would definitely be mystifying. So it is with trying to reconstruct the conditions of learning of people when we don't know what the cues are and why they provoke fear.

The basis of neurosis lies in the association of fear with cues that may be in the situation or may be internal (thoughts, physiological responses, other responses of the person). Fear motivates behaviour, and any response that effectively reduces it is reinforced. When acquired in the presence of a strong drive (fear), avoidance responses can be extremely persistent. Let's examine why it is that a person bedevilled by avoidance responses cannot use his mind to solve the problem, cannot master his fear and find more effective ways of dealing with the situations he is unable to face. We'll look at some of the reasons why, according to S-R theory, avoidance motivated by fear is so resistant to extinction despite the painful disruptions it can produce in people's lives.

Intense fear has as one of its effects the narrowing of attention, causing the person to focus on the immediate situation and on specific cues associated with fear arousal. Responses are less likely to be well thought out, and the fearful person doesn't notice other cues that might help him or her to choose a better approach. In situations of high fear, people are often apt to respond automatically to those few cues that stand out for them.

Fear originally aroused by cues in a particular situation can also be evoked by other, similar cues as a result of *stimulus generalization*. Fear may be stirred as well by thoughts of the fearful situation and the cues relevant to it. This occurs because of *secondary generalization*. Note that when fear is brought on by thoughts, it has become *anticipatory* to the situation itself. If the thought-produced fear is intense, the person avoids thinking; his or her thoughts are immediately deflected from the fear-evoking cues. This will tend to occur automatically, not as the result of deliberate choice.

Here's an example. A young boy is sharply punished by his mother for angry attacks on his younger brother. He is so severely punished that he comes to fear not only the provocations to anger toward his brother but the arousal of anger itself. His own anger arousal has thus become a cue for fear. The fear his mother arouses is so intense that even thinking angry thoughts or clenching his fist become cues capable of making him afraid. Because thinking tends to be anticipatory to action, we can expect exactly the following result:

because of secondary generalization, fear is aroused *before* the boy carries out any aggressive (and punishable) action. So, the distinction between thinking and acting has broken down; although the child's mother probably didn't intend to subject her child's thoughts to the same punishment as his actions, this is what has occurred. When we understand the psychological principles involved, we can see how the child's fear could generalize from punished actions to the cues produced by the arousal of his own angry feelings.

We have here Dollard and Miller's analysis of the defence of repression. Stopping oneself from thinking may be reinforced by an immediate reduction in fear. This must sound a bit odd—that interrupting an ongoing response is itself a response that can be reinforced—but Dollard and Miller argue that it can be just as much a fear-reducing response as an overt one. If the fear is intense, it may not require many experiences (trials) to acquire the stopping thinking–repression response. Once learned, repression will be evoked whenever the fear-producing cues are present, and this response will prevent any thinking and reasoning about the reason for one's fear. To follow our child who has been taught an anger–fear conflict and has come to repress awareness of his own anger arousal, the immediate effect of repression is to make him less fearful. A larger effect is to make the whole conflict unconscious, inaccessible to reasoning and problem solving. So, a second reason why neurotic conflicts are resistant to extinction is that responses learned to reduce fear interfere with thinking.

I have adopted Dollard and Miller's use of the term 'fear' for the powerful learned drive that motivates most defences and symptoms. Dollard and Miller, in turn, acknowledged Freud in distinguishing between fear and anxiety. Fear is aroused by situations and cues that can be identified: 'I'm afraid of the big dog down the street.' 'I'm afraid of bumpy rides in airplanes.' Freud (and Dollard and Miller) used the term 'anxiety' when the cues to fear are indistinct (a social situation, for example, that makes a person afraid, but she cannot point to anything specific) or have been buried by repression. We may think of anxiety as the experience of fear after repression or other defences have erased the awareness of eliciting cues.

There is a final question to answer in our discussion of fear (and anxiety). Why is it that fear is so often implicated in neurosis? No problem. Dollard and Miller said, 'There are three main reasons why fear is so important: because it can be so strong, because it can be attached to new cues so easily through learning, and because it is the motivation that produces the inhibiting responses in most conflicts' (1950, p. 190).

A Theory of Conflict

One of the most powerful features of S-R theory is its analysis of psychological conflict. Here is the state of a neurotic person as Dollard and Miller described it:

> . . . [T]he depth of the misery of the neurotic is concealed by his symptoms. Only when they are withdrawn does his true anguish appear. Occasionally the misery will be private, not easily visible to outside observers because friends and relatives are ringed around the neurotic person and prevent observation of his pain. In still other cases, the neurotic person is miserable but apathetic. He has lost even the hope that complaining and attracting attention will be helpful. However this may be, *if the neurotic takes the usual risks of life* he is miserable. He suffers if he attempts to love, marry, and be a parent. He fails if he tries to work responsibly and independently. His social relations tend to be invaded by peculiar demands and conditions. Neurotic misery is thus often masked by the protective conditions of life (as in childhood) and appears only when the individual has to 'go it on his own' (1950, p. 13).

This is terrible suffering, it is real, and it is caused by conflict between potent drives. On the one hand, there is strong motivation to approach certain goals (a sexual relationship, being assertive and standing up for oneself). On the other, there is intense learned fear. If this were a conscious conflict, we could certainly see how it could make someone feel wretched. The victim of such a conflict cannot do what he greatly wishes he could because when he tries he is driven off by fear. But it isn't conscious in the neurotic person. That makes it truly puzzling for the person himself (he may well think he's going crazy), others around him who would like to help but can't, and even the psychotherapist treating him, who will probably have to be very patient and persistent to be able to identify the source of the fear. The person in conflict vacillates at some distance from the goal (spatial, in time, or in a psychological sense), agonized and uncomprehending.

Let's follow Miller in making some assumptions about conflict. There are four of them.

1. The tendency to approach a desired goal increases as the person comes nearer to it. This is the *gradient of approach*, and you can see it plotted in Figure 12.2 as a straight, solid line rising with closeness to the goal. Dollard and Miller cited an extensive body of research confirming this and the next assumption (1950, pp. 353–5).

2. The tendency to avoid a feared goal increases with nearness to it. This is the *gradient of avoidance*, shown in the figure as a dashed line.

3. The gradient of avoidance is *steeper* than the gradient of approach. Why? We need to account for the vacillation, indecision, and misery of people suffering conflict involving *both* strong approach *and* strong avoidance motives. This assumption accomplishes that. If avoidance is stronger than approach near to the goal, the person will approach to the point at which the gradients intersect. Any nearer and fear overwhelms approach, compelling retreat. At the point of intersection, the conflict sufferer vacillates in misery.

4. The fourth assumption concerns the effect of increasing motivation to approach in situations of approach–avoidance conflict. Well-meaning friends often do this in the hope of encouraging the person in conflict to take that big breath and seize the sought reward. The effect, however, is likely to be disaster. As the strength of approach is increased and the person gets closer to the goal, so is the strength of

Figure 12.2 Miller's graphic representation of approach-avoidance conflict. (From S. Koch, ed., *Psychology: A Study of a Science, Vol. 2.* Copyright 1959 by The McGraw-Hill Companies. Reprinted with permission of the publisher.)

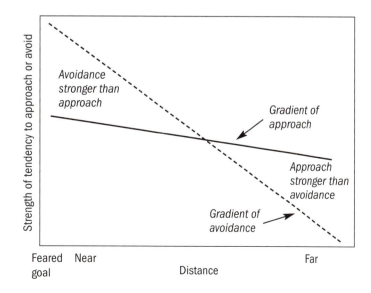

avoidance. Try this for yourself on the approach–avoidance graph, moving the gradient of avoidance upward. You can see that the point of intersection moves closer to the goal, and as it does fear is greatly intensified (measure the amount of fear elicited from the baseline of the graph to the avoidance gradient at the intersection shown and at the new intersection you have just created). Psychotherapists know that it is usually unwise to push patients in conflict. The effective therapeutic strategy, rather, is gradually to extinguish fear, thus lowering the avoidance gradient.

The case of Mrs A. in Perspective 12.2 is an excellent illustration of approach–avoidance conflict and its effects in creating a life seriously marred by symptoms.

Perspective 12.2 Dollard and Miller's Account of The Case of Mrs A

The Facts

Mrs A was an unusually pretty twenty-three-year-old married woman. Her husband worked in the offices of an insurance company. When she came to the therapist she was exceedingly upset. She had a number of fears. One of the strongest of these was that her heart would stop beating if she did not concentrate on counting the beats.

The therapist, who saw Mrs A twice a week over a three-month period, took careful notes. The life-history data . . . were pieced together from the patient's statements during a total of 26 hours. The scope of the material is necessarily limited by the brevity of the treatment. The treatment had to end when a change in the husband's work forced her to move to another city.

Her first neurotic symptoms had appeared five months before she came to the psychiatrist. While she was shopping in a New York store, she felt faint and became afraid that something would happen to her and 'no one would know where I was'. She telephoned her husband's office and asked him to come and get her. Thereafter she was afraid to go out alone. Shortly after this time, she talked with an aunt who had a neurotic fear of heart trouble. After a conversation with this aunt, Mrs A's fears changed from a fear of fainting to a concern about her heart.

Mrs A was an orphan, born of unknown parents in a city in the upper South. She spent the first few months of life in an orphanage, then was placed in a foster home, where she lived, except for a year when she was doing war work in Washington, until her marriage at the age of twenty.

The foster parents belonged to the working class, had three children of their own, two girls and a boy, all of them older than the patient. The foster mother, who dominated the family, was cruel, strict, and miserly toward all the children. She had a coarse and vulgar demeanor, swore continually, and punished the foster child for the least offense. Mrs A recalls: 'She whipped me all the time—whether I'd done anything or not.'

The foster mother had imposed a very repressive sex training on the patient, making her feel that sex was dirty and wrong. Moreover, the foster mother never let the patient think independently. She discouraged the patient's striving for an education, taking her out of school at sixteen when the family could have afforded to let her go on.

Despite the repressive sex training she received. Mrs A had developed strong sexual appetites. In early childhood she had overheard parental intercourse, had masturbated, and had witnessed animal copulation. When she was ten or twelve, her foster brother seduced her. During the years before her marriage a dozen men tried to seduce her and most of them succeeded.

Nevertheless, sex was to her a dirty, loathesome thing that was painful for her to discuss or think about. She found sexual relations with her husband disgusting and was morbidly shy in her relations with him.

The patient had met her husband-to-be while she was working as a typist in Washington during the war. He was an Army officer and a college graduate. Her beauty enabled the patient to make a marriage that improved her social position; her husband's family were middle-class people. At the time of treatment Mrs A had not yet learned all the habits of middle-class life. She was still somewhat awkward about entertaining or being entertained and made glaring errors in grammar and pronunciation. She was dominated, socially subordinated, and partly rejected by her husband's family.

When they were first married, Mr and Mrs A lived with his parents in a small town north of New York City and commuted to the city for work. Mrs A had an office job there. Later, they were able to get an apartment in New York, but they stayed with the in-laws every weekend. Although she described her mother-in-law in glowing terms at the beginning of the treatment, Mrs A later came to express considerable hostility toward her.

When she came to the psychiatrist, Mrs A was in great distress. She had to pay continual attention to her heart lest it stop beating. She lived under a burden of vague anxiety and had a number of specific phobias that prevented her from enjoying many of the normal pleasures of her life, such as going to the movies. She felt helpless to cope with her problems. Her constant complaints had tired out and alienated her friends. Her husband was fed up with her troubles and had threatened to divorce her. She could not get along with her foster mother and her mother-in-law had rejected her. She had no one left to talk to. She was hurt, baffled, and terrified by the thought that she might be going crazy.

Analysis in Terms of Conflict, Repression, Reinforcement

We have described Mrs A as of the moment when she came to treatment. The analysis of the case, however, presents the facts as they were afterward ordered and clarified by study.

Misery. Mrs A's misery was obvious to her family, her therapist, and herself. She suffered from a strong, vague, unremitting fear. She was tantalized by a mysterious temptation. The phobic limitations on her life prevented her from having much ordinary fun, as by shopping or going to the movies. Her husband and mother-in-law criticized her painfully. She feared that her husband would carry out his threat and divorce her. She feared that her heart would stop. She feared to be left all alone, sick and rejected. Her friends and relatives pitied her at first, then became put out with her when her condition persisted despite well-meant advice. Her misery, though baffling, was recognized as entirely real.

Conflict. Mrs A suffered from two conflicts which produced her misery. The first might be described as a sex-fear conflict. Thanks to childhood circumstances she had developed strong sex appetites. At the same time strong anxieties were created in her and attached to the cues produced by sex excitement. However, she saw no connection between these remembered circumstances and the miserable life she was leading. The connective thoughts had been knocked out and the conflict was thus unconscious. The presence of the sexual appetites showed up in a kind of driven behaviour in which she seemed to court seduction. Her fear was exhibited in her revulsion from sexual acts and thoughts and in her inability to take responsibility for a reasonable sexual expressiveness with her husband. The conflict was greatly intensified after her marriage because of her wish to be a dutiful wife. Guilt about the prospect of adultery was added to fear about sex motives.

Mrs A was involved in a second, though less severe, conflict between aggression and fear. She was a gentle person who had been very badly treated by her mother-in-law.

Resentful tendencies arose in her but they were quickly inhibited by fear. She attempted to escape the anger–fear conflict by exceptionally submissive behavior, putting up meekly with slights and subordination and protesting her fondness for the mother-in-law. She was tormented by it nevertheless, especially by feelings of worthlessness and helplessness. She felt much better, late in therapy, when she was able to state her resentment and begin to put it into effect in a measured way. (After all, she had the husband and his love, and if the mother-in-law wanted to see her son and prospective grandchildren she would have to take a decent attitude toward Mrs A.)

Stupidity. Mrs A's mind was certainly of little use to her in solving her problem. She tried the usual medical help with no result. She took a trip, as advised, and got no help. Her symptoms waxed and waned in unpredictable ways. She knew that she was helpless. At the time she came for therapy she had no plans for dealing with her problem and no hope of solving it. In addition to being unable to deal with her basic problems, Mrs A did many things that were quite unintelligent and maladaptive. For example, in spite of the fact that she wanted very much to make a success of her marriage and was consciously trying to live a proper married life, she frequently exposed herself to danger of seduction. She went out on drinking parties with single girls. She hitchhiked rides with truck drivers. She was completely unaware of the motivation for this behaviour and often unable to foresee its consequences until it was too late. While her behaviour seems stupid in the light of a knowledge of the actual state of affairs, there were many ways in which Mrs A did not seem at all stupid—for example, when debating with the therapist to protect herself against fear-producing thoughts. She then gave hopeful evidence of what she could do with her mind when she had available all the necessary units to think with.

Repression. Mrs A gave abundant evidence of the laming effects of repression. At the outset she thought she had no sex feelings or appetites. She described behavior obviously motivated by fear but could not label due fear itself. The closest she came was to express the idea that she was going insane. Further, Mrs A thought she had an organic disease and clung desperately to this idea, inviting any kind of treatment so long as it did not force her to think about matters which would produce fear. Such mental gaps and distortions are a characteristic result of repression. They are what produce the stupidity.

Symptoms. Mrs A's chief symptoms were the spreading agoraphobia which drove her out of theaters and stores and the compulsive counting of breaths and heartbeats. These symptoms almost incapacitated her. She had lost her freedom to think and to move.

Reinforcement of symptoms. An analysis of the phobia revealed the following events. When on the streets alone, her fear of sex temptation was increased. Someone might speak to her, wink at her, make an approach to her. Such an approach would increase her sex desire and make her more vulnerable to seduction. Increased sex desire, however, touched off both anxiety and guilt, and this intensified her conflict when she was on the street. When she 'escaped home', the temptation stimuli were lessened, along with a reduction of the fear which they elicited. Going home and, later, avoiding the temptation situation by anticipation were reinforced. Naturally, the basic sex–anxiety conflict was not resolved by the defensive measure of the symptom. The conflict persisted but was not so keen.

The counting of heartbeats can be analytically taken apart in a similar way. When sexy thoughts came to mind or other sex stimuli tended to occur, these stimuli elicited anxiety. It is clear that these stimuli were occurring frequently because Mrs A was responding with anxiety much of the time. Since counting is a highly preoccupying kind of response, no other thoughts could enter her mind during this time. While counting, the sexy thoughts which excited fear dropped out. Mrs A 'felt better' immediately when she started counting, and the counting habit was reinforced by the drop in anxiety. Occasionally, Mrs A would forget to count and then her intense anxiety would recur. In this case, as in that of the phobia, the counting symptom does not resolve the basic conflict—it only avoids exacerbating it.

Thus Mrs A's case illustrates the analysis of neurotic mechanisms. . . . Conflict produced high drives experienced as misery; repression interfered with higher mental processes and so with the intelligent solution of the conflict; the symptoms were learned responses which were reinforced by producing some reduction in the strength of drive. [*Personality and Psychotherapy* shows] how higher mental life can be restored and how actions which *will* resolve the poisonous conflict can be made to occur.

From J. Dollard & N.E. Miller, *Personality and Psychotherapy: An Analysis in Terms of Learning, Thinking, and Culture*, pp. 17–22. © 1950 by the McGraw-Hill Companies. Reprinted with permission of the publisher.

Approach–avoidance isn't the only kind of painful conflict. One may be caught between two feared alternatives. This is avoidance–avoidance conflict. An example: a child is afraid of the dark and is threatened with a spanking if she comes downstairs after being put to bed. In conflict situations of this sort, the person moves away from one feared alternative until the avoidance gradient of the other is met. With both situations eliciting fear, we should see retreat to the intersection, and then vacillation. The frightened child quietly creeps halfway down the stairs and huddles there hoping she won't be noticed. Sometimes, in such a conflict, there is a way to 'leave the field'. Halfway down the stairs isn't very comfortable and risks detection, but our fearful child might escape her twin terrors by coming downstairs to announce that she is sick. Figure 12.3 diagrams the avoidance–avoidance situation.

You will surely have a question about what happens when there is conflict between two approach motives. Well, any movement toward one results in stronger approach, and the choice is made. If the gradients in Figure 12.3 represent approach rather than avoidance, starting at point *P* means there really is no conflict: the person is already closer to one desired goal than to the other and goes for the hot fudge sundae at the Dairy Queen, not the beer at the pub.

Figure 12.3 Miller's graphic representation of avoidance-avoidance conflict. (From Dollard & Miller, p. 364.)

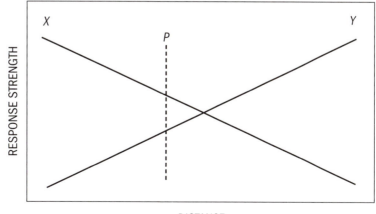

Personality Development

Dollard and Miller agreed with Freud that early childhood is critical in personality development. Normal personalities and those that will become neurotic both start with decisive experiences in early life. So, the basic conditions of learning in childhood are truly important. '[N]eurotic conflicts are taught by parents and learned by children'

A Fresh Look: Research Today

The motivational centerpiece of S-R theory is Miller's conception of approach–avoidance conflict. Take that conception, which identifies situations that arouse incompatible motives, and turn it into two enduring personality dispositions. This is just what Columbia University psychologist E. Tory Higgins and colleagues have done within Higgins's 'regulatory focus' theory (1997, 1998). Higgins proposes that two opposed motivational systems control all goal-seeking behaviour: a *promotion system*, which is oriented toward positive outcomes—generally, reward and pleasure—and a *prevention system*, which anticipates the negative outcomes of disappointment, failure, and punishment. The basic idea of approach and avoidance personality systems was in the air.

The late Jeffrey Gray, then professor of psychology at the Institute of Psychiatry in London, had argued that these systems are represented in brain structures that serve approach to reward (the Behavioural Activation System, BAS) and avoidance of threat (the Behavioural Inhibition System, BIS) and that they are responsible for consistent individual differences (see Gray, 1982, 1987, 1991). Higgins conceives of the BAS and BIS systems behaviourally and cognitively. We interpret our experiences to create a running history of success in approaching and attaining rewards (promotion focus) or in avoiding the possibility of unpleasant consequences (prevention focus). A promotion focus motivates 'eagerness means' to achieve the goal and results in 'promotion pride' in anticipation of its accomplishment. A prevention focus energizes caution—'avoidance strategic means' or 'vigilance means'—to ensure that one doesn't take on something too difficult and fail, expose oneself to punishment, get in so deep that extrication is impossible, and so on. Success in averting potential disasters gives the person 'prevention pride', the expectation that stopping at the yellow light in life will pay dividends.

Higgins and colleagues (Higgins, Friedman, Harlow, Idson, Ayduk, & Taylor, 2001) developed a personality measure to assess promotion and prevention orientations, the Regulatory Focus Questionnaire (RFQ). Here are sample items:

- Promotion: 'How often have you accomplished things that got you "psyched" to work even harder?' (scored on a five-point scale from 'never or seldom' to 'many times'; a promotion response would be toward many times).
- Prevention: 'Growing up, would you ever "cross the line" by doing things that your parents would not tolerate?' (scored on the same five-point scale; a prevention response would be toward the never or seldom).

In five experiments, Higgins et al. tested predictions from this approach–avoidance theory. Let's consider two of them.

Study 1 compared the decisions of promotion- and prevention-oriented participants on two difficult choices. The first was this:

Assume that you have spent $100 on a ticket for a weekend trip to Michigan. Several weeks later, you buy a $50 ticket for a weekend trip to Wisconsin. As you are putting your just-purchased Wisconsin trip ticket in your wallet, you notice that the Michigan trip and the Wisconsin trip are for the same weekend! It's too late to sell either ticket, and you cannot return either one. You must use one ticket and not the other. Which trip will you go on?

(1950, p. 127). It is a pity, said Dollard and Miller, that we don't really have a science of childrearing, and what dependable knowledge we do have is poorly taught to and learned by prospective parents. What is it that makes early childhood learning difficult—for the infant and for the parents? To begin with, the beginning of childhood is a period of helplessness and dependence, as we know and as other theorists have pointed out. At one and the same time, infant and small child have immense learning tasks to master and

And the second:

> As the president of an airline company, you have invested 10 million dollars of the company's money into a research project. The purpose was to build a plane that would not be detected by conventional radar, in other words, a radar-blank plane. When the project is 90 per cent completed, another firm begins marketing a plane that cannot be detected by radar. Also, it is apparent that their plane is much faster and far more economical than the plane your company is building. The question is: should you invest the last 10 per cent of the research funds to finish your radar-blank plane?

What will you choose? The error in the first dilemma would be to deny the greater pleasure of the Wisconsin trip because you had paid more for the Michigan ticket, an error of omission. If you are promotion-disposed, you should not make it; there's nothing you can do about the blown $100. Enjoying Wisconsin will be the most rewarding choice, and this is just what high-promotion participants elect. The second scenario's error would be to spend the remaining ten per cent, throwing good money after bad. In this case, the prevention focus on vigilance will urge you not to invest further in a lost cause, the choice prevention-oriented subjects were disposed to make.

The second of the studies involved people with long histories in their preferred motivational orientations. They were Columbia University alumni in their later years, aged from fifty to seventy. They completed the RFQ and a 'goals inventory', which asked participants to list major goals and means to achieve them. There was considerable agreement among the respondents on broad categories of goals—such things as family, health, growth, and learning—and on activities to meet them. The promotion- and prevention-oriented, however, differed in the number of means per goal: there was a significant positive relation between promotion scores and the number of means listed for each goal, and a negative one between prevention scores and listed means. Why? Those high in promotion-related eagerness would see a challenge in thinking about life goals and activities to reach them. Promotion pride would motivate them. Prevention vigilance and its conservative quest for the safe and secure would inhibit the search for goal-advancing means, limiting it to the known, tried, and true. These individuals, Higgins et al. suggest, would have experienced prevention pride.

Other experiments in the series further established the coherence and consistency of approach and avoidance personalities. We have moved in our generation away from Dollard and Miller's intent to account for the conditions that determine learning and how later conditions can revive it, and toward a conception that sees the outcomes of much earlier learning in childhood (and neurophysiological processes as well that may be inherited) incorporated in the motive systems of individuals. Dollard and Miller would have been delighted to see their work appear in the theory and research of succeeding scholars, and not entirely displeased, I think, with the new personality-focused application. After all, they might say, look what approach–avoidance conflict theory can do in commending therapists to extinguish anxiety in their patients, a principle no therapist can ignore. And, generously, they might congratulate regulatory focus theory for its implication that when therapists deal with patients who have failed in their goal-seeking pursuits they should be prepared to treat the promotion- and prevention-oriented differently. What will appeal to the one will not work with the other. You could not, they would acknowledge, suggest to the prevention-motivated person that he or she throw caution to the winds and just do it, any more than holding out the circumspect to one whose pleasure is in promotion.

must also tolerate strong states of tension and drive arousal. They depend on parents to be fed, cleaned, taken to bed, and comforted when they are in pain or are afraid. Much of the small child's learning is unlabelled or inadequately labelled because of the complexity of the learning (emotional experience, for example) and because language skills are far from developed. Generalization and discrimination are difficult. If parents who are well meaning but not very sensitive or skilful with their children fail to handle important aspects of their children's development thoughtfully, we may expect the consequences to be expressed in problem behaviour later on.

Four Child-Training Situations

Although there are no developmental stages in S-R theory, we will find a significant concern with the conditions of childhood learning. Dollard and Miller identified four critical child-training situations, acknowledging Freud's priority in recognizing them.

1. The Feeding Situation

Hunger is a strong drive, and parents may not appreciate just how intense it can be. Failing to understand that an infant is hungry and not just being 'difficult' exposes the child to extreme discomfort. Letting an infant 'cry itself out', as folk wisdom once advocated and some mothers continue to practice, may teach the infant the beginnings of apathy (no amount of crying brings relief) and apprehensiveness over the experience of hunger. It may also teach the infant to be afraid of being alone, since aloneness and fear are likely to become associated with the eventual reduction of very strong hunger drive stimuli when the mother finally arrives, and linked to the significant cues that are present. Through the mother's responsiveness to her infant, the feeding situation is the foundation from which sociability and love will develop. 'Since the mother or caretaker stands at the very head of the parade of persons who become "society" for the child, it is quite important that she evoke such benign and positive responses in the child' (1950, p. 133). Weaning, too, presents challenges to the mother. An infant refusing to take baby food is not obstinate, and letting her go hungry until she is willing to eat her Beech-Nut spinach is a strategy for creating conflict. 'There is hardly anything valuable that an infant can learn by punishment [for refusal to eat], and parents should take the greatest pains to avoid this' (1950, p. 134).

2. Cleanliness Training

Much of early learning occurs before children have developed language sufficient to understand their parents and to say what they feel and think. Cleanliness training is a major example. Freud was undoubtedly correct in pointing out that excretory and cleanliness training can have an importance in the development of personality that goes well beyond the civilizing of toilet habits. This is because Western culture generally prescribes powerful attitudes of secrecy, revulsion, and disgust over elimination that are often communicated by parents to their children and may be conveyed with angry feeling and accompanying punishment. Defecation and urination entail strong drives the expression of which must be modified and shaped into the rituals of adulthood largely without the aid that verbal instruction gives to learning. 'No child may avoid this training. The demands of the training system are absolute and do not take account of individual differences in learning ability' (1950, p. 136). It is no wonder that conflict between impulse and fear may develop from parental lack of understanding, impatience, and anger.

3. Early Sex Training

We know from the clinical study and treatment of adults that sex–anxiety conflicts are prominent in neurosis. Sex, as Dollard and Miller observed, is not the most insistent of drives, but it far surpasses stronger drives (hunger, for example) in the emotional intensity it can engender. We do not think of children as experiencing sexual arousal, and we view any sign with alarm and prohibition. Interest in genitals and masturbation is taboo, and sexual growing up and exploration often proceed in secrecy, accompanied by embarrassment and guilt inculcated by the moralistic stance of parents. Labelling of drives and feelings is made difficult.

4. Anger Management Training

The second of Freud's significant instincts was no less critical to Dollard and Miller. The conditions of learning to deal with angry feelings are frequently emotional and distressing for young children. Parents lose their tempers out of intolerance toward anger and tantrums. They may feel that getting angry and meting out punishment are justified because their children must be taught to inhibit rage. Such a reaction, however, may make it difficult for children to acquire control over their feelings because it creates fear and may cause resentment. Arousing fear may result in anger–anxiety conflicts that resentment only makes more difficult.

We want to be sure to understand that in singling out these four critical child-training situations, Dollard and Miller were specifying some potentially problematical conditions of learning in the early years of childhood. These are four situations that students of personality development definitely want to know about. We want to understand, too, that the conditions of developmental learning will in many cases be individual, and we are unlikely to be able to know about them. Thus, the cues eliciting behaviour in the adult may be truly obscure. They were salient aspects of long-lost childhood training situations, and they will have been modified by intervening years of experience.

The Damaging Effects of Mislabelling

We understand ourselves by being able to label our feelings, drives, and thoughts, and when we can't identify them we lose command of our behaviour. Cognitive omissions and distortions exact a big price, a toll that will begin in childhood, for which misguided parental teaching is responsible. Parents may reinforce the mislabelling of feelings, thoughts, and bodily functions, saying to children such things as 'You mustn't think that!' or 'That's a naughty thought!' or 'You're very bad to think that!'. If this is done with enough severity, it may lay the groundwork for repression. Or, consider this example. A mother finds her two boys fighting. She sternly admonishes them and tells them that they must put their arms around each other, apologize, and say that they love each other. What are they thinking at this point? Both are enraged and full of hateful thoughts and words. Their mother demands that they substitute for their present feelings something directly opposite. If she comes down hard enough, the result may be to teach the boys the defence of reaction formation. If fear is strongly aroused, and if this scene is a repeated one, the boys may learn to invert feelings of anger into an indefensible alternative. We should take note of the fact that small children *are* going to get angry, and they *are* going to repeat angry words they have heard. Parents, though, often don't appreciate that small children lack experience in identifying their feelings and in finding less direct and immediate ways of expressing them. Indeed, many parents aren't very good at that themselves.

Research

Dollard and Miller began by systematically reformulating psychoanalytic hypotheses in S–R terms and testing them in well-controlled laboratory experiments, in field studies, and in psychotherapy. Their participation in the work of the Institute of Human Relations studying racial discrimination in the southern US, imitation in social learning, and the role of frustration in provoking aggression was exemplary. As we noted earlier, Dollard, the authority on psychotherapy, collaborated with Auld and White in developing an extensive analysis of the steps in the process for the training of future psychotherapists in S-R theory technique. We have already considered some of this work. Let's examine two further areas of research—studies of conflict and of displacement.

Conflict

A series of experiments by Brown (1940), Miller's doctoral student, tested the assumptions of approach and avoidance gradients. Rats were trained to run down an alley for food in a goal box, under conditions of strong or weak hunger. They wore small harnesses attached to cords leading to a measuring device and were briefly restrained near to or far from the goal box where their strength of pull was recorded. To investigate avoidance, the rats were given electric shock at the same end of the alley, and their strength of pull (away from the shocked area) was measured near and far. There were clear approach and avoidance gradients. Miller and colleagues (Miller, 1944) then applied Brown's confirmation of the gradient assumptions to approach–avoidance conflict. Rats were trained to run down the alley for food and were then shocked in the goal box while eating. Tests using the harness were made without shock. The animals were placed at the start of the alley, and their strength of pull was recorded. Also, observations of conflict behaviour were recorded. 'The results', wrote Miller, 'confirm the deductions. The characteristic behaviour was to approach part way and then stop. The place at which the animals stopped was determined by the relative strength of the two drives. Stronger hunger or weaker shock caused the animals to come nearer to the goal before stopping' (1944, p. 437). It may seem a long way from rats in runways to people agonized by sex–fear or anger–fear conflicts, but Miller took the position that the laws of learning and of conflict behaviour equally apply. Moreover, he said, once the hypotheses about conflict behaviour (or any other derivation from the theory) are confirmed in simple situations, they can be tested in more complex ones with humans. Dollard and Miller:

> Thus, it can be seen that the subject should tend to remain trapped at an intermediate point where the two gradients cross . . . and [t]his is what occurs in experimental situations; the subject goes part of the way to the goal and then stops. If he is placed at the goal, he retreats and then comes part way back. The same thing is observed clinically; people in such a conflict seem to be unable to go forward far enough to reach their goals or away far enough to forget them (1950, p. 357).

Studies of Displacement

Freud had contended that when strongly motivated responses toward a target person are prevented, others will be directed to substitute targets, allowing the individual to gain some (though reduced) gratification and tension reduction from the new object choice. All our interests, creative achievements, and accomplishments are, ultimately, displacements of libido from original (and forbidden) objects. So, too, is much of our aggression. To Dollard and Miller, displacement could be seen as an instance of stimulus generalization, a concept in the psychology of learning with broad and very important applicability. Stimulus generalization can be used to understand how quite innocent minorities become targets of aggression that should really be directed at the true source of frustration; it thus provides an explanation of prejudice. Stimulus generalization can help us (and aggravated, bewildered parents) to see why a small boy after a particularly trying day at school attacks his little brother at home.

The process of displacement, as Dollard, Miller, and their Institute of Human Relations colleagues saw it, occurs when an initial response (aggression) is prevented because of fear, or because the target is inaccessible or so diffuse that aggression toward it is impossible (the heartless policies of a large industry or bank might be an example of an inaccessible target). Anger is instead aimed at the most similar target available. Now, the more intense the anger, the more likely it is that even relatively dissimilar stimulus persons may become aggression targets. Can you see in this the idea of a gradient of stimulus generalization? Displacement as stimulus generalization has been a very powerful hypothesis. Let's look at two experiments, one simple and one complex.

Two rats are placed in a small chamber with a grid floor to deliver electric shock. When shock is administered, one characteristic response of the rat (a response high in the animal's innate hierarchy) is to rear up on its hind legs, balanced by its tail. In the small enclosure, with both animals rearing and scrambling, they are likely to strike each other with their forepaws. As soon as this happens, shock is terminated, thus reinforcing the forepaw blows. Striking soon becomes a high probability response in the resultant (learned) hierarchies of the two animals. The rats ignore a small celluloid doll, about the size of a rat, placed in the cage with them. In the test of displacement, one rat is removed. Will the hitting response be generalized (displaced) to the substitute target? Yes, indeed. Displacement of the instrumental aggressive response does occur in this well-controlled experimental analogue (Miller, 1948b).

Miller and Bugelski (1948) had earlier tested the displacement hypothesis with humans. Their subjects were young men in an isolated camp (a Depression-era work camp, I believe). There was little to do after the day's hard labour; thus, the weekly 'bank night' at the movie theatre in town was eagerly anticipated. On one movie day, the investigators told the men that as a part of the camp educational program they would have to take a battery of tests. They weren't told at the outset that the tests would be extremely difficult and long, so long in fact that there would be no movie that night. Before the tests, a rating scale was handed out on attitudes toward two outgroups, Mexicans and Japanese. Then came the tests and the frustrating announcement. The evening ended, the men tight-lipped and sullen, with a second administration of the rating scale. 'After the frustration', wrote Miller and Bugelski, 'they attributed a smaller number of desirable traits and a larger number of undesirable traits to these foreigners who could not possibly have been to blame for the situation' (p. 441). Why? In the late 1930s when the experiment was conducted, the men would have known that anger directed toward the authorities in the work camp—even over unfair treatment—could bring down the heavy hand of discipline. What the men could do with the opportunity presented by the attitude scale was to displace their aggression to the target at hand—a group just similar

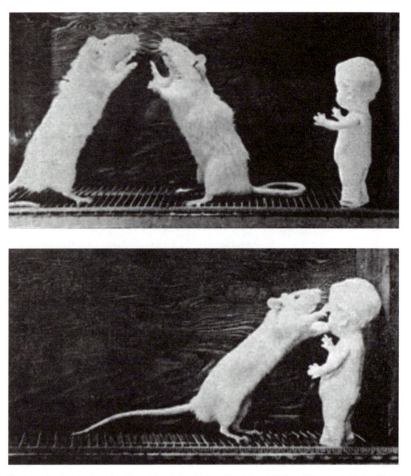

Top: Learned aggression toward another rat terminates shock and is reinforced. Bottom: Aggression is displaced to a substitute target. (From Miller, 1948b, p. 157, courtesy of the American Psychological Association)

enough to the frustrating camp authorities that stimulus generalization could do its work. Was this process of displacement conscious and deliberate? I doubt it.

The small sample of research I have given you in this chapter shows the elegance, care, and systematic approach of John Dollard, Neal Miller, and their collaborators and students. Virtually every major concept in S-R theory was examined by the theorists and their colleagues, beginning with elemental principles studied in animal experiments and extending to the human complexities of neurotic disorder and social behaviour. The most problematic aspect of the research of Freudian and Freudian-derived theories, reliance on the clinical study of persons, is not a question in evaluating S-R theory. Yes, many of the hypotheses came from Freud, but they were inventively translated into stimulus-response terms. Miller's long chapter in Volume 2 of *Psychology: A Study of a Science* (1959) testifies to the rigour behind the theory and the extent of its empirical support.

S-R Theory in Perspective

S-R theory is a whole generation and some behind us, but in our day it remains a theoretical system to contend with. Its concepts are the process concepts of the psychology of learning, thus making personality an integral part of one of the core areas of psychology. Psychoanalysis, even its liberalized neo-Freudian versions, and certainly Jung's analytic psychology, are all content theories with concepts strange to the ear of behaviourists and cognitive psychologists alike. It was a stunning achievement to take the clinical insights of Freudian theory and cast them in the process terms of Hullian learning theory. It took an exceptional breadth of view in the first place for Dollard, Miller, and other members of the Institute of Human Relations to immerse themselves in psychoanalysis and to learn it intimately. It would have taken the greatest determination and dedicated study to do that. Few psychologists of the era were so receptive, and very few universities provided the home for this kind of effort that the Yale Institute of Human Relations did.

Step by step, as the theory unfolded, its concepts were given detailed experimental scrutiny and applied to momentous questions of human behaviour, as in the studies making up the book *Frustration and Aggression*. Dollard and Miller provided a model of how to approach theory formulation and hypothesis testing. All of the learning theories of personality are outstanding in this respect, but these theorists came first and set the height of the bar.

S-R theory, though, did not want for critics. Dyed-in-the-wool behaviourists like B.F. Skinner, whose theory is next to come, found any inferences about covert processes that cannot be observed directly about as appealing as a mammoth spoonful of cod liver oil. To the radical behaviourist, S-R theory was badly mistaken. Inferences about drive states, even though tied to stimulus events evoking them and responses motivated by them, were entirely unnecessary. We could better, the extreme behaviourists said, study the observable (and manipulable) causes of behaviour and create the conditions for behaviour change. For them, personality, with its focus on the 'inner man', is not a scientifically useful way of thinking about the human individual. We'll see how Skinner developed this radical behaviourist approach and how far he took it.

Psychoanalytic critics found S-R theory oversimple in its account of neurosis, in its explanation of the afflictions of defences and symptoms, and in its characterization of human social behaviour. Remember, though, that psychoanalysts took the scientific validity of Freudian theory as a given and saw no reason to mess with it. In fact, Dollard and Miller gave many psychoanalytic concepts some good empirical ground to stand on (think of their analyses of repression, displacement, and conflict).

The emerging cognitive psychology also took aim at behaviour theory, likewise casting it—although for different reasons—as too simple. The cognitive psychologists were right. Even S-R theory, which took behaviourism a large step toward the new cognitive approach, stuck with behaviourism's traditional focus on discrete responses that might be linked in a complex chain but were still individual units of behaviour. Cognitive psychology liberalized psychology's approach to thinking, problem solving, memory, and perception. Learning came to focus on the acquisition and manipulation of concepts, not responses. As an illustration, consider the behaviourist and cognitive analyses of maze learning in the rat. Behaviourists claimed that the rat learns specific motor movements to guide it through correct alleys, avoiding the blind ones. Cognitive learning theorists showed convincingly that what the animal learns is a 'cognitive map', a conceptual representation of the maze (Dickinson, 1987; Olton, 1979). S-R theory was in many ways a bridge to cognitive psychology, but its approach was cumbersome and mechanical in its determined allegiance to the response. We want to acknowledge that Dollard and Miller certainly made room for implicit responses (in thinking, planning, and defending against anxiety), but they were still responses and not conceptual processes.

In the end, S-R theory emerged right at the transition from behaviourism to cognitive psychology, and it made significant contributions to the new developments. Dollard, Miller, and other Institute of Human Relations members, were not hidebound behaviourists but creative and imaginative ones. Their theory commands respect and can be read with profit for its insight into personality, neurosis, and psychotherapy. Anyone who wishes to learn how to conduct psychotherapy would do well to read the psychotherapy chapters in *Personality and Psychotherapy* and to pore over Dollard, Auld, and White's *Steps in Psychotherapy*.

SUMMARY

1. Dollard and Miller's stimulus-response theory grew out of the experimental psychology of learning, turned to the explanation of personality and complex social behaviour (social responses to frustration, for example). It found its hypotheses in psychoanalysis and in cultural anthropology, translating them into the S-R language of Clark Hull's theory of learning. Its intellectual home base was the Institute of Human Relations at Yale University, the members of which (experimental and social psychologists, sociologists, anthropologists, psychiatrists, lawyers) set out to find answers to major questions about human behaviour.

2. To understand S-R theory and the other learning theories that follow in the next three chapters requires a distinction between *content* and *process* theories. Psychoanalysis and its derivative theories are content theories. They propose structural concepts (id, ego, superego, self-dynamism, as examples) that are hypothetical components of personality, concepts that do not appear in other areas of psychology. These theories are concerned with the content of mental life, unconscious and conscious. Learning theories are concerned with process—how behaviour is acquired, maintained, and changed. Radical behaviourists (such as Skinner) focus only on observable behaviour; other learning theories of personality (S-R theory, the theories of Rotter and Bandura) make inferences to covert processes. Learning theories have profited from the clinical evidence of content theories on the nature of personality disorder, anxiety and defences against it, and details of child development.

3. The antecedents of S-R theory were Dollard's *Caste and Class in a Southern Town*, an analysis of black life in the deep South of the 1930s; *Frustration and Aggression*, by Dollard, et al.; and Dollard's *Social Learning and Imitation*. *Frustration and Aggression* introduced the approach, based on the assumption that understanding behaviour follows from knowing the principles and conditions of learning. *Frustration and Aggression* proposed that frustration is a significant condition for aggression. Many studies, animal and human, confirmed this basic relation. Dollard and Miller took the principles-conditions idea and the theory of learning to social psychology, studying imitation in the acquisition of social behaviour. In 1950, they turned to personality, disorders of personality, and the process (psychotherapy) by which normality is learned.

4. John Dollard was born in Wisconsin and received his BA from the University of Wisconsin. He was awarded the PhD in sociology by the University of Chicago in 1931, then received a fellowship to study psychoanalysis in Europe, where he underwent training analyses with notable psychoanalysts. He returned to join the Yale Institute of Human Relations as a research associate. He was an accomplished sociologist, anthropologist, psychologist, and psychoanalyst, an outstanding contributor to the research and theory building from which S-R theory emerged. Neal Miller, also born in Wisconsin, grew up in Washington, graduated from the University of Washington, received an MA from Stanford University and the PhD from Yale in 1935. He also studied psychoanalysis in Europe (a training analysis with Heinz Hartmann), and took up a position in the Yale Institute. His major contributions were in experimental psychology, testing fundamental assumptions

derived from the theory of learning and applying the concepts of the theory to such fundamental personality phenomena as conflict and displacement. From 1966 to 1985, he investigated the physiological basis of drives at Rockefeller University. Among other honours, he was named president of the American Psychological Association and was elected to the National Academy of Sciences.

5. S-R theory emphasizes four essential variables in learning: drive, cue, response, and reward. Drives motivate behaviour through the arousal of drive stimuli. Hunger, thirst, and sexual arousal are examples of *primary drives*. Many *secondary drives* are learned during early socialization—for example, approval, affection, and dependency. Fear is a notable secondary drive. Responses instrumental in reducing drive stimuli are reinforced and are likely to be repeated. This is the basis of reinforcement. Strong stimulation arouses both drive stimuli and internal responses. Instances of these are emotional responses, muscular contractions, and thoughts. There are *primary* and *secondary reinforcements*. Secondary reinforcements acquire their reinforcing ability through association with primary drive reduction in early childhood. Cues determine when and where responses will be made, and which responses will be chosen. Cues may be external stimuli or produced by the person (response-produced cues). Cue-producing responses direct much of our thinking and facilitate *generalization* and *discrimination*. Learning is systematic and involves the replacement of responses in an *initial hierarchy* by learned responses in a *resultant hierarchy*. *Learning dilemmas* cause nonreinforced responses to extinguish so that new responses may occur.

6. The basic concept in S-R theory is *habit*, a learned association between stimulus and response. The relation between drive and habit strength is multiplicative: R (response) $= D \times H$. This multiplicative relation is necessary since zero drive or zero habit strength do not produce responses.

7. Dollard and Miller followed Freud in using neurosis as a general model for personality processes. Thus, they adopted the *continuity assumption*. Psychotherapy affords a 'window to mental life', a way to look in on thinking, learning, unconscious processes, and child development. Necessarily, this must be done with neurotic patients.

8. Mowrer introduced the concept of the *neurotic paradox* for behaviour that is both self-perpetuating and self-defeating. The neurotic paradox is a particular problem for learning theories based on the reinforcement principle to explain. In neurosis, we have to account for: its persistence; how it generalizes; and why neurotic people can't use their minds to solve their problems.

9. The basis of neurosis lies in the association of fear with situational cues. Fear then may become attached to thoughts of the fearful situation and to emotional arousal to it. This is *secondary generalization*. Fear-reducing responses may include stopping thinking about the source of fear. This is S-R theory's analysis of repression.

10. Miller devised an experimental model of fear arousal and avoidance learning. A laboratory rat is shocked in one compartment of a two-compartment apparatus. It can escape through an open door and quickly does. Subsequently placed in this compartment without shock, it immediately escapes. In the next step, the animal must turn a small paddle wheel to escape the compartment; no shock is administered. It learns to do this to reduce *fear*. So, fear is a *learned drive*, fear reduction a *learned reinforcement*.

11. We can also teach animals or people (children) what *not* to do. This is *passive avoidance learning*. We train children to inhibit dangerous or hurtful responses. Passive avoidance learning can be very enduring if punishment is strong, and it can block normal behaviour. Dollard and Miller wrote that fear is important 'because it can be so strong, because it can be attached to new cues so easily through learning, and because it is the motivation that produces the inhibiting responses in most conflicts.'

12. Dollard and Miller presented a theory of psychological conflict, based on psychoanalytic hypotheses and studied experimentally. The most significant conflicts in neurosis are between fear and approach motivation (approach–avoidance) and between feared alternatives (avoidance–avoidance). Approach–avoidance conflict sufferers are unable to approach and vacillate in misery at a distance from the desired and feared goal. Faced with avoidance–avoidance alternatives, the person vacillates at a point equidistant from each feared possibility.

13. In Dollard and Miller's approach–avoidance conflict model there are four assumptions: (1) the tendency to approach a goal increases with nearness to it (gradient of approach); (2) the tendency to avoid a feared goal increases with nearness (gradient of avoidance); (3)

the gradient of avoidance is *steeper* than the gradient of approach; (4) increasing motivation to approach will increase conflict and misery.

14. Normal and neurotic personalities start early in life. Childhood learning is difficult, both for helpless and dependent infants and for parents who lack knowledge and skill. We don't have a science of childrearing that can be taught readily to parents. It is important to appreciate the degree to which learning in early childhood is challenging. Small children have major things to learn under conditions of strong drive and the absence of language. Essential generalization and discrimination are thus much harder. Four child-training situations are critical for personality development:

(1) The *feeding situation*. Hunger is a strong drive, and parents may not be alert to the intensity their infant's experience. Leaving an infant alone to 'cry itself out' is bad practice. Weaning presents difficulties for parents and infants. This is a critical period for socialization, and poor training can have disastrous and lasting consequences.

(2) *Cleanliness training*. Freud was correct in pointing out that the effects of cleanliness training go far beyond the learning of toilet habits. Cultural attitudes of revulsion tend to make parents impatient and angry. It is not surprising that frustrated and angry parents can create a power struggle and make their small children stubborn and defiant.

(3) *Early sex training*. Sexual exploration and sexual growing up often occur in a family atmosphere of secrecy. Labelling of drive arousal is difficult, emotional intensity may be high, and embarrassment and guilt may be inculcated by moralistic parents.

(4) *Anger management training*. Children will become angry, and parents are often intolerant of angry displays, creating fear and resentment. Correct labelling of feelings, drives, and thoughts is important, but parents sometimes teach their children to mislabel. Cognitive distortions and defences such as repression may be the result. Dollard and Miller singled out these four childrearing situations because they contain the seeds of problems that may appear in adult neurosis. It is essential to remember that to understand the personality development of children we need to know about the conditions of learning.

15. A significant feature of S-R theory is the amount of experimental and field research on its hypotheses. These are some examples:

- a major sociological study of racial discrimination in the US South
- experimental studies of the role of imitation in social learning
- the effects of frustration on aggression
- experimental studies of learnable drives, especially fear
- experimental tests of conflict theory assumptions
- establishing gradients of approach and avoidance, and a steeper avoidance gradient
- animal and human studies of frustration-induced displacement of aggression

16. In perspective, S-R theory is exemplary. It uses process concepts from the psychology of learning, casting the clinical observations of psychoanalysis in process terms. Concepts of the theory were examined in detail in experimental studies. It did have its critics. Radical behaviourists objected that Dollard and Miller made inferences to unobservable events and didn't stick to observable behaviour. Psychoanalysts thought it too simple in its analysis of neurosis, defences and symptoms, and social behaviour. Cognitive psychology thought the basic unit of S-R theory—the habit—too discrete and mechanical. The theory does not deal well with cognitive processes and concepts. S-R theory was a bridge to modern cognitive psychology and made significant contributions. Its analysis of psychotherapy is rich with ideas on how to approach and treat neurotic patients, and how their relearning proceeds.

TO TEST YOUR UNDERSTANDING

1. What do you think of Dollard and Miller's adoption of psychoanalytic concepts (for example, anxiety, defence mechanisms, displacement) and the clinical acumen of psychoanalytic theory as the basis for a learning theory account of personality and personality disorder? Do you see any significance in the fact that they chose process concepts from psychoanalysis? Did this choice advance S-R theory or hinder it?

2. A fundamental part of S-R theory is its analysis of drive and drive reduction as the basis of motivation and the fundamental mechanism of reinforcement. What are the possible flaws in the notion that all learning occurs because of the sudden reduction of drive stimuli? What are the strengths? What might contemporary cognitive theorists have to say about it?

3. Evaluate the frustration–aggression hypothesis. To the S-R theorist, it was *the* account of aggression. Do you think that all aggression has frustration as its antecedent? What other causes of aggression might there be? How does the S-R theorist explain the absence of observable aggression when frustration is known to have occurred?

4. Do you think the overall research strategy of Dollard and Miller was a fruitful one? What do you think of the use of animal experiments to test fundamental hypotheses of the theory? Did Dollard and Miller make a convincing case for the application of experimental findings from the laboratory to complex human behaviour?

CHAPTER THIRTEEN

Learning Theories of Personality: The Radical Behaviourism of B.F. Skinner

Introduction

In the early years of the twentieth century, psychology was the study of conscious experience. Since consciousness is private, psychologists from the time of Wundt in the last years of the nineteenth century turned to introspection to gain access to the mind. Their psychological method to study consciousness was to use trained subjects (observers) who described their own experience to sensory stimulation. Wundt also did this experimentally. Experimental participants were instructed to release a key on presentation of a light. Then, in a second condition, they had two keys, releasing one to a red light, the other to a green one. Wundt compared the reaction times of the two conditions and took the difference as the time required to make decisions about perceptual differences. This was 'mental chronometry', and it especially appealed to Wundt as an avenue to the speed of impulses within the central nervous system in attending, discriminating, and synthesizing. It put a clock on the activities of mind.

Wundt was circumspect in his use of introspection, recognizing as he did the subjectivity of the method. His student, Edward Bradford Titchener, later a professor at Cornell University, saw introspection grandly, as the Appian Way to all the elemental sensations, feelings, and images of which the human mind is capable, a kind of 'mental chemistry'. Titchener was bold and imaginative, no bean counter, but when he got through he had toted up 46,708 possible sensory experiences. Where could you go from there? His observers reported on sensory features from which the elements of mind could be derived—quality, intensity, clearness, and duration. As an example, these trained introspectionists would give their 'internal perceptions' of all the yellows that could be discriminated from each other. The goal was to analyze the structure of the generalized human mind, the mind of the species as Wundt had taught, finding the essence of mental experience according to principles of association, laws of colour mixture, and the like. To Titchener, this *was* psychology, and he called it *structuralism*.

No doubt you can immediately see what Titchener (and, to a lesser degree, Wundt) did not: since personal experience is private, the results produced by the observers, however trained, had a severe flaw. How could we confirm that what one of these

John B. Watson (Underwood and Underwood/CORBIS)

introspecting people reported was what actually occurred in his sensory processing? How could we be sure that the relation between a physical stimulus event and its psychological effect was usefully and accurately characterized by the observer?

Enter on this scientific scene a rebel, a man who regarded structuralism as sterile and fundamentally nonscientific. This was John B. Watson, a physiological psychologist and student of animal behaviour. At the start of his career, as a young professor at The John Hopkins University, he had to abandon his research in animal learning because the university could not provide him with space for his labs. He wouldn't have thought this propitious at the time, but it surely was. There was a foundling home and hospital nearby, and he turned to the study of learning and development in children. He was forced into a momentous decision, and it made him famous. Generations of children—not to mention psychologists—were influenced by his approach.

Watson was strongly impressed by Ivan Pavlov's discovery of the principles of classical conditioning, and he began to apply them to children's acquisition of behaviour. He wasn't a particularly good experimenter with children, being a little too glib and a little too careless with the niceties of experimental controls. But he sure could popularize ideas, and an entire school of psychology, behaviourism, grew from his writing to become the school that would dominate psychology for the next half-century. Watson made behaviourism accessible, writing articles for the *Ladies Home Journal* on child care, and set out behaviourism's scientifically proven (as he insisted) plan for childrearing in a widely read book, *Psychological Care of Infant and Child* (1928). He was, in behaviourism's heyday, its Dr Spock. How should children be raised? Not on mother love, as Watson warned:

> There is a sensible way of treating children. Treat them as though they were young adults. Dress them, bathe them with care and circumspection. Let your behavior always be objective and kindly firm. Never hug and kiss them, never let them sit in your lap. If you must, kiss them once on the forehead when you say goodnight. Shake hands with them in the morning (Watson, 1928, pp. 81–2).

Structuralism was an abomination, and to counter it Watson set out a credo for the scientific study of behaviour that banished the study of mind as unobservable and hence not a fit subject for psychological science to tackle. It was a strict and uncompromising declaration of independence from the psychology of Titchener. Instead of structuralism's self-limiting goal—to describe the contents of mind—the bold ambition of Watson's new psychology was to predict and control behaviour. We see behaviourism's principles in Watson's scientific credo for psychology:

> Psychology as the behaviorist views it is a purely objective natural science. Its theoretical goal is the prediction and control of behavior. Introspection forms no essential part of its methods, nor is the scientific value of its data dependent upon the readiness with which they lend themselves to interpretation in terms of consciousness. The

behaviorist, in his attempts to get a unitary scheme of animal response, recognizes no dividing line between man and brute. The behavior of man, with all its refinement and complexity, forms only a part of the behaviorist's total scheme of investigation (Watson, 1913, p. 158).

Watson was absolutely taken by Pavlovian conditioning, which he saw as the essential process in learning. If you understand how conditioning works and can manipulate its few variables, and if you can exercise control over the environment, any human behaviour is at your command. Apart from a very small innate repertoire, the human being is born a *tabula rasa*; experience—classical Pavlovian conditioning—writes everything, even modifying the reflexive to fit the dictates of the environment. He famously boasted:

> Give me a dozen healthy infants, well-formed, and my own specified world to bring them up in and I'll guarantee to take any one at random and train him to become any type of specialist I might select—doctor, lawyer, merchant-chief and yes, even beggar-man and thief, regardless of his talents, penchants, tendencies, abilities, vocations, and race of his ancestors (Watson, 1970, p. 104).

Perspective 13.1 The Conditioning of Little Albert

Watson badly needed an experiment to give his new behaviourism the credential it needed and to confirm that classical conditioning was the elemental basis of human learning. Demonstrating the acquisition of a 'conditioned emotional reaction' in a small child would do both. Little Albert would have the great honour of providing the evidence that behaviourism and the process of classical conditioning were dead right. He was the eleven-month-old son of a wet nurse in the foundling hospital, a 'stolid and phlegmatic' infant as Watson described him. Watson and his graduate student (and, later, wife) Rosalie Rayner set out to show how fear (there are but two inborn fears, he argued; one is of sudden loud sounds, the other loss of support) could become attached to neutral stimuli.

If infants are innately fearful of loud sounds and of being dropped, all we have to do to link one of the built-in fears (of loud sounds; better than dropping babies) to an environmental stimulus is to (1) show that the stimulus (a white rat), to which the infant will become fearful, does not initially evoke fear, and (2) produce the startling noise (hammer struck on a steel bar behind the infant's head) when the stimulus is presented. In short order, the innocent novel stimulus will be associated with the frightening clang. *Conditioned fear* to the white rat will be the result.

And so it was. In seven trials, Albert became distinctly afraid of the white rat. On the first trial, wrote Watson and Rayner, he 'jumped violently and fell forward, burying his face in the mattress' (1920, p. 4). Six trials later, 'The instant the rat was shown the baby began to cry. Almost instantly he turned sharply to the left, fell over on his left side, raised himself on all fours and began to crawl away so rapidly that he was caught with difficulty before reaching the edge of the table' (p. 5). Albert also showed fear, somewhat weaker, to a rabbit, a fur coat, and Watson in a Santa Claus mask. These demonstrated generalization.

What happened to Little Albert with his conditioned fur phobia? He was given back to his mother, fears and all, despite Watson's brash pronouncement on the durability of emotional conditioning. 'There is good evidence to show', he wrote much later, 'that such early built in fears last throughout the lifetime of the individual' (1928, p. 53). This was a bit of unwarranted braggadocio: it was not a great experiment, and over the years it has been severely criticized for methodological inadequacies and failure to replicate (Harris, 1979; Hilgard & Marquis, 1940; Samelson, 1980).

B.F. Skinner admired Watson, and we can place him directly in Watson's lineage except in one respect. Skinner saw classical conditioning as inconsequential beside the potent effects of the conditioning he described as 'operant'. At first captivated by Watsonian behaviourism and by Pavlov, Skinner came to reject **respondent conditioning**★ as basically limited and uninteresting. Little Albert may have been conditioned to fear furry animals and white beards, but there were more significant things in the lives of organisms for behaviourism to sink its teeth into. About Pavlovian conditioning, Skinner wrote in mid-career, 'I could not . . . move without a jolt from salivary reflexes to the important business of the organism in everyday life' (1959, p. 362). It is **operant conditioning**★ that reveals the potential and flexibility in *The Behavior of Organisms*, the title of his 1938 book.

If classical conditioning left him cold, he wholeheartedly endorsed Watson's principles of behaviourism, and formulated his own version of them, seen in Table 13.1. His behaviouristic view of human nature was unabashedly materialistic in its claim that humans, psychologically no less than physically, are lawfully regulated and mechanistic. He went on: human behaviour is both powerfully liberated and constrained by physiology, but because operant conditioning plays such a significant role it makes strategic and practical sense to study the variables of conditioning experimentally and to manipulate them intelligently in human affairs. Behaviour occurs in an environment, but the environment doesn't take sides. It is neutral. By neutrality, Skinner meant that it is organisms acting *on* the environment and the consequences those actions produce that determine which responses will be learned and which will be abandoned or suppressed. When we consider the whole of what we mean by 'environment'—the people, animals, objects that surround us, it cannot be that the environment chooses our behaviour. As he said, the environment 'does not push or pull, it *selects*' (Skinner, 1971, p. 25), and it does so by the consequences that greet action. We would make a serious mistake to regard the behaviourist's environment as some huge, amorphous hand behind the curtain, manipulating our behaviour as if we were puppets on strings.

To show the enormous potential of operant conditioning, Skinner set out to train a lab rat (christened Pliny the Elder, after the first-century Roman author, by students at the University of Minnesota, where he then taught) to pick up marbles and drop them in a chute for food, even saving them when it wasn't hungry to be cashed in later.

I decided to teach a rat to spend money. Poker chips [in a famous experiment, chimpanzees had been trained to work for poker chips, which they could spend in a

Table 13.1 Skinner's Behaviouristic Principles for Psychology

1. The human being is a complex machine.
2. Human behaviour is the product of learning.
3. The environment is neutral. It does not produce behaviour.
4. Behaviour is not immutable; it can change at any time in life.

Chimpomat for bananas and peanuts] would be hard to handle, and I chose glass marbles instead. The rat was to release a marble from a rack by pulling a chain, pick the marble up, carry it across the cage, and drop it into a tube standing about two inches above the floor. I could not, of course, wait for this complex sequence to appear before reinforcing it. I had to construct it step by step through 'successive approximation', each step being something the rat would do at the time so that it could be reinforced.

I began with a platform about a foot square. A bottomless wire cage was held far enough above it to permit a marble to roll off any edge. As the marble fell, it tripped a switch that operated a food dispenser in a corner of the cage. A number of marbles were put on the floor and any move the rat made that knocked one off the edge was reinforced. Moves of various kinds were strengthened. I then put a rim on three sides of the floor and the rat learned to push the marbles off the free edge, eventually quite quickly. A marble had meanwhile become a conditioned reinforcer, and when I added a rack and chain to the roof of the cage, the rat quickly learned to release a marble by pulling the chain (Skinner, 1979, p. 196).

Would your intelligence be insulted if I suggested that this is exactly the way your accomplishments develop—shaped by reinforcing consequences? Skinner didn't think this should be demeaning; it's just the way behaviour is controlled. Of course there were many whose image of Skinner's behaviourism was of automatons marching life's paces to the drumbeat of environmental control—a view, they said, that mocks human choice, freedom, and dignity. Skinner was an outspoken and undeviating determinist, but he wasn't blind to the issue. He had a ready reply in the significant control that people exercise over their own behaviour. One of the chapters in his book, *Science and Human Behavior* (1953), was titled 'Self Control'. In it, he argued that the individual person 'controls himself precisely as he would control the behavior of anyone else—through the manipulation of variables of which behavior is a function' (p. 228). Good behaviouristic language this, simply turned inward. He saw that inner states—forbidden territory to the behaviourist—could be scientifically useful. He wrote: 'What a person feels is a product of the contingencies of which his future behavior will also be a function, and there is therefore a useful connection between feelings and behavior. It would be foolish to rule out the knowledge a person has of his current condition . . . but we can nevertheless predict behavior more accurately if we have direct knowledge about the history to which feelings are to be traced' (Skinner, 1974, p. 230).

Behaviourism wouldn't be behaviourism without its familial ties to half a dozen other *isms*: associationism, functionalism, pragmatism, environmentalism, materialism, experimentalism. These were Skinner's *isms*, and in no small part he gained fame and popularity because his *isms* were our *isms*. *Associationism* provided the conceptual basis for the connection of experiences. The great animal behaviourist Edward L. Thorndike, whose studies of cats learning to escape from a 'puzzle box' gave behaviourism its starting push, used the term 'connectionism'—nice and explicit, but associationism had the hoary tradition of British and Scottish philosophers Locke, Hume, and the Mills on its side and won out. This was a happy idea for behaviourists. It provided the principle, contiguity, by which stimuli and responses are linked: occurring together, responses become associated with the stimuli present when they are made.

Associationism got rid of mentalisms and simplified the conception of mind. Its popular appeal came with the demystification of learning, which could now be seen to grow easily from elemental first steps to complex achievements. *Functionalism* in psychology had an eminent practicality in its emphasis on the ways organisms adapt to their environments, and nowhere was it better expressed than in the pragmatism of William James, which took as its data the usefulness or workability of ideas. *Pragmatism*, as historian Henry Steele Commager declared in his summing up of the influences on *The American Mind*, 'was as practical as the patent office' (1950, p. 95). Behaviourism's association with functionalism and pragmatism was parental. Watson, admired by Skinner, had taken his PhD with James Rowland Angell at Chicago. Angell had studied with William James at Harvard. Taken to heart, *environmentalism* flatly rejected the self, the person each of us thought resided within us, but in recompense it held out the prospect of bringing things we wanted to change—the problem behaviour of a child, for example—to heel. While the mechanistic stance of the *materialism* of mind was not very flattering and could seem a denial of human depth, in the approach of the behaviourists it promised that anyone could learn anything by the application of some simple principles. *Experimentalism*, of course, was an old American ideal.

Behaviourism did scare some people off, the conservative mostly. To them, it was too experimental, and in branding the inner person an idolatrous deceit it denied the God within us and became a radical and intolerable doctrine. Most, though, saw the opportunity and the optimism. Are elementary school classrooms routinized, inefficient, and boring? Skinner had an answer in programmed instruction, using simple teaching machines to present lessons in easy, incremental steps, each rewarded, at the individual child's own pace. Are institutions for the developmentally disabled and for long-term psychiatric patients insensitive to individual patients and mainly custodial? In their rigidity, do they stifle improvement and growth? Skinnerians developed the token economy, which uses operant methods to shape desirable behaviour, with patients earning tokens that could be redeemed for privileges or spent in the hospital store. Is psychotherapy unduly long, exacting, painful, and uncertain? Operant methods, one form of behaviour modification, are specifically directed at ridding patients of the troubling symptoms they came to psychotherapy for. They do so with anxiety symptoms in a fraction of the time that intensive psychotherapy requires at success rates that may be 80 per cent or better.

B.F. Skinner: Personal History

Burrhus Frederic Skinner was born in March 1904, in the northeastern Pennsylvania railway town of Susquehanna. His parents were highly intelligent and accomplished. His father was lawyer who, without a college education, had spent a year in law school and passed his bar exam. His mother was 'bright and beautiful' with many talents; she also imbued her son with strict rectitude. 'I was taught to fear God, the police, and what people will think. As a result, I usually do what I have to do with no great struggle' (Skinner, 1967, p. 407). Freudians have an easier time tracing the source of present behaviour in personal history than behaviourists. They can draw on a great store of psychoanalytic concepts to guide the search toward the deep roots of neurosis—or creativity—and in the end both outcomes have their origin in the vicissitudes of the id. To follow back the strands of a learning history to its beginnings—to discover the earliest

B.F. Skinner (© Bettmann/CORBIS)

shaping of a behaviourist by the behaviourist's own principles—is a formidable task (remember Dollard and Miller's cautionary words). We can only guess at the conditions under which learning occurred, and we cannot be sure that significant experiences have not been forgotten or that their recall preserves them in the original.

Skinner was smart and talented as a boy, a good student, both literary and musical, but we can point to only a few things that might have presaged his future greatness as a psychologist. An interest in animals, perhaps, and an astonishing mechanical curiosity and aptitude that would be expressed in the design of experimental apparatus like the famous Skinner box.

> I was always building things. I built roller-skate scooters, steerable wagons, sleds, and rafts to be poled about on shallow ponds. I made see-saws, merry-go-rounds, and slides. I made slingshots, bows and arrows, blow guns and water pistols from lengths of bamboo, and from a discarded water boiler a steam cannon with which I could shoot plugs of potato and carrot over the houses of our neighbors. I made tops, diabolos, model airplanes driven by twisted rubber bands, box kites, and tin propellers which could be sent high into the air with a spool-and-string spinner. I tried again and again to make a glider in which I myself might fly. I invented things, some of them in the spirit of the outrageous contraptions in the cartoons which Rube Goldberg was publishing in [the] *Philadelphia Inquirer* (to which my father, as a good Republican, subscribed). For example, a friend and I used to gather elderberries and sell them from door to door, and I built a flotation system which separated ripe from green berries. I worked for years on the design of a perpetual motion machine. (It did not work.) (1967, p. 388)

Despite the deviltry in his inventive exploits, which might seem to have left little room for intellectual pursuits, Skinner wrote poetry ('That Pessimistic Fellow', published when he was ten in the *Lone Scout* magazine), and a morality play and a novel, which were probably well left unpublished. He played piano and the saxophone in his high school dance band.

At eighteen, he was admitted to Hamilton College, where he had some exposure to biology in a course taught by an ex-student of Wundt, but majored in English. The deviltry found new expression in college writing—in parodies and caricatures of professors—and he wrote for the college newspaper, contributing as well to the literary and humour magazines. (For the humour magazine, he adopted the pseudonym Sir Burrhus de Beerus.) For all of that, he was also dedicated and serious. At the end of his third year, he took a summer workshop in writing, taught by, among others, Robert Frost, who told him, 'You are worth twice anyone else I have seen in prose this year' (Skinner, 1976, p. 249). On graduation, he determined to become a writer, settling in to an attic room in his parents' house to begin his new career. But it was, he wrote nearly fifty years later, his 'Dark Year', filled with loneliness and depression. And he couldn't write: 'The truth was, I had no reason to write anything. I had nothing to say, and nothing about my life was making any change in that condition' (1976, p. 264). Interludes in Greenwich Village and in Europe didn't help.

After reading philosopher Bertrand Russell on Watson (Russell thought behaviourism worth pursuing) and H.G. Wells on Pavlov, Skinner was provoked to read Watson and Pavlov. He was, almost at once, committed to becoming a behaviourist. He applied to Harvard for graduate study in psychology and was accepted in 1928. Harvard had no behaviouristic sympathies whatsoever; his adviser was an experimental biologist, and his

PhD thesis in 1931 was on the concept of the reflex. He was good, he was confident, and when one of the pillars of the psychology department sharply criticized his thesis, he stuck to his guns. Harvard awarded him a postdoctoral fellowship, and he spent five years working in his adviser's laboratory, three of them as a junior fellow, a prestigious appointment. He was fortunate, in the depths of the Depression, to get a job as assistant professor at the University of Minnesota, where he remained for nine years. He went to Indiana University as the chair of the department of psychology, and then returned to Harvard as professor.

Skinner staked out his position early and was soon recognized as a formidable—in fact, the foremost—behaviourist. His 1938 book, *The Behavior of Organisms*, gained him a loyal following among behaviouristic colleagues and students. He wrote a utopian novel, *Walden Two* (1948), about a behaviourally engineered world, that captured popular attention. A review in the *Chicago Sunday Times* said admiringly, '*Walden Two* is not a magic mountain, but it is a sunlit hill with an extensive view in many directions' (Skinner, 1979, p. 346). Others, though, saw in 'behavioural engineering' and especially in Skinner's liberal use of the word 'control' a calculated attack on the American ideals of freedom and independence. An editorial in *Life* magazine called *Walden Two* 'a slur upon a name, a corruption of an impulse'. The only freedom to be found in the novel's utopia, it said, 'is the freedom of those Pavlovian dogs which are free to foam at the mouth whenever the "dinner bell" invites them to a nonforthcoming meal' (Skinner, 1979, pp. 347–8). Skinner was quite aware of the danger. 'I knew the word was troublesome,' he wrote. 'Why not soften it to "affect" or "influence"? But I was a determinist, and control meant control, and no other word would do' (1979, p. 345).

One sure thing that set the critics to snarling and snapping was Skinner's belief that all of daily life should be conducted by observing learning principles, no less than laboratory experiments. Children, he thought, could be much more surely brought up to be happy and productive by the disciplined nurture of behaviour theory in action. Baby care could also be engineered to remove much of the drudgery. Skinner devised a 'baby tender' for his second child, a fully-enclosed, environmentally-controlled crib. With no small pride, he wrote about it in *The Shaping of a Behaviorist*.

> When Debbie came home, she went directly into this comfortable space and began to enjoy its advantages. She wore only a diaper. Completely free to move about, she was soon pushing up, rolling over, and crawling. She breathed warm, moist, filtered air, and her skin was never waterlogged with sweat or urine. Loud noises were muffled (though we could hear her from any part of the house), and a curtain pulled over the window shielded her from bright light when she was sleeping (1979, p. 276).

The *Life* editorial writer referred to 'the menace of the mechanical baby tender', and other critics alleged that Debbie would undoubtedly succumb to psychosis (she turned out to be a happy, healthy child and a well-adjusted adult).

After *The Behavior of Organisms* Skinner produced a number of books over the next forty-five years, among them *Science and Human Behavior* (1953), *Verbal Behavior*, (1957), *Schedules of Reinforcement* (with Ferster, 1957), *The Technology of Teaching* (1968), and *Contingencies of Reinforcement* (1969). In 1971, he published *Beyond Freedom and Dignity*, a controversial psychological philosophy in which he argued persuasively for a technology of behaviour to replace our cherished and timeworn notion of an inner, controlling, autonomous person.

It is in the nature of an experimental analysis of human behaviour that it should strip away the functions previously assigned to autonomous man and transfer them one by one to the controlling environment. The analysis leaves less and less for autonomous man to do. But what about man himself? Is there not something about a person which is more than a living body? Unless something called a self survives, how can we speak of self-knowledge or self-control? To whom is the injunction 'know thyself' addressed? . . . A self is a repertoire of behaviour appropriate to a given set of contingencies. . . . The identity conferred upon a self arises from the contingencies responsible for behaviour. . . . The picture which emerges from a scientific analysis is not of a body with a person inside, but of a body which *is* a person in the sense that it displays a complex repertoire of behaviour (1971, pp. 198–9).

Late in his career, Skinner and a co-author wrote *Enjoy Old Age: Living Fully in Your Later Years* (Skinner and Vaughan, 1983). In the same year, there was a general prescription, 'Intellectual self-management in old age', full of practical suggestions on what to do about such failings as forgetting, declining creativity, and the depression that comes with loss of friends. All the remedies have as their basis the development of new behavioural repertoires. Those who retire from teaching, for example, lose colleagues to challenge their thinking and lose their audiences. But one *can* find other complex and interesting old people, and regular afternoons or evenings can be devoted to good talk, even programmed for it. Although Western culture does not generously reinforce the elderly, they themselves can create many reinforcing contingencies.

There were other books and many an article in a long career, beautiful experimental articles, and lots of honours: the Distinguished Scientific Contribution Award of the American Psychological Association, membership in the National Academy of Sciences, and the President's Medal of Science. But not the presidency of the American Psychological Association. Was he too much the behaviourist, too straight-from-the-shoulder, too controversial? Skinner died in 1990 at the age of eighty-six, just days after the American Psychological Association had honoured him again with an award for Outstanding Lifetime Contribution to Psychology. To Ernest Hilgard, himself an outstanding psychologist, Skinner was nothing less than a hero (1987, pp. 196–7).

Emphases

The Control of Behaviour

The very first point to be made about Skinner's approach is that behaviour—human and other animal (we *are* animals, of course)—derives from environmental events that can be controlled. He argued that it is better to control behaviour rationally and intelligently than to deceive ourselves into believing that control is an evil thing. As he said, 'In its search for internal explanation, supported by the false sense of cause associated with feelings and introspective observations, mentalism has obscured the environmental antecedents which would have led to a much more effective analysis' (1974, p. 182). There are strong popular prejudices against the very idea of control of human behaviour, and it is commonly argued that it is better to be permissive, allowing children, for example, to make choices for themselves. But, as Skinner said, permissiveness is not a policy. It is the abandonment of policy, and its apparent advantages are illusory. To turn our backs on control is to leave it not in the hands of the person him- or herself, but to other parts of the social and nonsocial environments.

Control of Individual Behaviour

We demonstrate our scientific understanding of behaviour with our ability to bring it under control. Further, Skinner argued, we *really* demonstrate the prowess of psychological science when we bring the behaviour of *individuals* under the control of reinforcing stimuli. He wanted to see our understanding demonstrated in the individual case by changing situational or stimulus variables and reinforcing consequences to bring complex behaviour under stimulus control, and he dismissed probabilistic laws derived from groups of subjects. So, surprisingly, general laws (which we all seek) are tested and affirmed by the study of the *individual*. He wanted 'general applicability', established by this most rigorous application of control.

Functional Analysis

Skinner's beliefs about psychological science are captured by the term **functional analysis**★, the linking of behaviour to its antecedents, the establishment of cause-and-effect relationships. When we can link responses to their environmental causes—and especially when we can do that with the individual—we have a wholly sufficient psychological and scientific explanation and do not need to invoke internal (and unobservable) states. As Skinner said, 'The objection to the inner workings of the mind is not that they are not open to inspection but that they have stood in the way of the inspection of more important things' (1974, p. 182). Internal states—feelings and thoughts—exist, of course, but they are not explanatory. They are instead '*collateral products* of our genetic and environmental histories. They have no explanatory force' (Skinner, 1975, p. 43).

Skinner's 'Theory' Is Not a Theory

There is something slightly awkward we must do before we go further. We will talk about 'Skinner's theory', but simply as a convenience, a peg on which to hang his approach to behaviour and to personality. Let's try to keep this in mind. Skinner eschewed theory, arguing that theories are unnecessary. His 1950 article in the *Psychological Review*, 'Are theories of learning necessary?', made the point. Theory for him was purely descriptive. As Holland (1992) wrote, 'the goal of Skinner's science is the control, prediction, and interpretation of behavior. . . . When the description of the controlling functional relationship is complete, control is obtained and the goal of science is met' (p. 665).

What Is Personality?

We have to abandon almost all of what we have learned in the study of personality so far to appreciate Skinner's view. No more egos, superegos, selves, dynamisms, needs. No

"Well, you don't look like an experimental psychologist to me."

repression, and no anxiety to mobilize it. Skinner did recognize that some human behaviour is variable and modifiable while some is relatively consistent and unchanging. Our genetic endowments will make some behaviours difficult or impossible to alter, but a science of behaviour does not have to concern itself directly with them. A science of behaviour earns its spurs by predicting and controlling modifiable responses.

'Personality' refers to the *behavioural attributes* of a person. We may say that an individual is angry, and Skinner would do so. He did not, as other personality theorists, have in mind the individual's internal state, but the person's observable actions—muscles clenched, fierce disapproving expression, hostile verbal behaviour. We will find consistency in a person's behaviour—consistency, that bread and butter of personality theory—but we will not try to deal with it by inventing processes within the person. Consistent behaviour across many situations derives from genetic makeup and from environmental contingencies that reinforce and maintain learned (or what he called 'operant') responses. We might try to show off a behavioural science version of personality by constructing an operant history of significant behaviour, following the lead of traditional personality theorists. It will not be an easy job, as we know, to find how a person's behaviour has been shaped by experience. The reinforcement history may be buried and difficult to retrieve. We'll be better scientists in Skinner's view if we demonstrate that we can deal with behavioural attributes by modifying problem behaviour, for example, or by changing behaviour through intelligent control to more social and useful forms.

The Major Concepts of Skinnerian Behaviourism

Respondent and Operant Conditioning

When we think of conditioning, it is **Pavlovian★** or **classical conditioning★** we have in mind. A tone (Pavlov liked to use the tick of a metronome or the sound of water burbling) is closely followed by food in the mouth. The dog salivates to the food and presently, with repeated trials, to the tone. The events are **conditioned stimulus★** (tone), **unconditioned stimulus★** (food), **unconditioned response★** (the reflex salivation to food in the mouth), and **conditioned response★** (salivation to the conditioned stimulus). Skinner called this learning paradigm *Type S conditioning*, because reinforcement is correlated with the stimuli that produce it. The behaviour conditioned in this way is *respondent behaviour* because, in Skinner's view, it is elicited by and under the control of stimuli. We saw earlier his flat dismissal of elicited respondents as largely insignificant in the daily business of organisms. What matters to rats, pigeons, and people is the behaviour they emit, behaviour that results in reinforcing consequences. This is *Type R conditioning* because of the link between response and reinforcement. It is also *operant conditioning* because responses operate on the environment to produce reinforcing events.

It's essential to recognize that the operant is an emitted response not under the control of specific stimuli. The bar that the rat presses to get a pellet of food is not the specific stimulus that controls its behaviour. The response of pressing the bar produces the reward and comes under the control of the reinforcement. In this sense, operant conditioning is *instrumental conditioning* because responses are the instrument causing reinforcement to occur. So, another important point: Skinner started with an already behaving organism. As that organism acts within its environment, its actions cause consequences to follow, reinforcing stimuli that increase the probability of the responses that produced them. Operant behaviour is the real business of life, in the laboratory and without.

Shaping

Pliny was a very accomplished rat, but he didn't get that way because he was a rodent genius, grasping at once the connection between dropping marbles down the chute and getting fed. A remarkable achievement came about through **successive approximation★**, or **shaping★**, rewarding each acquisition in small steps. We choose responses that are very likely to occur, as Skinner would say of Pliny's training, rewarding them and gradually stepping up the requirements. How do we teach young children to read? With Shakespeare sonnets or with simple words accompanied by illustrative pictures—'See Jane jump. Jump, Jane, jump'?

But that's Pliny and small children. What about real people in real people situations? Is their behaviour controlled by reinforcing consequences? Is their behaviour shaped? Verplanck gave his students in an experimental psychology course the task of instrumentally conditioning novel behaviour in wholly uninitiated and naive volunteers. He started with simple motor responses.

> After finding a fellow student who was willing to be a subject, the experimenter [a member of the experimental psychology class] instructed him as follows: 'Your job is to work for points. You get a point every time I tap the table with my pencil. As soon as you get a point, record it on your sheet of paper. Keep track of your own points.' With these instructions, it seemed likely that a tap, a 'point', would prove to be a reinforcing stimulus. The method worked very well. Indeed, the experimenters were now able to condition a wide variety of simple motor behaviours, such as slapping the ankle, tapping the chin, raising an arm, picking up a fountain pen, and so on. They were further able to differentiate out, or shape, more complex parts of behaviour, and then to manipulate them as responses. The data they obtained included the results of the manipulation of many of the variables whose effects were familiar in operant conditioning of rats and pigeons. Despite the fact that the experiments were carried out in a variety of situations, the experimenters were able to obtain graphical functions that could not be distinguished from functions obtained on the rat or the pigeon in a Skinner box. . . . [Now the experimenters were given the task of shaping opinion statements.] The results of these experiments were unequivocal. In the first experiment, on opinion statements, every one of the 23 subjects showed a higher rate of giving opinion statements during the 10-minute period when the experimenter reinforced each of them by agreeing with it, or by repeating it back to him in paraphrase, than he showed in the first 10-minute period when the experimenter did not reinforce (Verplanck, 1955, pp. 598–600).

These classroom experiments assigned to Verplanck's students came from the heyday of behaviourism. What *couldn't* you do with operant methods? It would make behaviourism's claim even more irresistible, Greenspoon (1955) thought, to turn the shaping of human behaviour into something really simple. He showed with participants instructed to recite whatever words they thought of that a nod, half smile, and murmur of acknowledgement after each plural noun reliably increased the frequency of plurals over a baseline period in which the experimenter was silent and unresponsive. It was not exactly earth-shaking that the little gestures by which we convey approval would have such a reinforcing influence. The experiment went beyond the obvious and became a minor sensation with Greenspoon's report that his subjects were quite unaware of what they had done.

Behaviourists swarmed over the phenomenon, trying a variety of response classes (positive self-references, an operant elicited by having participants talk about themselves, was one of the most interesting). Several investigators administered personality questionnaires to the to-be-conditioned participants, predicting those who would be responsive. Bonnie Strickland and I carried out such an experiment; we found that only participants with a stronger than average need for approval produced more plural nouns to our Mm-hmms and head nods (Crowne & Strickland, 1961). Now a question for you: that wasn't at all Skinnerian to predict differential operant conditioning from a measure of an internal motive, i.e. a need for approval. Is there a way to make this more Skinnerian? Hint: What is reinforcing to one person is not necessarily reinforcing to another. Hungry rats and full ones will respond differently to food reinforcement, and responsiveness to *secondary reinforcement* (which we'll cover momentarily) will follow the rule.

The idea of reinforcing foolish responses in otherwise intelligent organisms immediately occurred to psychology undergraduates when they heard about Verplank's and Greenspoon's experiments. Inventive students often tried to shape the behaviour of their professors, nodding and smiling to get them to do something like moving far to the side of the room. All they needed was an operant (like pacing) with some reasonable probability of occurrence. Another question for you: does it work to reinforce people for doing what you want? Is this built into ordinary social behaviour, to people talking and listening to each other? Try it. Design a little experiment on the principles we've just been talking about and see.

The Control of Operant Responding

Operants are not just operants produced indiscriminately. The rat does not make bar pressing movements with its forepaws outside the Skinner box, the pigeon doesn't peck at spots on the wall, and we don't say a cheery good morning to get a wifely kiss at 2 a.m. Operant responses—especially the complex ones we're interested in—are *discriminative*. They are under the control of stimuli that tell us when and where to make them. When do we cross a busy road? When the walk light says so. When do we speak in class? When the professor acknowledges us. Lights, time of morning, and professorial acknowledgement have become discriminative stimuli, S with a D superscript (S^D). The aroma of dinner in the oven is a discriminative stimulus that informs us about a forthcoming reinforcing event and controls much of our pre-dinner and dinnertime behaviour. A small child who is angry may discern the scowl on his mother's face—a discriminative stimulus that tells him punishment is forthcoming. In response, he inhibits his angry display.

Responses may also be *differentiated*. We learn to make gentle pats on the shoulder, not great wallops, and murmur of our love, not bellow it. Responses generalize to situations similar to the ones in which they were acquired, to stimuli that partly share the attributes of the original. Entering different classes taught by different professors in different rooms, we do very much the same things. The joke we tell to a roommate we'll also tell to a group around the table at the pub, received in each case with a rewarding groan.

A Skinner box with a pigeon (Photograph by Robert W. Allan. Reprinted with permission.)

The Nature of Reinforcement

Some reinforcers are obvious—the kernel of corn dispensed to a pigeon or the food pellet to a rat. The basis of others is not so clearly evident. They require a conditioning history to become reinforcers. An 'A' on a test is just such a **conditioned reinforcer**. How did it get that way? Let's return to the rat for instruction. A green light accompanies every successful press of the bar for food, appearing just before the food pellet. The green light becomes a *secondary reinforcer* through this association and will itself support bar pressing—but only for a time if pairings with food pellets are completely withdrawn. As Skinnerians have said, 'A stimulus that is not originally a reinforcing one . . . can become reinforcing through repeated association with one that is' (Keller & Schoenfeld, 1950, p. 232). How did A's, praise, warmth and affection, Mm-hmms, disapproval and censure, and D's achieve the status of secondary reinforcers? Through a history of association with reinforcers that had a capacity all their own—*primary reinforcers*—to reinforce responses. These social reinforcers undoubtedly began their history through simpler associations with **generalized reinforcers** such as one's parents, particularly the main caregiver, mother.

It is the wisdom of the laboratory that responses to secondary reinforcers will extinguish if not at least occasionally paired with primary reinforcement. It is the wisdom of life in the real world that secondary reinforcers do not lose their ability to reinforce behaviour. We continue to respond positively to A's and negatively to D's even though A's are never accompanied by M&Ms nor D's by sharp blows on the palm with a ruler. Why? Likely, Skinner thought, because important secondary reinforcers are regularly accompanied by primary reinforcement. Money's a good example: it buys food, drink, and shelter. Also, such reinforcers as praise and affection are not always forthcoming; they are intermittent and, as we'll see, **intermittent** or **partial reinforcement** produces highly durable behaviour. Responses not followed by reinforcement extinguish. Responses learned to powerful reinforcers, however, are unlikely to extinguish in the absence of continued reinforcement, and responses rewarded on certain intermittent bases are exceptionally resistant to extinction. Stimuli associated with reinforcement take on reinforcing properties of their own, as I just said, and long chains of secondary reinforcement may be established. This *chaining* of responses routinely occurs. We go for a walk, and the stimuli we encounter may become associated with walks, perhaps with the time of year (the beauty of fall leaves, the heady aroma of spring), reinforcing our walking excursions and linking them in extended sequences. We look forward to and plan for them, and think pleasantly about them afterward. Elements in the chain will lead to others, anticipating them and sometimes modifying them. A lasting enjoyment of warm October Sunday afternoons may be a result.

Partial Reinforcement and Scheduling

In life, the continuous reinforcement of our responses is rare, and evolution must surely have adapted organisms to the periodic or intermittent occurrence of reinforcing stimuli. Only some of the responses we make to gain a given reinforcement are typically rewarded or punished; only some of the time a given response is made will it be reinforced. So we need to consider the way reinforcement is *scheduled*. Skinner showed in tightly controlled experiments how readily scheduling effects can be produced in experimental animals. He pointed out that they are easily gotten in humans and are part of the fare of daily life.

Some reinforcers occur at intervals. Responses produced outside the interval are not reinforced, so we learn to wait for the proper time. A rat in a Skinner box is reinforced if the bar is pressed at, let's say, ten-second intervals. The rat soon learns that bar-pressing is useless except during the brief period after every ten seconds, and it doesn't respond except at that time. We can see the pattern of its behaviour graphically thanks to a device called the cumulative recorder (now supplanted by the computer display of responses) seen in Figure 13.1. A roll of chart paper unrolls under a pen that steps from right (the bottom of the chart paper) to left (toward the top). If the rat isn't responding, the pen draws a straight line. If it is responding rapidly, the pen will draw a line that rises steeply. With this **fixed-interval schedule★**, the graphical picture we get is a scalloped slope. Can you see why? For us humans, there are many instances of behaviour rewarded on a fixed-interval basis: eating at certain times of the day, getting paid every two weeks, saying 'Good morning' and 'Good night' and being rewarded by reciprocal verbal behaviour. We don't say 'Thank God It's Friday' with great relief on Tuesday. Assignments and midterm exams in university are usually scheduled at regular intervals. We professors have come to expect a slackening of effort in the period after an assignment or exam is done—those of us, anyway, who are alert to fixed-interval behaviour. The reward of completed work is over and done with, and students are now in the nonreinforced interval.

Intervals between reinforcements don't have to be fixed. The reinforcer can arrive at irregular intervals, its timing unpredictable. Fishing is like this: we don't know how long we'll have to wait for a fish to bite. Our instructive Skinner box rat tells us that **variable-interval (VI) schedules★**—reinforcements averaging every 15 seconds but varying between 5 and 20—produce high rates of responding without the slack inter-interval period we see in the scalloped graph. This is all because the rat and the fisherman can't tell when the next reward is coming. A pigeon in a Skinner box is doing whatever it's doing when the food dispenser clicks, delivering a kernel of corn. Whatever it was that the pigeon was doing—ruffling its feathers or pacing around the box—has been reinforced and will be a more likely behaviour when the dispenser clicks again. There is no real causal relation here, but some response or other is now acquired by the bird. Skinner thinks superstitions

Figure 13.1 The cumulative recorder

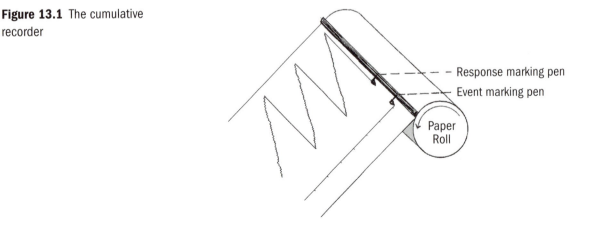

Response marking pen
Event marking pen
Paper Roll

"Maybe you're right, maybe it won't ward off evil spirits, but maybe it will, and these days who wants to take a chance?"

are learned in this way. Members of a preliterate tribe just happen to be singing and dancing when a long-awaited rain occurs. Result: a rain dance. Are prayers sometimes answered? What would Skinner say about the probability of praying? VI-scheduled reinforcement produces behaviour that is very resistant to extinction—the behaviour is likely to continue long after reinforcement is no longer forthcoming (see Research, below). Rain dances are not a good way to produce rain, but they are very persistent in the cultures that practise them.

Reinforcement may occur in relation to the number of responses made. This is the **ratio schedule**. If rewards come at some regular ratio to the number of responses, it is a **fixed ratio (FR)**★, and in laboratory animals we can stretch out the ratio so that a great many responses are required for a single reinforcement. Paradoxically, animals work harder for fewer rewards; the rate of bar pressing accelerates with increases in the ratio. Also, animals display a striking resistance to cease responding after the reward has been discontinued, persisting far longer in producing unrewarded responses than animals on a continuous, one-response-per-reward schedule. This experimental situation has a familiar ring. Ratio schedules are intrinsic to piecework; what one gets is determined by the rate of production. Farm workers know all about this—so many baskets of fruit or vegetables picked per unit of pay. Up to a point, ratio schedules stimulate work, but when the ratio becomes high we slacken and quit. So do rats in the Skinner box. We may make additional and more complicated human responses, rebelling at exploitation, joining together with fellow workers to try to compel a fairer rate in the schedule of pay. The essential features of fixed-ratio scheduled behaviour for humans and non-human animals, though, are much the same.

There is one more scheduling variation. It shares with the variable-interval schedule the attribute of unpredictability, this time by making the ratio variable. **Variable-ratio (VR) schedules**★ yield very high rates of behaviour and exceptional resistance to extinction. Gambling is controlled by exactly this kind of schedule, and the effect is so compelling that we think of compulsive gamblers as addicted. Interesting idea, this: is there an effect in the nervous system of the unpredictable ratio, the false tease of expectation that the next payoff is just around the corner? Go to a casino and watch the people depositing their hard-earned coins in the slots. I have a tale for you. My wife and I lived at the foot of Hampstead Heath, in Camden Town, during the time that she was completing medical school in London. Just around the corner from our flat was our local pub, the 'Washington, D.C.' No, not District of Columbia; the D.C. was for 'Drunks of Camden', as its denizens delighted in claiming. We would go round for a pint just before closing, a pleasant end-of-day ritual. The pub had a one-armed bandit, an expensive one that required 50p pieces, and it was always in use. One evening, the only place we could find to sit was right beside the slot machine, into which a middle-aged man was pouring his coins, one after the other, in regular rhythm to the pull of the arm. He beckoned his wife to fetch him another pint, his play uninterrupted. There was no interruption either when, to our horrified gaze, we saw a widening puddle at his feet. How strongly does the ratio schedule control behaviour?

Personality Development

Shaping Again

Skinner's behaviourism is tailor-made for an account of the development of personality. Heredity sets the parameters, and the people who make up an individual's environment— parents, siblings, peers, teachers, aunts and uncles—select the operants to be reinforced, shaping them gradually. Toilet training, teaching good table manners, coaching the development of motor skills (for riding a tricycle, later a bicycle), and teaching a child to read are excellent examples of how complex behaviour is shaped in children. No shaking your head and rolling your eyes at the comparison of teaching children with training rats to press bars or to drop marbles down a chute. Both rely on the step-by-step shaping of behaviour. An infant of a year or so says 'Mommy' to every human countenance, and her mother rewards her for her verbal performance, knowing that the process of language learning is one of gradually acquiring a more discriminated verbal repertoire. This is only one step in a very complicated and long-term process, one that won't end even with the last English course you take.

Punishment

In our consideration of reinforcing stimuli, we cannot neglect the role and effects of punishment. As Skinner sardonically wrote, 'if a man does not behave as you wish, knock him down; if a child misbehaves, spank him; if the people of a country misbehave, bomb them. Legal and police systems are based upon such punishments as fines, incarceration, and hard labor. Religious control is exerted through penances, threats of excommunication, and consignment to hellfire' (1953, p. 182). Education has given up slaps and swats but not the use of punishment, and childrearing is full of it. We do all of these things and numberless others with the aim of eliminating behaviour we don't want to see.

Does punishment work? Yes, of course. It has predictable effects in suppressing behaviour if administered immediately. But, as Skinner said, 'Reward and punishment do not differ merely in the direction of the changes they induce. A child who has been severely punished for sex play is not necessarily less inclined to continue, and a man who has been imprisoned for violent assault is not necessarily less inclined toward violence. Punished behaviour is likely to reappear after the punitive contingencies are withdrawn' (1971, p. 62). The trouble with punishment is that it also produces undesirable consequences, unwanted side effects. We punish children and, in addition to suppressing the punished behaviour (if we are successful), we may produce strong emotional reactions that can later substantially interfere with the child's responses in the punished situations and generalize to situations we hadn't thought of and didn't intend. We punish adults and get anger and resentment or other undesired consequences that might not be quite so evident in vulnerable children. So, Skinner argues, it is desirable to avoid the use of punishment and to try to bring behaviour under the control of positive reinforcers rather than aversive ones.

There are occasions, perhaps, when the use of punishment cannot be avoided, in which one needs a potent and commanding reinforcing stimulus to gain a child's attention—let's say, the attention of an autistic child to disrupt or inhibit some disturbing and persistent problem behaviour, evidently uncontrollable by other means. Example: the self-biting of a seven-year-old retarded boy. The clinician in this case effectively used electric shock, a mild but very insistent aversive consequence, in order to disrupt the self-biting. The child's mother was asked to say 'No!' in association with the shocks, and the result was a dramatic decline in self-mutilating behaviour. 'No!' became an effective secondary reinforcer. Then, other procedures, including positive reinforcement, were added to maintain the newly developed low rate of self-biting.

Language

Skinner's behaviouristic account of child training and the development of new responses is persuasive and useful. We can do much to foster healthy development in our children by operant methods. It fell flat on its face, though, in the operant analysis of language acquisition. Skinner's *Verbal Behavior* (1957) offered an elaborate story of language and language learning, including a set of terms for special language features. *Echoic responses* are repetitions of verbal behaviour, as when a mother says, 'Mummy loves you,' and the baby says 'Mum-Mum-Mum.' You can imagine the reinforcement that follows. *Mands* are verbal requests or commands that indicate the desired reinforcement ('Can I have some more mashed potatoes, please?') *Tacts* represent the correct naming of object or person. Holding the family cat, Baby Hermione says, 'Kitty,' and Mom reinforces.

Psycholinguists, especially Noam Chomsky (1959), had a collective seizure. Language, they argued, is far too complex to be reduced to such an impossibly simple basis. Its development is, they said, a biological necessity, and language learning is the acquisition of rules for word generation, grammar, and syntax (see Pinker, 1995). Children couldn't possibly acquire by operant means the nearly infinite number of sentences they can understand and produce. And no child was ever reinforced for saying, 'I goed to school today.'

Research and Applications

As the conditioning of Little Albert gave Watson the model for personality formation, so rat and pigeon in the Skinner box provided Skinner with the model for operant learning, by which all the significant voluntary behaviour of organisms (including you and me) is acquired, called into action by environmental circumstances, and changed when change is indicated. Skinner *was* interested in the learning of rats and pigeons, but from early on it was his intent to apply the principles of operant conditioning to the whole canvas of human behaviour.

To see the exceptional control of an individual animal's behaviour, let's consider a single experiment on variable-interval scheduling, one Skinner presented in his 1950 paper 'Are theories of learning necessary?' Figure 13.2 shows a cumulative record of the key pecking of a single pigeon reinforced at intervals averaging 5 minutes and ranging from 10 seconds to 21 minutes. Each sloping line represents 1,000 responses; at 1,000,

Figure 13.2 Cumulative record of a pigeon on a variable-interval schedule (From Skinner, 1950, p. 208.)

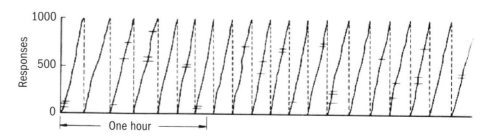

the pen resets to zero. Crosshatches are reinforcements, averaging about 12 per hour. There are 20,000 responses in the whole record, which covers approximately three hours. A very simple arrangement of environmental contingencies extracted a simply incredible amount of work from this pigeon.

Elsewhere, Skinner reported that 'Pigeons reinforced with food with a variable interval averaging five minutes between reinforcements have been observed to respond for as long as fifteen hours at a rate of from two to three responses per second without pausing longer than fifteen or twenty seconds during the whole period. It is usually very difficult to extinguish a response after such a schedule' (1953, p. 102). Such findings, he added, apply to humans: 'Many sorts of social or personal reinforcement are supplied on what is essentially a variable-interval basis, and extraordinarily persistent behaviour is sometimes set up' (1953, p. 102). The Christmas bonus, a fixed-interval reinforcement given to workers to get them to think well of their employer and work harder, has a diminishing return and can be improved on. 'An unpredictable bonus, given in smaller sums on a variable-interval schedule but in approximately the same amount annually, would have a much greater effect' (1953, p. 389). This is pure Skinner: show that an individual animal's behaviour can be controlled by varying interval-contingent reinforcement, and issue a challenge to accept the extension of it to the human arena.

Skinnerian behaviourism is rich in the possibilities it offers for the intelligent control of behaviour in a variety of life situations, applying an operant behaviour technology. Let's look at four of them.

Psychopharmacology

Psychopharmacology studies the effects of drugs on behaviour. It may use a sophisticated behaviour technology to carry out behaviour shaping and behaviour control. The general procedure is to train an operant response—let's say bar-pressing—in an animal and then to see how drugs may alter the response (suppress it, increase its rate, change its resistance to extinction) or modify the animal's endurance of pain or punishment to keep up its responding. The effects of pain-relieving drugs and of heroin have been investigated in this way. Many of the drugs used to combat anxiety, depression, and even schizophrenia began in laboratory experiments with animals, often with operant technology.

Behaviour Disorder

Skinnerians have been greatly concerned with behaviour disorder and its treatment. The general methods they have evolved are part of the body of techniques known as **behaviour modification**. Childhood autism and schizophrenia have received particular attention, not because Skinner and his followers believed they were abnormalities of learning but because the gravely disordered behaviour of their victims could be significantly altered. Operant techniques have been used to train autistic children in the use of language (at least some useful language), social responsiveness, self-care, and the minimization of self-destructive, self-damaging behaviour. Used properly, operant conditioning is highly effective with some truly refractory disorders. In the treatment of schizophrenia, for example, Skinnerian techniques have been developed for use in entire hospital wards. Early in this chapter, I mentioned the *token economy*, a treatment regimen for disturbed, disruptive behaviour. Its general principle is that tokens (positive reinforcers) are dispensed for specific desirable behaviour (keeping room and belongings neat, proceeding in a nice, orderly way to meals, doing laundry and washing dishes). Tokens are withheld from patients who do not produce the rewarded operants. The tokens can be exchanged for privileges (a pass giving access to the hospital grounds for thirty minutes, cigarettes and candy, an individual visit with the ward psychologist). To the criticism that the token economy is mechanical and artificial, Skinnerians explain that

> Token economies are not really unnatural. Indeed, any national economy with a currency system is in every sense a token economy: any currency consists by definition of token or symbolic 'reinforcers' that may be exchanged for items that constitute a more direct form of reinforcement. Whereas the individual in society works to earn tokens (money) with which he purchases his dwelling place, food, recreation, and so on, most institutions provide such comforts noncontingently and hence cease to encourage many adaptive behaviours that are appropriate and effective in the natural environment (Masters, Burish, Hollon, & Rimm, 1987, p. 222).

Token economies have produced marked changes in the disruptive behaviour of patients—often grossly inappropriate—in hospital wards. It is clear from the research, however, that rewards must be given consistently to reduce problem behaviour and increase the adaptive; the reinforcing staff members (attendants) must be well trained and alert to reinforcement opportunities. Further, the token economy has to be maintained. When a token economy is discontinued, its beneficial effects disappear. They don't generalize when patients go home, reside in community settings, or work in community workshops (Kazdin, 1977). Should we be asking if those who care for patients after they leave the hospital fail to keep up the reinforcement for good behaviour? Does changed situation plus no reward equal extinction, an unfortunate discrimination that discharged patients can all too easily learn? One final point. It will help if the token economy is subtle and not blatant, flexible and responsive to individual differences and not rigid.

Psychotherapy

Skinnerian psychotherapy focuses on the problem behaviour the patient seeks treatment for. Psychotherapy is inefficient and ineffective, Skinner argued, because it looks to change internal 'causes' instead of responses made to environmental ones. There are a number of 'behaviour therapies', of which operant techniques are only one instance, and they are especially effective in relieving fear-based avoidance behaviour. Operant therapy is fundamentally a matter of altering the environmental consequences of responses, ensuring that the undesirable ones are not reinforced and appropriate ones are. *Contingency management* sets up planned rewards and penalties for 'good' and 'bad' behaviour. For instance, a badly acting child might be given a 'menu' of behaviours earning rewards and penalties. The responsible adults (parents, teachers) keep track of the child's behaviour and administer the contingencies (Craighead, Craighead, Kazdin, & Mahoney, 1994).

Education

Skinner has had a substantial influence in education. He elaborated on my Ohio State University colleague Sidney Pressey's invention of the teaching machine, designed to shape, in graded steps, the individual child's (or adult learner's) acquisition of new skills and knowledge. The teaching machine minimizes failure by controlling the individual progress of learning. In a Skinnerian classroom, every child advances at his or her own pace, making gradual and progressive accomplishment without faltering. That, said Skinner, is the way learning should proceed; the teaching machine does not mechanize learning, and it is nothing more than a technological adjunct that makes the individual's achievement easier and virtually eliminates failure (Skinner, 1968).

Perspective 13.2 Mr Jones, the Slob

Bert Jones is a plumber, the stopped-up-toilet kind, who never had the ambition to be anything else. He is in his mid-forties, has a big, overhanging belly, and you'll always find him wearing dirty jeans and a checkered shirt. At the dinner table, he reaches to grab what he wants, fingers only, slobbers down his chin and wipes it off—spaghetti sauce, pea soup, bits of chicken that escaped his mouth—with his sleeve. Sloppy Joes would be the fitting meal for him. He belches loudly. He tosses scraps from his plate to Wolfie the family dog, an Irish Wolfhound-Beagle cross combining the Wolfhound's size and the Beagle's yappiness. Wolfie puts his huge paws on the table, begging for more, which makes Bert laugh and feed him another scrap. Mrs Jones is beside herself, completely revolted, and even their two boys, twelve and fourteen, are disgusted. Sunday afternoons he spends in front of the television watching football, beer in hand, a giant-size bag of chips at his elbow. There are great beer belches, and he passes gas. And this is not the half of it.

What is Mrs Jones to do? He was crude before they married, but she thought he was cute and funny, and by the time she realized he was a slovenly oaf he was too set in his ways. But now, she's got to do something. He's simply unendurable, 'a total pig' as she says to her girlfriend. She doesn't want to break up her family, but she can stand no more. She checks out introductory psychology texts from the library and pores over the personality and therapy chapters. The image of the stagnating lifestyle among Erikson's stages is her husband to a T, but it is one, she concludes, that even the very best ego analyst could do nothing about. Besides, what would Bert say to psychoanalysis? No hope there. In the chapters on psychotherapy, however, she finds the behaviour therapists, focused not on the underlying but the actual and visible, Bert's repulsive actions. Possible . . . maybe. A look in the telephone book finds a behaviour therapist, and a call books an appointment.

Dr Renovare doesn't look like someone Bert would take to—sports jacket and tie, clean-shaven—but he's attentive and hears her out. 'Can Bert change?' she asks at the end, her voice an anxious quaver. 'It's not going to happen overnight,' Dr Renovare says, 'but let's find a place to start. His table manners might make a good beginning. What's the worst thing he does?' 'Well,' replies Mrs Jones, 'his grabbing food with his hands and stuffing it right into his mouth. That's pretty awful. But aren't you going to see him? You're the doctor, after all.' 'That may not be necessary,' says Dr Renovare. 'You will be the actual therapist, and I'll guide you.'

The dinner table plan didn't come easily at first. Mrs Jones had trouble getting beyond the urge to give him severe whacks on his knuckles with the serving spoon, but soon saw that aversive measures would probably yield anger, retaliation, and no desirable effect. She swallowed hard over positive reinforcement but reluctantly saw its logic. Dr Renovare asked for a detailed description of Bert's food grabbing. It was appalling but useful. Out of that came a question: Was there any moment in the sequence from finishing the last bite to reaching across the table for a new fistful when a reinforcing stimulus could be inserted, forestalling the reach? Yes, she thought, there was. Could she, Dr Renovare wondered, quickly—it would have to be very quickly—hold the platter across the table and properly serve Bert another helping? 'Would you like some more, dear?' she was to say. Could it work?

Yes, it could and did. Bert was nonplussed, mumbled incoherently, but didn't reach. Not many dinnertimes passed before there was no more grabbing. He did belch, but that, too, was inhibited as Mrs Jones went round the table and held a napkin to his lips. He would now look at her expectantly to be served and put his hand over his mouth to stifle the belching. Dr Renovare pointed out that she couldn't possibly reinforce on every occasion. The real world, he said, just isn't like that. Moreover, putting Bert on a partial reinforcement schedule, serving him and bringing him the belch-drowning napkin only some of the time, would make his new politeness more lasting. What would Bert do? On his own, he began to reach for the platter and serving spoon. He did glare at his wife as if to say, 'What the hell's the matter with you? Ain't you gonna serve me?' but there wasn't any relapse, and Mrs Jones made sure that she did sometimes serve him, although with decreasing frequency.

Modifying those dreadful Sunday afternoons looked to be nigh impossible, but it wasn't. It was Mrs Jones's brainstorm to have some of Bert's hockey buddies from years past drop over to invite him to play. He grumbled but did go, and Sunday afternoon hockey games came to replace beer, flatulence, and football. He was sore and tired when he came home but in a good mood; in three months, he dropped twenty pounds.

Drugged and hogtied, you couldn't have gotten Bert Jones to a psychotherapist, so the therapy had to come to him. It was never labelled as therapy, and there was no confrontation over Bert's horrendous habits. True, Bert didn't understand what was happening to him and still doesn't, but he didn't have to. Changing behaviour was what this therapy was all about, and change behaviour it did. In many ways, Bert Jones remains a slob, but he's a slob Mrs Jones can live with, and her consultation with Dr Renovare gave her a way to deal with gross things that distressed her.

Radical Behaviourism in Perspective

Let's applaud Skinner's behaviourism with admiration: every one of the major concepts of the theory was developed on the basis of experimental research, almost all of it adhering to the principle that individual behaviour should be studied. The same can be said of most of the theory's applications. It joins the other learning theories on the honour roll of systematic research support.

Then, the questions begin to arise. Is Skinner's picture of human personality and social life 'a sunlit hill with an extensive view in many directions', as *Walden Two's* reviewer said, a slur on freedom and independence and a caricature, or is it simply a rosy but wholly impractical approach to human behaviour? The behaviour technology, based as it is on well-established principles of learning, obviously captures emitted behaviour and its reinforcement, and it is manifestly useful in many real-life settings. But is it too simple an account of complex organisms and their varied behaviour, too simple to be feasible as an approach to such applications of personality theory as psychotherapy, social aggression, or the rearing of children? When we get away from fairly straightforward things like the effects of variable-ratio schedules on gambling, does the edifice of Skinnerian behaviourism begin to crumble in our hands?

Observational learning, something a modern learning theory can't afford to ignore, slipped right by Skinner. His radical, stripped-to-the-bones science-of-behaviour approach is at odds with our vast and accumulating knowledge of cognitive life. We *do* feel, and do so intensely. We experience a variety of motives, act on them, are elated when we achieve their aims, and are downcast when we come up short. The modern details of memory, thinking, and language are not well served in the operant account. Can we substitute a search to find environmental causes for aspects of human life that

A Fresh Look: Application Today

A Contribution to the History of Behaviorism, 2004: Skinner's Epiphany in the Flour Mill

We can no more contemplate Skinner's operant behaviourism without the concept of shaping than we can imagine psychoanalysis without ego defences. How do we train organisms to do things not in their behavioural repertoires—pigeons pecking at illuminated buttons, Pliny the rat dropping marbles down a chute, children beginning to read, Bert the slob observing basic etiquette at the dining table? By shaping their behaviour little by little, beginning with a response likely to occur, rewarding it, and increasing the requirement when it has become established. Of course. But this wasn't always so. Skinner himself didn't fully appreciate the process and name it for years. Pliny didn't acquire his marble-dropping feat by shaping but by 'successive approximation', which meant having his behaviour largely constrained by the arrangement of the learning apparatus so that each new step would have to occur.

Skinner's realization, a true epiphany, happened one day in 1943, as Gail Peterson discovered from a serious dig into operant conditioning's forgotten past (Peterson, 2004). He was engaged in research for the Navy Department, which was trying to develop a guided bomb that could hone in, unerringly, on its target. Skinner was awarded a small amount of money by the government and by the food marketing giant General Mills, contracted to do war work, to study the feasibility of a pigeon guidance system for one of the bombs, codenamed the Pelican (Skinner, 1960). General Mills set him up with a lab on the top floor of its Minneapolis flourmill. The work ground along slowly, impeded by bureaucratic doubt, scoffing, and inefficient overseeing, and there was lots of time for Skinner and his graduate students to fool around. This is what he said many years afterward about how they filled the idle weeks.

In 1943, Keller Breland, Norman Guttman, and I were working on a war-time project sponsored by General Mills, Inc. Our laboratory was on the top floor of a flour mill in Minneapolis, where we spent a good deal of time waiting for decisions to be made in Washington. All day long, around the mill, wheeled great flocks of pigeons. They were easily snared on the window sills and proved to be an irresistible supply of experimental subjects. . . . This was serious research, but we had our lighter moments. One day we decided to teach a pigeon to bowl. The pigeon was to send a wooden ball down a miniature alley toward a set of toy pins by swiping the ball with a sharp sideward movement of the beak. To condition the response, we put the ball on the floor of an experimental box and prepared to operate the food magazine as soon as the first swipe occurred. But nothing happened. Though we had all the time in the world, we grew tired of waiting. We decided to reinforce any response which had the slightest resemblance to a swipe—perhaps, at first, merely the behaviour of looking at the ball—and then to select responses which more closely approximated the final form. The result amazed us. In a few minutes, the ball was caroming off the walls of the box as if the pigeon had been a champion squash player (1958, p. 94).

Amazed? How could that be? Well before this, Skinner had trained Pliny, devised the operant apparatus we know as the Skinner Box to bring the behaviour of legions of rats and pigeons under the control of a reinforcing environment, and published his first monument to operant learning, *The Behavior of Organisms*. He must have known about closely observing the activity of an animal, selecting proximate responses, and rewarding them by hand. Peterson, though, shows in her careful review of his writings that he didn't, that he had thought only of successively changing the mechanics of the apparatus to push the animal toward the next response requirement. In 1979, Skinner described the frivolous bowling experiment again, and the epiphany:

LEARNING THEORIES OF PERSONALITY: THE RADICAL BEHAVIOURISM OF B.F. SKINNER**373**

seem so important to us and that form such a great part of contemporary psychology? Skinner said that we can and persuasively argued that it would be worth our while to do so, to abandon 'autonomous man' and to use control wisely. So, you will have a problem in judging radical behaviourism. Skinner *does* make a case. What do you think of it?

Possibly our most impressive experiment concerned the shaping of behavior. I had used successive approximation in my experiments on the force and duration of lever-pressing, and we had seen how important it was in teaching a pigeon to peck hard. Pliny's complex behavior had been put together step by step by making slight changes in the apparatus. But one exciting day on the top floor of the flourmill we programmed contingencies by hand.

We put a pigeon in a large cardboard carton, on one wall of which was a food dispenser operated by a hand switch. We put a wooden ball the size of a Ping Pong ball on the floor and undertook to teach the pigeon to knock it about the box. We began by reinforcing merely looking at the ball, then moving the head toward it, then making contact with it, and eventually knocking it to one side with a swiping motion. The pigeon was soon batting the ball about the box like a squash player. We had shaped a very complex topography of behaviour through successive approximation in a matter of minutes, and we 'gazed at one another in wild surmise' [an allusion to a line in a Keats sonnet].

I remember that day as one of great illumination. We had discovered how much easier it was to shape behaviour by hand than by changing a mechanical device (p. 268).

Peterson shows that Skinner's research and writing shortly began to give evidence of just how illuminating the shaping of pigeon bowling (or was it squash?) had been. An understanding that the verbal behaviour of speakers is shaped by their listeners, the application of shaping to the education of children by the teaching machine, the estab-

lishment of token economies to get psychiatric patients to behave more normally, the retraining of speech in mute psychotics, indeed the appreciation that the virtual entirety of human social behaviour is shaped by the reinforcement of others—all of these Skinnerian contributions grew from extension of that day of astonishment in 1943. She concludes, 'In the more than 60 years that have transpired since then, shaping has come to be taken largely for granted, probably as much because of its intuitive appeal and sheer plausibility as for its demonstrated validity. It is hard to imagine a time in the formal field of psychology when the shaping process was essentially unknown, but that was clearly once the case' (p. 327).

Oh yes, and what happened to Pigeons in a Pelican? Despite an impressive ground simulation to Navy officials, they found the idea of pigeons guiding bombs by pecking at a screen showing the target silly and woolly-headed. They laughed off the birdbrained idea and closed down the research.

SUMMARY

1. Behaviourism began in scientific opposition to *structuralism*, a psychology based on introspection that sought to describe the contents of the generalized human mind. It used trained observers to report their sensory experience. John B. Watson, who introduced and championed behaviourism, regarded structuralism as scientifically sterile and invalid. Psychology should study only that which can be directly observed, ignoring inferences to covert processes. He held that humans and nonhuman animals learn and behave according to the same principles.

2. Watson was impressed by Pavlov's discovery of classical conditioning, and he saw it as the fundamental basis of learning and of personality development. The human being starts out with a repertoire of reflexes and primitive emotions. The emotions can become attached to new stimuli through conditioning; thus, the whole range of emotional experience represents the elaboration of conditioned associations. In a famous experiment with a small child, Watson attempted to show the conditioning of fear to a laboratory rat and its generalization to other furry objects. This extensively cited experiment, however, was badly flawed in its execution, and subsequent attempts to replicate it failed.

3. Watson launched a new movement in psychology, behaviourism, which dominated the field for half a century. It stood for objectivity and ruled out the study of processes that could not be directly observed. Behaviourists following Watson showed just how much could be done with a psychology that saw no scientific use for a concept of mind. The foremost of these was B.F. Skinner.

4. B.F. Skinner admired Watson and wholly endorsed behaviourism. He did not, however, agree with Watson on classical conditioning. Instead, he saw that emitted responses, strengthened and maintained by reinforcing consequences, represented the fundamental learning process in the lives of organisms—*operant conditioning*, not *respondent conditioning*. Watson's scientific credo for psychology met with his approval, and Skinner formulated a similar one of his own.

5. Six major ideas form the basis of behaviourism. *Associationism*, derived from the philosophers Locke, Hume, and the Mills, father and son, set the basis for the connection of experiences, providing the principle by which responses and stimuli are linked. From *functionalism* came an emphasis on adaptation to the environment. *Pragmatism* brought practicality to psychology. Behaviourism is nothing if not a practical approach to learning and to behaviour change. *Environmentalism* saw behaviour as controlled by the environment and thus readily modifiable. *Materialism* regarded mind as mechanistic matter. In the hands of behaviourists, there was nothing mystical and incomprehensible about the mind. Psychology simply had to focus on the mind's expression, behaviour. *Experimentalism* promised that anything can be solved by experimental trial. This is an ideal going back to the founding of America.

6. To psychology and to the public, behaviourism as Skinner developed and presented it held out appealing promises. It could improve classroom learning and make it interesting; turn mental institutions into flexible places of relearning; increase the efficiency of psychotherapy; and, greatest of all, put human social life on a rational basis.

7. Burrhus Frederic Skinner was born in 1904 in Susquehanna, Pennsylvania, to bright, talented parents. He was an inventive (and somewhat devilish) boy but a good student. After graduating from Hamilton College, where he majored in English, he determined to become a writer but failed. Reading about Watson and Pavlov turned him toward behaviourism. Admitted to psychology at Harvard, which had no behaviouristic interest, he completed his PhD in 1931 on reflexes under a biologist. He held a prestigious appointment at Harvard for five years, moved to the University of Minnesota, then Indiana University, before returning to Harvard as professor. Skinner is recognized as *the* major behaviourist. His career was established by two important early books, *The Behavior of Organisms* and a utopian novel, *Walden Two*, which created a storm. Many books followed: *Science and Human Behavior*, *Schedules of Reinforcement*, *Verbal Behavior*, *The Technology of Teaching*, *Contingencies of Reinforcement*, *Beyond Freedom and Dignity*, *Enjoy Old Age: Living Fully in Your Later Years*. He was greatly honoured as a psychologist but was never elected to the presidency of the American Psychological Association. He died at eighty-six in 1990.

8. Skinner strongly agreed with Watson that human behaviour, no less than that of animals, is controlled by events in the environment. Opposed to theory, he made his goal the control and prediction of individual behaviour. We proceed in psychology, as in other sciences, by *functional analysis*, linking behaviour to its causal antecedents. We study individual behaviour to ensure that we fully control environmental events, but we can discover general laws from the study of the individual subject.

9. Skinner saw personality as the study of the behavioural attributes of persons, in which inferred structures and processes have no place. We can best show our understanding of personality by bringing behaviour under control, using our knowledge of operants and the variables that determine them to change behaviour and improve learning. This is better than trying to probe the past of individuals to construct operant histories. The critical events and contingencies are likely to be poorly remembered many years later, their details blurred or erased.

10. The emitted response, the *operant*, is the major concept in Skinner's approach. He also called it *Type R conditioning*, the R recognizing the link of response to reinforcement. In classical conditioning, we would identify the bar in a Skinner box as the effective stimulus, but in operant conditioning it is the pressing of the bar that is the critical event. Reinforcement is not automatic; it can only occur when the response has been made. Responses cause consequences, reinforcing stimuli, that increase response probability. Repeated nonreinforcement results in *extinction*, but there are reinforcement contingencies that can make responses extremely resistant to extinction. Operants are often chained in long sequences: one response may produce another or others that alter variables controlling subsequent responses. Complex responses are developed gradually by a process of *successive approximation* or *shaping*. Learning to read is an example: we start children off with the simplest of words and sentences and increase the difficulty step by step.

11. Reinforcement refers to any event that increases (or decreases, in the case of punishment) the probability of a response. Skinner distinguished between primary (food and water, for example) and secondary reinforcers, but he really didn't care why a reinforcer is reinforcing. A reinforcer is a reinforcer because of its effects. Secondary reinforcers differ from primary ones in that they must be associated with primary reinforcers to gain their effects. Thus, secondary reinforcement is *conditioned reinforcement*. A host of secondary reinforcers control human behaviour. *Generalized reinforcers* have been associated with more than one primary reinforcer and may thus produce and maintain many responses under a variety of conditions.

12. One of the most significant of Skinner's contributions was his exploration of *intermittent* or *partial reinforcement*. Not every operant response in the lives of organisms is reinforced; reinforcement only some of the time is the rule. Intermittent reinforcement has some striking effects on response frequency and resistance to extinction. Skinner studied two types of reinforcement schedules, *interval* and *ratio*; each applies to a large array of human operant behaviour.

13. On interval schedules, behaviour is reinforced after a lapse of time that may be seconds to minutes in an animal experiment, or days, weeks, or months for the human. The interval may be a regular one (fixed interval), as is biweekly pay or the Christmas bonus, or irregular (variable interval), as in fishing. The fixed interval tends to produce an idle period after reinforcement (example: a student's slackened effort after an assignment is handed in); this is eliminated when the interval is variable, since the timing of reinforcement can't be predicted. The VI schedule results in a high response rate and resistance to extinction. Reinforcement may also be scheduled on a ratio. Skinner identified both *fixed-ratio* and *variable-ratio schedules*. Piecework—picking of fruit by farm workers, so much for each basket—is a fixed-ratio example; gambling exemplifies the variable ratio. Behaviour controlled by the variable ratio is often exceptionally difficult to extinguish.

14. Personality development shows the potential of Skinner's behaviourism. The child's developing repertoire of responses is acquired in small steps, reinforced by parents, teachers, siblings, and others. Skinner considered the use of punishment unwise. It can suppress unwanted responses but does so at the frequent cost of emotional responses and resentment. The behaviourist account of language development was, however, a significant mistake. The language of the child is not directly shaped by reinforcement; psycholinguists and cognitive psychologists have pointed out

that language acquisition involves the learning of rules for word generation, grammar, and syntax.

15. Like the other learning theories of personality, Skinner's radical behaviourism is solidly grounded in experimental research. Among the most important questions he has studied, one with far-reaching implications is the control of behaviour by intermittent reinforcement. Animal experiments on the effects of interval and ratio schedules have provided provocative interpretations of the determination of human behaviour by reinforcement schedules. VR-controlled gambling and the application of VI scheduling to worker productivity are two outstanding examples.

16. Skinner held out a behaviour technology with significant practical applications. Among them are contributions to the study of the behavioural effects of drugs (psychopharmacology), treatment of psychiatric patients and developmentally disadvantaged children by operant methods of behaviour modification, highly efficient psychotherapy, and individualized instruction of children by the teaching machine. All of these follow from the principles of operant conditioning.

17. The radical behaviourism of B.F. Skinner is a 'theory' based almost wholly in experimental research on the learning of rats and pigeons in automated experimental apparatus and extended to the individual and social behaviour of humans. Skinner's operant technology is eminently workable in many areas, and he passionately argued for its further extension to the design of society. There are a number of questions to be answered, however. Is it too utopian? Too simple? It doesn't recognize cognitive processes and fails to consider such modern questions as observational learning. How do we judge it as a contemporary personality psychology?

TO TEST YOUR UNDERSTANDING

1. What was it about classical conditioning as the model learning process that Skinner objected to? How was operant conditioning a better account of the important learning of organisms?

2. Explain behaviourism's basis in the following: associationism, functionalism, pragmatism, environmentalism, materialism, and experimentalism.

3. Is Skinner's operant conditioning view of human behaviour 'a sunlit hill with an extensive view in many directions', as an admiring reviewer of *Walden Two* said, or 'a slur upon a name, a corruption of an impulse', in the words of a critic? What's your view on Skinner and personality?

4. Design a small experiment to put operant conditioning to test in the control of an instance of social behaviour. How will you know that your conditioning worked? What controls will your experiment require?

CHAPTER FOURTEEN

Learning Theories of Personality: The Social Learning Theory of Julian Rotter

Introduction

Social learning theory shares with stimulus-response theory an origin in the application of the experimental psychology of learning to personality and disorders of personality. Unlike S-R theory, it departs from the core concepts of Hullian behaviourism. We won't find an emphasis on responses and habits as the basic units of the theory, nor is there any concept of drive and drive reduction as the basis of motivation. Instead, in social learning theory we find a thoroughly cognitive theory about people seeking to satisfy needs important to them and developing expectancies (beliefs) about their likelihood of gaining need satisfaction.

Dollard and Miller dedicated *Personality and Psychotherapy* to Pavlov, Hull, and Freud; notably, their acknowledgement as learning theorists was to behaviourists. Rotter owns to a behaviourist debt only in part. Those who influenced him, he has said, were Adler; the great learning theorist, social psychological theorist, and personality theorist Kurt Lewin; J.R. Kantor (about whom I'll have more to say shortly); Edward L. Thorndike, who was a founder of the experimental study of learning in animals; cognitive learning theorist Edward C. Tolman; and Clark Hull. Adler, Lewin, Tolman, and Kantor make prominent appearances in social learning theory.

Social learning is a name borrowed, as you surely have guessed, from Miller and Dollard. Of course, Miller and Dollard did not have a copyright, and Rotter was free to use a name he saw as especially apt. As he says, 'It is a *social* learning theory because it stresses the fact that the major basic modes of behaving are learned in social situations and are inextricably fused with needs requiring for their satisfaction the mediation of other persons' (Rotter, 1954, p. 84). Albert Bandura, whose theory we come to next, tried without grace or recognition of priority to appropriate the name exclusively for himself in 1963. His claim was that neither Rotter nor Miller and Dollard were sufficiently social in their theories, while his approach, based almost wholly at the time on observational learning—that is, learning from watching the behaviour of models—most assuredly was. Levy made a good point in saying, 'social learning theories are less a specific kind of theory than they are a declaration of intent by the theorist concerning the subject matter of his theory and a reflection of the contexts in which he gathers his data' (1970, p. 410). Rotter's theory definitely qualifies, but it is also correct to say that it is a cognitive theory of learning giving prime importance to the mental processes that shape our goal-seeking—the kind of social learning that personality psychologists are concerned with.

In the development of social learning theory (which we can abbreviate as SLT), Rotter did not so much reject S-R theory as attempt to bring it into the cognitive fold. He *was* influenced by Clark Hull's elegant and systematic theory of learning, but he is even more indebted to Edward Tolman's cognitive learning theory. Hilgard, a distinguished student of theories of learning, contrasted S-R theories like those of Hull with Tolman's approach:

> Stimulus-response theories, while stated with different degrees of sophistication, imply that the organism is goaded along the path by internal and external stimuli, learning the correct movement sequences so that they are released under appropriate conditions of drive and environmental stimulation. The alternative possibility is that the learner is following signs to a goal, is learning his way about, is following a sort of map. In other words, he is learning not movements but meanings. This is the contention of Tolman's theory of sign learning. The organism learns sign–significate relations. It learns a behaviour route, not a movement pattern (1956, p. 191).

Learning in this viewpoint is a matter of goal-oriented activity, the learner formulating hypotheses and acquiring meanings along the way. Although Dollard and Miller were also interested in how goal-oriented behaviour develops, they emphasized not so much meanings as the drives that impel behaviour and the stimuli and responses, both external and internal, that channel behaviour in one direction rather than another. Rotter's SLT brings the two 'cultures' of learning theory together: 'SLT may be regarded as one attempt to integrate two diverse but significant trends in American psychology—the "S-R" or "reinforcement" theories on the one hand and the "cognitive" or "field" theories on the other' (Rotter, Chance, and Phares, 1972. p. 1).

Julian Rotter: Personal History

Julian Bernard Rotter was born in October 1916 in Brooklyn, the third son of European immigrant parents. His father had a successful business until the Great Depression of the 1930s. Rotter traces his strong social interest to the devastating social effects of that decade. He studied chemistry at Brooklyn College, which provided free education to all, but switched to psychology after attending lectures by Alfred Adler, who had recently immigrated to the US. He wasn't supposed to be there, a young undergraduate student at seminars given for professionals, but he talked his way in. Adler's influence changed his major, his life, and, indirectly, clinical psychology and personality theory.

On graduation, Rotter pursued his master's degree at the State University of Iowa, where he took courses with Kurt Lewin and the renowned semanticist Wendell Johnson. In 1938–9, he completed one of the rare internships in clinical psychology at Worcester State Hospital in Massachusetts. It was there that he came under the influence of David Shakow, who

Julian Rotter (Courtesy Homer Babbidge Library, University of Connecticut)

strongly shaped his views about science in clinical psychology. He became a PhD student at Indiana University in 1939, taking courses with J.R. Kantor, an engaging and provocative behaviourist. From Kantor come some of the basic assumptions of SLT—importantly, that a psychological theory of personality does not depend on physiological concepts or the concepts of any other science. We'll see Kantor's influence in the next section, when we consider the emphases of the theory.

Rotter received the PhD in 1941, then served in the US Army during the war. In 1946, he joined the clinical psychology program at Ohio State University as a young assistant professor. His first years there were not easy. Ohio State in those days was infected by anti-Semitism (as were many universities), spread by a few of the older faculty serving out their time before retirement. The virulence of it was nasty and often explicit; many a tolerant man would have been moved to anger. It required all of Rotter's marvellous equanimity to keep his cool. He became director of the graduate program in clinical psychology, one that became a model throughout the country. In 1954, the major statement of SLT appeared in the book *Social Learning and Clinical Psychology*. The years from 1946 to 1963 were a rich period of research and theory building with students and colleagues; much of the experimental support for the theory appeared in his work and in the PhD dissertations of students during this extraordinary and exciting time. It *was* an exceptional time; I was there during the last five years of it. He left in 1963 to take up a professorship at the University of Connecticut, where he taught, directed the clinical psychology program, extended SLT research, and directed the theses of students until retirement in 1987. He has continued to teach as professor emeritus.

Influences on Julian Rotter (clockwise from top): Kurt Lewin, J.R. Kantor, Edward C. Tolman, Edward L. Thorndike, Clark Hull (Courtesy of the Archives of the History of American Psychology—The University of Akron)

Emphases

Rotter lays out the basic principles of SLT in a set of postulates. Let's look at them.

1. 'The unit of investigation for the study of personality is the interaction of the individual and his meaningful environment' (1954, p. 85). So, we start immediately by defining person–situation interactions rather than the internal characteristics of persons as the fundamental source of observation and what it is that we seek to understand. Rotter also points out that this is 'the basic postulate of a field theory' (p. 85)—that is, the type of theory that sees the behaving person in the context of an environment that will significantly affect him.

     Personality theory, moreover, is concerned with learned behaviour, behaviour that can be changed by experience. Investigating personality, we study the experience of the person historically, seeking to find the prior events responsible for present behaviour. This is analogous to Dollard and Miller's key point that we seek to understand the conditions of learning.

2. 'Personality constructs [concepts] are not dependent for explanation upon constructs in any other field, including physiology, biology, or neurology. Scientific constructs for one mode of description should be consistent with constructs in any other field of science, but no hierarchy of dependency exists among them' (1954, p. 88). Rotter means here that psychological concepts are independent of concepts in 'more basic' sciences such as physiology. It is wrong, in fact, to think of physiology as more fundamental than psychology. This is the essence of the point: each science tends to the events in its own backyard and is to be judged on how effectively it deals with them; there is to be no reaching over the fence for the better grounded account of a neighbour science.

3. The next postulate extends this elemental idea of concepts at different levels of explanation: 'Behaviour as described by personality constructs takes place in space and time. Although all such events may be described by psychological constructs, . . . they may also be described by physical constructs, as they are in such fields as physics, chemistry, and neurology. Any conception that regards the events themselves, rather than the descriptions of the events, as different is rejected as dualistic' (1954, p. 90). This principle and the preceding one say that we may develop concepts to explain particular events at a particular level: psychological; neurological (relating to the brain systems that regulate behaviour); biochemical (relating to the chemical transactions between neurons by which information in the brain is in part transmitted). It reminds us that explanations in different terms (psychological or physical) do not make the events themselves different. What differs is the nature of the concepts, which are specifically devised to predict and explain events at their own levels.

These three postulates all strongly reflect J.R. Kantor's influence on Rotter's thinking. Kantor was strongly insistent on the fundamental idea that a psychological level of explanation is no less scientifically useful for its purposes than, say, a neural one. If we can find neurological or genetic explanations for behaviour of interest to the psychology of personality well and good, but that does not diminish the scientific validity of the psychological.

4. 'Not all behaviour of an organism may be usefully described with personality constructs. Behaviour that may usefully be described by personality constructs appears

in organisms of a particular level or stage of complexity and a particular level or stage of development' (1954, p. 92). Personality concepts are not going to be useful in describing the behaviour of simple organisms. We would hardly think of bestowing personality attributes on Pliny the laboratory rat, nor would it be useful to try to use personality concepts intended to apply to the mature person to account for the behaviour of a newborn infant. Personality concepts are useful in describing the feelings, thoughts, and actions of people from the time socialization begins.

5.   This postulate and the two that follow expand the basis for the psychological study of persons. They state the fundamentals of personality study: 'A person's experiences (or his interactions with his meaningful environment) influence each other. Otherwise stated, personality has unity' (1954, p. 94). We are not just agglomerations of specific responses or habits acquired in relation to specific cues. There is a consistency and wholeness in personality. What we learn in one situation may have an important influence on how we feel, think, and act in other situations. How does Rotter deal with consistency in personality? Think for a moment: how would a learning theorist do that? Yep, that's right. He makes a very basic use of the principle of learned generalization across situations.

6.   'Behaviour as described by personality constructs has a directional aspect. It may be said to be goal-directed. The directional aspect of behaviour is inferred from the effect of reinforcing conditions' (1954, p. 97). Humans act purposefully. They pursue goals—all the meaningful behaviour we include under the term personality is goal-directed—that are defined by reinforcements.

7.   'The occurrence of a behaviour of a person is determined not only by the nature or importance of goals or reinforcements but also by the person's anticipation or expectancy that these goals will occur. Such expectations are determined by previous experience and can be quantified' (1954, pp. 102–3). Rotter, like the S-R theorists, thinks reinforcement is fundamental to acquiring, maintaining, and changing behaviour. Reinforcements become goals toward which people direct their behaviour, so we see a different emphasis than in S-R theory. SLT introduces another, distinctive concept, that of **expectancy★**. By expectancy, Rotter means a subjective probability that a particular behaviour will lead to particular reinforcing consequences. Remember that a given reinforcement may be desired, or it may be negative as in punishment. It's important to recognize a basic point here: to know whether a given behaviour will occur, we must know not only what the consequence (reinforcement) is and its value to the person, but also what the person anticipates—what his or her expectancy is of obtaining the desired reinforcement or avoiding the unpleasant one.

We need to consider three further points in setting out the basis of SLT. First, this is both a process theory and a content theory, but it is not a content theory that introduces structural concepts. As a process theory, it has concepts concerned with the learning and change of behaviour. It is a content theory in that it has concepts describing important individual differences. The process theory enables us to understand how new experiences modify behaviour and how behaviour is maintained. From it, we can apply general principles (laws) to persons. The content theory introduces variables such as needs or generalized expectancies by which we are able to characterize particular persons and groups of persons.

Second, Rotter does not accept the drive-stimulus reduction hypothesis of Hull that Dollard and Miller adopted. He argues instead that the kinds of reinforcements important in the learning of complex human social behaviour are acquired early in life and can be considered independent of primary drive states. He simply accepts as fact that certain stimuli can produce unlearned positive or negative reactions, the process that we call reinforcement. Other stimuli become reinforcers through their association with previously effective reinforcing stimuli. This is a highly empirical position about reinforcement based on Edward L. Thorndike's principle—the law of effect. Says Rotter: 'To define reinforcement in terms of movement toward a goal and then to infer goals from the effect of reinforcement seems wholly circular. [However,] as long as potential reinforcers may be identified and objectively described, there is no problem of circularity in the concept of reinforcement. When . . . reinforcers are described, predictions can be made even though these reinforcers or reinforcing conditions are first determined empirically' (1954, p. 98). This position requires that we identify the classes of reinforcements that affect behaviour. These are **needs**, and they are fulfilled by other people. Rotter sums this point up by saying, 'Recognition of the importance of others in the determination of goal acquisition leads to the conception of a social learning theory of personality. Initial psychological needs are inborn and are primarily satisfied by parents or parent surrogates. Mediation of our needs by others undoubtedly underlies the importance we humans place on such things as love and affection, recognition, status, and dependency' (Rotter, Chance, and Phares, 1972, p. 10).

A final point to bear in mind is that there is a strong emphasis in SLT on the development, beginning in early childhood, of a sense of competence or mastery—as SLT puts it, a generalized expectancy of success in attaining valued reinforcements. In the course of childhood experience, every individual develops expectancies that generalize across many specific situations, expectations about abilities and competence. Everyone first learns how to cope with failure in protected and secure family environments. Early in development, children pursue goals of love, praise, and approval, and the accomplishment of satisfying activities such as walking, making themselves understood, riding a tricycle. There will be many successes, but failures as well, buffered by understanding parents.

Not all children grow up in such favourable family environments. Some children may not develop high expectations of competence and mastery because their parents do not provide sufficient rewards of praise and approval. As we'll see, parents can expose their children to failure by setting goals for their accomplishment (in school, for example) that are too high. In this case, Rotter explains, a child may develop too high a **minimal goal**. This concept refers to that level of reinforcement on a continuum from negative to positive that is just barely rewarding. School grades are a good example. If a child learns through selective parental reward and praise that only an 'A' is an acceptable accomplishment (long faces and scowls of disapproval greet anything less), then it's likely that only A's or better will be positive reinforcements for him or her. Such an extreme minimal goal may doom this child to many later experiences of failure (feeling a 'B' to be not good enough, or even an A−). If a younger child in a family always has to be as strong, as fast, as quick-witted as an older sibling to be really noticed and praised, then the minimal goals that that level of expectation implies are going to mean a lot of struggle and probably a good deal of disappointment.

We should note the importance of siblings in the child's learning of expectancies. Older brothers and sisters provide models for the attainment of important satisfactions. A younger child may develop his or her own expectancies of success in gaining valued reinforcements partly from observing the success of older siblings. Children will develop expectancies of need satisfaction from their own special situations in the family. Only children and older children have family experiences that are very different from those of younger ones, as you will remember from Adler's concept of birth order and its developmental effects. Rotter has approached the study of siblings systematically, with concepts that enable us to predict more accurately just what the child learns from his or her family situation.

The Major Concepts of Social Learning Theory

SLT is a process theory, and it has a formal aspect. So, we're going to encounter some equations. Ugh! Nothing for it but to grit your teeth and sharpen your pencil. Ready?

SLT's fundamental aim is to predict behaviour, so we'll start with a probability concept—the probability that a behaviour will occur, which Rotter calls **behaviour potential (BP)**. The potentiality (a word Rotter likes better than probability) of occurrence of any behaviour is a function (f) of two variables, *expectancy* (E) and *reinforcement value* (RV):

$$BP = f(E \ \& \ RV)$$

The probability that a given behaviour will occur in a specific situation is a function of the person's expectancy that the behaviour will lead to a particular reinforcement and the value of that reinforcement (how much the person desires it or prefers it over other possible options). As I noted above, the reinforcement could be negative in value, and the behaviour could be avoiding an unpleasant consequence.

The two terms, *expectancy* and *reinforcement value*, are connected by an ampersand, not a multiplication sign. As Rotter explains, '. . . the sign & is used as the only indication of the nature of the mathematical relationship between expectancy and reinforcement value. The purpose of this is to avoid, for the time being, a more precise mathematical formulation because of an insufficient amount of experimental data. However, it seems fairly clear from the data available that this relationship is a multiplicative one' (1954, p. 108). If we hold one of the variables constant in experiments (as we typically do early in research on a theory), there is no problem. We don't have to specify the nature of the relation between them.

We might not act to obtain a particular reinforcement for either of two important reasons. First, the reinforcement isn't preferred; it just isn't a desirable goal to us. Second, we may have a low expectancy that the reinforcement can be obtained. It could be that in previous situations like the one we're considering we have failed to attain the reinforcement. A child doesn't do his homework, for example. The rewards are important (praise and approval), but in his experience they have not consistently followed his efforts; his expectancy of receiving reinforcement for doing his homework is therefore low.

The formula we're discussing is meant to represent the prediction of *specific* behaviour in *specific* situations. So, where's the situation? The psychological situation is represented right in the basic behaviour equation, but we have to complicate it to see where. Here's the expanded formula and the way to read it:

$$BP_{(x, s1, Ra)} = f(E_{(x, Ra, s1)} \ \& \ RV_a)$$

You're groaning again, but it's more straightforward than you think. The potentiality that our specific behaviour x will occur in situation *1* directed toward reinforcing event a is a function of the expectancy that behaviour x will lead to reinforcement a in situation *1* and the value of reinforcement *a*. So, thinking again of the child contemplating her home-work, the specific behaviour *x* is completing her homework on Sunday afternoon (*s1*) so that she will be allowed to watch an hour of television once she's finished (*Ra*). Whether or not she applies herself to completing her homework will depend on how likely she considers it that her parents will, as promised, let her turn on the TV when she's done, and just how much she prefers this outcome to the alternative, not watching television. Now, change the situation, and the expectancy that this behaviour will result in the same rein-forcement changes. We're no longer able to predict the occurrence of behaviour *x*.

Or are we? Sometimes, of course, expectancies that particular reinforcements will follow a given behaviour are specific to particular situations. Can you think of one in which you behave distinctively because you expect that what you do in that environ-ment alone is likely to gain a valued reinforcement? Far more often, though, we will have learned that there are similarities that many situations share; our expectancies for reinforcement are the same, and our behaviour is consistent. In a word, experience has taught us to **generalize★**, to respond in a number of situations as if they were the same. How about first dates as a class of situations that have a lot in common? Sure, we will adapt to each dating partner (that's a case of specificity in the psychological situation), but a lot of things we'll do with different partners will involve generalized expectancies about the reinforcing consequences of our behaviour. We'll be polite, show interest in the other person, try to anticipate what he or she would enjoy, inhibit bragging, and (hopefully) rein in our use of coarse words. All of these behaviours are, in the language of SLT, goal-directed; they seek such reinforcements as approval and affection.

The basic formula, then, needs to be extended further:

$$BP_{(x,\,s(1-n),\,R(a-n))} = f(E_{(x,\,s(1-n),\,R(a-n))} \; \& \; RV_{(a-n)})$$

In words: the potential for behaviour *x* to occur in situations *1* to *n* toward reinforce-ments *a* to *n* is a function of the expectancies for these reinforcements in these situations and the value of the reinforcements. Now, just one more step. We might wish to predict the occurrence of any of a number of behaviours directed toward a common group of reinforcements. So, the formula would now be

$$BP_{(x-n),\,s(1-n),\,R(a-n)} = f \cdots$$

and you will be able to fill in and say the rest.

In personality and clinical psychology, we often want to account for a person's behaviour in seeking broader goals in important classes of situations. That is, we want to predict *need-related behaviour*. In SLT, a group of functionally related reinforcements defines a need. Behaviours are functionally related to the degree that they are directed toward such broader goals—that is, needs. So, let's consider these clinical and personal-ity-oriented concepts of the theory—broad classes of reinforcements that Rotter calls needs (for example, affection, achievement, dependency, or independence), and expectancies generalized across a number of related situations.

For the prediction of the wider classes of behaviour with which personality study and clinical practice are concerned, we shall need some new terms. Here is the formula: **need potential** is a function of **freedom of movement** and **need value**:

$$NP = f(FM \; \& \; NV)$$

Need potential is the probability of occurrence of any of a given set of behaviours directed toward a particular need. It is like the concept of behaviour potential, but it specifies need-directed behaviour rather than specific reinforcement-directed behaviour. *Freedom of movement* means generalized expectancy. It refers to a person's generalized expectancy that any among a functionally related set of behaviours will lead to need satisfaction. Why the term freedom of movement? Rotter says,

> We have selected the term *freedom of movement* in order to convey the relationship of this concept to some of the frequently used concepts of maladjustment, since freedom of movement deals with expectancy for a variety of behaviours for positive satisfaction. High freedom of movement implies an expectancy of success for many different behaviours in different situations; low freedom of movement implies the opposite. *Freedom of movement* seems to be more similar in its connotations to concepts in other [theories] which are used to imply important aspects of adjustment, concepts such as *anxiety* and *inadequacy feelings* (1954, p. 194).

Low freedom of movement is likely to lead to avoidant, self-protective behaviour or to symbolic attempts to achieve goals that seem unattainable. The person tries to protect himself or herself from anticipated failure or punishment by whatever ways he or she has learned. A symbolic behaviour might be substituting the claim of high achievement in place of really trying. A braggart who tells fantastic stories of his successes but in reality doesn't try uses this defence, and we can infer from it his low freedom of movement. When freedom of movement is low and the goal (need) is highly valued, we have what Rotter means by *psychological conflict*. High need value keeps the person in the psychological situation, but low freedom of movement prevents realistic and appropriate goal-seeking behaviour because of the subjective risk of failure—that is, because of the person's generalized expectancy from previous experience that he is likely to fail or to be punished or experience some other aversive consequence. High freedom of movement means the person pursues satisfaction of the particular need with confidence.

Need value refers to the preference for or value of a related set of reinforcements. An example is affectional reinforcements, all the signs of caring that we may receive from others, or the recognition that comes from achievement—this is the level of generality or inclusiveness that Rotter has in mind.

Implications of the Theory

What is the nature of disturbed behaviour? The SLT approach stresses the possibility that neurotic behaviour may be in part goal-directed. That seems curious, but remember that we encountered this idea in Adler. Let's see how Rotter develops it. One may have learned that certain kinds of behaviour—behaviour that would be called neurotic and that other theories would consider to be based on anxiety—is actually reinforced, leading to valued satisfactions. We won't be surprised that a person who demonstrates such behaviour has low freedom of movement for more appropriate behaviour that would result in need satisfaction.

Consider this example. A wife exaggerates physical complaints. She is chronically tired; headache and backache trouble her constantly, and she frequently takes to bed. Her husband and children thus have to do a great many things for her, and they must keep up with running the household. Suppose her tiredness and other symptoms represent a way for her to satisfy dependency and protection needs. We discover that she has a very low expectancy that more appropriate behaviour would result in the same reinforcements. Her need value for dependency and protection is very high. She really wishes to lean on her husband and family; she desperately wants her family to surround her and give unending help and support. She can't ask for these things directly, however, because she expects that she will be rebuffed and made to feel foolish and over-demanding. She thus has to approach the satisfaction of those needs in a very backhanded and indirect way, an expression of her low freedom of movement in these need areas. She doesn't expect to be helped or nurtured; quite the contrary, she believes that demands will be placed on her without reward when she fulfills them.

How did she come to acquire such low freedom of movement? Looking into her history, we find that she was the unwanted child of rather cold and indifferent parents who often ignored and dismissed her needs. From childhood, she was made to feel that she had to work and be helpful, for which she received only minimal reward. There were threats of punishment if she didn't quickly do what was demanded. At one point, she became ill and was taken care of—grudgingly, but to a degree she hadn't experienced. This appears to be the root of her present symptoms. She sees illness and physical complaints as a way to achieve dependency goals, and they are also an expression to her husband and children of her resentful belief that they don't care enough for her. She doesn't suffer in silence. Her behaviour and her feelings are generalizations from childhood learning experiences in an unsympathetic family. Here are some of the things she repeats to herself and will occasionally say to her family and to others (women friends, her therapist): 'Nobody cares for you.' 'You (they) just want me to work myself to death.' 'You (they) make me feel like I'm no good.' Unfortunately, these claims are very alienating, distressing her husband and children with an unjust accusation and causing her friends to back away. You can see the strong Adlerian emphasis in this interpretation. Neurotic behaviour, like any other behaviour, is goal-directed. People may learn neurotic, inappropriate ways of striving (seeking need satisfaction) that provide some, but incomplete, gratification.

There is a very important implication in SLT for behaviour change. To get a reluctant child to learn a new behaviour, to change self-defeating behaviour in a psychotherapy patient, to correct problem behaviour in a delinquent adolescent, or to remedy poor achievement in a school-age child—in all of these cases we should try to modify expectancies. This will be a much more direct avenue to behaviour modification than trying to alter need values, which are unlikely to represent the difficulty. Further, need values are quite resistant to change, primarily because they are acquired so early in childhood. We can usually trace problem behaviour to low expectancies for appropriate choices in a given need area, or to high expectancies for unacceptable or deviant behaviour that has been rewarded.

Delinquency is a good example. Often, delinquent children will be found to have strong needs for recognition and status and for affection, needs that are surely not inappropriate. However, the delinquent has low freedom of movement for attaining satisfaction of needs like these from adults (parents and teachers, who are often angry and fed up) or from peers who conform to social norms. He discovers that a rebellious peer group, a gang, provides important reinforcements in these highly important need areas, and the peer group has needs and expectancies similar to his own.

If we want a young child to learn some new behaviour, we provide reinforcements we know the child values, and we try to give graduated experiences of success. We want to ensure the learning of a high expectancy that the new behaviour will succeed. This means that exposure to failure will occur only occasionally and will be followed by successes.

Perspective 14.1 gives us a clinical example of a case described by Rotter that will help us to see how the concepts of the theory may be applied.

Perspective 14.1 Robert: An SLT Analysis

Robert. Age 21, of medium height, good-looking, meticulous dresser, agreeable, and friendly. Family well off for the small midwestern community where he spent his childhood. Junior in college.

An only child, he described his childhood as being 'doubly pampered'. A younger sister of his mother lived with the family, and he reports that both mother and aunt would fight for the privilege of dressing him and taking him downtown. He slept with his mother usually and with his aunt when he did not sleep with his mother, at least to the age of six. Usually, he played alone and liked being with adults. His earliest memory was of having his hair cut for the first time while his mother and aunt cried. He went to kindergarten where his aunt was the teacher and from there to the first grade. Before he had progressed very far, he was taken out of school and taught at home (both his mother and his aunt were school teachers) during the first year and, subsequently, in the second, third, fifth, and one later grade. In high school, he received average grades. His choice of college was determined mainly by the presence of a speech clinic at [the State University of] Iowa, and he began work on his speech [impairment] immediately upon entering.

Speech History. Before entering the first grade, he was forewarned that his teacher was a 'holy terror', and he entered this class with considerable apprehension. He states, 'I was in constant fear of her. After about a month she slapped me when I did something wrong. What I did right then is rather vague, but I know that I thought I'd die on the spot.' Shortly after this his mother visited the school, and she describes the following episode: 'Robert talked very low and faltered several times. Not knowing what the trouble was, I took him to the family doctor and he advised taking him out of school immediately as he was in a nervous condition.' Of this year at home, Robert states that outside of the fact that he stopped stuttering he remembers very little. During the second year, when back in school, he began to stutter again but his teacher was very kind to him. On a day when the teacher was absent, a substitute teacher who was not acquainted with his difficulty called on him to read. The mother reports, 'When Robert read, she thought it was funny, so for her own amusement she had him read on. When he arrived home for lunch, he showed the reaction; he looked as if he had had all the life taken out of him.' Consequently, he was taken out of school again; and again, when home, he did not stutter. This procedure was continued in three later grades. In high school and grade school his mother would go to school before the beginning of each semester to register for him and to see all his teachers, the principal, and advisors to tell them that Robert needed special attention and care and should not be called upon in class.

One summer during high school he was taken to New York for treatment of his stuttering, the therapy showing little effect. During vacations his speech always improved. At the Iowa Speech Clinic he was subject to several therapies resulting in a diminution of the severity of the stuttering but no real cure. On one summer vacation during this period he stopped stuttering while on a job consisting mainly of reading numbers aloud in an accountant's office.

At the time of the first interview he was thoroughly convinced of the seriousness of his 'handicap'. He reported that on vacations, on dates, and when talking to inferiors he had less trouble than usual. His appearance was practically faultless; he was an active member of one of the leading social fraternities on the campus and was quite interested in dating. He played tennis well but reported that when he started to lose he would begin obviously to 'fool around' so that he could give the impression that he was not trying. In general, he reported that he did not mind discussing his stuttering with people; in fact that he rather enjoyed it (1954, pp. 146-7).

Robert began to stutter immediately after his mother visited the school, and the stuttering was exacerbated when the substitute teacher made him read aloud. We immediately think of a very overprotected child, fearful of school, a situation in which he felt overwhelmed. Now, what's likely to happen when someone (particularly a child) feels extremely apprehensive and overwhelmed? One thing that may well occur is difficulty in speaking. Robert had quite early on acquired the expectancy that when threatened and fearful, his mother (or aunt) would unfailingly come to help him. In fact, we can see two related expectancies: (1) His mother and aunt are sources of protection, and (2) nobody cares like mother and aunt do. His initial faltering and inability to speak were quite natural consequences of being intimidated, afraid, and likely crying. These anxiety symptoms brought dramatic results: he was immediately taken out of school. His mother established his expectation of criticism and punishment from his teachers, warning him before the first grade about the terrible teacher he would encounter. Time and again, his mother and aunt reinforced the expectancy that the only protection—protection he came to believe he could not do without—would come from them.

Stuttering thus became a help-seeking behaviour. His mother emphasized his dependence by going to school before each term to talk to his teachers. The speech impediment began when Robert, fearful, crying, and overcome by fright and self-pity, momentarily could not talk. The immediate consequence confirmed Robert's growing belief that he had a speech problem and that it needed mother's intervention.

From J. Rotter, *Social Learning and Clinical Psychology*, pp. 146–7. Reprinted by permission of the author.

The Psychological Situation

In reviewing the basic postulates of SLT at the beginning of this chapter, we found one principle specifically recognizing the unity of personality, an individual consistency principle. But human behaviour also varies as cues signal the behaviour called for, and SLT recognizes, as we have seen, the significance of the behavioural environment. Most of us are quiet and attentive in a classroom and boisterous on a baseball diamond. Individually, we share with most others in our society a great common ground of experience concerning important situations—classrooms, greeting and parting from others, casual social interchange, mealtimes, deference to authority. Indeed, I am only hinting at the range of shared situational knowledge and experience.

While we will think alike about many cues that direct our behaviour, however, each of us also learns some unique things about the situations we encounter. Examples: situations that evoke anger or fear or competitiveness, or arouse expectancies of failure; sexual situations; achievement situations; situations that provide opportunities for dependence on others; situations that encourage independence. Some are very powerful—that is, most people in a culture will experience them similarly—but even in the most compelling, there will be individual differences in experience. Others provide a wider variety of individual learning, particularly those that are open-ended, permitting different outcomes. Many social and achievement situations are just of this unbound sort, and as a result of differing experiences in them, individuals may pursue quite different goals and acquire quite different expectancies.

Consider the case of Robert in situational terms. How did Robert interpret speaking in public? Interactions with teachers? His relationship with his mother and aunt during childhood and adolescence? Remember that Robert acknowledged that he stuttered less when he felt superior to others.

Psychological situations are defined by cues that tell us what reinforcements may be expected to result from the behaviour possibilities we see. As Rotter says,

> From the SLT view, each situation is composed of cues serving to arouse in the individual certain expectancies for reinforcement of specific behaviours. For example, even though an individual may be described as possessing an extremely strong predisposition to aggressive behaviour, he will not behave aggressively in a given situation if the latter contains cues suggesting to him that aggressive behaviour is very likely to result in strong punishment. Meanings that cues acquire for the individual are based on prior learning history and can be determined in advance in order to help us predictively. Some of these meanings can be assumed on a cultural basis, but the possibilities raised by idiosyncratic life experiences must be recognized also' (Rotter et al., 1972, p. 37).

To understand individual behaviour thoroughly, we need to know how a person categorizes or interprets the behavioural environments in which we wish to predict. We need to know the expectancies the person has learned in those situations about the effectiveness of his or her behaviour in gaining potential reinforcements or avoiding unpleasant or punishing consequences. We also need to know the value or importance to the person of the potential reinforcements. A defiant schoolboy may think that a teacher's reprimand is trivial and value highly the approval of his peers for talking back.

Research

The psychology of learning brought an experimental approach to the study of personality and also a commitment to controlled research. SLT has followed the approach and observed the commitment. Much of the extensive work on hypotheses of the theory has been concerned with expectancy learning and changes in expectancy. Let's start our review of SLT research by considering a series of studies of expectancy carried out by Rotter, colleagues, and students. They began with experiments designed to manipulate expectancies of personal control, which they soon extended to studies examining individual differences in the belief that one has control over the outcomes of his or her behaviour.

The Locus of Control of Reinforcement

The core idea is that generalized expectancies about the control of reinforcement will have an influence over the behavioural choices people make. This expectancy concept is called

internal versus external control of reinforcement. Internal control is the expectancy that the important reinforcements in life are mostly determined by one's own behaviour. External control is the expectancy that rewards and punishments are beyond one's control, meted out by powerful and often capricious others or by fate or luck. It is important to understand that this is a continuous dimension, ranging from very strong belief in internal control at one end to very strong belief in external control at the other. It is not a typology.

Among the first studies of internal vs external control were experiments on learning in situations that were either visibly a matter of skill or clearly determined by chance (James and Rotter, 1958; Rotter, Liverant, and Crowne, 1961). These experiments showed that participants in skill or chance conditions differed strongly in how they behaved. When reinforcement for successful performance suddenly and without explanation ended, participants in the skill task took longer to quit; we could say that they were reluctant to abandon their expectancy—acquired in initial training trials—that they were skilful at the task. Those in the chance situation had the same success in the training phase but would have thought that their performance was just lucky. With a continuous string of failures, they readily extinguished. The most likely belief for them was that their luck had changed. In another pair of skill and chance conditions, participants succeeded on only half the training trials before reinforcement was again terminated. With this training experience of being correct only 50 per cent of the time, participants in the skill task stopped early. Their belief must have been, 'I'm failing because I'm not very good at this.' Those in the chance task, having had a number of encounters with failure in training, took longer to recognize that a situation over which they had no control had changed.

These promising studies clearly showed that we could teach laboratory experiment participants that their performance was under their own control or out of their hands, a matter of luck. The next step was to ask whether life situations teach us about the control of reinforcement and how instrumental we are in determining the things that happen to us. This step involved the development of a personality questionnaire to measure individual differences in expectancies of internal and external control. Thus, the concept became a dimension of personality, a content variable, and its implications were extended to a broad band of social behaviour and social learning. The test is in a format called forced choice: there are two alternatives for each question, and the respondent must chose one. Some sample items are in Table 14.1.

Generalized expectancies about causal relationships between behaviour and reinforcement are acquired as we meet a great variety of learning situations. We do not all acquire the same expectancies about how reinforcement occurs, even though we all go to school, have social relationships, succeed more or less at the myriad tasks that confront us, and have experiences with the accidental and unpredictable. Some people learn strong generalized expectancies of internal control, while others develop beliefs about the external control of reinforcements in the same situations. What experiences in childhood would cause children to begin to develop generalized expectancies of internal control? Of external control?

The Development of Internal Versus External Control Expectancies

The childhood origins of internal versus external control have been investigated by three procedures: retrospective reports by young adults of their parents' childrearing

Table 14.1 Sample Items from the Internal–External Control Scale

I more strongly believe that (choose *a* or *b* for each question):

1a. Many of the unhappy things in people's lives are partly due to bad luck.
1b. People's misfortunes result from the mistakes they make.

2a. No matter how hard you try, some people just don't like you.
2b. People who can't get others to like them don't understand how to get along with others.

3a. Sometimes I can't understand how teachers arrive at the grades they give.
3b. There is a direct connection between how hard I study and the grades I get.

4a. The average citizen can have an influence in government decisions.
4b. The world is run by the few people in power, and there is not much the little guy can do about it.

Source: From Rotter, 1966.

practices; interviews with mothers whose children who have been given an internal versus external control personality questionnaire; and observations of maternal and child behaviour. Interviews with mothers are better than adult recall of their parents' childrearing practices, and observational studies of mothers and children are better yet. Let's look at examples of the latter two.

Chance, who had been Rotter's PhD student, interviewed mothers of school children in grades three through seven, and she had the children complete a personality questionnaire measuring internal/external control (Chance, 1972). The interviews were carefully structured, and they yielded scores on maternal control, hostility/rejection, democratic attitudes, and independence training. She found that boys' expectancies of internal control were associated with earlier independence training and with less concern by their mothers about the need to control their sons' behaviour. The mothers of the internal boys also tended to be more highly educated. No significant relation between internal/external control and maternal attitudes turned up for girls. Chance had no explanation, and I'm afraid I can't say why either.

The second study was even more ambitious. Crandall and Crandall (1983) gave measures of internal/external control to young adults whose parents had been observed in home visits years earlier when their children were small. The observational data came from three periods in each child's life: birth to age three; age three to six; and age six to ten. The analysis consisted of correlations between ratings on each of the observational variables and the young adulthood scores of the offspring on two internal/external questionnaires. Crandall and Crandall found a different pattern of results for males and females, and the results from the two internal/external questionnaires were not identical. Virginia Crandall and

"Amazing, three failed marriages, scores of disastrous relationships, many financial reversals, and countless physical ailments, but through it all I've always had good luck parking."

her colleagues had earlier studied internal/external control in elementary school children, using the same sort of home-visit ratings, and had found maternal protectiveness, nurturance, affection, and approval associated with internal locus of control in the children (Katkovsky, Crandall, and Good, 1967).

In the study of young adults, however, intentional independence training was positively related to internal control, and maternal affection and approval were *negatively* related to internal control. That is, the more affectionate and approving the mothers were rated when their children were six and younger, the more their young adult offspring tended to have *external* expectancies. Crandall and Crandall offered a hypothesis to account for this genuine puzzle, suggesting that nurturance and warmth and the security they foster may be necessary for the development of internal expectancies only when children are very small. But for internal expectancies to become a stable and lasting feature of personality, a critical requirement is early and consistent independence training. In one way or another, mothers may need to say to their children, 'Now get out of my hair, dear, and go do something!' Mothers who teach their children to believe in internal control may insist as a matter of course that they encounter the reasonable consequences of their actions, both good and bad, a requirement leading to the development of the expectancy that their own behaviour makes a difference.

Internal Versus External Control in Adults

What are the consequences of beliefs in internal or external control of reinforcement in adults? The literature is now vast; there have been hundreds (more likely thousands) of experimental and field studies—research studying the relation of a great array of social behaviour to scores on the internal/external control questionnaire. Let me present a few of the outstanding examples.

Gore and Rotter (1963) did the trailblazing study of social action. Its setting was the deep South at the height of the civil rights movement. From the theory, commitment to protest for civil rights by blacks—by sit-ins, marches, voter registration—would be much more likely among those with more internal beliefs. They started by giving a number of personality questionnaires, including the internal/external control scale, to students at a southern black college. Weeks later, a student with no apparent connection to the questionnaires entered the classes in which the questionnaires had been administered to solicit volunteers for civil rights action. He ended his appeal by passing out forms on which students could indicate their interest in participating. There were five categories of commitment, from declining participation to strong forms of action to end discrimination.

Using the categories to classify their classroom participants, Gore and Rotter calculated the mean internal/external control scale score for each category. For those checking any of the strong categories, the mean score was significantly more internal than the mean score of the weak categories, alone or combined. Although this was a paper commitment, it did ask for personal identification at a time when it was dangerous to be known as a civil rights activist. Gore and Rotter pointedly noted: 'Shortly before the time of testing, a large number of [blacks] were arrested and placed in jail for a similar march on the state house of a nearby state' (p. 62).

Strickland, also a Rotter student, followed with a second civil rights study (1965). Her subjects were also black college students in the South, all of whom, like Gore and

Figure 14.1 The questionnaire asking for commitment to social action (From Gore and Rotter, 1963)

Students for Freedom Rally

Please check any or all aspects of our program in which you would be willing to participate.

I would be interested in: Check here:

(A) Attending a rally for civil rights.   _____

(B) Signing a petition to go to local government and/or news media calling
       for full and immediate integration of all facilities throughout Florida.   _____

(C) Joining a silent march to the capitol to demonstrate our plea for full
       and immediate integration of all facilities throughout Florida.   _____

(D) Joining a Freedom Riders Group for a trip during the break.   _____

(E) I would not be interested in participating in any of the foregoing.   _____

                    Signature _____

                    Address _____

                    _____

                    Telephone number _____

Rotter's research participants, had grown up with the bitter taste of segregation and the denial of basic rights. They differed among themselves, however, in one major respect: half of them were civil rights activists, members of the Student Nonviolent Coordinating Committee, and the others were students known to be uninvolved. The questionnaire scores of the SNCC members showed a far stronger belief in internal control than those of the inactive students. Internal control sustained the activists; most of them were paying a big price for their involvement. As Strickland wrote about them, 'Every active subject . . . had participated in some phase of civil rights protest, such as voter registration, sit-ins, and demonstrations. The mean number of arrests per person in conjunction with civil rights activities was about five, with a range of zero to 62. Nineteen . . . had received threats of violence directed either at themselves or their families' (p. 355).

This social action research led to further studies of beliefs about the control of reinforcement in black and white children, in the course of which these initial studies were replicated. The theory has been applied to the psychology of women, to depression, and to the way people preserve or endanger their health (Strickland, 1977, 1978). Belief that there are things one can do in unfair or stressful situations is an important antidote to despair and helplessness (Lefcourt, 1983), and those who think they can exercise some degree of control are less vulnerable to illness and to depression (Abramson, Seligman, and Teasdale, 1978).

Telling, real-life examples of helplessness are all around us. Let me cite one from Robert Coles's monumental study of American migrant families (Coles, 2003). You hear in this woman's story not only the despairing hopelessness, but also a deep-seated belief that reinforcement is controlled by others, that there is hardly anything she can do.

My children, they suffer, I know. They hurts, and I can't stop it. I just have to pray that they'll stay alive, somehow. They gets the colic, and I don't know what to do. One of them, he can't breathe right and his chest, it's in trouble. I can hear the noise inside when he takes his breaths. The worst thing, if you ask me, is the bites they get. It makes them unhappy, real unhappy. They itches and scratches and bleeds, and oh, it's the worst. They must want to tear all their skin off, but you can't do that. There'd still be mosquitoes and ants and rats and like that around and they'd be after your insides then, if the skin was all gone. That's what would happen then. But I say to myself it's life, the way living is, and there's not much to do but accept what happens. Do you have a choice but to accept? That's what I'd like to ask you, yes sir. Once when I was little, I seem to recall asking my uncle if there wasn't something you could do, but he said no, there wasn't, and to hush up. So I did. Now I have to tell my kids the same, that you don't go around complaining—you just don't (p. 153).

Sampling other findings, we discover just what we would anticipate as consequences of this generalized expectancy about the locus of control of reinforcement. People with internal beliefs are less likely to conform, particularly when there is something at stake such as a bet on the outcome of one's judgements (Crowne and Liverant, 1963). Those who believe in internal control are more likely to quit smoking; they resist others' attempts to influence them and are less inclined to submit unquestioningly to authority; they are more aware of important political happenings that could affect their lives; as hospital patients or reformatory inmates, they cope better with their situations, acquiring more relevant and useful information (Crowne, 1979; Rotter, 1966). The internal/external control expectancy concept has been robust, provocative of a vast amount of research, and durable (Lefcourt, 1992).

I need to issue a small caution. It's awfully easy to see people who hold internal expectancies as the heroes in the white hats, those with external beliefs as the bad guys with the black hats. Rotter is very explicit in saying that the extremes of *both* internal and external control may be maladaptive. In a world in which there are events beyond the possibility of one's control, to think that one can ward off all the bad happenings in society is to take internal control of reinforcement beyond a healthy limit. Reasonable care and self-protection, yes; an exaggeration of one's own potential influence, no. At the other end of the dimension, we fail to take a realistic personal hand in what happens to us when we believe that university grades, the possible effects of smoking, and the politics that affect our lives are just matters of luck, fate, or powerful others. But *some* recognition of happenstance is not psychologically unhealthy.

Finally, there are many offshoots of SLT research. Among them are applications to psychological testing, to learning theory, to problems in social psychology, to psychopathology, and to psychotherapy (Rotter, et al., 1972). SLT is a wellspring of well-conceived, theory-driven research.

Social Learning Theory in Perspective

Social learning theory has been the model—although often unacknowledged—for a number of present-day cognitive learning theories. Albert Bandura's social cognitive theory, which we take up next, is one of them. And it is no wonder that the theory has had widespread influence. SLT gave the psychological situation a centre-stage position in personality theory and made the prediction of behaviour more precise by introducing the expectancy concept as a significant determiner of need-related behaviour. Modern students of personality who emphasize the importance of the psychological situation (Mischel, 1968, 2003; Mischel and Shoda, 1995, for example) owe their situational thinking to Rotter and to SLT.

Classic psychodynamic personality theories have largely approached motivation as an internal process of drive (or instinct) arousal and satiation leading to quiescence, a conception that also appears in Dollard and Miller's S-R theory. Rotter gave motivation an altogether different focus by treating it in the context of goal-directed social behaviour. The goals important in personality are social goals, just as the behaviour we seek to predict is largely social behaviour. Cognitive psychologists were impatient with the old view of motivation, which they considered too confining. As Hilgard wrote in *Psychology in America* (1987), 'A problem with motivational theories was that, despite their authors' desire for universality, the starting point chosen [need and drive] was too narrow to cover the richness of human purposive, goal-seeking action' (p. 380). SLT gave an effective answer to the problem and to cognitive psychology's criticism.

From its very inception, SLT has been a research-based theory. The early research explored the concepts of expectancy and reinforcement value (or, in generalized form, freedom of movement and need value), establishing their usefulness in the prediction of a variety of behaviour. Then came applications to a wider range of social behaviour, such as the work on internal/external control, which took the process concept of expectancy and applied it to the study of individual differences.

SLT has had a significant clinical usefulness. It treats psychopathology (except for very serious disorders such as schizophrenia that, as we shall see, have a biological basis) as learned ways of reacting, and psychotherapy as a process of learning. A patient's symptoms are seen as efforts—not very rational and certainly self-defeating—to solve problems, and psychotherapy becomes a social encounter in which the therapist seeks to redirect the patient's thinking, to encourage the patient to attempt new ways of approaching difficult real-life situations, and to enhance problem-solving skills. In fact, says Rotter (1970), life situations, not the talking situation of psychotherapy, are the ultimate source of change. It is a long generalization from talking about problematical social relationships, for example, to confronting them face-to-face and actually changing behaviour in them. Psychotherapy initiates and guides the process.

Are there criticisms to make of SLT? Yes, of course. It is a relatively young theory, and there is much in personality psychology that it has not yet approached. New developments in behaviour genetics that implicate genes in such behaviour as risk-taking, and developments in the understanding of how children are socialized (the importance of peer learning, for example) need to be recognized and incorporated in the theory. It represents, however, a wonderful and highly promising step toward a true social learning theory of personality.

A Fresh Look: Research Today

Only a few years after the assassination of President John F. Kennedy, Rotter extended his study of generalized expectancies by developing a measure of interpersonal trust. It was certainly the time for it. Nearly a third of Americans believed that Lee Harvey Oswald could not have been the lone gunman—this wretched little man, radicalized but confused, whose motive for killing a president would never be certain—and they saw the conclusion of the Warren Commission on the Assassination of President Kennedy, appointed by President Johnson, as a coverup for a conspiracy. Whose conspiracy? Theories abounded: disbelievers in the commission's report had a large handful to choose from. Time did not allay doubt, and in 1991, 28 years afterward, Oliver Stone fanned public mistrust in the conclusion of a distinguished body of public figures headed by the Chief Justice of the United States in the film *JFK*, dramatizing the most prominent conspiracy theory of all.

The personality questionnaire of interpersonal trust (Rotter, 1967) strongly predicted belief (or disbelief) in the Warren Commission Report. Research participants holding the expectancy that 'the word, promise, verbal or written statement of another individual or group can be relied on' (Rotter, 1971, p. 444) were disposed to accept the commission's finding; distrustful participants decisively agreed with the statement 'I believe that there was, in fact, a conspiracy and information about it has been kept from the public' (Hamsher, Geller, & Rotter, 1968). More than a decade of experimental study contributed evidence on the validity of the expectancy concept of trust and its measuring instrument (see Rotter, 1980).

The timeframe for the study was a period pointedly identified by a *New York Times* editorial as an 'age of suspicion', suspicion manifested not only in popular distrust of government but in personality measurement as well. Hochreich and Rotter (1970) found a significant decline in Interpersonal Trust Scale scores in the six years following the beginning of interpersonal trust research. Well, the student of

SLT shouldn't be surprised. Change the situation, and we are likely to change behaviour (and belief), right? Right. Has the tide of mistrust risen again to darken the way we think of our own world? There is lots on the screen of contemporary events to excite suspicion that we are not given the whole truth by those governing our lives. Following is your chance to assess your own expectancy that others can be trusted, and an opportunity to see how it may relate to some issues in contemporary trustworthiness. Of course, you are an *N* of 1, not a research sample. I suggest that you show the trust items below to some friends and mark down their replies. Then ask them the trustworthiness questions you've just answered. Is the personality measurement of interpersonal trust related to contemporary belief in the words and actions of public figures?

The Interpersonal Trust Scale. There are twenty-five items in the original version of the scale, padded by fillers to disguise the purpose. I have chosen twelve, and there is no reason to try to put you on by masking the real aim of the scale. For each item, indicate the degree to which you agree with each statement, marking 1 for strong agreement, 2 for mild, 3 for neither agree nor disagree, 4 for mild disagreement, and 5 if you strongly disagree.

1. In dealing with strangers, one is better off to be cautious until they have provided evidence that they are trustworthy.
2. Fear and social disgrace or punishment rather than conscience prevent most people from breaking the law.
3. Using the honour system of *not* having a teacher present during exams would probably result in increased cheating.
4. The United Nations will never be an effective force in keeping world peace.

5. Most people would be horrified if they knew how much news that the public hears and sees is distorted.

6. If we really knew what was going on in international politics, the public would have reason to be more frightened than they now seem to be.

7. Many major national sports contests are fixed one way or another.

8. Most experts can be relied upon to tell the truth about the limits of their knowledge.

9. Most people can be counted on to do what they say they will do.

10. Most students in school would *not* cheat even if they were sure of getting away with it.

11. Most repairmen will not overcharge even if they think you are ignorant of their specialty.

12. A large share of accident claims filed against insurance companies are phony.

Scoring. We want higher scores to show greater interpersonal trust. Items 8–11 are stated in the trusting direction, so their scoring should be reversed (if you gave them a 1, score it 5; if you responded with 2, score 4, and so on). The average score of University of Connecticut students in 1969 was 66.6, approximately 2.6 on the five-point scale and mildly distrusting. On this twelve-item version, a corresponding average score would be 32.4. How did you fare?

Trust or Distrust in Today's World. Now just below you will find four questions about issues that confront North Americans in 2006. They are likely to be enduring, but even if they have faded from immediate concern you will know and hold beliefs about them. You could also devise your own questions about your government's handling of dominant issues at the time you are reading this. But let's try my issues.

1. I believe the present administration in the United States has truthfully presented the reasons for going to war with Iraq and for bringing a stable democratic government to the country.

2. I believe the policies of the American and Canadian governments to restrict the publication of photographs of the coffins of soldiers killed in combat in Iraq and Afghanistan are designed to keep from the public the cost in human life of the actions in these countries and to protect the image of the government.

3. I believe that the government spends tax dollars for appropriate purposes and is not covering up massive waste and fraud.

4. I believe private health care in the United States and the expansion of private health care in Canada are based less on the efficient delivery of medical services than on profit-motive interests.

Answer these questions with Yes or No. Notice that two of them, questions 1 and 3 are phrased in the trusting direction, numbers 2 and 4 in the direction of distrust. Do your answers show that you believe the government is trustworthy, or are you inclined to doubt? Were you consistent, or were your beliefs issue-specific? Does a personality disposition to trust or to mistrust lead to a general belief or disbelief in the trustworthiness of public officials, or do we repose trust issue by issue? I believe Rotter thinks the trust expectancy is widely generalized to many issues in public life. And, most important to our inquiry into the personality basis of trusting others, what is the relation between your Interpersonal Trust scale score and your answers to the issue questions? Do the scale responses of the friends you test predict their beliefs about public honesty or dishonesty?

SUMMARY

1. Social learning theory is a psychology of learning concentrating on significant social behaviour. It does not share S-R theory's emphasis on responses and habits, nor does it incorporate a drive-reduction motivation principle. Instead, it is a cognitive theory emphasizing goal-oriented behaviour, the meanings of situations to the person, and the concept of expectancy. It is, like Dollard and Miller's S-R approach, a reinforcement theory in its emphasis on the goals (reinforcements) people seek.

2. The term 'social learning' is borrowed from Dollard and Miller to make explicit the social nature of reinforcement in the acquisition and change of significant behaviour. It is important to recognize, however, that 'social learning' does not refer to a specific kind of theory; it is a term that expresses the context in which the learning of interest to the study of personality takes place.

3. Rotter was influenced by a number of distinguished theorists, among them Alfred Adler, Kurt Lewin, J.R. Kantor, Edward L. Thorndike, Edward C. Tolman, and Clark Hull. Their ideas can be seen in the social, cognitive, and learning emphases in SLT. The formal construction of the theory owes a debt to Hull.

4. Julian Rotter was born in Brooklyn to European immigrant parents. After graduating from Brooklyn College, where he attended seminars given by Adler, he went to the State University of Iowa for his MA, taking courses with Kurt Lewin. He received the PhD from Indiana University, taking courses with J.R. Kantor, whose behaviourist approach appears strongly in SLT. He taught at Ohio State University from 1946 to 1963 and thereafter at the University of Connecticut. A major book, *Social Learning and Clinical Psychology*, appeared in 1954. His theory and the research it has generated have had a major effect on personality psychology and have influenced the development of subsequent social learning and cognitive theories of personality.

5. The basic principles of SLT are stated in a set of seven postulates:
    - 'The unit of investigation for the study of personality is the interaction of the individual and his meaningful environment.'
    - 'Personality constructs [concepts] are not dependent for explanation upon constructs in any other field, including physiology, biology, or neurology. Scientific constructs for one mode of description should be consistent with constructs in any other field of science, but no hierarchy of dependency exists among them.'
    - 'Behaviour as described by personality constructs takes place in space and time. Although all such events may be described by psychological constructs, . . . they may also be described by physical constructs, as they are in such fields as physics, chemistry, and neurology. Any conception that regards the events themselves, rather than the descriptions of the events, as different is rejected as dualistic.'

    These three postulates reflect Kantor's insistence on the fundamental idea that a psychological level of explanation is no less scientifically useful for its purposes than, say, a physiological one.

    - 'Not all behaviour of an organism may be usefully described with personality constructs. Behaviour that may usefully be described by personality constructs appears in organisms of a particular level or stage of complexity and a particular level or stage of development.'
    - 'A person's experiences (or his interactions with his meaningful environment) influence each other. Otherwise stated, personality has unity.'
    - 'Behaviour as described by personality constructs has a directional aspect. It may be said to be goal-directed. The directional aspect of behaviour is inferred from the effect of reinforcing conditions.'
    - 'The occurrence of a behaviour of a person is determined not only by the nature or importance of goals or reinforcements but also by the person's anticipation or *expectancy* that these goals will occur. Such expectations are determined by previous experience and can be quantified.'

6. SLT is both a process and a content theory. Process concepts describe learning and change in behaviour. Content concepts characterize important individual differences. They represent dimensions along which individuals differ.

7. SLT rejects the drive stimulus reduction hypothesis of S-R theory in favour of the view that reinforcements

important in social life are established in early child-hood experience and become independent of primary drive states. This is an entirely empirical position on the nature of reinforcement and the effect of reinforcing stimuli. New stimuli can become reinforcers through association with reinforcers that already exist.

8. Expectancy learning begins early in childhood with the development of a sense of mastery and competence, a generalized expectancy of success. Learning to cope with failure is an important source of competence. Not all children are fortunate in acquiring strong expectancies of success. Poor parenting faces some children with damaging experiences of failure and criticism. One parental failing is to demand too much of children, setting a high *minimal goal* for their accomplishment. School grades are an example. Setting too high a minimal goal (by encouraging the belief that only 'A' grades are acceptable, for example) risks exposing a child to many experiences of failure.

9. SLT recognizes the importance of siblings as significant models in the development of expectancies. The theory also takes note of expectancy learning resulting from each child's special situation in the family. Rotter acknowledges the unique situations of only, older, and younger children in the family, an Adlerian concept.

10. The formal part of SLT consists of a set of behaviour formulas for the prediction of behaviour. These formulas may be applied both to simple situations involving a single behaviour and a single reinforcement, and to more complex situations involving a number of potential behaviours and reinforcements. The basic formula states that *behaviour potential = f(expectancy & reinforcement value)*, $BP = f(E \ \& \ RV)$. Subscripts in the formula represent the behaviour and the situation: $BP_{(x, s(1-n), R(a-n))} = f(E_{(x, s(1-n), R(a-n))} \ \& \ RV_{(a-n)})$. In words: the potential for behaviour *x* to occur in situations *1* to *n* toward reinforcements *a* to *n* is a function of the expectancies for these reinforcements in these situations and the value of the reinforcements. To be especially noted is the explicit recognition of the psychological situation, which is built right in to the behaviour equations. Note that a person might not seek a reinforcement for either of two reasons: he or she does not value the reinforcement or has a low expectancy of obtaining it.

11. To account for behaviour toward broader goals in a class of situations (that is, to predict need-related behav-

iour), SLT introduces new terms: *need potential, freedom of movement*, and *need value*, $NP = f(FM \ \& \ NV)$. Need potential is the probability of any of a related set of behaviours directed toward the satisfaction of a particular need. Freedom of movement is the generalized expectancy of satisfaction of the need, and need value is the importance of the need to the person.

12. Low freedom of movement will likely lead to avoidant, self-protective behaviour or to symbolic attempts to achieve the goal. The SLT analysis of conflict is low freedom of movement and high need value—a low generalized expectancy of satisfying an important need.

13. Among the implications of SLT is a view of disturbed behaviour that regards it as often purposive and goal-directed. Neurotic behaviour may directly satisfy important needs: it is often reinforced by others such as parents, spouses, and friends.

14. Problem behaviour is changed by modifying expectancies, not need values, which are hard to alter. Delinquency is a good example. The delinquent child is likely to have appropriate needs (for affection, recognition) that are gratified by a rebellious peer group. Delinquents learn expectancies that their nonconforming peers will satisfy important needs. We try to increase freedom of movement for need satisfaction from better sources.

15. There is individual consistency in personality (that's postulate 5), but behaviour also varies with situations. Situations are composed of cues that arouse expectancies for reinforcement (positive or negative). These cues are learned and may be unique to a specific person. To predict individual behaviour, we have to know the meaning of situations important to the person—that is, the significant cues and the expectancies they arouse.

16. SLT is a research-intensive theory. Because of the importance of the expectancy concept, much of the research on the theory has investigated expectancy learning and expectancy change. Among the most significant research is an application of the expectancy concept to the behaviour choices people make. This is research on the expectancy concept of belief in the *internal or external control of reinforcement*. Internal control is the generalized expectancy that one's own behaviour determines rewards and punishments. External control is the generalized expectancy that rewards and punishments are determined by

powerful others or by luck or fate. Note that this is a continuous dimension, not a typology. Expectancies of internal or external control are learned in early childhood experience, in school, and in social relationships.

17. Studies of the development of expectancies of internal or external control in children have used both maternal interviews and home visits. They find that early independence training and less maternal control are related to expectancies of internal control. In young adults, studied with their parents when they were children, intentional independence training is positively related to internal expectancies. Maternal affection appears to be needed for the development of internal expectancies in small children; for internal control to become a lasting part of personality, independence training is crucial.

18. Among adults, personality measures of internal/external control predict a range of social behaviour: social action by black college students to redress discrimination in the segregated south of the 1960s, responsibility for ensuring personal health, resistance to conformity pressures, and political awareness. The concept of internal versus external control is a robust personality variable with correlates that confirm the predictions of the theory.

19. SLT has been a model for other modern cognitive learning theories of personality, introducing the concept of expectancy to personality, giving the psychological situation a formal and central place in personality study, and broadening the concept of motivation in its emphasis on goal-directed behaviour. In addition to its strong research base, it has also shown important clinical usefulness.

TO TEST YOUR UNDERSTANDING

1. In what ways does SLT differ from S-R theory? How are the two theories similar?

2. What is it about SLT that makes it a cognitive learning theory? What cognitive processes are represented in its concepts, and what are their functions?

3. Put into words the formula, $NP = f(FM \ \& \ NV)$. Explain its meaning and give examples. Does this formula bring us closer to the meaningful experience of people? In what way? If not, why?

4. What does it mean to view disturbed behaviour as purposive and goal-directed? Does this mean that problem behaviour is no different from normal behaviour in its purposiveness and goal-direction? Think of some examples to illustrate your conclusion.

CHAPTER FIFTEEN

Learning Theories of Personality: The Social Cognitive Learning Theories of Albert Bandura and Walter Mischel

Albert Bandura

Introduction

In 1963, Albert Bandura, a young Stanford University professor, and Richard Walters, his first graduate student and later chair of the Department of Psychology at the University of Waterloo, published a small book titled *Social Learning and Personality Development*. Bandura and Walters resolved to take over the name 'social learning', and they staked their right to it with the naked acquisitiveness of a pair of claim jumpers in the Klondike. This was Bandura and Walters' opening argument:

> Previous attempts to conceptualize social phenomena, including deviant patterns of response, within the framework of modern learning theories have, generally speaking, relied on a limited range of learning-theory principles that have largely been developed and tested on the basis of studies of animal subjects and human subjects in one-person situations. Because of their neglect of social variables, these attempts have been particularly ineffective in accounting for the acquisition of novel social responses. Moreover, the exponents of learning-theory approaches to the problems of social and antisocial behavior have, for the most part, tacitly accepted the basic tenets and concepts of psychodynamic models and have merely translated these into terms familiar and acceptable to the learning theorist (pp. 43–4).

By the end of the 1950s, behaviourism was no longer the major force it had been in psychology. Its decline was the result of a constricting narrowness, especially when compared with the open-minded and liberating view of the new kid on the block, cognitive psychology. But behaviourism wasn't to be counted out yet. Social cognitive learning theory (which we'll abbreviate as SCLT) gave it a new life, or so the new social learning theorists claimed, and they accomplished the resurrection by demoting the reinforcement principle, thereby making behaviourism both social and cognitive. This—breathing life into a moribund school that had dominated psychology for half a century—was a very big deal, and it is hardly any exaggeration at all to say that Bandura and his students did it with a single experiment. We'll begin with that experiment, which borrowed heavily from Miller and Dollard's work on imitation and added a novel twist.

For imitation to occur, we have to have someone to imitate—a model—and we have to have a reason for imitation. *Reinforcement*★, you would have thought. Bandura and Walters noted that Miller and Dollard's experiments on imitative learning had reinforced subjects for reproducing the model's behaviour. They must have begun by wondering if direct reinforcement for imitation was necessary, as S-R theory claimed. This was the origin of the new take on the question. Suppose, they asked, children are exposed to the behaviour of a model and are then given an opportunity to reproduce it. The model does not receive any reward for her behaviour, and the children are not rewarded for imitating it. Would imitation occur?

An Observational Learning Experiment

In their experiment, Bandura, Ross, and Ross (1961) had nursery school children observe a model who either physically and verbally abused a large, inflated doll (Bobo) or else sat quietly and ignored the doll (the control condition). In the room were various aggressive implements (wooden mallet, for example), some of which the aggressive model used. We should note that the aggressive repertoire was unique; few of the things the model said or did could the children ever have witnessed. Then, each child was observed alone. The results were (pun intended) striking. Without seeing the model rewarded or being rewarded themselves, the children closely reproduced the aggressive acts.

A subsequent experiment compared the amount of modelled aggression witnessed in children exposed to abusive live models to the aggression seen in groups exposed to filmed humans and to a cartoon cat. After observing the model, the children were mildly frustrated by having the appealing toys they had been playing with taken away, then were observed alone, as in the original experiment. Frustration did increase the amount of aggression, but it was in the children who had seen the aggressive models. If we consider directly imitative responses *plus* other aggression toward Bobo that wasn't specifically imitative, the cartoon model elicited more aggression than the real model (Bandura, 1973). These findings are shown in Figures 15.1 and 15.2. Models who were rewarded (another adult praised the model and gave him or her pop and candy) elicited more imitation; imitation was greatly inhibited when children saw the model being punished (called a coward and a bully, spanked with a rolled-up newspaper, and threatened with a further beating for any more aggression).

Observational Learning and the Reinforcement Principle

What happened to the reinforcement principle? Bandura didn't throw it out, but he did insist on a major concession: that very significant behaviour could be acquired simply on the basis of observation. What must be recognized, he argued, is that reinforcement is effective only when the behaving or observing person notes the reinforcing contingencies (behaviour X followed by desirable or by negative consequences) and sees their relevance to situations he or she can anticipate. Reinforcement affects not acquisition but

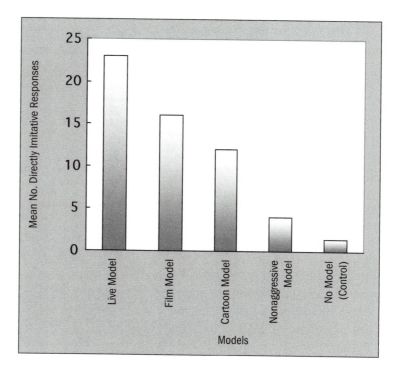

Figure 15.1 Direct imitation by children seeing an aggressive model (After Bandura, 1973.)

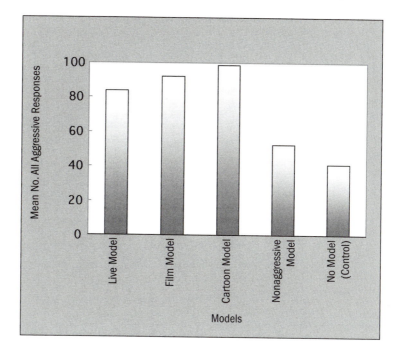

Figure 15.2 Aggression following frustration in children seeing aggressive and nonaggressive models. (After Bandura, 1973.)

performance of modelled learning. So, children seeing a model who is punished for striking Bobo show very little aggression, but this doesn't mean that they haven't learned it. Offered rewards for doing exactly what the model did, they imitate closely. You should puzzle a bit over how Bandura will deal with the reinforcement principle. Does reinforcement only affect performance? Or does it have another, less observable role?

One nursery school boy's imitation of the model's aggressive acts. Is the aggression real? Note the expression on the boy's face in the lower left panel. (Courtesy Dr Albert Bandura.)

We thus have two conclusions with far-reaching implications that form the underpinning for social cognitive theory. First, learning that forms the basis of personality is *social*. We learn from observing the behaviour of other people. And, we may add, the more significant those other people are to us, the more similar they are to us, the more they profit from (are rewarded for) the behaviour we see, and the more we are actually able to do what they do, the more likely it is that we will imitate them. This becomes in Bandura's hands a major developmental principle. Second, the learning of consequence to personality is *cognitive*. We see children as they observe the behaviour of others selecting important aspects of that witnessed behaviour, remembering them and thinking about them, and then reproducing them later in the right (as each child sees it) context. Children don't have to reproduce on the spot the behaviour they have just seen, and there is no inevitable link between learning and immediate reward. We grown-ups are no different.

Behaviourism thus got its reprieve, but it had to undergo some dramatic changes in approach, abandoning the tight S–R link and the S–R view of motivation. Figure 15.3 shows how differently S–R theory and social cognitive theory make use of the reinforcement principle in observational learning.

Albert Bandura: Personal History

Albert Bandura was born in the little Alberta town of Mundare in December 1925. His parents were of Polish descent, farmers, and his father operated a dray business. After graduating from Mundare's tiny high school, he spent a summer working on the Alaskan Highway. His co-workers were a motley lot, many of them less interested in highway construction and maintenance than in escaping, as Bandura said, 'creditors, alimony, and probation officers'. We'd rather profit from experiences we seek out, but

Figure 15.3 How reinforcement affects observational learning: S-R theory versus social cognitive theory (Bandura, A., *Social Learning Theory*, 1st edition, © 1977. Adapted by permission of Pearson Education, Inc., Upper Saddle River, NJ.)

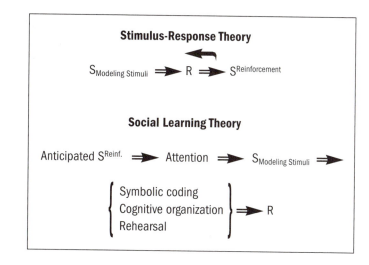

we do learn from unwanted ones; Bandura's colleagues, on the wrong side of banks, ex-wives, and the law, taught him 'a keen appreciation for the psychopathology of everyday life' (American Psychological Association, 1981, p. 28). He went to the University of British Columbia in 1946, majored in psychology, and graduated in 1949.

Bandura gained acceptance in the graduate clinical psychology program at the State University of Iowa, where he received the PhD in 1952. Iowa was noted for the strong influence of learning theory, notably Hullian; among its faculty were Yale graduates Kenneth W. Spence, Judson Brown, and Robert R. Sears. Spence, particularly, was an eminent learning theorist, arguably Clark Hull's most outstanding heir. Bandura spent a year on a clinical internship at the Wichita, Kansas, Guidance Center, and then joined the faculty of Stanford University. He rose quickly through the ranks and became the David Starr Jordan Professor of Social Science in Psychology in 1974. He was president of the American Psychological Association (1974), received its Distinguished Scientific Contribution Award (1980), and spent several years as chair of Stanford's Department of Psychology (sometimes an honour to be prized but more often, I suspect, a chronic pain). Apart from *Social Learning and Personality Development*, his books include *Adolescent Aggression* (1959), *Principles of Behavior Modification* (1969), *Aggression: A Social Learning Analysis* (1973), *Social Learning Theory* (1977)—a major statement of the theory—and *Social Foundations of Thought and Action* (1986), a more detailed exposition of social cognitive theory. He continues to teach at Stanford.

Emphases and Major Concepts of Social Cognitive Theory

The New Reinforcement Principle

We have already seen two of the notable emphases of the theory—its revision (or demotion) of the reinforcement principle, and the cognitive emphasis it gave to behaviourism. Let's just make sure that we're clear about the recasting of reinforcement. Of course, reinforcement increases the probability of behaviour, including the acquisition of new behaviour.

Albert Bandura (Courtesy Dr Albert Bandura.)

The development here is SCLT's claim that overt reinforcement isn't necessary to new learning. The observing child (or adult) *anticipates* (a cognitive process) the reinforcement he or she *will* receive for imitating a modelled act. Reinforcement may thus be given to oneself. This is **self-reinforcement★**, which can play a large role in observational learning. The observer sees an important, valued, interesting, similar-to-self model doing something (even something usually disapproved of, like aggression). He or she says, 'Wow! I can do that,' and is exhilarated by the imitation. Self-reinforcement is the subject of a later section.

People anticipate the outcomes of their behaviour. Says Bandura, 'By representing foreseeable outcomes symbolically, people can convert future consequences into current motivators of behavior. Most actions are thus largely under anticipatory control' (Bandura, 1977a, p. 18). Reinforcement, then, is 'an informative and motivational operation rather than . . . a mechanical response strengthener' (1977a, p. 21). The classical view of reinforcement, from the time of Thorndike's studies of animal learning before the turn of the twentieth century, holds that reinforcement is a consequence of a response and acts, we might say, backward to increase the probability of the response. Miller and Dollard applied this S-R view of reinforcement to imitative learning: the learner observes a model's response, repeats it, and is rewarded. The direct reinforcement acts exactly the way a pellet of food reinforces a rat's bar-pressing behaviour. Bandura makes the whole process of reinforcement anticipatory: observing a model's behaviour, learners anticipate reinforcement, attend to the modelling stimuli, represent the modelled behaviour to themselves (coding it symbolically and organizing their thinking about it, and rehearsing it), and then imitate. Reinforcement in this cognitive view is no longer the consequence of a response but an **antecedent** that guides subsequent behaviour.

Determinism

What determines behaviour? The great social, personality, and learning psychologist Kurt Lewin had defined the relation of behaviour to person and the meaningful contexts (the *field* or *environment*) in which behaviour takes place: $\mathbf{B} = f(\mathbf{P},\mathbf{E})$. Behaviour is a function of *both* person and environment. Change the attributes of person or situation, and the behaviour is different. Take especial note that person and environment are *independent* influences on behaviour. Bandura calls this person–situation interaction *unidirectional*. Example: an aggressive boy on a school playground joins a touch football game. The rough and tumble of the game makes him angry, and he strikes the boy who tagged him. Two effects on behaviour—aggressiveness in the boy and an aggressive game—operate independently to produce his behaviour.

Bandura points out that we could think of person and environment mutually influencing each other, with a *partially* bidirectional effect on behaviour. To use our current example, the aggressive boy induces the other boys in the game to play more roughly, and their increased aggressiveness magnifies his own anger. But this still isn't it. Bandura goes further to say that the relation between person and environment is one of **reciprocal determinism★**. It is not just person variables and environmental variables that determine behaviour; behaviour itself influences the person and situation, each of which in turn affects behaviour. Here is an example from Bandura:

[P]ersonal preferences influence when and which programs, from among the available alternatives, individuals choose to watch on television. Although the potential televised environment is identical for all viewers, the actual televised environment that impinges on given individuals depends on what they select to watch. Through their viewing behavior, they partly shape the nature of the future televised environment. Because production costs and commercial requirements also determine what people are shown, the options provided in the televised environment partly shape the viewers' preferences. Here all three factors—viewer preferences, viewing behavior, and televised offerings—reciprocally affect each other (1978, p. 346).

Returning to the angry boy and the football game, if we look for reciprocal determinism we will see an aggressive boy playing an aggressive game, making him more aggressive. His increased aggressiveness acts on the other boys in the game, making them more aggressive. In turn, their greater aggressiveness and his own aggressive behaviour arouse even greater aggression. Behaviour isn't disembodied, as Bandura observes; because of his intensified aggressive behaviour and that of the others, the boy thinks and fantasizes more aggressively (Bandura, 1999, p. 158). His thought and fantasy nourish his angry feelings and may lead him to seek other targets to vent his anger on. So person, environment, and behaviour mutually influence each other. Behaviour changes the environment and is in turn altered by the changes it produces. Since there is a person in this triadic equation, both behaviour and environment will change cognition and emotion—the boy's *thinking* about the outcomes of his behaviour, the other boys, and his relation to them, and his *feelings* about himself and the others. Bandura's diagram of the three approaches to determinism is in Figure 15.4. If you think that this is not at all simple, you are absolutely right.

Self-reinforcement

The behaviourist stance, most especially in its radical form (B.F. Skinner's version discussed in Chapter 13), contends that human behaviour, no less than the behaviour of animals, is controlled by reinforcing stimuli in the environment (so, also, thought the S-R theorists). Thus, it is the (external) reinforcement history that determines when and where a response will be performed, when and where it will be inhibited because it is inappropriate and will lead to negative consequences, or when and where it won't be

Figure 15.4 How behaviour is determined: Unidirectional, partially bidirectional, and reciprocal determinism (After Bandura, 1999, p. 157.)

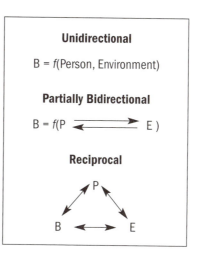

performed because discriminative cues in the situation don't call it forth. To be sure, our responses operate on the environment to produce reinforcement (that's why they're called **operants★**), but it's the environment that rewards or punishes them and thus determines their fate in our behavioural repertoire.

So are we no more than products of the environmental stimulation we've been exposed to? Bandura doesn't think so. Before we see how he deals with this reinforcement conundrum, I must add that what I've just said is a caricature of the behaviourist's (Skinner's) position. Skinner tried to clear up the misconception, noting that we can and do manage our own behaviour. We can and do choose our environments, and when we want to avoid engaging in some particular behaviour (we'd like, say, to quit smoking), we stay away from smoking situations. We don't go to bars where smoking is permitted, we don't linger over coffee after dinner, and we stay away from smoking friends until we have our addictive urge well under control. We create environments conducive to particular behaviour. Skinner and Charles Ferster wrote *Schedules of Reinforcement* in 1957, during the time that I was a graduate student. I and my fellow students all knew—although I can no longer recall how—that Ferster and Skinner had arranged to write in a 'writing environment', a room rich with writing cues—typewriter, paper, pencils; they worked there at the same time each day and maintained their productivity by self-reinforcement. The self-discipline was incredible to us. We did not recognize that we were surviving in graduate school on our own far less sedulous forms of it.

Bandura believes that behaviour is determined not only by external consequences (rewards and punishments) but *very* significantly by self-reinforcement. We learn standards that apply to the things we do and think; when we meet them, we are pleased and proud (these are two great reinforcers), and when we don't measure up (or do something that our internal standards tell us is bad) we are disappointed in ourselves, ashamed, or guilt-ridden. Of course, internal standards are learned in the course of development through rewards, withholding rewards, and punishment by important others. Dad and Mum are pleased as punch with the B's you bring home in the early grades in school and show you by praise. They have set a standard for you—B is a good achievement—and from that time on, when you get them, you experience the reward of self-administered praise. Do you recognize Rotter's concept of the minimal goal in this? We can learn standards through observational learning, as Bandura and Kupers (1964) have shown.

Self-regulation

This is all part of **self-regulation**, the determination of our behaviour by self-initiated cognitive acts. Most of our behaviour, Bandura argues, is self-regulated. Internal standards and goals profoundly influence how we think, feel, and act. As he says,

> One's previous behavior is continuously used as a reference against which ongoing performance is judged. In this referential process, self-comparison supplies the measure of adequacy. Past attainments affect self-appraisal mainly through their effects on standard setting. . . . After a given level of performance has been attained, it is no longer challenging, and people seek new self-satisfactions by means of progressive improvement. Hence, people tend to raise their performance standards after success and to lower them to more realistic levels after repeated failure (Bandura, 1986, pp. 347–8).

There are three processes in self-regulation, each with subprocesses.

1. **Self-observation** is the monitoring of one's own behaviour. We assess our performance (such aspects as quality, originality, sociability, morality), the regularity of what we do (getting up in time for every morning's class), and the accuracy of what we do. These are subprocesses.
2. We apply standards, or **judgemental processes**, both personal ones and ones that come from others. When we meet challenges (or sometimes fall short), we compare our performances to others and attribute our success or failure to internal or external causes. Subprocesses involve standards, comparison to others, and attribution of outcomes.
3. **Self-reaction** is the evaluation of oneself set in motion by self-observation and the judgemental processes. We evaluate ourselves and reward or punish. Reward may be in the form of a positive feeling of accomplishment. Self-punishment is likely to consist of painful feelings of failure. Rewards or punishments may also be tangible—giving oneself something especially desired as a reward for a real success, exposing oneself to criticism from others or even deliberately hurting oneself.

Bandura is well aware that we humans are capable of inhumane acts. How do our self-regulatory processes deal with behaviour that badly affects or injures others? He proposes a number of mechanisms by which we distance ourselves from the consequences of bad acts. Moral justification is one of them: it was right and proper to do what we did. Another is to identify (or label) our inhumane acts with euphemisms, as the Nazis did in hiding from themselves and from others the horror of genocide, cloaking mass murder in innocuous terms. They referred to the 'final solution', never using the explicit 'killing'. Another means of avoiding the implications of bad acts is to minimize or ignore their consequences. We may also dehumanize the people we hurt, attributing the blame to them. Remembering your Freud, these things will have a familiar ring; they are recognizable forms of ego defence. Evaluation and reactions to one's actions are the subprocesses.

The Person as Agent

Learning by observation alone; the future orientation of reinforcement; reinforcement of ourselves; regulation of our own behaviour; and the role of a thinking, feeling person in producing behaviour, reacting to the environment, and changing the environment—these all see the nature of the person in an **agentic** view of personality. Reinforcement doesn't just happen, strengthening the behaviour that led to it; we *anticipate* and *seek* rewarding events, control our own behaviour, refrain from acts that we are sure will lead to undesirable consequences. We *are* the agents of our actions and cognitive processes, and we shape and modify our environments. We don't simply step along to beats of the environmental drum.

> In the agentic sociocognitive view, people are self-organizing, proactive, self-reflecting, and self-regulating, not just reactive organisms shaped and shepherded by external events. To be agentic is to be an intentional doer selecting, constructing, and regulating one's own activity to realize certain outcomes. . . . People have the power to influence their own actions to produce certain results. The capacity to exercise control over one's thought processes, motivation, affect, and action operates through mechanisms of personal agency (Bandura, 1999, p. 154).

People as agents in charge of their own behaviour are architects of conscious choices and deliberate action. At the core of our experience of ourselves and the world around us, and central to a cognitive view of the human, is consciousness—not a weak and compromised consciousness, as classical psychoanalysis insisted, nor an epiphenomenal one, but one that is simply a byproduct of the processing of sensory and bodily information. Of course, we do things automatically on occasion, not thinking at all; sometimes, we may not understand the real basis of choices we make (Nisbett & Wilson, 1977). Neurosis may lay damaging claim to our cognitive deliberations. These, however, are not the mainstream of personality. A conscious agent of thought, feeling, and action is.

An important implication of the person as agent in action and choice is that brain development and the growth of brain cells (the neuronal basis of learning and memory) are significantly influenced by cognitive activity, exploring, and intervening in the environment. As Bandura says, 'By regulating their own motivation and the activities they pursue, people produce the experiences that form the neurobiological substrate of symbolic, social, psychomotor, and other skills' (Bandura, 1999, p. 155).

We must make sure that we don't pit the agentic view of personality against a straw man—a behaviourist caricature, as I suggested above, or a psychodynamic one, ego hemmed

A Fresh Look: Application Today

SCLT may be a spare theory, as I will say, that doesn't enable us truly to open the door on the mental life of another person, but its scope is remarkable. Bandura's transformation of the reinforcement principle, his treatment of observational learning, the far reach of his proposal that determinism is reciprocal, the concepts of self-regulation and self-efficacy, his bold application of modelling principles to psychotherapy have taken cognitive learning into new and exceptional realms.

The concepts of self-regulation make it possible for us to explain the terrifying actions of the modern terrorist, who is quite willing to sacrifice any number of wholly innocent people to attain religious and political objectives. How can the suicide bomber take his own life to kill others, who, entirely without malice, are not arrayed against him in his brutal struggle? This is a violently extreme act. What must the terrorist do to make it right and proper in his eyes and the eyes of his cohort? Suicide is a major sin in Islam, and Islam forbids harm to the innocent unless they are active in harming Muslims. Radical Islam turns suicide into heroism and makes the destruction of anyone in the path of its aims justifiable. What are the cognitive processes that make the ordinarily unthinkable worthy of the highest praise?

Bandura (2004) has expanded on earlier writings (see 1986, 1990) to show how self-regulatory processes, especially those in self-reaction, take the to-be terrorist from socialized and controlled adult to bombing and life sacrifice that appear to defy the precepts of his (or her) religion. He draws on a number of cognitive processes studied by social psychologists—for example, the cognitive mechanisms distancing the obedient perpetrator of injury from responsibility for harm to his victim shown by Milgram (1974)—and he casts them as processes of self-reaction. They co-opt guilty self-condemnation for the intent to commit an evil act by undercutting it, giving it no ground to stand on. Moral justification disengages self-sanction: one cannot feel morally despicable for being a martyred soldier in a holy war, a *jihad*. Instead, the terrorist yearns for his reward in paradise.

The cognitive mechanisms of moral disengagement are not the mind tricks of the evil. They are processes we all make use of in smaller measure to bring our thought and behaviour into conformity with the standards we've been taught. Caught doing something questionable? Compare what you did to similar but worse acts, an instance of social comparison that puts you in a better light. 'It's not like I robbed a bank; I just didn't declare this in by irreconcilable demands and hobbled in carrying out its tasks. We need, rather, to see the perspective of person-as-agent for what it is: a significant cognitive revision of some long-held views of the human animal's control of thinking and action. It's a revision that started with behaviour theory's reinforcement principle and advanced from there.

Expectancy

SCLT makes significant use of an expectancy concept, one that bears a close resemblance to expectancy in social learning theory. Bandura calls it **self-efficacy★**. We develop anticipations or expectancies about the possibilities of reinforcement in every situation in which we act. These expectancies are of two kinds.

1. **Outcome expectations** are the subjective probabilities we hold that a given outcome—a reinforcing event—will occur. One might conclude, for example, that an 'A' in a course taught by a tough and demanding professor is unlikely, or that an 'A' in a course taught by a friendly and helpful professor is quite possible.
2. **Efficacy expectations** are the expectancies a person has that he or she will be able to attain desirable outcomes (or avoid those that are unpleasant). The question set by effi-

income on my tax return.' You can also use euphemistic language to apply inoffensive and soothing terms to the unacceptable. In war, pilots are said to make 'clean, surgical strikes'; we have 'game plans' for the conduct of deadly military operations; we don't *aggress* against our marital partners but simply engage in a little family argument. Responsibility for harming another can be displaced: 'It was *his* fault'; 'I only did what I was told.' We may even attribute blame to the victim. We're all familiar with the effects of diffused responsibility. Someone else is pointed to as the person who did the wrong thing, failed to do the right thing, acted thoughtlessly or maliciously. Harmful consequences can be minimized or distorted. 'Aw shucks,' says the playground bully after knocking down a smaller child, 'I didn't really hurt him.' And, if we don't see the effects, the suffering of the person we injured will seem to be far less. We ourselves wouldn't dehumanize others, but we're familiar with the dehumanization inflicted on minority groups who may become, in the eyes of their tormentors, no more than animals.

These common cognitive transformations are escalated by the terrorist to absolve any possibility of guilt for acts of great cruelty. Bandura cites Osama bin Laden, whose inflammatory rhetoric illustrates *in extremis* what self-regulatory processes may accomplish:

'We will continue this course because it is part of our religion and because Allah, praise and glory be to him, ordered us to carry out jihad so that the word of Allah may remain exalted to the heights.' In the jihad they are carrying out Allah's will as a 'religious duty'. The prime agency for the holy terror is thus displaced to Allah. By attribution of blame, terrorist strikes are construed as morally justifiable defensive reactions to humiliation and atrocities perpetrated by atheistic forces. 'We are only defending ourselves. This is a defensive jihad.' By advantageous comparison with the nuclear bombing of Japan, and the toll of the Iraqi sanctions on children, the jihad takes on an altruistic appearance: 'When people at the ends of the earth, Japan, were killed by their hundreds of thousands, young and old, it was not considered a war crime, it is something that has justification. Millions of children in Iraq are something that has justification.' Bin Laden bestialized the American enemy as 'lowly people' perpetrating acts that 'the most ravenous of animals would not descend to.' Terrorism is sanitized as 'the winds of faith [that] have come' to eradicate the 'debauched' oppressors. His followers see themselves as holy warriors who gain a blessed eternal life through their martyrdom (2004, p. 125).

cacy expectations is *Can I do it? Am I smart, quick, determined, likeable enough to achieve X?* Here the chances of getting an 'A' on a particular course are evaluated not according to the demeanour of the instructor but according to the sense one has of one's own capabilities in the course. Of course, in any situation efficacy expectations will vary from person to person, and will vary in the same person from situation to situation. Efficacy expectations of failure will cause us not to try harder but to give up early and to avoid situations in which we believe we cannot succeed. As Bandura says, 'Given appropriate skills and adequate incentives, . . . efficacy expectations are a major determinant of people's choice of activities, how much effort they will expend, and of how long they will sustain effort in dealing with stressful situations' (Bandura, 1977b, p. 194). Some effects of positive and negative outcome and efficacy expectations are shown in Figure 15.5.

We develop efficacy expectations from previous accomplishments (or failures), from observational learning, from the verbal persuasion of others (encouragement or discouragement from those such as parents and teachers), and through experiences of emotional arousal. The arousal of anxiety, for example, may be the cue that makes us feel we cannot master a given task (doing well on an exam, say). Changing efficacy expectations is a major goal of psychotherapy. Instead of extinguishing anxiety, as S-R theory proposed, social cognitive theory focuses on changing expectations of failure, punishment, or other negative consequences. How would we treat a patient with a phobic fear of snakes? Change the person's expectancies of injury and of being unable to cope. How? By using a technique called **participant modelling***, which exposes the phobic patient to a model and also gets the patient to carry out graded tasks (from looking at snake pictures to approaching a snake to actually holding it). Participant modelling gives the person actual experiences of mastery that are very effective in teaching expectancies of control and success. More on this below.

Personality Development

The approach of social cognitive theory to personality development differs sharply from that of the psychodynamic content theories. Will we find here a conception of development over a series of stages? No indeed! This is a process theory, and so we will see per-

Figure 15.5 Effects of positive and negative outcome and efficacy expectations on behaviour (Bandura, Albert. 1982. 'Self-efficacy mechanism in human agency.' *American Psychologist*, 37, p. 140. Copyright 1965 by the American Psychological Association. Reprinted with permission.)

© Eric Sinkins

sonality development as the cumulative result of learning. Heredity will set possibilities for the developing child, to be shaped by the learning environment that will be determined by parents, siblings, peers, teachers, the culture, and economic conditions affecting the family. Reciprocal determinism will play a large role as others affect a child and the child's behaviour affects them. A child who is tense and anxious may create tension and anxiety in her parents that, in turn, make her more tense and anxious and may make her feel that she is not understood. Calm and reassuring parents can have a very different effect. We must understand that behaviour acquisition and change cannot be accounted for by motives in the child *or* features of the learning situations the child encounters. Personal characteristics of the child, significant aspects of the environment, and the child's own behaviour will mutually influence each other.

Children will acquire new behaviours by direct reinforcement, of course, but they will also learn vicariously by observing others—parents, siblings, playmates, adults, TV characters. Much of the significant social learning in childhood that will appear in adult personality is the result of observational learning. But we must recognize that children don't learn just what their parents want them to. The behaviour children acquire from their parents is often not intended by them. Many parents fail to understand all the ways in which they are models and are baffled. Bandura shows why this is so.

Outstanding among the learning accomplishments of childhood is the development of goals, internal standards, and efficacy expectations. Children will learn to regulate themselves, maturing in their abilities to self-observe, judge, and react to their achievements and failures. They will reinforce themselves as well as being reinforced by others, and they will in part acquire goals, internal standards, and efficacy expectations through observational learning.

The Psychology of Chance Encounters

Most personality theorists throw up their hands at accidental happenings and chance encounters. 'They're just noise in our predictive system,' they complain, 'and nothing we can account for.' The psychoanalysts are an exception. Freud, you remember, said that neurotic guilt could put us in harm's way, make us the victims of accidents that are really not accidents at all, but rather the price exacted by a tyrannical superego for unconscionable wishes and part of the covert agenda of the mind.

Bandura neither agrees with the complaining majority nor the analysts. Instead he offers a forthright attempt to deal with the problem without invoking hidden motives. Chance happenings and encounters cannot be specifically predicted, he acknowledges. Chance events follow their own causal sequence, one that intersects with personal attributes and life choices only accidentally. That's why they're called chance events. Bandura has a telling anecdote. He gave the presidential address to the Western Psychological Association, an address that drew a large audience. A psychology editor, keenly interested, took one of the few available seats in the hall near the rear, next to an attractive Stanford graduate who had recently completed her PhD. A year later, he called Bandura to tell him that he had married the woman he sat next to. Just imagine: a few seconds later and that seat might well have been taken by someone else; had he arrived earlier, many other seats would have been vacant. As it happened, the talk was on chance encounters and life paths! (Bandura, 1982a)

Chance encounters can dramatically alter our lives or affect us only slightly. A trivial event might have a major effect on a susceptible individual; a very significant and unfortunate one could leave a strong person relatively untouched. A chance meeting, or even exposure to a new idea or way of looking at things, can cause a major change in one's life path. Bandura points out that while psychological science cannot predict the unpredictable, it can have something to say about how people deal with impacts on their lives. Cognitive and emotional resilience, social skills (the ones needed to approach and establish relationships with others, for example), and personal standards are among the personality attributes that can determine our reactions to the unforeseen. He notes that a narrow, constricted life, one that keeps the door closed on new experiences, will limit the possibilities for chance encounters. A rich and varied life will enhance their likelihood. And, it is well to appreciate that a risky lifestyle increases the probability of chance happenings and outcomes one would wish to avoid. Trusting to luck is generally not a good idea.

The Major Concepts of Social Cognitive Theory: Reprise

On our tour through social cognitive theory, we've reviewed the principal process concepts and how they function in the theory. We've seen that these process concepts specify how behaviour is acquired (underlining the importance of observational learning), how behaviour changes, and how behaviour is self-reinforced and self-regulated. We've seen its complicated, reciprocal version of determinism.

1. It is very important to keep in mind that learning doesn't require reinforcement, and I take the liberty of repeating that point. Learning depends on a set of processes that begin with **observation**. The learner has to *attend to*, or observe, a model performing a given act. The model and modelled behaviour must have *significance* for the learner, and the learner must *remember* and *represent* in images and words the behaviour observed. If all of these occur, learning will surely take place. This doesn't mean that the learner will necessarily repeat the observed act; he or she may lack the skills or the confidence to do it, or else the external circumstances may not be favourable. But the new behaviour has been added to the person's potential repertoire.

    So, then, what *does* reinforcement do? All together now: reinforcement determines the *performance* of learned behaviour. Of course, direct reinforcement *can* produce learning, but when we note how much of learning in personality development and later occurs in the absence of reinforcing events, it's clear that it isn't a necessary condition.

2. A second, now familiar, modification of the reinforcement principle is that reinforcement may be self-administered. We react to what we do, evaluating our performances and feeling good (self-reinforcement) or bad (self-punishment, self-criticism, guilt). Bandura notes that external reinforcement is most effective when it supports our evaluations of ourselves. We not infrequently dismiss the reinforcing comments of others when we ourselves don't feel we did that well.

3. Reinforcement may also occur vicariously, as when we see someone else being rewarded (or punished) for a particular act. We anticipate similar consequences if we

repeat the same thing. So, we don't have to do anything except attend to the model, remembering and coding what we have observed.

The Self-system

Now, there is one more concept for us to add. It is a content concept, a cognitive behaviouristic version of the **self-system★**. Says Bandura, 'In social learning theory, a self-system is not a psychic agent that controls behaviour. Rather, it refers to cognitive structures that provide reference mechanisms and to a set of subfunctions for the perception, evaluation, and regulation of behaviour' (1978, p. 348). The self-system is thus an organization of cognitive processes by which self-observation, judgement, and self-evaluation are carried out. All the self-regulating processes and efficacy expectations are functions of this self-system.

Implications

Aggression

Freud, as we know, saw aggression as a human inevitability, the consequence of surrendering immediate instinctual gratification to the demands of social living. We are bound to be frustrated and bound therefore to be moved to anger, and the more civilized the society in which we live the more frustration we'll have to endure. Paradoxical, but there's no getting around it. Mostly, we let out our aggression in relatively small ways (verbal slights, for example, or badmouthing people behind their backs). We are also able to discharge tension vicariously by watching the aggression of others. Violent TV, hockey and football games, and even some of the more popular reality shows are in this sense good for us. They afford **catharsis★**, the reduction of tension, in socialized ways. These things reduce the probability that we'll act explosively, aggressively.

Except for the radical behaviourists and the revolutionaries of the nascent cognitive movement, psychology had largely taken on faith Freud's claim that vicarious aggression not only does no harm but is positively beneficial, draining off some of the tension from the accumulated frustrations of daily life. The implications of the observational learning experiments (particularly the experiments with film models) stunned us, and dozens of developmental, social, and personality psychologists began to pursue them, examining the effects on children of television's high-violence diet. If an experiment, which ordinarily pales in its authority over behaviour, could with the pittance of a grant budget, no special effects, and no cinematic expertise whatever induce young children to aggress simply by getting their attention and showing them the ropes, what must television be doing? It isn't as easy to study children watching TV in their homes and to follow their imitation into the schoolyard as it is to conduct an experiment in a controlled environment, but many investigators set out on this more challenging course. Over thirty years, a research literature numbering in a few dozen now counts in the thousands. Many of the studies have not shown the causal relation between observation and imitation demonstrated in the experiments of Bandura and his colleagues. They could not rule out the possibility that aggressive children have a preference for violent TV and watch more of it. But at least they established a correlation between a fist-in-the-mouth and bullet-in-the-head TV fare and aggression in its viewers. The best of them, in fact, could fairly claim that the connection is causal.

One of the good ones was the work of Friedrich and Stein, a 1973 experiment with nursery school children in a summer program. For a month during the nine-week session, Friedrich and Stein showed three television programs a week. Two classes saw *Batman* and *Superman* cartoons, each twenty minutes long and typical in their verbal and physical aggression. Two others watched episodes from *Mister Rogers' Neighborhood* to provide a 'prosocial' contrast. Children in four other classes were shown films that were not aggressive, nor did they emphasize thoughtfulness, helping, or co-operation. Observers rated both aggression and instances of reciprocity in each child during the course of classroom activities for three time periods—before viewing (to establish initial aggression and co-operativeness), during viewing, and after viewing. Children who were rated as initially above average in their aggressiveness behaved more aggressively toward others after watching the cartoons; nonaggressive children were unaffected. Those who saw *Mister Rogers* were a little more obedient to classroom rules and accepted waiting (for the teacher's attention, a pair of scissors, a crayon being used by another child) better than children in the neutral film classes. Moreover, children from families of lower socioeconomic status who saw the *Mister Rogers* episodes played more co-operatively and thoughtfully. Friedrich and Stein thus showed not only an antisocial outcome of a very short exposure to violent TV but some definite prosocial benefits from programs of a gentler sort.

Unremitting violence in the media and how it may affect children has occupied two generations of psychologists, as well as federal, state, and provincial legislatures, committees appointed by those legislatures, writers, critics, and television industry defenders of the status quo. Exposure to media violence was taken up years ago by the National Institute of Mental Health (1982) in a report concluding that violent television does indeed induce aggression in children. The consequences of watching violence in the media were taken up more recently in the National Television Violence Study (1998), which determined that modelling of violence, the observing of rewarded aggression, the absence of negative consequences for aggressive acts, and desensitization to the infliction of harm are the likely vehicles for training aggression. The Canadian House of Commons Standing Committee on Communications and Culture arrived at much the same conclusion (1993).

It is no longer in question that regular viewing of television violence by children increases their aggression, and the risk is greater for viewers with a high-violence diet, children under six, and children who are already disposed to act aggressively (Bushman & Huesmann, 2001). The causal effect is a modest one; a meta-analysis of many studies estimates a correlation of 0.31 (Paik & Comstock, 1994), but as Bushman and Huesmann sharply observe, 'The .31 correlation is equivalent to aggressive behaviour being exhibited by 65.5% of those above the median in exposure to media violence but only 34.5% of those below the median in exposure to media violence. This 31% difference hardly seems like a trivial effect' (p. 234). A colleague of mine points out to his classes that a modest association among the millions upon millions of television viewers does not really qualify as modest. Bandura's research and the theory that grew with it have had a major impact on our thinking about the mass media and their influence on developing minds (and older minds that are not fully developed and socialized). Not that we heed the message brought by some exceptional psychological research and theory. Freedom of speech is a more important principle than a sane influence on the young.

Perspective 15.1 Observational Learning, Mass Culture, and Violence in the Media

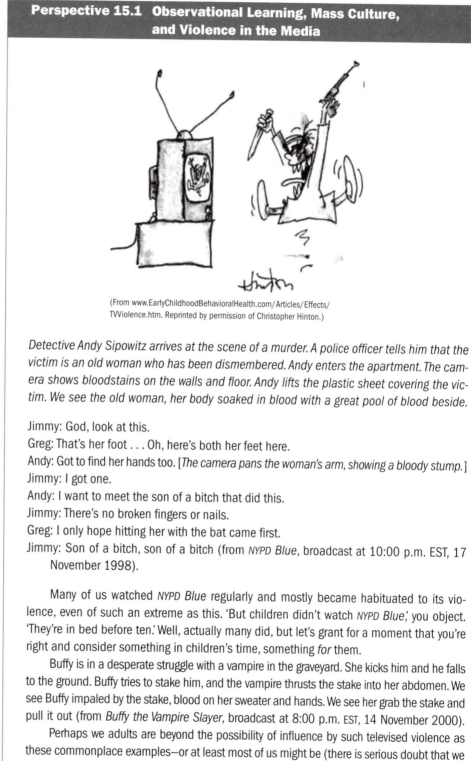

(From www.EarlyChildhoodBehavioralHealth.com/Articles/Effects/
TVViolence.htm. Reprinted by permission of Christopher Hinton.)

Detective Andy Sipowitz arrives at the scene of a murder. A police officer tells him that the victim is an old woman who has been dismembered. Andy enters the apartment. The camera shows bloodstains on the walls and floor. Andy lifts the plastic sheet covering the victim. We see the old woman, her body soaked in blood with a great pool of blood beside.

Jimmy: God, look at this.

Greg: That's her foot . . . Oh, here's both her feet here.

Andy: Got to find her hands too. [*The camera pans the woman's arm, showing a bloody stump.*]

Jimmy: I got one.

Andy: I want to meet the son of a bitch that did this.

Jimmy: There's no broken fingers or nails.

Greg: I only hope hitting her with the bat came first.

Jimmy: Son of a bitch, son of a bitch (from *NYPD Blue*, broadcast at 10:00 p.m. EST, 17
   November 1998).

Many of us watched *NYPD Blue* regularly and mostly became habituated to its violence, even of such an extreme as this. 'But children didn't watch *NYPD Blue*,' you object. 'They're in bed before ten.' Well, actually many did, but let's grant for a moment that you're right and consider something in children's time, something *for* them.

Buffy is in a desperate struggle with a vampire in the graveyard. She kicks him and he falls to the ground. Buffy tries to stake him, and the vampire thrusts the stake into her abdomen. We see Buffy impaled by the stake, blood on her sweater and hands. We see her grab the stake and pull it out (from *Buffy the Vampire Slayer*, broadcast at 8:00 p.m. EST, 14 November 2000).

Perhaps we adults are beyond the possibility of influence by such televised violence as these commonplace examples—or at least most of us might be (there is serious doubt that we are wholly immune). Children most certainly aren't, however, and their child's world of TV is hardly less filled with scenes of aggression, injury, and sometimes death than is the adult's. The research on observational learning and related theories—for example, desensitization theory, which proposes that aggression is easier as we become habituated to violence and its ugly consequences (see Huesmann, Moise-Titus, Podolski, & Eron, 2003)—and a very large literature on the effects of violence in the media tells us that the child looking in TV's window at aggression is likely to pick up an antisocial repertoire of schemas, attitudes, and biases.

Most of the research has assessed short-term effects, such as increased playground aggression, but there are a few longitudinal investigations that have followed children studied in the early years into later childhood, adolescence, and adulthood. These studies ask whether the frequency of watching violent television is related to aggressive behaviour in the longer run. Huesmann et al. (2003) carried out a remarkable fifteen-year follow-up of more than 500 Chicago area primary school children first studied at ages six to nine. Interviews with each child established TV viewing preferences, and peer ratings gave an index of each child's aggressive behaviour. Between 1992 and 1995, the investigators located 60 per cent of the original sample, interviewing them and a knowledgeable other (often a spouse) and collecting evidence of driving and other offences from public records.

There were three unambiguous findings. The viewing of TV violence between the ages of six and nine, the perception by child viewers that violent story plots are realistic and believable, and identification with same-sex aggressive characters were significantly correlated with violence in young adulthood. Those who regularly watched violent television programs as children were more likely to have engaged in a variety of adult aggressive actions—males pushing their wives, wives throwing things at their husbands, serious physical aggression toward other adults, criminal acts, and driving offences. Men and women were equally affected. The results held even when the initial peer-rated aggressiveness of the children, socioeconomic status, intelligence, and parenting practices were controlled. As the authors pointedly commented,

> The psychological laws of observational learning, habituation/desensitization, priming, and excitation are immutable and universal. It is not, as some have suggested, only the already violence-prone child who is likely to be affected. True, media violence is not going to turn an otherwise fine child into a violent criminal. But just as every cigarette one smokes increases a little bit the likelihood of a lung tumor some day, the theory supported by this research suggests that every violent TV show increases a little bit the likelihood of a child growing up to behave more aggressively in some situation. . . . What type of violent scene is the child most likely to use as a model for violent behavior? It is one in which the child identifies with the perpetrator of the violence, the child perceives the scene as telling about life like it is, and the perpetrator is rewarded for the violence (p. 218).

The pioneering experiments on observational learning decisively showed that modelled aggression could be immediately adopted by young children. We did not know that watching remote models, actors in often improbable roles, could have an enduring influence. Perhaps we failed to remember that subsequent aggression by the television viewer doesn't have to be directly imitative to be an observational learning effect. We really shouldn't have been surprised that modelling could be so effective. Nor should we find it surprising that TV viewing effects on individuals might have widespread social consequences affecting whole communities. Reporting on the results of a natural experiment, a Canadian study found that after the introduction of television to a British Columbia town that had not had it, children were significantly more verbally and physically aggressive than they were before television arrived (Joy, Kimball, and Zabrack, 1986).

Personality Development

If the greater part of what we learn is by observation of significant others, then the implications for childrearing are profound. Parents will, of course, teach their children many things deliberately, things they want them to learn. But as I noted above, parents, as models, will wind up teaching their children things they do not mean to and would not want them to learn. Verbal (and sometimes physical) aggression, crude and foul language, smoking—these are only obvious examples. Indeed, if parents physically punish their children or accompany their punishment with angry words, they are modelling physical and verbal aggression whether or not they succeed in their intended purpose to correct unacceptable behaviour. I suggest that you draw up two lists, one of desirable (prosocial, as we like to say) behaviour that parents wish to model for their children, and one of undesirable, antisocial behaviour that many parents will model unintentionally. When we considered S-R theory, I cited Dollard and Miller's admission that we are far from having a science of childrearing, and what we do have is not well taught to nor learned by parents. Bandura's theory and research have provided us with a sound empirical basis to understand how children learn and how modelled behaviour, attitudes, and standards become their own.

Psychopathology and Psychotherapy

Bandura and his colleagues have shown that classically conditioned responses such as phobic fears can be acquired by observational learning. It is conventional to think that phobic fears are learned by direct exposure to frightening stimuli, but this is not necessarily the case. Bandura and Rosenthal (1966) had experimental participants watch while a model, identified as a real subject, received repeated trials accompanied by the sound of a loud buzzer. The model grimaced and writhed in pain from ostensible electric shock accompanying the buzzer. When these observers were later exposed to the buzzer, they showed strong emotional (autonomic) responses despite the fact that they had not received any electric shocks. The conclusion: fear of dogs, insects, rodents, or flying need not be based on direct conditioning of emotional responses.

Psychotherapy has greatly benefited from the research on vicarious learning and from the concept of and research on self-efficacy. It is unusual, to say the least, for a personality theory to be based at every step in its development on experimental research. It is even more unusual for the psychotherapy derived from it to have the same kind of support. Both unusual, I should say, and highly commendable. Psychotherapy, as the S-R theorists saw it, is a process of extinguishing the anxiety that underlies psychological symptoms. The radical behaviourists, inspired by B.F. Skinner, see psychotherapy in strictly behavioural terms, with no inferences permissible to psychological events that can't be observed directly. Change problem behaviour, they say, and you have solved the problem the patient came to treatment for.

Social cognitive theory's approach to psychotherapy is without a doubt behavioural, but it is also firmly based in cognitive theory. It is cognitive behaviourism at work on psychological difficulties. Bandura's approach begins with a rejection of our classical views of anxiety, one based on psychoanalytic theory, and a parallel rejection of S-R theory's approach—that anxiety is a conditioned response to stimuli associated with frightening experiences. Instead, he argues that anxiety is a by-product caused by low efficacy expectations—the belief either that it would be futile to try because the environment will frustrate any effort (outcome expectation) or that one simply can't do it, that one

A severely snake-phobic young woman conquers her fear through participant modelling. (Courtesy Dr Philip G. Zimbardo.)

can't cope (efficacy expectation). As he says, 'In any given instance, behaviour would be best predicted by considering both self-efficacy and outcome beliefs' (Bandura, 1982b, p. 140).

What do we do in treatment, then? We make use of observational learning, modelling for patients how the difficult, fear-mobilizing activity can be accomplished. That helps, but not as much as invoking **performance accomplishment**. A major source of self-efficacy beliefs comes from experience of achievement. We learn how to do things and—just as important—we learn to believe in our abilities, skills, and coping. So, *doing* becomes an important aspect of treatment; we help patients to acquire feelings of mastery over deeds they formerly considered impossible by creating therapeutic opportunities for mastery experiences. This increases their efficacy expectations. An especially effective technique is **participant modelling★**. This begins, as we saw earlier, with observation of a model, proceeds to graded steps with the help of the model, and gradually withdraws the external help to give the patient successful experience on his or her own.

Bandura, Blanchard, and Ritter (1969) compared participant modelling, symbolic modelling (using a film model), and systemic desensitization (the counter-conditioning technique devised by Joseph Wolpe) in the treatment of severely snake-phobic adolescents and adults. There was also an untreated control group. Tests with a snake, grading the phobic person's closeness of approach, were given before and after treatment. The results showed that participant modelling far outstripped the film modelling and desensitization therapies, with film modelling and desensitization close in effectiveness (see Figure 15.6). A later experiment established that increased feelings of efficacy accompanied the behavioural mastery (actually handling snakes). Moreover, the strength of self-efficacy expectations was a strong predictor of snake handling in the post-tests (Bandura, Adams, & Beyer, 1977). There is now an extensive literature on

Figure 15.6 Modelling and behaviour therapy in the treatment of snake phobia (After Bandura, Blanchard, & Ritter, 1969.)

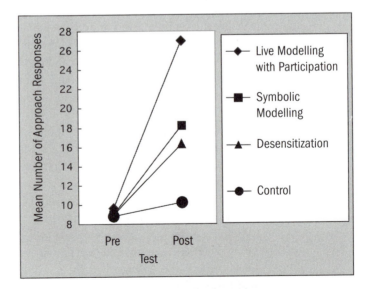

self-efficacy expectations and their role in shedding dysfunctional behaviour. Studies by Bandura and by many others repeatedly show the effectiveness of improving low efficacy expectations by modelling techniques, especially participant modelling.

Perspective 15.2   How to Cope When You Feel Anxious and Helpless and Don't Know What to Do: An SCLT Prescription

From time to time, many of us face personal difficulties that loom large and seem intractable. Our expectancies that we cannot do something about them are, as social cognitive theory says, **dysfunctional**. Feeling anxious and helpless, we don't try, and we become even more defeated. We need to believe that we *can* overcome whatever it is we face; we need to believe that we are competent.

This, of course, is self-efficacy, and the feeling that comes with it is empowerment. Professional help may not be readily available or ideally suited to solving the problem. A social cognitive behavioural therapist would be perfect, but one can't be found. What can we do?

Quite a lot, is the answer, and being able to see the possibility of remedies is a large first step. As agents in our own lives, not victims of internal states we are powerless to control, there are a number of self-help steps we can take. These are some of them.

1. First, we need to *think* behaviourally. Correcting the problem, whatever it is, does not have to do with ferreting out the source of anxiety. It is better thought of as discovering ways to behave differently in the stressful situation.
2. We need to *think* cognitively. Of course, that sounds foolish (How else *would* one think?), but it isn't. The real difficulty lies in the cognitive processes that determine our approach to and feelings about any situation—outcome expectancies and efficacy expectancies. What are the possibilities before us—good and bad—and what are our expectancies that we can carry out what we have to do? Thinking cognitively in this sense gets to the heart of the problem.
3. After sorting our thinking out, the very next thing is to begin to set goals. Looking into the far-off future and wishing for a dream outcome is not going to be helpful. The goals we set should be specific—that is, directed toward things to do (actual behaviour)—and measurable (we need to be able to mark our progress). Long-term goals are great to point us toward what we want to achieve, but they have to have the support of goals that can be accomplished in the short term. Being able to talk comfortably in front of a class is an excellent aim if we fear ridicule and believe we couldn't possibly speak to a group. We're going to get there by immediate measures, one at a time, starting with raising our hand to ask a question. Later, we'll take on the bigger challenge of commenting on a point made by the professor.
4. We'll look for opportunities to make use of observational learning. Modelling the behaviour of someone whose solution to our problem is effective and realistic for us will provide just what we need to work with. Our model should be reasonably close to us in age, abilities, and general situation. Adopting as a model a glamorous star who seems to navigate the crises of screen and TV with consummate ease won't have much effect on our shaky expectancies. Could I possibly be like Julia Roberts or Denzel Washington in a heroic role? No? Then, let's avoid the remote and fanciful and seek someone who has important resemblances to us.

5. What does the model do, specifically, in dealing with our problem? It will help to make a list of things we observe in our model that we think could help us. We could approach the model and ask how he or she prepares a class seminar. That would be hard, entailing more self-exposure than we would like, but it could pay significant dividends.

6. It's now time to put observational learning into practice. Remembering participant modelling, we want to do what the model does, taking small, graded steps to start. Here is the place for another list—of the modelled tasks we shall undertake. This list will help us keep track of our progress.

7. We'll reward ourselves as we achieve each goal, and alter what doesn't seem to work well (but not before we've given it a good chance). After all, not everything we adopt will be tailor-made for us. Some of the behaviour of the model will have to be adapted to fit our own style and ability.

8. Success will depend on rehearsal and practice of what we learned from our model. This is essential in participant modelling; we want to make sure that we have mastered each of our specific goals.

9. At this point, we're going to come to a conclusion we didn't think possible at the start: 'This wasn't as difficult as I thought, and I'm on the way to solving that insoluble problem.' And we won't forget to say in addition, 'Good for me!'

Research

Laboratory and clinical research has formed the basis of SCLT from the very beginning. Indeed, the theory was born with the experiment on observational learning with which we started. I have accordingly introduced Bandura's research as we have gone along instead of presenting it, as in other chapters, in a separate section. It is fair to say that in its short life SCLT has generated more solid experimental investigation of its propositions and implications than all but its sister learning theories. True, the research literature on psychoanalysis is vast, far and away exceeding the research on this theory, but there is the equivocal or negative, and the experimental study of psychoanalysis often does not follow a disciplined and organized path. SCLT research is unquestionably systematic in testing, step by step, the most important hypotheses of the theory, and it very largely affirms the claims of the theory. One possible exception is the causative role that Bandura attributes to self-efficacy expectations. In his view, efficacy expectations *cause* people to undertake activities or to quail before them. Critics have proposed that efficacy expectations are, instead, the *consequence* of succeeding or failing, not the antecedent of trying or giving up (Eastman & Marzillier, 1984; Hawkins, 1992). Bandura's claim is persuasive and he has strongly defended it (Bandura, 1991), but this is a difficult question to address, and it will need further experimental study. Confirming studies like that of Litt (1988), who found that self-efficacy expectations predicted pain tolerance, add importantly to Bandura's own findings.

Social Cognitive Learning Theory in Perspective

Bandura's theory has taken behaviourism a long way from what seemed its drooping last days in the late 1950s. Indeed, behaviourism is hardly recognizable in its modern cognitive form. Nowhere is this more evident than in the future-oriented transformation of the reinforcement principle: we act in anticipation of reinforcement, not because we have been reinforced.

Bandura has not shied away from the kind of big questions that have occupied psychoanalytic and neo-analytic theorists. Among them is the very concept of determinism, which he has ably analyzed and extended. He acknowledges the capacity of humans to inflict harm on others, and recognizes it in his development of self-regulatory processes. He makes room for our disengagement from the consequences of our bad acts, an imaginative inclusion in the theory. Self-efficacy is a potent concept, one that organizes striving and coping as well as failure avoidance and anxiety. Then, there are the startling data on observational learning, well established and incontrovertible, on which the theory's implications for the effects of mass media, personality development, and treatment are founded.

It is a powerful theory indeed, with its impressive empirical support, but there are some weaknesses that have been noted. Bandura does not deal in any thorough way with psychological conflict and the nature of motivation; his accounts of stress and emotional arousal are skeletal. He shies away from the neurophysiological basis of behaviour (but so does almost every other personality theorist), and he doesn't approach questions of the genetics of behaviour (neither do other theorists). The latter two may be unfair criticisms: a strictly psychological theory of personality is perfectly permissible and appropriate.

It could be argued that the richness, complexity, and power in psychoanalysis and psychoanalytic derivatives to help us appreciate great human turmoil and its self-destructive expression are missing from social cognitive theory. Instead, this is a spare, even stark theory, almost mechanical in its specification of the psychological processes of learning in personality development and change. We might say that SCLT doesn't help us to *imagine*. With further advances in the theory and its application, however, that could change. Social cognitive theory has made an outstanding start.

Walter Mischel

Introduction

In 1968, Walter Mischel's book *Personality and Assessment* told psychologists of personality exactly what they should have been attending to. His immediate target was the personality test, which had then been a disappointment for fifty years. The very best tests yielded correlations with criterion measures (validity coefficients) no better than .30 on average, accounting for 10 per cent (generously) of the variance. Try as assessment psychologists might, introducing techniques to identify and control for various result-distorting tendencies by research participants—lying, faking, agreeing with test items uncritically, responding in a socially desirable manner (Crowne & Marlowe, 1960; Crowne, 2000), and others—nothing improved prediction. Mischel didn't go after tests and testing, however, but took on the conceptual schemes on which tests were—and are—based. He had in mind as the real culprits theories of personality, responsible for the central notion in personality assessment: the personality disposition or trait. The intelligent approach was there all the time for you to see, he said. He might have sung (and maybe did), 'The answer, my friend, is blowin' in the wind, the answer is blowin' in the wind.'

What was it? What had personality psychologists been ignoring? The situation. He didn't say, 'The situation, stupid,' although psychologists of the psychodynamic and trait paradigms had been stubbornly resistant in holding to the belief that personality dispositions lead to behavioural consistency from one situation to another. A person whose motives dispose him to be aggressive, dependent, or power hungry, they held, consistently acts as his motives direct. He's aggressive in casual interactions and in the hockey rink, is forever leaning on others, and dominates his wife and his colleagues in the boardroom. As Mischel reviewed the evidence, however, an awfully large bundle of it pointed to the conclusion that one's behaviour varies as situations change despite the motives and attributes shown in one's tests. His forceful argument stirred up an outcry in the personality community and a person-versus-situation debate that continues to this day. Funder (2004) defends person consistency well, pointing out that from the standpoint of predictive utility the small correlation coefficients we obtain—not .30 but .40 (Nisbett, 1980)—are hardly small when we consider the improvement in prediction that correlations of this magnitude yield.

As Mischel's position evolved, he made two separate proposals. First, people *are* consistent, but over *time*, not over situations. So, the person who is aggressive is not necessarily so as he encounters one daily situation after another, but he is over the long run (Mischel & Peake, 1982). Second, people are very good at identifying the significant cues in situations and using them to categorize situations as similar (calling for similar behaviour) or different (posing distinctive behavioural demands). Does this sound to you very much like Rotter's situational analysis? It should; see below. Thus, to study personality, we must recognize person variables and situational variables, the latter consisting of cues interpreted by the person. From these nascent ideas came a cognitive social learning theory of personality, influenced strongly by Rotter and by Kelly, whose personal construct theory we took up in Chapter 11, and with a clear resemblance to Bandura's social cognitive theory.

Walter Mischel: Personal History

Walter Mischel (Courtesy of Dieter Hoppe, www.berlin-fotografie.de)

Walter Mischel was born in Vienna in 1930. Eight years later, his parents escaped in the exodus that followed the Nazi annexation of Austria, immigrating to the United States and settling in Brooklyn, New York. A Brooklyn upbringing is bound to leave a lasting imprint, and it did. In late career, he returned to New York and a professorship at Columbia University. Talented, he was originally attracted to art, studying painting and sculpture as well as psychology at New York University. He took to Freud and existentialism, turning away from the experimental S-R psychology of the late 1940s and early 1950s. Clinical psychology won over his other interests, and he completed a master's degree at the City College of New York in 1953. His experience working with impoverished and delinquent youth as a social worker convinced him that insight into their psychodynamics was of little use.

Mischel was accepted into the clinical psychology program at Ohio State University, where he took his PhD in 1956 with Rotter. Kelly taught him about *personal constructs*, the unique cognitions that each person develops to explain and predict the events of his or her life. After graduating, he taught first at the University of Colorado and then at Harvard University before joining Bandura at Stanford University in 1962. He remained at Stanford until 1983, when he moved to New York and Columbia University. The recipient of many honours, Mischel was elected to the National Academy of Sciences in 2004. He was named the Niven Professor of Humane Letters at Columbia in 1994.

Emphases and Major Concepts
of the Cognitive-Affective Personality System

The seed for the cognitive-affective personality system seems to have been the findings from two research programs—a large-scale study of Peace Corps volunteers, and a long series of experiments on delay of gratification in children. Seeking to predict the on-site success of young Peace Corps workers, Mischel and colleagues used interviews and expert clinical ratings, combining them with a measure of ethnocentric attitudes and with self-reports. The clinical techniques, which we may think of as global trait assessments, fared very poorly, despite the expertise on which they were based; self-ratings and the attitude scale were far more accurate (Mischel, 1965). Here was an eye opener. There was a lot of evidence on the failures of clinical person assessment (see, for example, the chapter, 'Some representative assessment programs', in Wiggins, 1973), but this was personal. Mischel had been a participant in the research project. If you think of the trait-based investigation of personality as the cross-situational study of persons, you have the first clue to the development of Mischel's thinking.

Mischel has been a close student of delay of gratification since the very earliest days of his career. He and colleagues have published dozens of experimental reports, reviews, and theoretical articles on the determinants of waiting for and pursuing larger rewards when a smaller reward could be had immediately, studies spanning nearly the entirety of his career. They stretch from 1958 to 2004. The experiments are to the cognitive-affective personality system (let's call it CAPS, as Mischel does) what the studies of observational learning have been to Bandura's social cognitive theory, defining the essential issues. In the basic experiment, which has now been conducted with hundreds of preschool children, an individual child is taught a game by the experimenter in which there are two possible rewards. One of them is large (two marshmallows or pretzels), the other small (only one). After the child 'wins', the experimenter says that she needs to leave the room for a while. If the child sits patiently, waiting for the experimenter to return, he or she gets the large reward. But, if the waiting gets to be too much, ringing a bell will summon the experimenter; then, it's the small reward. You can imagine that when the press hit upon this, they couldn't refrain from dubbing it the 'marshmallow test'. The dependent variable is time—how long the children wait before giving in and ringing the bell.

A number of manipulations are possible to find what it is in the situation—and, as Mischel discovered, what it is in the cognitive activity of the children—that enables them to delay gratification for a bigger reward. If the rewards are in view, surely the children would see the difference between them, opt for the larger reward, and stick it out. Not so. They tended to give in to temptation and ring the bell far earlier. This was an important clue to the cognition supporting delay. The rewards being in full view, it was very hard (but not impossible; see below) for the children to avoid attending to them, challenging and overwhelming their resolve to wait. Hiding the marshmallows or pretzels more than doubled the mean wait time.

Well, if looking at and thinking about the ever-so desirable marshmallow led to ringing the bell and taking the immediate reward, what about cognitive processes in the child that might make delay easier? Self-distraction, say? Thinking of 'fun things' enhanced delay, as did suggestions to think of the marshmallows as clouds or the pretzels as little brown logs (see Mischel & Baker, 1975; Mischel & Moore, 1973; Moore, Mischel, & Zeiss, 1976). Some children showed delay strategies of their very own. They covered their eyes, laid their heads down on their arms, talked or sang to themselves, played little physical games with hands or feet; one child even fell asleep. Indeed, there was a striking relation between the duration of waiting for marshmallows or pretzels in preschool children and their adolescent cognitive and intellectual competence. Those preschoolers who were good at delay in these experiments were rated by their parents in adolescence as more self-controlled, goal-directed, bright, and socially skilled, less easily distracted (Shoda, Mischel, & Peake, 1990). A startling result that caught the eye of the press was that pre-university SAT scores could be predicted from the few minutes these small children spent in the delay of gratification experiment (Shoda et al., 1990).

So, what is it that determines the likelihood that a child will tolerate waiting for a larger reward? Is it in the situation? Or is it in the child, a person variable? Situational manipulations clearly have big effects. So do attributes of the child, like spontaneously coming up with a strategy to make the frustration of waiting endurable. (Now, before we go any further, try not to think of that bag of crunchy, salty pretzels in the kitchen cupboard. How will you put off going to the cupboard now for just a couple when, if you finish this chapter, you can have a whole bunch?) These experiments confirmed the answer to Mischel. It is the cognitive activity and abilities of the person, stimulated and directed by the situation. That is the key to behaviour in a simple and apparently trivial experiment, and it is the key to personality.

The Reinforcement Principle

With Bandura, Mischel agrees that rewards and aversive events affect how we act, but they are not environmental controls on behaviour. Rather, it is individual cognitive processes that determine what is a reinforcement, positive or negative, whether it is to be pursued now or as a future goal, how long to wait for it, whether to accept a smaller substitute. Each person transforms reinforcing stimuli, giving them personal meaning and relevance. In Mischel's thinking, the reinforcement principle is actually replaced by a concept of **cognitive transformation**. Classical psychologists of learning had strongly asserted the stimulus control of behaviour. Mischel and colleagues, however, note that 'the perceiver's mental representations and cognitive transformations of the stimuli can determine and even reverse their impact' (Mischel, Shoda, & Smith, 2004, p. 272). The meaning of stimuli, situations, and reinforcement is, they say, in the head of the behaving person. I should really say, in the head of the cognizing, construing person, for it is the unique view of the individual person, expressed in his or her cognitions, that defines what stimuli and situations signify and what is rewarding or aversive. The occurrence of reinforcement is a moment-by-moment fact of life; why, then, invest a phenomenon that carries no individual information with psychological importance? This is a conclusion adapted from Kelly's psychology of personal constructs (see Chapter 11). It's not the environmental event on which personality study must focus, but what each person makes of it, how he or she construes life's reinforcing events.

Bandura's social cognitive theory and CAPS are kissin' cousins, in viewing reinforcement as anticipatory, self-administered, informative, activating, and an antecedent of and guide to future behaviour. Mischel goes further than Bandura, however, in his cognitive interpretation and emphasis; Bandura still retains a tie to his behaviouristic roots.

The Elements of the Cognitive-Affective Personality System

CAPS goes back to Mischel's 1973 article 'Toward a cognitive social learning reconceptualization of personality', which contains the emphases and most of the concepts of the present theory. Take note that in its title, CAPS features an affective component that was not a part of the earlier version. CAPS is a 'personality system', telling us that it concentrates on person variables. Its cognitive social learning forebear was person-centered too, but CAPS has amplified that emphasis. Then, there has been some rearrangement of the variables in the system; notably, competences are now part of a 'unit' in which there are also strategies and plans.

Cognitive and Affective Units in the Personality System

CAPS is Mischel's culminating effort to put personality dispositions (traits) in their proper place as person variables responsible for the goals we pursue and how we perceive ourselves, the situations we encounter, and ourselves in relation to them. In the theory, personality processes are represented by units or categories into which the cognitive activity and affect that determine behaviour may be cast. There are five units, which we see in Table 15.1. Let's look at them.

ENCODINGS

Encodings★ are the private meanings we all give to the features of our lives, including ourselves. They are private because our individual experience makes them so. Mischel surely chose the term 'encodings' to convey the sense of intimately personal, reflecting the phenomenological emphasis of his teacher and mentor, George Kelly. Encodings are not deliberately kept from others as the term could suggest (although all of us do shield aspects of our experience from view). They arise from learning histories and individual attributes, including genetically conferred traits, that make each of us unique. Thus, how we represent ourselves, other people, the happenings and situations in our lives—the categories, or constructs (Kelly's favoured term), we use for these things—come from the soil of our own personal experience. Of course, each of us will share encodings of important situations and even constructs of self with many people. Think of behaviour in the classroom, for example, or the worry we feel before an exam: most of us will hold a common (though not identical) view. A very significant implication: we cannot assume that even the most compelling situations will produce the same encodings in

---

Table 15.1   The Cognitive and Affective Units in CAPS

- **Encodings (Construals, Appraisals)**: Categories (constructs) for the self, people, events, and situations (external and internal).

- **Expectancies and Beliefs**: About the social world, about outcomes for behavior in particular situations, about self-efficacy, about the self.

- **Affects**: Feelings, emotions, and affective responses (including physiological reactions).

- **Goals and Values**: Desirable outcomes and affective states; aversive outcomes and affective states; goals, values, and life projects.

- **Competencies and Self-Regulatory Systems and Plans**: Potential behaviors and scripts that one can do, and plans and strategies for organizing action and for affecting outcomes and one's own behavior and internal states.

Source: From Mischel, 2004, p. 276.

everyone. We'll need to study the individual person; asking him or her is an effective strategy, says Mischel. People often can and will tell us about themselves and their take on situations and events (see Kelly on the person as informant in Chapter 11).

EXPECTATIONS AND BELIEFS

Expectancies and **beliefs** are the anticipations about what our behaviour, the situations in which we act, and the world around us will bring. The concept of expectancy comes directly from Rotter. It is parsed into two aspects that derive from Bandura: outcome expectations, called *behaviour-outcome expectancies* by Mischel, and *self-efficacy expectations*, the *can-I-do-it?* expectancies. We reviewed these earlier in this chapter. Mischel acknowledges Rotter's contribution and gives his Stanford colleague full credit for the two distinct aspects. Our experience teaches us about what to expect and believe, from our own abilities, from the settings in which we act, and from the larger contexts of community, nation, and world.

AFFECT

Humans are not coolly calculating cognitive organisms. Emotion is so much a part of us and our daily living that it cannot be omitted from theories of personality. So Mischel believes. Thus, he gives **affect**★ equal status with cognition in the name of the theory. There is little we think or do that is not accompanied by feeling, and many of our emotional reactions are immediate and automatic (Murphy & Zajonc, 1993; Niedenthal, 1990). Faces and facial expression, a sudden and momentary return of a disturbing memory, the sight of someone in pain or distress are examples we all know about; we've experienced affective responses and twinges like these over and over. None of us has to be told that affect colours and intensifies cognition, making thoughts—particularly those that are self-reflexive—'hot', emotional and changing the way we act (Metcalfe & Mischel, 1999). The thrill of a high mark on an essay may give added impetus to our effort in the course and in other courses and give a large boost to our confidence. We react happily to others and they, seeing us so, respond in kind, and they may carry something of our joy to the next people they encounter. 'You see,' Bandura might say, 'determinism really is reciprocal.' It is important to remember that situations and events are not the only sources of feelings. Enduring personality dispositions, based on genetic traits or learning histories, shape our affect in major ways.

GOALS AND SUBJECTIVE STIMULUS VALUES

The concepts of **goal** and **value** in CAPS are very similar to—indeed, derived from—Rotter's treatment of needs and need value. Goals are the long-term aims we pursue, the motives that channel our thought, feeling, and action. Mischel does not directly subscribe to Rotter's list of needs, preferring, I think, to leave the questions of the number of human motives and the desires they represent open. Goals—seeking power or affection, say—affect the value we place on reinforcing events, **subjective stimulus value** in Mischel's terminology. The qualifier 'subjective' is important; it emphasizes the unique, personal nature of our preferences and aversions. The power-oriented businessman strives to gain and exercise control over colleagues and subordinates and experiences success as rewarding. But remember that he must encode situations he encounters as relevant; we'll not be surprised that in many contexts his power goal will not be dominant because they are not 'power' situations to him.

COMPETENCIES AND SELF-REGULATORY SYSTEMS AND PLANS

What we set out to do, how we undertake it, and how well we manage will involve our abilities, talents, and skills, the knowledge we have acquired, the adequacy of our planning, and how well we monitor and regulate our activity and achievement. Take your own case as a university student. You have to stick out a long course of study, delaying many gratifications for years. You must be bright, diligent, and self-directed, keeping the goal in mind and disciplining yourself to study when giving in to temptations of the moment would be much the more pleasurable. You have to add hugely to your knowledge base, make use of it, and show what you can do. You will set standards—performance goals—to strive for and perhaps adjust them according to your successes or failures. And you will feel, probably very keenly, the delight of succeeding and the pangs brought by falling short. I have used you as an example of the **competencies**, **self-regulating abilities**, and **planfulness** required over a quest that takes years to complete. Recognize, though, that these things come into play in the short term as well and may involve other goals. At a party, you may find yourself asking, 'Do I have the social skills to make new friends here?' And, 'How will I do it? What resources do I have to call on? Is there anything about me that I will have to discipline, hold in check—maybe a tendency to make funny remarks at someone else's expense?' Competencies and self-regulatory systems and plans are intrinsic to thought and action. You can't do without 'em.

IF . . . THEN CONTINGENCIES

Expectancies, both outcome and self-efficacy, answer the question, 'What shall I do in this situation? Shall I seek the reward it offers, or avoid it because the outcome is disagreeable or because I have no hope of reward?' Our expectancies in the myriad situations of our lives are in a very important way *predictive*: We anticipate and act accordingly. '*If* this situation offers thus-and-so, *then* I will act in such-and-such a way.' Mischel introduced the *if . . . then* to capture expectancy-determined consistency in behaviour, *behavioural signatures* in our personalities. In the same kinds of situations (as each of us construes them), we act consistently; when situations are different, our behaviour changes. I am shy (do you believe that?) in meeting new people and tend to hold back, not knowing what to say. With friends, I am outgoing, conversing easily and comfortably. As an exercise, think of behavioural signatures of your own—the situations in which you act similarly and how, with variation in the situation, your behaviour is different.

The Cognitive-Affective Personality System in Perspective

We can think of CAPS as the theoretical distillate of social cognitive learning theories—Rotter's and Bandura's—and the phenomenology of George Kelly. Its outstanding accomplishment is the offer of a solution to the person–situation controversy. It credits the person with the consistency that has been a hallmark of personality theories, and it makes the necessary room for situational variation. CAPS does this via person variables interacting with the behavioural context through *if . . . then* contingencies. The person variables—all except competencies, which are individual attributes—are process concepts. They are scientifically powerful in making precise hypothesis formation and test possible.

Mischel has tried to flesh out the dry-bones view of the person that has been attributed to the social cognitive theories. CAPS seeks a richer view, one including the clinical characterizations of personality types from the psychodynamic approaches. Mischel has given cognitive accounts of distinctive personalities such as the narcissistic and rejection-sensitive, and a 'triple typology' of the hostile person based on person attributes, behaviour, and situations (Mischel, Shoda, & Smith, 2004). He has not succumbed to the cross-situational consistency argument of personality disposition theorists, however. Personality types in the CAPS framework are the expression of behavioural signatures. It is only in specifically evocative situations that a type will appear.

CAPS is a bravely inclusive effort toward a rapprochement with psychodynamic and trait theories. The friendly relations will be on Mischel's terms, however. Classical theories are acceptable only if they acknowledge the point he has been making for nearly half a century: a workable theory of personality must incorporate the situation, recognizing that people are exquisitely sensitive to situational variation, their thought, feeling, and behaviour reflecting their appreciation of the contexts in which they find themselves. We should note, finally, that CAPS is a theory that invites research. Mischel and colleagues have produced a large body of findings important to the theory, and they have been at pains to interpret research from other theories in person variable–situation terms.

SUMMARY

1. As the 1950s ended, behaviourism was on the way out, a casualty of its narrow approach to psychology and the obvious promise of cognitive psychology, which did not abolish mind as a legitimate scientific subject and had a vigorous and probing research program. Behaviourism was resurrected by the research and theory of Albert Bandura, who demoted the established principle that behaviour acquisition depends on immediate reinforcement. A more social and cognitive behaviour theory was the result.

2. Experiments on imitation (called 'observational learning' by Bandura) were responsible for the rescue and established SCLT. In the basic experiment, young children were exposed to an adult model who performed novel aggressive acts on a large inflated doll. Later, alone, the children spontaneously reproduced the aggressive repertoire. Subsequent experiments showed that filmed and cartoon models elicited the same vicarious learning of aggression.

3. Albert Bandura was born in 1925 in Mundare, Alberta, a small farming community. His father was a farmer and operated a dray business. A summer spent after graduating from Mundare's tiny high school working on the Alaska Highway with tough co-workers, many there to avoid the law, taught Bandura about 'the psychopathology of everyday life'. It was a rude introduction to the field he would take up. He entered the University of British Columbia, graduating in psychology, and went on to the State University of Iowa, which had a strong behaviouristic tradition. He received the PhD in 1952. After a clinical internship, he joined the Stanford University psychology department, where he remains the David Starr Jordan Professor of Social Science. He published a major book, *Social Learning and Personality Development*, in 1963, announcing the theory's basic ideas. Among other significant books are *Adolescent Aggression*, *Principles of Behavior Modification*, and *Social Foundations of Thought and Action*. He is indefatigable and creative in his research and has been the recipient of many honours and awards, including the presidency of the American Psychological Association and the Distinguished Scientific Contribution award by the American Psychological Association.

4. SCLT is based on a significant revision of the reinforcement principle. Reinforcement increases the probability of behaviour (including new learning), but it isn't necessary. The learner *anticipates* reinforcement to be received from imitating a model. There is also *self-reinforcement*. We reward (or punish) ourselves for good or bad behaviour. In contrast to the classical view, which holds that reinforcement acts directly on responses to increase the likelihood that they will be repeated, Bandura argues that reinforcement is

informative and *motivational* and not automatic in its effects. It is an *antecedent*, guiding future behaviour, not the consequence of behaviour directed toward it. In observational learning, anticipated reinforcement channels attention to models, whose actions are coded, organized, and rehearsed by the learner.

5. Bandura greatly extended the understanding of psychological determinism, going well beyond Kurt Lewin's influential formulation **B = *f*(P, E)**, or behaviour as a function of *person* and *environment*. Behaviour and environment are independent in their effects on behaviour; this is *unidirectional determinism*. A modified view, *partially bidirectional determinism*, sees person and environment mutually influencing each other. A complete picture is given by *reciprocal determinism*, which recognizes characteristics of the person (personality attributes), the person's behaviour, and the environment all reciprocally affecting each other.

6. The classical behaviouristic argument is that behaviour is controlled by reinforcing stimuli in the environment, making humans the behavioural products of environmental stimulation. This is an extreme characterization, a caricature, that Bandura uses to contrast the position of SCLT. Behaviour, he insists, is controlled through self-regulation and self-reinforcement, and there are three processes. Self-regulation and self-reinforcement start with *self-observation*, the monitoring of one's own behaviour. We apply *judgemental standards*, both personal and those that come from others, in regulating our behaviour. The final self-regulating process is *self-reaction*, evaluating ourselves, rewarding or punishing, and sometimes evading bad implications of our behaviour.

7. The future orientation of reinforcement, self-regulation, self-reinforcement, and the fact that behaviour is produced by thinking and feeling humans who react to and change their environments add up to a perspective that Bandura calls an *agentic* view of personality. Humans are the agents of their actions and cognitive processes, not simply creatures controlled by environmental contingencies. At the core of the theory is a picture of people as conscious beings, agents of their own thought, feeling, and action.

8. SCLT makes significant use of an expectancy concept, one similar to the concept of expectancy in social learning theory. There are two kinds of *expectations*, as Bandura prefers to call them. *Outcome expectations* are subjective probabilities that a given outcome, a reinforcing event, will occur. We anticipate reinforcement (positive or negative) in the situations we encounter and adapt our behaviour to outcome expectations. *Efficacy expectations* ask, 'Can I do it? Can I cope, gain reinforcement X, avoid aversive consequence Y?' They vary from person to person in any given situation and will vary from situation to situation in a single person. Efficacy expectations are learned from past performance, from observation of others, from verbal persuasion (as from parents or teachers), and from experiences of emotional arousal that may tell us that we are too anxious to do well. Self-efficacy holds a major implication for psychotherapy: we will not try to reduce the anxiety of a distressed patient but instead concentrate on changing his or her expectations, increasing self-efficacy. The most effective therapeutic technique is *participant modelling*, which combines observational learning with experiences of mastery of the problem.

9. As a process theory, SCLT views personality development as the result of learning. Development is continuous and does not proceed by stages. Heredity sets the possibilities for the developing child, to be shaped by learning environments determined by family, school, culture, and economic conditions. Reciprocal determinism will play a large role, as others affect a child and the child's behaviour affects them. Direct reinforcement of the child's behaviour will be important, but even more significant will be observational learning, both intended by parents and others and unintended (the modelling of aggression or the breaking of rules, for example). Acquiring goals, internal standards, and self-efficacy expectations are major learning tasks in personality development. Children learn self-regulation and will acquire abilities to self-observe, judge their own behaviour, and react to their accomplishments and failings.

10. Chance encounters cannot be predicted; the fact that they happen to a person at a particular time and place is accidental and beyond the possibility of science to account for. How chance encounters affect individuals, however, is a legitimate question for a science of personality. Whether one is overwhelmed by a chance event or masters it will be determined by personality attributes of the person. People who insulate themselves within constricted lifestyles will reduce (but not

eliminate) the possibility of chance happenings; those who habitually make risky choices are likely to expose themselves to unwanted chance occurrences.

11. A major part of SCLT is the content concept of the *self-system*. It is an organization of cognitive processes by which self-observation, judgement, and self-evaluation are conducted. Self-regulating processes and efficacy expectations are functions of the self-system.

12. SCLT contrasts sharply with psychoanalysis in its portrayal of the antecedents of aggression. The psychoanalytic hypothesis of *catharsis* is strongly contradicted by the hypothesis and evidence that aggressive behaviour may be acquired by observing models. Research on the effects of the mass media establishes that viewed violence increases the probability of aggression by the viewer, and this is especially the case in children.

13. There are important implications of the theory for psychopathology and for psychotherapy. Such symptoms as phobic fears, which are traditionally regarded in behaviour theory as classically conditioned responses acquired by exposure to frightening stimuli, may be developed through observation of the fear-inducing experience of others. There is strong experimental evidence that phobic-like fear may be learned vicariously. Phobic avoidance of dogs or of flying may be learned by observing frightened models. Effective psychotherapy is directed toward providing experiences of mastery over problem situations, increasing self-efficacy. Modelling is a helpful technique, but even better is *participant modelling*.

14. SCLT is almost entirely research-based. Its major propositions have been systematically investigated in experimental studies and consistently confirmed. It is also a theory with significant implications for social behaviour, social influence, personality development, psychopathology, and psychotherapy. SCLT is, however, a spare theory that doesn't fully help us to grasp human complexity.

15. A number of years ago, Walter Mischel chided the personality community for the emphasis, common to nearly every theory, on cross-situational dispositions (traits). People are consistent in their motive-relevant behaviour over *time* but not over situations. They are finely attuned to situational similarities and differences, adapting their behaviour to cues that tell them what will be rewarded, ignored, or met with disapproval. Out of this proposition, and from extensive research on the cognitive activity in children that enables them to delay gratification, grew a person–situation theory, the *cognitive-affective personality system*, adapted from the social cognitive theories of Rotter and Bandura and the cognitive phenomenology of George Kelly.

16. CAPS consists of five person variables:
    - *encodings*, how people construe themselves, others, and events;
    - *expectancies and beliefs* about situational outcomes and self-efficacy;
    - *affects*, the emotional responses that activate and colour cognition;
    - *goals and values*, both long-term aims and more immediate *subjective stimulus values*; and
    - *competencies and self-regulatory systems and plans*, the abilities possessed by an individual and the cognitive activity that anticipates and accompanies action.

17. To account for situational variation, CAPS introduces the concept of *if . . . then contingencies*. These are the thoughts, associated affect, and action called up by situations: if Samantha sees Bert as critical, demeaning, and demanding on their date, then she will . . . What Samantha does will be typical of her, a *behavioural signature*.

18. CAPS is a comprehensive theory consisting of process variables that are open to hypothesis formation and test, and there is an appreciable body of evidence to support its concepts.

TO TEST YOUR UNDERSTANDING

1. This chapter argues that a single experiment is the basis of SCLT. Review that experiment and explain how it could form the underpinning of an entire personality theory. What principles did it establish?

2. Think of some examples of behaviour you've observed and account for them in the terms of reciprocal determination. How does your explanation go beyond attributing the cause of behaviour to the person or to the person in a situation?

3. How does Bandura's agentic view of personality differ from other theories—from Freud, the neo-Freudians, or other learning theories? Is this a novel conception, or was it anticipated by other personality theorists? Do you agree with it, or do you see human behaviour controlled by forces within the person or in the environment?

4. What is the most effective psychotherapy as SCLT sees it? What makes this psychotherapeutic procedure so successful? What principles in the theory is it based on? What kinds of behaviour problems is it best suited for?

5. Henry is very sweet and gentle to his wife, Henrietta. With his employees in the office, though, he is a tyrant, boiling over in anger over the slightest, most trivial mistake. His employees fear and hate him. Explain Henry's 'inconsistency' in CAPS terms, using CAPS concepts and variables.

CHAPTER SIXTEEN

Genes, Behaviour, and Personality

Introduction

Let's begin by imagining a king in ancient times, deeply troubled by doubtful allegiance among his subjects. He summons his court psychologist, Master Shrink (that was his name, Shrink). 'Tell me, Master Shrink, why it is that only some of my subjects are loyal and true, and all the others—far, far too many, I warrant—are shifty and untrustworthy, and would overthrow me in a minute if they had a chance?'

'I do not know, Sire,' says Shrink. 'My duty is to your mental health, not to answer imponderables. Would you like some psychotherapy now, perchance?'

'No!' snaps the king. 'Sometimes you try my patience too much. I want an answer to a question that rankles me. Now Shrink, we are going to do something for which there is no precedent. We are going to conduct an experiment, a word I have borrowed from the Latin. It means—you would know if you were more of a scholar—*to try*. We are going *to try* to find out whether my subjects act as they do because of their upbringing or because of inheritance from their parentage. You will bring me two healthy infants, one from a duty-abiding family and one from a family of the other kind, disloyal and deceitful. We will switch these infants so that each is brought up by the other's family. In twelve years' time, Shrink, you will remind me and bring the youths back before me. We shall endeavour to determine how they are going to turn out as adults. If the youth of good parentage raised in the troublesome family shall turn out badly, while the infant of the bad parents shall bear the signs of a good subject, we will know that rearing—the nurture of children—is the key. If, however, each shows the traits of the family of its birth, it will be clear that it is nature itself that makes one either good, loyal, and true or else born to be unworthy.'

You might like to think about the bygone king's experiment, its good points and its faults (do, though, be kind to the king, for after all he thought of this long before science existed). The story of the king introduces us to this chapter and to ideas that figure prominently in the study of the inheritance of human traits.

Behaviour genetics has hardly figured at all in the study of human personality. Until recently, personality psychologists knew and cared little about the inheritance of human characteristics. Yes, they were aware of grave genetic disorders like Huntington's disease, but they did not consider at all that *personality* characteristics might be inherited. Even schizophrenia, for which we now have significant evidence of its genetic basis, was considered to be an acquired disorder. Disruptive families, 'schizophrenogenic mothers', weak and fragile egos, chronic exposure to intolerable, conflicting, and inescapable parental communications in childhood—these were the origins of schizophrenia that generations of psychologists were nurtured on. Personality theorists regarded experience as personality's tutor. Sophisticated theorists who understood the person–situation interaction would find that experience in the family. Theorists like Freud looked to experience that determined how instinctual life was socialized. As we saw, Freud (1915) always wanted to know about 'the vicissitudes of instincts' in the origin of personality and personality disorders.

The inheritance of personality features is not incompatible with most personality theories. It's just that theorists haven't been concerned with the ways in which their variables might be influenced by characteristics that nature has provided. In this chapter, we're going to explore a bit of the modern world of behaviour genetics. We'll go over some basic concepts and look at mechanisms of inheritance.

It will be helpful for us to review the Augustinian monk Gregor Mendel's experiments with pea plants in the 1850s and 1860s, which could have illuminated the processes underlying natural selection if Darwin had troubled to look at the paper on the genetics of inheritance, cast unread into a drawer, that Mendel sent him. We'll consider single-gene transmission in animals and humans, applying Mendelian principles directly to behaviour and to disorders. Most personality characteristics, however, are not the result of single-gene transmission. They occur as the result of genes at many loci— they are *polygenic*. So, we'll look at some multiple-gene effects on human behaviour, and we'll consider the research methods used to establish them.

What Is a Gene?

'Genes', say Plomin, DeFries, and McClearn in their excellent *Behavior Genetics: A Primer* (1990),

> . . . are blueprints for the assembly and regulation of proteins, which are the building blocks of our bodies, including the nervous system. Each gene codes for a specific sequence of amino acids that the body assembles to form a protein. If even the smallest part of this chain is altered, the entire protein can malfunction. . . . Genes do not magically blossom into behaviour or anything else. They are stretches of chemicals that code for protein production or regulate the activities of other genes. . . . There is no gene or protein, for example, that repeatedly causes a person to lift shot glasses and perhaps become an alcoholic. Proteins interact with other physiological intermediaries . . . , which may be other proteins, such as hormones or neurotransmitters, or may be structural properties of the nervous system (p. 7).

A small part of the genetic blueprint might, for example, cause neural sensitivity to alcohol, resulting in alcoholism in a person who has become a drinker. Alcoholism may be an effect of a number of genes, brain chemistry and structure, and the environment (adolescent and young adult peers who influence the genetically susceptible person to take up drinking).

Genes★ are biochemical substances. They are segments of chromosomes that carry an element of genetic information and determine heredity. Genes control the development and metabolism of organisms. Their second function is to transmit genetic information to the next generation.

The gene is the genetic material of **chromosomes★**, threadlike structures found in the nuclei of cells. Each species has a definite number of chromosomes—39 in the dog, 7 in the grasshopper, 6 in spinach, 23 in the human (and also the privet shrub, but the similarity doesn't make the privet shrub human). The number of chromosomes in a species is the *monoploid* (or *haploid*) number. Mammalian organisms, however, have twice the haploid number of chromosomes, one haploid set from each parent; we call this the *diploid* number. Each parent contributes a haploid set of chromosomes, giving the diploid complement of each cell. These paired chromosomes determine the bodily characteristics of the organism, such as eye and hair colour in the human. Of the 23 paired chromosomes in the human, 22 are identical in males and females and are called **autosomes★**. In the twenty-third pair, however, is a chromosome that determines sex. Normal females have two similar chromosomes in pair 23; they are called X chromosomes. Normal males have one X chromosome in pair 23 and one that is different, the Y chromosome. So, it is the presence or absence of the Y chromosome that says you're a male or a female. The sex chromosomes determine sex and carry genes for sex-linked traits. Much of this was known at the end of the first half of the twentieth century, but the structure of genetic material and how it transcribes the genetic code were mysteries.

The DNA Code

At Cambridge University in 1953, an American, James Watson, and an Englishman, Francis Crick, proposed a hypothesis to account for the nature and molecular structure of genetic material. Elements of the idea were in the wind and others were close, but it was Watson and Crick who put the evidence all together. Their hypothesis, which research confirmed, was that deoxyribonucleic acid (DNA) is the physical basis of the genetic code, and its molecular structure is a double coil or helix.

The structure of DNA consists of two twined strands of phosphate and sugar groups held in place at a fixed distance from each other by base pairs of nitrogenous material. Figure 16.1 shows a schematic DNA segment. There are four bases: adenine, thymine, guanine, and cytosine. Adenine pairs with thymine, guanine with cytosine, forming bonded pairs. The sequence of these four bases is the code of a gene. During the process of cell division, the coils of the DNA molecule unwind, the base pairs separate, and each strand acts as a template for the structuring of a new strand. Within the nucleus of the cell will be one of the four bases, a deoxyribose sugar, and a phosphate. These nucleotides pair with the bases of the unwound helices and go on to form a new strand with each of the original strands. We now have two molecules of DNA. This is genetic replication, or copying.

Only seldom in nature are there errors of replication. When errors (mutations) happen, they are random copying errors that might occur, say Plomin et al. (1990), once in several million replications. Mutations are most often damaging to the survival and development of the organism, but on rare occasions they may produce genetic changes that favour adaptation to an organism's environment (Plomin et al, 1990). There are occasional mutations that produce organisms with distinctive characteristics, and we can use them to study genetic transmission. An example: the Waltzer mouse. A mutant mouse strain was imported by mouse fanciers to Europe and North America in the 1890s, a mouse with strange, 'waltzing' behaviour. These mice do not make the rhythmic twirls their name suggests; rather, they rapidly turn in circles, shake their heads from side to side and up and down, and are easily irritated. When Waltzer males are crossed with Waltzer females, all of their offspring show the trait, implying that this is a true-breeding

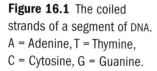

Figure 16.1 The coiled strands of a segment of DNA. A = Adenine, T = Thymine, C = Cytosine, G = Guanine.

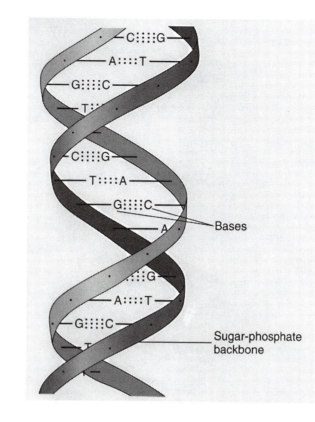

population. When Waltzers are crossed with non-Waltzers, none of the pups shows the behaviour pattern; waltzing thus appears to be a recessive trait. We can also induce mutations by mutagenic substances that alter DNA.

Some Genetic History

Charles Darwin's *The Origin of Species*, published in 1859, set out the process by which evolution takes place. Within each species, many individual organisms in each generation fail to survive to reproductive age. There is, secondly, great variation among the individual members of a species, and at least some of that variation is due to heredity. Now, if the probability of survival to reproductive age is affected, even in a very small way, by the heritability of a characteristic, the progeny of the survivors (possessors of the characteristic that reproduced) will display more of the trait than the parental population. Little by little, then, the population changes, and in time the original population and the later one might be very different. The evolution of Darwin's finches by adaptation to the food available in local habitats is the classic example (see Figure 16.2).

The most widely accepted theory of heritability in Darwin's time took as its basic datum the observation that children show some of the characteristics of both their parents. So, the theory went on, parental attributes were merged, or *blended*, in their offspring. A very awkward consequence of the genetic blending hypothesis was that blending would greatly reduce (halve, in fact) the variability in each succeeding generation. It would not take many generations for genetic variability to reach zero, a disastrous implication for Darwin's theory.

Figure 16.2 Darwin's finches. (a) Woodpecker-like finch using twigs to get insects from tree bark. (c–e) Insect eaters. (f–g) Vegetarians. (h) Cocos Island finch. (i) Lives on hard seeds; not strong beak. Other birds on ground mainly eat seeds. (From D. Lack, *Darwin's Finches*. Reprinted with permission of Cambridge University Press.)

Darwin struggled with this problem but could not satisfactorily resolve it (if only he had looked in that drawer!). His attempts involved the idea that environmental events could alter genetic material, a Lamarckian notion that *acquired* characteristics can be inherited. This theory, known as *pangenesis*, claimed that bodily cells in addition to self-replication gave off 'atoms' (molecules) of cellular material, called gemmules. These gemmules would multiply and combine in the course of development. At the right time, they would cause the development of new bodily organs like those of the parents. Pangenesis was clever but flat wrong and, entailing no place for genetic variation, truly problematical.

Darwin was at least partly persuaded. He noted the common belief that sailors had longer legs and shorter arms than soldiers and proposed: 'Whether the several foregoing modifications would become hereditary [longer legs, shorter arms], if the same habits of life were followed during many generations, is not known, but it is probable' (Darwin, 1871, p. 418). So, a family of sailors would show over its generations progressively longer legs and shortened arms as a result of the family occupation.

Gregor Mendel

Gergor Johann Mendel. (© Bettmann/CORBIS)

Gregor Mendel was the son of peasant farmers. He was an outstanding student, but his parents could not afford to send him to university. He entered an Augustinian order and was presently sent to the University of Vienna, training to become a high school teacher of science. Unfortunately, however, he got the jitters and failed his university examinations. Returning to the monastery at Brunn, Austria, he became a substitute teacher, but he also took up research into plant genetics in the monastery garden. It was this at which he excelled. Mendel was not, as we would now say, a rocket scientist, but he was consummately diligent and a first-rate experimenter.

By an exceptionally fortunate choice—one, however, that seems to have been thought out and deliberate—Mendel crossed garden peas, examining seven really simple qualitative characteristics (round versus wrinkled seeds, green versus yellow, short versus tall, for example). Others interested in heredity had crossed different species of plants. The offspring of these crosses are usually sterile, so the results of crosses could not be studied in succeeding generations. Mendel discovered that crossing true-breeding pea plants (that is, plants that invariably yield the same characteristics when crossed with the same kind of plant) that had round seeds with true-breeding wrinkled-seed plants yielded seeds that were *all round* in the new generation (called F_1, the first *filial* generation). There was no blending. What had happened to the wrinkled attribute? Now Mendel crossed plants in the F_1 generation to see what might happen in the next, F_2. The result? There were both round and wrinkled seeds in a 3:1 ratio (see Figure 16.3). Whatever it was that determined 'wrinkledness' in some of the parent plants was unscathed in the F_1 generation.

Mendel's deduction from these findings was that each individual plant had two heritable factors, as he called them. We now call them *alleles*, which are alternate forms of a gene. Parents have two alleles, passing only one to offspring. Secondly, one allele could *dominate*. In the F_1 generation, the offspring will have one allele from each parent (we'll call these A_1 and A_2). With A_1 as a dominant allele, all F_1 plants produce round seeds. In the F_2 generation, we have A_1A_2 crossed with A_1A_2. One-quarter of the F_2's are A_1A_1, one-half A_1A_2, and one-quarter A_2A_2. Since A_1 is dominant over A_2, then A_1A_2 should have round seeds just like A_1A_1. We could just as well say that A_2 is a recessive allele. We might have complete dominance (or recessiveness), as above, or partial dominance (or recessiveness), in which case what we would observe would fall somewhere between the values for the two hetereozygotes (that is, plants having the two alleles).

Figure 16.3 Mendel's basic findings. (After Plomin et al., 1990, p. 39.)

	Observed	**Hypothesized**
Truebreeding Parents	Truebreeding Round X Truebreeding Wrinkled	$A_1 A_1$ X $A_2 A_2$
F_1	All Round	All $A_1 A_2$ (A_1 dominant)
F_2	$3/4$ Round, $1/4$ Wrinkled	$1/4$ $A_1 A_1$, $1/2$ $A_1 A_2$ Round $1/4$ $A_2 A_2$ Wrinkled

Huntington's Disease

Our major purpose in this chapter is to study the inheritance of personality characteristics. Mendel's groundbreaking experiments gave us the principles to work with. Let's now apply them to humans—to a disorder affecting movement and personality that is caused by a single, dominant gene.

Huntington's disease, first described by New York physician George Huntington in 1872, is severe, degenerative, and ultimately fatal. As a signature, it produces strikingly abnormal involuntary movements of limbs or parts of limbs. It used to be called Huntington's chorea, from the Greek for 'dance'; the movements aren't, however, gracefully dance-like. They start with ceaseless fidgeting and progress to incessant, exaggerated twitching and flailing of entire extremities. There are memory and cognitive impairments plus emotional and personality changes (anxiety, depression, manic behaviour, and symptoms resembling schizophrenia). Onset of symptoms occurs typically in midlife, between the ages of 30 and 50, and death ensues fifteen to twenty years after the disease first makes its appearance. The most famous sufferer was the folksinger and songwriter Woody Guthrie, whose story is told in Perspective 16.1. Indeed, Huntington's disease is sometimes called Woody Guthrie's disease.

Huntington's disease is a condition we can trace back to 1630 and to the village of Bures in England. Entire afflicted families were accused by their neighbours and tried as witches. Some of those who suffered from or carried the disease left with the Puritan fleet of John Winthrop in 1630 and settled in the Massachusetts Bay Colony. One of them was tried and hanged for witchcraft in 1653, her strange behaviour attracting the mass hysteria of this exceptionally intolerant time in colonial America. The incidence of Huntington's disease in populations of white European origin is 1 in 15,000, and considerably lower among Asians and blacks.

The offspring of two unaffected parents will, of course, have no risk of the disorder. The offspring of an unaffected parent and a parent who has one of the alleles (a *heterozygote*) have a 50 per cent chance of developing it. If both parents are heterozygotes, each having the gene from one of their parents, the probability of afflicted offspring will be 75 per cent. And the offspring of a Huntington's victim with alleles from both parents (a *homozygote*) and an unaffected parent will *all* have the disorder.

Figure 16.4 The genetic risks of Huntington's disease. (After Plomin et al., 1990.)

		Unaffected Parent	
		a	a
Unaffected Parent	a	aa	aa
	a	aa	aa

a. Neither parent is affected by the disease.

		Affected Parent (Heterozygote)	
		A	a
Unaffected Parent	a	Aa	aa
	a	Aa	aa

b. One parent is unaffected; the other is a heterozygote.

		Affected Parent (Heterozygote)	
		A	a
Affected Parent (Heterozygote)	A	AA	Aa
	a	Aa	aa

c. Both parents are heterozygotes.

		Unaffected Parent	
		a	a
Affected Parent (Homozygote)	A	Aa	Aa
	A	Aa	Aa

d. One parent is unaffected; the other is a homozygote.

Perspective 16.1 Woody Guthrie

Woody is just Woody. Thousands of people do not know he has any other name. He is just a voice and a guitar. He sings the songs of a people and I suspect that he is, in a way, that people. Harsh voiced and nasal, his guitar hanging like a tire iron on a rusty rim, there is nothing sweet about Woody, and there is nothing sweet about the songs he sings. But there is something more important for those who will listen. There is the will of the people to endure and fight against oppression. I think we call this the American spirit (John Steinbeck 1967).

(© John Springer Collection/CORBIS)

Woody Guthrie was born in the small Oklahoma town of Okemah in 1912. His father was a successful land speculator and tried his hand at politics. When Woody was a young boy, the family's newly built house burned down. Then his father, the victim of cutthroat speculators, lost everything. 'A little bit of bad luck', Woody called it, but it was followed by two tragedies. His fourteen-year-old sister, kept home for the day, either set herself on fire to scare her mother or her clothes accidentally caught fire while ironing. She died the next day. Woody's mother, already moody, distressed, violent, and notably strange in her behaviour, became yet more seriously disturbed and was committed to a mental hospital, where she spent the rest of her life. The aggravating cause wasn't the death of her daughter, though, as Woody would think until late in his life; it was Huntington's disease, undiagnosed. As if this weren't enough, Woody's mother either set his father on fire or, in despair over his ruination, he did it to himself. Woody's remembered version of events was the latter. Their world in tatters, the Guthries moved to the Texas panhandle town of Pampa, where Woody completed his growing up.

He had been a happy child in Okemah, musical, the class clown, and not a very good student. Not that he lacked the essentials of learning; in Pampa, he read almost every book in the library and wrote one that the librarian placed on the library shelves in the psychology section. He had a huge talent for music and from boyhood could make up songs on the spot. But he was also, people said, a bit odd—funny, with a capacity for childlike absorption, restless, somewhat impulsive and erratic, careless of his appearance, nothing exactly you could quite put your finger on. Remember this: we'll reflect on these traits and what they might mean shortly. He was also lovable. He charmed three women into marrying him and became an inspiration to the dispossessed and downtrodden.

In Pampa, he married the sister of a close friend, and they had three children. A settled family life wasn't for him, though, and it was the time of the Great Depression. There were no jobs, and the dust storms of the mid-1930s ruined the farms. Woody left his young family at home and set out for the southwest, riding the rails; he began to write and sing songs, a lot of them songs of protest and outrage over the oppression of the poor and the exploited.

This would be the pattern of his life—roaming, picking crops, singing and writing, great songs flowing ('This Land Is Our Land' is a memorable one), family life endlessly disrupted. Finally, his wife had had enough and they divorced. He married again; soon there were more children. He joined the Merchant Marine and was later drafted. After the war, signs of trouble—the personality kind—began to appear. He was violent with his wife and became a serious problem drinker. He checked himself into a hospital for treatment of alcoholism, and was shortly transferred to a psychiatric hospital, where the diagnosis of Huntington's disease was made.

On his release, he set off again. An especially ill-advised trip to California and Mexico got him a Mexican divorce and a new young wife and, before long, another daughter. Back in New York, he was readmitted to the psychiatric hospital; this or other hospitals would be home for his remaining thirteen years. Often, when he was allowed out, he suffered the indignity of arrest by the police for being a drunken or schizophrenic nuisance. He had the uncontrollable choreic movements, a staggering gait, slurred speech. He was difficult to understand, and he might have shown something like the disordered thought of the schizophrenic. So, off they would take him to the police station or to the admitting department at the nearest psychiatric hospital. He did have visitors—his second wife and the children, devoted to him, and occasional others who looked on him as a folk hero. One of those was the young Bob Dylan. There is a moving biography of Woody by Klein (1980).

What happened to Woody's children? Three of them died in childhood or adolescent accidents, so we can't tell how the roll of the Huntington's dice would have turned out for them. Two developed the disorder, and three (including Arlo, his folksinging son, now in his late fifties) appear not to have inherited the gene.

I said that we would consider the possible implication of Woody's behaviour from childhood on. Were the things that people pointed out—the oddness, the distinctive and frequently troublesome characteristics that in part made Woody the person he was—an expression of his upbringing, including the family calamities he endured, or were they early and subtle signs of Huntington's? Some authorities think the latter is a real possibility (Gusella, 1987, p. 505). We have a genetic disease, on the one hand, with an inevitable final course and outcome. Is it, though, totally silent until the fourth decade, only then emerging with a visible progression of symptoms? Or, is it lifelong but shown only quietly, inscrutable except to those who might have an idea about what to look for? This is the case in schizophrenia, which can make itself known in small but telling ways in childhood (Grimes & Walker, 1994). On the other hand, we have an upbringing marred by some of the most horrific and tragic environmental events that could befall a child. What did they do to Woody's personality development? How did they shape him? But we are not limited to one of two alternatives. Could genetic disease in its earliest form have *interacted* with environment—dysfunctional family, tragedy, and all—to result in personality attributes that neither alone might have produced? I have no answer. I pose these possibilities for you as worth thinking about.

Research Methods in the Genetics of Personality

With single-gene disorders we can, with knowledge of Mendelian genetics, trace family history. A family pedigree will reveal the incidence and conformity to the influence of an autosomal dominant gene. However, personality traits and intelligence are not discrete **phenotypes★** (round versus wrinkled, have the symptoms of the disease versus don't have them) stemming from single genes. Their phenotypes are continuous (low to high in intelligence or on a personality trait). If they are heritable, they are *polygenic*—outcomes of many genes. So, pedigrees are not helpful, and we have to turn to other research methods to establish the genetic basis of personality characteristics, just as we have with intelligence. There are three basic methods: family studies, twin studies, and adoption studies. We'll look at each of these in turn.

First, though, a note about the limits of this kind of research. If we scientists were not bound by the rules of civilized society and could carry out human studies of inheritance as we would with mice, we'd recruit samples of people varying in the personality characteristics we wanted to investigate—aggressiveness, say, as an example. We'd form a group of very aggressive people and one of nonaggressive people, and in each group we'd ask them to breed. This would be a very long research program, since we would have to elicit breeding and test for aggressiveness over several generations. Only the psychologists many generations hence would get to see the results. Well, of course, we'd wait in vain for volunteers, and ethics committees would run us out of town on a rail. So, the three methods we have are default methods, what we have to fall back on to answer our heritability question.

Family Studies

If genetic factors influence personality, then we must necessarily find similarity in personality characteristics among family members. To be sure, we may also find environmental similarity. If we take a personality characteristic and examine familial resemblances—the correlations of scores on a measure of the characteristic between family members with varying degrees of genetic relationship—what we find will tell

JIMMY, SIXTH-GENERATION PAIN IN THE ASS

us whether there is any basis to consider a genetic contribution. You might object that we have not distinguished between genetic and environmental influence, and you are absolutely correct. All we have is evidence that is or is not *compatible* with a genetic hypothesis. If we find no familial similarity, we have to consider the possibility that there are neither genetic nor environmental influences.

Some Evidence

Loehlin (1987) analyzed the data of several research projects using scales from a personality questionnaire, the Thurstone Temperament Schedule. The definition of the trait 'sociable' and some sample items are shown in Table 16.1. Table 16.2 shows the correlations of 'sociable' between family members of varying genetic relationship. Note that there is an adoption study in these data. The correlations for the identical twin pairs are higher than the correlations for fraternal twins or for any other family relationship, and environmental similarity doesn't seem to have much influence, since the correlations of adopting parents and their children and adopted children pairs are essentially zero. We can conclude that these data support the possibility that some of the variability in this sociability trait is genetic.

Evidence on Schizophrenia

Worldwide, the incidence of schizophrenia in the general population is about 1 per cent (Gottesman, 1991). But in Table 16.3 we see that schizophrenia runs in families: the percentage of schizophrenic patients whose parents are schizophrenic is 5.6, more than five times greater than the probability of schizophrenia in the population at large. Look at the risk statistic for siblings: the probability of schizophrenia for a sibling of a schizophrenic patient is ten times that of randomly selected persons from the general population. These data suggest that a genetic influence is at work, but they don't help us to

Table 16.1	The Definition of the Trait *Sociable*, and Some Sample Items from the Thurstone Temperament Schedule

Thurstone's "Sociable" Trait

"Persons with high scores in this area enjoy the company of others, make make friends easily, and are sympathetic, cooperative, and agreeable in their relations. Strangers readily tell them about their troubles."

You start work on a new project with a great deal of enthusiasm.	YES ? NO
You are often low in spirits	YES ? NO
Most people use politeness to cover up what is really "cutthroat" competition.	YES ? NO

Source: From L. Thurstone, *Thurstone Temperment Schedule: Examiner's Manual*, 2nd ed. Copyright 1953 by Science Research Associates. Reprinted with permission of the McGraw-Hill Companies.

Table 16.2 Sociable Trait Correlations for Twin and Adoptive and Natural Pairings

Pairs	Correlation	No. of Pairs
Identical Twins (Michigan)	0.47	45
Fraternal Twins (Michigan)	0.00	34
Identical Twins (Veterans)	0.45	102
Fraternal Twins (Veterans)	0.08	119
Father - adopted child	0.07	257
Mother - adopted child	-0.03	271
Father - natural child	0.22	56
Mother - natural child	0.13	54
Adopted - natural child	-0.05	48
Two adopted children	-0.21	80

Source: After Loehlin, 1987.

disentangle genetic and environmental influences. Don't forget, though, what we said about the purpose of family studies. They are a start, not the whole story.

By far the greatest likelihood is that even with the most extreme familial risk, schizophrenia will not occur in the relatives of schizophrenics, meaning that *nongenetic influences* are chiefly responsible. We think that schizophrenia must involve a genetic predisposition *and* significant exposure to stress, either neurodevelopmental or environmental, or both (Cornblatt & Erlenmeyer-Kimling, 1985). This is a **diathesis–stress model**. No one becomes schizophrenic without the predisposition, but a great proportion with predisposing genes will not develop the disease because they are fortunate in not having to endure serious developmental stressors.

Table 16.3 The Risk of Schizophrenia in the General Population and Among Family Members of Schizophrenics

Group	Percent
General population	1.0
First-degree relatives	
Parents of schizophrenics	5.6
Siblings of schizophrenics	10.1
Children of schizophrenics	12.8
Second-degree relatives	3.3
Third-degree relatives	2.4

Source: After Gottesman & Shields, 1982.

Twin Studies

In the 1870s, Charles Darwin's cousin Francis Galton (later, Sir Francis, knighted at the age of 87 in 1909) studied two groups of twins—twin pairs who from birth highly resembled each other physically and behaviourally and twin pairs who were dissimilar. He thought he might be able to determine if environmental influences could make similar twins different and twin pairs who were different more similar. His study of the life histories of these two groups led him to believe that 'there is no escape from the conclusion that nature prevails enormously over nurture . . .' (Galton, 1875, p. 576). Although Galton knew that there were both identical and fraternal twins, the one fertilized from the same egg (**monozygotic★**) and genetically identical and the other no more similar in inheritance than siblings (**dizygotic★**), he failed to obtain the obvious data. He might have thought to identify identical and fraternal twins (in responses to questionnaires that he devised and from biographical data) but he didn't, simply assuming that 'similar' twins would have to be identical and 'different' twins fraternal. Fifty years later, Merriman (1924) studied the intelligence of 'duplicate' (identical) and fraternal twins and found evidence compatible with a genetic hypothesis.

Twin studies provide us with a powerful way to estimate the heritability of characteristics that we can measure—intelligence, a number of personality attributes, cognitive abilities, and serious disorders of personality such as schizophrenia. We compare identical and fraternal twins on the measures we're interested in, and a greater similarity in identical twins implicates the heritability of the trait. 'Not so fast,' you say. Identical twins look more alike than fraternals, sometimes to the point that even their parents have difficulty in telling them apart. They may well be treated more similarly than fraternal twins, and this similarity of experience could account for the closeness of their scores on our test measures. You're right to object, and this has been a serious issue to students of the heritability of behaviour.

There are, however, some things we can do to establish whether the environments of identical and fraternal twins really differ in their effect on behaviour. Thus, we can *test* the critical assumption that the environments of identical and fraternal twins are equal—an assumption we must be able to make and defend with evidence if we are to draw any conclusions about the heritability of behavioural traits.

The Equal Environments Assumption

Identical and fraternal twins are not always correctly identified, either by themselves or their parents. If you and your parents *thought* you and your twin were identical twins when you were fraternals, you might very likely have been raised and treated according to belief, not genetic reality.

Let's consider some data on 400 twin pairs studied in a Philadelphia research project (Scarr & Carter-Saltzman, 1979). The investigators (who knew the zygosity of the twins) asked them if they were identical or fraternal. Forty per cent (!) were wrong. The investigators compared these wrongly self-identified twin pairs on cognitive and personality tests. The outcome favoured a genetic interpretation: identical twins who believed they were fraternal were only slightly more different than identicals who thought they were identical. And, fraternals who thought they were identical weren't any more alike than fraternals who correctly identified themselves.

We can *measure* features of the environments of identical and fraternal twins to see whether the equal environments assumption is defensible. When we do this we find that identical twins dress alike (i.e. their parents choose identical clothes), study together, share more friends. *But*, do similarities such as these affect important traits like cognitive abilities, intelligence, or personality characteristics? Some evidence shows that parents treating identical twins similarly are responding to their children's behaviour, not creating it (Lytton, Martin, & Eaves, 1977).

Even better is to determine whether differences in family experience between identical and fraternal twins actually influence behaviour. A way to do this is to *correlate* measures of differences between identical twins (on cognitive and personality measures in one important investigation) with measures of similarity in the treatment of the twins. The data from a large study by Loehlin and Nichols (1976) show that similarity of experience in the family is not correlated with measures of differences between twins in cognition, personality, and social behaviour. Examined closely, it appears that the equal environments assumption is a fair one.

Among a rapidly growing list of findings of heritable personality characteristics from twin studies are the following:

- Psychopathology: *schizophrenia* (identical twin concordance of 50+ per cent; fraternal twin or sibling concordance about 15 per cent; identical twins reared apart, 58 per cent concordance, Faraone, Taylor, & Tsuang, 2002). Concordance is the percentage of twins sharing the diagnosis—here, schizophrenia. It is the statistic of choice when we have categories (schizophrenia versus normal) and not a continuously distributed variable.
- 'Big Five' traits—*agreeableness, conscientiousness, openness to experience* (identical twin correlations average .45; fraternal twin correlations average .20, Loehlin, 1992). You will recall that the Big Five is a set of personality test factors describing five traits that cover, according to its proponents, the entire range of personality.
- *Extraversion* (identical twin correlation = .51; fraternal = .18); *neuroticism* (identicals = .46, fraternals = .20, Plomin & Caspi, 1999). Extraversion reflects sociability, impulsivity, and liveliness; neuroticism is a measure of moodiness, anxiety, and vulnerability. Another name for neuroticism might be emotional stability versus instability. Extraversion and neuroticism are part of the Big Five.

Table 16.4 Testing the Equal Environments Assumption: Correlations Between Cognitive-Personality Measures and Similarity of Experience in Identical Twins

Measure	Correlation	No. of Twin Pairs
Cognitive Abilities	-0.06	276
Personality Test Scores	0.06	451
Vocational Interests	0.01	276
Interpersonal Relationships	0.05	276

Source: After Loehlin and Nichols, 1976.

- *Alcohol consumption* (identical twin correlation = .64, fraternal correlation = .27; among identical and fraternal twins reared apart the correlations are .71 and .31, Pedersen, Friberg, Floderus-Myrhed, McClearn, & Plomin, 1984)
- *Vocational interests*, measured by the Strong Vocational Interest Blank (average identical twin correlation from two twin studies = .50; average fraternal twin correlation = .25, Plomin et al., 1990). The Strong Vocational Interest Blank yields scores for vocational types—realistic, intellectual, social, enterprising, conventional, artistic—and the genetic effect is about the same for all of these.
- *Traditional attitudes* (identical twin correlation = .63, fraternal correlation = .46, Martin, Eaves, Heath, Jardine, Feingold, & Eysenck, 1986). Traditional attitudes favour conservatism, conforming to authority, observing rules, and holding high standards of behaviour.

These findings are summarized in Table 16.5.

Estimating Genetic and Environmental Effects: Twins in Germany and Poland

Studying twins reared together, identical and fraternal, gives us the opportunity to estimate not only genetic contributions to personality but the role of the environment as well. In personality psychology, we are thoroughly accustomed to thinking of the environment that affects development as the family environment, or **shared environment★**, as it is called. There are, however, environmental influences that are unique to individual children in any family; these constitute the **nonshared environment★**.

We'll consider shared and nonshared environments in more detail below. For the present, let's suppose we could estimate the influences of genetics and environment separately. Riemann, Angleitner, and Strelau (1997) did just that in a massive study of identical and fraternal twins normally reared in their birth families. Their measures were the Big Five factor scales of personality traits—extraversion, neuroticism, agreeableness,

Table 16.5 Twin Study Findings of Genetic Influence

Personality Measure	Heritability Finding	
	Identical	Fraternal
Schizophrenia	Concordance = 50+%	Concordance = approx. 15%
Agreeableness, Conscientiousness, Openness to Experience	*r*'s average 0.45	*r*'s average 0.20
Extraversion	*r* = 0.51	*r* = 0.18
Neuroticism	*r* = 0.46	*r* = 0.20
Alcohol Consumption	*r* = 0.64	*r* = 0.27
Vocational Interests	*r* = 0.50	*r* = 0.25
Traditional Attitudes	*r* = 0.63	*r* = 0.46

conscientiousness, and openness to experience. Each twin participant followed the normal course of completing the questionnaire, answering the questions to describe himself or herself. Afterward the same questionnaire was filled out by two friends of each twin, describing the twin participant. These were peer ratings, personality measures not dependent on self-report. Heritability was estimated by doubling the difference between identical twin and fraternal twin correlations for each Big Five trait, a standard statistical technique in behaviour genetics research. So, for example, if the correlation of identical twin scores on extraversion is 0.51 and the correlation of fraternal twins is 0.18, the difference would be .33; doubling the difference will give us a heritability in excess of 65 per cent. The technique is called Falconer's estimate (Falconer, 1981) or, as it is usually cited, h^2:

$$h^2 = 2(r_{MZ} - r_{DZ})$$

We are after the percentage of variance in a trait that is explained by genetic predisposition, so our index will be h^2, not h, the trait-genetic correlation. What is available to measure is observed (test) behaviour, the monozygotic (MZ) and dizygotic (DZ) twin correlations. For the monozygotic twins, the genetic contribution to one is the genetic contribution to the other, but because the dizygotic twins share on average half their genes, their shared genetic contribution to the r_{DZ} correlation will be only half that of r_{MZ}. Algebraically, $r_{MZ} - r_{DZ} = .5h^2$; accordingly, h^2 equals twice the monozygotic–dizygotic difference. You need to accept that this mathematical procedure for estimating heritability is not statistical mumbo jumbo (Falconer would be very insulted if you thought it was) but a well-justified way of approximating the heritability of traits. It does critically depend on the assumptions that the environments of identical and fraternal twins are equal (environment is thus cancelled out in the equation) and that genetic variance is additive (see below). A more complete derivation of this heritability formula is given in the appendix.

Environment is customarily that variance remaining after heritability is accounted for, and as a component of the total variance it includes errors of measurement. In the Reimann et al. data, environment was separated into shared and nonshared estimates. Shared environment is given by the difference between the identical twin correlation and the heritability value; the remainder is the nonshared environment. Figure 16.5 shows the percentage of genetic, shared environment, and nonshared environment variance for both self-report and the peer ratings. It makes strikingly clear that there are two big sources of influence on these personality measures, heritability and the nonshared environment, and a very minor one, the environment shared within the family. Note that the heritability in the peer ratings, although somewhat less than in the self-reports, is still substantial. This research unmistakably shows that the inheritance of the same personality attributes can be shown by self-report questionnaires *and* by the ratings of observers.

In behaviour genetics research on twins, the very best thing to do, of course, would be to study identical twins *reared apart*. Now there can be no environmental similarity, assuming that the twins had no contact with each other from an early age and that selective placement (putting the twins up for adoption in homes closely alike in major respects) did not play a role. Twin birth is a rare event. Twins occur in one of 83 births in North America, and only one-third are identical (this number drops to about one-fourth after childhood because identical twins are less likely to survive than

Figure 16.5 Genetic, shared-environment, and nonshared-environment contributions to Big Five self-report and peer ratings (From R. Plomin & A. Caspi, "Behavioral Genetics and Personality" in L.A. Pervinand O.P. John (Eds.), *Handbook of Personality Theory and Research*. Reprinted by permission of the Guilford Press.)

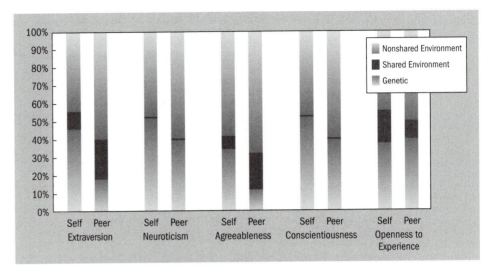

singletons or fraternal twins). So, locating identical twins reared apart is exceptionally difficult. Perhaps 300 pairs worldwide are known to us. More separated pairs certainly exist, but we haven't been able to find them. There are some modern studies on the known pairs; we'll consider two in particular.

The Minnesota Study of Twins Reared Apart

This research has been in progress since 1979. It came into being with headline news of the reunion of separated twins Jim Springer and Jim Lewis after a 39-year separation. Thomas Bouchard, Jr, professor of psychology at the University of Minnesota, appreciated the rich mine of data the Jims represented and arranged to bring them to the university for study. The number of Minnesota twin pairs has since increased steadily (135 pairs as of 1999), and findings are accumulating. Data from a major study examining identical twins reared apart, adopted children, and identical and fraternal twins reared together show substantial identical-twin correlations on a number of personality measures; the average correlation is .54, and the average heritability coefficient is .50 (Tellegen, Lykken, Bouchard, Wilcox, Segal, & Rich, 1988). These correlations are shown in Table 16.6.

Swedish Twins and Big Five Variables

A large-scale study in Sweden examined identical twins reared apart and together on the variables of extraversion and neuroticism (Pedersen, Plomin, McClearn, & Friberg, 1988). Like the Minnesota research, it found significant heritability. For extraversion, the correlation of identical twins reared apart was 0.30; the correlation of fraternal twins reared apart was 0.04. The corresponding correlations for identical and fraternal twins reared together were 0.54 and 0.06. There were similar findings for neuroticism. The data of the four twin groups suggested to the investigators that the heritabilities of these variables were approximately 40 per cent for extraversion and 30 per cent for neuroticism. However, the correlations of identical twins reared together were larger, giving greater heritability estimates; this might have occurred because of similarities in the environments of the twins in the same family. If so, this would be a violation of the equal environments assumption. Accordingly, we have to ask whether heritability is overestimated in twin studies, actually accounting for

Table 16.6   Correlations of Personality Test Scores for Monozyotic and Dizygotic Twins Reared Together and Apart

Personality Scale	Monozygotic Reared Apart	Dizygotic Reared Apart	Monozygotic Reared Together	Dizygotic Reared Together
Well-being	0.48	0.18	0.58	0.23
Social Potency	0.56	0.27	0.65	0.08
Achievement	0.36	0.07	0.51	0.13
Social Closeness	0.29	0.30	0.57	0.24
Stress Reaction	0.61	0.27	0.52	0.24
Alienation	0.48	0.18	0.55	0.38
Aggression	0.46	0.06	0.43	0.14
Control	0.50	0.03	0.41	-0.06
Harm Avoidance	0.49	0.24	0.55	0.17
Traditionalism	0.53	0.39	0.50	0.47
Absorption	0.61	0.21	0.49	0.41
Positive Emotionality	0.34	-0.07	0.63	0.18
Negative Emotionality	0.61	0.29	0.54	0.41
Constraint	0.57	0.04	0.58	0.2

Source: From Tellegen et al., 1988. Personality similarity in twins reared apart and together. *Journal of Personality and Social Psychology, 54,* p. 1035. Copyright 1988 by the American Psychological Association. Reprinted with permission.

a smaller proportion of the variance, not the average heritability of 40 per cent or more that the Minnesota group has proposed. The equal environments assumption is not easy to satisfy, and there are not enough cases of identical twins reared apart to help settle the issue. There may also be a problem of nonadditive genetic variance, which does not affect the similarity of identical twins but will result in lower fraternal twin resemblance since nonadditive effects contribute less than additive effects to genetic similarity (see below).

Another issue we need to take note of is so important that all the research on the heritability of personality is affected by it. This is the question of the validity of the personality measures taken on twins and other family members. We simply must have evidence that a personality test actually measures what it purports to measure. Without solid validity data, we don't know what our twin correlations or any heritability estimates based on them mean. We don't know, in other words, just what behavioural characteristic is inherited. There are a few studies in which personality characteristics have been assessed by behavioural observations, and they tend to confirm the personality test data (Plomin et al., 1990). This is encouraging evidence, as are the peer ratings of Riemann et al. that we have just reviewed.

Perspective 16.2 Identical Twins Reared Apart: Twin Data, Remarkable Coincidences, and the Question of What Is Inherited

Separating twins in infancy for adoption in different families seems a harsh solution, and we would like to think that it isn't done any longer. Thirty or forty years ago, however, the separation of twins was sometimes—although not often—practised in adoption agencies when families could be found for each of the twins but not both together. This heartrending severance is mostly how separated twins are available for us to study (Segal, 1999). We are less likely now to find new cases, both because we better understand how sad a thing this is to do and because there are simply fewer adoptions. In our time, abortion reduces the number of potential adoptees, and single mothers are more likely to keep their children.

We have seen some of the inherited similarity in personality of identical twins reared apart, but in a sense data like these just tease us. How alike, *really*, are those twins who have spent their formative years in other people's families and much of their adulthood in complete ignorance of someone who is a genetic copy? To ask that question is to move from the world of measurement, quantifiable variables, and statistical inference to a non-metric one in which the evidence is anecdotal. This is a big problem for the scientist, and some behaviour geneticists shy away from it. Others, though, can't resist a look at just how similar those separated twins are. Let's join the ones who have succumbed to temptation and see what twin anecdotes might reveal. Let's do so with the recognition that when we find similarities, even dramatic ones, we must somehow hold them up to the probability that any two people selected at random might be just as similar.

The two Jims, reunited at age 39, had been adopted in infancy and reared by different families in Ohio. As small children, each had been told that he was a twin, but as one of them said, 'it never soaked in'. Representatives of various media—the press, television, and popular magazines—picked up their story, dramatizing it and presenting exaggerated claims of their similarities. At the University of Minnesota, investigators, careful and circumspect, confirmed many startling resemblances (Segal, 1999):

· Each Jim had married and divorced, the first time to a wife named Linda, the second to one named Betty.
· Growing up, each had had a dog named Toy.
· As adults, they had vacationed in Florida at the same beach, never encountering each other.
· Each arrived for his vacations driving a light blue Chevrolet.
· They both smoked Salem cigarettes and drank Miller Lite beer.
· They bit their fingernails and suffered from tension and migraine headaches.

Jim and Jim weren't unusual among separated identical twins; many coincidences of choice and behaviour could be found. Jerry Levey and Mark Newman, another separated twin pair from the Minnesota study, were both volunteer fire fighters; both wore large belt buckles and carried big key rings, and both were Budweiser drinkers, each hooking his little finger under his beer can as he drank.

What do we make of shared choice and behaviour in the absence of any opportunity to learn together or for one twin to imitate the other? We can say, to begin with, that randomly chosen individuals will have attributes in common at probabilities above zero. Budweiser and Miller Lite are popular beers, many women are named Linda and Betty, and biting the fingernails is a common habit. When the coincidences pile up in individual separated twin pairs, we find it more improbable that the popularity of beers and women's names and the frequency of indulgence in a bad habit could be the explanation.

The two Jims. Their similarities were remarkable. Both were part-time deputy sheriffs, took their holidays in Florida, drove Chevrolets, married first wives named Betty and second wives named Linda, named their sons almost identically (James Alan and James Allen) and their dogs Toy, and had highly similar medical histories. A $64,000 question: how can their identical genes account for these similarities? (© 2006 Bob Sacha)

This is, however, a quantitative nightmare, since in each twin case the similarities are different; how would we come up with the categories in which to place specific coincidences, categories by which to simplify our similarity data? Most of our twin pairs will not show up in many categories, since the similarities are unique to individual pairs. It helps that coincidences of choice and behaviour appear more often in separated identical twin pairs than in separated fraternal twin pairs (Segal, 1999)—that is a point for heredity. But are we any closer to the truly important question: what is it that is inherited? We would do well to curb our enthusiasm for unique anecdotal data of this sort and to concentrate on measures we can quantify, such as those generated by well-established personality tests. We stand a better chance of finding the genetic basis of extraversion, neuroticism, and the other traits of the Big Five, and it is for that reason that behaviour geneticists use tests and behaviour ratings and avoid becoming captivated by unique patterns of coincidence. Studies searching for specific genes that may be responsible for novelty or sensation seeking, described later in the chapter, are a promising beginning.

Adoption Studies

The simplest and most straightforward research design for examining the relative contributions of nature and nurture is the adoption study. It enables us to hold genetic influence constant by randomizing its effect, thus studying family influence on children who have been adopted. We can examine genetic influence independent of family environment by looking at the correlations between children who have been adopted and their birth parents (usually mothers).

What do we have to worry about in adoption designs? If we wish to generalize to genetic and environmental influences in the general population, we have to be concerned with the **representativeness**⋆ of our samples of adopted children, their adopting families, and the parents giving up their children for adoption. If, for example, mothers giving up their infants for adoption are not representative of the general population in some important ways (they might, for instance, be of below-normal intelligence or be drug and alcohol abusers whose habits have deleterious effects on their children), adoption-study data would be biased—unrepresentative and potentially inapplicable to the population at large. Second, you can see that if we study children who were **selectively placed** so that they would wind up in families with important resemblances to their birth parents, we will have a possible built-in correlation between birth parent and child. This might be a concern with intelligence, since adoption agencies do have information about the education, occupation, and social class of birth parents and adopting parents (intelligence will be correlated with these). On the other hand, agencies typically know little or nothing about the personalities of birth and adopting parents and wouldn't be able to place selectively on these grounds even if they wanted to. So, representativeness of samples is a genuine issue, while selective placement isn't. It appears, however, that representativeness is generally not a problem, and if it is of potential concern, measures can be obtained from adoption samples to determine the extent of biases that may be present and these can be dealt with in the interpretation of findings (Plomin et al., 1990).

Among the results of adoption studies we find that the adopted offspring of schizophrenic birth mothers are at significantly higher risk. There is no evidence that rearing in an adopting family with a schizophrenic parent will produce the disorder (Plomin et al., 1990). Plomin et al. draw a striking conclusion from the adoption-study research on schizophrenia:

> . . . all of the familial resemblance for schizophrenia is due to heredity, and . . . none is due to between-family environmental influences, whose hypothesized role in the etiology of schizophrenia had seemed so reasonable. . . . This does not mean that the environment is unimportant in triggering schizophrenia. However, it does indicate that the environmental culprit that we have traditionally blamed for schizophrenia (between-family influences) is actually blameless (p. 360).

A disturbed family environment or cold and distant parents may set off a schizophrenic psychosis, but these environmental events are not the root cause.

Depressive disorders also display significant genetic influence, although the heritability may be lower than with schizophrenia (Plomin et al., 1990). In one of the most careful studies, Wender and colleagues (1986) studied 71 depressive or bipolar disorder adoptees and 70 controls free of the disorder. Depressive or bipolar disorder was found in 5.2 per cent of biological relatives of the depressive sample and 2.4 per cent of the controls. Alcoholism similarly has a genetic influence in adoption studies. In a Swedish study, 22 per cent of the sons of alcoholic fathers, given up for adoption in infancy, were alcoholic (Cloninger, Bohman, & Sigvardsson, 1981).

Extraversion and neuroticism show genetic influence in adoption studies, but it is smaller than we find in twin studies (Plomin & Caspi, 1999). The probable reason is

nonadditive genetic variance, which will decrease genetic correlations in relatives but not in identical twins. Nonadditive genetic variance results when the effects of genes at a single locus (called *dominance*) or at different loci (*epistasis*) are not simply additive but interact. This means in effect that a parent's genotypic contribution to a given trait will be affected by a particular combination of alleles (genes) at a particular locus or, in the case where many loci are involved, a particular combination at different loci. Thus, we can't predict exactly from parent to offspring. As Plomin and Caspi (1999) put it,

> Additive genetic effects refer to independent effects of genes that 'add up' to influence a trait, in contrast to nonadditive genetic effects in which genes interact. Identical twins are identical for all genetic effects whether additive or nonadditive. Fraternal twins, however, resemble each other 50% on average for additive effects of genes, but nonadditive effects only contribute slightly to the resemblance of fraternal twins and other first-degree relatives (p. 255).

If there is a substantial nonadditive contribution to a given trait, a fraternal twin correlation will be an underestimate, thus exaggerating the identical–fraternal genetic difference.

By a great margin, there are fewer adoption studies than twin studies, despite the advantages of the design. We can conclude our discussion of this smaller literature with a brief summary:

- Schizophrenic and depressive disorders: there is risk of heritability from birth parents
- Alcoholism: 22 per cent of adopted-away sons of alcoholic fathers were alcoholic
- Extraversion and neuroticism: heritability is lower than in twin studies; this is likely due to *nonadditive genetic variance* (interactive combinations of genes)

Personality Theory, Genetics, and Environment

When we review the evidence on the heritability of personality characteristics, it is inescapable that genetic contributions far outweigh those of the shared family environment. We saw this in the important results of the research carried out by Riemann et al. Thus, children growing up in the same family will for the most part resemble each other behaviourally because they are related genetically, not because of common experience in the family. Environmental effects (to the degree that we have studied them) act on children *individually*. In adoption studies, for example, we find that genetically unrelated children in the same adopting family do not resemble each other. The personality correlations between adopted children in the same family average 0.05 (Plomin et al., 1990). This upsets our traditional understanding of the effects of families on children, but a growing behavioural genetics literature bears it out. Environmental influences on children come mainly from the nonshared environment, experiences specific to each child in the family. Within the family, birth order (which we examined when we studied Adler), sex differences, or the serious illness of one child may make each child's family experience different. Outside the family, each child will have different friends, teachers, success in activities such as sports—and these nonshared experiences can have major effects.

The Importance of the Nonshared Environment

In a 1998 book that created a storm, *The Nurture Assumption: Why Children Turn Out the Way They Do*, Harris argues on the basis of considerable evidence that parents have only small influence on their children (apart from the genes they transmit, we have to note). She focuses on nonshared environmental influences—especially the influence of peers—in shaping personality. You can imagine that some developmental psychologists objected strenuously to Harris's review of the literature and her conclusion, and they have a point. 'Excuse me,' they said, 'but don't you know about the generations of developmental psychologists who reported on the effects of childrearing on development?' Now, these traditional findings are confounded by the fact that parents and children share approximately half of their genes, but there *are* shared-environment influences that are independent of heredity. An example: in experiments in which we teach parents how to do a better job of rearing their children, the behaviour of the children changes. They behave better and are more in control of their emotions (Eisenberg, Spinrad, & Cumberland, 1998). A number of shared-environmental effects have come from behaviour genetics research. Among

A Fresh Look: Research Today

The cutting edge: Molecular genetics

Developments in molecular genetic analysis have made it possible to search for and identify specific genes affecting personality. The results so far are limited because of the sheer difficulty of the task. Personality traits are not produced by single genes; they are, as we have seen, the outcomes of many genes, each with a small effect. Molecular geneticists hope to find some among the number of genes that determine a trait. These genes with minor effects—accounting for, say, a fifth of the genetic variance in the trait—are called **quantitative trait loci**, QTLs for short, and geneticists assume that their individual effects are independent—that is, additive. The trick, Plomin and Caspi say, '. . . is to find QTLs for personality . . . [by investigating] allelic association using DNA markers that are in or near genes thought to be relevant to the trait. Allelic association refers to a correlation between alleles of a DNA marker and trait scores across unrelated individuals. That is, allelic association occurs when individuals with a particular allele for the marker have higher scores on the trait' (1999, p. 262). What is required is a valid measure of the trait (a very large requirement) and an exceptionally good guess about its physiological basis, say a neurotransmitter system.

The first link of a QTL with a personality trait came in 1996 with the report by Cloninger, Adolfsson, and Svrakic of three studies independently confirming an allelic associa-

tion between a trait called novelty-seeking and a gene for a receptor of the neurotransmitter dopamine. Both Cloninger and Zuckerman (1994a) have investigated much the same trait; it is 'novelty-seeking' to Cloninger and 'sensation-seeking' to Zuckerman. (Sensation-seeking has been extensively studied by Zuckerman and colleagues, who have produced a significant body of psychological, neurophysiological, and genetic evidence. We'll review it in Chapter 17.) Cloninger, Svrakic, and Przybeck (1993) have proposed a four-trait theory of temperament, one of the traits in which is novelty-seeking. Novelty-seekers, they point out, are impulsive and inclined to be exploratory; they seek thrills and are excitable. A variety of evidence, psychological and biological, pointed to the dopamine neurotransmitter system as an underlying basis of novelty/sensation-seeking. There are several dopamine receptors, and the gene coding for one, D4DR, concentrated in the limbic system, appeared to be a likely candidate. D4DR may appear as one or the other of two alleles; these are short (few repetitions of a base-pair sequence) or long (more repetitions). The receptors coded by short alleles are more efficient in taking up dopamine.

The hypothesis, thus, is that persons inheriting the less effective long-repeat allele are dopamine-starved (an exaggerated way of saying it, but you get the idea) and seek novel and exciting experiences that will enhance dopamine transmission. In each of the three studies, parthem are juvenile delinquency (Rowe, Rodgers, & Meseck-Bushey, 1992), aggression (Miles & Carey, 1997), positive emotionality (Tellegen et al., 1988), and the conduct of loving relationships (Waller & Shaver, 1994). The shared environment *does* matter, but not to the degree and in the way we thought it did in shaping personality.

A Final Word

It's clear that personality and developmental psychologists have their work cut out for them in coming to grips with the genetics of behaviour and development. They will have to reconcile the assumptions of personality and developmental theory and all the evidence we have accumulated with genetic influences on behaviour. Behaviour geneticists also have a long row to hoe. For example, divorce shows a genetic influence (McGue & Lykken, 1992). We know how foolish it would be to believe that there is a gene (or a number of genes) for separating from a marital partner. There must be some third variable, or maybe there are several. Consider some possibilities: novelty-seeking

ticipants with the long-repeat D4DR allele had significantly higher scores on the personality-test measure of novelty-seeking but did not differ on measures of the other three traits (Cloninger, Adolfsson, & Svrakic, 1996). Other independent studies confirm Cloninger et al. (for example, Ebstein, Novick, Umansky, Priel, Osher, Blaine, Bennett, Nemanov, Katz, & Belmaker, 1996), including a few failures of replication that may have been due sample sizes too small to detect differences (see Ebstein & Belmaker, 1997). There is the possibility that the D4DR gene may be more strongly associated with specific aspects of novelty-seeking—lack of inhibition or easily becoming disinhibited, experience- and thrill-seeking, and readily becoming bored (Plomin & Caspi, p. 266). Ultimately, we stand to reap an enormous yield from this molecular research in more detailed understanding of both personality measures and the genetics of their biological bases.

Molecular genetics has also tackled schizophrenia, using a technique known as **linkage analysis** to probe for genes that may be implicated. The closer two genes are located on a chromosome, the more likely it is that they are inherited together. This co-inheritance is exceptionally useful to the discovery of genes implicated in disease or behaviour. If an unknown gene for a particular disease is linked to a known site (that is, co-inherited), one that represents a DNA marker with an established locus on a chromosome, geneticists can use the marker to identify the unknown gene. The likelihood of linkage between markers

and a trait are computed, and conventional statistical decision rules tell us whether the association is significantly beyond chance expectancy.

Genes with a possible involvement in schizophrenia have been investigated by linkage analysis, and loci on a number of chromosomes have been found (Faraone et al., 2002). The technique works best with single-gene transmission; it is problematical with multiple-gene disorders like schizophrenia in which individual gene effects are small. So, unfortunately, positive findings are routinely followed by failures to replicate.

A promising study has found stronger evidence implicating anomalies in a gene located on chromosome 6 that encodes a protein named dysbindin (Straub et al., 2002), found in brain structures thought to be involved in schizophrenia. The level of dysbindin was significantly reduced in an intensively studied population of Irish schizophrenics and their nuclear family members, and a number of other schizophrenic samples have yielded similar results (Talbot et al., 2004). Straub et al. acknowledge '. . . the possibility that this is a false-positive result, due to any of several possible artifacts. . . . However, given the internal consistency and strength of the results, we think that genetic variation in dysbindin influences the risk of schizophrenia . . .' (p. 345). The dysbindin gene, confirmed in eleven studies, is one of the most promising among a number of schizophrenia susceptibility genes. This research stands out as a model for the study of other potentially involved genes.

(a trait characterized by impulsivity and jumping at new, untried experiences), social remoteness (which would impair intimacy), alcoholism, depression, schizophrenia . . . Any of these might increase the probability of divorcing.

With most personality variables, just what it is that is inherited still needs to be established. To complicate matters, there are also heritability–environment interactions, or the possibility of them anyway. Let's take a boy who is of slightly below-average intelligence and is physically clumsy. These are heritable traits, but they also make him vulnerable to teasing by his peers. The result is a genetic–environment interaction that may cause him to behave and develop differently than if he weren't teased or didn't have those genetically given attributes. Or consider novelty-seeking, which leads a teen to experiment with drugs. The novelty-seeking is genetically influenced. Drug experimentation, an environmental variable, leads him into the drug culture, with potentially huge consequences on his development and personality.

SUMMARY

1. Behaviour genetics has largely been unrecognized by personality theorists, most of whom have built theories on the role of psychological factors and the family environment in personality development. This is so despite the fact that behaviour genetics and psychological theories of personality are not inevitably incompatible. Even serious disorders of personality like schizophrenia, known for many years to have genetic and neurochemical origins, were considered to be psychological, rooted in personality dynamics or damaging families.

2. Single-gene transmission provides a model of genetic effects, and the principles discovered by the Austrian monk Gregor Mendel can be applied to human disorders and to the inheritance of behavioural characteristics. Personality, however, does not result from single-gene transmission. Attributes of personality are influenced by many genes; they are polygenic.

3. Genes determine how sequences of amino acids of proteins are assembled. Proteins, in turn, are responsible for virtually all cellular activities, regulation of cellular functions, and determination of developmental pathways. Defects in proteins due to gene mutations lead to abnormal traits.

4. Chromosomes are threadlike structures of nucleoproteins that contain genes and are found in the nuclei of cells. Every species has a specific number of chromosomes (23 pairs in the human). Gametes (sex cells) have 23 chromosomes—that is, the *haploid*

number. Somatic cells have twice the haploid number of chromosomes, the *diploid* number. Each parent contributes a haploid set of chromosomes to an offspring. The combining of chromosomes from each parent gives the diploid complement of each cell.

5. Genes consist of complementary strands of phosphate and sugar groups secured at a fixed distance from each other by base pairs of nitrogenous material. There are four bases: adenine, thymine, guanine, and cytosine, and they form pairs—adenine with thymine, and guanine with cytosine. During cell division, the coils of the DNA molecule unwind. The base pairs separate, and one of each pair remains attached to each strand. Within the nuclei of cells will be one of the four bases, a deoxyribose sugar, and a phosphate. These are nucleotides that pair with the bases of the unwound strands and form new strands with each of the original strands. There are now two molecules of DNA. Mutations are copying errors, and they are rare. Only very infrequently are mutations adaptive.

6. The process of evolution, as laid out by Darwin, is based on two principles: first, many individuals within each species do not survive to reproduce; second, individual members of a species vary widely, and some of that variation is due to heredity. If the probability of survival to reproduce is influenced by the heritability of some characteristic, offspring of the survivors will show more of the characteristic than their parents. With enough repetitions over many generations, the

species changes. Despite the brilliance of his theory of evolution, Darwin did not have a satisfactory theory to account for the mechanism of inheritance.

7. Mendel experimented with garden peas, studying seven qualitative characteristics (e.g., round versus wrinkled exterior of seeds). He crossed true-breeding plants of one type (round) with plants of the other (wrinkled) type, which resulted in seeds that were all round. He then crossed plants in this new F_1 generation to produce a second F_2 generation, this time yielding round and wrinkled seeds in a 3:1 ratio. Mendel concluded that each plant had two heritable factors, now called *alleles*, which are alternate forms of genes. Parent plants pass along one of their two alleles to their offspring. If round is dominant, the F_1 generation will all have round seeds. The F_2 generation shows the 3:1 ratio.

8. A grave and ultimately fatal human disorder, Huntington's disease, which affects movement and personality, is the result of Mendelian transmission of a single gene. The offspring of an affected parent (heterozygote) and an unaffected one will have a 50 per cent chance of developing the disorder. If both parents inherited the gene from one of their parents (heterozygote × heterozygote), the probability of having an affected offspring will be .75, and *all* the offspring of an affected parent with alleles from both parents (homozygote) and an unaffected parent will develop the disorder.

9. We rely on three methods to study the potential genetic basis of personality characteristics. Family studies examine the similarity of members of families according to genetic relationship. If a trait is genetic, similarity should increase with degree of genetic similarity. Family studies do not distinguish between genetic and environmental effects; they provide evidence that is or is not *compatible* with a genetic hypothesis. In a study of family resemblance in the personality trait 'sociable', the correlations of identical twins in two studies greatly exceeded the correlations of fraternal twins, siblings, or parents with children. Adopted children's scores were more closely related to scores of natural than to scores of adopting parents. These data suggest that the trait 'sociable' is heritable, but they don't rule out environmental influence. In the case of schizophrenia, family studies show a strong family influence. For example, siblings

of schizophrenic patients have a likelihood of being schizophrenic themselves that is ten times the incidence of the disorder in the general population.

10. Family studies and the other two methods commonly used depend on the statistical technique of correlation. A far more powerful method is the study of twins in which we compare identical and fraternal twins on measures of interest. Because identical twins may receive more similar treatment than fraternals, we cannot be certain that we have shown a genetic effect. We can, however, test the assumption that the environments of identical and fraternal twins are equal. This is done by *measuring* environmental features to see if they are comparable or, even better, determining whether differences in family experience between identical and fraternal twins affect behaviour. One large study shows that similarity of family experience is not correlated with measures of differences in cognition, personality, or social behaviour.

11. There are many twin studies of heritable personality characteristics. Among the variables showing substantial heritability are schizophrenia; the traits of agreeableness, conscientiousness, openness to experience, extraversion and neuroticism; alcohol consumption; vocational interests; and traditional attitudes.

12. Ideally, twin research would study identical twins reared apart, so that if separation is complete and early there can be no environmental influence. Identical twins separated early in life are rare, but modern studies in Minnesota and in Sweden have unearthed a sizeable number of adults who have had no contact with their twins until they were discovered. These studies find substantial twin correlations on a variety of personality measures. However, there may be a question about whether they have met the *equal environments assumption*. When twin correlations of identical twins reared apart are compared to the correlations of identical twins reared together, heritability estimates from reared-together twins may appear to be larger because of similarities in the environments of the twins in the same family.

13. A critical issue in behavioural genetics research is the validity of the personality test measures on which heritability estimates are based. If personality tests do not specifically assess the traits they are claimed to measure, we cannot be sure of the meaning of twin correlations or estimates of heritability.

14. Adoption studies represent the least complicated research design for investigating genetic and environmental contributions to personality. Genetic contributions are held constant by randomizing their effects (adopting parents have no genetic resemblance to biological parents), so the effects of family environment can be studied on their own. Genetic effects appear in the correlations between children who have been given up for adoption and their birth parents. There are two major concerns in adoption studies. One is the *representativeness* of samples of adopted children, adopting families, and biological parents. As a rule, this is not a problem. *Selective placement* of children in adopting families that resemble the birth parents will, if true, result in a correlation between birth parent and adopted-away child. Placement agencies don't try to place selectively and would not have data to place by personality attributes.

15. Adoption studies find a significant genetic component for schizophrenia and for depressive disorders. Adopting parents, even if schizophrenic or depressed, do not produce schizophrenia in their adopted children. Genes passed along by biological parents do. Adoption studies show a genetic influence for alcoholism and for personality traits such as extraversion and neuroticism. In adoption studies of twins reared apart, *nonadditive genetic variance* may inflate differences between identical and fraternal twins. Nonadditive effects do not influence identical twin correlations (since their genes, additive and nonadditive, are identical), but will reduce the similarity of fraternal twins since nonadditive genetic effects contribute less.

16. Behavioural genetics research makes clear that genes make a far greater contribution to personality than the *shared family environment*. Environmental influences on children come mainly from the *nonshared environment*, consisting of experiences that are individual and specific to each child. The nonshared environment includes outside-the-home influences such as different friendships, schoolteachers, and activities; among nonshared environment influences in the home are order of birth, sex differences, and serious illness of one child. Developmental psychology has been challenged by the claim that nonshared environmental effects outweigh the influence of the shared environment, and the full story is not yet in. There are very important shared-environment effects, including parental influences on children, juvenile delinquency, aggression, positive emotionality, and the shaping of loving relationships.

17. The effects of individual genes on personality are studied using molecular genetics. These are the effects of many genes on a particular personality trait; the genes are called **quantitative trait loci** (QTLs). They are found by using identified sites (DNA markers) that are at or near the loci of genes believed to be implicated in the trait. Investigators look for the association of alleles of a DNA marker and scores on the personality trait. A major study of a QTL and a personality trait found an allelic association between a trait called novelty-seeking and a gene coding for a receptor of the neurotransmitter dopamine. This gene may appear as one or the other of two alleles (short base-pair sequence or long sequence); the receptor coded by the short allele is more efficient in taking up dopamine. It was hypothesized that individuals inheriting the long-sequence allele would be dopamine-deficient and would seek experiences (novelty, excitement, relief from boredom) to enhance dopamine transmission. Several studies have confirmed the hypothesis. There are also studies searching for genes involved in schizophrenia. They employ a technique called **linkage analysis**, which is based on the likelihood that genes located close together on a chromosome will be inherited together. Thus, DNA markers can be used to identify unknown genes of interest. A series of promising studies has found evidence implicating a gene located on chromosome 6 encoding the brain protein dysbindin in schizophrenia.

TO TEST YOUR UNDERSTANDING

1. What is heritability? Define the term and be exact in your definition. What cautions do we have to observe in studying the inheritance of personality characteristics?

2. Imagine that you are a behaviour geneticist interested in the heritability of personality attributes. Describe how you would go about studying the genetic basis of personality. What would your basic procedure be? What measurement issues would you face? How much would you draw on psychological theories of personality? Which theories?

3. Despite all the shared experiences among members of individual families, the nonshared environment appears to contribute more to many personality traits. So, when we look at family resemblance for a given personality trait, we are likely to find that it is genetic and not due to shared experience. Develop a hypothesis to account for these findings. Are you satisfied that behaviour geneticists and developmental psychologists like Judith Harris have got it right?

4. Using the formula on page 449, calculate the heritability coefficients for monozygotic twins reared apart and reared together on each of the personality variables in Table 16.6 (page 451). What do these values say about the heritability of these attributes? Give your answer in proper behaviour genetics language. What possible limitations are there on your interpretation?

CHAPTER SEVENTEEN

Personality Theory
in Perspective

Introduction

Most of the personality theories we have considered belong to a distinctive period in the history of personality psychology, dating from the early Freudian days up to about 1955 or so. Exceptions include Bandura's social cognitive theory, later developments in Cattell's and Eysenck's trait theories, Big Five theory, and of course the recent work in behaviour genetics, and there are some minor ones we did not take up. But the late nineteenth century and first half of the twentieth was a heady time, a span of seventy years that Sigmund Koch, in an epilogue to a massive study of psychology as a science commissioned by the American Psychological Association, characterized as 'The Age of Theory'. Short-lived as ages go, Koch's age included theories not just of personality but of learning as well—the formulations of Hull, Tolman, Guthrie, Skinner, and, before them, Thorndike and Watson.

The Age of Theory

This fertile conceptual era was marked by the flourishing of **hypothetico-deductive systems**★, psychological systems comprising sets of intervening variables (theoretical concepts) that could be linked to observable events—both antecedents and consequents. This was the personality theorist's home territory, where intervening variables were seen as providing the bridge between pivotal happenings in personality development and the behaviour of the adult. Freud formally did this: significant events in the life of the infant and young child represent the antecedent conditions for the emergence and early growth of the ego and the differentiation of the superego following on the resolution of the Oedipus complex. Childhood beginnings will have their imprint on instinctual life and the developing ego, laying the groundwork for ego development, and how the Oedipus complex is resolved will decisively affect the nascent superego. The concepts of the theory are tied on the consequent side to observable (or potentially observable) events—the development of particular forms of neurosis, say. In these principles of theory formation, Hull followed the same course with the theory of learning that Dollard and Miller adapted as the S-R approach to personality. The theorists we've reviewed may differ in the rigorousness of their definitions of theoretical concepts and the explicitness and precision of linkages to antecedent conditions and the consequents in adult personality, but (the radical behaviourist Skinner aside) they all share this focus on intervening variables.

Koch saw an unavoidable conclusion emerging from *Psychology: A Study of a Science*—that 'the intervening variable paradigm and much of the associated doctrine [is called] sharply into question . . . in almost every sense in which questioning is possible' (Koch, p. 735). This was tough language and a drastic indictment of a paradigm that, all along, had been irresistible to producers and consumers of theory alike and seemed so promising. As Koch wrote in setting up his stern judgement,

> The appeal of the intervening variable paradigm to the Age of Theory systematists was twofold. First, the criterion of 'firm anchorage' of hypothetical theoretical concepts *via* explicit functional relations to 'antecedent' and 'consequent' *observables* seemed neatly to fill the strong requirement of the age for a theoretical *decision procedure*. If inferred explanatory concepts were to be unequivocally *linked* to observables, no longer need there be fear of irresponsible constructions whose role within the theory is instant to the whim of the theorist (what Hull called 'anthropomorphism . . . in behaviour theory'). At the same time, the paradigm seemed to render into orderly and intelligible terms the *problems* confronting the psychological theorist: . . . he needed three classes of variables [antecedents, theoretical concepts, and consequents]. . . . (1959, p. 734)

Koch, though, wasn't about to back away from the demolition of a theoretical schema honoured by nearly everyone. Looking at 'grand design' theories from Freud to Hull, in between and beyond, he could see only that they had fallen short in their objective. The linkages to observables had been incomplete, he said, and theoretical concepts had been inadequately specified. In attempting to do so much—here, he surely had personality in mind—theories had supplied no answer to the critical question of dealing precisely, operationally, with behaviour. He commandeered the words of one of the theorists in question, Neal Miller, to make the point:

> In general [Miller had written], stimulus–response psychologists have tended to bypass problems of . . . [defining *S* and *R*]. By intuition and trial and error, they have concentrated on experimental situations in which the stimulus and response were so simple and manageable that the lack of more precise definitions or laws concerning these variables was not a practical problem. Using such situations, stimulus–response psychologists have concentrated on determining the laws governing the connections of responses to stimuli. *Thus, stimulus–response psychologists may be said to know and care relatively little about either stimuli or responses; they are specialists on the hyphen between the S and R and could more aptly be called 'hyphen psychologists'*, or to use Thorndike's term, 'connectionists' (Koch, 1959, p. 755).

Freudians, neo-Freudians, and ego psychologists were guilty of the same offence. They were too preoccupied with *concepts* and too blasé, too casual, about establishing strict links to observables. Ergo, claimed Koch, the Age of Theory was dead. R.I.P.

One of the major contributors to the demise of formal theory as Koch thought was the *liberalization* of the approach to theoretical concepts. Koch saw in this two effects, which Miller fully acknowledged and regarded as necessary: first, an easing and broadening of the definitions of antecedents and consequents (*S* and *R*, for Miller); and second, a greater concern with empirical questions, with a behaviour analysis not involving formal inference to intervening variables, with experience. Liberalization was not a good thing, thought Koch. It gained psychologists some freedom from the strict demands of good theory and a little space, but liberalization was motivated by the fact that theoretical psychologists *couldn't* cope with the rigours of formal theory construction and testing. Koch saw theories becoming 'models', *guides* to thinking about intervening variables and their relations to observable events, the inference process much looser and more easily influenced by new data.

But did liberalization of the constraints on theoretical definition actually lure theory down a path to self-destruction? Consider: a liberalized view of unconscious processes, one not fully dependent on the psychoanalytic conception of a storehouse of unconscionable material, has led to an extraordinarily rich literature on a cognitive unconscious, one we sampled—for example, on memories that affect conscious thought and behaviour without our awareness of them, and on other implicit memory processes. Bandura may not have pursued his studies of observational learning without reinforcement if the old formalisms about learning and reinforcement had dominated his thinking. Surely a liberalized view of learning and a broader approach to the stimulus situation teamed up to launch this productive and influential research that formed the very core of a theory of personality not in existence when Koch made his critique.

At the time Koch's epilogue appeared in *Psychology: A Study of a Science* it was already evident that theoretical development had markedly slowed, and many thought it was likely at an end. Rotter's social learning theory and Kelly's personal construct theory appeared to be the last of the line. That, however, was a premature conclusion. New theories *did* emerge, and the connection of concepts to antecedent and consequent observables did not turn out to be as mountainous an obstacle to useful theory as Sigmund Koch's disparaging vision made it appear. The sky *wasn't* falling in, Henny-Penny.

Other liberalizing changes in psychology accompanied those in the psychologies of personality and learning. In clinical psychology, there was a movement toward a pragmatic behaviourism—a focus on the behaviour of the patient, on the symptoms brought to treatment—instead of the probing for anxiety, conflict, and causative history that were the bread-and-butter of the analytic and neo-analytic depth approaches. Behaviour modification liberated psychotherapy from the antecedent conditions–intervening concepts–consequent behaviour paradigm. Then, there was the development of community psychology, which has been highly untheoretical and so practical and eclectic in its orientation that it takes from anywhere the guides for practice and is sometimes found at the outer edge of psychological intervention, far from the centre. One could ask, as John Dollard and Neal Miller might have asked, that community psychology turn to sociology and to political science for content-oriented concepts and to psychology for process concepts to deal with individual behaviour change, individual–social matrix relations, and social change.

Paradigms in Personality: Reprise and Prospects

It is time to chalk up the scores of the seven paradigms. How have they succeeded as personality theories in the years since they first became serious theoretical competitors? How do they compare, each to the others? Which are likely to command increasing respect and attention, yielding significant personality research and fostering improved treatment methods for personality disturbance?

For five of the seven, the exhilarating period of theoretical development and con-firmation—the time of asserting their place in the sun—is long over. Most paradigms are in a stable period, established and settled, the burghers of the personality community. But are they just tottering along, past their prime, no longer vigorous and active in fur-thering the growth of the psychology of the person? Let's look at them, one by one, and see where they stand.

Psychodynamic

Psychoanalysis could easily have expired decades ago, done in by the deficiencies we have reviewed. With no Freud, no determined old father, to defend it and to set the crit-icisms down as ill informed and without merit, it might well now be no more than a historical curiosity.

But that isn't the case, thanks to revisionists mostly loyal to the master, who saw the flaws in classical analytic theory, saw that they could be mended, and carried out the necessary repairs. We know the major changes they argued for, and when psychoanalysis absorbed them, it was like a patient on the critical list drawing the breath of life.

As we saw at the end of Chapter 3, Freudian theory could not go on sidestepping the role of the family in personality development, and had to give honest weight to society and culture. Its view of aggression as displacement of a death instinct was untestable; psychoanalysts themselves saw the psychoanalytic psychology of aggression as a theoretical dead end. Freud's ego, that 'poor creature', beleaguered in waking life and forced into the role of dream sentry during sleep, could do no more than try to make the best of a bad deal. The ego is far more than that, said the critical ego psychol-ogists. It is master in its own house, an explorer in every person's world, sometimes bul-lied but certainly not a mere servant. And then, there's the discreditable and discredited psychology of women, so rightly and fiercely damned by Horney.

The biggest contributions to a workable psychodynamics came from ego psychol-ogy, which not only enlightened the concept of the ego but in the process gave an understanding of parental roles, society's hand in the family, and culture's prescriptions. Present-day psychodynamic theories—modified psychoanalysis, ego psychologies, and psychoanalytic derivatives like the theory of object relations—have embraced and thrive on experimental research. Without the controlled study of personality that Freud disdained, the psychodynamic paradigm would inevitably become weaker and weaker, and theorists know it. Psychodynamic research has gone beyond personality to enliven cognitive psychology, although a number of cognitive psychologists are at pains to deny psychodynamic—particularly psychoanalytic—influence.

An exception to the liveliness of psychoanalysis and psychoanalytic ego psychology is Jung's analytic psychology. Jungian psychotherapists treat patients, the theory is taught in institutes around the world, scholars have not given up mining the wealth of Jung's ideas, and it has some important adherents in intellectual circles and among the very wealthy. By my reading, however, analytic psychology has changed little from Jung's time. It survives on the respect accorded the astonishing breadth and depth of Jung's scholarship—perhaps, too, on the appeal of its mysticism?—but in science this is thin ice to be skating on. With no research, there is no possibility of confirming the theory's far-reaching claims, and in the end, without going beyond the consulting room and the world of the ancient and mystical, analytic psychology will become just old history. That, I'm afraid, is the way it is.

Meanwhile, the psychodynamic paradigm is in the best of health and a significant influence in personality psychology. We shall have to keep our eye on it, however, to see if it can continue to compete successfully with paradigms that more fully account for the person–situation interaction (family, society, and culture; learning and personality), that are in the main current of contemporary cognitive psychology (learning and personality, especially social cognitive theory), and that reach out for a bridge to behaviour genetics (the trait paradigm).

Family, Society, and Culture

After Freud, there were outstanding disciples to take up the creative task. There were none, however, to step in where Adler, Fromm, Sullivan, and Horney left off. Followers certainly carried on with the practice of psychotherapy and with the training of new therapists and teachers. But there were no minds like Erikson's to lead these theories in directions only imagined by their founders. The paradigm is still viable; there is much to commend in it, as Chapters 5 through 7 showed, but it hasn't the momentum of advances in thought and research of its modern rivals. The learning and personality paradigm, especially in its social learning theories, well represents many of the principal views of the family, society, and culture group.

Learning and Personality

Learning theories of personality span an exceptional range, more than we see in any other paradigm. They extend from the most uncompromising radical behaviourism to a sophisticated attempt to frame the concepts of psychoanalysis in a classical theory of learning to modern cognitive theories of social learning. Behind these theories are revered names in the psychology of learning—Watson, Hull, and Tolman among them—and the highest authorities in the experimental approach to personality, notably Dollard, Miller, and other members of the Yale Institute of Human Relations. Much of the ground for developments in personality study has been marked out by these theories.

The architects of learning theories did not introduce situation to personality theory, but they shaped and honed the context of behaviour to a fine understanding, represented in its most advanced form by the reciprocal determinism of Bandura. Learning theories of personality brought process concepts to replace psychodynamic content variables. If process concepts seemed strange at first, hardly suited to take the place of ego, id, self, and their content brethren, they gave the ready possibility to translate the abstract into credible and workable operations. The pragmatism and laboratory experience of experimental psychologists in formulating and testing hypotheses in carefully designed experiments brought a welcome and much needed research tradition to personality, one now widely emulated. Psychodynamic concepts—conflict, frustration and aggression, and displacement—became part of mainstream psychology as a direct result of the work of learning theorists, and the radical behaviourists demonstrated how the environment may be manipulated to produce new or altered behaviour. They haven't ruled out any behavioural repertoires as impossible to tackle and change. Cognitive psychology gave learning theories new approaches to attention, memory, thought, and motivation, which produced the exceptionally fruitful concepts of expectancy and efficacy, and a goal-oriented view of motivation. One of the consequences was the study of observational learning and a whole new way of looking at reinforcement.

Learning theories are still rather barren when it comes to conveying the depth, the intensity, and the intricacies of thought, feeling, and motive. For that, we look to psychodynamics and phenomenology/humanism (think Rogers and Maslow). From the process concepts of the learning and personality theories emerges a stark etching of what it's like to be a person. Perhaps a scientific theory doesn't need to be filled in with colour and detail; what really matters is the formation of accurate predictions of what people will do. Then again, a well-scribed portrait can help our understanding, and may be an additional source of hypotheses to explore.

Psychological theories of personality can stand on their own. The personality psychologist does not have to hanker after 'basic' concepts at the level of neurophysiology to underpin behavioural ones. One of Rotter's postulates made this point forcefully, as we saw in Chapter 14. We need to be clear, however, that recognizing the independence of psychological concepts does not mean prohibiting the neurophysiological investigation of personality processes where that is possible. This is not better; it's interesting and potentially valuable. It's hard to imagine how an ego or a self might be inherited and what its representation in the nervous system might be, although Jung tried to convince us that elemental structures in personality evolve through a collective mechanism. It is far easier to develop an account of the neural processes in learning (a number of them have been proposed) and their genetic basis. Learning theories are well poised for fruitful intercourse with neurophysiology, but we need to appreciate that simple biological systems are mostly studied. Genetic investigations of the neural processes involved in learning are well underway. Learning theories of personality, genetics, and neurophysiology are not at the marriage age, but the psychology of learning and personality can meaningfully contribute process concepts of behaviour acquisition and change to sister disciplines.

Phenomenology and Humanism

What do you do these days if you are a phenomenologist and humanist? I expect we're not going to find you slumped on the couch before the TV watching soap operas. You're more likely to have a clinical practice or participate in the work of a humanist institute like those in which Rogers spent his last years, teaching, offering workshops, or conducting group psychotherapy. You might even be an inspirational speaker to audiences of business professionals. But it's less likely that you will be in the lab generating new hypotheses and designing experiments to test them. That's a pity, because there are impressive findings confirming Rogerian propositions, as we saw in Chapter 11. The business of scientific theories is the production of new knowledge; there really isn't any standing pat.

On the other hand, you might have become a positive psychologist, devoting yourself to studying the variables that contribute to healthy growth and the attainment of the highest potential. Chapter 11 concluded with a review of the origins of positive psychology and its full-steam development. Here, in fact, is where phenomenological personality theory and the humanist perspective have wound up in the twenty-first century. What they have bequeathed to psychology, especially personality psychology, is huge: rejection of the preoccupation with failure in life—all the forms of neurosis—that for a century has dominated the study of the person; a boundless faith in human possibility and finding the means to nurture its achievement; an expanded program of research reaching well beyond mental health into culture, psychophysiology, neuro-physiology, and even evolutionary processes. Phenomenologists taught us to listen to people and to respect without question the validity of each individual's experience, and that's no small gift. Their bequest is an even bigger one. The phenomenology/humanist paradigm lives on in positive psychology.

Existentialism

As a paradigm in psychology, existentialism is a movement, not a body of theory. It is a psychology for those who are overwhelmed by a raw deal in life, authored by them-selves or by implacable forces, or for people who see life as hopeless and without mean-ing. It doesn't offer solace but instead a kind of tough love, an unblinking analysis of the nature of human existence and a prescription for coming to grips with terror, misery, and despair. Recognize, as Sartre said, that not to make choices is itself a choice; don't give in to fear of freedom but exercise it, and take seriously your personal responsibility; fight nothingness with the best choices you can make; and give up the conceit that the end of the rainbow is just over the next hill.

Traits

The trait paradigm is the easiest of the seven to grasp, because every single person in the world is involved in it. All people have the tools to label consistencies in the behaviour of others—the trait words of our languages. There are thousands of them, understood and applied to others (including ourselves). As a source of traits, languages are easily accessible and represent the research contribution of millions upon millions of subjects and observers. There is one small difficulty, not hard to overcome: too many trait-like words. We could not begin to describe people using such a large library of terms, and predicting behaviour would be a nightmare. Reducing them to a manageable number (by eliminating synonyms, for example) is a straightforward task. Then there is the ques-tion of how many basic traits make up personality, but this is answered by the statistical procedure of factor analysis.

So off we skip down the Yellow Brick Road, devising trait measures (rating scales, personality questionnaires), testing large samples of subjects, carrying out factor analy-ses, and testing the implications of what we've found. The Wizard in the Emerald City has been good to us. He has rewarded all of our hop-skipping and good old-fashioned hard trudging with a small set of factors that *might* be the fundamental dimensions of personality. Are they real? If we pinch ourselves, will the dream bubble burst? Well, our bubble might not burst, but what we've been given won't be all of what we asked the Wizard for. We didn't get humbug, but neither did we get everything we sought. How many traits should there be? The Wizard didn't pin that down. Well, maybe sixteen, maybe three, he said; maybe five. What *are* the traits? 'You're going to have to go back and figure them out. What'd you put into those rating scales and questionnaires, any-way?' Persons in situations? No answer at all.

Those traits from the Wizard, though, have really paid off. They do predict hand-somely, and the variety of behaviour they account for seems to fit with them and make perfect sense. Traits based on North American research appear in widely differ-ent cultures whose languages have highly distinct ways of saying things. And, by golly, traits are heritable and strongly so. We don't know just what it is that's inherited when we find a significant heritability coefficient for a trait and its behavioural expressions, but that journey to the Emerald City was sure worth it. Pretty good Wizard! Pretty good paradigm!

The Inheritance of Behaviour

In the long history of the idea that the determinants of human behaviour might be inherited, finding evidence of confirmation was not possible until controlled methods appeared. As you remember from Chapter 16, twenty years before Freud's first major publication on neurosis (*Studies on Hysteria*, with Breuer, in 1895), Galton had proposed the twin-study method—staple of modern behaviour genetics—to distinguish 'the Relative Powers of Nature and Nurture' (1875). He thought his data on identical and fraternal twin pairs affirmed beyond doubt the dominant role of nature, but the study was badly flawed and the conclusion impermissible. It remained for scientists of the twentieth century to conduct twin studies properly and demonstrate convincingly that many attributes of personality show significant heritability. They have done so by teaming up with trait psychologists, using well-grounded measures of basic personality dimensions. The importance of this collaboration cannot be overestimated.

The advances in behaviour genetics have been remarkable. Investigators have capitalized on methods to control genetic influence, notably twin and adoption studies, and with persistence and ingenuity have located substantial samples of the most critical and informative group of twins: identical twins reared apart. Hot on the heels of these studies is research on molecular genetics, seeking to identify specific genes involved in personality traits and personality disorders. This is the current cutting edge of genetic research in personality.

While behaviour genetics research goes on apace, there are signal challenges that must be answered. Genetic influences on personality, like personality traits, take little account of the situation. The interaction of person and situation in virtually every behaviour is still foreign territory, though it shouldn't be. Personality traits are not inflexible dispositions to act; they are aroused by cues, they appear in varying strength as situations call for, and they are subject to reciprocal influences as others are affected and as the person reacts to the effects of his or her own behaviour. Traits that are in part genetically based are likely to cause people to choose trait-relevant environments and to influence what happens in those environments. Thus, we should expect that the heritability of traits will contribute to environmental measures. The complexity of this question is a barrier to working out gene-based trait–situation interactions, but it is not an insurmountable one. A second challenge is the thorny matter of what is inherited. To find significant heritability coefficients for divorce or conservative and conforming attitudes is a start, but we must find the gene-influenced processes that are responsible. Contemporary research in behaviour genetics is not blind to the issue, and there are highly promising research approaches now disclosing such possibilities as the effects of neurotransmitters on traits showing genetic influence. We review one of them in the next section.

Behaviour genetics is an entirely research-based paradigm with a growing body of methods to study personality inheritance. Investigators point to hard facts (coefficients of heritability, the quantitative measures of molecular genetics) and do not make the extravagant claims, made by earlier genetic enthusiasts, of nature's dominance over nurture. It has no overarching theory to guide (or constrain) research; genetic researchers are perfectly content to pursue an empirical program, raking in the facts as they are determined. A genetic theory of personality, they say, will come.

Marvin Zuckerman (Courtesy of Marvin Zuckerman, Professor Emeritus, University of Delaware.)

An Alternative: Miniature Theories

Personality psychologists have shown strong interest in developing **miniature theories**★ to provide a way of thinking about a limited set of events, a conceptual scheme for a restricted range of phenomena. Instead of trying to tackle everything, covering the whole person, and perhaps not all but a great deal of what he might think, feel, do, and get in neurotic trouble over, miniature theories take on smaller questions and try to secure a theoretical and experimental basis for them. The theorizing is less strict and is often guided by developments in the research as it progresses.

Sensation-Seeking

A fine example is the trait of sensation-seeking that I mentioned in Chapters 9 and 16. Investigated by Marvin Zuckerman over a period now of more than forty years, sensation-seeking is '. . . defined by the seeking of varied, novel, complex, and intense sensations and experiences, and the willingness to take physical, social, legal, and financial risks for the sake of such experience' (Zuckerman, 1994a; Zuckerman & Kuhlman, 2000, p. 1000). The overall trait involves four contributing factors: looking for adventure and thrills, desire to pursue new experiences (those that are novel, high-risk, daring), disinhibition (leading to socially uncontrolled behaviour and activities such as drinking), and susceptibility to boredom. Zuckerman began with the development of a sensation-seeking personality questionnaire (Zuckerman, Kolin, Price, & Zoob, 1964) and the search for the behavioural correlates of the trait (1978, 1979, 2000). Among the findings: people high on sensation-seeking drive faster and more recklessly, and are more likely to smoke and to use drugs and alcohol, to engage in extreme sports like sky diving, and to indulge in high-risk, antisocial behaviour. They have more sexual experience but are less satisfied in close relationships. Sensation-seekers tend to choose risky occupations, have convictions for criminal offences, and like to gamble. All in all, they are not only drawn to exciting, intense, and novel experiences but are strikingly impulsive as well, so much so that Zuckerman has recognized the affinity, collapsing two traits into one 'supertrait', *impulsive sensation-seeking* (Zuckerman, 1994b; Zuckerman & Kuhlman, 2000).

Perspective 17.1 Sensation: To Seek Or Not To Seek . . . .

The week was not atypical for Artie. He was tired out from Sunday night's party, which broke up at four in the morning. He had casual sex with a girl he had just met, persuading her that precautions were stupid and unnecessary. After all, each could see that the other was OK. A lot of beers—rather more than he could remember—and some ecstasy were part of it; he couldn't recall just when the sex happened. He slept in and missed his morning Psych class, a review for the midterm on Wednesday.

That was nothing to worry about. Psych was boring anyway, and a review was going to be worse. Plenty of time to get out the textbook (also boring) on Tuesday evening and go over a few chapters. No sweat. He'd do all right, maybe even ace the dumb exam. On Tuesday afternoon, a friend who wasn't a student came by to ask Artie if he'd like to go to the casino, an hour's drive away, to play the slots. 'I've got some money,' he said. 'We could clean up.'

'Aw,' said Artie, 'I've got a Psych exam I oughta study for.' Then, 'Geez, why not? I can get through that old exam easy. I'll look at the book in the morning before class.' He banged his fist hard on his desk. 'Let's go.' Ben, Artie's roommate, his studying interrupted, issued a caution, waved off impatiently.

They stayed until the wee hours, blowing the friend's stake and all that Artie had as well. On the way home, sleepy, full of beer, and driving too fast, they ran a red light and were stopped. Blowing over the limit and tossing out some smart remarks did it—they were arrested and jailed for the night. Artie's parents, somewhat less than pleased, had to bail them out. It was afternoon before they got back to town, too late for the exam. Artie found Professor Crowne in his office on Thursday. He entered with uncharacteristic diffidence, managing an expression both sad and apologetic. 'I'm very sorry, sir. I missed the midterm. My mother was hurt in an automobile accident.' There was a raised eyebrow in response, but also an appointment to write a make-up on Friday. Outside the door and a barely safe distance down the hall, Artie couldn't resist a fist pump and a small yelp of triumph.

The exam was in the morning, before class. Despite the reprieve, the extra time to study, and a promise to Ben that he would, Artie disappeared on Thursday evening to join a pick-up hockey game, in which he fired one improbable shot after another, never passing to an open teammate. There were a lot of questions unfamiliar to Artie on the exam, but he didn't take any time to try to figure them out. No, best guess would do, the first thing that comes to your mind is the only way. He was through in thirty-five minutes. Friday afternoon from two till six he set aside for study. Textbooks piled at his elbow, highlighter in hand, he opened the one at the top—Psych, wouldn't you know it!—finding a chapter he didn't think he'd read. Picking out sentences, he highlighted them furiously for the next few minutes. The ones with boldfaced words were always good, and that sure made it easier. Underneath the table, his leg jiggled constantly. He got up and went to the Coke machine, then outside for a cigarette. So passed his afternoon of hard study, two till almost five. He'd gotten through the chapters for three of his courses and felt virtuous. Such dedication shouldn't go unrewarded; he began to think about what he would do that evening.

Ben broke in while Artie was running through ideas about something cool for Friday evening. 'Hey, Artie, how'd you like to come with me and my girlfriend to the movies and a beer at the campus pub after?' Artie dismissed him. 'Naw, I got something better to do.' He didn't, really, but then he had it—Roseanne's, the strip joint at the edge of town. Grab a burger and some beers while he watched the girls. Wait a minute, though. A sudden and highly urgent realization. He'd have to score some pot first. Roseanne's wouldn't be any fun without getting high.

Now, I've told you about Artie, and it's your turn. On the next page is a set of items from Zuckerman's Sensation Seeking Scale. For your part, answer them as Artie would. You will need to take what Artie's week says about him and put yourself in his shoes—or, more exactly, in his head.

Figure 17.1 Items from the Zuckerman Sensation Seeking Scale, Form IV (From Zuckerman, M. 2002. Zuckerman-Kuhlman Personality Questionnaire (ZKPQ): An alternative five-factorial model. In B. De Raad and M. Peruginini (Eds.), *Big Five Assessment*. Seattle, UH: Hogrefe & Huber. Reprinted with Permission of John Wiley & Sons,Inc., and M. Zuckerman.)

INTEREST AND PREFERENCE TEST

DIRECTIONS: Each of the items below contains two choices, A and B. Please indicate on your answer sheet [a sheet of paper will do perfectly] which of the choices most describes Artie's likes or the way Artie feels. In some cases you may find items in which both choices describe his likes or feelings. Please choose the one which better describes his likes or feelings.

1. A. I would like a job which would require a lot of travelling.
    B. I would prefer a job in one location.

2. A. I can't wait to get into the indoors on a cold day.
    B. I am invigorated by a brisk, cold day.

3. A. I dislike all body odors.
    B. I like some of the earthy body smells.

4. A. I get bored seeing the same old faces.
    B. I like the comfortable familiarity of everyday friends.

5. A. I would not like to try any drug which might produce strange and dangerous effects on me.
    B. I would like to try some of the new drugs that produce hallucinations.

6. A. I would like to take off on a trip with no pre-planned or definite routes, or timetable.
    B. When I go on a trip I like to plan my route and timetable fairly carefully.

7. A. The most important goal of life is to live it to the fullest and experience as much of it as you can.
    B. The most important goal of life is to find peace and happiness.

8. A. I would like to try parachute jumping.
    B. I would never want to try jumping out of a plane with or without a parachute.

9. A. I enter cold water gradually giving myself time to get used to it.
    B. I like to dive or jump right into the ocean or a cold pool.

10. A. I prefer friends who are excitingly unpredictable.
    B. I prefer friends who are reliable and predictable.

11. A. A good painting should shock or jolt the senses.
    B. A good painting should give one a feeling of peace and security.

12. A. People who ride motorcycles must have some kind of an unconscious need to hurt themselves.
    B. I would like to drive or ride on a motorcycle

Scoring. These items come from the General Sensation Seeking Scale. The sensation-seeking alternatives are as follows:

1. A   2. B   3. B   4.A   5. B   6.A   7.A   8.A   9. B   10. A   11. A   12. B

Count one point for each of Artie's sensation-seeking responses.

How did Artie come out? If his score was close to 12, you have accurately read him as a sensation-seeker on items from the General Scale of the Sensation Seeking Questionnaire. There are four factor scales in addition that measure more specific aspects of sensation-seeking. These are the factors and an illustrative item from each.

- **Thrill and adventure seeking.** 'I sometimes like to do things that are a little frightening.' Alternative: 'A sensible person avoids activities that are dangerous.'
- **Experience seeking.** 'I like to have new and exciting experiences and sensations even if they are a little frightening, unconventional or illegal.' Alternative: 'I am not interested in experience for its own sake.'
- **Disinhibition.** 'I like "wild" uninhibited parties.' Alternative: 'I prefer quiet parties with good conversation.'
- **Boredom susceptibility.** 'I get very restless if I have to stay around home for any length of time.' Alternative: 'I enjoy spending time in the familiar surroundings of home.'

It shouldn't be difficult to answer these factor scale items as Artie would have responded. I deliberately tried to include characteristics of each factor as I imagined Artie's week.

The Psychobiology and Genetics of Sensation Seeking

Zuckerman has extended his research to brain biochemistry. Scores on the sensation-seeking scale are correlated *negatively* with the level of an enzyme, *monoamine oxidase* (MAO), that deactivates monoamine neurotransmitters. (Its concentration in blood platelets, presumably reflecting the amount present in the brain, makes measurement easy.) The smaller the amount of MAO, the greater the availability of dopamine, and the higher the sensation-seeking questionnaire score and the quest for thrills, new experiences, and relief from boredom. Sensation-seekers are also lower in the concentration of norepinephrine, which results in reduced arousal. Their quest for excitement is a behavioural compensation (Zuckerman, 1994a, 1995).

Sensation-seeking also has strong genetic links, one of which we saw in Chapter 16. Investigators have discovered a gene, related to the level of MAO, that is associated with aggressive and impulsive behaviour, attributes of the extreme sensation-seeker (Manuck, Flory, Ferrell, Mann, & Muldoon, 2000). Earlier in the research, Zuckerman and colleagues found a high heritability coefficient (.58) in twins reared in their own families (Fulker, Eysenck, & Zuckerman, 1980), closely replicated by Hur and Bouchard (1997) in samples of identical twins raised together and apart. In these studies, no shared family environment influence surfaced. Environmental effects on sensation-seeking are non-shared (in particular, through peers), and any family resemblance is genetic.

From Miniature Theory to Personality Theory

Impulsive sensation-seeking proved to be so powerful a trait behaviourally, biochemically, and in genetically, and the convergence of evidence so impressive, that it became the cornerstone in a five-factor theory rivalling the Big Five. Zuckerman greatly expanded the biological model of sensation-seeking in his 1991 book, *Psychobiology of Personality*, in which he introduced the larger theory. Zuckerman calls it the 'Alternate Five', and its traits are derived from factor analyses of personality scales that have significant psychobiological findings. The Alternate Five traits are

- impulsive unsocialized sensation seeking,
- sociability,
- neuroticism-anxiety,
- aggression-hostility, and
- activity.

Except for activity, you can see parallels to Big Five factors. There is a test to measure them, the Zuckerman–Kuhlman Personality Questionnaire (Zuckerman, 2002). The Alternate Five has, along with its conceptual godfather, Eysenck's type-trait theory, and the Big Five, contributed in a very large way to the revitalization of personality theory, giving renewed vigour to our enterprise of accounting for the broad band of human behaviour.

The Achievement Need

Another exceptional miniature theory is the psychological approach to the study of a particular motive taken by the theorist–investigators David McClelland and John Atkinson. The motive in question is the need for achievement. McClelland and Atkinson started with a conception of needs and their expression (borrowed from Harvard psychologist and personality theorist Henry Murray) and simplified. The research strategy was inventive and far-reaching, and extensions of the theory and methods to explore them were stunning, even audacious.

What Is a Need?

A need, Atkinson said, is a 'disposition to strive for a particular kind of goal-state or aim' (1958, p. 596), developed early in childhood and highly resistant to change. Needs are aroused by situational cues, thoughts, or fantasies, which trigger the emotion and cogni-

David C. McClelland
(www.dushkin.com/connectext/psy/ch09/bio9b.mhtml)

John W. Atkinson (Courtesy Dr Melvin Manis)

tion associated with a need state and focus on the goal. You want to take note, then, of a motivationally determined relation among thought, fantasy, and action.

McClelland and Atkinson were strongly influenced by Murray, and they set out to study *Motives in Fantasy, Action, and Society* (the title of a 1958 book edited by Atkinson on achievement and other motives). What motives? Murray had proposed a tentative list of twenty psychological needs in *Explorations in Personality*, a seminal book on personality and personality research published in 1938. The needs ranged from abasement ('To submit passively to external force . . . To surrender . . . To admit inferiority, error, wrongdoing, or defeat.') to understanding ('To ask or answer general questions. To be interested in theory. To speculate, formulate, analyze, and generalize.'). In between were needs for achievement, affiliation, and power that especially interested McClelland and Atkinson.

The Measure of Needs

The study of needs had to go beyond just asking people about their motives. McClelland and Atkinson appreciated Murray's point that many psychological needs are beyond the consciousness of the person, and they saw in the Thematic Apperception Test developed by Murray a way to get at needs the person can't directly reveal. The TAT, as you recall from Chapter 3, is a story-telling measure of fantasy production. Since the TAT story is the respondent's creation, its elements must be his or her *projections*. It is the respondent who, motivationally, is the central character.

The surest way to start is to put first things first. Get the basics out of the way by putting a straight question. If you are hungry, will your fantasies reveal it? In the experiment designed to find the answer, Atkinson and McClelland (1948) tested groups of men after one, four, or sixteen hours without food. The test was the TAT. You might think that food-related *themas* (need and related environmental forces—called *press*—acting together) would increase with hours of food deprivation, but that was not the case. Very hungry participants did not tell more stories with direct reference to food or eating. But there were more food deprivation themas—hunger-thwarting barriers, the steak for dinner falling off the kitchen counter to be gobbled up by the family dog—and more instrumental attempts to deal with the source of the deprivation. This was highly encouraging. A basic motive state *did* appear in fantasy in a form that could be recognized and scored.

The next step was to choose a psychological motive and see if TAT stories would contain fantasy evidences of it. Sex and aggression were obvious candidates, but both presented a complication: because of strict socialization, they are sources of anxiety and conflict for many people, which might obscure the motive of interest. A less inhibited motive would be better to study and no less informative. McClelland and colleagues (McClelland, Clark, Roby, & Atkinson, 1949) then made the choice that would decide a whole research future: they picked Murray's need for achievement. Now, the hunger-fantasy experiment had used the expedient of assessing fantasy when the research participants were not at all, moderately, or very hungry, a simple physiological manipulation of motivation that laid the psychological ground for fantasy. This was just the sort of thing an experimental psychologist might have done in studying the effect of drive intensity on learning in the lab rat. McClelland et al. understood at once that there was no way to deprive subjects of their need for achievement, but they thought they might very well be able to contrive a manipulation that would engage it, arouse it.

The experiment would require the TAT, of course, and for need arousal there was a series of short tasks, presented under four motivational conditions. In a relaxed condition, the tasks were 'just some tests' being tried out by 'some graduate students', and there

*"O.K., so I dig a hole and put the bone in the hole.
But what's my motivation for burying it?"*

would be no scrutiny of the individual subjects. They came before the TAT. A second, neutral condition was formal and classroom-like, but not specifically achievement arousing. The other conditions were notably different, one involving failure and the other failure after initial success. The tasks were 'tests of a person's general level of intelligence', on which the whole group of participants was informed that they had failed (after brief success in the fourth condition). The TAT, given next, was described as a test of 'creative imagination'. The two failure conditions were designed to sensitize the participants to achievement, arouse it, and get them to worry about it. The relaxed and neutral conditions provided baselines. TAT stories were scored for achievement imagery, themas or plots, deprivation or failure, direct statements ('He wants to be a doctor.'), instrumental activity, and several other variables in a quite complex scheme. Then, the mean need for achievement scores in the four experimental conditions were compared. The findings were straightforward and very convincing: scores on need for achievement (it's time you learned that it's familiarly called *n*Ach—that's 'en-atch') in the failure and success–failure groups were significantly higher than in the neutral group, which in turn exceeded the relaxed group. The success–failure condition didn't turn out to be any more or less arousing than failure alone.

A very large number of experimental studies followed. Here's a basic list of findings. Experimental participants with high *n*Ach scores take moderate risks, neither foolishly high nor ridiculously easy (Atkinson & Litwin, 1960; McClelland, 1958); they perform better under competition (Ryan & Lackie, 1965); when matched on intelligence test scores with low *n*Ach participants, they get better grades (McClelland, Atkinson, Clark, & Lowell, 1953; Schultz & Pomerantz, 1976); they work harder and more persistently on verbal and mathematical tests and are more successful (McClelland et al., 1953); they choose as work partners people described to them as successful rather than people depicted as friendly (French, 1956); they are willing to delay gratification, waiting for a larger reward instead of taking a smaller immediate one (Mischel, 1961); and they tend to choose occupations in business, ones involving challenging risks they feel equipped to handle (McClelland, 1961).

In their childhood development, high-*n*Ach persons grow up in families, societies, and cultures that place value on striving and accomplishment. Their parents teach them self-reliance and give them the opportunity to set their own goals. Coming from a family in which the father is engaged in an entrepreneurial occupation helps to foster a high need for achievement (McClelland, 1961; Winterbottom, 1958; Rosen & D'Andrade, 1959). But, as social psychologist Roger Brown cautioned, 'A mother who . . . decided to produce a highly [achievement] motivated son by expecting her son to "know his way around the city", "do well in competition", and "make his own friends" before he was eight years old might be disappointed by the results. Motive creation cannot be that simple' (1965, p. 448).

In all of this, there were two strong hints that entrepreneurship matters. The first related to choice of occupation in achievement-oriented university students, the second to the facilitating effect of an entrepreneurial father. McClelland now took a big step, opening the lens wide to look at the achievement attributes of *societies* rather than individuals. But how could we measure in a whole society a motive that characterizes an individual? 'It's a tough job, but somebody's got to do it,' McClelland surely said to his colleagues and students.

'I'll try, sir,' said Elliot Aronson, bravely volunteering. Well, something like that. Aronson (1958) chose an aspect of expressive behaviour: graphic expression. Why, I don't know; he may simply have been fishing. He got participants for whom nAch scores had been obtained to reproduce from memory an abstract design, briefly shown, and then scrutinized the productions of the high and low groups for systematic differences. We might call this the 'doodle method', and it did distinguish between subjects high and low in nAch. High-need persons drew more discrete (versus fuzzy, overlaid) lines, left less space at the bottom of the page, drew more diagonal lines and figures and more S-shaped figures and multiwave lines. It is something of a stretch, but here was a possible alternative to the verbal measurement of nAch, one that could be applied to artistic productions of people no longer present. Brown noted: 'The problem is to project a modern measure backward in time' (1965, p. 459), and Aronson's method promised to solve it.

In ancient Greece, urns to transport wine and olive oil were decorated with designs, and those designs could be scored by treating them like Aronson's doodles. Greece traded all around the Mediterranean, and many urns have been found and dated. Is it not a reasonable hypothesis that a wider dispersion of the urns might reflect greater economic activity, greater entrepreneurship, and in the background, greater nAch? That was McClelland's dazzling idea, and a test of it—scoring the patterns scribed on urns, establishing the era of their production, and estimating from the spread of urn finds the extent of commerce—revealed an increase in achievement motivation (shown by high-nAch designs) approximately a generation before an epoch of extensive trade. A similar study of funerary urns from pre-Incan Peru found two timespans of high-achievement motivation followed by cultural expansion (seen in greater construction of public buildings) and two low-nAch periods that preceded the conquest of Peru by invading peoples. Said Brown, 'Believe it or not' (1965, p. 460). The credibility of these extraordinary investigations rests on a strong relation of the doodle method to traditional nAch measurement. If it isn't a strong one, we will not really know what to make of the urn design relationships. If it is strong, the entrepreneurial hypothesis is more believable. The correlations are moderate but not whopping. What *do* we make of that?

Next, a new tack. Take economic development in modern societies, some industrialized, some not (the US, Sweden, Canada, Great Britain; Greece, Argentina, Uruguay, Spain). Develop indices of economic growth such as national income and amount of electricity generated, and find a national, cultural measure of achievement motivation. Here again, the nAch measure was bold and imaginative. Rate stories for children in second, third, and fourth grade schoolbooks on expressed motivation for achievement, obliterating all references to national identity. We wouldn't have any trouble with 'The Little Engine that Could', and the raters readily spotted achievement imagery or the lack of it in the whole set of stories. Two story samples were taken—in 1925 and in 1950. The 1925 readers, then eight to ten, grew up and took their places in the economy. If their achievement motivation reflected their culture's, economic activity in 1950 should have benefited from a culture-wide achievement orientation. Cultures not imbued with nAch wouldn't tell achievement stories to their children, and their economic progress would lag behind. A story sample taken in 1950 should show no relation to economic development, since motivation must precede entrepreneurial activity. The findings confirmed the relationship between the nAch–entrepreneurship measure and rate of economic gain.

Out of achievement motive theory grew an even more ambitious hypothesis linking values of effort and hard work (the Protestant work ethic) to childrearing, the development in children of the achievement need, and a capitalist ideal. There are vastly more studies than I have reviewed, some of them uncertain, but a great many confirmatory. I think the need-for-achievement research is a model for what can be done with a miniature theory. In summing it up, Brown wrote:

> Since there is no single clear criterion against which to validate a measure of achievement motivation, . . . the validation process amounted to a demonstration that scores on the measure related to other kinds of behaviour in such a way as to satisfy our intuitive notions of achievement motivation. In the end, however, something more than this has come of the very numerous studies relating Achievement Motive scores to other data. The scores are higher for managers than for other sorts of professional men; they are related to economic growth; they go with a taste for moderate risks, long range planning, and tasks that involve clear criteria of success and failure. The process of validation has turned into a process of reconceptualization. The measure now seems to be primarily concerned with motivation for economic achievement rather than with achievement motivation in general (1965, pp. 473–4).

Study of the motive has extended to further and no less provocative applications—a remedial treatment for underachieving schoolboys, creating a motive where it didn't exist (Kolb, 1965), and the entrepreneurial training of industrial managers (McClelland, 1965).

Some Concluding Thoughts about Personality Theory

Why is there such a number of personality theories? Are there so many facets to the human animal that we are like the blind men feeling the elephant, unable to make out the whole idea of the thing? Or, perhaps, coming from different perspectives, each theorist is predetermined to see personality in his or her own framework—a dynamic, depth, clinical one; a dynamic, depth, clinical one modified by a keen appreciation of society and family; an approach coming from the experimental psychology of learning with some strong notions about the unimportance of reinforcement; an existential and despairing view of humankind's prospects; a sophisticated statistical taxonomy of traits based on everyday language. . . . I think the latter of these is the more correct. We see what the conceptual schemes we bring along point us toward.

In an important way, the psychology of personality has been well served by the large number of competing theories. They have enriched our perspectives and caused us to think more carefully about the essential attributes of the person. New kids on the block have supplied necessary correctives to theories with too narrow a focus, as the neo-Freudians did in stressing to the psychoanalysts the roles of society, culture, and family in personality formation and expression, and in holding up to the analysts a better psychology of women. Some theories have shown us that we must think of individual personality *and* situation in the determination of behaviour, and one in particular, social cognitive theory, has taken the person–situation interaction to a highly sophisticated level.

In a sense that is equally important, the multiplication of theories has been a disadvantage, fracturing personality study into a number of camps, often keenly adversarial. As a result, we do not have a coherent personality literature. Given the theoretical diversity, will we see the merging of theories—weaker ones lacking testable concepts and without major research support fading away, and the more viable ones moving toward a common base? As an example, think of S-R theory's recasting of psychoanalytic concepts in the form and language of Hullian learning theory.

The answer is, I believe, probably not, at least for a long time. There are just too many conflicting ideas and approaches to make a theoretical amalgam possible. Social cognitive theory and psychoanalysis don't have much in common, and trait theory is far from dealing well with the process concepts of learning theories, the role of the situation, or significant variables in personality development. We shall continue to need to learn our Freud, neo-Freudians, ego and analytic psychologies, varieties of learning theory, trait theories, and existentialism. We'll want to watch developments in behaviour genetics very closely to see what theory or theories the inheritance of personality attributes favours, and keep up with miniature theories. And you, like all students of personality, will have to take a stance and declare for yourself which theory you find most compelling.

SUMMARY

1. The great era from the time of Freud to the mid-1950s is sometimes called the 'Age of Theory', when both personality and learning theories (those of Hull and Tolman, for example) flourished. The emphasis was on *hypothetico-deductive systems* consisting of intervening variables linked to antecedent conditions and consequent (adult) behaviour. Although differing in rigour, the major personality theories were all of this sort.

2. The Age of Theory, said Sigmund Koch in a massive study of psychology as a science, is dead. The grand personality theories (and learning theories as well) had failed. Their theoretical concepts were poorly described, not well defined operationally, and not clearly linked to observables. To cope with the difficulty of specifying links to antecedents and consequents, theories were liberalized, loosening and broadening the definitions of concepts.

3. Koch claimed that the liberalization of theory and theoretical concepts was harmful. But was it? There were, in fact, some major benefits. For example, a liberal definition of unconscious processes led to a large amount of research on the cognitive unconscious. Also, Bandura's studies of observational learning without reinforcement grew from a liberalized approach to reinforcement and resulted in novel findings and a new social learning theory of personality. Because grand theories were no longer strict and uncompromising, the age of their development, so the argument went, had come to an end. Were theories of the 1950s the last of the line?

4. A theoretical age wasn't dead. Consider social learning theory, social cognitive theory, and the trait theories. It turned out that the connection of concepts to antecedent and consequent observables was not such a huge problem. The sky wasn't falling in. There were other liberalizing changes in psychology, among them a pragmatic behaviourism in clinical psychology and the development of a largely atheoretical community psychology.

5. The seven paradigms into which the twenty-two theories of this book fall all survive and have their adherents. Among the *psychodynamic* theories, psychoanalysis and the ego theories (particularly Erikson's) thrive. Research is vigorously pursued, and it is far more sophisticated than earlier work. Erikson's ego psychology has served psychoanalysis well with its developmental, social, and cultural emphases. The *family, society, and culture* paradigm has enthusiastic followers, and institutes that train new practitioners. There is no research base, however, to test important hypotheses and lay the basis for theoretical advances. *Learning and personality*, with its strong experimental and research tradition, has produced major advances in the study of the person. It has shown the personality community how critical it is to recognize the variability of behaviour from situations, and its modern form, the social cognitive theories, has established cognitive processes as essential to learning and to personality development and adult expression. The radical behaviourists have shown the way to manipulating the

environment to produce remarkable changes in behaviour. *Phenomenology* and *humanism* have made a great contribution to personality psychology in their emphasis on truly listening to people and accepting without question each person's own experience. While the heyday of phenomenological research has passed, this paradigm lives on in positive psychology, which emphasizes human possibility and the nurturing of its achievement, and it is deeply involved in research on how accomplishment and health are attained. *Existentialism* is not theory but instead a philosophical movement that has become psychological. Its message for anxious and desperate people—and for anyone who struggles with the meaning of life—is difficult, a kind of psychological tough love. The *trait* paradigm has a ready source of trait terms in the common language and powerful methods to extract the essential traits that define personality. There is some disagreement over the number of traits and their description, but the knowledge base from many all-out research programs is increasing at a fast pace. *The inheritance of behaviour* is another paradigm advancing rapidly. It has capitalized on twin and adoption studies, establishing the heritability of major personality traits, and it now has the most sophisticated molecular genetic methods to find individual genes involved in traits and personality disorders. Genetic research in personality, however, is not ready for a theory to incorporate its findings, and it has not yet dealt with the person–situation interaction or the difficult question of what, specifically, is inherited.

6. Miniature theories deal with limited sets of events. The theorizing is often less strict and demanding and may take more explicit form as research progresses. The study of sensation-seeking by Zuckerman is an excellent example. Sensation-seeking comprises four distinct factors: adventure and thrills, new experiences, disinhibition, and susceptibility to boredom. There is a personality questionnaire to measure the general trait and factors.

7. Sensation-seekers are characterized by a number of behavioural attributes. They drive faster, use illicit drugs and alcohol, engage in high-risk sports and risky antisocial behaviour, have more sexual experience, and are easily bored. There are, as well, neurochemical characteristics: investigators have found a *negative* correlation between sensation-seeking and monoamine oxydase (MAO), a brain enzyme that deactivates monoamine neurotransmitters (dopamine, norepinephrine). Researchers have found a gene regulating MAO that is associated with behavioural characteristics of sensation-seeking. Further, there is twin study evidence on the heritability of the trait. Impulsive sensation-seeking has become part of a more inclusive theory of personality, the Alternate Five-Factor model.

8. Another exceptional miniature theory is part of a contemporary study of the achievement motive by McClelland and Atkinson. They consider a need as a 'disposition to strive for a particular kind of goal-state or aim'. Needs affect behaviour, cognition, and fantasy, develop early in childhood, and do not readily change. Needs in the individual reflect family and cultural values.

9. An initial experiment showed that hunger was expressed in a fantasy measure, the Thematic Apperception Test (TAT). Would the TAT reveal psychological motives like the need for achievement (*nAch*)? A first step was to arouse the need and see if fantasy scores would follow. They did. An extensive series of studies established the characteristics of people with high *nAch*.

10. High-*nAch* scorers take moderate—not extremely high or low—risks, get better grades, work harder on challenging tasks, choose effective work partners, are willing to delay gratification for larger rewards, and tend to choose business careers involving challenging risks within their capabilities. As children, they experienced independence training early in childhood, grew up in families and societies that valued striving, and were raised by fathers who tended to be in entrepreneurial occupations.

11. A graphic expression measure was developed that correlates significantly with the fantasy measure. It was applied to Greek urns of the classical period, scoring their designs for *nAch*. Achievement-related designs preceded expansion of Greek commerce throughout the Mediterranean by a generation. There was a similar finding in pre-Incan Peru: achievement designs on funerary urns anticipated an increase in the construction of public buildings, and the absence of them a decline in that civilization.

12. Economic development in modern society was investigated by examining the relation between children's stories and economic growth. Societies in which chil-

dren's stories contained achievement themes ('The little engine that could') had higher rates of economic development. The need for achievement has become part of a larger theory of values, childrearing, achievement motive, and capitalism.

13. Why are there so many personality theories? Is personality too big a question to grasp, or does the large number reflect the influence of the prior perspectives of the theorists? The proliferation of theories has had a beneficial influence. The appearance of new ones has been a corrective to narrow older theories (seen, for example, in the introduction of family and social

dynamics to psychoanalysis by the neo-Freudians). Other theories have made clear the importance of the person–situation interaction, to the benefit of theories failing to give it full recognition. Theory proliferation has also been a disadvantage, breaking up personality study into rival camps. It is unlikely that there will be a significant merger of personality theories in the foreseeable future, given the substantial differences among them. It will be important to watch developments in behaviour genetics, to keep up with miniature theories, and to be sure that we understand the major theories.

TO TEST YOUR UNDERSTANDING

1. When Sigmund Koch judged the success of personality theories, he set the bar for the intervening variable paradigm on which nearly all of them depend at a very high level. They failed abjectly, he determined, because—in a word—they cheated. Personality theories invented concepts—within-person structures and processes such as ego and defence mechanisms—that they could tie only loosely to behaviour and very inconclusively to supposedly causal events in childhood. Theorists fell in love with their concepts and dismissed the need for strict verification. This was theoretical 'liberalization', as Neal Miller put it, arguing that at the present stage in psychological science a lower bar would pay off in theoretical advances. Who was right—Koch or Miller? Would you like to see the high scientific standard or one that realistically adapts to the difficulty of confirming hypothetical concepts?

2. Do you think contemporary theories—Bandura's social cognitive learning theory, for example, or Big

Five theory—represent an advance over older, classical theories? In what way? Are there unresolved deficiencies that remain in them? What are they, and how might they be remedied?

3. Is sensation-seeking a good miniature theory? What makes it good? What do you think of the theoretical and empirical progress made by Zuckerman and colleagues in establishing sensation-seeking? Have they overlooked anything? If so, what?

4. The motivational theory of need achievement has a long psychodynamic heritage. Trace its history. Where do its fundamental ideas come from? How do they represent an improvement over their theoretical ancestors? Need achievement principally rests on a fantasy measure. What do you think of its logic and method? Do you think the leap to decorations on commercial urns and funerary urns and to stories told to children truly reflect achievement motivation in society and culture, or are you dubious?

Appendix

The following is a more complete explanation of the formula to derive heritability from monozygotic twin and dizygotic twin correlations. It comes from my colleague Dr Erik Woody, to whom go my great thanks and admiration.

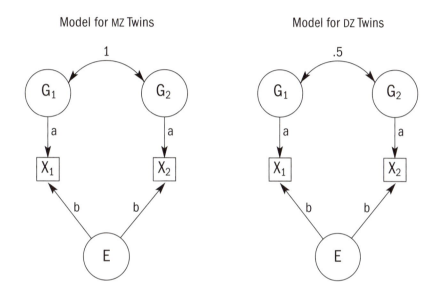

The twins are represented by the X subscripts 1 and 2. The G's represent genetic predispositions. MZ twins have the same genetic complement, so the correlation of their genetic predispositions is set to 1.0. DZ twins share half their genetic complements, so the correlation of their genetic predispositions is set to 0.5. (The proportion of variance *shared* by two variables is equal to their correlation. An example would be that the correlation of alternate forms of a test is also an estimate of their reliability, or the proportion of variance they share in common. In contrast, a squared correlation is the proportion of variance in one variable that can be *predicted or explained* by the other.) The X's represent behaviour (X_1 for twin 1 and X_2 for twin 2), and the coefficient a represents the correlation of genetic predisposition with behaviour. The E's represent the environment, and the coefficient b represents the correlation of environment with behaviour.

There are at least three important assumptions in these models.

1. There are no important factors omitted from them, such as gene-by-environment interactions.
2. The effect of the environment (E) is the same for MZ and DZ twins, as represented by the equality of b across the two models.
3. The X_1's and X_2's are measured without error (i.e. with virtually perfect reliability and validity).

More complex models can be proposed that relax these assumptions; they will yield somewhat different values for heritability than the simple models here.

The G's and E's are latent variables that are assumed to exist but are not directly measured. In contrast, the behaviours—the X_1's and X_2's—can be directly measured. In particular, from data we can calculate the correlation between X_1 and X_2 for MZ twins, r_{MZ}, and the corresponding correlation for DZ twins, r_{DZ}.

What we want to know is heritability, which is a^2. Because a represents the correlation of genetic predisposition with behaviour, a^2 is the proportion of variance in behaviour that is explained by genetic predisposition. Assuming that the two models above are correct, we can use the two correlations to calculate heritability.

Specifically, it can be demonstrated algebraically that according to the foregoing models, the correlations are equal to the following linear combinations of coefficients a and b:

$$r_{MZ} = a^2 + b^2$$
$$r_{DZ} = .5a^2 + b^2$$

In other words, the environment makes equal contributions to each of the correlations, but heredity makes twice as big a contribution to the MZ correlation as to the DZ correlation.

Taking the difference between the correlations,

$$r_{MZ} - r_{DZ} = a^2 + b^2 - (.5a^2 + b^2)$$
$$r_{MZ} - r_{DZ} = .5a^2$$

and thus

$$a^2 = 2(r_{MZ} - r_{DZ}).$$

Glossary

acquired drive   another term for **secondary drive**.

affect   emotion or subjectively experienced feeling, such as happiness, sadness, fear, or anger.

aggression   behaviour intended primarily or solely to injure another, either physically or psychologically. Kelly considered aggression a natural consequence of an attempt to test and expand one's construct system.

anima   (in analytic psychology) the feminine principle as represented in the male unconscious; an archetype forming part of the collective unconscious, representing the feminine aspect of human nature, characterized by imagination, fantasy, and play.

animus   (in analytic psychology) the masculine principle present as an archetype in the female collective unconscious, characterized by focused consciousness, authority, and respect.

antecedent   (esp. in behaviour genetics and personality theory construction) the cause or source of a particular trait. Also, part of the intervening variable paradigm; intervening variables (concepts) are tied to observable antecedents and consequents.

anti-cathexis   (in psychoanalysis) the unconscious process by which repressed ideas that are threatening to break through into consciousness are prevented from doing so by an equal force operating in the opposite direction (compare **defence mechanism**).

anxiety   a state of uneasiness, accompanied by signs and symptoms of tension, focused on apprehension of possible failure, misfortune, or danger. In person-centred theory, anxiety results when threat is perceived and symbolized.

archetype   (in analytic psychology) an inherited mental structure or pattern forming part of the collective unconscious, observable through its manifestations in behaviour, especially that associated with ancient and universal experiences such as birth, marriage, motherhood, and death.

attitude   a pattern of affective, cognitive, and behavioural responses towards a person, object, or issue.

autosome   any chromosome that is not a sex chromosome.

behaviour shaping   another term for **successive approximation**.

biophilous   having a love of life; the term was coined by Fromm to describe the productive character type (see **productive character**; compare **necrophilous character**).

case study   the detailed investigation of one particular case or individual.

catharsis   a term originating with Freud, meaning generally the discharge of affect and tension; more specifically, the reduction of aggressive urges resulting from exposure to violence enacted in TV shows, movies, or video games.

Aristotle first used the term to denote the purging of emotions that results from watching a staged tragedy.

cathexis   (in psychoanalysis) an investment of energy in an object associated with instinctual gratification.

chromosome   a thread-like structure of nucleic acids and protein found in the nucleus of most living cells, carrying genetic information in the form of genes.

classical conditioning   the learning process through which an initially neutral stimulus such as the ticking of a metronome comes to elicit a particular response, such as salivation, as a consequence of being paired repeatedly with an unconditioned stimulus, such as food (also called **Pavlovian conditioning**).

clinical method   an approach to psychological research based on the assessment and treatment of mental disorders and disabilities (see also **case study**).

collective unconscious   (in analytic psychology) an unconscious part of personality distinct from the personal unconscious, containing memories, instincts, and experiences shared by all people.

compensation   a process by which one attempts to redress a perceived deficiency that cannot be eliminated, such as a physical defect or painful feelings of inferiority, by excelling in some other way.

complex   an organized collection of ideas, emotions, impulses, and memories that share a common emotional tone and that have been excluded either partly or entirely from consciousness but continue to influence a person's thoughts, emotions, and behaviour.

condensation   (in psychoanalysis) the representation of several chains of mental associations by a single idea, especially in dreams, jokes, and other manifestations of unconscious activity.

conditioned response   (in classical conditioning) a learned response that follows a conditioned stimulus.

conditioned stimulus   (in classical conditioning) a stimulus such as the ticking of a metronome that is initially neutral but that comes to elicit a particular response such as salivation only as a consequence of being paired with an unconditioned stimulus such as food.

conscience   an acquired mental framework for making judgements about the moral rightness or wrongness of actions; Fromm preferred this to the Freudian term **superego**.

content theory   any of a number of theories that propose structural concepts, such as ego, superego, and id, that are hypothetical components of personality; psychoanalytic theory is an example (compare **process theory**).

continuity assumption   the assumption that differences in degree, not differences in kind, distinguish normal and psychologically disturbed persons. Most personality theories make and depend on this assumption.

control   manipulate a variable to study it experimentally or hold it constant.

control group   a group in an experiment that is used for comparison with the experimental group.

conversion   (in psychoanalysis) the process by which unconscious conflict capable of arousing anxiety is expressed symbolically, the repressed idea or wish being transformed into a physical symptom. A **conversion disorder** is a physical disorder characterized by such a physical symptom, often pain or sexual dysfunction, brought about as a result of conversion (*see also* **hysteria**).

countertransference   (in psychoanalysis) the analyst's emotional reactions to the patient and to the patient's transference, influenced by the analyst's unconscious needs and conflicts (*compare* **transference**).

cue   an attribute of an object or event to which an organism responds, simple examples being the size or shape of a visual stimulus to which a response may be conditioned.

deduction   the process of drawing inferences or hypotheses from general principles, i.e. theory (*compare* **induction**).

defence mechanism   (in psychoanalysis) the process by which the ego protects itself from the anxiety produced by inadmissible wishes or urges, memories, or feelings (such as sexual arousal, aggression); defence mechanisms banish the frightening material from consciousness (*compare* **anti-cathexis**).

denial   (in psychoanalysis) a defence mechanism in which thoughts, memories, or feelings that would be painful or unacceptable are immediately excluded from consciousness. Examples: the smoker or alcoholic denies that he has an addiction that may harm him; a patient in psychoanalysis denies that she was sexually aroused by someone wholly inadmissible (such as a parent, a sibling, or a psychoanalyst).

depersonalization   the action of divesting someone or something of human characteristics or individuality; emotional detachment or estrangement that causes one to regard others as things.

despised self   a conception of oneself comprising all of one's failures or shortcomings, real or imagined (*compare* **idealized self**, **real self**).

determinism   the scientific assumption that all events, including human action, are ultimately determined by heredity, past history, immediate environment, present behaviour. This assumption is opposed by the doctrine of free will.

dethronement   (in individual psychology) the ouster of an eldest child from his or her position as the only child once siblings are born.

developmental line   developmental sequences, proposed by Anna Freud, that plot the course of a child's growth from helpless dependence and total self-absorption to greater maturity and independence.

dichotomy   a division or contrast between two things that are opposed or entirely different. Fromm identified **existential dichotomies** (life *vs* death) and **historical dichotomies** (the era of one's birth; peace *vs* war), which he considered inescapable.

displacement   (in psychoanalysis) a defence mechanism that involves the redirection of emotional feelings from their original object to a substitute object related to the original one by a chain of associations. Displacement is process involved in aggression toward a substitute target when the original target cannot be attacked.

dissociation   a partial or total disconnection between memories of the past, awareness of identity and of immediate sensations, and control of bodily movements, resulting from traumatic experiences, intolerable problems, or deeply disturbed relationships.

dizygotic   denoting twins derived from two separate ova, who are therefore not identical (*compare* **monozygotic**).

dream censor   (in psychoanalysis) the sleep-relaxed ego as it transforms the latent content of a dream into its manifest content, thereby making the expression of the instinctual urging harmless.

dream work   (in psychoanalysis) all of the processes employed by the ego to transform the latent content of a dream into its manifest content, concealing its meaning from the dreamer and thus allowing undisturbed sleep to occur.

dynamism   (in interpersonal theory) the basic unit of personality, responsible for organizing and channelling energy into behaviour; they are evident in interpersonal relations (*see also* **self dynamism**).

ego   (in psychoanalysis) one of three components of personality, which deals with external reality and controls the instinctual urges of the id.

ego ideal   (in psychoanalysis) part of the superego, an internal notion of personal perfection serving as a model to which one strives to conform, derived from early identification with one's parents, especially the parent of the same sex.

empathy   the capacity to understand and enter into another person's feelings and emotions or to understand another's experience as if it were one's own.

empiricism   the view that all knowledge is derived from sense experience, that knowledge is gained by the study of observable events.

encoding   a representation of sensory information stored in memory; the ways in which we represent the features of our lives.

engulfment   an existential term for the fear that in any relationship one will lose one's autonomy and thus one's individual identity.

entropy, principle of   (in analytic psychology) the theory that energy use seeks a balance, flowing from strong structures, values, or activities to weaker ones; one of two principles governing the psychodynamics of libidinal energy, derived from the first and second laws of thermodynamics in physics (compare *equivalence, principle of*).

epigenesis   (in ego psychology) a model of psychological development according to which specific characteristics appear at certain stages of development, a theory based on the way an embryo develops progressively from an undifferentiated egg cell.

equivalence, principle of   the theory that energy withdrawn from an activity is not lost but will be expended elsewhere in personality; one of two principles governing the psychodynamics of libidinal energy, derived from the first and second laws of thermodynamics in physics (compare *entropy, principle of*).

erogenous zone   any of several specific areas of the body that, when stimulated, give a sexualized pleasure.

existential dichotomy   *see dichotomy*.

expectancy   (in social learning theory) a subjective probability that a particular behaviour will lead to particular reinforcing consequences.

exploitative character   (in neo-Freudian theory) Fromm's term for a character type who uses others and takes things from others by force and cunning (compare *hoarding character, marketing character, necrophilous character, productive character, receptive character*).

expression in opposites   (in psychoanalysis) a mechanism of the dream work, in which forbidden wishes are replaced by their opposites. Example: a feeling of sexual attraction is replaced by disgust or revulsion.

externalization   a defence mechanism noted by Horney in which a person unconsciously attributes inner impulses to the outside world, as when a child converts unconscious angry impulses into a fear of monsters.

external validity   the extent to which the conclusions of an empirical investigation remain true when different research methods and research participants or subjects are used.

facet   an aspect or feature; in Big Five measurement the term refers to a lower-level trait.

falsifiability   the property of a hypothesis, or the truth claim of a theory, that is capable of being disconfirmed or disproven by empirical evidence if it is wrong.

fictional finalism   (in individual psychology) the characteristic form of human motivation, driven by striving after goals that may be unreachable.

fixation   (in psychoanalysis) the failure to progress from an earlier stage of psychosexual development, such as the oral stage, anal stage, or phallic stage, or an earlier relationship (compare *regression*).

fixed-interval schedule   (in operant conditioning) a simple reinforcement schedule in which reward follows the first response that the organism makes after a predetermined time interval (compare *fixed-ratio schedule, variable-interval schedule, variable-ratio schedule*).

fixed-ratio schedule   (in operant conditioning) a simple reinforcement schedule in which reward is delivered after the organism has made a specified number of responses (compare *fixed-interval schedule, variable-interval schedule, variable-ratio schedule*).

fixed-role therapy   (in personal construct theory) a form of psychotherapy in which the patient is given a role to play that will entail developing new constructs and abandoning ones that fail to predict.

free association   (in psychoanalysis) a clinical method in which the patient is encouraged to relate, uncensored, all thoughts, feelings, memories, and images that come to mind, however trivial they may seem.

functional analysis   the linking of behaviour to antecedents; the establishment of cause-and-effect relationships.

gene   a segment of chromosomes that carries genetic information and determines heredity. Genes code for sequences of amino acids that form proteins and in so doing control development and metabolism.

generalization   the process by which a learned response is elicited by stimuli dissimilar to the stimulus that originally elicited it. **Response generalization** occurs when different responses are made to the same stimulus situation.

genotype   the genetic constitution or blueprint of an organism (compare *phenotype*).

guilt   a feeling of having committed a wrong or of having failed in an obligation. In psychoanalysis, the experience of guilt is produced by the superego. According to personal construct theory, guilt is aroused when we violate the terms of constructs that define our relationships.

habit   an association between a stimulus and a response. The habit is a product of learning; responses followed by reinforcements become habits.

historical dichotomy   *see dichotomy*.

hoarding character   (in neo-Freudian theory) Fromm's term for a character type who derives security from saving and holding onto possessions and whose miserliness extends to feelings as well as to material things (related to Freud's anal character) (compare *exploitative character, marketing character, necrophilous character, productive character, receptive character*).

hostility   aggressive behaviour marked by unfriendliness or opposition. Kelly saw hostility as an attempt to find evidence of validation of a construct that is a failure.

hypothetico-deductive systems   theoretical systems comprising sets of intervening variables (theoretical concepts) that may be linked to observable events, both antecedents and consequents.

hysteria   a once popular name for a mental disorder characterized by emotional outbursts, fainting, and conversion symptoms such as paralysis. The term has been supplanted in our modern psychiatric lexicon by the term **conversion disorder** (*see* **conversion**).

id (in psychoanalysis) one of the three components of the human mental apparatus. The id is the motivational part of personality and is entirely unconscious. Psychologically, it demands immediate gratification of its wishes to reduce tension and is regulated by the ego.

idealized self a conception of oneself as one would most like to be, in contrast to how one actually is or sees oneself. In the neurotic person, the idealized self is impossibly demanding and submerges the real self (*compare* **despised self**, **real self**).

identification (esp. in psychoanalysis and social cognitive learning theory) the adoption—deliberate or unconscious—of another person's behaviour or ideas. Identification of the child with the same-sex parent is the Freudian basis of the development of the superego.

identity an individual's sense of self. Erikson identified as the major task of adolescence the establishment of a stable sense of identity embodying commitments to an occupation, life with an intimate partner, and an ideology that will underpin the mature developments in personality.

ideology a comprehensive belief system that guides one's life, containing core beliefs about religion, politics, personality morality, and the authorities one recognizes.

idiographic the study of the individual person, stressing the uniqueness of every individual; contrasted with the search for general laws based on the study of many individuals (*compare* **nomothetic**).

implosion an existential term for a feeling of emptiness accompanied by a fear that one will be overwhelmed by reality 'exploding inward'.

inception (in ego psychology) a sex-typed genital sexuality identified by Erikson, occurring in girls and representing a less aggressive way of relating than is seen among boys (*compare* **phallic intrusiveness**).

induction the process of deducing general principles from a series of specific instances (*compare* **deduction**).

inferiority feelings that arise out of the condition of helplessness and dependence that characterizes every human, and that drive efforts to compensate that may be social and appropriate or else neurotic.

inferiority complex (in individual psychology) a neurotic pattern manifesting pervasive feelings of inadequacy, worthlessness, and helplessness.

irrational not based on or using reason or logic. In Freud's view, the neurotic patient's account of his or her symptoms is irrational, since it fails as a rational explanation.

latency (in psychoanalysis) a period of development from the resolution of the Oedipus complex at the end of the phal-lic stage until the onset of the genital stage at puberty, characterized by a decrease in sexual interest.

latent content the instinctual wish as expressed in a dream (*compare* **manifest content**).

L-data Cattell's term for 'everyday-life' data; these are factual data (such as academic or police records) and the observations of others (*compare* **Q-data**).

learned acquired through learning; both habits and drives may be learned.

learned drive a drive such as fear that is acquired through learning and can motivate a variety of behaviour.

learning any lasting change in behaviour resulting from experience. In classical learning theory, the specific processes will be those of conditioning.

lexical hypothesis (in trait theory) the claim that the folk wisdom of languages contains everything we could want to know about personality dimensions.

libido sexual desire; in psychoanalysis, the term refers to the energy of the sexual instinct.

limbic system a set of structures in the brain involved in emotion but also in the regulation of motivated behaviour generally (that is, the four *F*s: fighting, fleeing, feeding, and sexual behaviour).

manifest content the dream as it is experienced and remembered by the dreamer (*compare* **latent content**).

manipulate alter an experimental condition or variable to see how these changes affect the variable under study.

marketing character (in neo-Freudian theory) Fromm's term for a character type who acts as if personality were a commodity to be bought and sold and who moulds him- or herself to fit whatever qualities are demanded by others, with consequent superficiality and lack of individuality (*compare* **exploitative character**, **hoarding character**, **necrophilous character**, **productive character**, **receptive character**).

masculine protest (in individual psychology) beliefs and attitudes in either sex that represent overcompensation for feelings of inferiority arising from perceived lack of masculine attributes and prerogatives.

mechanism (in psychoanalysis) one of two processes in psychoanalysis to account for the development of a neurosis such as hysteria: a motive and a mechanism by which the symptoms become the expression of psychological conflict.

miniature theories any of a number of conceptual schemes devised to account for limited sets of events or restricted sets of phenomena; sensation-seeking is an example. Contrast with inclusive personality theories.

modality (in Erikson's ego psychology) the ways in which societies and cultures shape the modes of expression of psychosexuality in each bodily zone.

mode (in Erikson's ego psychology) each of five **modes of expression** of the erogenous zones of the body: two are incorporative, one is retentive, one is eliminative, and one is intrusive.

monozygotic   denoting twins derived from a single ovum, who are therefore identical (*compare* **dizygotic**).

moral anxiety   the form of anxiety produced by the super-ego, experienced as guilt (*compare* **neurotic anxiety, reality anxiety**).

motivation   the driving force or forces responsible for the initiation, persistence, direction, and vigour of goal-directed behaviour.

motive   the driving force responsible for the occurrence and strength of behaviour.

necrophilous character   (in neo-Freudian theory) Fromm's term for a narcissistic and aggressive character type who has a love of or attraction to death (*compare* **exploitative character, hoarding character, marketing character, productive character, receptive character**).

neurosis   a once common term for a broad category of mental disorders without organic origin, causing crippling anxiety, guilt, and guilt-based symptoms; neurotic disorders include *depression, hysteria, obsession,* and *phobia.* Today the term has been replaced by such terms as *conversion disorder, anxiety disorder,* and *obsessive-compulsive disorder.*

neurotic anxiety   (in psychoanalysis) the anxiety experienced by the ego when dangerous instincts of the id are poised to break through (*compare* **moral anxiety, reality anxiety**).

nomothetic   having to do with the study or discovery of general scientific laws (*compare* **idiographic**).

nonproductive character   (in neo-Freudian theory) Fromm's term for each of five character types who are socially disordered and dependent on mechanisms of escape: the **exploitative character**, the **hoarding character**, the **marketing character**, the **necrophilous character**, and the **receptive character** (*compare* **productive character**).

nonshared environment   the set of environmental influences that are unique to individual members of a family or group (*compare* **shared environment**).

Oedipus complex   (in psychoanalysis) the attachment of the boy of three or four to his mother, childishly sexual, accompanied by wishes to have his father out of the way. This central feature of the phallic stage is resolved by the boy's fear of castration and his renunciation of his sexual interest in his mother; identification with the father and the superego are the result. In the girl, it is the threat not of castration but of *perceived castration* when she becomes aware of her lack of a penis and turns to her father to have vicariously that which she lacks. This resolution is more gradual and less anxiety-inducing than for the boy. Accordingly, the consciences of men and women differ.

ontological insecurity   absence of confidence in one's sense of being or in the reality of one's experience; Laing considered this as a fundamental feature of schizophrenia.

ontological security   confidence in one's sense of being or in the reality of one's experience.

operant   the form of conditioning considered fundamental by Skinner, in which responses act (operate) on the environment to produce reinforcement. **Operant conditioning** is the learning process whereby the frequency of a response increases as a result of reinforcement that is contingent on the response being emitted. What is learned is the relation between the response and its reinforcement (*compare* **classical conditioning, respondent conditioning**).

paradigm   a pattern or example, a framework of assumptions or beliefs within which a particular item of knowledge is located; in personality theory, each of the seven established sets of ideas offering contesting views of the origin and organization of human behaviour.

parataxic distortion   (as seen in Sullivan's theory) the process in which the patient attaches to the analyst attitudes and feelings based on an erroneous identification of the analyst with significant others in the patient's experience.

parataxic thinking   a primitive form of thinking that sees connections between events, though these connections are not linked logically and may be perceived causal connections between events that have simply occurred sequentially and have no real relationship (*compare* **prototaxic thinking, syntaxic thinking**).

participant modelling   (in social cognitive learning theory) a psychotherapy treatment for overcoming fear and achieving self-efficacy, in which the patient begins with observation of a model, proceeds to graded steps with the help of a model, and gradually undergoes the experience on his or her own, without external help.

passive avoidance learning   learning to inhibit a particular response in order to avoid a punishing or aversive stimulus.

Pavlovian conditioning   *another term for* **classical conditioning**.

penis envy   (in psychoanalysis) the sense of deprivation supposedly felt by females upon discovering the anatomic differences between the sexes, developing, during the Oedipal phase, into a desire for a penis (*see* **Oedipus complex**).

permeable   (in personal construct theory) accessible to change when experience shows the way. **Permeable constructs** can be extended to adapt to and incorporate new evidence.

persona   (in analytical psychology) the mask or face that a person presents to others; a 'necessity for social living' that the ego can invest in too heavily to the detriment of personality.

personal unconscious   (in analytic psychology) the name for an individual unconscious containing forgotten or repressed material. It adjoins the conscious ego and may vie with it for control. It is distinguished from the collective unconscious (*compare* **unconscious, collective unconscious**).

personification   (in interpersonal theory) an image, attitude, or interpretation, acquired parataxically, that reflects one's experience in satisfying needs and maintaining security;

personifications associated with positive experiences in need satisfaction will likewise be positive, though they may be oversimplifications or distortions of reality.

petrification   in existential theory, the fear of being turned into something dead or just robotic, without being.

phallic intrusiveness   (in ego psychology) a sex-typed genital sexuality identified by Erikson, developing in boys in the third early childhood stage and representing a more aggressive way of relating than is generally seen among girls of the same age (*compare **inception***).

phenotype   the set of observable characteristics of an individual resulting from the interaction of its genotype with the environment (*compare **genotype***).

pleasure principle   (in psychoanalysis) the governing principle of the id, according to which psychological processes and actions are governed by the gratification of instincts and the avoidance or discharge of unpleasurable tension (*compare **reality principle***).

positivism   The view that every rationally justifiable assertion can be verified scientifically, and that the sciences must be strictly empirical, relying for explanation on processes established by experience.

potentialities   the motives, attributes, and processes that determine behaviour.

pride system   a process of defence that operates by falsely giving oneself status, prestige, or recognition for accomplishments that are not genuine.

primary drive   any innate physiological motive, such as sex, hunger, or self-preservation, that impels an organism to pursue a goal or satisfy a need (*compare **secondary drive***).

primary process   (in psychoanalysis) the primitive mental processes present in the id from birth and seen in the way the unconscious is expressed (*compare **secondary process***).

opposites, principle of   (in analytic psychology) the principle that processes and structures in personality each have their opposites (e.g. consciousness *vs* the unconscious; rational *vs* irrational functions). For normal development, balance is required.

person–situation interaction   see *situation–person interaction*.

process theory   any of a number of theories concerned with studying how behaviour originates, what maintains it, and what factors are responsible for its change; Dollard and Miller's S-R theory is an example (*compare **content theory***).

productive character   (in neo-Freudian theory) Fromm's term for a character type who is loving, committed, ethical, striving, and unwilling to surrender to mechanisms of escape (*compare **nonproductive character***).

projection   (in psychoanalysis) the attribution to others of wishes and feelings that are intolerable to one's own ego, making them appear as external threats that can be defended against.

prototaxic thinking   the initial mental activity of the infant that consists of undifferentiated stream-of-consciousness sensation, without organization or connection (*compare **parataxic thinking**, **syntaxic thinking***).

psychic energy   the energy behind thought, feeling, and action.

psychosocial   having to do with the interrelation of social factors and individual thought and behaviour.

psychoticism   (in Eysenck's type-trait theory) a personality type characterized by traits such as aggressiveness, coldness, impulsiveness, and weak socialization.

P-technique   an idiographic approach to multi-trait personality theory, in which a single subject is studied over many occasions (*compare **R-technique***).

Q-data   Cattell's term for data obtained from responses to questionnaires, subjected to factor analysis (*compare **L-data***).

Q-sort   a test in which the respondent classifies self-descriptive statements into categories ranging from 'most like me' to 'least like me'.

Q-technique   a method of studying the self-concept using the Q-sort; it was adopted by Rogers from a more extensive methodology to study the individual person proposed by Stephenson.

quantification   the process of measuring data and mathematically analyzing them to determine the probability that research findings are not determined by chance.

rational   thinking or behaving reasonably or logically; using or involving deliberate cognitive processes. In analytic psychology, the term denotes functions that call on reasoning, judging, evaluating, abstracting, and generalizing.

reaction formation   (in psychoanalysis) a defence mechanism in which intolerable feelings are made harmless by being turned into their opposites.

reality anxiety   (in psychoanalysis) any anxiety resulting from an external danger that poses a real threat (*compare **moral anxiety**, **neurotic anxiety***).

reality principle   the governing principle of the ego, exercising control over behaviour to meet the conditions imposed by external reality, thereby acting as a moderating influence on the pleasure principle (*compare **pleasure principle***).

real self   a conception of self that is healthy and robust, with an aim toward self-realization (*compare **despised self**, **idealized self***).

receptive character   (in neo-Freudian theory) Fromm's term for a character type who leans on authority for knowledge and help, and on people in general for support, and who usually has a chronic inability to say no to requests and an inordinate fondness for food and drink (*compare **exploitative character**, **hoarding character**, **marketing character**, **necrophilous character**, **productive character***).

reciprocal determinism   (in social cognitive learning theory) the relationship between person and environment, in which behaviour itself influences the person and situation, each of which affects behaviour.

reflex action   a mechanism for discharging tension by means of automatic reflexes, including sucking, sneezing, and coughing.

regression   (in psychoanalysis) a return to an earlier stage of psychosexual development, such as the oral stage, anal stage, or phallic stage, by a child or adult who is traumatized by anxiety (compare *fixation*).

reinforcement   (in Skinnerian behaviourism and in the social learning theories) an event that increases the probability of occurrence of the response preceding it. In S-R theory, reinforcement reduces the stimuli of a drive state.

relatedness   the condition of belonging with or feeling connected to others in a community or group; Fromm saw human existence as a lifelong search for relatedness (compare *rootedness*).

replication   the repetition of an experiment or other research procedure to check the external validity of the results.

representativeness   the degree to which a research sample is typical of the larger population.

respondent conditioning   Skinner's term for *classical conditioning*.

response   any physical or psychological reaction of an organism to a stimulus. Responses are linked to stimuli by reinforcement or (in social cognitive learning theory) the anticipation of reinforcement.

ritual   a strictly defined, meaningful pattern of behaviour, carried out according to rules defined by society and culture, with significant social meaning in a well-defined context.

ritualism   a pathological excess of ritualization that is not mutual and serves only the needs of the individual; adulation of a cult figure is one example.

ritualization   a formalized sequence or pattern of interactions, or a stereotyped behaviour that characterizes interaction, such as the interaction between a mother and her infant.

rootedness   the condition of belonging with or feeling connected to a particular place; Fromm associated the human need for rootedness with the need for *relatedness*.

R-technique   a method of multi-trait personality assessment that measures people on many variables to carry out trait discovery and confirmation (compare *P-technique*).

secondary drive   any acquired non-physiological urge, such as the need for achievement or for affiliation, that impels an organism to pursue a goal or satisfy a need (also called *acquired drive*; compare *primary drive*).

secondary process   (in psychoanalysis) a process that invokes reality testing by means of realistic and appropriate means of attaining need satisfaction (compare *primary process*).

security   comfort and relief from the disapproval of others, achievement of which is the task of the self-dynamism (or self-system).

selective inattention   a defence mechanism that operates by directing attention away from experiences—sounds, sights, words, and ideas—that carry an anxious meaning.

self   (in analytic psychology) the driving force behind behaviour, found midway between the ego and the unconscious; it does not appear until other aspects of personality develop fully and become individuated. In Rogers' person-centred theory, the self consists of perceptions of oneself, one's life and achievements, and the people and situations one encounters, together with the values those things represent to the person.

self-actualization   the motive to realize one's latent potential, understand oneself, and establish oneself as a whole person; Maslow considered it the highest level of psychological development. This is the only motive in Rogers' person-centred theory.

self-concept   (in person-centred theory) one's concept of oneself (see *self*).

self dynamism (also **self system**)   (in Sullivan's theory) the dynamism involved in the organization of all interpersonal behaviour in the pursuit of security, which develops in infancy with the first awareness of approval and disapproval (see also *dynamism*).

self-effacement   the process of seeking affection with behaviour that is endlessly good, loving, and undemanding, as a defence mechanism.

self-efficacy   (in social learning theory) the expectancy that one has the ability to attain desired reinforcements (or avoid unpleasant consequences).

self-reinforcement   (in social cognitive learning theory) reinforcement that is self-administered as we evaluate what we do, feeling good (self-reinforcement) or bad (self-punishment) as a consequence.

sense of identity   one's sense of personal being or independence that emerges (if not blocked by a denying society) as one gains freedom from family in the process of growing up. Identity is a developmental task of adolescence and consists of commitments to an occupation, life partner, and an ideology (see *identity*).

shadow   (in analytic psychology) the part of personality that contains animal instincts that go back to prehistoric origins; these instincts are both evil and vital—they cannot be denied and must be disciplined.

shaping   another term for *successive approximation*.

shared environment   the set of environmental influences affecting all members of a family or group (compare *non-shared environment*).

situation   the specific context in which behaviour takes place.

situation–person interaction   the interaction between one person and another or others in a specific interpersonal situation that will have a unique bearing on the personalities of those involved. Sullivan was among the first to suggest that personality can be observed only in such interactions and is thus not a fixed, inherent property of the person. Social learning theories emphasize that situations strongly influence behaviour, interacting with person variables.

social interest   (in individual psychology) one of two broad kinds of compensation, shown in children who have been taught the importance of co-operation and productive accomplishment (the other is neurotic compensation).

social stimulus value   the effect an individual has on others. Personal impressions of others (their social stimulus value) are not a good basis for personality theory.

stimulus   any event, agent, or influence—internal or external—to which an organism attends and may respond.

style of life   (in individual psychology) each person's unique approach to superiority striving and compensation in living and pursuing goals.

sublimate   (in Sullivan's theory) the child's combining of anxiety-inducing thoughts and behaviour (e.g. bad things they think of doing) with thoughts and acts that gain approval.

substitution   (in psychoanalysis) a defence mechanism that operates by replacing an unattainable or unacceptable instinctual object with one that is more accessible or tolerable; this is a mechanism of the dream work (*see* **dream work**).

successive approximation   a technique in operant conditioning that involves gradually building up a complex response by selectively reinforcing closer and closer approximations of it, beginning with existing elements in the subject's behavioural repertoire, until the required responses are learned (*also called* **shaping**).

superego   (in psychoanalysis) one of three components of the human mental apparatus, it is the moral agency of personality, emerging with the resolution of the Oedipus complex.

syntality   (in Cattell's trait theory) the behaviour of a particular group, as determined by subjecting measures taken on a neighbourhood, society, or nation to factor analysis.

syntaxic thinking   mental activity that is logical, operational, and confirmable by the experience of others (*compare* **parataxic thinking, prototaxic thinking**).

T-data   Cattell's term for data obtained from responses to objective tests, which he considered less susceptible to the inaccuracies produced by the questionnaires used to obtain Q-data. Sources of T-data are tests that disguise what they measure.

teleology   the explanation of phenomena by the purpose they serve rather than by postulated causes.

threat   a feeling of vulnerability to physical or psychological harm. In person-centred theory, threat results when experiences are incongruent with the self.

trait   a consistent pattern of behaviour that a person possessing the characteristic would be likely to display in relevant circumstances. Traits are *dimensional*: they are seen in varying degrees among people.

transcendence   (in Fromm's theory) the need to rise above an animal level of existence and improve life and environment.

transference   the redirection of emotions and attitudes from their original instinctual object to a substitute. In psychoanalysis, the term refers specifically to the transfer of child-like feelings for a parent to the analyst, an essential part of the psychoanalytic process.

type   categories into which we may place people. Introversion and extraversion refer to personality *types*; however, we treat personality types as traits.

unconditioned response   (in classical conditioning) a response such as salivation that occurs automatically to an unconditioned stimulus such as food without any prior process of conditioning.

unconditioned stimulus   (in classical conditioning) a stimulus such as food that automatically elicits an unconditioned response such as salivation without any prior process of conditioning.

unconscious   (in psychoanalysis) a part of the mind containing the instincts and their representative wishes, ideas, and images that are not accessible to consciousness (*see also* **collective unconscious, personal unconscious**).

undoing   (in psychoanalysis) a defence mechanism that neutralizes an unconscionable idea or act by following it with another that negates the first, as if it had never happened.

validation   the act of making something valid, ratifying it, or checking that it satisfies certain standards or conditions. In personal construct theory, validation occurs when predictions of events are confirmed.

variable-interval schedule   (in operant conditioning) a reinforcement schedule in which reward follows the first response that the organism makes after a random time interval (*compare* **fixed-interval schedule, fixed-ratio schedule, variable-ratio schedule**).

variable-ratio schedule   (in operant conditioning) a reinforcement schedule in which reward is delivered after the organism has made a random number of responses. Gambling is based on variable-ratio schedules (*compare* **fixed-interval schedule, fixed-ratio schedule, variable-interval schedule**).

will   the belief that a person decides on and initiates his or her own action; also, the self-determination and understanding that one can make choices.

References

Abramson, L.Y., Seligman, M.E.P., & Teasdale, J. Learned helplessness in humans: Critique and reformulation. *Journal of Abnormal Psychology, 87*, 49–74.

Adler, A. 1927. *Understanding Human Nature*. Longond: G. Allen & Unwin.

———. 1929. *Problems of Neurosis*. London: Kegan Paul.

———. 1930. Individual psychology. In C. Murchison (Ed.), *Psychologies of 1930*. Worcester, MA: Clark University Press.

———. 1931. *What Life Should Mean to You*. New York: Putnam.

———. 1979. *Superiority and Social Interest*. 3rd edn. H.L. & R.R. Ansbacher, Eds New York: Norton.

Adorno, T.W., Frenkel-Brunswik, E., Levinson, D.J., & Sanford, R.N. 1950. *The Authoritarian Personality*. New York: Norton.

Allport, G.W. 1928. A test for ascendence-submission. *Journal of Abnormal and Social Psychology, 23*, 118–36.

———. 1937. *Personality: A Psychological Interpretation*. New York: Holt, p. 295.

———. 1954. *The Nature of Prejudice*. Cambridge, MA: Addison-Wesley.

———. 1955. *Becoming: Basic Considerations for a Psychology of Personality*. New Haven: Yale University Press.

———. 1961. *Pattern and Growth in Personality*. New York: Holt, Rinehart and Winston.

———. 1965. *Letters from Jenny*. New York: Harcourt, Brace Jovanovich.

———. 1967. Autobiography. In E.G. Boring & G. Lindzey (Eds), *A History of Psychology in* Autobiography. Vol. 5. New York: Appleton-Century-Crofts. Excerpts printed with permission of Robert Allport.

Allport, G.W., & Odbert, H.S. 1936. Trait-names: A psycho-lexical study. *Psychological Monographs, 47*, 211, 1–71.

Allport, G.W., & Ross, J.M. 1967. Personal religious orientation and prejudice. *Journal of Personality and Social Psychology, 5*, 432–43.

Allport, G.W., Vernon, P.E., & Lindzey, G. 1960. *A Study of Values*. 3rd edn. Boston: Houghton Mifflin.

American Psychiatric Association. 1980. *Diagnostic and Statistical Manual for Mental Disorders*. 3rd edn (DSM-III). Washington, DC: American Psychiatric Association.

American Psychiatric Association. 1994. *Diagnostic and Statistical Manual of Mental Disorders*. 4th Edn. (DSM-IV). Washington, DC: Author.

American Psychological Association. 1981. Awards for distinguished scientific contributions: 1980. *American Psychologist, 36*, 27–42.

Anderson, C., John, O.P., Keltner, D., & Kring, A.M. 2001. Who attains social status? Effects of personality and physical attractiveness in social groups. *Journal of Personality and Social Psychology, 81*, 116–32.

Andersson, O. 1979. A supplement to Freud's case history of 'Frau Emmy v. N.' in Studies on Hysteria. *Scandinavian Psychoanalytic Review, 2*, 5–15.

Aronson, E. 1958. The need for achievement as measured by graphic expression. In J.W. Atkinson (Ed.), *Motives in Fantasy, Action, and Society*. Princeton, NJ: Van Nostrand.

Atkinson, J.W. (Ed.) 1958. *Motives in Fantasy, Action, and Society*. Princeton, NJ: Van Nostrand.

———. 1958. Thematic apperceptive measurement of motives within the context of a theory of motivation. In J.W. Atkinson (Ed.), *Motives in Fantasy, Action, and Society*. Princeton, NJ: Van Nostrand.

Atkinson, J.W., & Litwin, G.H. 1960. Achievement motive and test anxiety conceived as motive to approach success and motive to avoid failure. *Journal of Abnormal and Social Psychology, 60*, 52–63.

Atkinson, J.W., & McClelland, D.C. 1948. The projective expression of needs. II. The effect of different intensities of the hunger drive on thematic apperception. *Journal of Experimental Psychology, 38*, 643–58.

Auden, W.H. 1976. *Collected Poems*. London: Faber and Faber.

Bak, S. 2002. Lecture to the International Colloquy about the Holocaust, at the European Parliament, Strasbourg, France.

Bandura, A. 1959. *Adolescent Aggression*. New York: Ronald.

———. 1969. *Principles of Behavior Modification*. New York: Holt, Rinehart, and Winston.

———. 1973. *Aggression: A Social Learning Analysis*. Englewood Cliffs, NJ: Prentice-Hall.

———. 1977a. *Social Learning Theory*. Englewood Cliffs, NJ: Prentice-Hall.

———. 1977b. Self-efficacy: Toward a unifying theory of behavioral change. *Psychological Review, 84*, 191–215.

———. 1978. The self system in reciprocal determinism. *American Psychologist, 33*, 344–58.

———. 1982a. The psychology of chance encounters and life paths. *American Psychologist, 37*, 747–55.

———. 1982b. Self-efficacy mechanism in human agency. *American Psychologist, 37*, 122–47.

———. 1986. *Social Foundations of Thought and Action: A Social Cognitive Theory*. Englewood Cliffs, NJ: Prentice-Hall, pp. 347–8.

———. 1990. Mechanisms of moral disengagement. In W. Reich (Ed.), *Origins of Terrorism: Psychologies, Ideologies, Theologies, States of Mind*. Cambridge, UK: Cambridge University Press.

———. 1991. Human agency: The rhetoric and the reality. *American Psychologist, 44*, 1175–87.

———. 1999. Social cognitive theory of personality. In L.A. Pervin & O.P. John (Eds), *Handbook of Personality: Theory and Research*. New York: Guilford.

———. 2004. The role of selective moral disengagement in terrorism and counterterrorism. In F.M. Moghaddam & A.J. Marsella (Eds), *Understanding Terrorism: Psychosocial Roots, Consequences, and Interventions*. Washington, DC: American Psychological Association.

Bandura, A., Adams, N.E., & Beyer, J. 1977. Cognitive processes mediating behavioral change. *Journal of Personality and Social Psychology, 35*, 125–39.

Bandura, A., Blanchard, E.B., & Ritter, B. 1969. The relative efficacy of desensitization and modeling approaches for inducing behavioral, affective, and attitudinal changes. *Journal of Personality and Social Psychology, 13*, 173–99.

Bandura, A., & Kupers, C.J. 1964. The transmission of patterns of self-reinforcement through modeling. *Journal of Abnormal and Social Psychology, 69*, 1–9.

Bandura, A., & Rosenthal, T.L. 1966. Vicarious classical conditioning as a function of arousal level. *Journal of Personality and Social Psychology, 3*, 54–62.

Bandura, A., Ross, D., & Ross, S.A. 1961. Transmission of aggression through imitation of aggressive models. *Journal of Abnormal and Social Psychology, 63*, 575–82.

———, ———, & ———. 1963. Imitation of film-mediated aggressive models. *Journal of Abnormal and Social Psychology, 66*, 3–11.

Bandura, A., & Walters, R.H. 1963. *Social Learning and Personality Development*. New York: Holt, Rinehart and Winston.

Battista, J., & Almond, R. 1973. The development of meaning in life. *Psychiatry, 36*, 409–27.

Begg, L., Armour, V., & Kerr, T. 1985. On believing what we remember. *Canadian Journal of Behavioral Science, 17*, 199–214.

Benjamin, Jr, L.T., & Dixon, D.N. 1996. Dream analysis by mail: An American woman seeks Freud's advice. *American Psychologist, 51*, 461–8.

Berger, R. 1977. *Psychosis: The Circularity of Experience*. San Francisco: Freeman.

Berndt, T.J. 1986. Children's comments about their friendships. In M. Perlmutter (Ed.), *Cognitive Perspectives on Children's Social and Behavioral Development: The Minnesota Symposium on Child Psychology*. Vol. 18, pp. 189–212. Hillsdale, NJ: Erlbaum.

Bettelheim, B. 1983. *Freud and Man's Soul*. New York: Knopf.

Binswanger, L. 1963. *Being-in-the-World: Selected Papers of Ludwig Binswanger*. New York: Basic Books.

Block, J. 1978. *The Q-sort Method in Personality Assessment and Psychiatric Research*. Palo Alto, CA: Consulting Psychologists Press. First published in 1961.

———. 1995. A contrarian view of the five-factor approach to personality description. *Psychological Bulletin, 117*, 187–215.

Block, J., Block, J.H., & Keyes, S. 1988. Longitudinally foretelling drug usage in adolescence: Early childhood personality and environmental precursors. *Child Development, 59*, 336–55.

Block, J., Gjerde, P.F., & Block, J.H. 1991. Personality antecedents of depressive tendencies in 18-year-olds: A prospective study. *Journal of Personality and Social Psychology, 60*, 726–38.

Bonebright, C.A., Clay, D.L., & Ankenmann, R.D. 2000. The relationship of workaholism with work–life conflict, life satisfaction, and purpose in life. *Journal of Counseling Psychology, 47*, 469–77.

Bonss, W. 1984. Critical theory and empirical social research. In E. Fromm, *The Working Class in Weimar Germany*, W. Bonss (Ed.). Cambridge, MA: Harvard University Press.

Borgatta, E.F. 1964. The structure of personality characteristics. *Behavioral Science, 12*, 8–17.

Boring, E.G. 1950. Great men and scientific progress. *Proceedings of the American Philosophical Society, 94*, 339–51.

Bottome, P. 1939. *Alfred Adler*. New York: G.P. Putnam's Sons.

Bowers, K.S. 1984. On being unconsciously influenced and informed. In K.S. Bowers & D. Meichenbaum (Eds), *The Unconscious Reconsidered*. New York: Wiley-Interscience.

———. 1987. Revisioning the unconscious. *Canadian Psychology, 28*, 93–104.

Bowers, K.S., Farvolden, P., & Mermigis, L. 1995. Intuitive antecedents of insight. In S.M. Smith, T.M. Ward, & R.A. Finke (Eds), *The Creative Cognition Approach*. Cambridge, MA: MIT Press.

Bowers, K.S., Regehr, G., Balthazaard, C., & Parker, K. 1990. Intuition in the context of discovery. *Cognitive Psychology, 22*, 72–110.

Bretherton, I. 1993. From dialogue to internal working models: The co-construction of self in relationships. In C.A. Nelson (Ed.), *Minnesota Symposium on Child Development: Memory and Affect in Development*. Vol. 26. Hillsdale, NJ: Erlbaum.

Breuer, J., & Freud, S. 1955. *Studies on Hysteria*. In S. Freud, *Standard Edition*. Vol. 2. London: Hogarth. First published in 1895.

Brody, N. 1988. *Personality: In Search of Individuality*. San Diego: Harcourt Brace Jovanovich.

Brown, A.S., & Halliday, H.E. 1990. Crypomnesia and source memory difficulties. Paper presented at meeting of the Southwestern Psychological Association.

Brown, J.S. 1940. Generalized approach and avoidance responses in relation to conflict behavior. Unpublished PhD dissertation, Yale University.

Brown, R. 1965. *Social Psychology*. New York: The Free Press.

Bushman, B.J., & Huesmann, L.R. 2001. In D.G. Singer & J.L. Singer (Eds), *Handbook of Children and the Media*. Thousand Oaks, CA: Sage, pp. 223–54.

Bushnell, I.W.R., Sai, F., & Mullin, J.T. 1989. Neonatal recognition of the mother's face. *British Journal of Developmental Psychology, 7*, 3–15.

Buss, D.M. 2000. The evolution of happiness. *American Psychologist, 55*, 15–23.

Butler, J.M., & Haigh, G.V. 1954. Changes in the relation between self-concepts and ideal concepts consequent upon client-centered counseling. In C.R. Rogers & R.F. Dymond (Eds), *Psychotherapy and Personality Change: Coordinated Studies in the Client-Centered Approach.* Chicago: University of Chicago Press.

Cameron, N. 1959. Paranoid conditions and paranoia. In S. Arieti (Ed.), *American Handbook of Psychiatry.* New York: Basic Books.

Canada. Parliament. House of Commons. Standing Committee on Communications and Culture. 1993. *Television Violence: Fraying Our Social Fabric—Report of the Standing Committee on Communications and Culture.*

Caplan, P.J. 1979. Erikson's concept of inner space: A data-based reevaluation. *American Journal of Orthopsychiatry, 49*, 100–8.

Carlson, R. 1980. Studies of Jungian typology. II. Representations of the personal world. *Journal of Personality and Social Psychology, 38*, 801–10.

Carlson, R., & Levy, N. 1973. Studies of Jungian typology. I. Memory, social perception, and social action. *Journal of Personality, 41*, 559–76.

Cattell, R.B. 1943. The description of personality: Basic traits resolved into clusters. *Journal of Abnormal and Social Psychology, 38*, 476–506.

———. 1944. *The Culture Free Test of Intelligence.* Champaign, IL: Institute for Personality and Ability Testing.

———. 1946. *The Description and Measurement of Personality.* New York: World Book.

———. 1949. *An Introduction to Personality Study.* London: Hutchinson's University Library.

———. 1950. *Personality: A Systematic, Theoretical, and Factual Study.* New York: McGraw-Hill.

———. 1957. *Personality and Motivation Structure and Measurement.* New York: World.

———. 1959. Personality theory growing from multivariate quantitative research. In S. Koch (Ed.), *Psychology: A Study of a Science.* Vol. 3. New York: McGraw-Hill.

———. 1965. *The Scientific Analysis of Personality.* Baltimore, MD: Penguin.

———. 1973. *Personality and Mood by Questionnaire.* San Francisco: Jossey-Bass.

———. 1979. *Personality and Learning Theory: The Structure of Personality in its Environment.* Vol. 1. New York: Springer.

———. 1980. *Personality and Learning Theory: A Systems Theory of Maturation and Structured Learning.* Vol. 2. New York: Springer.

Cattell, R.B., Blewett, D.B., & Beloff, J.R. 1955. The inheritance of personality. *American Journal of Human Genetics, 7*, 122–46.

Cattell, R.B., Eber, H.W., & Tatsuoka, M.M. 1977. *Handbook for the 16 Personality Factor Questionnaire.* Champaign, IL: IPAT.

Cattell, R.B., Saunders, D.R., & Stice, G.F. 1953. The dimensions of syntality in small groups. *Human Relations, 6*, 331–56.

Cattell, R.B., & Wispé, L.G. 1948. The dimension's of syntality in small groups. *Journal of Social Psychology, 28*, 57–78.

Chamberlain, K., & Zika, S. 1988. Religiosity, life meaning, and well-being: Some relationships in a sample of women. *Journal for the Scientific Study of Religion, 27*, 411–20.

Chamove, A.S., Eysenck, H.J., & Harlow, H.F. 1972. Personality in monkeys: Factor analysis of rhesus social behavior. *Quarterly Journal of Experimental Psychology, 24*, 496–504.

Chance, J.E. 1972. Academic correlates and maternal antecedents of children's belief in external or internal control of reinforcement. In J.B. Rotter, J.E. Chance, & E.J. Phares (Eds), *Applications of a Social Learning Theory of Personality.* New York: Holt, Rinehart and Winston.

Chomsky, N. 1959. Review of Skinner's *Verbal Behavior. Language, 35*, 26–58.

Claridge, G.S. 1967. *Personality and Arousal.* Oxford: Pergamon.

Clark, L.A., Kochanska, G., & Ready, R. 2000. Mothers' personality and its interaction with child temperament as predictors of parenting behavior. *Journal of Personality and Social Psychology, 79*, 274–85.

Cloninger, C.R., Adolfsson, R., & Svrakic, D.M. 1996. Mapping genes for human personality. *Nature Genetics, 12*, 3–4.

Cloninger, C.R., Bohman, M., & Sigvardsson, S. 1981. Inheritance of alcohol abuse: Cross-fostering analysis of adopted men. *Archives of General Psychiatry, 38*, 861–69.

Clower, C.E., & Bothwell, R.K. 2001. An exploratory study of the relationship between the Big Five and inmate recidivism. *Journal of Research in Personality, 35*, 231–7.

Coles, R. 1970. *Erik Erikson: The Growth of His Work.* Boston: Little, Brown.

———. 2003. *Children of Crisis. Selections from the Pulitzer Prize-Winning Five-Volume Children of Crisis Series.* Boston: Little, Brown.

Commager, H.S. 1950. *The American Mind.* New Haven: Yale University Press.

Coolidge, F.L., Moor, C.J., Yamazaki, T.G., Stewart, S.E., & Segal, D.L. On the relationship between Karen Horney's tripartite neurotic type theory and personality disorder features. *Personality and Individual Differences, 30*, 1387–1400.

Cornblatt, B., & Erlenmeyer-Kimling, L.E. 1985. Global attentional deviance in children at risk for schizophrenia: Specificity and predictive validity. *Journal of Abnormal Psychology, 94*, 470–86.

Costa, P.T., Jr, & McCrae, R.R. 1978. Objective personality assessment. In M. Storandt, I.C. Siegler, & M.F. Elias (Eds), *The Clinical Psychology of Aging.* NY: Plenum.

———, & ———. 1992. *Revised NEO Personality Inventory (NEO-PI-R) and NEO Five-Factor Inventory (NEO-FFI)*

Professional Manual. Odessa, FL: Psychological Assessment Resources, Inc.

Craig-Bray, L., & Adams, G.R. 1986. Different methodologies in the assessment of identity: Congruence between self-report and interview techniques? *Journal of Youth and Adolescence, 17*, 173–87.

Craighead, L.W., Craighead, W.E., Kazdin, A.E., & Mahoney, M.J. (Eds). 1994. *Cognitive and Behavioral Interventions: An Empirical Approach to Mental Health Problems*. Boston: Allyn and Bacon.

Crandall, V.C., & Crandall, B.W. 1983. Maternal and childhood behaviors as antecedents of internal–external control perceptions in young adulthood. In H.M. Lefcourt (Ed.), *Research with the Locus of Control Construct. Developments and Social Problems*. Vol. 2. New York: Academic Press.

Crowne, D.P. 1962. Review of S. Schachter, *The Psychology of Affiliation. Journal of Individual Psychology, 18*, 92–4.

———. 1979. *The Experimental Study of Personality*. Hillsdale, NJ: Erlbaum.

———. 2000. Social desirability. In American Psychological Association, *Encyclopedia of Psychology*, A.E. Kazdin (Ed.). New York: Oxford University Press.

Crowne, D.P., & Liverant, S. 1963. Conformity under varying conditions of personal commitment. *Journal of Abnormal and Social Psychology, 66*, 547–55.

Crowne, D.P., & Marlowe, D. 1960. A new scale of social desirability independent of psychopathology. *Journal of Consulting and Clinical Psychology, 24*, 349–54

Crowne, D.P., & Strickland, B.R. 1961. The conditioning of verbal behavior as a function of the need for social approval. *Journal of Abnormal and Social Psychology, 66*, 395–401.

Darwin, C. 1871. *The Descent of Man and Selection in Relation to Sex*. London: John Murray.

Deal, J.E. 1996. Marital conflict and differential treatment of siblings. *Family Process, 35*, 333–46.

Debats, D.L., van der Lubbe, P.M., & Wezeman, F.R.A. 1993. On the psychometric properties of the Life Regard Index (LRI): A measure of meaningful life. *Personality and Individual Differences, 14*, 337–45.

Deci, E.L., & Ryan, R.M. A motivational approach to self: Integration in personality. In R. Diestbier (Ed.), *Nebraska Symposium on Motivation: 1990*. Lincoln, NE: University of Nebraska Press.

———, & ———. 2000. The 'what' and 'why' of goal pursuits: Human needs and the self-determination of behavior. *Psychological Inquiry, 11*, 227–68.

deWaal, F.B.M. 1996. *Good-Natured: The Origins of Right and Wrong in Humans and Other Animals*. Cambridge, MA: Harvard University Press.

Dickinson, A. 1987. Animal conditioning and learning theory. In H.J. Eysenck & I. Martin (Eds), *Theoretical Foundations of Behavior Theory*. New York: Plenum.

Diener, E. 2000. Subjective well-being. *American Psychologist, 55*, 34–43.

Digman, J.M. 1990. Personality structure: Emergence of the five-factor model. *Annual Review of Psychology, 41*, 417–40.

Dollard, J. 1942. *Victory over Fear*. New York: Reynal & Hitchcock.

———. 1943. *Fear in Battle*. New Haven: Yale University Press.

———. 1957. *Caste and Class in a Southern Town*. 3rd edn. New York: Doubleday Anchor. First published in 1937.

Dollard, J., Auld, F., & White, A.M. 1953. *Steps in Psychotherapy*. New York: Macmillan.

Dollard, J., Doob, L.W., Miller, N.E., Mowrer, O.H., & Sears, R.R. 1939. *Frustration and Aggression*. New Haven: Yale University Press, 1939.

Dollard, J., & Miller, N.E. 1950. *Personality and Psychotherapy. An Analysis in Terms of Learning, Thinking, and Culture*. New York: McGraw-Hill. Excerpts reprinted by permission of the publisher.

Du Caju, M., Fraile, J.C., Gonzalez de Chavez, M., and Gutierrez, M. 2000. Comparative study of the therapeutic factors of group therapy in schizophrenic inpatients and outpatients. *Group Analysis, 33*, 251–64.

Dunn, J., & Plomin, R. 1990. *Separate Lives: Why Siblings Are So Different*. New York: Basic Books.

Eastman, C., & Marzillier, J.S. 1984. Theoretical and methodological difficulties in Bandura's self-efficacy theory. *Cognitive Therapy and Research, 8*, 213–29.

Ebstein, R.P., & Belmaker, R.Y. 1997. Saga of an adventure gene: Novelty seeking, substance abuse and the dopamine D4 receptor (D4DR) exon III repeat polymorphism. *Molecular Psychiatry, 2*, 381–4.

Ebstein, R.P., Novick, O., Umansky, R., Priel, B., Osher, Y., Blaine, D., Bennett, E.R., Nemanov, L., Katz, M., & Belmaker, R.Y. 1996. Dopamine D4 receptor (D4DR) exon III polymorphism associated with the human personality trait novelty seeking. *Nature Genetics, 12*, 78–80.

Einstein, A. 1933. *Why War?* Letter to Professor Freud. International Institute of Intellectual Cooperation, League of Nations.

Eisenberg, N., Spinrad, T.L., & Cumberland, A. 1998. The socialization of emotion: Reply to commentaries. *Psychological Inquiry, 9*, 317–33.

Ellenberger, H.F. 1970. *The Discovery of the Unconscious: The History and Evolution of Dynamic Psychiatry*. New York: Basic Books.

Erikson, E. 1949. Ruth Benedict. In A.L. Kroeber (Ed.), *Ruth Fulton Benedict, A Memorial*. New York: Viking Fund, pp. 14–17.

———. 1958. *Young Man Luther*. New York: Norton.

———. 1963. *Childhood and Society*. 2nd edn. New York: Norton. Excerpts Copyright 1950, © 1963 by W.W. Norton & Company, Inc., renewed © 1978, 1991 by Erik

H. Erikson, used by permission of W.W. Norton & Company, Inc.; reprinted by permission of the Random House Group Ltd.

———. 1964. *Insight and Responsibility.* New York: Norton.

———. 1966. The ontogeny of ritualization in man. *Philosophical Transactions of the Royal Society of London*, Series B, Vol. CCLI, No. 772.

———. 1968. *Identity: Youth and Crisis.* New York: Norton.

———. 1969. *Gandhi's Truth: On the Origins of Militant Nonviolence.* New York: Norton.

———. 1975. *Life History and the Historical Moment.* New York: Norton.

———. 1977. *Toys and Reasons: Stages in the Ritualization of Experience.* New York: Norton.

———. 1985. *The Life Cycle Completed.* New York: Norton.

Erikson, E., Erikson, J., & Kivnick, H. 1994. *Vital Involvement in Old Age.* New York: Norton.

Evans, R.I. 1966. *Dialogue with Erich Fromm.* New York: Harper & Row.

Eysenck, H.J. 1947. *Dimensions of Personality.* London: Routledge & Kegan Paul.

———. 1952. *The Scientific Study of Personality.* London: Routledge & Kegan Paul.

———. 1953a. *The Structure of Human Personality.* London: Methuen. (Revised, 1970).

———. 1953b. *Uses and Abuses of Psychology.* Baltimore: Penguin.

———. 1957a. *Sense and Nonsense in Psychology.* Baltimore: Penguin.

———. 1957b. *The Dynamics of Anxiety and Hysteria: An Experimental Application of Modern Learning Theory to Psychiatry.* New York: Praeger.

———. 1967. *The Biological Basis of Personality.* Springfield, IL: Charles C. Thomas.

———. 1972. *Psychology Is About People.* New York: Penguin.

———. 1980. Autobiographical essay. In G. Lindzey (Ed.), *A History of Psychology in Autobiography.* Vol. 7. San Francisco: W.H. Freeman.

——— (Ed.). 1981. *A Model for Personality.* Berlin: Springer-Verlag.

———. 1982. Autobiography. In H.J. Eysenck (Ed.), *Personality, Genetics, and Behavior: Selected Papers.* New York: Praeger, pp. 287–98.

———. 1991. Dimension of personality: 16, 5, or 3?—Criteria for a taxonomic paradigm. *Personality and Individual Differences, 12,* 773–90.

Eysenck, H.J., & Eysenck, M.J. 1983. *Mindwatching: Why People Behave the Way They Do.* New York: Garden/Doubleday.

———, & ———. 1985. *Personality and Individual Differences.* New York: Plenum.

Eysenck, H.J., & Eysenck, S.B.G. 1969. *Personality Structure and Measurement.* San Diego: Robert R. Knapp.

———, & ———. 1975. *Manual of the Eysenck Personality Questionnaire.* London: Hodder & Stoughton (San Diego: Edits, 1975).

———, & ———. 1976. *Psychoticism as a Dimension of Personality.* New York: Crane, Russak.

Falconer, D.S. 1981. *Introduction to Quantitative Genetics.* London: Longman.

Faraone, S.V., Taylor, L., & Tsuang, M.T. 2002. The molecular genetics of schizophrenia: an emerging consensus. Expert reviews in molecular medicine, 23 May, http://www.expertreviews.org/02004751h.htm.

Feldman Barrett, L., Williams, N.L., & Fong, G.T. 2002. Defensive verbal behavior assessment. *Personality and Social Psychology Bulletin, 28,* 776–88.

Ferster, C.B., & Skinner, B.F. 1957. *Schedules of Reinforcement.* New York: Appleton-Century-Crofts.

Fiske, D.W. 1949. Consistency of the factorial structures of personality ratings from different sources. *Journal of Abnormal and Social Psychology, 44,* 329–44.

Fowler, J.C., & Perry, J.C. 2005. Clinical tasks of the dynamic interview. *Psychiatry, 68,* 316–36.

Frankl, V. 1963. *Man's Search for Meaning: An Introduction to Logotherapy.* New York: Washington Square Press.

Franks, C.M. 1956. Conditioning and personality: A study of normal and neurotic subjects. *Journal of Abnormal and Social Psychology, 52,* 143–50.

———. 1957. Personality factors and the rate of conditioning. *British Journal of Psychology, 48,* 119–26.

———. 1963. Personality and eyeblink conditioning seven years later. *Acta Psychologica, 21,* 295–312.

Freese, J., Powell, B., & Steelman, L.C. 1999. Rebel without a cause or effect: Birth order and social attitudes. *American Sociological Review, 64,* 207–31.

French, E.G. 1956. Motivation as a variable in work-partner selection. *Journal of Abnormal and Social Psychology, 53,* 96–9.

Freud, A. 1946. *The Ego and the Mechanisms of Defense.* New York: International Universities Press, 1946. First published in 1936.

———. 1965. *Normality and Pathology in Childhood.* In *The Writings of Anna Freud.* Vol. 6. New York: International Universities Press.

———. 1966a. *The Ego and the Mechanisms of Defence.* Rev. edn. New York: International Universities Press. First published in 1936.

———. 1966b. Links between Hartmann's ego psychology and the child analyst's thinking. In R.M. Loewenstein, L.M. Newman, M. Schur, & A.J. Solnit (Eds), *Psychoanalysis—A General Psychology.* New York: International Universities Press.

Freud, E.L. (Ed.). 1961. *Letters of Sigmund Freud, 1873–1939.* London: Hogarth.

Freud, S. 1953a. Three essays on sexuality. In S. Freud, *Standard Edition.* Vol. 7. London: Hogarth. First published in 1905.

———. 1953b. *The Interpretation of Dreams.* In S. Freud, *Standard Edition.* Vol. 4. London: Hogarth. First published in 1900.

———. 1955. Analysis of a phobia in a five-year-old boy. In S. Freud, *Standard Edition.* Vol. 10. London: Hogarth. First published in 1909.

———. 1957. On the history of the psycho-analytic movement. In S. Freud, *Standard Edition.* Vol. 14. London: Hogarth. First published in 1914.

———. 1959a. Why war? Letter to Professor Einstein. In J. Strachey (Ed.), *Collected Papers of Sigmund Freud.* Vol. 5. New York: Basic Books.

———. 1959b. The question of lay analysis. In S. Freud, *Standard Edition.* Vol. 20. London: Hogarth. First published in 1926.

———. 1961a. *The Ego and the Id.* In S. Freud, *Standard Edition.* Vol. 19. London: Hogarth Press. First published in 1923.

———. 1961b. Letter to the Burgomaster of Příbor. In S. Freud, *Standard Edition.* Vol. 21. London: Hogarth. Original dated October 25, 1931.

———. 1962a. Further remarks on the neuro-psychoses of defence. In S. Freud, *Standard Edition.* Vol. 3. London: Hogarth. First published in 1896.

———. 1962b. Screen memories. In S. Freud, *Standard Edition.* Vol. 3. London: Hogarth. First published in 1899.

———. 1964a. Analysis terminable and interminable. In S. Freud, *Standard Edition.* Vol. 23. London: Hogarth. First published in 1937.

———. 1964b. The question of a *Weltanschauung. New Introductory Lectures on Psycho-Analysis.* In S. Freud, *Standard Edition.* Vol. 22. London: Hogarth. First published in 1932.

———. 1964c. *An Outline of Psychoanalysis.* In S. Freud, *Standard Edition.* Vol. 23. London: Hogarth. First published in 1940.

———. 1971. *The Psychopathology of Everyday Life.* Trans. by A. Tyson. New York: Norton. First published in 1901.

Friedman, I. 1955. Phenomenal, ideal and projected conceptions of self. *Journal of Abnormal and Social Psychology, 51,* 611–15.

Friedrich, L.K., and Stein, A.H. 1973. Aggressive and prosocial television programs and the natural behavior of preschool children. *Monographs of the Society for Research in Child Development, 38,* (4, Serial No. 151).

Fromm, E. 1947. *Man for Himself.* New York: Rinehart.

———. 1951. *An Introduction to the Understanding of Dreams, Fairy Tales, and Myths.* New York: Holt, Rinehart, & Winston.

———. 1955. *The Sane Society.* New York: Rinehart.

———. 1956. *The Art of Loving.* New York: Bantam.

———. 1968. *The Revolution of Hope.* New York: Harper & Row.

———. 1969. *Escape from Freedom.* New York: Avon. First published in 1941. Excerpts © 1941, 1969 by Erich Fromm, reprinted by permission of Henry Holt and Company.

———. 1970. *The Crisis of Psychoanalysis: Essays on Freud, Marx, and Social Psychology.* Greenwich, CT: Fawcett.

———. 1973. *The Anatomy of Human Destructiveness.* New York: Holt.

———. 1976. *To Have or To Be.* New York: Harper and Row.

———. 1984. *The Working Class in Weimar Germany: A Psychological and Sociological Study.* W. Bonss (Ed.). Cambridge, MA: Harvard University Press. Trans. by B. Weinberger.

———. [with H.J. Schultz] 1986. *For the Love of Life.* New York: Macmillan.

Fromm, E., & Maccoby, M. 1970. *Social Character in a Mexican Village. A Sociopsychoanalytic Study.* Englewood Cliffs, NJ: Prentice-Hall.

Fulker, D.W., Eysenck, S.B.G., & Zuckerman, M. 1980. The genetics of sensation seeking. *Journal of Personality Research, 14,* 261–81.

Funder, D.C. 2004. *The Personality Puzzle.* 3rd edn. New York: Norton.

Funder, D.C., Block, J.H., & Block, J. 1983. Delay of gratification: Some longitudinal personality correlates. *Journal of Personality and Social Psychology, 44,* 1198–213.

Galton, F. 1875. The history of twins as a criterion of the relative powers of nature and nurture. *Fraser's Magazine, 92,* 566–76.

———. 1884. Measurement of character. *Fortnightly Review, 36,* 179–85.

Gay, P. 1988. *Freud: A Life for Our Time.* New York, Norton.

Geen, R.G. 1984. Preferred stimulation levels in introverts and extraverts: Effects on arousal and performance. *Journal of Personality and Social Psychology, 46,* 1302–12.

Gendlin, E.T., & Tomlinson, T.M. 1967. The process conception and its measurement. In C.R. Rogers, E.T. Gendlin, D.J. Kiesler, & C.B. Truax (Eds), *The Psychotherapeutic Relationship and Its Impact: A Study of Psychotherapy with Schizophrenics.* Madison: University of Wisconsin Press.

Glucksberg, S., & King, L.J. 1967. Motivated forgetting mediated by implicit verbal chaining? A laboratory analog of repression. *Science, 158,* 517–19.

Goldberg, L.R. 1981. Language and individual differences: The search for universals in personality lexicons. In L. Wheeler (Ed.), *Review of Personality and Social Psychology.* Beverly Hills, CA: Sage.

———. 1993. The structure of phenotypic personality traits. *American Psychologist, 48,* 26–34.

Goldstein, K. 1939. *The Organism.* New York: American Book.

Gore, P.M., & Rotter, J.B. 1963. A personality correlate of social action. *Journal of Personality, 31,* 58–64.

Gottesman, I.I. 1991. *Schizophrenia Genesis: The Origins of Madness.* New York: W.H. Freeman.

Gottesman, I.I., & Shields, J. 1982. *Schizophrenia: The Epigenetic Puzzle.* Cambridge: Cambridge University Press.

Gray, J.A. 1982. *The Neuropsychology of Anxiety: An Inquiry into the Functions of the Septal-Hippocampal System.* Oxford: Clarendon.

———. 1987. Perspectives on anxiety and impulsivity: A commentary. *Journal of Research in Personality, 21,* 495–509.

————. 1991. The neuropsychology of temperament. In J. Strelau & A. Angleitner (Eds), *Explorations in Temperament: International Perspectives on Theory and Measurement*. New York: Plenum.

Greenspoon, J. 1955. The reinforcing effect of two spoken sounds on the frequency of two responses. *American Journal of Psychology, 68*, 409–16.

Grimes, K., & Walker, E.F. 1994. Childhood emotional expressions, educational attainment, and age at onset of illness of schizophrenia. *Journal of Abnormal Psychology, 103*, 784–90.

Gusella, J.F. 1987. Huntington's disease (HD). In G. Adelman (Ed.), *Encyclopedia of Neuroscience*. Vol. 1. Boston: Birkhäuser Boston.

Hall, C.S., Lindzey, G., & Campbell, J.B. 1998. *Theories of Personality*. 4th edn. New York: Wiley.

Hall, C.S., & Nordby, V.J. 1973. *A Primer of Jungian Psychology*. New York: New American Library.

Hamsher, J.H., Geller, J.D., & Rotter, J.B. 1968. Interpersonal trust, internal–external control, and the Warren Commission report. *Journal of Personality and Social Psychology, 9*, 210–15.

Harlow, L.L., Newcomb, M.D., & Bender, P.M. 1986. Depression, self-derogation, substance use, and suicide ideation: Lack of purpose in life as a mediational factor. *Journal of Clinical Psychology, 42*, 5–21.

Harrington, D.M., Block, J.H., & Block, J. 1987. Testing aspects of Carl Rogers' theory of creative environments: Child-rearing antecedents of creative potential in young adolescents. *Journal of Personality and Social Psychology, 52*, 851–6.

Harris, B. 1979. Whatever happened to little Albert? *American Psychologist, 34*, 151–60.

Harris, J.R. 1995. Where is the child's environment? A group socialization theory of development. *Psychological Review, 102*, 458–89.

————. 1998. *The Nurture Assumption: Why Children Turn Out the Way They Do*. New York: Free Press.

Hartmann, H. 1958. *Ego Psychology and the Problem of Adaptation*. New York: International Universities Press. First published in German in 1939.

Hawkins, R.M. 1992. Self-efficacy: A predictor but not a cause of behavior. *Journal of Behavior Therapy and Experimental Psychiatry, 23*, 251–6.

Hearnshaw, L.S. 1979. *Cyril Burt: Psychologist*. Ithaca, NY: Cornell University Press.

Herrnstein, R.J., & Murray, C.A. 1994. *The Bell Curve: Intelligence and Class Structure in American Life*. Cambridge, MA: Free Press.

Higgins, E.T. 1997. Beyond pleasure and pain. *American Psychologist, 52,* 1280–300.

————. 1998. Promotion and prevention: Regulatory focus as a motivational principle. In M.P. Zanna (Ed.), *Advances in Experimental Social Psychology* (Vol. 30). New York: Academic Press.

Higgins, E.T., Friedman, R.S., Harlow, R.E., Idson, L.C., Ayduk, O.N., & Taylor, A. Achievement orientations from subjective histories of success: Promotion pride versus prevention pride. *European Journal of Social Psychology, 31*, 323.

Hilgard, E.R. 1965. *Hypnotic Susceptibility*. New York: Harcourt Brace Jovanovich.

————. 1987. *Psychology in America: A Historical Survey*. San Diego: Harcourt Brace Jovanovich.

Hilgard, E.R., & Marquis, D.G. 1940. *Conditioning and Learning*. New York: Appleton-Century.

Hilts, P.J. 1997. Group delays achievement award to psychologist accused of fascist and racist views. *The New York Times*, 15 August, p. A10 y.

Hochreich, D.J., & Rotter, J.B. 1970. Have college students become less trusting? *Journal of Personality and Social Psychology, 15*, 211–14.

Holland, J.G. 1992. B.F. Skinner (1904–1990). *American Psychologist, 47*, 665–7.

Holmes, D.S. 1990. The evidence for repression: An examination of sixty years of research. In J.L. Singer (Ed.), *Repression and Dissociation: Implications for Personality Theory, Psychopathology, and Health*. Chicago: University of Chicago Press.

Horney, K. 1924. On the genesis of the castration complex in women. *International Journal of Psychoanalysis, 5*, 50.

————. 1937. *The Neurotic Personality of Our Time*. New York: Norton.

————. 1939. *New Ways in Psychoanalysis*. New York: Norton.

————. 1942. *Self-Analysis*. New York: Norton, p. 54.

————. 1945. *Our Inner Conflicts*. New York: Norton.

————. 1946. What Does the Analyst Do? In K. Horney (Ed.), *Are You Considering Psychoanalysis?* New York: Norton.

————. 1950. *Neurosis and Human Growth: The Struggle Toward Self-Realization*. New York: Norton.

Hunt, E. 1998. The Cattell affair: Do hard cases make poor lessons? *History and Philosophy of Psychology Bulletin, 10*, 26–9.

Hur, Y.-M., & Bouchard, T.J., Jr. 1997. The genetic correlation between impulsivity and sensation seeking traits. *Behavior Genetics, 27*, 455–63.

Jacobi, J. 1942. *The Psychology of C.G. Jung*. London: Kegan Paul.

James, W. 1890. *Principles of Psychology*. Vol. 1. New York: Holt.

James, W.H., & Rotter, J.B. 1958. Partial and 100 per cent reinforcement under chance and skill conditions. *Journal of Experimental Psychology, 55*, 397–408.

Jenkins, J.J., & Russell, W.A. 1960. Systematic changes in word association norms: 1910–1952. *Journal of Abnormal and Social Psychology, 60*, 293–304.

Jensen-Campbell, L.A., & Graziano, W.G. 2001. Agreeableness as a moderator of interpersonal conflict. *Journal of Personality, 69*, 323–62.

John, O.P. 1990. The 'Big Five' factor taxonomy: Dimensions of personality in the natural language and in questionnaires. In L.A. Pervin (Ed.), *Handbook of Personality: Theory and Research*. New York: Guilford.

Johnson, C.S. 1941. *Growing Up in the Black Belt: Negro Youth in the Rural South*. Washington, DC: American Council on Education.

Jones, E. 1955. *The Life and Work of Sigmund Freud*. Vol. 2. *The Years of Maturity, 1901–1919*. New York: Basic Books.

———. 1957. *The Life and Work of Sigmund Freud*. Vol. 3. *The Last Phase, 1919–1939*. New York: Basic Books.

Jones, H.E. 1933. Order of birth. In C. Murchison (Ed.), *The Handbook of Child Psychology*. Vol. 2. New York: Russell & Russell.

Joy, L.A., Kimball, M.M., & Zabrack, M.L. 1986. Television and children's aggressive behavior. In T.M. Williams (Ed.), *The Impact of Television: A Natural Experiment in Three Communities*. Orlando, FL: Academic Press.

Jung, C.G. 1928. *Contributions to Analytical Psychology*. London: Kegan Paul.

———. 1929. Ziele der psychotherapie. In *Die gesammelten Werk von C.G. Jung, X*. Zurich, p. 49.

———. 1953. *The Psychology of the* Unconscious. In C.G. Jung, *The Collected Works of C.G. Jung*, Vol. 7. Princeton, NJ: Princeton University Press.

———. 1956. *Symbols of Transformation*. In *Collected Works*, Vol. 5. Princeton, NJ: Princeton University Press.

———. 1964. *Man and His Symbols*. London: Aldus Books.

———. 1966a. On the psychology of the unconscious. In *Collected Works*, Vol. 7. Princeton, NJ: Princeton University Press. First published in 1943.

———. 1966b. The relations between the ego and the unconscious. In *Collected Works*. Vol. 7. Princeton, NJ: Princeton University Press. First published in 1928.

———. 1968. *Psychology and Alchemy*. 2nd edn. Princeton, NJ: Princeton University Press. First published in 1944.

———. 1971. A psychological theory of types. In *Collected Works*. Vol. 6. Princeton: Princeton University Press. First published in 1931.

———. 1973. *Memories, Dreams, Reflections*. Recorded and edited by Aniela Jaffé (Translated from the German by R. & C. Winston). New York: Pantheon Books.

———. 1978. Woman in Europe. In *Collected Works*. Vol. 10. Princeton, NJ: Princeton University Press. First published in 1927.

Kaitz, M., Good, A., Rokem, A.M., & Eidelman, A.I. 1987. Mothers' recognition of their newborns by olfactory cues. *Developmental Psychology, 20*, 587–91.

Katkovsky, W., Crandall, V.C., & Good, S. 1967. Parental antecedents of children's beliefs in internal–external control of reinforcements in intellectual achievement situations. *Child Development, 38*, 765–76.

Kazdin, A. 1977. *The Token Economy: A Review and Evaluation*. New York: Plenum.

Keller, F.S., & Schoenfeld, W.N. 1950. *Principles of Psychology*. New York: Appleton-Century-Crofts.

Kelly, G.A. 1955. *The Psychology of Personal Constructs*. New York: Norton.

———. 1963. *A Theory of Personality: The Psychology of Personal Constructs*. New York: Norton.

———. 1964. The language of hypotheses: Man's psychological instrument. *Journal of Individual Psychology, 20*, 137–52.

———. 1969. The autobiography of a theory. In B.A. Maher (Ed.), *Clinical Psychology and Personality: Selected Papers of George Kelly*. New York: Wiley.

———. 1980. A psychology of the optimal man. In A.W. Landfield & L.M. Leitner (Eds), *Personal Construct Psychology: Psychotherapy and Personality*. New York: Wiley.

Kernberg, O. 1975. *Borderline Conditions and Pathological Narcissism*. New York: Jason Aronson.

———. 1984. *Severe Personality Disorders: Psychotherapeutic Strategies*. New Haven, CT: Yale University Press.

Kihlstrom, J.F. 1999. The psychological unconscious. In L.A. Pervin & O.P. John (Eds), *Handbook of Personality: Theory and Research*. 2nd edn. New York: Guilford.

King, J.E., Weiss, A., & Farmer, K. 2005. A chimpanzee *(Pan troglodytes)* analogue of cross-national generalization of personality structure: Zoological parks and an African sanctuary. *Journal of Personality, 73*, 389–410.

Kirschenbaum, H. 1979. *On Becoming Carl Rogers*. New York: Dell.

Klein, J. 1980. *Woody Guthrie: A Life*. New York: Knopf.

Koch, S. 1959. Epilogue. In S Koch, (Ed.), *Psychology: A Study of a Science*. Vol. 3. *Formulations of the Person and the Social Context*. New York: McGraw-Hill.

Kohut, H. 1977. *The Restoration of the Self*. New York: International Universities Press.

Kohut, H., & Wolf, E. 1978. The disorders of the self and their treatment: An outline. *International Journal of Psycho-analysis, 59*, 413–25.

Kolb, D.A. 1965. Achievement motivation training for under-achieving high-school boys. *Journal of Personality and Social Psychology, 2*, 783–92.

Kosselyn, S.M., & Rosenberg, R.S. 2001. *Psychology: The Brain, the Person, the World*. Boston: Allyn and Bacon.

Krapelin, E. 1905. *Lectures on Clinical Psychiatry*. 2nd rev. edn. London: Baillière, Tindall & Cassell.

Kris, E. 1964. *Psychoanalytic Explorations in Art*. New York: Shocken. First published in 1952.

Lack, D. 1953. *Darwin's Finches*. Cambridge: Cambridge University Press.

Laing, R.D. 1961. *Self and Others*. London: Tavistock Publications.

———. 1964. *Sanity, Madness, and the Family*. New York: Basic Books.

———. 1967. *The Politics of Experience and the Bird of Paradise*. London: Penguin.

———. 1969. *The Divided Self*. New York: Pantheon Books. First published in 1960. Excerpts © 1960 Pantheon Books. Reprinted by permission of Taylor and Francis.

———. 1970. *Knots*. New York: Pantheon Books.

———. 1985. *Wisdom, Madness, and Folly: The Making of a Psychiatrist, 1927–1957*. London: MacMillan. Excerpts reprinted by permission of the publisher.

Lauter, E., & Rupprecht, C. (Eds). 1985. *Feminist Archetypal Theory: Interdisciplinary Re-visions of Jungian Thought*. Knoxville: University of Tennessee Press.

Lefcourt, H.M. 1983. The locus of control as a moderator variable: stress. In H.M. Lefcourt (Ed.), *Research with the Locus of Control Construct. Developments and Social Problems*. Vol. 2. New York: Academic Press.

———. 1992. Durability and impact of the locus of control construct. *Psychological Bulletin, 112,* 411–14.

Lerner, I.M. 1968. *Heredity, Evolution, and Society*. San Francisco: Freeman.

Lewin, K. 1935. *A Dynamic Theory of Personality*. New York: McGraw-Hill.

Levy, L.H. 1970. *Conceptions of Personality: Theories and Research*. New York: Random House.

———. 1947. Frontiers in group dynamics. Part 2. Channels of group life: Social planning and action research. *Human Relations, 1,* 143–53.

Lewin, K., Lippett, R., & White, R. 1939. Patterns of aggressive behavior in experimentally created 'social climates'. *Journal of Social Psychology, 10,* 271–99.

Lilienfeld, S.O., Gershon, J., Duke, M., Marino, L., & de Waal, F.B.M. 1999. A preliminary investigation of the construct of psychopathic personality (psychopathy) in chimpanzees *(Pan troglodytes)*. *Journal of Comparative Psychology, 113,* 365–75.

Litt, M.D. 1988. Self-efficacy and perceived control: Cognitive mediators of pain tolerance. *Journal of Personality and Social Psychology, 54,* 149–60.

Loehlin, J.C. 1987. *Latent Variable Models: An Introduction to Factor, Path, and Structural Analysis*. Hillsdale, NJ: Lawrence Erlbaum Associates.

———. 1992. *Genes and Environment in Personality Development*. Newbury Park, CA: Sage.

Loehlin, J.C., & Nichols, R.C. 1976. *Heredity, Environment, and Personality*. Austin: University of Texas Press.

Loftus, E.F. 2002. Memory faults and fixes. *Issues in Science and Technology, 18,* 41–50.

———. 2003a. Our changeable memories: Legal and practical implications. *Nature Reviews: Neuroscience, 4,* 231–4.

———. 2003b. Make-believe memories. *American Psychologist, 58,* 867–73.

Loftus, E.F., & Ketcham, K. 1991. *Witness for the Defense*. New York: St Martin's Press.

——— & ———. 1994. *The Myth of Repressed Memory: False Memories and Allegations of Sexual Abuse*. New York: St Martin's Press.

Lyons, D. 1997. The feminine in the foundations of organizational psychology. *Journal of Applied Behavioral Science, 33,* 7–26.

Lytton, H., Martin, N.G., & Eaves, L. 1977. Environmental and genetical causes of variation in ethological aspects of behavior in two-year-old boys. *Social Biology, 24,* 200–11.

McAdams, D.P. 1987. A life-story model of identity. In R. Hogan and W.H. Jones (Eds), *Perspectives in Personality* (Vol. 2, pp. 15–50). Greenwich, CT: JAI Press.

McAdams, D.P., & Pals, J.L. 2006. A new big five: Fundamental principles for an integrative science of personality. *American Psychologist, 61,* 204–17.

McCleary, R.A., & Lazarus, R.S. 1949. Autonomic discrimination without awareness. *Journal of Personality, 18,* 171–9.

McClelland, D.C. 1958. Risk taking in children with high and low need for achievement. In J.W. Atkinson (Ed.), *Motives in Fantasy, Action, and Society*. Princeton, NJ: Van Nostrand.

———. 1961. *The Achieving Society*. Princeton, NJ: Van Nostrand.

———. 1965. Toward a theory of motive acquisition. *American Psychologist, 20,* 321–33.

McClelland, D.C., Atkinson, J.W., Clark, R.A., & Lowell, E.L. 1953. *The Achievement Motive*. New York: Appleton-Century-Crofts.

McClelland, D.C., Clark, R.A., Roby, T.B., & Atkinson, J.W. 1949. The projective expression of needs. IV. The effect of the need for achievement on thematic apperception. *Journal of Experimental Psychology, 39,* 242–55.

Maccoby, M. 1976. *The Gamesman: The New Corporate Leaders*. New York: Simon and Schuster.

———. 1981. *The Leader: A New Face for American Management*. New York: Simon and Schuster.

———. 1995. *Why Work: Motivating and Leading the New Generation*. 2nd Edn. Alexandria, VA: Miles River Press.

———. 2002. Toward a science of social character. *International Forum of Psychoanalysis, 11,* 33–44.

McCrae, R.R., & Costa, P.T., Jr. 1985. Openness to experience. In R. Hogan & W.H. Jones (Eds), *Perspectives in Personality* (Vol. 1). Greenwich, CT: JAI Press.

———, & ———. 1986. Personality, coping, and coping effectiveness in an adult sample. *Journal of Personality, 54,* 385–405.

———, & ———. 1996. Toward a new generation of personality theories: Theoretical contexts for the five-factor model. In J.S. Wiggins, Ed., *The Five-Factor Model of Personality: Theoretical Perspectives*. New York: Guilford Press.

———, & ———. 1997. Personality trait structure as a human universal. *American Psychologist, 52,* 509–16.

———, & ———. 2003. *Personality in Adulthood: A Five-Factor Theory Perspective*. New York: Guilford.

McCrae, R.R., Terracciano, A., & 78 members Of the Personality Profiles of Cultures Project. 2005. *Journal of Personality and Social Psychology, 88*, 547–61.

McCrae, R.R., Yik, M.S.M., Trapnell, P.D., Bond, M.H., & Paulhus, D.L. 1998. Interpreting personality profiles across cultures: Bilingual, acculturation, and peer rating studies of Chinese undergraduates. *Journal of Personality and Social Psychology, 74*, 1041–55.

McGue, M., & Lykken, D.T. 1992. Genetic influence on risk of divorce. *Psychological Science, 3*, 368–73.

McLaughlin, R.J., & Eysenck, H.J. 1967. Extraversion, neuroticism, and paired-associate learning. *Journal of Experimental Research in Personality, 2*, 128–32.

Mailer, N. 2003. *The Spooky Art: Some Thoughts on Writing*. New York: Random House.

Manuck, S.B., Flory, J.D., Ferrell, R.E., Mann, J.J., & Muldoon, M.F. 2000. A regulatory polymorphism of the monoamine oxidase-A gene may be associated with variability in aggression, impulsivity, and central nervous system serotonergic responsivity. *Psychiatry Research, 95*, 9–23.

Marcia, J.E. 1980. Identity in adolescence. In J. Adelson (Ed.), *Handbook of Adolescent Psychology*. New York: Wiley.

Marcia, J.E., Waterman, A.S., Matteson, D.R., Archer, S.L., & Orlofsky, J.L. 1993. *Ego Identity: A Handbook for Psychosocial Research*. New York: Springer-Verlag.

Martin, N.G., Eaves, L.J., Heath, A.C., Jardine, R., Feingold, L.M., & Eysenck, H.J. 1986. Transmission of social attitudes. *Proceedings of the National Academy of Sciences, USA, 83*, 4364–8.

Maslow, A. 1970. *Motivation and Personality*. 2nd edn. New York: Harper & Row.

Massimini, F., & Delle Fave, A. 2000. Individual development in a bio-cultural perspective. *American Psychologist, 55*, 24–33.

Masson, J.M., Ed. 1985. *The Complete Letters of Sigmund Freud to Wilhelm Fliess, 1887–1904*. Cambridge, MA: Belknap Press.

Masters, J.C., Burish, T.G., Hollon, S.D., & Rimm, D.C. 1987. *Behavior Therapy: Techniques and Empirical Findings*. 3rd edn. Orlando, FL: Harcourt Brace Jovanovich.

Mehler, B. 1997. Beyondism: Raymond B. Cattell and the new eugenics. *Genetica, 99*, 153–63.

Merriman, C. 1924. The intellectual resemblance of twins. *Psychological Monographs, 33*, 1–58.

Metcalfe, J., & Mischel, W. 1999. A hot/cool system analysis of delay of gratification: Dynamics of willpower. *Psychological Review, 106*, 3–19.

Miles, D.R., & Carey, G. 1997. Genetic and environmental architecture of human aggression. *Journal of Personality and Social Psychology, 72*, 207–17.

Milgram, S. 1974. *Obedience to Authority: An Experimental View*. New York: Harper & Row.

Miller, A. 1949. *Death of a Salesman*. New York: Viking.

Miller, N.E. 1944. Experimental studies of conflict. In J. McV. Hunt (Ed.), *Personality and the Behavior Disorders*. Vol. 1. New York: Ronald, pp. 431–65.

———. 1948a. Studies of fear as an acquirable drive: I. Fear as motivation and fear-reduction as reinforcement in the learning of new responses. *Journal of Experimental Psychology, 38*, 89–101.

———. 1948b. Theory and experiment relating psychoanalytic displacement to stimulus response generalization. *Journal of Abnormal and Social Psychology, 43*, 155–78.

———. 1959. Liberalization of basic S-R concepts: Extensions to conflict behavior, motivation and social learning. In S. Koch (Ed.), *Psychology: A Study of a Science*. Vol. 2. New York: McGraw-Hill.

———. 1982. Obituary. John Dollard. *American Psychologist, 37*, 587–8.

Miller, N.E., & Bugelski, R. 1948. Minor studies in aggression: II. The influence of frustrations imposed by the in-group on attitudes expressed toward out-groups. *Journal of Psychology, 25*, 437–42.

Miller, N.E., & Dollard, J. 1941. *Social Learning and Imitation*. New Haven: Yale University Press. Excerpts reprinted by permission of the publisher.

Mischel, W. 1961. Delay of gratification, need for achievement, and acquiescence in another culture. *Journal of Abnormal and Social Psychology, 62*, 543–52.

———. 1965. Predicting the success of Peace Corps Volunteers in Nigeria. *Journal of Personality and Social Psychology, 1*, 510–17.

———. 1968. *Personality and Assessment*. New York: Wiley.

———. 1973. Toward a cognitive social learning reconceptualization of personality. *Psychological Review, 80*, 252–83.

———. 2003. *Introduction to Personality*. 7th edn. New York: Wiley.

Mischel, W., & Baker, N. 1975. Cognitive transformations of reward objects through instructions. *Journal of Personality and Social Psychology, 31*, 254–61.

Mischel, W., & Ebbesen, E.B. 1970. Attention in delay of gratification. *Journal of Personality and Social Psychology, 16*, 329–37.

Mischel, W., Ebbesen, E.B., & Zeiss, A.R. 1972. Cognitive and attentional mechanisms in delay of gratification. *Journal of Personality and Social Psychology, 21*, 204–18.

Mischel, W., & Moore, B. 1973. Effects of attention to symbolically-presented rewards on self-control. *Journal of Personality and Social Psychology, 28*, 172–9.

Mischel, W., & Peake, P.K. 1982. Beyond déjà vu in the search for cross-situational consistency. *Psychological Review, 89*, 730–55.

Mischel, W., & Shoda, Y. 1995. A cognitive-affective system

theory of personality: Reconceptualizing situations, dispositions, dynamics, and invariance in personality structure. *Psychological Review, 102*, 246–68.

Mischel, W., Shoda, Y., & Smith, R.E. 2004. *Introduction to Personality: Toward an Integration.* 7th edn. Hoboken, NJ: Wiley.

Moore, B., Mischel, W., & Zeiss, A.R. 1976. Comparative effects of the reward stimulus and its cognitive representation in voluntary delay. *Journal of Personality and Social Psychology, 34*, 419–24.

Mowrer, O.H. 1950. *Learning Theory and Personality Dynamics.* New York: Ronald.

Mullahy, P. 1948. *Oedipus—Myth and Complex. A Review of Psychoanalytic Theory.* New York: Hermitage House.

———. 1953. *Oedipus: Myth and Complex. A Review of Psychoanalytic Theory.* New York: Hermitage House.

Mullan, B. 1995. *Mad to be Normal: Conversations with R.D. Laing.* London: Free Association Books.

Munroe, R. 1955. *Schools of Psychoanalytic Thought.* New York: Holt, Rinehart and Winston.

Murphy, S.T., & Zajonc, R.B. 1993. Affect, cognition, and awareness: Affective priming with optimal and suboptimal stimulus exposures. *Journal of Personality and Social Psychology, 64*, 723–39.

Murray, H.A., Barrett, W.G., Homburger, E., et al. 1938. *Explorations in Personality: A Clinical and Experimental Study of Fifty Men of College Age.* New York: Oxford University Press.

Myers, D.G. 2000. The funds, friends, and faith of happy people. *American Psychologist, 55*, 56–67.

National Institute of Mental Health. 1982. *Television and Behavior: Ten Years of Scientific Progress and Implications for the Eighties. Summary Report.* Vol. 1. Washington, DC: US Government Printing Office.

National Television Violence Study. 1998. *National Television Violence Study.* Vol. 3. Santa Barbara, CA: University of California, Santa Barbara Center for Communication and Social Policy.

Niedenthal, P.M. 1990. Implicit perception of affective information. *Journal of Experimental Social Psychology, 26*, 505–27.

Nisbett, R. 1980. The trait construct in lay and professional psychology. In L. Festinger (Ed.), *Retrospections on social psychology.* New York: Oxford University Press, pp. 109–30.

Nisbett, R.E., and Wilson, T.D. 1977. Telling more than we can know: Verbal reports on mental processes. *Psychological Review, 84*, 231–59.

Norman, W.T. 1963. Toward an adequate taxonomy of personality attributes: Replicated factor structure in peer nomination personality ratings. *Journal of Abnormal and Social Psychology, 66*, 574–83.

Olton, D.S. 1979. Mazes, maps, and memory. *American Psychologist, 34*, 583–96.

Page, K. 1999 (May 16). The graduate. *Washington Post Magazine, 152*, 18, 20.

Paik, H., & Comstock, G. 1994. The effects of television violence on antisocial behavior: A meta-analysis. *Communication Research, 21*, 516–46.

Palermo, D.S., & Jenkins, J.J. 1963. Frequency of superordinate responses to a word association test as a function of age. *Journal of Verbal Learning and Verbal Behavior, 1*, 378–83.

Paris, B.J. 1994. *Karen Horney: A Psychoanalyst's Search for Self-Understanding.* New Haven: Yale University Press.

Pavlov, I.P. 1927. *Conditioned Reflexes: An Investigation into the Physiological Activity of the Cortex.* Trans. by G.V. Anrep. New York: Dover.

———. 1928. *Lectures on Conditioned Reflexes.* Vol. 1. Trans. by W. Horsley Gantt. New York: International Publishers.

Pedersen, N.L., Friberg, L., Floderus-Myrhed, B., McClearn, G.E., & Plomin, R. 1984. Swedish early separated twins: Identification and characterization. *Acta Geneticae Medicae et Gemellologiae, 33*, 243–50.

Pedersen, N.L., Plomin, R., McClearn, G.E., & Friberg, L. 1988. Neuroticism, extraversion and related traits in adult twins reared apart and reared together. *Journal of Personality and Social Psychology, 55*, 950–7.

Perry, J.C. 1994. Assessing psychodynamic patterns using the Idiographic Conflict Formulation (ICF) method. *Journal of Psychotherapy Research and Practice, 4*, 238–51.

Perry, J.C., Fowler, J.C., & Semeniuk, T. 2005. An investigation of tasks and techniques associated with dynamic interview adequacy. *Journal of Nervous and Mental Disorders, 193*, 136–9.

Perry, H.S. 1962. Introduction. In H.S. Sullivan, *Schizophrenia as a Human Process.* New York: Norton.

———. 1982. *Psychiatrist of America: The Life of Harry Stack Sullivan.* Cambridge, MA: The Belknap Press.

Pervin, L.A., Cervone, D., & John, O.P. 2005. *Personality: Theory and Research.* New York: Wiley.

Peterson, C. 2000. The future of optimism. *American Psychologist, 55*, 44–55.

Peterson, G.B. 2004. A day of great illumination: B.F. Skinner's discovery of shaping. *Journal of the Experimental Analysis of Behavior, 82*, 317–28.

Pinker, S. 1995. Why the child holded the baby rabbits: A case study in language acquisition. In L.R. Gleitman & M. Liberman (Eds), *Language: An Invitation to Cognitive Science.* 2nd edn, Vol. 1. Cambridge, MA: MIT Press.

Plomin, R., & Caspi, A. 1999. Behavioral genetics and personality. In L.A. Pervin & O.P. John (Eds), *Handbook of Personality Theory and Research.* 2nd Edn. New York: Guilford.

Plomin, R., DeFries, J.C., & McClearn, G.E. 1990. *Behavioral Genetics: A Primer.* 2nd edn. New York: W.H. Freeman.

Premack, D. 1988. 'Does the chimpanzee have a theory of mind?' revisited. In R.W. Byrne & A. Whiten (Eds),

Machiavellian Intelligence: Social Expertise and the Evolution of Intellect in Monkeys, Apes, and Humans. Oxford: Clarendon.

Raimy, V.C. 1948. Self-reference in counseling interviews. *Journal of Consulting Psychology, 12,* 153–63.

Riemann, R., Angleitner, A., & Strelau, J. 1997. Genetic and environmental influences on personality: A study of twins reared together using the self- and peer report NEO-FFI scales. *Journal of Personality, 65,* 449–75.

Roazen, P. 1976. *Erik H. Erikson: The Power and Limits of a Vision.* New York: Free Press.

———. 1980. Erik H. Erikson's America: The political implications of ego psychology. *Journal of the History of the Behavioral Sciences, 16,* 333–41.

Roberts, B.W., & Robins, R.W. 2000. Broad dispositions, broad aspirations: The intersection of personality traits and major life goals. *Personality and Social Psychology Bulletin, 26,* 1284–96.

Rodgers, J.L. 2001. What causes birth order—intelligence patterns? *American Psychologist, 56,* 505–10.

Rogers, C.R. 1938. *Clinical Treatment of the Problem Child.* Boston: Houghton Mifflin.

———. 1942. *Counseling and Psychotherapy, New Concepts in Practice.* Boston: Houghton Mifflin.

———. 1959. A theory of therapy, personality, and interpersonal relationships, as developed in the client-centered framework. In S. Koch (Ed.), *Psychology: A Study of a Science.* Vol. 3. New York: McGraw-Hill. Excerpts reprinted by permission of the publisher.

———. 1961. *On Becoming a Person: A Therapist's View of Psychotherapy.* Boston: Houghton Mifflin.

———. 1966. Client-centered therapy. In S. Arieti (Ed.), *American Handbook of Psychiatry.* Vol. 3. New York: Basic Books, pp. 189–90.

———. 1967. Autobiography. In E.G. Boring & G. Lindzey (Eds), *A History of Psychology in Autobiography.* Vol. 5. New York: Appleton-Century-Crofts.

———. 1973. My philosophy of interpersonal relationships and how it grew. *Journal of Humanistic Psychology, 13,* 3–15, p. 3.

———. 1980. *A Way of Being.* Boston: Houghton Mifflin.

Rogers, C.R., & Dymond, R.F. (Eds). 1954. *Psychotherapy and Personality Change: Coordinated Studies in the Client-Centered Approach.* Chicago: University of Chicago Press.

Rogers, C.R., Gendlin, E.T., Kiesler, D.J., & Truax, C.B. 1967. *The Therapeutic Relationship and its Impact: A Study of Psychotherapy with Schizophrenics.* Madison, WI: University of Wisconsin Press.

Rosen, B.C., & D'Andrade, R.G. 1959. The psychosocial origins of achievement motivation. *Sociometry, 22,* 185–218.

Rothlisberger, F.J., & Dickson, W.J. 1939. *Management and the Worker.* Cambridge, MA: Harvard University Press.

Rotter, J.B. 1951. Word association and sentence completion methods. In H.H. Anderson & G.L. Anderson (Eds), *An Introduction to Projective Techniques.* Englewood Cliffs, NJ: Prentice-Hall.

———. 1954. *Social Learning and Clinical Psychology.* New York: Prentice-Hall. Excerpts reprinted by permission of the author.

———. 1962. An analysis of Adlerian psychology from a research orientation. *Journal of Individual Psychology, 18,* 3–11.

———. 1966. Generalized expectancies for internal versus external control of reinforcement. *Psychological Monographs, 80,* No. 1 (Whole No. 609).

———. 1967. A new scale for the measurement of interpersonal trust. *Journal of Personality, 35,* 651–65.

———. 1970. Some implications of a social learning theory for the practice of psychotherapy. In D.J. Levis (Ed.), *Learning Approaches to Therapeutic Behavior Change.* Chicago: Aldine.

———. 1971. Generalized expectancies for interpersonal trust. *American Psychologist, 26,* 443–52.

Rotter, J.B., Chance, J.E., & Phares, E.J. 1972. *Applications of a Social Learning Theory of Personality.* New York: Holt, Rinehart and Winston.

Rotter, J.B., Liverant, S., & Crowne, D.P. 1961. The growth and extinction of expectancies in chance controlled and skilled tasks. *Journal of Psychology, 52,* 161–77.

Rowe, D.C., Rodgers, J.L., & Meseck-Bushey, S. 1992. Sibling delinquency and the family environment: Shared and unshared influences. *Child Development, 63,* 59–67.

Rubins, J.L. 1978. *Karen Horney: Gentle Rebel of Psychoanalysis.* New York: Dial.

Rudikoff, E.C. 1954. A comparative study of the changes in the concepts of the self, the ordinary person, and the ideal in eight cases. In C.R. Rogers & R.F. Dymond (Eds), *Psychotherapy and Personality Change: Coordinated Studies in the Client-Centered Approach.* Chicago: University of Chicago Press.

Rumbaugh, D.M., & Savage-Rumbaugh, E.S. 1994. Language in comparative perspective. In N.J. Mackintosh (Ed.), *Animal Learning and Cognition.* San Diego: Academic Press.

Ryan, D.E., & Lakie, W.L. 1965. Competitive and noncompetitive performance in relation to achievement motive and manifest anxiety. *Journal of Personality and Social Psychology, 1,* 342–5.

Ryan, R.M., & Deci, E.L. 2000. Self-determination theory and the facilitation of intrinsic motivation, social development, and well-being. *American Psychologist, 55,* 68–78.

Salovey, P., Rothman, A.J., Detweiler, J.B., & Steward, W.T. Emotional states and physical health. *American Psychologist, 55,* 110–21.

Samelson, F. 1980. J.B. Watson's Little Albert, Cyril Burt's twins, and the need for a critical science. *American Psychologist, 35,* 619–25.

Sarbin, T. 1986. The narrative as a root metaphor for psychology. In T. Sarbin (Ed.) *Narrative Psychology: The Storied Nature of Human Conduct*. New York: Praeger.

Sartre, J.-P. 1956. *Being and Nothingness: An Essay on Phenomenological Ontology*. Translated from the French by H.E. Barnes. New York: Philosophical Library.

Scarr, S., & Carter-Saltzman, L. 1979. Twin method: defense of a critical assumption. *Behavior Genetics, 9*, 527–42.

Schaar, J.H. 1961. *Escape from Authority: The Perspectives of Erich Fromm*. San Francisco: Jossey-Bass.

Schachter, S. 1959. *The Psychology of Affiliation*. Stanford, CA: Stanford University Press.

Schacter, D.L. 1987. Implicit memory: History and current status. *Journal of Experimental Psychology: Learning, Memory, and Cognition, 13*, 501–18.

Schultz, T.R., & Pomerantz, M. 1976. Achievement motivation, locus of control, and academic achievement behavior. *Journal of Personality, 44*, 38–51.

Schwartz, B. 2000. Self-determination: The tyranny of freedom. *American Psychologist, 55*, 79–88.

Segal, N.L. 1999. *Entwined Lives: Twins and What They Tell Us about Human Behavior*. New York: Dutton.

Seligman, M.E.P. 1971. Phobias and preparedness. *Behavior Therapy, 2*, 307–20.

Seligman, M.E.P., & Csikszentmihalyi, M. 2000. Positive psychology: An introduction. *American Psychologist, 55*, 5–14.

Shedler, J., & Block, J. 1990. Adolescent drug use and psychological health: A longitudinal inquiry. *American Psychologist, 45*, 612–30.

Shedler, J., Mayman, M., & Manis, M. 1993. The illusion of mental health. *American Psychologist, 48*, 1117–31.

Sheldon, K.M., Houser-Marko, L., & Kasser, T. 2006. Does autonomy increase with age? Comparing the goal motivations of college students and their parents. *Journal of Research in Personality, 40*, 168–78.

Shoda, Y., Mischel, W., & Peake, P.K. 1990. Predicting adolescent cognitive and self-regulatory competencies from preschool delay of gratification: Identifying diagnostic conditions. *Developmental Psychology, 26*, 978–86.

Shorter, E. 1992. *From Paralysis to Fatigue: A History of Psychosomatic Illness in the Modern Era*. New York: Macmillan Free Press.

Singer, J.A. 2004. Narrative identity and meaning making across the adult lifespan: An introduction. *Journal of Personality, 72*, 437–59.

Skinner, B.F. 1938. *The Behavior of Organisms*. New York: Appleton-Century-Crofts.

———. 1948. *Walden two*. New York: Macmillan.

———. 1950. Are theories of learning necessary? *Psychological Review, 57*, 193–216.

———. 1953. *Science and Human Behavior*. New York: Macmillan.

———. 1957. *Verbal Behavior*. New York: Appleton-Century-Crofts.

———. 1958. Reinforcement today. *American Psychologist, 13*, 94–9.

———. 1959. A case history in scientific method. In S. Koch (Ed.), *Psychology: A Study of a Science*. Vol. 2. New York: McGraw-Hill.

———. 1960. Pigeons in a pelican. *American Psychologist, 15*, 28–37.

———. 1967. Autobiography. In G.E. Boring & G. Lindzey (Eds), *A History of Psychology in Autobiography*. Vol. 5. New York: Appleton-Century-Crofts.

———. 1968. *The Technology of Teaching*. New York: Appleton-Century-Crofts.

———. 1969. *Contingencies of Reinforcement: A Theoretical Analysis*. New York: Appleton-Century-Crofts.

———. 1971. *Beyond Freedom and Dignity*. New York: Knopf.

———. 1974. *About Behaviorism*. New York: Knopf.

———. 1975. The steep and thorny way to a science of behavior. *American Psychologist, 30*, 42–7.

———. 1976. *Particulars of My Life*. New York: Knopf.

———. 1979. *The Shaping of a Behaviorist*. New York: Knopf. Excerpts used by permission of Alfred A. Knopf, a division of Random House, Inc.

———. 1983. Intellectual self-management in old age. *American Psychologist, 38*, 239–44.

Skinner, B.F., & Vaughan, M.E. (1983). *Enjoy Old Age: Living Fully in Your Later Years*. New York: Warner.

Smith, M.B. 1971. Peasant characterology: Method vs insight? *Contemporary Psychology, 16*, 635–37.

Snygg, D., & Combs, A.W. 1949. *Individual Behavior: A New Frame of Reference for Psychology*. New York: Harper.

Spielmann, J. 1963. The relation between personality and the frequency and duration of involuntary rest pauses during massed practice. Unpublished PhD dissertation, University of London.

Stanton, A.H., & Schwartz, M.S. 1954. *The Mental Hospital: A Study of Institutional Participation in Psychiatric Illness and Treatment*. New York: Basic Books.

Steger, M.F., Frazier, P., Oishi, S., & Kaler, M. 2006. The Meaning in Life Questionnaire: Assessing the presence of and search for meaning in life. *Journal of Counseling Psychology, 53*, 80–93.

Stein, H.T. 2000. Dealing effectively with children's mistaken goals. Handout from a course in Classical Adlerian Child and Family Therapy in the Distance Training Program of the Alfred Adler Institute of San Francisco.

Steinbeck, J. 1967. Introduction. In W. Guthrie, *Hard Hitting Songs for Hard-Hit People*. New York: Oak Publications.

Stelmack, R.M., & Stalikas, A. 1991. Galen and the humour theory of temperament. *Personality and Individual Differences, 12*, 255–63.

Stephenson, W. 1953. *The Study of Behavior: Q-technique and its Methodology*. Chicago: University of Chicago Press.

Straub, R.E., Jiang, Y., MacLean, C.J., Ma, Y, Webb, B.T., Myakishev, M.V., Harris-Kerr, C., Wormley, B., Sadek, H., Kadambi, B., Cesare, A.J., Gibberman, A., Wang, X., O'Neill, D.W., & Kendler, K.S. 2002. Genetic variation in the 6p22.3 gene DTNBP1, the human ortholog of the mouse dysbindin gene, is associated with schizophrenia. *American Journal of Human Genetics, 71,* 337–48.

Strickland, B.R. 1965. The prediction of social action from a dimension of internal–external control. *Journal of Social Psychology, 66,* 353–8.

———. 1977. Internal–external control of reinforcement. In T. Blass (Ed.), *Personality Variables in Social Behavior*. Hillsdale, NJ: Erlbaum.

———. 1978. I–E expectations and health-related behaviors. *Journal of Consulting and Clinical Psychology, 46,* 1192–211.

Sullivan, H.S. 1938. Introduction to the study of interpersonal relations. *Psychiatry, 1,* 123n.

———. 1950. Tensions interpersonal and international: a psychiatrist's view. In H. Cantril (Ed.), *Tensions that Cause War*. Urbana, IL: University of Illinois Press.

———. 1953a. *Conceptions of Modern Psychiatry*. Washington, D.C: William Alanson White Foundation. Paperback edition: Norton, 1953. First published in 1947.

———. 1953b. *The Interpersonal Theory of* Psychiatry. New York: Norton.

———. 1954. *The Psychiatric Interview*. New York: Norton.

———. 1956. The paranoid dynamism. In H.S. Sullivan, *Clinical Studies in Psychiatry*. New York: Norton.

———. 1964. *The Fusion of Psychiatry and Social Science*. New York: Norton.

———. 1972. *Personal Psychopathology: Early Formulations*. New York: Norton.

Sulloway, F.J. 1996. *Born to Rebel: Birth Order, Family Dynamics, and Creative Lives*. New York: Pantheon.

Talbot, K., Eidem, W.L., Tinsley, C.L., Benson, M.A., Thompson, E.W., Smith, R.J., Hahn, C.-G., Siegel, S.J., Trojanowski, J.Q., Gur, R.E., Blake, D.J., & Arnold, S.E. 2004. Dysbindin-1 is reduced in intrinsic, glutamatergic terminals of the hippocampal formation in schizophrenia. *Journal of Clinical Investigation, 113,* 1353–63.

Taylor, S.E. 1989. *Positive Illusions: Creative Self-deception and the Healthy Mind*. New York: Basic Books.

Taylor, S.E., Kemeny, M.E., Reed, G.M., Bower, J.E., & Gruenewald, T.L. 2000. Psychological resources, positive illusions, and health. *American Psychologist, 55,* 99–109.

Tellegen, A., Lykken, D.T., Bouchard, T.J., Wilcox, K., Segal, N., & Rich, S. 1988. Personality similarity in twins reared apart and together. *Journal of Personality and Social Psychology, 54,* 1031–9.

Theophrastus. 1831. *The Characters of Theophrastus*. Translated with Physionomical Sketches by Francis Howell. Boston, MA: Frederick S. Hill.

Thompson, C. 1962. Harry Stack Sullivan: The Man. In H.S. Sullivan, *Schizophrenia as a Human Process*. New York: Norton.

Thurstone, L. 1953. *Thurstone Temperament Schedule: Examiner's Manual*. 2nd edn. Chicago: Science Research Associates.

Tillich, P. 1952. *The Courage to Be*. New Haven: Yale University Press.

Trobst, K.K., Herbst, J.H., Masters, H.L. III, & Costa, P.T. 2002. Personality pathways to unsafe sex: Personality, condom use, and HIV risk behaviors. *Journal of Research in Personality, 36,* 117–33.

Vaihinger, H. 1927. *The Philosophy of 'As If'*. New York: Harcourt, Brace & World.

Vaillant, G.E. 2000. Adaptive mental mechanisms: Their role in a positive psychology. *American Psychologist, 55,* 89–98.

van den Daele, L. 1987. Research in Horney's psychoanalytic theory. *American Journal of Psychoanalysis, 47,* 99–104.

Van Hooff, J. 1971. *Aspects of Social Behavior and Communication in Humans and Higher Nonhuman Primates*. Rotterdam: Bronder.

Van Kaam, A. 1966. *Existential Foundations of Psychology*. Pittsburgh: Duquesne University Press.

Verplanck, W.S. 1955. The operant, from rat to man: An introduction to some recent experiments on human behavior. *Transactions of the New York Academy of Science, 17,* 594–601. Excerpts reprinted by permission of Blackwell Publishing.

Waller, N.G., & Shaver, P.R. 1994. The importance of nongenetic influences on romantic love styles: A twin-family study. *Psychological Science, 5,* 268–74.

Watson, J.B. 1913. Psychology as the behaviorist views it. *Psychological Review, 20,* 158–77.

———. 1928. *Psychological Care of Infant and Child*. New York: Norton.

———. 1970. *Behaviorism*. New York: Norton. First published in 1924.

Watson, J.B., & Rayner, R. 1920. Conditioned emotional reactions. *Journal of Experimental Psychology, 3,* 1–14.

Watson, J.D. 1968. *The Double Helix*. New York: Atheneum.

Weinberger, D.A. 1995. The construct validity of the repressive coping style. In J.L. Singer (Ed.), *Repression and Dissociation: Implications for Personality Theory, Psychopathology, and Health*. Chicago: University of Chicago Press.

Weinberger, D.A., Schwartz, G.E., & Davidson, R.J. 1979. Low-anxious, high-anxious, and repressive coping styles: Psychometric patterns and behavioral and psychological responses to stress. *Journal of Abnormal Psychology, 88,* 369–80.

Wender, P.H., Kety, S.S., Rosenthal, D., Schulsinger, F., Ortmann, J., & Lunde, I. 1986. Psychiatric disorders in the biological and adoptive families of adopted individuals with affective disorders. *Archives of General Psychiatry, 43,* 923–39.

Westen, D. 1998. The scientific legacy of Sigmund Freud: Toward a psychodynamically informed psychological science. *Psychological Bulletin, 124,* 333–71.

Westen, D., & Gabbard, G.O. 1999. Psychoanalytic approaches to personality. In L.A. Pervin & O.P. John (Eds), *Handbook of Personality: Theory and Research.* 2nd edn. New York: Guilford.

Whyte, L.L. 1962. *The Unconscious Before Freud.* Garden City, NY: Doubleday.

Wiggins, J.S. 1973. *Personality and Prediction: Principles of Personality Assessment.* Reading, MA: Addison-Wesley.

Winterbottom, M.R. 1958. The relation of need for achievement to learning experiences in independence and mastery. In J.W. Atkinson (Ed.), *Motives in Fantasy, Action, and Society.* Princeton, NJ: Van Nostrand.

Woodworth, R.S. & Schlosberg, H. 1954. *Experimental Psychology.* Rev. Ed. New York: Henry Holt.

Youniss, J. 1980. *Parents and Peers in Social Development.* Chicago: University of Chicago Press.

Zajonc, R.B. 1976. Family configuration and intelligence. *Science, 192,* 227–36.

———. 2001. The family dynamics of intellectual development. *American Psychologist, 56,* 490–6.

Zuckerman, M. 1978. Sensation seeking. In H. London & J.E. Exner, Jr (Eds), *Dimensions of Personality.* New York: Wiley.

———. 1984. Sensation seeking: A comparative approach to a human trait. *Behavioral and Brain Sciences, 7,* 413–471.

———. 1991. *Psychobiology of Personality.* Cambridge: Cambridge University Press.

———. 1994a. *Behavioral Expressions and Biosocial Bases of Sensation Seeking.* New York: Cambridge University Press.

———. 1994b. Impulsive unsocialized sensation seeking: The biological foundations of a basic dimension of personality. In J.E. Bates & T.D. Wachs (Eds), *Temperament: Individual Differences at the Interface of Biology and Behavior.* Washington, DC: American Psychological Association.

———. 1995. Good and bad humors: Biochemical bases of personality and its disorders. *Psychological Science, 6,* 325–32.

———. 2002. Zuckerman-Kuhlman Personality Questionnaire (ZKPQ): An alternative five-factorial model. In B. DeRaad & M. Peruginini (Eds), *Big Five Assessment.* Seattle, WA: Hogrefe & Huber.

Zuckerman, M., Kolin, E.A., Price, L., & Zoob, L. 1964. Development of a sensation seeking scale. *Journal of Consulting Psychology, 28,* 477–82.

Zuckerman, M., & Kuhlman, D.M. 2000. Personality and risk-taking: Common biosocial factors. *Journal of Personality, 68,* 999–1029.

Index

abreaction, 34
achievement: need for, 474–8; societies and, 476–8
achievement motive theory, 474–8
Adler, Alfred, 5, 88, 93, 104, 114–41, 377, 378; emphases of, 120–2; Freud and, 135–7; Freud and Jung and, 117–20; major concepts of, 122–30; personal history of, 115–17
adolescence: Erikson's view of, 204, 206–8, 211, 216–18; Sullivan's view of, 154–5
adoption: genetics research and, 444, 453–5; selective placement and, 454
adults: Erikson's view of, 208–9, 211–12; Freud's character structure of, 60–1; internal and external control in, 392–4; Jung's view of, 106–7; Sullivan's view of, 155
affect, 428
affective units, 427–9
affiliation: fear and, 133–4
agent: person as, 409–11
Age of Theory, 462–4
aggression: Dollard's study of, 318–19; Kelly's view of, 306; as instinct, 50; observational learning and, 402, 403; psychoanalysis and, 70; SCLT and, 415–18; S-R theory and, 343
agreeableness, 254
alcoholism: genetics and, 448, 454, 455
Alexander, Franz, 162
alleles, 439
Allport, Gordon, 1, 224, 225, 226–31, 242, 260; personal history of, 226–8
Alternate Big Five, 473–4
American Indians: Erikson's study of, 213–14
anal stage, 55–6
analytic psychology, 88–113, 465; concepts of, 96–107; current application, 98–9; emphases of, 93–5; major concepts of, 95–107; personality development and, 106–7; research and, 107–10; structural parts of, 95–102
anger: S-R theory and, 341, 343

anima, 98, 99–100
animus, 98, 99–100
Anna O. (Breuer's case), 34–5
Ansbacher, Heinz and Rowena, 124
antecedents: consequents and, 462–4; reinforcement as, 406; traits and, 226
anthropology, 213–14
anti-cathexis, 51
anticipation: reinforcement and, 406
anxiety: basic, 163, 165 ; birth order and, 133–4; experiments on, 74–5, 78–9; fear and, 332; Freud's types of, 51; Horney's view of, 163, 165; neurotic, 51; ontological insecurity and 273–4; Rogers' view of, 289–90; Sullivan's view of, 148, 149, 157
approach–avoidance conflict, 333–7, 338–9
approach gradient 333–4, 342
approximation, successive, 361–2, 372–3
archetypes, 92, 97–102
Aristotle, 224, 225
Aronson, Elliot, 476–7
arousal, 247, 249–51
ascending reticular activating system (ARAS), 250
association: free, 35, 37, 38; learned, 323; S-R theory and, 328
associationism, 354–5
associative meditation, 74
assumptions: personality theory and, 23; science and, 9–14
Atkinson, John, 474–8
attitudes: Jung's view of, 104–5; traits and, 236–7; twins and, 448
Auden, W.H., 71
authoritarianism, 189–90
autism, 368
autonomy, 205–6
autosomes, 436
avoidance–avoidance conflict, 337
avoidance gradients, 333–4, 342
avoidance learning, 329–32

'baby tender', 357
Bak, Samuel, 265–6
Bandura, Albert, 5, 377, 395, 401–23,

424, 429; emphases and major concepts of, 405–15; personal history of, 404–5
'basic anxiety', 163, 165
'basic evil', 165
'basic hostility', 165
behaviour: change in, 385; control of, 358–9; S-R theory and, 326
Behavioural Activation System (BAS), 338
Behavioural Inhibition System (BIS), 338
behaviour genetics, 4, 8, 241, 434–61; assessment of, 467, 469–70; see also genetics
behaviourism, 77, 464; SCLT and, 401–2, 404; see also radical behaviourism
behaviour modification, 368–9, 464
behaviour potential (BP), 383–5
behaviour theories, 22
beliefs: CAPS and, 428
Bettelheim, Bruno, 48
Big Five Theory, 253–9; genetics and, 447, 448–51, 473
Binswanger, Ludwig, 267
biophilous character, 184
birth order, 127–30, 133–5
black people: Dollard's study of, 317–19
Bleuler, Eugen, 91
Block, J., 259
Bowers, K.S., et al., 77
boys: Erikson's view of, 206, 212–13; genital stage and, 59–60; phallic stage and, 56–9; see also children
Breuer, Josef, 33–5
Brody, Nathan, 253
Brown, J.S., 342
Brown, Roger, 58, 476, 477–8
Brücke, Ernst, 29, 30–1
Burt, Sir Cyril, 11–12, 242, 245
Bushman, B.J., and L.R. Huesmann, 416
Butler, J.M., and G.V. Haigh, 297–8

Cameron, N., 21–2
Camus, Albert, 267
care: Erikson's view of, 209
Carlson, R., and N. Levy, 109–10
case study, 15

catharsis, 415

cathexis, 51, 53

Cattell, Raymond, 1, 226, 230, 231–42, 260; major concepts of, 234–8; personal history of, 233–4

causality: existentialism and, 267

chaining: responses and, 363

Chance, J.E., 391

chance encounters, 413–14

character orientations: Fromm's view of, 178, 179, 184–5, 190–3

character structure: Freud's view of, 60–1, 184

Charcot, Jean Martin, 29, 31–3, 40

childhood: Erikson's view of, 205–6, 211; Freud's view of, 38, 40, 46–7, 48; Jung's view of, 106; Sullivan's view of, 153–5

childrearing: behaviourism and, 351–3, 357, 366–7; individual psychology and, 128–9; person-centred therapy and, 299; SCLT and, 419; SLT and, 390–2; S-R theory and, 338–41

children: birth order and, 127–30; factor analysis and, 238; A. Freud and, 198, 199; Fromm and, 188–9; gratification and, 425–6; individual psychology and, 127–30, 131; observational learning and, 402–4; person-centred theory and, 284, 294–5, 296, 299; play of, 212–13; 'problem', 128–9; psychology of, 198; SCLT and, 412–13; SLT and, 382–3; television and, 415–18, 419; see also boys; girls

chimpanzees, 259

Chomsky, Noam, 367

chromosomes, 435–6

cleanliness training: S-R theory and, 340–1

client-centred therapy, 284–5, 296–9; see also person-centred therapy

clinical method, 15–17; psychoanalysis and, 71–4

Cloninger, C.R., R. Adolfsson, and D.M. Svrakic, 456–7

cognition: Sullivan's view of, 150–1

cognitive-affective personality system (CAPS), 425–30; elements of, 426–9; emphases of, 424–6

cognitive psychology: S-R theory and, 345–6

cognitive transformation, 426

cognitive units, 427–9

Coles, Robert, 394

Commager, Henry Steele, 355

communication: Sullivan's view of, 151

compensation, 122–3

competencies: CAPS and, 429

complexes, 96, 102, 108; mother, 96, 130

condensation: dreams and, 64

conditioning: classical, 352–3, 360; instrumental, 360–1; operant, 353–4, 360; Pavlovian, 352–3, 360; respondent, 353, 360; Type R, 360; Type S, 360

conditions of learning, S-R theory and, 331

conditions of worth, 289, 294–5

conflict, psychological: Dollard and Miller's theory of, 332–7, 342; experiments on, 342; Freud's view of, 47; SLT and, 385

'confluence model', 135

congruence, 289

conscience, 53, 58–9, 179

conscientiousness, 254

conscious ego, 121

consequents: antecedents and, 462–3

consistency, 424

constructs: permeable, 304; personal construct theory and, 302–4; personality and scientific, 380; preverbal, 304; submerged, 304; suspended, 304

content: latent/manifest, 57, 63

contingencies: if . . . then, 429; management of, 369

continuity assumption, 21–2, 325

control: internal vs external, 389–94; operant responding and, 362; principle of, 11–14, 17; Skinner's view of, 358–9

control groups, 13–14, 296

control of reinforcement, 389–90

correlations, 230

Costa, Paul T., Jr, 253–9

countertransference, 34

Crandall, V.C., and B.W. Crandall, 391–2

creative self, 126

creativity: person-centred theory and, 298–9; psychoanalysis and, 69–70

crises, psychosocial, 202, 204–9, 216–19

Crowen, John H., 17–19

cues: CAPS and, 424; SLT and, 388–9; S-R

theory and, 322, 327, 328–9

culture: behaviour and, 319–20; personality and, 176, 177–84; traits and, 258–9, 260

cumulative recorder, 364

Darwin, Charles, 435, 437–9

Deci, Edward, and Richard Ryan, 310

deduction, 13

defence mechanisms: dreams and, 64–5; A. Freud's view of, 198; Freud's view of, 47, 51–2, 64–5, 78–9; Rogers' view of, 290; S-R theory and, 331, 332

dehumanization, 409, 410

denial: 41, 'to awareness', 290

deoxyribonucleic acid (DNA), 436–7

depersonalization, 273–4

description: scientific method and, 12–13

desensitization theory, 415–16, 420

despair, 209

despised self, 163, 168

determinism: 9–10; denial of, 295; reciprocal, 406–7; SCLT and, 406–7

dethronement, 127

developmental lines, 198, 199

Diagnostic and Statistical Manual, 40

diathesis-stress model, 445

dichotomies, existential and historical, 180

dimensions: testing, 247; type-trait theory and, 242–4

disassociation, 149

discoverability, 11

disorders: anxiety, 33, 40; behaviour, 368–9; conversion, 32, 38, 40; depressive, 454; obsessive-compulsive, 33, 40; panic, 33; personality, 5–6; study of, 16, 21–2

displacement: dreams and, 65; S-R theory and, 342–3

dispositions: cardinal, 229–30; central, 230; secondary, 230

DNA (deoxyribonucleic acid), 436–7

doctor–patient relationship: Horney's view of, 163–5; Sullivan's view of, 146–7

Dollard, John, 5, 16, 317–20, 322–49, 377–8, 406; emphases of 322–3; major concepts of, 323–42; personal history of, 320–1 dominance: genetics and, 439

'doodle method', 477

dream censor, 63

dreams: Adler's view of, 130–2; Freud's view of, 62–9; Fromm's view of, 188; Sullivan's view of, 151

dream theory, 65

dream work, 63, 64–5

drive reduction hypothesis, 327

drives: acquired, 326; learned, 325; primary, 322–3, 326; secondary, 322–3, 326; S-R theory and, 322–3, 326–7; stimuli of, 322–3

Dunn, J., and R. Plomin, 135

dynamic adaptation, 188–9

dynamisms, 158–60, 161; lust, 147, 155; paranoid, 150; self, 147, 149, 153, 154, 162; sub-, 160

dysthymia, 246

echoic responses, 367

education: person-centred theory and, 296; Skinner's view of, 369–70; *see also* learning

efficacy expectations, 411–12, 419–21, 422

ego: Adler's view of, 121; conscious, 121; Erikson's view of, 202; Freud's view of, 39, 42, 47–8, 50–3, 63; Fromm's view of, 179; Horney's view of, 167–9; individual psychology and, 121; Jung's view of, 94, 95, 103; neo-Freudians and, 115

ego ideal, 53

ego identity, 207, 216–19

ego psychology, 197–223, 465; A. Freud's, 197–9; Erikson's, 200–20; Hartmann's, 198–200

'eight ages of man', 204–9

Einstein, Albert, 70

élan vital, 94

Elisabeth von R. (Freud's case), 35–8

Ellenberger, Henri, 88, 89, 92

Emmy von N. (Freud's case), 35

'empathetic understanding', 287, 291, 292

empathy: Sullivan's view of, 151, 153

empiricism, 88

encodings, 427–8

engulfment, 273

environment: behaviourism and, 353; equal, 446–8, 450–1; genetics and, 443–61; nonshared, 448–50, 456–7; person and, 406–8; shared, 448–50; *see also* situation

environmentalism, 354, 355

epigenesis, 202–3

epochs, Sullivan's, 152–5

Epstein, Raissa, 116

equal environment assumption, 446–8, 450–1

eras, Sullivan's, 152–5

ergs, 236–7

Erikson, Erik, 198, 200–20; emphases of, 202–4; major concepts of, 204–12; personal history of, 200–1; research and, 212–18

erogenous zones, 55; Erikson's view of, 203–4

euphemisms, 409, 411

euphoria, 147–9

evil, basic, 165

evolution, 437–9

excitation, 247–50

existentialism, 6–7, 265–80; assessment of, 468; current research in, 278–9; European, 276; North American, 276; personality theory and, 267

expectancies: change in, 389–94; control, 389–94; disturbed behaviour and, 385–7; generalized, 382, 384, 396–7; SCLT and, 411–12; SLT and, 381, 382, 383–5

expectancy (E), 383–5

expectations: CAPS and, 428; outcome, 411; self-efficacy, 421

experience: Rogers's use of, 287

experimentalism, 354, 355

experiments, scientific, 13–15

exploitive character, 184, 192–3

expression in opposites, 65

externalization, 169

extraversion, 99, 104–6, 109–11, 224, 254; excitation-inhibition and, 248–51; genetics and, 447, 454, 455; type, 244, 246–7, 252

Eysenck, Hans J., 109, 224, 225, 242–53; major concepts of, 246–51; personal history of, 245–6

Eysenck Personality Questionnaire, 256

facets, 254

factor analysis, 230–3, 242

factor-analytic trait theory, 231–42

factor loadings, 230–1

factors, 230–1; 'first-order', 235

Falconer's estimate, 449

falsifiability, 24

family: individual psychology and, 121–2, 126–30; neo-Freudians and, 114–15; person-centred theory and, 294–5, 296; schizophrenia and, 272–3

'family constellation', 126

family, society, and culture paradigm, 5, 466

family studies: genetics and, 443–5

fantasies: Freud and, 41; needs and, 475–6

father archetype, 102

fear, 325, 329–32; anxiety and, 332; birth order and, 133–4; conditioned, 352–3; phobic, 419; thought-produced, 331–2

feeding, child-: S-R theory and, 340

Feldman Barrett, Lisa, Nathan Williams, and Geoff Fong, 78–9

feminism: Jung and, 98–9

fiction: theory and, 23–4

fictional finalism, 121, 125

field: person and, 406–7; *see also* situation

Fields, Mary, 66–9

Fiske, Donald, 253

Five-Factor Model (FFM), 257–9, 260

fixations, 53, 55, 61

fixed-role therapy, 306–7

foreclosure, 207, 216–18

Fowler, J. Christopher, 158–9

frame of orientation, 182

Frankl, Viktor, 265, 276

Franks, C.M. 249

free association, 35, 37, 38

freedom of movement (FM), 384–5

Freese, J., B. Powell, and L.C. Steelman, 134

Freud, Anna, 51, 53, 58, 197–8, 320

Freud, Sigmund, 4, 10, 28–45, 46–87, 104, 197–8, 199, 340, 342; Adler and, 116–20, 121, 135–7, 435; Allport and, 226–7; chance and, 413; first discoveries of, 38–42; Fromm and, 176, 178, 181, 188, 191; Horney and, 169, 170; Jung and, 91–2, 121; learning theory and, 316; neo-Freudians and, 114–15; personal history of, 29–38; women and, 81, 98

Freudian 'left', 115

Freudian slip, 42

Friedman, I., 300

Friedrich, L.K., and A.H. Stein, 416

Fromm, Erich, 5, 115, 176–97; dreams and, 188; emphases of, 177–9; major concepts of, 179–85; personal history of, 176–7; research and, 189–93

Fromm-Reichmann, Frieda, 16–17

frustration, 317–19

fully functioning person, 295

functional analysis, 359

functionalism, 354, 355

Funder, D.C., 424

Galton, Sir Francis, 8, 96, 225, 242, 469, 446

galvanic skin response (GSR), 108

Gandhi, Mohandas K., 214–16

Gay, Peter, 1, 39, 62, 116–17, 171, 214

generalizations: learned, 381; secondary, 329, 331; stimulus, 331, 343

generativity, 209

genes: definition of, 435–6

genetic blending hypothesis, 437, 439

genetics, 4, 8, 241, 467, 469–70; behaviour and, 434–61; current research in, 456–7; history of, 437–43; research and, 443–55; transmission and, 436–7

genital stage, 59–60

genotypes, 244

Gershwin, George and Ira, 117–20

girls: Erikson's view of, 206, 212–13; phallic stage and, 59–60; see also children

Glucksberg, S., and L.J. King, 74–5

goals, 395; CAPS and, 428; future, 121, 125; internal, 408–9; minimal, 382; -seeking, 378

Goldberg, L.R., 253

Goldstein, Kurt, 282

Gore, P.M., and J.B. Rotter, 392

graphic expression: achievement and, 476–7

gratification: delay of, 425–6

Gray, Jeffrey, 338

Greenfield, Josh, 177

Greenspoon, J., 361

groups: control, 13–14, 296; factor analysis and, 239

guilt: Erikson's view of, 206; Kelly's view of, 306

Guthrie, Woody, 440, 441–3

habits, 323; traits and, 229

Hall, C.S., G. Lindzey, and J.B. Campbell, 56, 121, 126, 155

Hall, C.S., and V.J. Nordby, 97

hallucinations, 49, 62

Harrington, D.M., J.H. Block, and J. Block, 299

Harris, J.R., 134, 456

Hartmann, Heinz, 115, 198–200, 320

Heidegger, Martin, 7, 267, 281

heredity, 238, 241; traits and, 235, 236; see also genetics

heritability formula, 449, 483–4

Herrenstein, R.J., and C.A. Murray, 11

Higgins, E. Tory, 338–9

Hilgard, Ernest, 161, 378, 395

Hilts, P.J., 234

Hippocrates, 242

hoarding character, 184

Hochreich, D.J., and J.B. Rotter, 396–7

Holmes, D.S., 76

Horney, Karen, 5, 161–71, 177, 320; emphases of, 162–5; feminine psychology and, 169–70; major concepts of, 165–9; personal history of, 161–2

hospitals, psychiatric, 157–60

hostility: basic, 165; Kelly's view of, 306

Hull, Clark, 249, 317, 323, 378

humanism, 309–10; assessment of, 467–8; as paradigm, 6

humanistic communitarian socialism, 183–4

human nature, 2–9

humour: psychoanalysis and, 71

Huntington's disease, 440–3

Husserl, Edmund, 267, 281

hypnosis, 32–4, 36

hypotheses, 24; lexical, 225–6, 247; testing of, 252

hypothetico-deductive systems, 462–4

hysteria, 31–8, 246; origin of, 40

id, 47–8,

idealized self, 163, 167–8

ideas: Jung's view of, 96

identification: psychoanalytic concept of, 58

identity: crisis of, 216–19; Erikson's view of, 206–8, 216–19; Fromm's view of, 182; negative, 207–8

identity achievement, 216–19

idiographic approach, 228–9

if . . . then contingencies, 429

imitation: learning by, 402; social behaviour and, 319–20

implosion, 273

inception, 206

incongruence, 289, 291

individual psychology, 120–43; current practice of, 128–9; emphases of, 120–2; major concepts of, 122–30; personality development and, 126–30; practicality of, 120; psychoanalysis and, 135–7; research and, 133–5

induction, 13

industry, 206

infancy: Erikson's view of, 204–5, 210; Sullivan's view of, 152–3

inferiority, 121, 123, 206

inferiority complex, 120

inheritance of behaviour paradigm, 8

inhibition, 247–50; reactive, 249–50

initiative, 206

instincts: death, 49–50, 70; Freud's view of, 42, 47, 49–50, 70; Fromm's view of, 176, 178, 179, 181; Jung's view of, 100; life, 49–50; neo-Freudians and, 114; sexual, 88

Institute of Human Relations, 320, 321, 345

integrity, 209

intelligence: birth order and, 134–5; fluid/crystallized, 236

interpersonal theory of psychiatry, 144, 145–61; current practice in, 158–9; emphases of, 145–7; major concepts of, 147–51; personality development and, 152–5; research and, 155–60

Interpersonal Trust Scale, 396–7

intervening variables paradigm, 462–4

interview, psychiatric, 156–9

intimacy, 208–9

introspection, 350–1

introversion, 99, 104–6, 109–11, 224; excitation-inhibition and, 248–51

introversion–extraversion dimension, 243–4, 246–51

isolation, 208–9
it-terms, 270

James, William, 76, 150, 230
Janet, Pierre, 33, 76, 91
John, O.P., 259
judgemental processes, 409
Julie (Laing's patient), 272–3
Jung, Carl, 88–113, 224, 465; Adler and
Freud and, 117–20; Eysenck and,
243; personal history of, 88–93

Kant, Immanual, 242
Kantor, J.R., 377, 379, 380
Kelly, George, 6, 22, 282, 300–9, 424,
426, 429; personal history of, 300–2;
research of, 307–8
Kernberg, O., 81
Kierkegaard, Søren, 266–7, 268
Kihlstrom, John, 77, 80
King, J.E., A. Weiss, and K. Farmer, 259
Kirschenbaum, H., 283
Koch, Sigmund, 462–4
Kohut, Heinz, 81
Kraepelin, Emil, 270–1
Kris, Ernst, 69

Laden, Osama bin, 411
Laing, R.D., 266–80; major concepts of,
270–5; personal history of, 267–70
Lamarckism, 94, 98, 438
Langfield, Herbert, 226, 227
language: behaviourism and, 367;
everyday, 7; objective, 23; scientific,
12–13; traits and, 225–6, 247, 252,
254, 256–7, 260
latency period, 59–61
L-data, 232–3
learning: avoidance, 329–32; cognitive,
404; Kelly's view of, 304, 306;
observational, 402–4; operant,
367–8; passive avoidance, 330;
personality types and, 247–9;
principles and conditions of, 322;
skill vs chance and, 390; social, 404
learning dilemma, 327
learning paradigm, 5–6
learning theories: assessment of, 466–7;
radical behaviourism, 350–76; social
cognitive learning theories (SCLT),
401–33; social learning theory (SLT),
377–400; S-R theory, 316–49

Levy, L.H., 377–8
Lewin, Kurt, 73, 99, 230, 377, 378, 406
lexical hypothesis, 225–6, 247
liberalization: theoretical concepts and,
463–4
libido: Freud's view of, 49–50, 60;
Fromm's view of, 179; Jung's view
of, 94, 102–3
life force, 94
limbic system, 250
linkage analysis, 457
Litt, M.D., 422
Little Albert (Watson's case), 352–3
Little Hans (Freud's case), 57–8
Loehlin, J.C., 444;
Loehlin, J.C., and R.C. Nichols, 447
Loftus, E.F., 42
logical inference, 13
lust dynamism, 147, 155
Lyons, D. 99

McCleary, R.A., and R.S. Lazarus, 290
McClelland, David, 78–9, 474–8
Maccoby, Michael, 191, 192–3
McCrae, Robert, 253–9
McLaughlin, R.J., and H.J. Eysenck,
250–1
Mahler, Gustav, 72
Mailer, Norman, 71
mandala, 100, 101
mands, 367
manifest content, 57, 63
manipulation: experiments and, 13–14
Marcia, J.E., 216–18
marketing character, 184–7
'masculine protest', 124
Maslow, Abraham, 6, 282, 309–10
materialism, 354, 355
May, Rollo, 265, 282
Mayo, Elton, 99
Mead, George Herbert, 146
Meaning in Life questionnaire, 276–7
mechanisms: 'of escape', 183, 184, 185;
Freud's view of, 38; see also defence
mechanisms
meditation, associative, 74
Mehler, B., 234
memory: earliest, 132; false, 42;
implicit/explicit, 77; racial, 94, 96–7
men: animus and anima and, 98, 99–100;
individual psychology and, 124, 125
Mendel, Gregor, 435, 439

mental health: positive psychology and,
311
mentalisms, 355
Merriman, C., 446
methods: adequacy of, 17; science and,
11–17
Meyer, Adolph, 145
Miller, Arthur, 185–7
Miller, N.E., 5, 16, 317, 322–49, 377–8,
406, 463; emphases of, 322–3; major
concepts of, 323–42; personal history
of, 320–1
Miller, N.E., and R. Bugelski, 343
miniature theories, 470–8
Mischel, Walter, 5, 423–30; personal
history of, 424–5
mislabelling, 341
mistrust, 205
modalities and modes: Erikson's view
of, 203–4
modelling: participant, 412, 420;
symbolic, 420
molecular genetic analysis, 456–7
moral anxiety, 51
moral justification, 409, 410
moratorium, 207, 216–18
mother archetype, 101
mother complex, 96, 130
motivation: Kelly's view of, 304, 306;
Rogers's view of, 290–1; Rotter's
view of, 395
motives: achievement and, 474–8;
Freud's view of, 38; implicit/
explicit, 78–9
Mowrer, O. Hobart, 324
Mullahy, Patrick, 101–2, 152, 267, 268
Mullen, Bob, 266
Multiple Abstract Variance Analysis
(MAVA), 238
Munroe, R., 94, 97, 100, 132, 147, 149,
199
Murray, H.A., 475
mutations, genetic, 436–7
Myers-Briggs Type Indicator (MBTI),
109–10

nAch score, 476–8
National Institute of Mental Health, 416
National Television Violence Study, 416
necrophilous character, 185
need potential (NP), 384–5
need-related behaviour, 384–5

needs: definition of, 474–5; Fromm's view of, 176, 179, 180–2; Horney's view of, 165, 166–7; McClelland and Atkinson's view of, 474–8; measurement of, 475–8; noninstinctual, 181–2; SLT and, 382, 384–5; Sullivan's view of, 147, 148
need value (NV), 384–5
neo-Alderians, 115
neo-Freudians: Adler, 114–41; Fromm, 176–96; Horney, 161–71; Sullivan, 142–61
NEO Personality Inventory, 254–7
neurophysiology, 467
neurosis: Charcot and, 31–5; Freud's theories of, 40–2; Horney's view of, 161, 165–7; origin of, 40; SLT and, 385–7; S-R theory and, 329–37; symptoms of, 46–7
neurotic anxiety, 51
neuroticism, 254; genetics and, 447, 454, 455; type, 244, 246–7, 252
neuroticism–normality dimension, 243–4, 246–51
'neurotic paradox', 323–5
Nisbett, R.E., and T.D. Wilson, 77
nomothetic approach, 228–9
nonproductive character, 184–5
normality: neurosis and, 243–4, 245–51, 325
novelty-seeking: genetics and, 456–7; *see also* sensation-seeking

object: instincts and, 49
object relations, 81–2
observables: links to, 462–4
observation, 402–4; scientific method and, 12–14; SCLT and, 414
observational learning, 402–4
obsessive-compulsive disorder, 33, 40
occupations: factor analysis and, 239–41; genetics and, 448
Odbert, H.S., 225
Oedipus complex, 55–60, 130, 169, 170; Fromm's view of, 189
ontological insecurity, 271–4
ontological security, 272
openness to experience, 254
operants, 407–8
operationalism, 12
oral dynamism, 149, 153
oral stage, 54–5

organ inferiority and compensation, 122–3
organism, 282
organizational psychology, 99

pampering: in childhood, 126
pangenesis, 438
'pansexualism', 114
Pappenheim, Bertha, 34–5
paradigms, personality, 3–8; assessment of, 464–9
parataxic distortion, 146–7
parataxic thought, 146–7, 150, 151
partially bi-directional person–situation interaction, 406
participant modelling, 412, 420
passive avoidance learning, 330
Pavlov, Ivan, 247, 351
peer ratings, 449, 451
penis envy, 59, 171
perceptual defence, 290
performance accomplishment, 420
Perry, Helen Swick, 142–3, 144
Perry, J. Christopher, 158–9
Perry, Ralph Barton, 230
person: as agent, 409–11; fully functioning, 295; situation and, 406–7; *see also* person-centred theory; person–situation interactions
persona, 98, 100
personal construct theory, 6, 300–9; postulate and corollaries of, 302–4; psychotherapy and, 306–7
personality: agentic view of, 409–11; definitions of, 1, 19; interpersonal theory of psychiatry and, 146; Skinner's view of, 359–60
personality assessment: Kelly and, 306
personality change: Rogers's view of, 286–7, 291–4
personality development: Adler's view of, 126–30; behaviourism and, 366–7; Cattell's view of, 238–9; Erikson's view of, 204–9; Freud's view of, 48, 54–61; Fromm's view of, 188–9; Horney's view of, 163, 169; individual psychology and, 126–30; Jung's view of, 106–7; psychosexual stages of, 54–61; Rogers's view of, 294–5; SCLT and, 412–13, 418; S-R theory and, 338–41; Sullivan's view of, 152–5

personality inventory (PI), 254
Personality Profiles of Cultures Project, 258–9
personality–society–culture relation, 177–9
personality structure, 252, 254, 257–9
personality theory: beginnings of, 28–45; nature of, 22–4
person-centred theory, 6, 282–301; conditions of therapy, 291–2; emphases of, 286–7; major concepts of, 287–91; outcomes of, 292–3; processes of, 292; psychotherapy and, 286–7, 291–4
personification, 151
person–situation interactions, 20–1, 146, 380, 406; factor analysis and, 238; type-trait theory and, 253
person-society theory, 121
Pervin, L.A., D. Cervone, and O.P. John, 1
Peterson, Gail, 372–3
petrification, 273
phallic intrusiveness, 206
phallic stage, 56–9
phenomenology, 6, 266, 267, 277–8, 281–315; assessment of, 467–8; current research in, 310–11; North American, 281–2
phenotypes, continuous, 443
phobias, 33, 419
planfulness, 429
'play age', 206, 211
pleasure principle, 49
Plomin, R., and A. Caspi, 455, 456
Plomin, R., J.C. DeFries, and G.E. McClearn, 435, 454
positive psychology, 309–12; assessment of, 467–8
positive regard, 288–9, 291, 294–5
positive self-regard, 288–9
positivism, 30
potential human benefit, 11–12
potentialities, 19
pragmatism, 354, 355
predictability: science and, 10
predisposition, genetic, 445
prevention system, 338–9
pride system, 169
primary process, 49
principle of entropy, 102–3
principle of equivalence, 102–3
principle of opposites, 104–5

process concepts, 5
processes: judgemental, 409; primary, 49
    secondary, 50–1
process theories, 317
productive character, 184–5
professors: trait profile of, 239–42
projections, 52
promotion system, 338–9
prototaxic thought, 150
proximate responses, 372–3
psychiatry: American, 145–6;
    interpersonal theory of, 144, 145–61;
    interview technique in, 156–9; Jung
    and, 91; Laing and, 268–71
psychic energy, 10; Jung's view of, 94, 102
psychoanalysis, 3–4, 28–9, 35, 46–87,
    201, 320, 321; assessment of, 465–6;
    critics of, 88, 114–15; current
    research and, 78–9; ego psychology
    and, 197, 218–20; emphases of, 46–8;
    Eysenck and, 245–6; Fromm and,
    176–7; historical figures and,
    214–16; implications of, 69–71;
    individual psychology and, 135–7;
    Jung and, 91–2; major concepts of,
    48–61; modern revisions of, 80–2;
    research and, 71–80; S-R theory and,
    316–17, 345; validity of, 72–4
psychodynamic paradigm, 4; assessment
    of, 465–6
psychohistory, 214–16
psychology: cognitive, 345–6;
    community, 464; feminine, 171–2;
    personality theory and, 2, 9–14;
    positive, 309–12; social, 142; 'third
    force', 282; see also analytic
    psychology; ego psychology;
    individual psychology
psychopatholgy: genetics and, 447
psychopharmacology, 368
'psycho-politics', 269–70
psychosocial crises, 202, 204–9
psychotherapy: neurosis and, 324; SCLT
    and, 412, 419–21; Skinner's view of,
    369; SLT and, 395
psychoticism (P) type, 244, 247, 252
P-technique, 232–3
punishment, 366–7

Q-data, 232–3
Q-sort, 288, 298, 299–300
Q-technique, 288

quantification, 14
quantitative trait loci (QTLs), 456
questionnaires: clinical interpretation of,
    189–91; Eysenck and, 246; genetics
    and, 444, 449, 451; Meaning in Life,
    276–7; Regulatory Focus, 338–9;
    sensation-seeking and, 470–4; 16PF,
    232, 234, 238, 239–41; SLT and, 390,
    391, 392, 396–7; S-R theory and,
    338–9; see also tests

radical behaviourism, 19, 350–76;
    applications of, 367–71; current
    application of, 372–3; emphases of,
    358–60; major concepts of, 360–5;
    personality development and, 366–7;
    research and applications, 367–71;
    S-R theory and, 345–6
Raimy, V.C., 296–7
Rank, Otto, 281
reaction formation, 52, 65
reality anxiety, 51
reality principle, 50–1
receptive character, 184
recessiveness, 439
reflex action, 49
regression, 53
regulatory focus theory, 338–9;
    Questionnaire (RFQ), 338–9
Reichmann, Frieda, 176
Reimann, R., et al., 455
reinforcements: behaviourism and, 354,
    363–5; CAPS and, 426; classes of,
    382, 384; conditioned, 363; disturbed
    behaviour and, 385–7; generalized,
    363; intermittent, 363–5; internal vs
    external control of 389–94; Kelly's
    view of, 306; locus of control of,
    389–90; partial, 363–5; primary, 363;
    scheduled, 363–5; SCLT and, 402–4,
    405–6, 407–8, 414; secondary, 363;
    SLT and, 381–2, 383–7; S-R theory
    and, 322–3, 327–8
reinforcement value (RV), 383–5
rejection, childhood, 126
relatedness: Fromm's view of, 178, 179,
    181
religion: Adler and, 117; Jung and, 94,
    107
repetition compulsion, 49
replicability, 17; psychoanalysis and, 72–3
representation, 23

representativeness: adoption studies and,
    454
repression: defence of, 332; experiments
    on, 73–4; Freud's view of, 39, 41, 42,
    51–2
Rep Test, 305, 307–8
resistance: Freud's view of, 38–9
respondent behaviour, 360
response-produced cues, 328–9
responses: chaining of, 363; conditioned,
    360; differentiated, 362; echoic, 367;
    internal, 323; S-R theory and, 322,
    327; unconditioned, 360
rewards: S-R theory and, 322, 323
Riemann, R., A. Angleitner, and J.
    Strelau, 448–50
ritual, ritualism, ritualization: 209–12
Roazen, P., 220
Rodgers, J.L., 135
Rogers, C.R., 6, 281, 309–10; personal
    history of, 282–6; person-centred
    theory of, 282–301; research of,
    297–300
Rogers, C.R., and R.F. Dymond, 296
role confusion, 207, 216–18
Role Construct Repertory Test, 305,
    307–8
rootedness: Fromm's view of, 181
Roth, Philip, 177
Rotter, Julian, 5, 108, 377–400, 424, 429;
    major concepts of, 383–5; personal
    history of, 378–9
R-technique, 232–3
Rudikoff, E.C., 299

Sachs, Hanns, 177, 201, 320
Sartre, Jean-Paul, 267, 281
Scarr, S., and L. Carter-Saltzman, 446–8
Schacter, S., 13, 133–4
schedules: fixed-interval, 364; ratio, 365;
    reinforcement and, 363–5; variable-
    interval (VI), 364–5, 367–8;
    variable-ratio (VR), 365
schizophrenia, 144, 156, 160, 368;
    genetics and, 434–5, 443, 444–5,
    447, 454, 455, 457; Laing and,
    275–6, 269–73; Rogers and, 285–6
science: assumptions of, 9–14;
    existentialism and, 267; methods of,
    11–17; personality theory and, 2,
    9–17; phenomenology and, 286
scientific method, 11

security: Horney's view of, 166–7; Sullivan's view of, 147, 148

selective inattention, 149

self: Adler's view of, 126; Cattell's view of, 237; despised, 163, 168; embodied/unembodied, 274, 275; Fromm's view of, 179; Horney's view of, 163, 167–9; idealized, 163; Jung's view of, 93, 94, 100; real, 163, 167; Rogers's view of, 287–8; Sullivan's view of, 147

self-actualization, 6 , 290–1, 294–6, 310

self-concept, 287–8

self-consciousness, 274

self-determination theory, 310

self dynamism, 147, 149, 153, 154, 161

self-effacement, 169

self-efficacy, 411–12

self-efficacy expectations, 421

self-esteem: client-centred therapy and, 297–8

self-experience, 288–9

self-observation, 409

self-reaction, 409, 410

self-realization, 93

self-reference, 296–7

self-regard, 288–9

self-regulation, 408–9, 410, 429

self-reinforcement, 406, 407–8, 414

self system, 149, 415

Seligman, M.E.P., 97

sensation seeking, 253, 470–4; genetics and, 456–7

sentiments: traits and, 236–7

sex: as instinct, 49–50; S-R theory and, 341

sexual abuse, 33–4, 41–2

sexuality: Erikson's view of, 203–4; infantile, 48, 54–61; Jung's view of, 91–2; neo-Freudians' view of, 142

sexual seduction: Freud's view of, 33–4, 40–2, 37

shadow, 100

shame, 205–6

shaping, 361–2, 366, 372–3

Sheldon, K.M., L. Houser-Marko, and T. Kasser, 310–11

siblings: SLT and, 382–3

situations: person and, 406–7, 423–4, 430; SLT and, 383–5, 388–9; trait theory and, 260

16 Personality Factor (16PF) Questionnaire, 232, 234, 238, 239–41

Skinner, B.F., 1, 5, 317, 345, 353–76; emphases of, 358–60; major concepts of, 360–5; personal history of, 355–8; 'theory' of, 359

Skinner, B.F., and Charles Ferster, 408

Snygg, D., and A.W. Combs, 281–2

sociability, 444–5

social cognitive learning theories (SCLT), 401–33; current application of, 410–11; emphases and major concepts of, 405–15; implications of, 415–22; research and, 422

social cognitive theory, 395

social learning theory (SLT), 5–6, 377–400; current research in, 389–94; emphases of, 380–3; implications of, 385–7; major concepts of, 383–5; research in, 389–94

social selection, 192

social stimulus value, 19

society: Fromm's view of, 182–4; individual psychology and, 125–6; neo-Freudians and, 114–15; personality and, 176, 177–84; sane, 183–4

Society for Individual Psychology, 117

sociology: psychiatric hospitals and, 157–60; psychiatry and, 145–6

Spearman, Charles, 233, 242

specification equation, 237–8

Spence, Kenneth W., 405

Spielmann, J., 249

S-R theory, 316–49, 463–4; conflict and, 332–7; current research in, 338–9; major concepts of, 323–42; neurosis and, 329–37; principles and conditions of, 322; research and, 342–4; SCLT and, 404, 405; variables in, 326–9

stagnation, 209

standards, internal, 408–9

Standing Committee on Communications and Culture, 416

Steger, M.F., et al, 276

Steinbeck, John, 441

sten, 240

Stephenson, William, 288

stimulus: conditioned, 360; discriminative, 362; generalization of, 331, 343; unconditioned, 360

stimulus-response theory; see S-R theory

Straub, R.E., et al., 457

Strickland, Bonnie, 362, 392–3

structuralism, 350–1

'style of life', 121, 124–5, 130–2

subception, 290

subjective stimulus value, 428

sublimation, 154

substitution: dreams and, 64

successive approximation, 361–2, 372–3

Sullivan, Henry Stack, 1, 5, 142–61, 177; personal history of, 143–5

Sulloway, F.J., 134

superego, 47–8, 53–4; Fromm's view of, 179

superfactors, 244, 246–7, 252

superiority striving, 123–4

symbolic expression, 62–9

symbolic modelling, 420

symbolism, dream, 63–4

symptoms: as behaviour, 60–1; as sexual activity, 47; Freud's view of, 39, 47, 60–1; irrationality of, 39; meaning of, 132

synchronicity, 94

syntality, 239

syntaxic thought, 150, 153

tacts, 367

T-data, 232–3

teaching machine, 369–70

teleology, Jung's, 88, 93

television: aggression and, 415–18

temperament, 236–7; type-trait theory and, 242–4

tension, 147–8

tests: personality 109–10, 230, 232, 423, 451; Role Construct Repertory, 305, 307–8; TAT, 78, 475–6; word association, 107–9; see also questionnaires

Thematic Apperception Test (TAT), 78, 475–6

Theophrastus, 224, 225

theories: achievement motive, 474–8; behaviour, 22; cognitive, 377, 378; content/process, 316–17, 381; desensitization, 415–16, 420;

factor-analytic trait, 231–42; fiction and, 23–4; field, 378, 380; miniature, 470–80; multiplication of, 478–9; personal, 302; person-society, 121; process, 317; regulatory focus, 338–9; reinforcement, 378; scientific, 3; self-determination, 310; social cognitive, 395; type-trait, 242–53; *see also* learning theories; personal construct theory; person-centred theory; social cognitive theory; social learning theory; S-R theory; trait theory

therapies: client-centred, 284–5, 296–9; fixed-role, 306–7; operant, 369; person-centred theory and, 291–2; *see also* psychotherapy

'third force psychology', 282

Thompson, Clara, 143, 145, 177

Thorndike, Edward L., 284, 355, 377, 381

threat, 289–90

Thurstone Temperament Schedule, 444, 445

Tillich, Paul, 267

Titchener, Edward Bradford, 227, 350

token economy, 368–9

Tolman, Edward C., 377, 378

trait paradigm, 7–8; assessment of, 468–9

trait ratings, 230

traits, 224–6; common, 229–30; dynamic, 236–7; heritable, 447–51; individual, 229–30; personality, 423; source, 235–8; surface, 232, 235, 236; temperament, 236–7; types of, 229–30

trait theories, 224–64; Allport's, 226–31; Alternative Big Five, 473–4 Big Five, 253–9; Cattell's, 231–42, 247; current

research and, 258–9; Eysenck's 242–53; factor-analytic, 231–42

transcendence, 181

transference, 34, 70–1

traumatic episodes, 33–4, 40–2, 46–7

trust, 205; measurement of, 396–7

truth claims, 24

twins: dizygotic, 446; fraternal, 446; identical, 446; monozygotic, 446; nonshared environment and, 449–53; studies of, 444, 446–53, 483–4

types: causes of, 247–51; Eysenck and, 242–4, 246–51; Jung and, 104–6, 107

type-trait theory, 242–53

typologies, personality, 104–6

unconscious: cognitive, 80, 464; collective, 88, 93–4, 96–102; Freud's view of, 39, 42, 47; motivational, 78; personal, 95–6, 103; processes of, 76–80

undoing, 53

unidirectional person–situation interaction, 406

Vaihinger, Hans, 125

validation: Kelly's view of, 306

validity, external, 13

variability, genetic, 437–8

variables: experiments and, 13–14; intervening, 462–4; person and situation, 424

variance, genetic: additive, 456–7; nonadditive, 454–5

Verplanck, W.S., 361

'vicious circle', 165–6

violence: mass media and, 415–18

Walden Two, 357

Walters, Richard, 401

Watson, James, and Francis Crick, 12, 436

Watson, John B., 351–2

Wednesday Psychological Society, 116

Weinberger, D.A., 75

Wender, P.H., et al., 454

Westen, D., and G.O. Gabbard, 81, 82

White, William Alanson, 144, 145

white people: Dollard's study of, 317–19

Whyte, L.L., 39

will: Erikson's view of, 206; free, 10; Rogers's view of, 281

wishes, instinctual, 42; *see also* instincts

wit: psychoanalysis and, 71

women: animus and anima and, 98, 99–100; Freud and, 81, 98; individual psychology and, 124, 125; psychology of, 163, 169–70

Woodworth, R.S., and H. Schlosberg, 108

Woody, Erik, 483–4

word association test, 107–9

Wundt, Wilhelm, 242–3, 350–1

Yerkes-Dodson law, 250, 251

Zajonc, R.B., 135

Zeitgeist, 28

zones: Erikson's view of, 203; erogenous, 55, 203–4

Zuckerman, Marvin, 253, 456, 470–8

Zuckerman-Kuhlman Personality Questionnaire, 474

Zuckerman Sensation Seeking Scale, 471–3